# Women Writing Africa
## THE NORTHERN REGION

# The Women Writing Africa Project

A Project of The Feminist Press at The City University of New York
Funded by the Ford Foundation and the Rockefeller Foundation

Women Writing Africa, a project of cultural reconstruction, aims to restore African women's voices to the public sphere. Through the publication of a series of regional anthologies, each collecting oral and written narratives as well as a variety of historical and literary texts, the project will make visible the oral and written literary expression of African women. The definition of "writing" has been broadened to include songs, praise poems, and significant oral texts, as well as fiction, poetry, letters, journals, journalism, and historical and legal documents. The project has been undertaken with the expectation that the publication of these texts will allow for new readings of African women's history.

### PROJECT CO-DIRECTORS AND SERIES EDITORS

Tuzyline Jita Allan, Department of English, Baruch College, CUNY
Abena P. A. Busia, Department of Literatures in English, Rutgers University
Florence Howe, emerita, Department of English, The Graduate Center, CUNY, and publisher, The Feminist Press at CUNY

### EXECUTIVE COMMITTEE

Anne Adams, Cornell University
Diedre L. Badejo, Kent State University
Ann Biersteker, Yale University
Debra Boyd, Winston-Salem State College
Judith Byfield, Dartmouth College
Frieda Ekotto, University of Michigan
Thomas A. Hale, Pennsylvania State University
Peter Hitchcock, Baruch College, CUNY

Nancy Rose Hunt, University of Michigan
Marjolijn de Jager, New York University
Eileen Julien, Indiana University
Judith Miller, New York University
Angelita D. Reyes, University of Minnesota
Joyce Hope Scott, Wheelock College
Marcia Wright, Columbia University
Louise Allen Zak, Marlboro College

### BOARD OF ADVISORS

Jacqui Alexander, Barbados
Belinda Bozzoli, South Africa
Boutheina Cheriet, Algeria
Johnnetta B. Cole, United States
Carolyn Cooper, Jamaica
Fatoumata Sire Diakite, Mali
Nawal El Saadawi, Egypt
Aminata Sow Fall, Senegal
Wanguiwa Goro, Kenya
Asma Abdel Halim, Sudan
Charlayne Hunter-Gault, United States
Adama Ba Konaré, Mali
Joy Kwesiga, Uganda
Françoise Lionnet, United States

Marjorie Oludhe Macgoye, Kenya
Mbulelo Mzamane, South Africa
Lauretta Ngcobo, South Africa
Kimani Njogu, Kenya
Asenath Bole Odaga, Kenya
Mamphela Ramphele, South Africa
Sandra Richards, United States
Fatou Sow, Senegal
Filomena Steady, Sierra Leone
Margaret Strobel, United States
Susie Tharu, India
Nahid Toubia, Sudan
Ngugi wa Thiong'o, Kenya
Aminata Traore, Mali

◆

**Volume 1: The Southern Region** (Botswana, Lesotho, Namibia, South Africa, Swaziland, Zimbabwe)

**Volume 2: West Africa and the Sahel** (Benin, Burkina Faso, Côte d'Ivoire, Gambia, Ghana, Guinea-Conakry, Liberia, Mali, Niger, Nigeria, Senegal, Sierra Leone)

**Volume 3: The Eastern Region** (Kenya, Malawi, Tanzania, Uganda, Zambia)

**Volume 4: The Northern Region** (Algeria, Egypt, Mauritania, Morocco, Sudan, and Tunisia)

# Women Writing Africa

## THE NORTHERN REGION

The Women Writing Africa Project, Volume 4

Edited by Fatima Sadiqi, Amira Nowaira,
Azza El Kholy, and Moha Ennaji

ASSOCIATE EDITORS: Fatima Bouabdelli, Abena P.A. Busia, Sahar Hamouda,
Nadia El Kholy, Marjorie Lightman, Zahia Smail Salhi, and Khadija Zizi

CONTRIBUTING EDITORS: Mohamed El-Sayed Abd-el-Ghani,
Ali Ouahidi, Heba Sharobeem, and Zakia Iraqui-Sinaceur

TEXT EDITOR: Florence Howe

The Feminist Press at The City University of New York
New York

Published by The Feminist Press at The City University of New York
The Graduate Center, 365 Fifth Avenue, New York, NY 10016
www.feministpress.org

First edition, 2009

13 12 11 10 09     5 4 3 2 1

Library of Congress Cataloging-in-Publication Data
Women writing Africa, the Northern region / editors, Fatima Sadiqi . . . [et al.].
p. cm. — (Women writing africa project ; vol. 4)
Includes bibliographical references and index.
ISBN-13: 978-1-55861-589-2 (pbk. : alk. paper)
ISBN-13: 978-1-55861-588-5 (hardcover : alk. paper)
1. North African literature—Women authors—Translations into English. I. Sadiqi, Fatima.
PN849.A3552W66 2009
808.8'035861—dc22
2008009279

Publication of this volume is made possible, in part, by funds from the Ford Foundation and the Rockefeller Foundation.

Cover art: Huda Lutfi, "The Secrets of Silence", 1998. Acrylic, handprints on paper, 90 x 64 cm. Courtesy of the artist and The Third Line.

Printed in Canada on acid-free paper by Transcontinental Printing

# Contents

## ISLAM: SEVENTH CENTURY TO EIGHTEENTH CENTURY

## NINETEENTH CENTURY TO EARLY TWENTIETH CENTURY

## MID-TWENTIETH CENTURY

## LATE TWENTIETH CENTURY

# A Note on the Women Writing Africa Project

The first conversation about this project took place when Tuzyline Jita Allan spoke with Florence Howe at the 1990 meeting of the Modern Language Association. Allan was responding to the recent publication by The Feminist Press of the first volume of *Women Writing in India: 600 B.C. to the Present*, edited by Susie Tharu and K. Lalita. Referring to this landmark publication as a striking example of the untapped potential of international feminist scholarship, Allan pointed to the need for a similar intervention in Africa. Both Allan and Howe knew that a project for Africa like one that the Press had begun for India could testify to the literary presence and historical activity of African women. While Howe did not want to assume responsibility for such a project, she agreed to discuss it at a meeting of the Publications and Policies Committee of The Feminist Press held in February 1991. All present understood that so massive a project would need funding. Howe expected that the Africans interested in such a volume would prepare a grant application, organize the work, and, when it was ready for publication, offer it to The Feminist Press.

Later that year, when Howe was delivering the volume of *Women Writing in India* to the Ford Foundation to thank it for its small grant in support of that project, Alison Bernstein said, "Africa has to be next." A small group—Abena P. A. Busia, Chikwenye Ogunyemi, Peter Hitchcock, Allan, and Howe—met with Bernstein to discuss the possibility of and support for a planning meeting to follow the meeting of the African Literature Association (ALA) in Accra, Ghana, in April 1994. We are grateful to Johnnetta B. Cole, then president of Spelman College, who opened that meeting and testified to the need for such a project and to the commitment of The Feminist Press to publishing women's lost voices. Susie Tharu, who grew up in Uganda, Abena P.A. Busia, and Florence Howe also spoke with enthusiasm about the importance of such a project. They were joined by Margaret Busby and Bella Brodsky, who shared their experiences of editing individual volumes on women in Africa and around the world. In addition, some forty members of the ALA attended these two-day meetings, including Judith Miller, who has been an important member of the committee for the West/Sahel region ever since.

Three primary considerations guided the preliminary discussions of the project. First, in spite of their overlapping agendas, Women Writing Africa could not be an exact replication of *Women Writing in India*. Africa's entrenched oral traditions called for a different response to the discursive modes of expression on the continent. To this end, reconceiving the notion of "writing" marked a conceptual breakthrough in determining how to name a project aimed at capturing African women's creative landscape. "Writing" in Women Writing Africa metonymically suggests a blend of verbal and written forms of expression embodying the experience of African women in envisioning their lives in relation to their societies. The project's matrix of spoken and scripted words represents the creative interaction between living women in the actual world and the flux of history: in short, African women "making" a world.

Women Writing Africa, therefore, became a project of cultural restoration that aims to restore African women's voices to the public sphere. We are publishing several volumes documenting the history of self-conscious expression by African women throughout the continent. This expression is both oral and written, ritual and quotidian, sacred and profane. We are as interested in dance songs and private letters as in legal depositions and public declamations. We hope to foster new readings of African history by shedding light on the dailiness of women's lives as well as their rich contributions to culture. In the end, seeing through women's eyes, we expect to locate the fault lines of memory and so change assumptions about the shaping of African knowledge, culture, and history.

A second consideration focused on the establishment of a framework for conducting research on the continent, and here two hard questions presented themselves: how to think of Africa regionally rather than nationally, and how to set up working groups in those regions and also in the United States. We originally projected five volumes, but conditions in the countries of central Africa led to the decision to produce four representative, rather than all-inclusive, volumes—from Southern Africa, from West Africa and the Sahel, from Eastern Africa, and from North Africa.

Following the Ghanaian planning conference, Abena P. A. Busia joined Allan and Howe as co-directors of the project. Together we formed an Executive Committee of U.S.-based Africanist scholars to serve as a resource and review board for the project's articulated goals, and an Advisory Committee of prominent scholars and writers in the field. Together we planned how to organize both regionally and nationally in the field: Allan would find the scholars in the Southern region; Busia would do the same in the West/Sahel region. For their help with this phase of the project, thanks are due to Debra Boyd and Joyce Hope Scott, who attended the Accra meeting and have continued to make contributions to the project. Then, with Africa-based colleagues, both Allan and Busia began the work of developing research teams in their assigned regions, first by locating national coordinators who would work as a team with their regional counterparts. Later, we proceeded in a somewhat similar manner in the East and the North.

The third consideration essential to realizing the project's promise was funding. The three co-directors wrote the first grant proposal to the Ford Foundation, and within two years, another to the Rockefeller Foundation. Florence Howe then continued the process, writing other grant proposals to Ford and Rockefeller, as well as annual reports to them and to the Board of Directors of The Feminist Press. At Ford, we wish to acknowledge specifically the instigating interest of Alison Bernstein and the support of our several program officers—Janice Petrovitch, Margaret Wilkerson, Geraldine Fraser, and Irma McLaurin. At Rockefeller, we wish to acknowledge the interest and support of Lynn Szwaja, our program officer.

We would like to thank both Lynn Szwaja and Morris Vogel for their support of the French editions of all four volumes. We are also grateful to the Rockefeller Foundation for five Team Awards to its Bellagio Study and Conference Center, where we worked with the editorial teams of the Western/Sahel and the Eastern volumes, and where we wrote drafts for this Note. We want to thank especially Susan Garfield for her administrative support, and Gianna Celli, the director of the Bellagio Center, for her continued interest in our work. We wish to acknowledge Pilar Palacia, who became director of the Bellagio Center during the period of the Northern Region's Team Award. The time spent in Bellagio was invaluable for editors and consultants, all of whom live in different countries and would not ordinarily have had an opportunity to work together on their volumes for an extended period of from two to four weeks.

Without the commitment of the staff and Board of Directors of The Feminist

Press, we could not have done this work. Florence Howe wants to acknowledge the whole staff during the years 1997 to 2000, when she was the publisher/director of The Feminist Press, especially for their support during the weeks when she was holding meetings in Africa. In addition, she wants to acknowledge similar support during the years when she was again, publisher/director (2005) and then publisher (2006–2007).

In particular, and with respect to this volume, we note with thanks Jean Murley's early typing of the manuscript. We want to acknowledge Cary Webb for her painstaking work seeking permissions; Anjoli Roy for her administrative sagacity in trafficking the manuscript and bringing in material from the editors; Jean Casella for her editorial work; Hadassah Gold for her proofreading; Michael Clark for his assistance; and Pascale Burkart for type setting. We are grateful too for the work of publicist Franklin Dennis, and the marketing strategies of Jeannette Petras, as well as Paul Pombo's careful attention to the myriad financial details of this project. We appreciate the continuing faith in this project of the Board of Directors of The Feminist Press, our executive director, Gloria Jacobs, and, finally, we wish to express our thanks to friends and colleagues in the African Studies Association and the African Literature Association for their continuing interest and support.

We want particularly to thank the editorial team of the Northern volume for their patience and understanding as a series of interruptions—some caused by world affairs, others by internal constraints within The Feminist Press—slowed their project's original trajectory.

As always Abena Busia wishes to acknowledge the nearly two decades of support from the Department of English at Rutgers University; especially chairpersons Barry Qualls, Cheryl Wall and Richard Miller for flexible teaching schedules that allowed for extensive travel in Africa. She is grateful for the support of several Rutgers University graduate students, past and present: Carol Allen, Ronal Tyson, Kimberly Banks, Shalene Moodie and Nia Tuckson for assistance of various kinds through years, including teaching and monitoring classes during her absences for editorial board meetings, some of which they also helped plan. For her work on the continent she would like to acknowledge the companionship and guidance of Leila Hessini with whom she journeyed through Morocco, Algeria and Tunisia in 1999 to establish the project in the Maghreb. For the work they did to make those exploratory journeys successful, she would like to thank Fatima Sadiqi and Moha Ennaji in Fez, Louisa Ait-Hamou and Djamila and Daho Djerbal in Algiers, and Nabila Hamza in Tunisia. Her thanks also go to Margot Badran for accompanying her to the Ford Foundation offices in Cairo to ensure the support for this volume, and in planning the first meeting of the Egyptian team. Though not all the people we worked with on that first journey could stay with the project, through them we met most of the women who have, and for that we are grateful. Finally she would like to give her heartfelt thanks to Majorie Lightman for her lessons in diplomacy through the often difficult work on this volume. Her sustaining wit and wisdom at the many editorial meetings frequently made the difference between going to sleep troubled, and going to sleep rejuvenated to face the work of another day.

Florence Howe would like to thank Feminist Press Board members, Helene D. Goldfarb, Mariam K. Chamberlain, Judith Miller, and Shirley L. Mow for their extraordinary support of her work. She would also like to thank Amira Nowaira for her special contributions to this volume. In addition to writing major portions of the Introduction, Amira Nowaira also provided an eagle's eye on the text, as well as help on permissions and on art for the cover. All who have worked on the entire project will be forever grateful to Christiane Owusu-Sarpong for the exemplary translations into French of each of these volumes. The French versions of these volumes are being published by Editions Karthala Press in Paris.

At the end of an intellectual endeavor that began nearly two decades ago, Tuzyline Jita Allan and Florence Howe would like to express once more a genuine sense of gratitude to the scholars in and outside Africa who helped to bring this project to fruition. All four volumes of Women Writing Africa also tell the story of the scholarly vision and dedication that went into providing this bit of essential knowledge about Africa – from grueling travels and field work to compelling theoretical reconfigurations of African women's lives. Finally, for the energy, passion, and celebrated expertise of the Feminist Press editorial team which worked tirelessly to open up a new world of letters that both delights and instructs, Allan is eternally grateful.

We are aware that Women Writing Africa represents the largest undertaking of our lives, a responsibility to set the reality of African women's lives in history and in the present before a world that is only just waking up to their importance. It is our continuing hope that these volumes will give birth to hundreds of others.


Tuzyline Jita Allan
Abena P. A. Busia
Florence Howe
*Project Co-Directors and Series Editors*

# PREFACE

Work on the fourth and final volume of Women Writing Africa has filled a continuous, though often subterranean, stream since 1996. It ran through the peaks that came with publication of volumes I (2003), II (2005), and III (2007); proceeded slowly, with its own eddies and swirls, around the critical boulders that stood in its path; and, as with the other volumes, flowed most smoothly at those moments when we could sit around a table together in Fez (1999, 2001), Malaga (2003), Alexandria (2004), Bellagio (2005), and Washington, D.C. (2007). Between these regional meetings, smaller organizational and national groups convened in different cities of Morocco for the Maghreb, and in Cairo and Alexandria for Egypt and the Sudan.

These smaller gatherings represent the logistical reality of our work. While one of the rewards of the work has been witnessing the commonalities in the lives of women across this broad regional sweep, stretching from the Atlantic to the Suez Canal and from the Mediterranean across the Sahara Desert, the logistics of our lives have meant that in practical terms we have labored in the twin contexts of "Morocco and the Maghreb" and "Egypt and the Sudan." This North African volume comprises a selection of women's writings and orature from six countries: Algeria, Egypt, Mauritania, Morocco, Tunisia, and Sudan. These countries, historically and today, represent a variety of cultures, political systems, and societies; together they include an important segment of Africa's population. In this volume, women in very diverse settings—and over five thousand years of history—express views of themselves and their worlds.

Defined as the coastal region from Egypt to Mauritania, North Africa was historically linked to sister cultures farther south on the continent. At the same time, the region was also celebrated in Western tradition for its Mediterranean and Middle Eastern civilizations. One aspect of the region that singles it out as distinct from other areas of Africa is its long tradition of written records. These writings form a rich inheritance for the modern world, even as they emphasize the distinctiveness of the coastal cultures of North Africa. With regard to the history of women, however, commonalities are as numerous as differences between sub-Saharan cultures and the Northern region's civilizations.

The North has been washed by the waves of the world's great civilizations and empires: Egyptian and Carthaginian; Greek, Roman, and Byzantine; Arab and Ottoman Turk; Spanish, French, Italian, and British. Through the long swing of history, indigenous peoples—Berbers, Egyptians, Coptic Christians—resisted or accommodated themselves to invaders and visitors, sharing their worlds with Andalusians entering the region from Spain, with Jews from across the Mediterranean world, with others from the Levant, with Tuaregs crossing the Sahara and Nubians coming up the Nile.

Over the centuries, North Africa has been home to Christianity, Judaism, and Islam. Although the region has been foundational to the history of Christianity, today all six countries are predominantly Islamic, and all identify themselves as members of the Arab League. Nonetheless, Christians and Jews still live side by side with Muslims in some of the countries of the region. Morocco, for example, counts more than five thousand Jews among its inhabitants, and Egypt has an important population of Coptic Christians. To these, we may add the Hispano-Moorish cultures, with their complex history of religious coexistence and willing or forced conversion, which have immensely enriched dialogue among different communities in Morocco, Algeria, and Tunisia.

Regional conquests and migrations have given North African countries a relatively common history and culture, despite marked differences in certain aspects of their institutions and cultures. In the most recent pre-independence history, for example, Morocco, Algeria, Tunisia, and Mauritania were occupied by France, with the inevitable imposition of French language and culture. Similarly, Egypt and the Sudan were colonized by the British.

The vast majority of the region's population is Arab, though there are groups and communities in the region who may speak Arabic but who do not necessarily define themselves as Arabs. In Morocco and Algeria, where a majority of the population is of Berber descent, some 20 million people speak Berber languages, and they exert significant social and cultural influence.

Today, one can map three major social classes in North Africa: the upper class (rich businessmen, landowners, government officials, and army generals), the middle class (doctors, engineers, university teachers, pharmacists, schoolteachers, and other professionals), and the working class (workers, peasants, shopkeepers, craftspeople, and others). Of the three groups, the working class is the largest, representing the vast majority of the population; the middle class is much smaller, making up less than a quarter of the population; and the upper class accounts for less than 10 percent of the population, although it controls most of the national wealth.

Although the overall rate of those attending school in North Africa has risen remarkably since independence, the attendance rate of girls is still low. In Morocco, for example, it remains 50 percent lower than that of boys, and only one percent of girls who attend elementary school graduate from university (Ennaji 2005, 220). Despite efforts by the state and by civil society, women's social situation is still more precarious than men's. Unemployment is higher among women. Economic and political crises— ranging from deep state indebtedness and instability to military coups and short-term civil violence to civil wars in Algeria and Sudan—usually foster pressures on women to leave employment and stay "safely" at home. As in the rest of Africa, elite women in the Northern region may hold high office or higher education degrees; they may make public political statements and attempt to resist male rule. On the other hand, less fortunate women may be sold into slavery. Historically, as in all of Africa, Northern women worked alongside men to resist colonialism, after which they were urged to return to their former subordinate status; but here, as elsewhere, women have fought for their own right to education, and eventually to suffrage and to elected or appointed office.

One strong distinction in the Northern region is language. Unlike sub-Saharan Africa, where hundreds of native languages coexist (three hundred in East Africa alone), North Africa has relatively few languages. The texts in this volume were translated into English from Hieroglyphic, Hittite, Greek, Latin, Arabic, Berber, Portuguese, and French, with several written originally in English. Though the vast majority of texts were written in Arabic, the official language of all the countries represented, Berber—spoken in Morocco, Algeria, Tunisia, Libya, and Mauritania, as well as in Mali, Niger, and Chad—is the mother tongue of most of the earliest inhabitants of North Africa. Today, about 50 percent of the population speaks Berber in Morocco, 25 percent in Algeria, and one percent in Tunisia. While it is still a vital and living language, many native Berber speakers and progressive forces in the region believe that Berber ought to be codified, standardized, and taught. Recently, in Morocco and Algeria, teaching Berber language has been recognized as important to literacy and basic education (see Ennaji 1997), as well as an important tool for preserving and disseminating popular and women's culture in the region. The wealth of Berber songs in this collection, on subjects from love to military resistance, attests to this reality.

Differences between classical and colloquial Arabic need to be noted. As in the rest of the Arab world, there are at least two varieties of Arabic in North Africa: the classical (or its contemporary version, Modern Standard Arabic), which is used in writing and some formal speaking, and colloquial Arabic, which is spoken by the vast majority of the population across the region, with national differences and other differences reflecting urban and rural usage. As the language of Islam, classical Arabic is a language of high status; the Qur'an was revealed in classical Arabic, which supports great literary and religious traditions. The allegedly "low" status of various national and regional forms of colloquial Arabic can be ascribed to the fact that they are neither codified nor standardized. These distinctions have not been inconsequential for our work, for in some countries, such as Mauritania, the social sanctions against women mastering classical Arabic have been, and remain, strong. The use of classical Arabic can therefore become a highly charged political and ideological issue in the struggle for women's liberation.

## THE FORMATION OF THE NORTHERN AFRICA COMMITTEE OF SCHOLARS

An American scholar of Northern Africa and longtime resident of Egypt, Margot Badran, was on the Publications and Policies Committee of The Feminist Press when the Women Writing Africa project first began, and was among the first group of scholars named to the project's Advisory Board. Early in the 1990s, she visited various archives where women's texts resided and, using her extensive contacts in Egypt and Sudan, she began to identify resources and people with access to them. She also advised that the work was too vast, and the region too disparate, to be the work of one coordinator, and suggested for the purposes of organization and collection that Egypt and Sudan be organized as the eastern sector of the region, and the Maghreb as the western. This suggestion was prescient: Most work on this volume has moved forward from that idea.

The first meeting between Margot Badran and the core of the Egyptian team—Sahar Hamouda, Azza El Kholy, and Amira Nowaira—took place during the Lawrence Durrell conference held in 1996 in Alexandria. Badran presented an overview of the project, and from that time forward several meetings were held to discuss and organize the work. By the spring of 1997 she had also managed to find national co-coordinators to embark on retrieving women's oral histories in the Sudan. Unfortunately, that work could not be sustained and we have since relied on the Egyptian team for those texts we have from the Sudan. Nevertheless, we are grateful to Balghis Badri and Nafissa Abd al-Rahman for those early efforts.

In March 1998, Abena Busia traveled to Cairo to join Margot Badran for a workshop on the ideas and methodologies of the project. What the meeting made clear was the significance of North Africa to the overall project intellectually, logistically, and strategically, as we rethought women's contributions to African history. We had to make clear why the inclusion of North Africa had always been integral to our conception of Women Writing Africa, despite the resistance to what we perceived as an essentially colonialist divide between sub-Saharan and Northern Africa. Our defiance of that divide remains controversial among some communities to this day.

The people assembled at the first Egyptian meeting of the project, held at the American Resource Center in Cairo on 29 March 1998, included Hibba Abugideiri (Georgetown University), Aida Addelmoneim (American University in Cairo), Zubeida Atta (Melwan University), Marilyn Booth (University of Illinois), Laila Abdel Gamad (Cairo University), Hala Halim (Al-Ahram Weekly), Sahar Hamouda (Alexandria University), Taef Kamal (Helwan University), Azza El Kholy (Alexandria University), Nadia El Kholy (Cairo University), Fatma Moussa (Cairo University), and Amira Nowaira (Alexandria University), . Although many of the team from Cairo University subsequently withdrew from the project, we remain grateful to them for their early support and their willingness to place on the table issues that have remained central to our concerns around organizing in the region. Badran also helped recruit Leila Hessini, who at the beginning of 1998 began to search for people in the Maghreb.

The first important meeting of the people who at the time formed the core of the Northern Africa Committee—Margot Badran, Leila Hessini, Amira Nowaira, and Fatima Sadiqi—took place on 10–13 March 1999 at the African Literature Association conference in Fes, Morocco, where they were observers at a combined meeting of the West Africa and the Sahel and Southern Africa committees. This was a landmark meeting in the history of the project, as the two quite separate groups of scholars, from countries in the South and in the West and the Sahel, met to share accounts of their very different kinds of progress. The Southerners had emphasized the location of historical texts, for example, while the Westerners and Sahelians had been collecting oral songs and accounts. These early members of the Northern Africa Committee heard in-depth discussions of these different strategies. The experience offered a sense both of the intellectual excitement and the logistical challenges of this project.

In November 1999, Abena Busia and Leila Hessini traveled to Algeria, Tunisia, and Morocco to meet with those they hoped would head the national committees for the Maghreb. In Morocco, they held a number of meetings with diverse individuals from Rabat, Fes, and Meknès, all invited by Fatima Sadiqi. They included Leila Abouzeid, Najia Ajraoui, Najia Al-Alami, Aicha Belarbi, Khadija Bentouhami, Rahma Bourquia, Fatima Bouzenirh, Annisa Benzakour-Chami, Layla Chaouni, Moha Ennaji, Fouzia Ghissassi, Fatima Hajjarabi, Fatima Harrak, Leila Hessini, Fatima El-Kannoui, Noufissa Lahmil, Hasna Lebbady, Amina Lemrini, Mohammed Monkachi, Rkia El-Mossadeq, Fatima Mouaid, Rabia Naciri, Malika Ben Radi, Linda Rashidi, Fouzia Rhissassi, Fatiha Sadass, Najet Sebti, Souad Slaoui, Nadia Tahri, Zohra Tamouh, and Latifa Toujani. Most of the attendees represented research groups working in such areas of interest to the project as women's written and oral histories and women's literature. During one of the final meetings, a diverse steering committee was established, including Moha Ennaji, Mohammed Monkachi, Fatima Sadiqi, and Najet Sebti.

In Algeria and Tunisia, Busia and Hessini also held several meetings with small groups and individuals, among them Djamila, Daho Djerbal and Louisa Ait-Hammou. Despite the initial enthusiasm of this group, we never managed to establish a continuous working group in either country, nor in Mauritania. We were very fortunate that Fatima Sadiqi invited Algerian scholar Zahia Smail Salhi, professor of English literature and gender at the University of Leeds in Great Britain, to join our team. Similarly, we owe it to the exceptional organizing skills of Moha Ennaji and Fatima Sadiqi that Tunisian and Mauritanian scholars contributed texts to the volume.

The first truly regional meeting of the Northern Committee was held in Fes in May 2001. Florence Howe met with some thirty scholars from Morocco, Tunisia, and

Egypt, most of them coming together for the first time. The Algerians sent texts, though they were not permitted to travel. Some brought texts by men about women and needed to be told that we were searching for the "voices of women." So informed, one of the elderly male Moroccan scholars returned the following day with ancient texts by women. The meeting proceeded rather slowly, since the Egyptians and most of the Americans knew no French, and some of the Moroccans and all of the Tunisians knew no English.

We had planned another regional meeting to be held in Cairo at the end of February 2002, but external conditions began to slow us down. The 11 September 2001 terrorist attacks on the United States had devastating consequences on the whole world, from which the committees of Women Writing Africa were not exempt. These attacks profoundly affected relations between the Muslim world and the West, as have subsequent terrorist attacks in Morocco, Algeria, Tunisia, Mauritania, and Egypt. The launching of the U.S. war on Iraq in March 2003 derailed a joint meeting of the Northern and Eastern committees planned to follow the African Literature Association's conference in Alexandria that March. In addition, Rafik Hariri, Prime Minister of Lebanon, was assassinated while the committee was meeting in Bellagio in 2005. Many other events have affected the project's calendar and timing, including earthquakes in the north of Morocco and in Algeria, regime change in Mauritania, the end of civil war in Algeria, and democratic changes in the region.

## WORKING PROCEDURES

The central objectives of all meetings were choosing texts, meeting the challenges of translation, and preparing headnotes. International scholarly collaboration and deep friendships developed among participants, along with the skills of research, writing, and translation. Team members were conscious that texts should represent the diversity of women in the region. The network of scholars and activities thus created to sustain work on the volume met locally and regionally as often as possible to present their preliminary findings, draw on each other's comments and critiques, share their commitment to the project, and deepen personal bonds with one another. The editors, associate editors, and contributing editors corresponded for years in preparation for this volume.

Two goals guided our search for contributors who would be working members of the team. First, we wanted to create a network of scholars and activists interested in women's voices and agency. Toward that end, we aimed to find English-speaking scholars at various points in their careers. No decision shaped the course of the project as much as this one. To locate editors and authors of texts, we contacted individuals through lists provided by colleagues and friends in the academy. We also contacted a number of nonnative experts who generously forwarded to us the names of in-country colleagues.

## FINAL MEETINGS

In Fes, a Maghreb meeting in 2002 gathered researchers from Morocco, Algeria, Tunisia, and Mauritania. Present were Zoubida Achahboun, Fatima Amhannad, Fouzia Baddouri, Fatima Bouabdelli, Moha Ennaji, Nadia Laachiri, Abdennour Kharraki, Ali Ouahidi, Fatima Sadiqi, Souad Slaoui, Zakia Iraqui-Sinaceur, and Khadija Zizi, from

Morocco; Yansarha Bent Mohamed from Mauritania; Khadija Arfaoui, Nadia Arfaoui, Yamna Benmilad, and Dalinda Largueche, from Tunisia; and Maryam Bouzid, Aicha Ghattas, and Zahia Smail Salhi from Algeria. Similar meetings and seminars were held in Alexandria among the Egyptian colleagues, who by now included Radwa El Barouni, Carole Saad-Escoffey, Mohammed Abd El Ghany, Sahar Hammouda, Laila Helmi, Azza El Kholy, Nadia El Kholy, Amira Nowaira, Hassan El Saady, Heba Sharobeem, and Shadia El Soussi, as well the Sudanese Nada Mustafa Ali. The Egyptian team continued to assume responsibility for finding texts from the Sudan.

The third regional meeting in May 2003—which was held in Malaga, Spain, rather than in North Africa because of security concerns following the 9/11 terrorist attacks—brought together all the current researchers and editors. The meeting's focus was, first, the selection of texts submitted by many colleagues and second, a plan for the research needed to write an introduction to the volume. In February 2004, we gathered again in Alexandria, to examine new texts and do the rigorous selection necessary to whittle down the mass of material we had gathered. The editorial team was both excited and sobered as we finished the selection of texts, prepared the first draft of a table of contents for the volume, discussed a few remaining lacunae, and began initial assignments for the writing of the introduction.

The Northern editors held what we believed would be our last meeting in Bellagio, Italy, in February 2005, our goal being to rewrite headnotes, refine translations, and most significant of all, plan and write a first draft of the introduction. Over endless cups of coffee, we worked out timetables and charted the table of contents, as well as the conceptualization, collaboration, writing, and editing of the introduction. Those two weeks together consolidated the intellectual groundwork for the book. The core editorial board in Bellagio—consisting of Fatima Bouabdelli, Abena Busia, Moha Ennaji, Sahar Hammouda, Florence Howe, Azza El Kholy, Nadia El Kholy, Marjorie Lightman, Amira Nowaira, Fatima Sadiqi, Zahia Smail Salhi, and Khadija Zizi—also divided responsibilities for continuing the search for still missing texts.

The final work on this volume was disrupted and delayed by certain internal constraints at The Feminist Press. Therefore, it was not until May 2007, when several of the editors were going to be in the United States, that these editors, together with Abena Busia, Florence Howe, and Marjorie Lightman, were able to meet for three days in Washington D.C. Abena Busia, Moha Ennaji, Florence Howe, Nadia El-Kholy, Marjorie Lightman, Amira Nowaira, and Fatima Sadiqi reviewed a dozen new texts brought in by the editors, discussed the status of other texts and headnotes, and reviewed assignments for the writing of the preface and introduction. This group also confirmed a schedule that would quickly move this volume into print.

## THE COMMITTEE

During the project's nine years, many changes have occurred in the lives of its participants. Two authors have died: Malika El Fassi and Lalla Amina Lamrania. There have been many job changes, two retirements, one wedding, and two divorces, and Abena Busia spent almost eight of those nine years battling to get her Ghanaian daughter admitted into the United States. Many editors and authors have faced serious illnesses or surgeries. Khadija Zizi lost both parents in 1999, and Moha Ennaji and Fatima Sadiqi lost their fathers in 2006 and 2005 respectively. Many of the editors still bear heavy responsibilities for the care of elderly parents, small children, or other family members. But through all of this, the commitment to the work of this volume has remained firm.

For us—and we speak for all the members of the team—working on this project has been a source of joy and inspiration. It has been a unique, challenging, and gratifying experience to be able to immortalize the voices and contributions of North African women, many of whom have, through the centuries, been forgotten or neglected by patriarchal societies, but who have, nonetheless, shown resistance and resilience, standing strong to create change and demand respect.

The names that appear on the title page of this book represent those of us who worked on the project through to its completion. For a host of different personal and professional reasons, we lost a number of people on the way; we have tried to acknowledge all of them here. If we have omitted any of their names, we wish nevertheless to thank them sincerely for their contributions. Our sincere expressions of gratitude go to all our colleagues on the national committees for starting the work of collecting, translating, and editing the immense number of texts from which we were able to select the texts published in this volume. Their initial work was crucial to writing and annotating the headnotes. In particular, our heartfelt gratitude for the early work of Margot Badran and Leila Hessini, who laid the ground for the work we have been able to do. This volume would not have seen the light of day were it not for the constant enthusiasm and scholarly efforts of Tuzyline Jita Allan, Abena Busia, and Florence Howe, to whom the entire editorial board is grateful for initiating the project and for bringing it to completion.

We are extremely grateful to the funders and sponsors of the project, namely the Rockefeller Foundation and the Ford Foundation. We would like to thank very warmly the Rockefeller Study and Conference Center at Bellagio, Italy, as well as The Feminist Press at the City University of New York for their support of this project. Finally, we recognize the positive impact and encouragement of our sisters and brothers in the Southern, Western and Sahel, and Eastern African volumes, whose work was published before ours and who served as a source of inspiration and motivation for us to carry on with our own tasks. This is indeed an achievement of which we as a team can be very proud.

Moha Ennaji
Abena P. A. Busia

# INTRODUCTION

This fourth volume of Women Writing Africa portrays the ebb and flow of women's lives in North Africa over the course of more than five thousand years. Over the millennia, from Egypt and the Sudan to Morocco and Mauritania, women sometimes ruled empires and sometimes ruled the men who ruled empires. From Pharaonic ancient Egypt through to the rise and fall of the Greco-Roman world and the advent of Islam, women challenged the proscriptive limits of custom and female propriety to lead armies, accumulate wealth, and exercise authority over kin and public affairs. Some were merchants engaged in international trade; some owned vast swaths of land in multiple provinces of their empires. At all times and throughout the region—as in all of Africa— women farmed. Many also sold produce in village stalls or from baskets balanced on their heads. More often than not they were unpaid workers on the land and in their households. And many were slaves. A few women were literate; most were nonliterate.

Rich, poor, well-connected, orphaned, free, and slave women in North Africa participated in the greatest cultural transformations of recorded history. The poets, scholars, and religious teachers among them documented the emotions and conflicts of their times. Nonliterate singers of songs and tellers of tales who were respected and even feared in communities where the written word was rarely invoked have preserved an oral tradition of intergenerational transfer that has assured the continuity of women's memories. Together, they have left a body of literature about the momentous events in women's lives, from marriage songs, laments, and celebrations of valor to women's yearnings and religious rites. They have left a record of women who celebrated Isis and women who led the first ascetic movement into the Egyptian desert to foster the early Christian search for salvation. And in the seventh and eighth centuries, when poverty and tribalism supplanted the institutions of civil authority across North Africa, women's stories tell of joining the new conquerors from Arabia, who brought Islam with them.

With the advent of Islam, a new society emerged from the older Greco-Roman–dominated world. As in preceding eras, class and race, along with ethnicity and religion, controlled women's lives. Land remained the basis of wealth and status. Islam incorporated advanced ideas about women's independent ownership of property, which were also at the center of Roman statutory law. Islam also intensified and codified ideas about women's seclusion and about men's right to polygamy, both practices that shifted relationships between women and men. While Islamic conventions with regard to literacy redefined women's possibilities for achievement, especially among the wealthy and those who might manifest political influence, the greatest number of women continued, as they had for millennia, working the land in households that suffered the vagaries of floods, famines, tax collectors, and invading armies.

In the nineteenth century, Europeans colonized North Africa. Women gained a new self-consciousness that transformed their efforts for enlightenment and empowerment from individual achievement to collective action. A fervent sense of nationalism combined with the quest for self-empowerment, turning women into members of an organized resistance to colonial power. Education became the avenue to a new articulation of women's place in the public spheres of North African society. During the later twentieth century, in their newly independent nations, women struggled to change the social order in accord with their own altered consciousness, which demanded equity and equality. The twenty-first century finds their efforts unfinished, but still moving forward.

This book is not the first effort to give North African women a voice—nor, we hope, will it be the last. Nonetheless, it is unique. Its geographical and chronological scope allows an unusually long perspective that suggests both continuity and change. Insights about social class, family organization, literacy and orality, education, autocracy and democracy, colonialism and postcolonial independence wrap around female experience with sorrow, fear, loss, and pleasure to mark moments in time and place. Often, these North African women also transcend their own time and place, and illuminate for all women their past and, possibly, their future as well.

## THE ANCIENTS, FIFTEENTH CENTURY BCE TO FOURTH CENTURY CE: FROM THE PHARAOHS TO THE ROMAN EMPIRE

From the Nile valley in the east to present-day Mauritania in the west, Punic, Egyptian, and Greco-Roman cities and cultures thrived. In the centuries before Islam, the North African coast was also a center of early Christianity. In the texts that open this volume, women's own words provide glimpses into the worlds in which they lived, worked, ruled, and worshiped in ways that have sometimes been forgotten, although today they may also seem at times surprisingly familiar. These early texts cover a period from the fifteenth century BCE to the fourth century CE. Some explore the relationships between life and death. One contains a series of love poems. Two contain petitions for redress. Others are private letters, and several reflect aspects of ancient law that affected the lives of women. Few in number, they can do no more than suggest a variety of experiences, an array of emotions, and the kinds of relationships that dominated lives in the distant past and, in some measure, contribute to the present.

### Death and Birth

The early texts reveal a consciousness about the world that marked ancient times as significantly different from the more recent past. Societies across the millennia, in the ancient world of North Africa before Islam, wrestled with death's heavy presence. Death was everywhere visible as an ever-present and immediate threat. Open sores or lingering colds often led to opportunistic secondary infections, and rendered fatal a minor injury or a malady that would be easily eradicated in modern times. Infections from water, poorly cleaned food, or intimate contact with animals were endemic among the wealthy, the well-born, and the poor alike. In the first century BCE, when the Latin poet Catullus described a beautiful woman, he noted her full set of teeth, uncrossed eyes, skin clear of pock marks, and straight limbs—all attributes that in many parts of the world in the twenty-first century are simple measures of good health (Catullus 86).

Just as intimacy with death was the leitmotif of life, the ancients sought to preserve the presence of their lives long after death. Hatshepsut, the pharaoh who ruled during the famous Eighteenth Dynasty of Egypt, proclaimed her accomplishments "for all eternity" in an inscription to celebrate the restoration of a temple and the revival of its rites. (See "My Falcon Rises High," fifteenth century BCE.) She stared death in its face, and left behind a legacy that reaches across time. Unabashedly, she reveled in her deeds that brought good fortune to her people and security to her reign. It was no accident, however, that Hatshepsut chose to restore a temple and endow its performance rites. Fortune was fickle. Since neither goodness nor effort might alone ensure good luck, it was wise to appease the gods with attention and obeisance. Only a performance of respectful rites would earn the reward of good fortune. This "do ut des"—give and get— was everywhere the sought-for bargain between apparently frivolous gods and vulnerable people.

The search for good fortune was matched by awe for the mysteries of birth and rebirth. In a world that lived only one harvest away from starvation, even in the best of times, the annual Nile flood that fertilized the soil was essential for the next year's crops. Similarly, the vagaries of annual rainfall determined the availability of food in Carthage and all along the coastal areas of North Africa. Women's fertility was a mirror of the awesome mystery of the annual renewal of the earth. Conception was a mystery to the ancients—and indeed, remained so well into the modern period. Clearly, new life was created between a man and woman, but what exactly happened inside the body of a woman? What assured people that it would continue to happen?

These questions and fears informed ancient religious practices, among which were the rites of Isis. From the Old Kingdom of Egypt in the third millennium BCE to the fourth century CE, Isis was at the center of a powerful and widespread religion. The songs of Isis belong to the genre of poetic lamentation that women sang throughout the ancient world, and still sing upon life's momentous occasions in North Africa. Lamentations link women, fertility, and the life of the community. They speak to a world in which personal grief merges with communal burdens of sorrow and regret. They reflect the ancient belief that if women were able to bring forth life, then they were also best able to mourn its end.

The rites celebrate death and resurrection in the story of Isis, her husband and lover Osiris, his violent death at the hands of Seth, and the amazing birth of Horus. Although the story grew in complexity and developed an extraordinary number of variants over the course of the centuries, the central tale of Isis collecting the pieces of Osiris's body and making him whole so that he could father Horus was never lost. Nor did the narrative lose the centrality of women in the performance of the rites. This volume includes a section of one variant. (See "Lament of Isis and Nephtys," c. 300 BCE.) Following the text of the lament sung by Isis and her sister Nephtys as they collect the body parts of Osiris are instructions for the women who would have been the actors in a ceremonial reenactment (Cumont 1956, 72–102).

Respect and honor for the dead, however, consisted of more than rites and lamentations. For the ancients through the early Christian period, the dead were never quite severed from the living. They remained very much a part of everyday life and obligated their descendants to ritual practices and emotional connections. An inscription on a flat stone of a tomb in ancient Mauretania (on the coast of present-day Morocco), erected by a daughter for her mother, captures a sensibility about life and death widespread for many centuries, and perhaps not unfamiliar today. (See "To the Memory of Aelia Secundula," 299 CE.) The mother died at the age of seventy-two, and the stone tablet was added to her tomb some time after her death. It marked the occasion, following the family's most acute period of sorrow and lament, when the dead and the living could once again share food. The last line reads, "Yes, she who once fed us is now done with food forever" (Hedlund 1966, 49).

## Rules and Family Networks

Vulnerabilities that made death a daily companion also encouraged the formation of rules, possibly to provide at the least an illusion of order and control. Ancient societies had rules for everything, since every action of daily life was fraught with danger. Which foot you first put across the lintel of the doorway and on which side of the street you walked, whom you greeted and how they greeted you—all were circumscribed by rules to avoid the "evil eye" and gain favor with the gods. Today, in countries on both sides of the Mediterranean, the blue-eyed talismans to ward off the "evil eye" are readily available in the markets, and the residue of ancient beliefs clings to stories of black cats, walking under ladders, or killing a ladybug.

Rules framed the organization of social relationships. By and large, societies along the North African coast have always revolved around families, organized into networks bound by blood, contract, and service. These networks assured that people had food, that land had seed, and that in both good and bad times, friendship and allegiance to one another would remain secure. The networks were hierarchical, with lesser families and individuals, including ex-slaves, allied with more powerful families. At the apex of family networks were a small group of families that, regardless of the city's form of civil authority, constituted a controlling oligarchy (Veyne 1987, 71–94; Syme 1960, 10; Dixon 1992, 161–63).

Women were critical to these family networks. A code of honor regulated relationships within the family and with dependents and patrons. Laws upheld honor with procedures and sanctions. Since women were the primary means for the intergenerational transfer of wealth and honor, law paid them special attention. By the time of the Romans, there were multiple sophisticated civil codes among peoples living in the cities of North Africa. Different tribes and various ethnic, national, and religious groups domiciled in the same city had their own codes of law and court systems. Sometimes individuals could seek judgments under the legal system most advantageous to their situation. The relationship between place and law changed after the beginning of the third century, when the emperor Caracalla extended Roman citizenship to most categories of peoples resident in the empire. Thereafter, except for some few exempt categories, anyone could choose to claim rights under Roman civil law. Thus, some form of legal marriage, inheritance rights, and personal control over wealth became available to most women (Schulz 1969, 102–41).

## Inscriptions and Marriage Contracts

In Roman times, many women exercised independent control over small farms or vast landholdings that spread across the provinces of the empire. Elite women, who influenced politics throughout the ancient period, appear in men's histories, letters, and speeches. Such women are admired or vilified in men's poetry and plays. Inscriptions, especially on tombstones and often in women's words, also offer insights into the lives of the less wealthy (Fantham et al. 1994, Index). Since the late nineteenth century, scholars have collected and studied thousands of inscriptions about both women and men, from every part and period of the ancient Greco-Roman Empire, and published them in the *Corpus Inscriptionum Latinarum* and in the *Corpus Inscriptionum Graecae*. Additional specialized collections include inscriptions from early Christianity and the Byzantine period. Newly explored sites continue to contribute to the ever-increasing number of tributes to virtue and valor in memorial and funerary inscriptions, which, although often brief and usually formulaic, praise rich and poor women alike for modesty and faithfulness and praise men for strength of character and valor. Fabia Bira Izelta, for example, inscribed on a statue in 54 CE a tribute to her husband, Marcus Valerius Severus, a prominent figure and army commander in the city of Volubilis, in present-day Morocco. She noted that her husband, a Roman soldier, had married her, a local woman without Roman citizenship. Later their marriage was recognized under Roman law and the title to his land assured. As a widow with marital contract in hand, she was a Roman citizen landowner.

At all times and throughout the cities on the coast, the social order was hierarchal and inclusive, and the types of socially acceptable sexual unions differed in accord with the partners' personal status. Marriage contracts were restricted to the propertied classes, which were concerned with the control, ownership, and transfer of property to the next generation. Such contracts also included the terms of marital dissolution, since divorce was always a possibility and the early death of one of the spouses a probability. Two fragments from an extraordinary correspondence about marriage were written some time in the fourteenth century BCE by Ankhesen-pa-Atun, who had been widowed at an early age by the pharaoh Tutankhamun, and who was eager to arrange for her future. Caught in the crosscurrents of domestic political struggles, she twice approached the ruler of the Hittites, a potential invader of Egypt, with a proposal of marriage to one of his sons. She stated her reason clearly: She had no sons of her own, and needed to ensure succession. (See "A Proposal of Marriage," fourteenth century BCE.) Ankhesen-pa-Atun was a daring woman who gambled in foreign policy, and she lost when the son the Hittite king sent to her died mysteriously, perhaps at the hands of her enemies in court.

Centuries later, when the Greeks ruled Egypt, another woman, Olympias, set out the terms by which she would agree to a marriage. Separated from Ankhesen-pa-Atun by status and by more than a millennium, Olympias was a woman of some wealth but by no means among the elite, let alone a ruler. Her terms, however, had the quality of a ruler's self-assurance. She offered her prospective husband a measure of her wealth, but she would brook no other woman in her house or in her man's life, neither as second wife nor as mistress. Moreover, her husband-to-be had to agree never to father a child with another woman. Effectively, she demanded fidelity in exchange for her goods, her bearing of his children, and her proper behavior as his wife. Unlike Ankhesen-pa-Atun, Olympias appears to have succeeded, although it is possible that we simply have no record of her divorce.

The two examples cited are markedly different, although both portray men and women in relationships identifiable as marriage, and notable for their focus on legitimate lineage and property. The inscriptions also suggest that, in the absence of property or the need to insure a legitimate line, there may have been no reason for a marriage contract. Those who had no property, often freed slaves or their children, were the most numerous members of the population in ancient cities from Alexandria to Rome. They bore children, lived together, and died, recognized as a couple within their communities. The collections of inscriptions from gravestones throughout the Greco-Roman Empire, including North Africa, indicate that social custom affirmed stable relationships, despite the absence of legal contracts, and that widespread monogamous and caring relationships existed among people who, before 212 CE, lacked the right to connubium under Roman law, and possibly the equivalent right under local law as well (Schulz 1969).

### Slavery and Families

Almost by definition, civil codes organized around the family in ancient societies attended to rules about slavery (Dixon 1992, 2–5; Schulz 1969, 33–48). Slaves were not only a fact of life, owned by men and women alike, but were often the measure of wealth. The terms of slavery in these societies were harsh: Slaves could not engage in actions or relationships recognized by law, and children of a slave woman were slaves of her master or mistress regardless of their paternity. But slavery was not determined by either race or ethnicity. In a world in which war was prevalent, life fragile, and the spoils of war included human beings, slavery was largely viewed as an accident of fate.

Ancient literature contains many examples of well-educated slaves who held administrative positions and who worked with independence and authority, sometimes as guardians for women. By the first century BCE, the transformation of guardian into agent was already well under way. The elite-born Roman Terentia, who brought into her marriage with Cicero the wealth he needed for a public career, ran the family's business affairs, using a Greek slave as her agent (Lightman and Lightman 2007, 308–09). Not a century later, Tacitus's history of Rome under the Julio-Claudian Dynasty exhibited a high-born Roman's scorn of an imperial civil service filled with slaves and ex-slaves, including both men and women. Little did he know that only a couple of centuries more and ex-slaves could become emperors (Tacitus 1982, passim).

Most of the legal codes, and certainly Roman law, allowed for the manumission of slaves as far back as we have legal information. Roman law also accounted for the integration of former slaves into the larger family after they were freed. The continued relationship was essential, since nowhere in the ancient world was there an impersonal labor market of any size. The networks of families, whose wealth rested on landed estates, were the society. Belonging to a family of status—or marrying into one—was the preeminent social determinant. In the ancient imagination, family was understood as the only significant form of social order.

Hence, freed men and women joined together to establish associations—called collegia in Latin—which functioned like families. Adapted from the practices of elite communities, collegia were primarily burial societies, which assured that the proper rites would be practiced even with limited resources and in the absence of blood kin. Collegia also provided such other services as regular dinners, loans, and, just as important, personal relationships with other people who shared a common place of birth or affiliation in a specific household, or who found themselves alone and domiciled in the same town (Schulz 1969, 95–102).

### The Status of Women and Literacy

In the ancient world it was better to be a wealthy woman than a poor man. On the other hand, far more than men, women suffered the fecklessness of fate. Along with widows, many married women were left on their own for long periods of time to maintain the family and the family business and to negotiate their way through law and social custom. Men had to travel, and travel was slow and dangerous. In the first century BCE, the Roman statesman Cicero wrote letters to his wife and daughter over several years during a single business trip. Nor was that unusual or restricted by class, as one private letter from Ptolema to her brother indicates. (See "Letter to a Brother," second century CE.) In the letter, she describes all she has done with regard to their fields and crops, but she clearly needs him for the family's business before officialdom, and urges him to return from his travels as swiftly as possible.

Ptolema's letter is unusual not because she is a woman, but because it has survived. In the literature of the ancient world, the loss of the female side of many correspondences is common, and maddening. Yet, despite all the losses, it is possible to affirm women's literacy and active participation in literature, since men's surviving correspondence makes clear that the women they wrote to read and responded with letters of their own. The existence of literate women in North Africa, moreover, reaches back to the Old Kingdom and the first of the female pharaohs, in the third millennium BCE.

From the seventh century BCE, a letter to Sappho of Lesbos, written by her brother, who was visiting Naucratis, Egypt, suggests the frequency of travel and the breadth of trade, as well as the existence of women's literacy. Aspasia, the friend, lover, and wife of the great fifth-century Athenian Pericles, was said to have a circle of women friends interested in the study of philosophy, belying the usual portrait of Athenian women. In the third century BCE, Cornelia, the mother of the Gracchi brothers, who sought to promote land reform in Italy, was described by men as literate. Cicero's regular correspondents included his wife Terentia and his daughter Tullia. The Latin love poets from Catullus to Ovid addressed women in their poems. Included in a collection of Tibullus's poetry from the first century BCE was a book of poems by Sulpicia, a young woman of his circle. A large trove of correspondence, either addressed to women and/or with references about other women who could read and write, dates back to the beginning of the Roman Empire. Livy, the historian of the first century CE, noted the correspondence that passed between North African women and Livia, an independently powerful woman who was also the wife of Augustus. In the second century, the younger Pliny wrote letters to women as he traveled across the empire on imperial business. At the end of the fourth century CE, the Christian saint Augustine, bishop of Hippo, near Carthage, corresponded with women in the region and beyond; another saint, Jerome, traveled widely and maintained a mammoth correspondence that included letters to dozens of women (Lightman and Lightman 2007, passim). The examples are so abundant that one may conclude that literacy was no less widespread among women than among men.

## *Papyri and the Letters of Ordinary Women*

Beyond such evidence, we may want to attach special importance to the letters of ordinary women engaged in the everyday struggles of life. Written on papyrus, many of these letters were the detritus of a literate world, thrown away onto garbage heaps and remaining buried for centuries. In excavations of Greco-Roman settlements in the Fayum, near the Nile in Egypt, during the early decades of the twentieth century, these papyri began to surface. Thousands of fragments were recovered and more continue to appear. A consortium of Western universities bought those available from Egyptian bazaars, while others rest in Egypt's museums and libraries, untranslated and separated from matching pieces that may have gone to other libraries and museums around the world.

This volume has been enriched by the inclusion of several texts from papyri that have already been studied and translated. Aurelia Thaisous, for example, writes to the prefect of Egypt, requesting the right of independent control over her affairs. (See "A Mother Seeks Legal Independence," 263 CE.) Proudly she notes that she is literate and can write. The laws upon which she bases her request were the Lex Iulia de Maritandis or Julian laws (18 BCE) and the Lex Papia Poppaea (9 CE), both enacted during the reign of the first Roman emperor, Augustus (Schulz 1969, 105–08).

Aurelia stands, in this volume, as the modern woman of the ancient world, a Roman citizen entitled, through the ius tria liberorum (three live births) section of the Julian law, to independent legal personhood after giving birth to three live children. Bearing three live children was no small feat in a world in which a woman faced death each time she gave birth and in which a successful live birth was less frequent than a miscarriage. Just as important, for the first time among Mediterranean cultures, the Augustan laws allowed women to attain legal independence in a manner analogous to men's coming of age. While there are no substantial data to suggest that, as a result of this law, the population actually increased, Aurelia's papyri provides evidence that women acted to gain this freedom, which by the third century CE became widely available throughout the empire and could often be obtained even without the prerequisite number of children.

Until the middle of the 1960s, conventional scholarly wisdom routinely ascribed the genesis of these marriage laws to Roman women's reluctance to bear children, beginning sometime in the first century BCE, when a population decline in Italy became evident after a century or so of civil wars (Balsdon 1963, passim). While more recent revisionist scholars have found little evidence that women avoided childbearing, they have found ample evidence that women successfully executed new responsibilities. Using such evidence as the Laudatio Turiae, a long Italian funerary inscription from the late first century BCE by a husband about his wife, as well as the letters of Cicero and the histories of Livy and Tacitus, scholars have concluded that women increasingly gained a public face during the years of revolution and the emerging empire. Further evidence also suggests that the new independence of women extended to cosmopolitan cities on the North African coast. Alexandria in the east and Carthage in the west were powerful and wealthy centers of population with extensive hinterlands that were the agricultural breadbasket for Italy (Lightman and Lightman 2007, 189).

### Sex and Sensuality

Between law and religion, there was pleasure. Sex was the electricity of the ancient world. The pleasures of sex were no less mysterious than the mysteries of fertility. Sex was, however, both immediate and available everywhere, free and for a price. In the corners around the stadium, which was a fixture of every city and even any town of size, were prostitutes who charged as little as the entrance ticket. In the bordellos found throughout the cities were partners costing more or less. But the pleasures of sex were not a male preserve. Women's sexuality was central to rites that celebrated Bacchus or Dionysus, which were practiced throughout the ancient world, following the path of Greco-Roman rule and urban culture (Otto 1973, 174).

What little women's poetry we have from these times exudes sensuality. Sappho, in the seventh century BCE, reveled in the beauty of women's bodies. Marriage songs, sung by young women before their weddings, celebrated touch, smell, and sound (Fantham et al. 1994, 13). In the first century CE, Sulpicia, a young well-born Roman, wrapped her poems around a longing for Cerinthus, her lover. Similarly, in the love songs included in this volume—far older poems from Egypt under the pharaohs—the voices of young women express sensual pleasure.

> My longing for you is my eye-paint;
> When I see you my eyes shine.
> I press close to you. . . .
> (See "Love Songs," 14th–12th centuries BCE.)

The everyday language of cosmetics, as well as images borrowed from the wind and from flowers in the garden, becomes the language of eroticism. Above all, such ancient poetry by women captures a pursuit of pleasure marked by exuberance and an absence of either inner guilt or fear of the gods.

### Early Christianity and Monasticism

Into this sexually unrestrained world Christianity came early to North Africa. But even as the littoral areas welcomed Christianity, the prosperity that had made the region the breadbasket of the Mediterranean began to decline. Centuries of exploitation by absentee landowners, complicated by warfare and perhaps also a change in the patterns of precipitation, had seriously eroded the fertility of the land. A bifurcated society soon emerged. On one side were extremely wealthy families who owned vast tracks of land, worked by thousands of slaves or dependent farmers. These rich families, often a mixture of Christian women and pagan relatives, were cosmopolitan travelers with connections at the highest levels of imperial society. On the other side were local populations, who suffered severely (Brown 2000, 285–96).

In the late fourth and early fifth centuries CE, preaching and writing in Hippo, not far from Carthage, in today's Tunisia, Augustine described the Christian world, in which he was a political force and theological giant. He offered insights into the growing divide between the Latin and Greek parts of the Roman Empire; the new possibilities Christianity offered women; and the divide between rich and poor in North Africa. His own orthodoxy engaged him in constant disputes with Christian sects that surfaced in North Africa. In his youth a Manichean, he attacked the Donatists and the Pelagians, whose adherents were especially numerous in North Africa and at one time or another challenged the domination of the Roman Church. Both groups also attracted women, especially wealthy women who retreated to North Africa in the fifth century as the Germanic Goths advanced on Rome. Melania, Albina, and Proba, who were among the wealthiest women in the empire, went from Rome to estates that bordered Augustine's bishopric, where he vainly sought to redirect their faith away from personal salvation through asceticism to the acute economic distress around them (Lightman and Lightman 2007, 14, 216, 275 ).

In his Confessions, Augustine wrote about his mother, Monica, a devout Christian married to a pagan, and about the consort and friend with whom he spent fifteen years before his own conversion and baptism by Bishop Ambrose of Milan. He also wrote about women domiciled in his household who carried out the daily work of the monastery in which he lived in Hippo, as well as the disbursing of charity throughout the area. Above all, however, Augustine wrote about his love for God. In the most powerful section of his Confessions, he described the discovery of love as essential to the search for spiritual purity that would bring him closer to God.

### Voices of a New Female Consciousness: Perpetua and Syncletica

Before Augustine returned to North Africa from Italy and became a bishop, Perpetua, a young Punic Roman, wrote—while in prison—the earliest extant account by a woman of her "passion" for God. (See "I Am a Christian," 203 CE.) She had stood firm as a Christian, refusing to make the traditional offerings before the statue of the emperor. Despite the pleadings of her father and the call of her newborn son, she went willingly into the arena to die. What Augustine presented in the Confessions with elegance and subtlety, Perpetua captures with blunt naïveté. She records three visions. Using the language of love and sensuality, borrowed from pagan poetry, she mixes everyday images with literary references, many from the Bible, to describe her passionate commitment to the Lord. Her Christian commitment insists on a willingness to die, since only through death can she find true union with God.

Perpetua willingly surrenders her infant son out of a devotion to God, her eternal lover. While her determination may have perplexed most of her contemporaries, one cannot overestimate the historical importance of Perpetua's restatement of the relationship between death and love, which had been a constant in literature throughout the long history of North Africa. In abandoning her child, Perpetua's action tears in two the historical relationship between women and fertility that had grounded ancient religion, law, and social custom. Over the course of the next three centuries, a Christian vision would largely supplant paganism along the coast of North Africa. At the same time, however, the action also would reveal a new set of possibilities for women's lives.

Among the new possibilities opening for Christian women were lives of celibacy, perhaps the first widely available alternative to life in conjugal families. By the fifth century, circles of women who lived together, practiced a modest lifestyle, studied Christian texts, and engaged in good works could be found from Rome to Constantinople, and in the cities and towns of North Africa. The center of the emerging monastic phenomenon was in the Egyptian desert, where men and women retreated to live alone and in like-minded communities, formulating rules translated and adapted by travelers and pilgrims who spread them to other parts of the world.

Christian women began to choose celibacy as early as the first century BCE. We have many examples, including Thecla, who was converted to Christianity by the Apostle Paul, and Petronilla, who is regarded as the spiritual daughter of the Apostle Peter and Irene. During the second, third, and fourth centuries, women who wanted to remain celibate could become reclusive in at least three different ways. Some continued to live with their families but in rooms of their own; others lived together in what were known as houses of virgins. And still others established their living quarters on the outskirts of a city or ventured out of the city by going to the desert. According to Jo Ann McNamara, "Clearly the real virginal life was only fully sanctioned by Orthodox writers after women made it a practical reality" (1985, 1).

Syncletica was such a Christian woman. Born into an Alexandrian family that appeared to have been comfortably situated, she was said to have distributed her inheritance among the poor and taken herself and her blind sister to live in the desert. Over a long life as an anchorite Christian, she spoke about women's struggle for salvation. While condemning none, she urged women to choose communion with God and to seek salvation through a focus on the spirit and not on the material goods of life. (See "Let Women Not Be Misled," fourth century CE.)

Syncletica's sayings have been read continuously as part of a rich Coptic Christian literature. Among the earliest Christians, Coptic communities in Egypt claim a continuous existence since their establishment by the Apostle Mark in the middle of the first century CE. Their historical experience of Christianity included not only the monasteries founded by Anthony and Pachomius, but also the coenobitic communities of women. Syncletica's sayings belong to the tradition of the Desert Fathers, a revered group of early monastic Christians. Collected into a standard work, the Apophthegmata Patrum (Sayings of the Elderly Fathers), these have been widely available in the Coptic Church and to scholars throughout the last millennium. Syncletica's sayings were spoken in the Coptic language, the language of the Egyptian desert, but some were collected and written in Greek by Egyptians such as Athanasius; in the sixth century, they were translated from Greek into Latin. Only recently, however, have Syncletica's sayings, as well as those of other women who chose asceticism, become widely available in the west, as part of a more gender-inclusive study of early Christianity, which now includes the "Desert Mothers" of North Africa (Clark 1983, 115–53).

The women of the fifth and sixth centuries are present in the works of such churchmen as Jerome, the archbishop of Constantinople John of Chrysostom, Gregory of Nyssa, Paulius of Nola, and Palladius (Clark 1983, 204–45; Lightman and Lightman 2007, 241, 198). Collectively, their references contribute to an understanding of the friendships between elite Christian men and women, as well as the frequency with which these men and women traveled across the Mediterranean from Italy to Egypt, as well as to Palestine and Constantinople. The elder Melania and her granddaughter, the younger Melania, as well as Paula and Eustochium—all from Rome—visited the desert in Egypt and lived for some part of their lives in North Africa, establishing and endowing monastic houses that opened their doors to men and women from across the empire (Lightman and Lightman 2007, 213, 216, 129, 248).

### The Christian World Before the Advent of Islam

As early as the second century CE, Clement of Alexandria, one of the leaders of the new Catechetical School in Alexandria—which was meant to supplant the older pagan Museum and Library, and to which Syncletica was affiliated for a short time—freely accepted women students. Despite physical differences between men and women, they were spiritually equal, Clement wrote: "As when there is sameness, as far as respects the soul, she will attain the same virtue," and yes, they may both "equally philosophize, whether male or female in sex" (Clement, Stromata IV, 59, 4–60, as quoted in Meskeen 1997, 54–55).

Perpetua and Syncletica represent, for this volume, voices of a new female consciousness. The personal autonomy and control over wealth enjoyed by citizen women rested on changes in Roman civil law and on social mores given shape by their Christian vision. For many Christian women, the heavy burdens of work, family obligations, and death, felt for thousands of years, became transformed into a joyous pursuit of personal salvation that nourished the spiritual life of their historically evolved civil autonomy.

More than two centuries ago, in his famous *History of the Decline and Fall of the Roman Empire* (1776), Gibbon placed responsibility for the fall of the empire on the altar of Christianity. He believed that Christianity's promise of resurrection, and its pacifism, sapped the civic energies of pre-Christian Rome. No feminist, he shared with other scholars the view that the great republican women of ancient Rome had given way to lustful women in search of pleasure and power. Today, while one may easily demolish his antiquated views of women's lives, one must also note his essential insight: Christianity altered the construction of women's lives and changed the balance of gender in the ancient world. When Clement was once mocked because he admitted women to study, and then mocked again with the charge that Christianity was "a philosophy of women," his response was, "Yes, Christianity is a philosophy of women as much as it is a philosophy of men, for Christ came to save all people alike" (quoted in Masry 1979, 10).

### The Transition from Christianity to Islam

After the sack of Rome by the Visigoths in the early fifth century, North African migrants who returned to Rome included very wealthy Christian women. Such an influx of wealth, however, failed to ease the distressed economy, and resident populations were unable to rise above economic disaster. Poverty and subsistence farming brutalized life, and the mitigating institutions of schools, churches, and public charity were also insufficient to ameliorate the distress.

Germanic invaders from the north claimed the mantle of Roman control over North Africa during the sixth and seventh centuries. But the civic culture that had defined ancient urban life—from communal baths to libraries—failed to regain vibrancy under their authority. Roads and irrigation systems in the countryside disintegrated and the coastal region west of the Nile valley, which had once helped feed the population of Italy across the sea, could barely feed itself. Similarly, in the rich Nile valley, famine became a frequently recurring reality of life. Increasingly, over the next several centuries, tribal and family associations became the bulwark against roaming hordes that threatened settled life. Christianity ceased to expand. The Christian search for salvation faltered in the face of violence and starvation.

Into this dispirited region came the Arabs, repeatedly invading until they conquered. They triumphed not only over military resistance, but also over Christianity. They carried Islam with them, and made Islam the basis for a security that promised to tame warfare, brute force, and increasingly widespread human slavery. The success of Islam in North Africa, inseparable from the search for order, led the victorious Arabs to invent a new society.

## ISLAM, SEVENTH CENTURY TO EIGHTEENTH CENTURY: DISCONTINUITIES AND CONTINUITIES

The Arab conquest of the whole of North Africa, which began with Egypt in the year 636, brought about profound and far-reaching changes in social structure, as well as in the basic concepts and assumptions governing gender relations. The societies to which the Arabs brought their Islamic creed were by no means liberal or broad-minded with regard to women. Compared to the Arab newcomers, according to Leila Ahmed, the prior societies were "more restrictive toward women and more misogynist; at least their misogyny and their modes of controlling women by law and by custom were more fully articulated administratively and as inscribed code" (1993, 67). The new religion, far from challenging the existing patriarchy, came instead with a new set of patriarchal rules that harmonized with—and gave a new impetus to—the subordinate status of women. In fact, the ease and rapidity with which the mores of the conquering minority were adopted by the majority of the population, especially in Egypt, would suggest the presence of continuities rather than a sudden rupture with the Greco-Roman and Christian past, particularly in the ways women were situated within society and the family.

It would be misguided, therefore, to view the early centuries of Islam in the northern region of Africa as introducing a misogynous mind-set, despite the presence of gender segregation and the stereotyping that went largely, though not wholly, unchallenged. Women across the region maintained a degree of autonomy that found expression not only in their ability to inherit property, carry out monetary transactions, and emancipate slaves, but also in their literacy. Women continued to be actively engaged in the cultural and religious lives of their communities. On the other hand, women were now defined primarily by their sex and their relationships in marriage, rather than by their own occupations or wealth. And while their presence may have been felt in decision-making processes, women were not often openly acknowledged as having political influence.

### Economic Hardship and Protest

Women suffered acutely during the famines that frequently struck northern Africa during the early Islamic period. Commander Amr Ibn Al-'as's conquest of Egypt in the seventh century turned the region into a province of the vast Islamic empire. As in Roman times, it would soon serve as a breadbasket for the whole empire. The hardships of Egyptian life during the Umayyad and Abbasid periods are clearly reflected in a letter written by Om Makina when she apologizes that "a shortness of money" has prevented her from sending certain objects to her friend. (See "Letter to a Woman Friend, eighth century.) Another letter makes a more urgent case: "Please tell my father," a woman urges her brother, "to send me some clothing fast, since by God Almighty, I am going about unclothed." She also adds that she is hungry and even thirsty. (See "A Plea for Money," c. 9th to 10th century.) Such letters are but a few of the historical sources documenting the series of economic crises Egypt suffered from the seventh to the eleventh centuries, due in part to shallow Nile flooding but more significantly, perhaps, to the mismanagement and internal feuding of the ruling powers (Nariman Ahmed 1999, 92–93).

The chronicles of the period include reports of women voicing their grievances openly, even challenging authority. During a severe famine in the eleventh century,[1] for example, one woman decided to take a precious necklace to the market to barter it for flour. While she was on her way home after accomplishing her mission, a group of people gathered around her and tore away most of the flour, leaving her with only a handful. Once she had baked it into a tiny loaf, she went back to the market, stood close to Bab Zoueila, one of the gates of Cairo, and raised the loaf high for people to see, screaming loudly: "To the people of Cairo, praise is due to our ruler Al-Mustanssir, who turned our life into paradise. May he always shine on all of you. It is thanks to him that I managed to get this tiny loaf of bread for a thousand dinars." The woman was neither too frightened nor too repressed to air her grievances, with bitter irony, in public. In response to her public complaint, the story goes, the caliph ordered that wheat be taken out of storage and sent to the markets, which immediately reduced the price of flour (Nariman Ahmed 1999, 95).

During the fifteenth and sixteenth centuries, severe famines, natural disasters, and political instability also hurt the Maghreb, and drove many to flee their countries for Spain and Portugal. This was the heyday of the Inquisition, when many Muslim migrants were forced to renounce their religion and adopt Catholicism. The testimony by Ana de Melo documents the coercion exercised by the Catholic Church in Portugal on Muslims, under threat of punishment and death. (See "Escaping the Inquisition," 1559.) De Melo's voice resounds emotionally with submission to an authority that could not be confronted or challenged openly.

### Veiling, Seclusion, and Polygamy: Sharp Turns in Women's Lives

The parameters around which women could exert influence were shaped in part by the degree of their seclusion. The veiling and segregation of women were formally adopted by Islam around the end of the eighth century. Directed toward urban women of propertied families, the requirement that they cover their bodies, hair, and faces marked their status as different from poor and working-class women and slaves. Veiling as an aspect of class distinction evidenced by dress was not a new phenomenon in the ancient world. The stola of Roman matrons was an analogous symbol of social distinction. A plethora of visual artifacts, moreover, suggest that ancient women across Mediterranean cultures frequently covered their heads when outdoors, and in some other circumstances. Jewish women covered their hair routinely for ritual acts, and into the modern period some shave their hair and wear wigs after marriage. But on the whole, the formal adoption by Islamic society of women's veiling—and its required extent—marked a significant change from the past.

Also different was the degree of seclusion for women in Islamic society. Elite Athenian women in the fifth century BCE were encouraged to remain within the family compound, although their presence at religious festivals—and, by the fourth century BCE, in courts of law—suggests that the limitations on their urban movements may have been exaggerated by Thucydides in his report of Pericles's oration about women. Similarly, in the early centuries of the Roman Empire, elite women were encouraged to remain at home, remembering that "home" was, in the Marxian sense, the center of production, and that the core of a city-state's social and economic life rested on a household economy. But by the sixth century CE women were not restricted or secluded, although city streets were not generally considered a safe place for women, nor was travel between cities safe. Still, the Islamic introduction of seclusion as a class marker was new, and served to limit women's geographical universe. While the domestic sphere had always been a gendered space, seclusion turned it into the only sphere of elite women's lives.

Similarly, polygamy, which allowed men to marry several wives at a time, was not entirely new to ancient cultures. Although both ancient Athens and Rome held marriage to be a monogamous relationship, ancient Persia did not, nor were the royals of Egypt, before or after the advent of the Greeks, monogamous. Polygamy, formally instituted by Islam as it was practiced by the Prophet Muhammad and sanctioned by Qur'anic utterances, was also conditional: Men were forbidden to marry more than one woman if they might prove not able to be fair to any of their wives.

Men in the ancient world were always free to engage in sexual relationships with slaves, providing they owned them or had the agreement of the slave's owner, since they were, by definition, property. Similarly, under Islam's polygamy, it was possible for men to have sexual relations with slave women captured in war or purchased. At no time before Islam, however, was it usual for slave or free women concubines and wives to share domestic space. The Roman matron ruled her house, and no other wife or concubine was welcome. Indeed, she could get a no-fault divorce and the return of her dowry plus interest if her husband brought another woman into her house without her consent.

### In the Corridors of Power: Contesting Political Authority

Despite—or perhaps because of—the twin institutions of veiling and polygamy, many women were able to wield political power, both covertly and openly. Numbers of renowned women in the region influenced political affairs, as mothers, sisters, wives, slaves, or concubines of ruling men. In the eleventh century, Sitt al-Mulk (The Lady of Power), for example, the daughter of Imam Al-Aziz and the older sister of the Fatimid ruler, Al-Hakim bi-Amr Allah, ruled both directly and indirectly. Born in Morocco in

970, she was reported to have been endowed with an overpowering, even ruthless, personality. She never married, and dedicated her life to politics as adviser to her brother, who came to power fairly young. Like many other women exercising power in the Fatimid period, she interceded on behalf of others, and also had agents who worked for her in regions abroad that were affiliated with the Fatimid Caliphate, and briefed her on political and economic situations in these regions.

While historians have accused Sitt al-Mulk of plotting with a senior statesman to murder her brother, little evidence supports this accusation. Her management of state affairs after the disappearance of the caliph in February 1020, however, suggests the extent of her control. By keeping her brother's disappearance a closely guarded secret, she succeeded in safeguarding the stability of the country. Until the declaration of the death of the caliph and the appointment of Al-Hakim's son, Ali Al-Zhahir, as the new caliph, she remained sole ruler of Fatimid Egypt. Even after the appointment, she retained full control, since the new ruler was young and inexperienced. As regent to the young Al-Zhahir, she carried out virtually all the functions of caliph, directing the affairs of the empire effectively as regent, holding the formal title of "Naib Al Sultan," or Deputy to the Sultan (Nariman Ahmed 1999, 196–201).

While Sitt al-Mulk's father was a Muslim imam, her mother was a Christian of Byzantine origin, and she was proud of her dual heritage. Indeed, her regard for Christians and Jews at times endangered her life. Once, reports have it, she delivered a speech to the people of Egypt promising justice and equality. She also allowed women to go out of their homes to manage their own affairs, despite injunctions forbidding such activity that had been handed down by her eccentric brother. She was also keenly aware of the political climate, and intelligent and careful enough not to violate any important rules. It is to her credit that by the time she died, in 1024, she had brought order and stability to the state.[2]

### A Slave Turned Ruler and Other Politicians

Of all the successive rulers of Egypt and neighboring areas during the Islamic period, one name towers above others: Shajarat Al-Durr, whose name means "tree of pearls," was one of the very few women in Islamic history to ascend to the throne. Originally a slave of Turkoman descent, she became the wife of Sultan Al-Salih Najm Al-Din Ayyub (Jackson 1999, 181). Although she ruled Egypt only for eighty days in her own name, Shajarat Al-Durr held virtual power for seven years. Her life story epitomizes the violence and challenges facing women who sought and wielded power at a time when power was deemed the exclusive right of men. In the course of her political career, she was a military leader, a mother, a sultana or empress, and a conspirator.

In 1249, the crusading French army under Louis IX attacked Egypt. Shajarat Al-Durr organized the defense of the realm, acting as regent for her husband, the last ruler of the Ayyubid Dynasty, while he was away in Damascus. Soon after Al-Salih Ayyub's return, he died, but Shajarat Al-Durr decided to conceal the fact of his death, saying that he was ill and sending food to his tent. She was thus able to continue to lead in his name. After her husband's death was announced in 1249, his son Al-Muazzam Turanshah became ruler. Shajarat Al-Durr retained control, however, and defeated the crusaders at Damietta. The leaders of the army plotted against Turanshah and had him murdered, and on 2 May 1250, the army put Shajarat Al-Durr on the throne, thus beginning the Mamluk Dynasty.

As Sultana, Shajarat Al-Durr had coins struck in her name, and was mentioned in weekly prayers in mosques: "May God bless and keep Salih's consort, the Queen of all Muslims, the inviolable Lady of Earth and Heavens, the one with the beautiful veil and venerable stature, the mother of the late Khalil, and the wife of Sultan Al-Salih Najm Al-Din Ayyub." This suggests that the religious establishment in Egypt looked with favor on the accession of a woman to the throne, in view of her extraordinary talent at rallying the forces of the nation around her at a time of crisis and foreign invasion. Gender was temporarily overlooked in the interest of national unity. But the Abbasid Caliph in Baghdad, who still held power over Egypt in matters of state, took a very different position. Upon learning of the appointment of a woman as Sultana, he sent a famous message: "If there are no longer any men left among you, let us know and we will send you one." The message convinced Shajarat Al-Durr to marry and turn over power to her husband, at least ostensibly, in a strategic attempt to secure the caliph's recognition of the Mamluk Dynasty. Historical accounts of Shajarat Al-Durr's life vary a great deal in their treatment of her; her story has become the stuff of legends, to the point where it is almost impossible to disentangle myth from fact.[3]

Another imposing female figure in the political history of North Africa is Assayida al-Hurra. Born in 1493 to a family of Muslim exiles who returned to North Africa, along with thousands of others, after the Christian reconquest of Andalusia, she was the daughter of the governor of Chefchaouen, a small town in the north of Morocco. Al-Hurra married another prominent exile, Al-Mandri, who oversaw the rebuilding of the city of Tétouan, earlier destroyed by the Spanish. When he died, Assayida al-Hurra had served as the governor of Tétouan for more than thirty years. She led a large fleet in the western Mediterranean, with which she fought the Spanish and the Portuguese. In 1520, she captured a governor's wife and caused great damage to Portuguese shipping. According to Ibn Azzouz-Hakim, she was "the only woman to have had almost sovereign power in Morocco" (1982, 128).

Assayida al-Hurra's second marriage was also unconventional, since widowed women were seldom sought after by men, unless they were powerful in their own right and capable of providing wealth and security along with power (Louh 1975, 164). Sultan Ahmad Al-Wattasi of Morocco needed al-Hurra's ability to defend the Northern region, and he needed her diplomatic experience and skill (Véronne 1956, 225). Their wedding took place in her hometown of Tétouan, away from the capital in Fes. After the ceremony, she reportedly remained in her political position in Tétouan, while her husband returned to the capital.

Lalla Khnata Bint Bakkar was an equally formidable woman, who, as wife of the great Sultan Moulay Ismail, who reigned from 1672 to 1727, was active politically. Like Sitt al-Mulk, Shajarat Al-Durr and Assayida al-Hurra before her, she wielded tremendous power and was intimately involved in the affairs of state. Her commanding and imperial voice may be heard in two letters in this volume, addressed to the Flemish state and to the people of Oujda. (See "Two Political Letters," 1729, 1736.) These letters were written during the turbulent years following her husband's death (which included multiple brief reigns by the son who did not take her counsel) and before the ascension of the grandson she nurtured, Mohammed III, who took the throne in 1757 and laid the foundations of modern Morocco. Signed by herself in her capacity as "Mother of Our Sovereign," the letters clearly demonstrate the ability of an eighteenth-century Muslim woman to control not only her domestic world but also some aspects of foreign policy. She addresses the people of Oujda with a great deal of self-assurance, allaying their fears in the face of threats from invading Turks. "In any case, you are our subjects," she reassures them. "So don't fear anyone." In her letter to the Flemish, she confidently negotiates peace with a foreign state.

Another woman wielded tremendous power from behind the scenes in late eighteenth-century Morocco. Shehrazad, one of the widows of Sultan Sidi Mohamed Bin Abdellah, who was the grandson of the writer of the previous letters, was greatly involved in the struggle for succession. She managed to protect the throne for her son, who became Sultan Suleiman. He ruled from 1792 to 1822, and consolidated the modernization work of his father. The letter to her son, Salama, included in this volume, was written sometime during the two years it took to settle the issue of the successor. It is a document that combines the personal and the public: She tries to give sound advice to her son by reminding him that they must submit to the will of God. "Should the throne become yours," she tells him with a great deal of conviction, "no one will take it away from you, but if it goes to somebody else, then you will not have it." (See "Struggle for the Throne," 1792.) This is the voice of a mother fearing for the life of her son, as well as the voice of a seasoned politician who is well aware that one should never overreach, and that accepting the status quo may at times be the only reasonable option.

## *The Tradition of Female Scholarship*

In spite of the various restrictions imposed on women during many centuries of the Islamic period, available information suggests that many upper-class women were literate, wrote poetry, harbored literary ambitions, and competed with men as scholars in their own right. Women were educated initially in the family, but they could have access to male scholars and teachers later on in life (Leila Ahmed 1993, 113). Outstanding women became teachers themselves, instructing both men and women on various subjects such as Hadith (the Prophet's sayings), fiqh (jurisprudence), and poetry. One such woman was Hajjar, a renowned Hadith scholar born in 1388. In her advanced age, Hajjar taught without a veil, a phenomenon perhaps suggesting that women were not always segregated. Although it is evident that scholarly interactions between men and women were fairly common, it is not clear where and how this kind of interaction took place (Leila Ahmed 1993, 114).

Generations of scholars of the Islamic past, however, have generally ignored the existence of women scholars and turned a blind eye to their contributions. This omission seems particularly striking since medieval Muslim writers wrote extensively on the subject (Hambly 1999, 4). In the fourteenth and fifteenth centuries, Al-Haafidh Shihabuddin Abul-Fadl Ahmad ibn Ali ibn Muhammad, better known as Ibn Hajar Al-Asqalani, and Shams El Din Muhammad bin Abdel Rahman Al-Sakhawi both wrote biographical accounts of many of the eminent women of their times and described their intellectual contributions, particularly to the field of religious teaching. Ibn Hajar Al-Asqalani, the author of renowned Hadith commentaries and biographical dictionaries, was married to Anas Khatun, who was a Hadith expert in her own right, having been granted an *Ijaza*, or certificate, from the well-known scholar Zayn al-Din al-'Iraqi.[4] She gave celebrated public lectures to crowds of learned men, including Al-Sakhawi, who, describing how students congregated around her, also expressed his pride at having had the chance to study with her (Abdel Razik 1999, 31–35). In *Al-Durrar Al-Kamina* (Hidden Jewels), Ibn Hajar mentions fifty-three women Hadith scholars with whom he had studied, while Al-Sakhawi notes that he had received sixty-eight *Ijazas* from women teachers.[5]

This volume includes a striking example of the tradition of female scholarship in the poetry of Fatma-Setita, born in Cairo in 1451. (See "Consolation and Other Poems," 1492–1494.) She had a unique friendship with Al-Sakhawi, with whom she exchanged poems and letters expressing her views of current events. He included these verbatim in his volume of biographies of famous women. In one of her letters to him, confessing her dismay about gossip circulating about her, she responds with a line of poetry, underscoring not only her defiance but her unflinching self-assurance and unswerving confidence.

What would it matter to the Euphrates
If some worthless dogs waded in? (Abu Bakr 1998, 135)

By comparing herself to the Euphrates River, she highlights her dignity and intellectual richness. For an inhabitant of sixteenth-century Cairo, a reference to the Nile might have been more immediate and intuitive; but an allusion to the Euphrates points clearly and forcefully to her embrace of the whole legacy of Arab culture, acknowledged to emanate from Baghdad, for centuries regarded as the center of Arab enlightenment and culture. This legacy, she implies, is as accessible to her as it is to men of letters.

### Oral Islamic Teaching for Nonliterate Women

The transmission of Islamic teachings across the North African region has always been polyvocal. One common means for ensuring the proliferation of oral texts was popular Sufi poetry in local vernaculars (Schimmel 1982, 21). Only recently have scholarly studies begun to explore and acknowledge the significance of women's participation in the oral transmission of Islamic teachings (Berkey 1992, 29). In the Sous region of southwestern Morocco, for example, women have been significantly involved in the teaching of Islamic rituals through chanting and poetry. The Berber text in this volume, recorded in 2004, may stretch back through many centuries. In this chant, women first offer allegiance to Muhammad, whom they praise as "O Master of Lights, O Flower of everyone who is born." (See "The Flower of All Earthly Creatures," 2004.) They go on to portray themselves—"the women of the world"—as "standing at the gate" of paradise. Conscious of their status, even proud of it, they chant, "We are better than those who always have what they need." They add to their prayers the work they do: the grinding of grain, the bearing of and caring for children, even the water they draw for others. The specificity of their chant, which adds their domestic lives to the tradition of Islam, provides still another example of women insisting they be heard.

### Legal and Economic Agency

Researchers of the pre-modern period in North Africa have often confronted the unfounded assumption that the drive toward women's emancipation and participation in public life was altogether a Western import. Emerging evidence, however, suggests that for many centuries, women across the region functioned more autonomously than previously assumed.[6] Numbers of women throughout the medieval period worked as peasants, matchmakers, nannies, midwives, bath attendants for other women, beauticians, tattoo-makers, and singers. Because Islamic law permits women to own and inherit property, middle-class women were often engaged in buying and selling their own real estate, renting out shops, and lending money at interest (Leila Ahmed 1993, 110). They were often recorded as contributing to public life "in terms of participation in the marketplace as buyers, sellers, and investors" (Marsot 1995, 134).

Extant documents from the period also confirm that upper-class women could own and emancipate slaves, without permission from other members of their families. In a document included in this volume, Astour Heyoh, a Coptic Christian living in eleventh-century Egypt, chooses to free her own slave. Hers is the only signature on the document, officially registered as a legal proof of emancipation that cannot be contravened or revoked at a later date. (See "Freeing a Slave Woman," 1003.)

## Ottoman Court Registries

The court registries of the Ottoman period in Egypt, roughly spanning the sixteenth through the eighteenth centuries, contain a huge number of documents pertaining to the daily social and economic lives of Egyptians and such other citizens as Syrians, Moroccans, Mamluks, Turks, and Greeks. These Ottoman court registries, moreover, are especially valuable as a source of information about the legal and economic status of women and attitudes toward gender in general. Many of these records pertain to commercial transactions, wills, religious endowments, and social interactions. They often show the process of justice, in which the plaintiff, male or female, appeared before a denominational judge. In the absence of a secular, civic legal code, judgments were based on, and derived from, the principles and precepts of one of the four major sects of Sunni Islamic thought and jurisprudence (Hanafi, Hanbali, Maliki, and Shafi'i).

In all these documents, we see women resorting to legal action to obtain and safeguard their rights. Women appear to have had ready access to the legal system, in which they could succeed in making their voices heard. In one document, for example, two women file a complaint against a man who owes both of them money, which the court orders him to repay. When he refuses, he is put into prison at the behest of the women. In another document, Om-el-kheir, the daughter of Mansour, agrees to become the financial guarantor of her husband.

> She pledged to guarantee her husband's payment of his debt to Sheikh Abdel Kader son of Aly, son of Moussa. . . . Her husband, Ibrahim, son of Khalil, son of Mohamed . . . owed Sheikh Abdel Kader nine hundred coins [nisf] of a legally documented original amount of two thousand and six hundred coins. Sheikh Abdel Kader granted her the extension she asked for provided she guarantees, by legal decree, that the husband will pay him half a pound daily because she cannot guarantee payment otherwise. . . . Should she fail to continue the payment for thirty consecutive days, her right to an extension will become null and void, and she will have to pay the whole sum immediately. (Court Registry 1566)

Although in North Africa, where Islam predominates, the right to initiate divorce was, and still is, a male preserve, a woman's right to severance—becoming legally divorced from her husband—is supported by Islamic Shari'a law, with the proviso that she return to the husband the dowry and gifts that he had given her on marriage. In a document from eleventh-century Egypt, Sara, daughter of Abboud Al-Nahid, a married woman with a young child, requests and obtains the right of severance from her husband. (See "Using the Right to Severance," 1069.) She clearly indicates that her request does not result from any ill treatment by her husband, but simply from her feelings of "aversion for his person." Since both she and her husband are "afraid of inviting God's wrath in disobeying His precepts," a tacit reference to the possibility of engaging in extramarital relationships, she therefore renounces her financial severance rights, such as alimony and back dowry.

In another document taken from an Ottoman court registry, Fatima, daughter of Salem Ben Aly, seeks divorce and obtains it by returning to her former husband all the money he had spent on her. In this case, while the marriage contract had been signed and was therefore legally binding, the marriage itself had not been consummated.

> Fatima, the virgin daughter of Salem Ben Aly, better known by the name of El-Zeidaq, asked her husband Shehab El Din, known as Shoheib El Etkawy, to divorce her by making a first-time divorce pronouncement, before consummating the marriage. This divorce would be granted on the condition that she return the alimony he had paid her which is twenty-five dinars. He complied and gave her the divorce she asked for under the financial conditions agreed upon. She has thus become legally divorced from him, and is now free to take control of her life. Consequently, she will not remarry him except by a new contract with new legal terms. . . . (Court Registry 1595)

## Philanthropy

Women's intimate involvement in the affairs of North African societies may also be noted through their numerous contributions to the *waqf*, deeds of endowment or financial donations in support of the building of mosques, shops, and other charity projects. Afaf Lutfi Al-Sayyid Marsot, who studied endowments and estates registered in the registry office in Cairo over the forty-year period from 1749 to 1789 found that 30 to 40 percent of *waqfs* were made out in the name of women (1995, 55). Similarly, hundreds of women's *waqf* documents can be found in the Beylic registers, the Beit Al-Mal, or the "Money House," and the legislative Court of Algiers.

Many women donated huge sums of money for specific public purposes—especially for the *waqf* of the "Great Mosque," and especially to the "Haramayn" or Mecca *waqf*, and the *waqf* of Saints' Tombs and Zaouias, with the "Haramayn" contributions being most substantial.[8] All such documents attest to the fact that women of the region were more autonomous and respected for their financial power than has been widely acknowledged. By the nineteenth century, according to Marsot, women of almost all social groups "had access to all forms of property. Neither gender nor the seclusion of the elites prevented women from participating in the economic life of the country" (1995, 134).

## Slavery

During the sixteenth and the seventeenth centuries, two powerful, religion-backed empires, the Ottoman and the Spanish, competed for territory and military supremacy in the Maghreb. Within this period, many male and female Maghrebians were captured and made slaves (Ennaji 1999, xxii, 166). While historical documents abound with stories of Christian renegades, very little has been recorded about female slaves of the Maghreb, the great majority of whom were Berber and Muslim.

The 1568 Morisco Revolt—launched by the Muslims of southern Spain who had been forced to convert to Christianity—and the battles that followed filled Spanish markets with Berber women slaves. Both men and women of wealth traded in female slaves. Trade contracts and franchising charters, as well as records of baptisms, marriages, and deaths in the archives of Granada for the years 1560–1579 attest to the existence of these slave women. The Maghrebian cities cited in the documents as sources for the enslaved North Africans are Oran, Tlemcen, Algiers, Mostaganem, Constantine, Birzete, Tunis, and Melilla (Majalla Al-Manahil 1981, 87). Oran, where the Spanish presence lasted from the beginning of the sixteenth century until the end of the eighteenth, is the city most often cited.

The majority of female slaves were captured when they were children, six to twelve years old. By the time they were eighteen or twenty, these young girls had been turned into "obedient" Christians. No slave could marry without a certificate of baptism. Few rebelled by escaping, for they faced imprisonment if they were caught. Occasionally such rebellion was violent, and the punishment equally so: In 1631, one Berber woman slave who had tried to kill her masters was hanged publicly in a square in Granada (Majalla Al-Manahil 1981, Volume 21, 29).

The issue of slavery runs like a subterranean current through the life of this region throughout the millennia. The dearth of texts of the nineteenth century also means there is a dearth of references to this subject precisely at the moment when it was once again shaping the life of the region, becoming racialized in ways it may not have been in the Classical Age. It was a controlling reason behind both the Mahdist revolt of 1881–1899, between the Sudanese on one side and the Egyptians and then the British on the other, and it leaves its lasting legacy in the split between the North and the South in Bilad-al-Sudan—the "Land of the Blacks." The existence of slaves at this juncture in the nineteenth century would influence a range of issues governing the establishment of early education for girls, whether secular or religious, and this historical undercurrent persists to this day in such crises as the current turmoil in Darfur (Green 2007).

### The Personal, the Passionate, and the Intimate

During these long centuries, just as they had in the Classical period, women expressed passionate and intimate feelings through writing both poetry and letters, and, for those without literacy, through song. Some of the written texts have survived. Mahriyya Al-Aghlabiya, for example, mourns her dead brother in a manner reminiscent of al-Khansaa, the classical poet of seventh-century Arabia renowned for her great elegies. (See "Two 'Lost' Poets," ninth century and eleventh century.) In memorable lines, she describes the depths of her desperate grief.

> As the earth eats away
> the dead, so
> does sorrow eat
> loving women away.

Similarly, Khadija Bint Kalthoum writes of the man she loves, whom her brothers have rejected as her suitor: "They drove us apart," she says, and "tore us to pieces."

In Andalusian Spain during the tenth and eleventh centuries, when Muslims controlled large portions of the Iberian Peninsula, Muslim and Jewish women poets "thrived," according to Abdulla al-Udhari (1999). While in the eastern areas of the Islamic empire the freedom and equality of women were being seriously challenged, in Andalusia they could break taboos, certainly in their poems, and perhaps in their lives as well. Love and passion were central in the poetry of these women. The tenth-century Muslim woman Hafsa Bint Hamdun, for example, wrote:

I have a lover who thinks the world of himself, and when he sees me off
he cocks up: "You couldn't have had a better man."
And I throw back: "Do you know of a better woman?"
(Al-Udhari 1999, 156)

The eleventh-century Jewish poet Qasmuna Bint Isma'il ibn Yusuf ibn Annaghrila described her fear of missing her opportunity for sexual experience.

I see a garden ripe for picking, but no picker's hand reaching for it.
It's painful to watch my youth passing me by, leaving the
unmentionable untouched.
(Al-Udhari 1999, 178)

Also in the eleventh century, Wallada Bint al-Mustakfi, a daughter of the Umayyad Caliph Mustakfi and one of the most beautiful women of her time, is both witty and scornful about her lover's infidelity:

If you were faithful to our love you wouldn't have lost your head over my maid.
You dropped a branch in full bloom for a lifeless twig.
You know I am the moon yet you fell for a tiddly star.
(Al-Udhari 1999, 188)

The eleventh-century poet I'timad Arrumaikiyya is explicitly erotic as she implores her lover to fulfill her desires.

I urge you to come faster than the wind to mount my breast and firmly dig and plough my body, and don't let go until you've flushed me thrice.
(Al-Udhari 1999, 196)

In this volume, the twelfth-century poet Hafsa Al- Rakuniya, who left Spain to settle in Marrakesh, celebrates carnal love in exquisite language. "I praise those lips," she writes, "From them I've drunk nectar / more delicious than wine." (See "Love Poems," 1160.)

### Marriage and Love: Convergence or Divergence
Marriage as the socially legitimized outlet for feelings and passions during the medieval period was, in practice, often based on material considerations and sometimes even on coercion. Younger women were frequently given in marriage to older men, which resulted in increased cases of infidelity. In his fifteenth-century work, *The Bright Light Concerning the People of the Ninth Century*, Shams El Din Al-Sakhawi describes an encounter with a dissatisfied wife who admits to him that she is physically attracted to handsome young men, especially when she thinks of her older, quite repulsive husband. When Al-Sakhawi asks this woman why she "hated going out to market," she replied, "When I look at all those good-looking men there, I feel drawn to them. When I get home, I cannot bear to look at my husband any longer."

Although the woman's words have come to us filtered through the consciousness of Al-Sakhawi, the narrative provides a rare glimpse into women's daily lives in the region during the middle ages. Perhaps women were not as segregated and confined to the home as is generally agreed. The woman's frankness breaks another stereotype, for she is astonishingly unapologetic about her fascination with the beauty of men and proclaims, "Just as men feel attracted to beautiful women, so are women equally attracted to handsome, clean-shaven young men."[9]

## NINETEENTH CENTURY TO MID-TWENTIETH CENTURY: COLONIAL OPPRESSION AND "WOMEN'S AWAKENING"

By the early nineteenth century, when Napoleon's campaign against Egypt came to an end, all of North Africa, except for Morocco, was under Ottoman rule. For much of the century, Algeria and Morocco were dominated by tribal conflicts and a war against the French occupation of Algeria, which began in 1830. From 1830 to 1847, Morocco joined Algerian nationalists in fighting the French, and for the rest of the century, Morocco's tribal structure and religious tradition ruled when it could, for there were continual conflicts between the Ottoman sultan and Berber tribes.

We have found no nineteenth-century North African women's texts surviving, at least in part because most women were nonliterate and, we speculate, elite women, who may have been literate, were confined to the harem. We speculate also, as many historians have, that the nineteenth century was much harder on women—and not only in Egypt—than earlier centuries, when seclusion was perhaps not as strictly enforced and education not as thoroughly forbidden.

Thus, we can only glimpse, from accounts by men or by European women, the activities of some North African women in the nineteenth century. For example, a young Algerian Berber woman, Laila Fatma N'soumer, born about 1830, led a wide-scale rebellion against the French army in the middle of the nineteenth century. We do not have her view of this action, though she was an educated woman as well as a religious and national leader, because after her arrest the French burned down her library and confiscated all her possessions. She died in prison at the age of thirty-three.

### Oral Texts in Berber and Arabic
The Arab conquest included the homelands of the Berbers, present from the earliest histories of the region. Multilingual, often nomadic, and at varying times embracing pagans, Christians, and Jews, a well-preserved Berber oral tradition includes, for example, the sixth-century story of Kahina, a woman warrior from the Aures Mountain area of present-day Algeria, who fought the invading Arabs to a standstill in 690. Within five years, however, when the fragile coalition she controlled fell apart, Kahina committed suicide, commending her sons to the Arab camp with instructions to adopt Islam.

The oldest oral texts in this volume probably date from the early nineteenth century, although they were first discovered in the 1920s by an intrepid Moroccan scholar Mohammed al-Fassi, who produced a small collection of these songs in French. The songs were called La'rubiyat, a metathesis of Al-Ruba'iyat, the classic Arabic Bedouin poetic genre. They comprise an exclusively female poetic genre that originated in Fes, Morocco, and continues to be performed. (See "La'rubiyat, or Women's Songs," early nineteenth century.) During the nineteenth century, the countries of the Maghreb maintained strong cultural links with the former Islamic kingdoms of Andalusia in Spain, strengthened by the mass emigration of Muslims and Jews fleeing the Christian Reconquista of Spain and settling in Fes and other urban and rural areas in North Africa. Situated only seven miles from Europe, Morocco was open to the external world but closed to anything that would shake its internal political and social stability. Thus, it was in the carefree city of Fes that the songs of La'rubiyat could be born.

These songs, sung in colloquial Moroccan Arabic where women gathered, were passed down from mothers to daughters. Countless and nameless generations of women memorized, changed, and added to them. The audience for such songs was other women, probably in seclusion. Their subjects ranged over such domestic themes as love and bereavement, including at least allusions to their setting in seclusion.

> Sing, oh bird, since you are so lucky.
> You have water and grain in your cage.

At the other end of the spectrum of nineteenth-century women's lives in North Africa are the political songs of Kharboucha, often referred to as "sheikha," or leader of her tribe in a region of Morocco called Abda in Doukkala. Kharboucha invented a form of singing now called "Aita," a call to action, sung exclusively by Moroccan women or by men dressed as women. She composed and sang songs in Arabic to urge the people's militant opposition to the state's agent, Aissa Ben Omar, whose armies had killed ruthlessly. (See "Aissa the Fox," 1895.) In one of her songs, she anticipates her own death at Aissa Ben Omar's hands, and asks a moving question of her countryman.

> Oh gray-haired old man! Treachery is bad.
> Where are you from? Where am I from?
> Are we not from the same place?
> Nothing lasts forever.

Other oral texts in this volume include Berber and Arabic songs and stories, lullabies and wedding songs, as well as folktales. While many of these texts depict the lives of women inside families, some songs also express anticolonial resistance, a fierce sense of independence, and an urgent desire for political rights.

### Early Schools for Girls

At the end of the nineteenth century, North African women, like their sisters in sub-Saharan Africa and elsewhere in the world, began their struggle for equality by calling for women's right to education. The path toward education was neither direct nor unswerving.

The first school for women in the region was established in Egypt in 1832, not because Egypt's ruler, Mohammed Ali, believed in women's education per se, although he was interested in preserving the image of an enlightened ruler, but because he needed nurses for the increasing numbers of his soldiers infected with syphilis, supposedly caught from prostitutes in Cairo. Since foreign nurses were expensive, he ordered the establishment of a school for nurses and midwives (Fahny 1998, 46; in Abu-Lughod). Not surprisingly, given the general resistance of well-to-do Egyptians to female education, the Egyptian government was unable to fill the school with young women. Hence, government officials went to a local slave market and bought ten young Abyssinian and Sudanese girls, who became the first students at the school, attached to a military hospital in Abu Zabal outside Cairo (Badran 1995, 8–10). Eventually, orphaned girls born at the Abu Zabal Hospital were also admitted to this school, which was to become the first state school for nonelite girls. In time, other girls from poor families were willing to enroll, since they could earn a stipend, and after graduation they could be appointed as midwives or doctor's helpers. The curriculum consisted of the basics of Arabic, obstetrics, public health, and child care (Khalifa 1973, 102–05). It is interesting to note that the first woman journalist in the region, Galila Tamerhan, was a graduate of the Abu Zabal Nursing School (Abou Ghazi and El Saddah 2001, 29).

During the same period, some upper-class and middle-class girls attended foreign religious schools that were established between 1830 and 1870. The Anglican Missionary School was founded in 1835; the French also founded a girls' school in 1845, followed by a Franciscan school for slave girls, initially to prepare liberated slaves for domestic work. In 1875, the establishment became a regular girls' school (Khalifa 1973, 99–101). The Catholic Franciscan Order founded many other schools in Upper Egypt, which expanded throughout the country. All of these schools primarily served the daughters of foreigners living in Egypt. The few Egyptian girls enrolled in these schools were Christian, since most Muslim fathers feared sending their daughters away from Islamic traditions. Egyptians held more tolerant attitudes toward schools set up by Protestant missionaries, assuming that they were not interested in converting Muslims. The Coptic Christian and Muslim communities also opened schools in 1855 and 1878, respectively. In all cases, it is important to note, the purpose of these institutions was to prepare women to be good wives and mothers. A woman's first duty was to care for her husband's happiness, not her own (Khalifa 1973, 99–101; Atiya 1991, 678).

In general, the movement to found state schools for girls grew slowly throughout the region. In Egypt, the El Siyufiya School for girls was established in 1873 with a contribution from, and under the patronage of, the wife of Khedive Ismail. In 1889, El Siyufiya, renamed El Saneya School, offered primary education to girls, and later certificates in pedagogy and eventually secondary school education (Abou Ghazi & El Saddah 2001, 27). In the opposite corner of the region, the first girls' school in Morocco opened in 1862 in Tétouan and was attended mainly by Jewish girls and a small number of Muslims (Daoud 1993, 243). By 1932, some three thousand girls were enrolled in schools in Morocco, and in 1943 fifteen girls graduated with a certificate from primary school (Dafali 2001, 225). Beginning in 1945, many more schools for girls were founded.

Between 1882 and 1884, the French colonizing forces in Algeria closed down the Qur'anic schools as potential resistance locations and set up secular schools for boys and missionary schools originally intended for orphaned girls. One such school was the famous Taddert-ou-Fella village school run by the French Madame Malaval, from which Fatma Ait Mansour Amrouche graduated. (See "Outcast and Exile," 1968.) In her memoir, Amrouche would later write: "My memories are vague up to 1888. In October of that year, I was put up into the big girls' class. There were four of us little ones: Alice, Inés, Blanche and myself, Marguerite. We had all been given French names, as there were too many Fadhmas, Tassâdits and Dahbias" (Amrouche 1988, 11–12). Even if such schools did not teach Christianity—and many of them did—the Algerian Ulamaa, the community of leading Muslim scholars, believed that such practices as giving Christian names to young girls would erode Algerian identity. Hence they opened several madrasas, Islamic schools designed to teach Arabic and religion to children during the day and to men in the evening.

Children's classes included some girls, who were allowed only basic education, with no opportunities for secondary or higher education. In rural areas, there was little or no schooling for girls. In the cities of Algeria and Morocco, French schools were established both for French and North African girls alike. In Tunisia, the first girls' school was founded in Tunis in 1900 with ten students enrolled. Similarly, the French founded religious schools attended by middle-class girls in the capital city (Daoud 1993, 43).

## Advocating Education for Women

In 1899, a well-known Egyptian scholar, Qasim Amin (sometimes spelled "Kassem Amin"), broke new ground when he advocated women's education in a book called *Tahrir al-Mar'a* (The Liberation of Women). Similarly, other early-twentieth-century male leaders interested in reform—including Mohammed Allal al-Fassi in Morocco, Abd al-Hamid Ibn Badis in Algeria, and Tahar Haddad in Tunisia—argued on behalf of women's emancipation within the cultural and religious values of their societies. These leaders linked social development and modernization with women's education. It was a first step, since Amin, for example, called only for primary education, the conception of which was male-centered: "It is the wife's duty," he wrote, "to plan the household budget . . . to supervise . . . to make her home attractive to her husband, so that he may find ease when he returns to it and so that he likes being there. . . . And it is her duty—and this is her first and more important duty—to raise the children, attending to them physically, mentally, and morally" (Qasim Amin 1976, 31). Clearly, Amin would be both hero and nemesis for the women's movement for many years to come: The existence of an important male champion for a feminist cause was important at the time. Similarly, it was helpful also that Amin's views provoked opposition and more radical positions from some already educated women.

One of these women was the renowned journalist and novelist Labiba Hashim, who encouraged women to put their education to useful purpose, to abandon imposed domesticity, to become role models for their sisters, and to get involved in the social and intellectual life of their country. (See "The Eastern Woman," 1898.) Hashim emphasizes her belief in women's abilities as she concludes: "We certainly have the capacity and the potential to shine."

Another woman who became a significant role model for others of her generation—and for generations to come—was Nabaweya Moussa who rejected the salient proverb at the time: "Teach girls to spin but don't teach them to write." (See "Yes to Education and No to Marriage," 1937.) When her brother threatened to disown her if she persisted in her plan to continue school, she declared defiantly: "Never mind! I'll have one family member fewer, then!" Determined to achieve her goal, she also dismissed her mother's refusal to help her, stole her mother's seal, and set out to apply for admission at the Saneya School on her own. In her memoir, she describes her dissatisfaction with the basic education she had been permitted, and how she had to struggle by herself to prepare for the admission exam as well as to write with a totally unfamiliar pen, without previous practice. Once admitted, she had to defy her mother again with a threat that she would apply to become a boarding student if she were prevented from attending school. Moussa's courage in pursuing her own education against all odds, as well as her subsequent efforts to support women's education, made her a model for other women to emulate.[10]

Another story of heroism comes from Morocco, where Khnata Bennani, an unsung, nonliterate mother with five daughters, risked her husband's displeasure to secure her daughters' education. One of these daughters, Khadija Zizi, an associate editor of this volume, describes her mother's rebellious acts with regard to her eldest daughter in the early 1950s:

My father had decided that my eldest sister would not go to secondary school. So on the day of the entrance exams, my mother, pretending to send my sister to run an errand, sneaked her out of the house and off to school. When she passed her exams with high grades, my father finally approved and allowed her to go on with her education.

Zizi's eldest sister is now an internationally known molecular physicist, and all five sisters have earned graduate degrees. It should be noted that for the family's two sons, access to secondary school was never in question.

In Algeria, male education was the prime platform used by the *Ulema*, or political nation, to restore the identity of Algerians and to oppose and counterbalance French education. Education, they thought, was a dangerous weapon of the colonists that targeted Algerians' Muslim and national identity. Although some classes admitted girls, the political program opposed the mixing of sexes, rejected the idea of legal equality for men and women, and supported veiling. Segregated female education, including literacy, was viewed as necessary only for producing better mothers who could help educate their own children to build a better nation. All political parties agreed that female education was not intended to enable women to enter the world as skilled workers. The so-called "women's question" was, in that milieu, irrelevant to nonliterate Algerians.

## *Journalism and Journals*
The first monthly women's periodical in Egypt was Hind Nawfal's *Al-Fatat* (The Young Woman), founded in Alexandria in November 1892. A rich variety of women's publications followed, publishing essays by women on marriage, polygamy, veiling, as well as the rights to education and employment, and marking a period of transformation and change. As Beth Baron notes, "The sense of progress and possibility was summed up by a phrase that recurred throughout the women's press: al-nahda al-nisa'iyya ("women's awakening") (2005, 2). Labiba Hashim, whose fervent feminist essay "The Eastern Woman" was first published in one of these new periodicals, had by 1906 established her own magazine, *Fatat Al-Shark* (The Girl of the East), in which she continued to emphasize the importance of education for women. In 1908, a group of Egyptian Muslim women formed the Society for Women's Progress and issued a monthly journal under the same name—*Jam'iyyat Tarqiyat al-Mar'ah*—to promote women's rights within the context of Islam. Its chief editor was Fatima Rashid. At the end of 1908, Malaka Sa'd, an Egyptian Copt, launched *Al-Jins Al-Latif* (The Gentle Sex) and encouraged women to address both gender and political issues. Malak Hifni Nassef was a major contributor to the journal's publication (Baron 2005, 29–30).

This volume includes several essays first published in these early journals, and discussed elsewhere in this Introduction. But it is important to mention that, as early as 1910, Malak Hifni Nassef (writing under the pseudonym of Bahithat al-Badiya) published an essay critiquing men's abusive practice of polygamy in *Al-Jarida*, the liberal newspaper belonging to the secular *Umma* Party. (See "Polygamy," 1910.) In 1925, Mounira Thabet, the feminist editor of *Al-Amal* (Hope), the women's journal of the Wafd, Egypt's first political party, wrote on the abuse of financial rights granted to women under Shari'a law. (See "Women's Rights," 1925.)

Through the 1930s and 1940s, women journalists in Morocco expressed themselves on questions of women's rights, and the need for the education that would help women gain those rights. Some newspapers and magazines cooperated. *Majallat Al-*

*Maghrib* (Morocco's Magazine), for example, published an essay, possibly written by Malika Al-Fassi, under the pseudonym "Al Fatat." (See "On Young Women's Education," 1935.) In 1940, the same magazine published a weekly special ten-page supplement on women's issues, including arguments about whether women should wear only the *haïk* or the *jellaba* as well (Aouchar 1990, 60). By 1946, *Le Jeune Maghrébin* (The Young Maghrebi), a weekly independent newspaper, called for women's emancipation, unveiling, and "modernizing" (Lamouri et al. 1994, 29).

In Algeria, on the other hand, women did not enter the field of journalism until after independence. The exception was Djamila Débêche who, in 1947, launched *L'Action*, a feminist review that served as a platform for Muslim Algerian women in the 1940s to debate questions about women's emancipation and advancement. As an independent publication, *L'Action* called for Algerian women to contribute to the development of their country by adopting the example of such other Muslim nations as Egypt and Turkey. The review also published selected essays and literary texts by Western writers.

### Debates About the Purpose of Women's Education

In the opening years of the twentieth century, a number of forces combined to propel discussions about women's education. While many believed that women's education should be confined only to primary school, teachers were needed for that purpose. Thus, even primary education demanded more advanced training and paid employment for at least some women. In 1900, the Saneya School began a teacher training program, followed by others, in both Cairo and Alexandria, during the first two decades of the twentieth century. In addition, Egyptian and Maghreb nationalists, keen to promote progress, founded independent schools for girls in many provincial areas. Secularization of the curriculum had begun earlier, when Egyptian ruler Muhammad Ali took over the control of Al-Azhar University, the prestigious institution of Egyptian higher education, during the first half of the nineteenth century. Some religious leaders, including the Islamic reformer Mohammed Abdou, had also called for the right of women to study religious matters independently as part of their education (Badran 1995, 8–10).

All this activity, quite naturally, fomented debate, which continued well into the twentieth century (Khalifa 1973, 112–115). Reactionary and conservative Islamists who insisted on keeping women at home and depriving them of proper education were attacked by women writers who saw these attitudes as harmful not only to women, but to the nation's progress as a modern state. Writing in *Al-Amal*, Helmeya Yousry criticizes conservatives who misuse Islam to achieve their goal of suppressing women and depriving them of their right to education and freedom. (See "Response to Reactionaries," 1925.) Knowing full well that the 1923 Egyptian Constitution had declared education a national priority, and that in 1924 the government decreed primary education compulsory for girls and boys (Khalifa 1973, 124), Yousry attacked reactionaries with full force, declaring vehemently that educating women meant educating the nation: "Women are half the world and the mothers of the other half, and thus in their education lies the education of the whole population, and in their deterioration, the misery and backwardness which will befall all people."[11]

A shift in female consciousness—brought about, at least in part, by the urge toward nationalism and the resistance to colonialism—encouraged the desire of many women to leave seclusion and claim public space through education, philanthropy, and political activism, all primary means of self-improvement for women, regardless of social class or religion. Women both liberal and conservative, and both secular and religious, began to recognize common goals: education and the right to a new public voice. In 1908, Fatma Rashid founded *Jam'iyyat Tarqiyat al-Mar'ah* (The Society for Women's Progress) and the journal of the same name. She encouraged women to use their real names when writing rather than employing pseudonyms to protect their reputations (Abu Ghazi & El Saddah 2001, 58). In 1908 also, the renowned and influential Princess Fatima, daughter of Khedive Ismail, encouraged, sponsored, and funded the establishment of the first national university, and continued to support it for many years.

In 1934, the *Comité d'Action Marocaine*, Morocco's first political party, presented a reform plan demanding compulsory education for both sexes from ages six to twelve.[12] In 1931, the first school for elite girls was founded in Salé, and in 1937, in Fes (Daoud 1993, 243). By 1938 there were eight schools for Moroccan girls. It is important to mention here that journalism played a major role in promoting girls' education and emancipation. Between 1931 and 1936, *Al-Maghrib*, a nationalist newspaper, called for the opening of schools and women's right to education. (In 1963, education would become compulsory for both girls and boys in Morocco.) Similarly, a call for girls' education was becoming popular in Tunisia, and parents were no longer reluctant to send their daughters to school. By 1939, primary schools for girls had 6000 pupils in Tunisia (Daoud 1993, 48).

Like their Egyptian sisters, Moroccan nationalist women undertook the task of educating other women, and often used the progress of Egyptian women as a model. In 1944, Lalla Radia Ouazzani Chahdi, a wealthy woman, religiously educated but illiterate, was moved by Malika El-Fassi to buy a house in which to set up informal classes for women. Volunteer teachers and other donations kept the school going. On Moroccan Independence Day in 1955, a group of five women teachers, who owed their education to this school, wrote a letter of thanks to Lalla Radia Chahdi (See "To Lalla Radia: Our Eternal Lighthouse," 1955.) and enclosed sums of money with which to carry on the work of fighting illiteracy among women.

But the struggle for women's education was also a struggle for the right to work, and not only in the classroom, but also, for example, in journalism. In a 1942 newspaper essay, Malika Al-Fassi, a leading woman in the nationalist movement, celebrated the graduation of girls from primary school and called upon the nation to encourage further female education. The goal of education, she insisted, was to produce not only wives, but citizens of "virtue and success" who understood their "duty to society," and who wished "to turn ideas into realities." (See "An Important Step for Girls' Education," 1943.)

Similarly, in the first general assembly of the *Akhawat Al-Safa* (Sisters of Purity) association, Morocco's first women's association, president Habiba Guessoussa argued that educating women would save them from the "darkness of ignorance" and lead them to "the light of knowledge and prosperity." (See "An Opening Speech," 1947.) Speaking for national policy, Princess Lalla Aisha, daughter of Morocco's sultan (later king) Mohamed V and a great champion of women's education, declared in a renowned public speech that her father was " expecting all Moroccan women to invest in their education and to expend all their efforts to gain an education, which is the standard by which a nation's civilization and progress can be measured." (See "A Princess Speaks, Unveiled," 1947.)

# Mid-Twentieth Century: Liberating Nations, Liberating Women

From the beginning of the nineteenth century well into the twentieth, all of North Africa was subject to colonization by European powers. While the countries of the Maghreb—Morocco, Algeria, Tunisia, and Mauritania—endured French colonial domination, Libya was colonized by Italy, and Egypt by the British Empire. Furthermore, while Algeria and Libya fell before colonial armies, following a long period of armed resistance, Morocco and Tunisia, without invasions by foreign armies, became protectorates. Hence, in each area, the process of gaining liberation varied, from political maneuverings to armed revolt. None of this was easy. In Algeria, for example, deadlocked political negotiations led to lengthy armed struggle: The Algerian War of independence lasted from 1954 to 1962, and has been described by Benjamin Stora as "one of the two cruelest wars of French decolonization in this century: the other was the war in Indochina (1946–1954)" (Stora 2001, 29–30).[13] In Morocco, the battle shifted from armed resistance in rural areas to political struggle and then back to further armed struggle in some urban areas.

## Struggles for National Independence

In Morocco in the early 1920s, a blind, Berber orphan woman named Tawgrat Walt Aissa N'Ait Sokhman sang oral poems urging women's resistance to the colonizers and demonizing cowardly men. She calls on "women to carry the flag," and she decries the men:

> Shame on you; you have no manhood,
> For you love to be the slaves of the unfaithful."
> (See "Resistance," early 1920s.)

Rabha Moha, another verbally talented Berber woman, recording memories of the past for her descendants, sang of the "big buildings/The French have built/in Meknes city," and recommends "eat[ing] soup since/They give it to us/For free." In a darker vein, she sings also about the French killing "civilian women," and about sons forced to carry water for the French, and she vows:

> I will not have children any more
> Who will work for the French
> When they grow up.

Another militant Moroccan, Rabéa Qadri, is more angry still. In a song from the 1950s, she cries:

> Bring me De Gaulle's head—
> I shall burn it.
> Bring me De Gaulle's head—
> I shall grill it.[14]

By its nature, colonialism threatens national and cultural identities, often focusing on women as the vulnerable carriers of culture. Thus women were caught between the nationalists' endeavors to protect them from cultural contamination and the colonizer's quest to "civilize" women as the most effective way to "civilize" the whole society. Inevitably, as this effort met patriarchal resistance, many women became increasingly secluded in their homes and villages and thus excluded from public discourse and action.

Several women, nonetheless, led regional rebellions against the colonizers, and many others participated in them. We have already mentioned the legendary Algerian Fatma N'Soumer who, in the middle of the nineteenth century, led an army of men and women in a rebellion against the forces of occupation, and rallied to her cause the mosques and zawiyas, or religious schools, of the Kabyle region in northern Algeria, which gave her their full support. Her resistance brought the French troops under General Randon several defeats—notably, in the battle that took place on 18–19 July 1854, in which the colonizers lost 800 men, including 56 officers. Injured were 371 others.[15]

On 16 March 1919, several hundred Egyptian women demonstrated on behalf of the Wafd Party leader Saad Zagloul, who had been exiled to Malta. This demonstration, which was part of a nationwide uprising that came to be known as the Egyptian Revolution of 1919, marked a historic moment for middle- and upper-class, veiled women, placing them firmly in the public world as part of the nationalist struggle. In Cairo, the march was led by Saphia Zagloul, wife of the exiled leader, and by Huda Shaarawi, the organizer of the Egyptian Feminist Union, among others. In Alexandria, Fayyum, and elsewhere, hundreds of other veiled women marched. Later, thousands of teachers and students, workers, lawyers, and government employees marched through sections of Cairo, where they were joined by thousands more, ignoring British attempts to block their progress. And again, similar demonstrations occurred in other cities of Egypt.

While Saphia Zagloul was later allowed by the British to join her exiled husband. (See "Letter from Exile," 1922), other women continued to organize strikes and other demonstrations, as well as boycotts of British goods. They wrote petitions denouncing British authorities and deploring their own ill treatment during demonstrations: Several women had been killed alongside men when the British opened fire during some of the 1919 protests. Shafika Mohammed, shot dead on 16 March, was declared the first woman martyr of the revolution; others followed, including Fahima Riad, Aisha Omar, and Hamida Khalil (Subki 1986, 18–19). Women also used the press to circulate pamphlets and statements throughout the country and abroad. Outside urban centers, other women cut rail lines, destroyed telegraph lines, and assisted militants engaged in other acts of resistance (Subki 1986, 21–30).

Similar marches were organized by the women of Morocco in protest against the French protectorate in their country. In August 1952, women textile workers in Rabat joined a strike that lasted for an entire month, and in Casablanca women joined the general strike and demonstrations that took place in December of the same year. Several women and men were killed during these demonstrations by police willing to shoot unarmed demonstrators. In response to these demonstrations, the French colonialists moved to eliminate communists and members of the nationalist Istiqlal Party across Morocco. But, when the French then decided to send the sultan, Mohammed V, into exile in 1953, men and women in almost equal numbers filled urban streets and began an armed struggle that primarily targeted Moroccan collaborators and French police and soldiers.

Women's relationship to their deposed monarch was labeled "Yusefism" and compared to the psychoanalytic idea of transference. According to this theory, Moroccan women were able to identify with the sovereign not as majestic and remote, but rather as weak and abandoned. The sultan had become a "father figure," thanks to his misfortune, and women wanted to protect and save him. When tens of thousands of women gathered on their terraces, they even experienced a collective hallucination: Many saw the figure of Mohammed V on a white horse, appearing in the moon! Touria Chaoui, the first woman pilot, flew over the Royal Palace, dropping leaflets celebrating the glory of Mohammed V (Rivet 1991, 373–76).

As Alison Baker explains, when it came to resisting colonialism, gender barriers simply collapsed. After Mohammed V was sent into exile, she writes, "men and women took to the streets spontaneously in mass demonstrations in cities all over Morocco. Women who had never before gone out of their houses came out to join these demonstrations" (1998, 27). During this period of resistance, women carried arms in their handbags and under their veils. They worked as liaison agents, hiding militants in their homes and gathering necessary intelligence to help the resistance (Lakthiri 2002, 3–8). As Malika El-Fassi later described, "Housewives in Fes gathered in crowds on their terraces and used as weapons all kinds of household objects: flower pots, hot water basins, large stones" (1992, 22). Morocco's urban armed struggle continued until the return of Mohammed V from exile in November 1955.

He returned as liberator: Everywhere he went, men and women came out in huge crowds, chanting such slogans as "Long live the king, long live independence!" Women's presence on these occasions was highly visible; their nationalist feelings and their work for the independence of Morocco could not be denied. As a result, in its 21 November 1955 meeting, the Istiqlal Party declared Moroccan women equal to men and called for their emancipation. Several women took part in this congress, but one who stood out was Zhor Lazraq, a twenty-one-year-old woman from Fes who defended women's rights with great ardor.[16] Moroccan women were demonstrating for their personal freedom along with that of their nation.

Similarly, Algerian women, seeking to liberate both themselves and their country, joined the ranks of the armed struggle for independence. On 1 November 1954, all Algerian nationalists joined forces under the leadership of the *Front de Libération National* (FLN), or National Liberation Front, a party organized for the purpose of driving out the French colonizers. At the start of this war, the Algerian women's movement suspended all social activities to join forces with the FLN. They believed that personal independence for women could not be achieved under a colonized nation. Nafissa Hamoud, the leader of the *Association des Femmes Musulmanes Algérienne* (Algerian Muslim Women's Association), was the first woman doctor to join the freedom fighters, in 1955; a number of nurses followed her example. Fatima Benosmane, the leader of the *Union des Femmes d'Algérie* (Union of Algerian Women), also joined the resistance, and was arrested and tortured in 1957. Women were among the university students who took part in the May 1956 strike organized by the *Union Générale des Etudiants Musulmans d'Algérie* (General Union of Muslim Algerian Students). Forty-nine women were among the 1010 first *moudjahiddine*, or freedom fighters, according to a census conducted in August 1956 during the Soummam Congress, the first congress of the FLN (Daoud 1993, 140).

By the end of the revolution the number of *moudjahidat*, or women freedom fighters amounted to 10,949, of whom 1,755 were in the ranks of the *Armée de Libération*

*National* (ALN), the National Liberation Army. To this number one might add the 2,388 women who served as *fida'iyat*, or liaison workers, who worked to link the various factions of the ALN; to smuggle arms and money; and to facilitate the movements of the *moudjahiddin*, especially in urban centers, where women were of paramount importance. For their massive participation in the revolution, the FLN declared officially, "Algerian women won their rights by their participation in the war."

Joining the revolution represented an extraordinary leap forward for Algerian women. Their participation empowered them to move from private to public spheres and to defy major social taboos. At the same time, Algerian men had to take a pragmatic—if ultimately temporary—view of women's behavior, accepting change that they might have resisted in less exigent circumstances. Women who joined the ranks of revolutionaries were then not seen as breaking any code, although most of them were high school or university students. They entered revolutionary actions as minors, without the consent of their parents. Baya Hocine, whose letter from prison is included in this volume, joined the ranks of the FLN at age fifteen, and was arrested and tortured while still a minor at seventeen. She became the youngest person sentenced to death during the liberation struggle, although the sentence was never carried out because of her age. (See "Sentenced to Death," 1957.) She wrote to her mother from prison:

> Mother darling, I am writing to you for the first time after my death sentence. My sisters and I received the sentence with calm and dignity. I hope you will have the same attitude. . . I have immediately asked for an appeal; you know now that I will sit for another trial.

### The Veil at War

As a key identifying device for women, the veil in all its forms has been used metaphorically in as many variant ways. When Mohammed V returned to Morocco from exile, for example, women removed their *lithams*, the thin piece of fabric with which they covered their faces, as a gesture meant to symbolize their liberation from the protectorate. Similarly, but in contradiction as well, for long years before the war of independence, the *haïk*, or full-length covering, was used as a means of cultural resistance against colonialism. And quite complexly during the armed liberation struggle, the *haïk* became an instrument of combat and a tool of camouflage. Under their veils women hid messages, money, and weapons. Covered with their *haïks*, women could avoid being searched by French soldiers, since no man was allowed to touch a veiled Muslim woman. At the peak of the Battle of Algiers, some revolutionary male fighters resorted to the veil to cover their movements between quarters of the Casbah, but were often identified as male by the way they walked. Eventually, all were searched and identified at checkpoints. Unable to hide under their veils, Algerian women fighters resorted to dressing as Europeans so that they might enter the European quarter of the city to deposit explosives.[17] To many in the FLN, urban terrorism seemed the only option remaining as a response both to the execution by guillotine in Algiers's Barberousse Prison of the national heroes Ahmad Zabane and Abelkader Ferradj, and to the devastating bomb deposited by colonists in the Rue Thèbes, in the heart of the Casbah, which killed some seventy innocent civilians. These two events encouraged many women and men to see armed struggle as the only means to end French colonialism. More and more women joined the revolution to take on dangerous tasks.

The names of women fighters appeared in the international media, and helped to garner sympathy and support for the Algerian cause from such French intellectuals as Simone de Beauvoir, who wrote a preface to a volume in which war hero Djamila Boupacha described the hideous torture she endured in prison in 1960, including water-boarding, electric shocks, and the "bottle treatment":

> First they tied me up in a special posture, and then they rammed the neck of a bottle into my vagina. I screamed and fainted. I was unconscious, to the best of my knowledge, for two days." (See "Testimony of Torture," 1960.)

In the narratives of Algerian women prisoners tears are absent. Despite intense trauma, their ordeals served to strengthen their commitment to their mission. They knew they were imprisoned not as criminals, but as soldiers serving what they believed to be a noble cause. The poet Zhor Zerari, who was also arrested, tortured, and permanently maimed, dreamed of an independent future for her country in the poems she wrote in prison.

> The children of today
> Do not study in the classroom.
> They are writing the history
> Of a Free Algeria.
> (See "Two Poems," 1960.)

Beyond this handful of powerful narratives, women's accounts of their work for the liberation of their countries from colonialism remain relatively scarce. Their absence contributes to the loss of memory about the vital part women played in securing freedom for the nations of North Africa. In fact, the most celebrated popular account of their struggle, dramatized in Gillo Pontecorvo's remarkable1965 film, "Battle of Algiers," gives visual representation to the nuanced racialized boundaries that women's bodies in colonized Islamic societies could engender. The film pays tribute to the women's heroism, but is silent on their torture. Its opening is framed by the representation of the meaning of torture for the male body in the context of nationalist struggle, but is silent on the torture of female bodies. Not until Assia Djebar's 2001 film, "La Nouba des Femmes du Mont-Chenoua" (The Nouba of the Women of Mount Chenoua), do we get a woman's perspective on this struggle in all its rich, engendered complexity, in a work that addresses not only the stories of heroism, but those of torture as well—and significantly, the question of silence.

### Building Nation States with Women as Citizens

Although largely ignored in official recorded histories of the region, women contributed significantly to the political and social construction of the modern countries of North Africa. They fought for independence, entered into the work of political parties, initiated or joined in activism, infiltrated academe and international organizations, and boldly combated religious fanaticism. Throughout the period that extends from colonization through independence and state-building to the era of democratization, women worked throughout the public sphere. While women's movements first focused on their rights to education and legal status, they moved quickly into social activism during the wars of liberation, and then into the efforts to establish, in each country, a civil society that included acceptable rights for women, always understanding that the environment had to include Islam.

The period during which the countries of North Africa became nation states extended from 1922 (Egypt) to 1956 (Morocco and Tunisia) to 1962 (Algeria). Despite the span of forty years, many similarities can be found among women's activities in the region, especially because the goals of Egyptian nationalists were not satisfied by the unilateral declaration of Egyptian independence. After the 1919 Revolution calling for democracy and independence from British occupation, Egypt's status as a protectorate was terminated and the country was declared a sovereign state, although the British still retained a military presence and strong influence, especially over foreign policy. Following this declaration, a new constitution was adopted in April 1923, approved by a thirty-member legislative committee. Although the new constitution made the cabinet accountable to parliament, it gave the king the right to dissolve parliament. None of this satisfied many reformers, including those in leading women's groups, who continued their efforts on behalf of Saad Zagloul, who would be elected prime minister in 1924. Women's organizations also objected strenuously to the fact that the new constitution did not offer women the same civil and political rights as men.

In May 1923, Huda Shaarawi, under the banner of the newly formed Egyptian Feminist Union, attended an international meeting in Rome, along with Saiza Nabarawi, her friend and protégé, and Nabaweya Moussa. At the conference they called for the restoration of rights women once enjoyed during the Pharaonic and Islamic periods. Upon their return to Egypt, as they stepped off the train in Cairo, Shaarawi and Nabarawi, in a symbolic act of emancipation, removed their veils. From that point forward, two Egyptian organizations—the Wafdist Women's Central Committee (WWCC) and the Egyptian Feminist Union (EFU)—continued a tradition of independent, organized feminist struggle, aimed at least in part to amend the new Egyptian constitution and bring women truly equal rights in the political, economic, and social spheres. Egyptian women began to attend European conferences on women's rights and, at home, to agitate for those rights. With Huda Shaarawi as their leader, the Wafd Central Committee for Women demanded political rights for women, including the right to attend parliamentary celebrations in 1924. When they were refused, they demonstrated and issued a declaration denouncing this refusal.

In 1946, Huda Shaarawi wrote to the prime minister, urging him "to grant women their full political rights," in accordance with a United Nations resolution that had just been passed, to which Egypt had bound itself. (See "Letter to the Prime Minister," 1946.) Shaarawi, who had herself built bridges to other women's movements in the Arab world and beyond, reminded the prime minister that women's rights would enhance Egypt's stature in the eyes of the UN and the larger international community. The following year EFU issued a booklet listing women's demands, including as most important the necessity of changing the voting law to give all women the right to vote and to take seats in parliament and positions on local councils. The booklet was sent to all members of parliament, the media, and to the speaker of the House. Mounira Thabet was an important leader in this effort. She published a book on women's political rights and wrote a letter to Saad Zagloul and the parliament, attacking the 1923 Constitution for neglecting women's political rights. Thabet continued to lobby for women's suffrage and even attacked Saad Zagloul for forming a cabinet that did not represent the population correctly. She said that excluding women was a violation of the United Nations Charter and a violation of the UN General Assembly's Declaration of Human Rights issued on 10 September 1948.

Women continued to press for suffrage and to demand a place in political life. With the advent of the 1952 Revolution, which issued the 1956 Constitution that gave women the right to vote and run for parliamentary office, political equality was formally established in Egypt. In the 1957 parliamentary elections, five female candidates presented themselves, and two of them won seats: Rawya Shams El Din and Amina Shokry (Koura 1996, 22–23).

During the 1930s and 1940s, in other North African countries not yet free of colonialism, pioneer women's organizations were created by educated urban elite women: Akhawat al-Safaa (Sisters of Purity) in Morocco, the *Association des Femmes Musulmane Algérienne* (Algerian Muslim Women's Association), and the *Union des Femmes Tunisiennes* (Tunisian Women's Union). While many of their members had connections to larger national liberation movements, these organizations did not focus on women's rights per se, believing that the independence of their countries would bring about their emancipation. Their aim was to make women aware of their own social importance as potential citizens; their function was to train them to be active participants in the public life of their countries.

Thus the activities of these organizations and their members included writing for journals and even publishing their own, as well as organizing and speaking at meetings in which the importance of women's education and women's participation in the struggle for independence were key. Delivering formal public speeches became an important strategy for women's emancipation, in that it brought women's voices into the political arena. For example, when the writer and activist Bchira Ben Mrad celebrated, in a public speech, the first Tunisian woman doctor, the event indirectly marked the entrance of women's voices to the public sphere. (See "Honoring Dr. Tawhida Ben Cheikh," 1937.)

Such speeches as a means of self-assertion in public spaces characterize the beginnings of women's liberation movements in the countries of the Maghreb, just as they had in Egypt. In these speeches, pioneer women's movements associated emancipation with the independence of their countries. As noted, journalism also contributed by promoting the importance of education, the visibility of women, and fostering the idea of women's responsible citizenship.

### Islamic Fundamentalists, Family Codes, and Religious Texts

Following the independence of the countries of the Maghreb in the 1950s and early 1960s, the new ruling elites sought to reestablish a narrow version of Islam in their social and legal institutions through family laws based on the Muslim law of Shari'a. Women's movements were quick to see in this a betrayal of their cause. Only in Tunisia was the post-independence family law progressive. To move discussion forward, women activists organized themselves within "women's sections" of leftist political parties, using this space to challenge the "reactionary" establishment and to call for human rights. Writers depicted women's painful disillusionment and the helplessness of women in the face of powerful governments that had betrayed them.

In Morocco, for example, women's activism was particularly fueled by a bitter realization that family laws in the newly independent nation relegated women to home and hearth, distanced from public life. From the late 1940s, when efforts were initiated by the Akhawat Al-Safaa (Sisters of Purity), through the 1990s, the women's movement in Morocco was focused on the revision of the family law, or *Mudawana*. These energies culminated in the One Million Signatures petition for the reform of the *Mudawana*, led by the *Union de l'Action Féminine* (Women's Action Union), and strongly opposed by the Minister of Islamic Affairs and by Islamic religious authorities. (See "One Million Signatures," 1992.) Key elements of the petition called for the abolition of polygamy and the establishment of age of majority rights, child care rights, divorce rights, and employment rights for women equal to those of men. The petition itself, widely circulated in 1992, was only the first step towards the reform of Moroccan family law, announced by the king in Parliament on 17 October 2003.

Women have also struggled for the revision of the family laws in Algeria and Tunisia. The Tunisian family law was amended in 1965, 1966, and 1981. Algeria, on the other hand, was an exception, since it did not possess a Shari'a-based family code until 1984. Throughout the 1970s, conservative elements in the Algerian government and society had presented several drafts of a family code, based on the teachings of the Maliki school of Shari'a, but President Houari Boumedienne postponed the passage of such a law. After Boumedienne's death in 1978, the same group finally succeeded in passing a new family law in 1984, with the agreement of President Chadli Bendjedid, who needed their support to stay in office. This code's 224 articles were repressive blows dealt to Algerian women. They represented reactionary misogynist policies of a culture determined to subjugate women by rendering them minors under the law.

Determined to challenge the new family code, the women of Algeria embarked on a long and lonely battle. As Khalida Messaoudi asserted, "Men were painfully absent from our struggle. This reinforced my conviction that Algerian women could expect salvation only from themselves" (Messaoudi and Schemla 1998, 56). Since 1984, women war veterans and younger feminists have joined together to protest ceaselessly against the legislation that has codified women's subordination.

In the summer of 2004, the government appointed a commission of lawyers, activists, and academics to draft a proposal for the amendment of the family code. Despite the fact that President Bouteflika insisted that the proposed reforms do not target Islamic law, but rather codified social custom, such Islamist parties as the *Mouvement pour la Société et la Paix* (Movement for Society and Peace) strongly opposed the changing of many essential articles in the code. After lengthy and heated parliamentary debate, a preliminary draft of amendments to the family code was presented to the Algerian government and approved on 22 November 2004. Although these changes were derided as timid by many feminist groups, they represent at least the first steps towards further changes to come.

Perhaps just as important as reforms of the family law are the attempts by women to lift the male control of sacred Islamic religious texts. Increasingly, women in North Africa and throughout the Muslim world have called for opening these texts to reinterpretation from feminist perspectives. Such critiques as those from Fatima Mernissi, for example, question the use of religion to control women politically, even in Islamic countries that have announced the rights of their populations to universal suffrage. Mernissi discusses what she calls "political Islam"—as distinct from the true religion of Muhammad—in which the oppression of women finds its parallel in the repression of the will of the people.

> Universal suffrage tears away two veils, two veils that give substance to the two thresholds of political Islam in its cosmic architecture: the hijab of women and that of the caliph. For, paradoxical as it may seem, women are not the only ones to hide themselves behind a hijab. The Muslim caliph, the ultimate concentration of all the wills of the faithful, of those who choose submission, who choose negation of the will for the benefit of the group, needs more than anyone else to protect himself.

The hijab of the caliph, his veil, is an institution just as fundamental to political Islam as is the veil of women, and if it is never directly invoked in the desperate cry of the return of the veil, it is because it hides the unmentionable: the will of the people, the will of the '*amma*, the mass, which is just as dangerous as that of women. (See "Women and Political Islam," 1990.)

## The Slow Road to Higher Education for Women

As early as 1934, shortly after the first small group of women had graduated from an Egyptian university, Asma Fahmy wrote in a cultural weekly of the need for women to gain college and university degrees. (See "Higher Education for Women," 1934.) She argued that women needed such education even more than men, for they had been deprived of it for millennia. She saw such education fulfilling both personal and social purposes: It would "both improve their minds and allow them to serve in the field of social reform." Thus, it was clear that higher education must serve a purpose far beyond the creation of obedient wives and caring mothers. Indeed, Fahmy insists that while society will benefit from "the excellent children who can only be produced by a highly educated woman," it will also benefit from educated women who choose not to marry, and instead serve "in a direct manner: through scientific and practical means and by helping improve society." She concludes with a jibe to the "selfish" men who would deny women an education because they fear competition in the workplace. "Men's opposition to women's higher education," she declares, "hardly compliments their integrity or chivalry."

In spite of such spirited arguments, the opening of universities to women was painfully slow in coming. A few privileged women continued to go abroad to Europe for university degrees. But even privileged women needed the permission of conservative fathers to pursue higher education and professional work. The plight of many of these women is poignantly represented in a poem by Nahed Taha Abdel Ber, whose father denied her such opportunities.

> Crushed by ungratified desire
> Night after night my feeble body lies sleepless,
> Yet dreaming of all I want,
> Of a life in that great place of learning.
> Of a life of study and fruitfulness.
> (See "The Lost Hope," 1936.)

One of the factors preventing parents from sending their daughters to universities was coeducation. In 1929, five women were admitted to university in Egypt, though not until 1930 were they allowed to enroll in the Faculty of Science. It is important to mention that studying Arabic in those years had both national and feminist significance, since the field had been a closely held male domain, especially dominated by graduates of Al-Azhar. Similarly, archeology was both a male and a Western domain. In 1939, when Afifa Iskandar wanted to study Egyptology, she was permitted to enroll in courses, but not allowed to pursue a degree. In the area of medicine, the first female graduates in 1936 were not allowed to work at the university hospital. Similarly, when the faculties of commerce, agriculture, and engineering were founded in Egypt, women were allowed only into commerce.[18]

No doubt the hostility to women's entering heretofore male fields had to do with competition in the workplace, as Fatma Ne'mat Rashed indicates in the essay in this volume on women's admission to the famous Al-Azhar University. (See "Should Women Enter Al-Azhar," 1946.) Rashed was writing a response to an essay in a journal by Abdel Hamid Bek Saleh, a member of parliament who strongly opposed the admission of women, partly on the grounds that Islam forbade women's mingling with men. Rashed takes the view that all people must earn their livelihoods, and, further, that divorced or widowed women especially need to support themselves. Ultimately she argues that all women should be allowed "the right of choice": "Allow them to choose either to be mothers and housewives, or engineers, physicians, and lawyers." She adds, "After all, women are human beings, are they not?"

Prior to independence in Morocco, there were few colleges and less than two thousand college students. In 1946, Moroccan Al Qarawiyine University enrolled young women, six of whom graduated in 1955. In 1959, the first modern university in Morocco, Mohammed V University, was founded as a coeducational institution, though some women continued to pursue higher education in Paris. The enrollment of women was one percent in 1956. It continued to increase gradually, and by 2002, the figure was 44 percent (Zouaoui 2005, 167–72).

From the mid-1990s onward, women's movements have been greatly enhanced by the creation of centers and groups for academic research on gender and women's studies, especially those in university graduate units. These graduate units have produced, for example, the first cohorts of M.A. and Ph.D. holders in women's and gender studies in Morocco. They have also been instrumental in researching and publicizing the early history of women during the colonial years. National and international colloquia continue to be devoted to women's history and politics, using new scholarship on women appearing in books and journals.

## LATE TWENTIETH CENTURY: SHIFTING SOCIAL AND POLITICAL LANDSCAPES

### Colonialism and the Question of Class

While the colonization of North Africa, as we have already noted, took various shapes and forms, the question of class was often bound up with the nature of the colonial encounter. In places where the colonizing force took root and established a permanent, visible presence, the local inhabitants were relegated to a social and economic position inferior to that of the occupier. Some of the Berber songs by Rabha Moha, for example, reveal resentments felt against the colonizer, not only as exercising political dominance, but perhaps more important as wielding economic power and controlling the livelihood of the indigenous population. (See "I Want to Tell You," 1977.) Moha makes clear through defiantly sarcastic pronouncements that her spirit will remain untouched, even when her body may succumb.

To understand how far back a colonial presence controlled some aspects of life in North Africa, one must recall that Muhammad Ali, the acclaimed founder of modern Egypt who ruled from 1805 to 1849, encouraged foreigners to settle in the country in order to accelerate its modernization. To encourage them to immigrate and to extend to them a sense of security, he instigated several changes. He opened the western port of Alexandria to Christian ships. He gave foreigners several privileges: tax exemptions, customs reductions, consular protection, and trials in mixed courts. Foreigners from all around the Mediterranean and from as far away as Russia were encouraged to migrate to Egypt. The reigns of consecutive khedives that followed were also conducive to such immigration and growth. Khedive Ismail, who ruled from 1863 to 1879, announced that Egypt had turned its face to Europe, and he set about Westernizing it.

Hence, some European foreigners initially settled in the region not as colonizers but as a foreign community, occupying a distinct space and inaugurating forms of belief that were distinguishable from those of the indigenous masses. They formed an elitist culture that held allegiance to and prided itself upon an affiliation with European culture. The recently published memoir of Eugenie (Janie) Sinano Horwitz, for example, embodies the spirit of these Europeanized classes and reveals their predominant discourse. (See "Tales from the Zogheb Family Saga," 1949.) The memoir, written in French, chronicles the economic rise of a family of Levantine immigrants arriving in Alexandria in the mid-nineteenth century in search both of livelihood and security from persecution. The narrative describes the kind of life they and their descendants made for themselves up to the aftermath of the 1952 Revolution, when suddenly the whole mood of the country became nationalistic and hostile to all foreign presence.

Originally a Catholic Syrian, the patriarch of the Zogheb family, Joseph de Zogheb, the author's grandfather, made an enormous fortune on the cotton exchange and was ennobled.[19] In a society where money and prestige reigned supreme, an ennobled family, not surprisingly, could and did forget that their ancestors had been impoverished, had not always spoken French or worn European clothes, then hallmarks of class superiority. It was also not surprising that the descendants of established foreign communities became more concerned with a search for roots, origins, and identities than with issues of social and political rights. This "identity issue that obsesses so many non-Egyptian Alexandrians" (Mabro 2002, 244) separates the narrative of Eugenie Sinano Horwitz from those of the Muslim Egyptian women fighting feminist and nationalist battles. The "cosmopolitan" women, in the main Christian foreigners, did not suffer the seclusion imposed upon their Muslim counterparts, and had none of the material concerns that plagued the lives of other local women. Questions of origin and identity worried Horwitz, rather than questions of liberation, whether from male or colonial oppression. The British bombardment of Alexandria in 1882 held no significance for her in terms of the nationalist revolt of Orabi or the occupation of Egypt, but only in the fact that the palatial residence of her grandfather in the Place des Consuls, which was strictly limited to the foreign consuls and the elite of the city and was off limits to Egyptians, had been burned down. The British occupation had no negative impact either on the wealth or the social status of her family.

### Narratives of Class in the Fifties, Sixties, and Seventies

For Egyptian women, the nationalist 1952 Revolution was comparable in its transforming effects to the struggles for independence in Tunisia, Algeria, and Morocco. Under the leadership of Gamal Abdel Nasser, the Free Officers who carried out the revolution in Egypt, many of whom belonged to far from affluent social classes, altered the country's structure of wealth and power—although ultimately, their policies served merely to change the membership of the elite, rather than eradicating the class altogether. The revolution removed the king from power, and in theory at least proposed an ambitiously radical agenda for redistributing wealth. It promised people a more egalitarian society based on justice rather than on inherited wealth and titles. The Land Reform Law, issued in September 1952, limited land ownership to two hundred feddans (1.038 acres) and gave five feddans to hitherto landless peasants. The implications of this for both men and women were huge. Perhaps for the first time in the history of Egypt, the ordinary person, man or woman, felt a new sense of dignity and pride.

With the embrace of a brand of "Arab Socialism," adapted to the needs and ideology of an Islamic Arab society, women seemed to have attained a status hitherto denied to them, and were, at least in theory, free to pursue their goals and ambitions in life. Socialism also meant that traditional interpretations of Islam were quietly and discreetly being bypassed in support of a more liberal and liberating mode of thinking, especially with regard to women. Arguments were put forward that Islam was the first truly socialist creed, created centuries before Marx.

This optimistic embrace of the ideology of Arab Socialism was not, however, wholeheartedly shared by all. Leila Ahmed, in her autobiography *A Border Passage*, presents a moving and articulate analysis of this dilemma. On the subject of the ideology of being an Arab, she devotes her chapter "On Becoming an Arab" to a recollection of her childhood in Alexandria, amid a thriving polyglot community of Jews, Copts, and Muslims, who were Egyptian Nationalists without being required to claim "Arabness." She lays out the shift in ideology, through propaganda, which saw the Jews of Egypt— some of them Zionists who had supported the independence of Egypt from the British, and who had helped to articulate and to bankroll the revolution—being cast out after the 1952 Revolution (1999, 243–70). Ahmed holds equally nuanced views of Marxism, having learned in exile to recognize its appeal, yet wary, from experience of its own pitfalls, of dogma and tyranny.

Those aristocratic families of the "ancient regime," whose monopoly on privilege and wealth had been taken for granted for centuries, were understandably distressed when their property and lands were confiscated and later nationalized by the Nasser regime in the early 1960s. To this class belongs Nadine, the narrator of Samia Serageldin's narrative. (See "Love is Like Water," 1999.) While Nadine mentions that Gamal Abdel Nasser sent a representative to the funeral of her grandmother as an act befitting the family's importance, she later expresses her relief that her grandmother had escaped the period's harrowing events: "Dying when she did, she was spared the worst of what was to follow: her sons sent into political exile; her family's fortune expropriated and nationalized."

Consciousness of class also permeates Wadida Wassef's rare account of upper-class Coptic life in mid-century Egypt, though with no mention of religion. (See "Aunt Noor," 1975.) Though thirty years separate her life from that of Eugenie Sinano Horwitz, author of "Tales from the Zogheb Family Saga," Wadida Wassef could claim an upbringing just as refined and surroundings equally cosmopolitan. But questions of origin did not weigh heavily on Wassef as they had on the Levantine Horwitz, for Egyptian families kept in touch with their past, even when it lay in the countryside. Wassef's narrative also testifies to Egyptians' fealty to the inherited customs of extended families, their origins and traditions, regardless of contemporary—and possibly Western— lifestyles.

"Tales from the Zogheb Family Saga" and "Aunt Noor" are both unpublished memoirs of family history written by Christian women. While the first cosmopolitan account offers an anxious quest for origins and an urgent need to write the record before it disappears forever, the second Egyptian history presents a soothing narrative of cyclical female time and comfortable, known space. The figure of the grandfather whose portrait adorns every house looms large in Horwitz's memoir, while men are missing entirely from "Aunt Noor." The young Wadida Wassef may feel oppressed by the notions of propriety and respectability that dominate her family's mystique, and she may feel rather embarrassed by her Aunt Noor, who still dresses like a peasant. Yet the narrator, looking back, appreciates that an attachment to traditions sustains family life and defines identity. Her narrative revolves a round the female world of cooking and nurturing that not only keeps the family together but also maintains the links between city and country, from which origins are derived, even though the former may be regarded with unapologetic admiration and awe while the latter is viewed as shabby, unsophisticated, and irredeemably inferior.

Class is also at the heart of the story by Aisha Abdel Rahman, written one year after the 1952 Revolution in Egypt. (See "The Heiress," 1953.) The story gives voice to the resentments harbored by a domestic servant, Zoheira, who is turned out of her old employer's home by his son, a doctor who fears his father will marry the young woman, since she is beautiful as well as virtuous. Almost as in a fairy tale, the fortunes of Zoheira change until she is in a position of power over that same doctor and able to take her revenge. The fact that Zoheira is a woman highlights the intersection of class and gender, her revenge appearing as an attempt to even the score in a society that has abused her as a woman as well as a person of low social position.

### Escaping Class Through Marxism

In the middle of the twentieth century, many women in the region expressed their resistance to colonialism by embracing Marxist ideology. In "Prison," for example, Saida Menebhi, a Moroccan activist jailed for voicing dissident views, wrote a letter in the form of a poem in which she proudly declares that she is a "communist," a word that has resonated negatively within the traditional, religious-conscious societies of North Africa, where it has often been equated with atheism. Menebhi, however, expresses her determination to forge ahead with her struggle against the harsh regime of King Hassan—who ruled Morocco from 1961 to 1999 and was ruthless in suppressing dissent—even if it means death for her. The struggle, she writes, "runs in our blood" and "comes from the people." (See "Two Poems," 1977.)

Many Egyptian women also embraced Marxist ideology as a form of resistance to social injustice and in the hope of forging a better future. Latifa Al-Zayyat, for example, recalls the 1940s, when she was still an undergraduate at Fouad I University (now Cairo University). She vividly charts the two intellectual currents dominant during the period, radical Islam and Marxism. (See "In Her Own Mirror," 1993.) The women involved in the communist movement in particular envisioned a classless society that could fulfill their dreams of justice, equality, and freedom from foreign domination. The "ideal of equality among human beings, women and men alike," she writes, "regardless of color, sex, or creed, fired my imagination." As Al-Zayyat captures the contemporary mood, voicing a popular optimism then prevalent because of victories scored against Nazism and Fascism, she also highlights women's political awareness, which was international as well as local.

### Female Empathy Across Class Differences

Women's consciousness of class differences may be noted in the short story by Amina Arfaoui, in which a first wife, in order to shame her husband for his infidelity and perhaps undermine his plans to take a second wife, insists on meeting his "other" woman. (See "The Gramophone," 1987.) The encounter, however, does not turn out as she had expected. The wife observes that her husband's mistress, far from being the stereotypical "vulgar, outrageously made up woman" she had anticipated, is disarmingly and pathetically "sad-looking" and "very thin," a foreigner and an orphan. The woman she meets clearly belongs to a lower stratum of society, and instead of resentment, she evokes pity. It is interesting to note that Arfaoui's character equates plumpness with good living, and thinness with inferior economic status.

Another variety of social empathy between women of different classes appears in Saida Menebhi's poem "The Prostitutes." (See "Two Poems," 1977.) The poet describes the scarred faces of the young women "that people call prostitutes," their heavy breasts looking ironically like "two cathedrals," which bear the signs of ageing. The poem evokes a sense of injustice that comes out as a scream of protest against the poverty compelling such women to sell their "kisses, / Just like the flower-shop girl / Sells flowers."

### Shifting Class Patterns in the Eighties and Nineties

From the 1980s onward, the new accumulating oil wealth in the Gulf States, and to a lesser extent in Libya, directly affected social structures in North Africa, especially since countless numbers of men from this region traveled for employment to oil-rich countries.[20] The consequences for women of such temporary migrations were immense: They needed to run households on their own, with all the attendant turmoil and triumph that such activity may portend. It also meant that, for a large number of working-class and lower-middle-class families, a new economic prosperity was possible. Salwa Bakr's short story can be read as a document detailing a young woman's sensitive reaction to the rapid increase of personal wealth that came with employment in places outside Egypt. (See "Worms in the Rose Garden," 1992.) Her sense of revulsion becomes translated into repellent images of humans turning into worms eating enormous quantities of food and growing fatter and fatter. Her family is totally oblivious to her psychological and spiritual needs, as well as to her growing madness. Instead, they are bent on satisfying her material needs as an end in itself. Thus they want her to eat with them, and thus they want to marry her off to a rich man regardless of her feelings, marriage in their view being the fulfillment of physical needs, pure and simple. The short story can be read as an expression of resistance against the increasing influence of newly wealthy societies that may have eschewed rules for enforced segregation and veiling, yet have not in any meaningful way adopted liberal attitudes toward women.

## INTO THE TWENTY-FIRST CENTURY: PROBLEMS AND EXPECTATIONS

As the twentieth century drew to a close and a new century began, women in North Africa continued their work in the public sphere as well as their efforts to establish a more balanced domestic life. They continued to be firmly outspoken—through both their own publications and general media outlets, books, and public speeches—taking on a legacy of hard-core prejudices and seemingly insurmountable problems, many of them centuries in the making. These problems include such social and cultural ills as prostitution and trafficking in women, female genital mutilation, violence in the home, discriminatory legislation, and inadequate family codes as well as wartime violence against women. Women in the Sudan, in particular, have suffered especially gravely as marauding official and unofficial military bands have raped women and killed them and their children. Other human rights violations, in which women are often disproportionately represented among the victims, include abductions and forced displacements.

## The Political Process

While North African countries have granted women the right to vote and to stand for election, only very recently have there been significant signs of progress with regard to parliamentary representation. In Morocco, for example, where women have been able to vote and run for office since 1962, only in 2002 were thirty parliamentary seats reserved for women. In that year, thirty-five women held parliamentary seats; in 2007, there were 24. While such quotas allow for representation numerically, they do not address various social, cultural, and psychological obstacles. Women have begun to develop strategies to overcome the pervasive masculine culture of parliamentary politics. In terms of female representation in politics, Morocco ranks sixty-ninth internationally, surpassed by Tunisia, where 14 percent of legislators are women, and by Mauritania.

In Mauritania today, there are three female ministers, five undersecretaries, two ambassadors, and two governors of provinces. In the last election, women gained 20 percent of the parliamentary seats, the highest percentage in the Arab world. In the municipal council, Mauritanian women occupy 1,120 seats out of a total of 3,699, or 37 percent (Nelson and Chowdhury 1994). During the 1980s, the Mauritanian government established a ministry of women's affairs and, at the end of that decade, appointed Khadija Bint Ahmed as Minister of Industry and Commerce (Daoud 1993).

## Prostitution and Trafficking

Although prostitution is recognizably one of the bitterest challenges that continues to confront North African women, during the last few decades it has taken on new and more ugly forms, especially when combined with trafficking in women. Young women, sometimes teenagers, seemingly offered employment or training for employment or marriage, are lured into foreign journeys at the end of which is a life of forced prostitution, often accompanied by physical violence—in other words, a life of enslavement. The stories of Berber slave women included in this volume testify to the dangerous—and occasionally brave—lives of these prostitutes, which are sometimes additionally complicated by racism. (See "Two Slaves" and "Love and Militancy," 2001.)

The sudden and unexplained death of Aicha Mekki, a well-known Moroccan journalist who wrote exposés of wealthy pimps and the corruption behind prostitution, suggests that this is a social illness that will not be eradicated simply or swiftly. (See "On Prostitution," 1980.) An earlier poem by Saida Menhebi called simply "The Prostitutes" vividly provides a perspective on the economic needs of such lives:

> I think of them
> When they take off their clothes
> And then quickly dress again
> For they don't want to miss the next customer
> Or the bus,
> Since they need to keep feeding their children.
> (See "Two Poems," 1977.)

## Female Genital Mutilation (FGM)

Despite the early and brave anti-FGM work of Egypt's Nawal El Saadawi and others, and despite the continued and relentless agitation of various nongovernmental organizations and governmental bodies through much of the twentieth century, FGM remains a serious problem in North Africa, particularly in Egypt and Sudan.[21] A powerful evocation of its continuing presence as a necessity for male sexuality appears in a story by the Sudanese author Buthayna Khadr Mekky. (See "Rites," 1996.) The married woman at the center of the story, who has not undergone FGM, attends a wedding in the northern Sudanese village home of her husband, where screams of pain on the bride's wedding night shock and mystify her. Her husband tells her that sex for women who have been circumcised becomes extraordinarily painful, while for men the practice provides additional pleasure.[22] Her husband has an agenda to which his wife—in order to keep her marriage—eventually submits.

Mekky's story highlights not only male ruthlessness about women's pain, but also the seemingly unstoppable power of collective thinking. The rites referred to by the title suggest the magical intensity of ancient sacred ritual, difficult for an individual to challenge. Village women accept as fact that their pain is the sine qua non of male pleasure. The heroine's final remark—"I have lost forever the beloved who resided in my heart and soul, despite having gained a man: my husband"—is bitter news, for she is an educated woman and from an enlightened culture in southern Sudan.

While "Rites" is a shocking piece of fiction, a real incident that took place in 2007 in one of the small towns of Upper Egypt has brought renewed outrage and public scrutiny to the practice of FGM. Following the death of a twelve-year-old named Bodour during a circumcision operation, scores of articles in the daily press and a large number of television programs focused on the case, making it one of the most widely publicized events of 2007 in Egypt. In one of the articles inspired by the young girl's death, Mona Abousenna argues cogently and forcefully that the practice has no religious roots, but is in fact a social custom that should be completely eradicated. She calls upon the intellectual elite to speak publicly and responsibly against the practice in order to break the vicious circle from which the child—like millions of girls and young women before her—has no power to extricate herself. (See "Girls' Honor and Intellectuals' Shame," 2007.)

For a time, at least, it seemed as though the child's death would produce some results. Certainly all of Egypt seemed outraged by such needless death, and many government agencies, nongovernmental organizations, and some religious leaders were united in their determination to curb the practice. Soon after the girl's death, activists launched a campaign against the practice in several cities and towns. As a result, the Minister of Health issued a decree prohibiting FGM operations in all public and private clinics and hospitals, although the decree did not criminalize such operations. A new bill criminalizing and outlawing the practice was presented to parliament as part of more comprehensive legislation to protect children, and was passed in June 2008.[23] This was announced in April 2008 by Moushira Khattab, president of the National Council for Childhood and Motherhood, in a speech in which she also indicated that a study conducted in ten governorates in Egypt showed that between 2003 and 2007, the percentage of girls' undergoing FGM had dropped 3 percent (Rashwan 2008, 5).

## Writing as One Strategy of Survival

In spite of persistent problems, women's energies remain undaunted. With vigor and determination, they have continued devising new strategies; among these is a flood of writing in various forms, much of which responds to age-old challenges. An increasingly huge stream of fiction, autobiography, journalism, and poetry produced by women in the region continues to emphasize the importance of women's rights and of writing as a tool not only of self-expression but of social change. The important autobiographical essay, included in this volume, by pioneering Egyptian feminist Nawal El Saadawi, for example, analyzes the relationship between freedom and creativity. (See "Writing and Freedom," 1993.) Her assertion that "writing has become the only way I can survive" in fact echoes the sentiments of many creative women in the region, who have discovered that writing is synonymous with existence, while silence and voicelessness are sure signals of death.

Tassadit Yacine, an Algerian who has focused on the anthropology of suffering among Berber women, offers a similar perspective for women of a traditional society, who "increasingly feel the need to express themselves. . . even more than their more fortunate sisters. . . born to lives supposedly more favorable to women's emancipation." Yacine describes an orphan named Nouara "who has lived through several marriages and divorces," and continues to live a peasant life controlled by Islam. Poetry and her journal remain a refuge for a woman, who is "neither totally and openly emancipated nor traditional. . . . This notebook. . . has now become her faithful companion." (See "Why Some Women Write Poetry," 1995.)

The lives and writing of poets attest over and over again to this need to write in resistance to, or defiance of custom. The life of Khadija Bent Abdelhay of Mauritania is exemplary in this instance. An award-winning young scholar who passed away just before the approval of her M.A. on the Mauritanian short story at the University of Algiers, she left behind one published collection, *Inscriptions on the Walls of a Bus* (2002) and an unfinished manuscript of poems in Arabic. One of these poems, "I am Drunk With Poetry," on the very subject of writing poetry, was deliberately composed in Classical Arabic, for in Mauritania, the social sanctions against women mastering Classical Arabic have been, and remain, strong. The use of Classical Arabic can therefore become a highly charged political and ideological issue in the struggle for women's liberation. Her use of Classical Arabic for a poem containing a debate between an old man instructing a woman that the language of poetry was too grand to be wielded by women, and a woman defiantly claiming the muse of poetry for any subject she chooses, becomes part of the ethics of liberation for the woman writer.

Some writers use fiction to express their defiance. In Azza Filali's story, for example, the heroine manages to keep her sanity by refusing to submit to the psychological pressures of her husband's continued state of rage, which he maintains for seemingly no reason. Her creative solution is laughter: "Now, he speaks and she laughs. She laughs without being able to stop." Through laughter she breaks free of his dominance and reasserts her freedom and independence. (See "Duo," 2003.)

## The Past: Dead Weight or Inspiration

For a large segment of women in the region, recent decades have brought a new dynamic into their outlook on, and relationship with, their history and cultural heritage. In *Granada*, a fictional trilogy, Radwa Ashour, for example, reconsiders some aspects of Islamic history previously ignored. Inspired by a view of Islamic civilization as a site of rationality, tolerance, and human decency, Ashour presents women characters as admirable, rational beings who contribute constructively to the welfare of their communities. Ashour's view sharply challenges prevalent views of former Islamic societies and the position of women in them. Set in Andalusia after the fall of Granada in 1492 and the forcible conversion of Muslims to Catholicism, the text selected for this volume portrays the plight of one Muslim woman hounded as a witch and thrown into prison by a ruthlessly fanatical Catholic inquisition. (See "Accused of Heresy," 1994.) The character Salima Bint Jaafar, an intellectual and a medical practitioner, carries within her the legacy of learning and scholarship of her learned father. She "read books, treated patients, and removed all thought of Castilian oppression from her mind. When she walked in the streets, she did not get distracted by the markets, like other women. She imagined the face of the woman whom she had not been able to treat with her medicine."

For Ashour as author, the Muslim heritage embodies all the human values that are enshrined in, and advocated by, the Universal Declaration of Human Rights proclaimed by the United Nations in 1948. These values, according to Ashour, are not imports from other civilizations but are homegrown and indigenous to Islamic culture. The women of the region only need to dig deep into their history to find them.

## Veiling Revisited

For many North African women, this reconsideration of history has meant a return to their cultural heritage as Muslims, stated visually in the adoption of Islamic dress on the streets throughout most of the region. Some modern North African feminists no longer seek to shed their own heritage, or modify it in favor of a more secular and modernized approach, as did some of their grandmothers in feminist movements during the early years of the twentieth century. Instead, these contemporary feminists now seem willing to go back to the roots of their cultural heritage and to adopt not only the dress code but, more important, a new view of past centuries. In fact, some young women who consider themselves both feminists and Islamists are now promoting a new view of Islamic thought that takes into account women's aspirations and problems while at the same time reinstating Islamic teachings and precepts.

The women of early twentieth century liberation movements were mainly secular in their outlook, believing that to accomplish gender equality and establish justice, it was necessary to reinvent Islam in modern gear. In contrast, contemporary Islamist women activists at the end of the twentieth century and the beginning of the twenty-first have decided that Islam does not in any way contradict the notions of justice and equality. "Representatives of Islamist movements," as Omayma Abdellatif and Marina Ottaway argue, "now invariably proclaim their commitment to the rights of women—as long as those rights are interpreted and recast in an Islamic framework" (Abdellatif and Ottaway 2007, 6).

The mass adoption of the Islamic dress code represented either by the headscarf or the overall veiling that covers the whole body is often dismissed as a natural reaction to such rampant economic problems as poverty and unemployment. It would be rather simple-minded, however, to dismiss the movement toward Islamization in North African societies as mere reaction. The roots of the movement seem to go deeper than this view suggests, and may be related to the ways in which women view their relationships to tradition as well as their attempts to establish feminist identities markedly different from Western models. For such women in the region, the past is not conceived of as a dead weight holding down women's progress, but rather as an inspiration to be consulted, negotiated, and used to further women's quest for a fairer deal in society.

> Islamist women are doing more than questioning their role in the movements. They have also initiated a far-reaching debate about women's roles, concerns, and rights from within an Islamist frame of reference, which challenges both dominant interpretations of Islamic views of women and the Western view of a universally valid definition of women's rights. In other words, Islamist women activists are seeking to derive the answers to the questions posed by women's organizations throughout the world by working from within the Islamic tradition rather than by embracing the Western tradition. (Abdellatif and Ottaway 2007, 10).

It would be premature to conclude that a full-fledged Islamist paradigm for addressing women's lives has established itself, as Abdellatif and Ottaway suggest, but one may note as ongoing such attempts to develop one.

Indeed, we can point to a recent essay by Ekbal Baraka included in this volume, written without an Islamist agenda, but recognizing that a sharp departure from Islamic precepts will be counterproductive and produce negative results. (See "So As Not to Forget the Dreams of Qasim Amin," 2002.)

> Enough harm has been done already to Egyptian women and our feminist movement by interfering colonial powers during the first half of the twentieth-century. In fact, the first enlightened Egyptian feminist leaders faced much perverseness. They were accused of being foreign agents, deserters of Islam, and followers of Lord Cromer, the emissary for the British ambassador in Egypt.

Baraka recognizes that in order for a strong feminist movement to grow in North Africa, and to rally support, it cannot ally itself closely with a Western model or agenda, but must promote a view of Islam which is not inimical to women's rights.

For many, the issue of veiling has grown still more complex. To men, Islamist or not, the veil remains a sign of Islamic affiliation and traditional piety. For many women, however, the veil is a token of liberation, an indication that they have engaged publicly to announce their own sense of religious practice. Liberal North African feminists understand this use of the veil, having encouraged dialogue with women who hold such views. Other signs of cooperation among these groups of women may be noted, including an increasing use of Arabic rather than French; discussions that incorporate real knowledge of Islamic scripture; and the recognition that Islam, as women understand it, may remain distinct from traditional practices.

### Political Work Continues

Actions to revise and improve Family Codes continue to engage feminists across North Africa. Some of these revisions have led to other progressive reforms, as, for example, the right of a woman to pass her citizenship on to her children. Currently, the Tunisian and Moroccan family codes are the most progressive in the region. While Morocco's revisions to the Mudawana in 2004 grant women many significant rights, the government's commitment to implementation remains untested, nor have political elites and other members of civil society, including ordinary people, shown strong interest in these changes.

Among a series of significant political rights is the legal protection of a woman's children, especially when paternity is at issue. A provision of Morocco's law gives judges the right to order a DNA paternity test when a woman can establish her formal engagement to a particuar man. Such identified fathers must provide financial and psychological support; and such fathers being identified may allow a woman her family's forgiveness. One must admit, however, that judges have applied this law only rarely, given the difficulty of proving the existence of a formal engagement.

In a speech to Morocco's House of Representatives on the first day of parliamentary discussion of the Mudawana, Nouzha Skalli-Bennis, an important Moroccan political figure, emphasizes the importance of granting women their legal rights, and exhorts male members of parliament to endorse the new law. (See "Progress for Women Is Progress for All," 2004.) She describes the family as "the first cell of society," and asks, "how can we aspire to a just and democratic society . . . providing a fair socializing environment for our children, within a unit based on inequality, discrimination, and violence?" She also claims that the new family law "highlights the core values of Islam: justice and equality. It has allowed us to show to the whole world that Islam is perfectly compatible with the values of equality and human rights." Echoing a century of feminist women's voices in the region, she adds that promoting and empowering women is "a strong way of inscribing our country in modernity, in progress, and in development."

Similarly, the Egyptian parliamentarian Mona Makram-Ebeid, the first woman to head a political party in the Arab world, writes to invoke the importance of women as half the members of the Arab world, even as she also hearkens back more than a century to claim women as "the mothers and educators of the nation," as well as "the partners of men." But in the twenty-first century, she can also claim women as "warriors in search of prosperity and development." (See "Rights of Political Representation," 2007.) Boldly, she states, "Women are the foundation of the transformation under way in Arab societies." What she wants is a quota system that would grant women fair representation in political parties and political bodies. She concludes by reminding her audience of early feminist struggles for women's suffrage.

> Let us remember that thanks to Doria Shafik, the courageous political activist and her supporters, women won the right to vote in 1956. Can we expect that her daughters and granddaughters be as courageous as she?"

### Dislocated Psyches and Transplanted Minds: The Experience of Exile

Many women originally from North Africa address themselves to memory amid the trauma of dislocation. Faiza Shereen, for example, recreates the past as both ever-present and a healer of current woes. (See "Gifts of Time," 2003.) Shereen looks back with a sense of loss and nostalgia for a past that has disappeared forever. She uses her father's watch, whose value she had not initially been aware of, to indicate the richness of her roots and their continued impact on her life. Finding the lost watch becomes symbolic of an ability to retrieve and enjoy her past as a positive force of reconciliation and harmony.

Yaëlle Azagury's text, in which she revisits a lost homeland, is also replete with nostalgia. (See "A Jewish Moroccan Childhood," 2007.) Although she had left Morocco while still a child, certain memories remain indelible in her heart and color her imagination. For her, Morocco is an enchanted land, "a magical kingdom where palm trees cede ground to deliciously smelling pines, where two continents—Europe and Africa—stare at each other, where East flirts with West." Her journey back celebrates the hybrid co-existence of roots and realities, creating a fluid identity.

> I have always felt I was made of endless crystallization, layers brought by winds and oceans, built through gradual accumulation, and then shattered by landslides collapsing my epicenter. And finally, after the turmoil, it is as though I had been swallowed by seas, and granted a patient reappearance, a delivery in a new shape, as an island or perhaps a volcano.

Azagury's views may resonate for many dislocated women: "Perhaps I am just made with pieces to be grafted together and voids to be filled," she writes. "But in the end, I like to think of myself as an all-inclusive structure, an ever-changing ocean's surface echoing the glittering kisses of Tangiers' sun."

### *What's in a Name?*

A North African woman's name is her identity, her home. She lives in it and carries it throughout her life. Unlike her Western counterparts, a North African woman has never been bound socially or legally to take her husband's name after marriage. But her father's name is a badge she carries through life. Integral to the supremacy of maleness over femaleness in North African societies is the exclusive right of all men to have their names carried by subsequent generations of offspring. This right has been inscribed not only in traditions and customs, but by the law itself. It is also a right with especially unfortunate effects on children born out of wedlock. If denied recognition by their biological fathers, these children will go through life without a surname; they may simply be branded "illegitimate" on their birth certificates, and will carry the stigma like a heavy weight all their lives. Defenders of such practice have argued that granting a name to such children will conceal their mothers' shame and therefore promote women's immoral behavior. None seem to care about the children's welfare, nor do they acknowledge that a large percentage of their mothers were victims of rape—nor, of course, is there any shame to be worn by the fathers.

In one of the final texts in this volume, Mona Nawal Helmi, as she now calls herself, decides that she will begin to use the name of her mother, Nawal El Saadawi. (See "From this Day Forth I Shall Carry My Mother's Name," 2006.) Carrying a mother's name, she argues, should be the proper tribute to the sacrifices and selfless devotion offered by mothers to their children. Helmi exposes the social hypocrisy that urges devotion to mothers while denying them proper recognition. Using media to reach a large audience, Mona Nawal Helmi has made appearances on television, stating her case and defending a person's right to choose a name. She has also addressed the taboo subjects of illegitimate children and rape, including incestuous rape, a problem rarely mentioned.

## CONCLUSION

Despite the persistence of inequalities for women in the countries of Northern Africa, we believe that women will continue to fight for their human rights. We conclude by quoting Nawal El Saadawi's recent words addressed to Bodour, the twelve-year-old Egyptian victim of FGM, and to her family, emphasizing the certain triumph to be achieved in the fight against ignorance and injustice, against silence, submission, and indifference:

Yes, Bodour, they grabbed you and tied you up like a chicken and slaughtered you on the altar of their superstitions, ignorance, and fear of this little piece of flesh in your body that threatens their shaky dominance based on illusions throughout the ages.

I say to Bodour's family, let their daughter's spilt blood turn into a beacon of light for the minds. They should never resort to silence and forgetfulness, under any temptation or threat. They should raise their voices high in the sky, to make of Bodour's case a national concern that is not any less important than the issue of liberating the land and the country. A nation without reason is bound to vanish into oblivion. A land without humanity is bound to go with the wind. (El Saadawi 2007)

It is up to the women of North Africa to reinstate humanity and reestablish reason. It is up to them to turn the negatives into positives. They are intent on facing up to the challenge.

Amira Nowaira
Azza El Kholy
Marjorie Lightman
Zahia Smail Salhi
Fatima Sadiqi
Khadija Zizi
Moha Ennaji
Nadia El Kholy
Sahar Hamouda

# NOTES

1. This famine was dubbed the Mustansiri Slump, in reference to the ruler Al-Mustansir Biallah. It continued unabated for seven years, from 1065 to 1071, but reached a peak in 1069.

2. For an interesting biographical account of Sitt al-Mulk, see Fatima Mernissi 1993, 238. According to Mernissi, the Sitt al-Mulk story is a study in the ambiguities of female influence in the medieval world—capable but untitled, depending upon her private connections to make a public impact, poised among the Christian, Jewish, and Islamic communities of Cairo, always in a delicate balance between forces she hoped to manipulate without becoming subordinate to them. On the surface, the rather ruthless Sitt al-Mulk outwitted the traps that normally ensnared women of her class and background, but as her name, which means "Lady of Power," implies—and as Mernissi states—she was unique. Her successes, such as they were, only underscore the conditions under which most women achieved little, if any, independence.

3. The melodrama of Shajarat Al-Durr's life, her involvement in palace intrigues, her alleged murder of her husband, and her own grisly murder—bludgeoned with

wooden clogs at the hands of another woman—somehow shift the emphasis away from the strength of her personality, the significance of her political career, and her success in fending off the danger of the crusading campaign against Egypt. For an account of the various historical treatments of Shajarat Al-Durr, see Duncan 2000.

4. *Ijaza*, literally translated, means "license" or "certificate." This was a proof of attendance and proficiency granted by a well-known teacher to a student who is deemed by the teacher to have attained knowledge in a particular book or area of religious study. The process of teaching and learning was carried out as follows: First, the teacher, male or female, read the original text of a particular book, with comments and explanations by the teacher himself/herself. Second, the student read the text and recounted the book to the teacher in the presence of other students and received comments and corrections from the teacher. Third, the teacher might allow the student to copy out the book or parts thereof. Fourth, the teacher granted the student an *Ijaza*, which is the equivalent of an academic certificate testifying to the student's ability and the fact that he or she has read and understood a certain book under the tutelage of the teacher. This Ijaza is also a permission for the student to go on to teach the same book or area of knowledge (Abu Bakr 1998, 129).

5. For a detailed and reasoned account of Al-Sakhawi's book, *Kitab Al-Nisa* (The Book of Women), see Huda Lutfi 1981, 104–24.

6. This is the argument persuasively put forward by Afaf Lutfi Al-Sayyid Marsot in her 1995 book *Women and Men in Late Eighteenth-Century Egypt*.

7. The document is dated the 16th of Dhee Al Hijja at the end of the Hijira Year 1056 (22 January 1647). The text records that the judge "accepted the women's petition and ordered the defendant to pay the sum of eighteen *nisf* and three quarters in accordance with religious/legal requirements. The man, however, did not pay. So the aforementioned women chose that he be arrested and placed in prison. This was carried out by the command of the aforementioned judge. . . ."

8. Women donated 187 *waqfs*, that is, 22.86 percent. These contributions included property (26 full shops, 72 houses, 14 stores, 8 little houses, 18 upper parts of houses, and 8 stables). The rest was made up of women's shares or inheritance. In 1752, 23 women's *waqfs* were documented. The Haramayn mosque alone got three quarters of the *waqf* and many civil servants were hired to manage it. Documents show that it was the Turks and the Andalusians who, in most cases, were in charge of the money. For example, in 1653, Mohamed Agha Bin Hassan Al-Turqi and Ali Agha Bin Mahmoud Al-Turqi and the two merchants Al-Hajj Ali Klato Bin Mussa Al-Andalusi and Al-Hajj Mohamed Bin Fateh Al-Andalusi were in charge of the contributions. These contributions were managed by a board of trustees in the presence of the Haramyn executive committee, the Maliki and Hanafi Muftis, the Maliki and Hanafi judges, and the chief of the tribe, the president of the board of trustees, in addition to a military committee. All this took place under the supreme supervision of the highest executive power: the pasha or the *bey*. The *waqfs* did not benefit only the poor of Medina and Mecca, but also the civil servants, and a big part of the money was allocated to the maintenance of the offered houses and other buildings. The remainder was distributed annually as alms to the poor; this was known as *surra*, a bag full of money, which the finance officer used to take with him to distribute to the poor when accompanying princes to Hajj. Of the distinguished rulers who accompanied the Hajj procession we find Cheikh Al-Mawhub in the year 1707, Bu Tiba Al-Lamadani before 1758, Al-Hajj Mohamed Bin Al-Wahid Bin Sidi Al-Khalladi, and one of the grandsons of Sidi Ahmed Bin Yussuf in the year 1761.

9. The woman continued, according to Al-Sakhawi: "'I was once at the Warrakeen market where I met a young man who simply captured my heart. After going home, my husband seemed in my eyes to be no better than a blue fly, a monster, an ogre, or an unattractive bull. Just as men feel attracted to beautiful women, so are women equally attracted to handsome, clean-shaven young men. On another occasion, I was looking out of the window with my husband when I saw a man. I began to compare the beauty of his beard, his face, and his eyes to my husband's unkempt beard, his huge teeth, his enormous nose, his beady eyes, his rough skin, the ugliness of his attire, his uncouthness, and the nauseous smell reeking from his mouth and armpits, in addition to his insipid conversation. I was but enamored of the man I saw. But,' she continued, 'I have repented and decided never to go to the public baths or to go visiting any more. In this way, my husband turned into a swan in my eyes'" (Quoted in Abdel Razik 1999, 123).

10. See Khalifa 1973, 117–22. Moussa continued to call for women's right to get an education and started her own school, *Madrasat Tarkeyat Al-Fatah* (School for the Development of Girls), which became *Banat El Ashraf* School. She then she founded several other schools in Cairo and Alexandria. Moussa also called for ending the discrimination between boys' and girls' curricula and demanded the unification of course descriptions. She also contributed to women's education by taking up teaching as a profession and by giving public lectures to women at the university as early as 1908.

11. See Khalifa 1973, 124. Statistics of girls' education in Egypt in 1923:

| Type of School | Date of Founding | Number of Girls |
| --- | --- | --- |
| Kindergarten | 1918 | 306 |
| Elementary | 1909 | 22,335 |
| Primary | 1882 | 247 |
| Secondary | 1920 | 72 |
| Teacher Training Schools | 1903 | 917 |

12. See Daoud 1993, 244. The reform platform of the *Comité d'Action Marocaine* called for:
Compulsory education for children ages 6 through 12, including girls Pedagogy to be adapted to Arabic and Muslim culture
A Moroccan *baccalauréat* (high school diploma)
Institutions of higher education
Literacy and unemployment programs
Health policy focused on maternity

13. For more detail, see Julien 1956 and 2002 and Troutt Powell 2003.

14. The song was sung on 4 April 2002 for the recorder, Abdennour Kharraki. It was first sung in colloquial Moroccan Arabic in the early 1960s, according to the singer and the recorder.

15. For more details see Bitam 2000. Unfortunately, because the French eventually imprisoned Fatma N'Soumer, killed her, and burned her library and papers, we have no text from her.

16. Zhor Lazraq began her political career at twelve when she joined the Istiglal Party (Akharbach and Rerhaye 1992, 48).

17. Frantz Fanon glorified the new lives of these women in the following terms: "Carriers of machine guns, hand-grenades, hundreds of forged identity cards, or bombs, the unveiled Algerian woman swims like a fish in the Western waters. The military, the French patrols smile at her as she passes, compliment her on her physical appearance, but no one suspects that in her briefcase lies the machine gun, which in a short while will be used to shoot four or five members of a patrol" (2002, 4).

18. It is important to point out here that, despite all pressures and constraints, women's enrollments at Egyptian universities continued to increase, and by 1947, the number of women with university degrees had reached 4,033 (Khalifa 1973, 125). This is less than twenty years from the time when the first five women fought to be admitted into a university.

19. Great fortunes were made on the Alexandria Cotton Exchange during the nineteenth century. The American Civil War, in particular, had the effect of making the price of Egyptian cotton skyrocket, which allowed cotton merchants in Egypt—mainly foreigners—to acquire vast fortunes.

20. The rapid change in social structure and the increasing rate of social mobility may be attributed to a number of factors including, but not confined to, the labor market in the Gulf States. Another factor is the liberalization and privatization of the economy. Sadat's open-door policies in the seventies had the effect of bringing about a rate of social mobility probably greater than anything Egypt has experienced in its modern history, with all the attendant problems that this brings (Amin 2000, 177).

21. According to a World Health Organization report, between 100 and 140 million girls and women in the world are estimated to have undergone female genital mutilation, and 3 million girls are estimated to be at risk of undergoing such procedures every year. See WHO 2006. The practice of female genital mutilation/cutting (FGM/C) in Egypt dates back to more than two thousand years. Today, it is almost universal: An authoritative survey conducted in 2003, according to UNICEF, showed that 97 per cent of Egyptian women of reproductive age had been subjected to the practice, while eight out of ten mothers had either circumcised their daughters or intended to have a daughter circumcised in the future.

22. The WHO/UNICEF/UNFPA Joint Statement published in 1997 classified female genital mutilation into four types, ranging from a mild excision of the clitoris to type four, which involves the pricking, piercing, or incising of the clitoris and/or labia or the introduction of corrosive substances or herbs into the vagina to cause bleeding or for the purpose of tightening or narrowing it.

23. Neither the decree nor the law criminalizes the private practice of using unlicensed midwives to perform the procedure.

## WORKS CITED AND SELECTED BIBLIOGRAPHY

Abdel Razik, Ahmed. 1999. *Al-Mar'a fi Misr Al-Mamloukia.* Cairo: General Egyptian Book Organization.

Abdellatif, Omayma and Marina Ottaway. 2007. *Women in Islamist Movements: Toward an Islamist Model of Women's Activism.* Carnegie Papers 2 (June). Beirut: Carnegie Middle East Center, Carnegie Endowment for International Peace.

Abou Ghazi, Emad, and El Saddah, Hoda. 2001. *The Path of the Egyptian Woman: Landmarks and Situations, Volume I.* Cairo: National Council for Women.

Abouzeid, Leila. 1992. In *Femmes et Media,* ed. Latifa Akharbach and Narjis Rerhaye, 38–47. Casablanca: Editions le Fennec.

Abu Bakr, Omaima. 1998. "Female Scholars in Islamic History: 14th and 15th Centuries" *Hajir: Kitab Al-Mar'a* 5/6: 125–40. Cairo: Nossous Publishing House.

Ahmed, Leila. 1993. *Women and Gender in Islam: Historical Roots of a Modern Debate.* Cairo: American University in Cairo Press.

Ahmed, Nariman Abdel Kerim. 1999. *Al-Mar'a Fi Misr Fi Al-'Asr Al Fatimi.* Cairo: General Egyptian Book Organization.

*Aissa Ben Omar wa Fadaiihi*. Manuscript 463. Sbihi Library, Salé.

Akharbach, Latifa and Narjis Rerhaye. 1992. *Femmes et Politique*. Casablanca: Editions Le Fennec.

Al-Asqalani, Ibn Hajar (Al-Haafidh Shihabuddin Abu'l-Fadl Ahmad ibn Ali ibn Muhammad). *Al-Durrar Al-Kamina*.

Al-Sakhawi, Shams El Din Mohamed bin Abdel Rahman. c. 1492–1494. *Al Daw' al-Lami li-Ahl al-Qarn al-Tasi*, Vol. 12.

Amin, Galal. 2000. *Whatever Happened to the Egyptians? Changes in Egyptian Society from 1950 to the Present*. Cairo: American University in Cairo Press.

Amin, Qasim. 1976. "Tahrir Al-Mar'a." In *The Complete Works of Qasim Amin, Volume II*, ed. Amara Muhammad. Beirut: Al Mu'assasa al-'arabiyya lil-dirasat wa'l nashr.

Amrane, Djamila. 1991. *Les Femmes Algériennes dans la Guerre*. Paris: Plon.

Amrouche, Fadhma Ait-Mansour. 1988. *My Life Story: The Autobiography of a Berber Woman*. Trans. Dorothy Blair. London: The Women's Press.

Aouchar, Amina. 1990. *La Presse Marocaine dans la Lutte pour l'Indépendance 1933–1956*. Casablanca: Wallada.

Atiya, Aziz, ed. 1991. *The Coptic Encyclopedia*. New York: Macmillan Publishing Company.

Badran, Margot. 1995. *Feminists, Islam and the Nation*. Princeton: Princeton University Press.

Bahraoui, Hussein. 2003. "*Fenn al Aita fi l'Maghrib*." *Al Ayam* (June): 19–25.

Baida, Jamaa. 1996. *La Presse Marocaine d'Expression Francaise des Origines à 1956*. Rabat: *Faculté des Lettres et des Sciences Humaines*.

Baker Alison. 1998. *Voices of Resistance: Oral Histories of Moroccan Women*. SUNY Series in Oral and Public History. Albany: State University of New York Press.

Balsdon, J.P.V.D. 1963. *Roman Women*. New York: John Day.

Baron, Beth. 1994. *The Women's Awakening in Egypt*. New Haven and London: Yale University Press.

———. 2005. *Egypt as a Woman: Nationalism, Gender, and Politics*. Berkeley: University of California Press.

Belarbi, Aicha. 1989. "*Mouvements de Femmes au Maroc*." *Annuaire de l'Afrique du Nord* 28: 455–65.

Benjelloun, Mohammed. 2001. "*Malamih 'an Mussahamat Almar'a Almaghribya fi Malhamat Alistiqlal wa Lwahda*." In *Nadwa Ilmiya. Dawr Lmar'a Almaghribya fi Malhamat Alistiqlal wa Lwahda. Nashr Almadubiya Assaamiya Liqudama' Almuharibine wa 'Aadaa' Jaysh Attahrir, 58*. Rabat: Matbaâat Bani Isnassen.

Bennani, Farida and Zainab Maadi. 2000. *Sélection de Textes Sacrés sur les Droits Humains de la Femme en Islam*. Rabat: Friedrich Ebert Stiftung.

Bennouna, Khenatha. 1992. In *Femmes et Média*, ed. Latifa Akharbach and Narjis Rerhaye, 77–86. Casablanca: Editions le Fennec.

Bennouna, Mehdi. 2004. Attajriba Assahafiya. *Al'ahdat Almaghribiya* (Rabat), September 10.

Bennoune, Mahfoud. 1988. *The Making of Contemporary Algeria: 1830–1987*. Cambridge: Cambridge University Press.

Berkey, Jonathan P. 1992. *The Transmission of Knowledge in Medieval Cairo: A Social History of Islamic Education*. Princeton: Princeton University Press.

Bernal, Martin G. 2006. Black Athena: The Afroasiastic Roots of Classical Civilization. Vol. 3, *The Linguistic Evidence*. New Brunswick, N.J.: Rutgers University Press.

Bessie, Sophie and Souhayr Belhassen. 1992. *Femmes du Maghreb: L'Enjeu*. Paris: Eddif.

Bitam, Boukhalfa. 2000. *Fadhma N'Soumer: Une Autre Lecture du Combat de l'Illustre Fille de Werja*. Tizi-Ouzou: Aurassi.

Boogert, Nico van den. 1997. *The Berber Literary Tradition of the Sous*. Leiden: Nederlands Instituut voor het Nabije Oosten.

Bourquia, Rahma, ed. *Etudes Féminines*. Rabat: *Faculté des Lettres et des Sciences Humaines*.

Boutaleb, Brahim. 1982. "Lalla Knatha Bent Bakkar." In *Le Mémorial du Maroc*, ed. Larbi Essakali, 86–87. Rabat: Nord Organisation.

Brown, Peter. 2000. *Augustine of Hippo*. Berkeley: University of California Press.

Chucri, Mounir. 1991. "Cyril IV." In *The Coptic Encyclopedia*, ed. Aziz Atiya, Vol. 3, 678. New York: Macmillan Publishing Company.

Clark, Elizabeth. 1983. *Women in the Early Church.* Collegeville, Minn.: Liturgical Press.
Collectif 95 Maghreb Egalité. 1995. *Women in the Maghreb: Change and Resistance.* Rabat:
　　Friedrich Ebert Stiftung.
———. 1999. *Les Maghrébines entre Violences Symboliques et Violences Physiques (Algérie, Maroc,
　　Tunisie).* Rabat: Friedrich Ebert Stiftung.
Court Registry, Old Quarter Courthouse, Cairo. 1566. 17 October (3 Rabie' Akhar 974 AH).
　　Egyptian National Library and Archives, Cairo.
Court Registry, Rachid Courthouse. 1595. 12 June (4 Shawal 1003 AH). Egyptian National
　　Library and Archives, Cairo.
Court Registry, Qausoon Courthouse. 1647. Register No. 268, 22 January (16 Dhee Al Hijja
　　1056 AH). Egyptian National Library and Archives, Cairo.
Cumont, Franz. 1956. *Oriental Religions in Roman Paganism.* New York: Dover Publications.
Dafali, Mohamed Maârouf. 2001. *"Alharaka Alwataniya wa Mas'alat Taâlim Lamar'a."* In *Nadwa
　　Îlmiya. Dawr Lmar'a Almaghribiya fi Malhamat Listiqual wa Lwahda. Nashr Almandu-
　　biya Assaamiya Liqudama' Almuharibine wa "Aâdaa" Jaysh Attahrir,* 215–32. Rabat :
　　Okad: Matbaâat Bani Isnassen.
Daoud, Zakya. 1993. *Féminisme et Politique au Maroc. Soixante Ans de Lutte.* Paris: Ediff.
———. 2007. *Les Années Lamalif* 1958–1988, *Trente Ans de Journalisme.* Casablanca and
　　Mohammedia: Tarik Éditions and Senso Unico Éditions.
Débêche, Djamila. 1950. *Les Musulmans Algériens et la Scolarisation.* Algiers: Charras.
Dixon, Suzanne. 1992. *The Roman Family.* Baltimore: Johns Hopkins University Press.
Duncan, David J. 2000. "Scholarly Views Of Shajarat Al-Durr: A Need For Consensus." *Arab
　　Studies Quarterly* 22(1): 51–70.
"The Last FGM Victim?" 2007. *Egypt Today* (Cairo), August, http://www.egypttoday.com/arti-
　　cle.aspx?ArticleID=7607.
El Afiya, Abdelkader. 1989. *Amirate Aljabal. Alhorra Bent Ali Ben Rachid.* Tétouan: Nour Printing.
———. 1999. *A Border Passage.* New York: Penguin Books.
El Bouih, Fatna. 1987. *"A S'y Brûler les Ailes." Kalima* 18: 38.
El-Fassi, Malika. 1992. In *Femmes et Politique,* ed. Latifa Akharbach and Narjis Rerhaye, 22–26.
　　Casablanca: Editions Le Fennec.
El-Fassi, Mohammed. 1934. *"Poemes Maroccains (Aroubis de Fes)." Cahiers du Sud* 21: éme année:
　　189–91.
———. 1957. *Chants Anciens des Femmes de Fes.* Paris: Seghers.
———. 1972. *Rubaiyat Nissa' Fass (Alarubiyates).* Fes: Matbaat Mohammed V.
El Khayat. Ghita. 1992. *Le Maghreb des Femmes. Les Femmes de l'Umma.* Casablanca: Eddif.
El Meskeen, Matta. 1997. *Women: Their Rights and Obligations in Social and Religious Life in the
　　Early Church.* Cairo: Monastery of St. Macarius.
Ennaji, Moha. 1999. "The Arab World (Maghreb and Near East)." In *Handbook of Language and
　　Ethnic Identity,* ed. Joshua A. Fishman, 382–98. New York: Oxford University Press.
———. 2005. *Multilingualism, Cultural Identity and Education in Morocco.* New York: Springer.
———, ed. 2008. *Language and Gender in the Mediterranean Region.* Special Issue of *Interna-
　　tional Journal of the Sociology of Language* 190. Berlin: Mouton de Gruyter.
Ennaji, Mohammed. 1999. *Serving the Master: Slavery and Society in Nineteenth-Century Morocco.*
　　Trans. Seth Graebner. New York: St. Martin's Press.
Fanon, Frantz. 1959/2001. *L'An V de la Révolution Algérienne,* Repr. Paris: La Découverte.
Fantham, Elaine, Helene Peet Foley, Natalie Boymel Kampen, Sarah B. Pomeroy, and H.A.
　　Shapiro. 1994. *Women in the Classical World.* New York: Oxford University Press.
Ferchiou, Sophie. 1996. *"Féminisme d'Etat en Tunisie: Idéologie Dominante et Résistance Féminine."*
　　In *Femme, Culture et Société au Maghreb,* Vol. 2, ed. Rahma Bourqia, Mounira M.
　　Charrad, and Nancy Gallagher, 134–38. Casablanca: Afrique-Orient.
Finley, M.I. 1960/1964. *Slavery in Classical Antiquity: Views and Controversies.* New York: Barnes
　　and Noble.
Fnitir, Mustapha. 1988. *Quwad Aljanub Alkibar: Namuwdaj Alqa'id Aissa Ben Omar Laabdi.*
　　Unpublished M.A. thesis, Faculty of Letters, Rabat.
Gibbon, Edward. 1776–1788. *History of the Decline and Fall of the Roman Empire.* London.
Green, Dominic. 2007. *Three Empires on the Nile: The Victorian Jihad, 1869–1899.* New York:
　　Free Press.

Halimi, Gisèle. 1973/1992. *La Cause des Femmes*. Repr. Paris: Gallimard.

Hambly, Gavin R. G. 1999. "Becoming Visible: Medieval Islamic Women in Historiography and History." Introduction to *Women in the Medieval Islamic World (The New Middle Ages)*, ed. Gavin R. G. Hambly, 3–27. New York: Palgrave Macmillan.

Hanna, Nelly. 2003. *In Praise of Books: A Cultural History of Cairo's Middle Class, Sixteenth to the Eighteenth Century*. Cairo: American University in Cairo Press.

Hoexter, Miriam. 1998. *Endowments, Rulers and Community: Waqf Al-Haramayn in Ottoman Algiers*. Leiden: Brill Academic Publishers.

Ibn Azzouz-Hakim, Mohammed. 1982. "Sida al–Horra *Exceptionnelle Souveraine*" *Le Mémorial du Maroc*, ed. Larbi Essakali, 128–35. Rabat: Nord Organisation.

Ibn Khaldun, Abd al-Rahman Bin Muhammad. 1377/1967. *The Muqaddimah: An Introduction to History*, 3 vols. Bolligen Series XLIII. Trans. Franz Rosenthal. Princeton, N.J.: Princeton University Press.

Jackson, Peter. 1999. "Sultan Radiyya Bint Iltutmish." In *Women in the Medieval Islamic World*, ed. Gavin R. G. Hambly, 181–98. New York: Palgrave Macmillan.

Jalal, Oum. 2004. "*Femmes Célèbres: Entretien avec* Malika Al Fassi." *L'Opinion* (Rabat). 10 January.

Jbabdi, Latifa. 1987. In *Al-Sahafa Al-nisa'iga fi Maghrib. Namudhaj Jaridat 8 Maris* by Khadija El Bab, 27. Unpublished M.A. thesis, *Institut Supérieur de Journalisme*, Rabat.

Julien, Charles-André. 1952/2002. *L'Afrique du Nord en Marche: Algérie, Tunisie, Maroc, 1830–1952*. Repr. Paris: Omnibus.

———. 1966. *Histoire de L'Afrique du Nord: Tunisie, Algérie, Maroc*. Paris: Payot.

Kapchan, Deborah A. 1996. *Gender on the Market: Moroccan Women and the Re-voicing of Tradition*. Philadelphia: University of Pennsylvania Press.

Khalifa, Iglal. 1973. *The Modern Women's Movement: The Story of the Arab Woman in Egypt*. Cairo: Modern Arab Press.

Koura, Nadia Hamed. 1996. *The History of Women's Parliamentary Life in Egypt: From 1956 to 1995*. Cairo: General Egyptian Book Organization.

Lagace, Hélène and Nadia Lamhaidi. 2006. *Programme à Moyen Terme pour l'Institutionalisation de l'Egalité entre les Sexes dans le Secteur de la Communication*. Rabat: Ministry of Communication with the support of the Canadian International Development Agency.

Lahjomri, Abdeljahl. 2001. *Pleure Aïcha, Tes Chroniques Egarées*. Casablanca: Malika Editions.

Lakthiri, Mustapha. 2002. "*Taqdeem. Almar'a Almaghribiya fi Malhamat Listiqlal wa Lwahda. Tarajim an Hayat Lmar'a Almuqawima. Aljuz'u L'awal.*" In *Nadwa Ilmiya. Dawr Lmar'a Almaghribya fi Malhamat Alistiqlal wa Lwahda. Nashr Almadubiya Assaamiya Liqudama' Almuharibine wa "Aâdaa" Jaysh Attahrir*, 3–8. Rabat: Okad: Matbaâat Bani Isnassen.

Lamouri, Mohammed, Nadia Lamhaidi, Myriam Monkachi, and Abdelouhab Errami. 1994. *Rapport Femmes et Médias au Maroc*. Rabat: UNESCO/*Institut Supérieur de Journalisme*.

Lightman, Marjorie and Benjamin Lightman. 2000. *Ancient Greek and Roman Women*. New York: Facts-on-File.

Lihamba, Amandina, Fulata L. Moyo, M. M. Mulokozi, Naomi L. Shitemi, and Saida Yahya-Othman. 2007. *Women Writing Africa: The Eastern Region*. New York: Feminist Press at CUNY.

Louh, Amina. 1975. "Amiraat Al'arsh Almaghribi 'Abra Attarikh." Al Funun Assana athaniya 9–10 (July-August): 158-164. Rabat: Ministry of Culture.

Lutfi, Huda. 1981. "Al-Sakhawi's *Kitab Al-Nisa'* as a Source for the Social and Economic History of Muslim Women during the Fifteenth Century A.D." *The Muslim World* 71(2): 104–24.

Mabro, Robert. 2002. "Nostalgic Literature on Alexandria." In *Historians in Cairo: Essays in Honor of George Scanlon*, ed. Jill Edwards, 237–66. Cairo: American University in Cairo Press.

*Majallat Al-Manahil*. 1981. Vol. 21.

Marsot, Afaf Lutfi Al-Sayyid. 1995. *Women and Men in Late Eighteenth-Century Egypt*. Austin: University of Texas Press.

Masry, Iris Habib el. 1979. *Al Mara'Al Asria fi Mowagahat al Massih.* Cairo: Kamal Yussef Printing House.

McNamara, Jo Ann. 1985. *A New Song: Celibate Women in the First Three Christian Centuries.* London: Routledge.

Mdidech, Jaouad. 2002. "Malika El Fassi, *La Passionaria du Nationalisme Marocain.*" *La Vie Economique,* 15 November.

Menebhi, Saida. 2000. *Poèmes – Ecrits — Lettres de Prison.* Rabat: Edition Feed-Back.

Mernissi, Fatima. 1975. *Beyond the Veil: Male-Female Dynamics in a Modern Muslim Society.* New York: Schenkman Publishing.

———. 1993. *The Forgotten Queens of Islam.* Trans. Mary Jo Lakeland. Minneapolis: University of Minnesota Press.

Messaoudi, Khalida and Elizabeth Schemla. 1998. *Unbowed: An Algerian Woman Confronts Islamic Fundamentalism.* Trans. Anne C. Vila. Philadelphia: University of Pennsylvania Press.

Morsy, Magali. 1983. "Lalla Knatha *Reine du Maroc.*" In *Les Africains,* Vol. 1, 171–98. Paris: Editions Jeune Afrique.

Naciri, Rabéa. 2002. "Genre, Pouvoir et Prise de la Décision au Maroc." In *Disparité Entre Femmes et Hommes et Culture en Afrique du Nord,* 25–40. Tangier: United Nations Economic Commission for Africa, *Centre de Dévelopement Sous-Régional pour l'Afrique du Nord.*

Naji, Jamal Eddine. 2006. *Profession: Journalisme Maghrébin au Féminin.* Rabat: UNESCO.

Najmi, Hassan. 2007. *Ghinaa' alaita.* Vols. 1/2. Rabat: Dar Toubkal.

Nelson, Barbara J. and Najma Chowdhury. 1994. *Women and Politics Worldwide.* New Haven: Yale University Press.

*La Parole Confisquée: Textes, Dessins de Prisonniers Politiques Marocains.* 1982. Paris: L' Harmattan.

Rafouq, Fatima. 1983. *Ishtighal Almar'a bi Assahafa fi Almagrib* (Women Working in the Press in Morocco). Rabat: *Institut Supérieur de Journalisme.* M.A. thesis.

Rashwan, Hoda. 2008. "According to Moushira Khattab, FGM Dropped by 3% in 4 Years." *Almasry Alyoum* (Cairo). 2 April.

Rausch, Margaret. 2006. "Ishelhin Women Transmitters of Islamic Knowledge and Culture in Southwestern Morocco." *Journal of North African Studies* 11(2), 173–92.

Rivet, Daniel. 1991. *Le Maroc de Lyautey à Mohammed V. Le Double Visage du Protectorat.* Paris: Editions Denoël.

Saadawi, Nawal El. 2007. "Nawal El Saadawi Writes, Inspired by the Image of Bodour, the Egyptian Girl Murdered in a Clinic at the Hands of a Woman Doctor." *Almasry Alyoum* (Cairo), 28 June.

Sadiqi, Fatima. 1997. *Grammaire du Berbère.* Paris: L'Harmattan.

———. 2003. *Women, Gender and Language in Morocco.* Leiden and Boston: Brill Academic Publishers.

———. 2006. "The Impact of Islamization on Moroccan Feminisms." *Signs: Journal of Women in Culture and Society.* Autumn Issue. 32(1): 32-40.

Sadiqi, Fatima, and Moha Ennaji. 2006. "The Feminization of Public Space: Women's Activism, the Family Law, and Social Change in Morocco." *Journal of Middle East Women's Studies* 2(2): 86–114.

Schimmel, Annemarie. 1982. *As Through a Veil: Mystical Poetry in Islam.* New York: Columbia University Press.

Shulz, Fritz. 1969. *Classical Roman Law.* London: Oxford University Press.

Sikainga, Ahmad Alawad. 1998. "Slavery and Muslim Jurisprudence in Morocco." *Slavery and Abolition: A Journal of Slave and Post-Slave Studies* 19(2): 57–72.

Stora, Benjamin. 2001. *Algeria 1830–2000: A Short History.* Trans. Jane Marie Todd. Ithaca: Cornell University Press.

Subki, Amal Kamel Al. 1986. *Al-Haraka Al-Nisa'eya fi Misr.* Cairo: General Egyptian Book Organization.

Syme, Ronald. 1960. *The Roman Revolution.* New York: Oxford University Press.

Tacitus. 1896–1907/1982. *Annals of Tacitus*, ed. Henry Furneaux. 2 vols. Repr. Oxford: Clarendon Press.

Tibullus, Albius. 1973. *Dionysus, Myth and Cult.* Trans. R. Palmer. Bloomington: Indiana University Press.

Troutt Powell, Eve M. 2003. *A Different Shade of Colonialism: Egypt, Great Britain and the Mastery of the Sudan.* Berkeley: University of California Press.

Van der Meer, F. and Christine Mohrmann. 1966. *Atlas of the Early Christian World,* 3rd ed. Trans. Mary Hedlund and H.H. Rowley. London: Thomas Nelson and Sons.

Véronne, Chantal de la. 1956. "Sayda El-Horra, La Noble Dame." *Hespéris* 43: 221–25.

Veyne, Paul, ed. 1987. *A History of Private Life,* Vol. I: *From Pagan Rome to Byzantium.* Trans. Arthur Goldhammer. Cambridge, Mass.: Harvard University Press.

World Health Organization. 2006. *Progress in Sexual and Reproductive Health Research,* no. 72. Geneva: World Health Organization.

Yacine, Tassadit, ed. 1987. *L'Izli oul l'Amour Chanté en Kabylie,* Publication de Centre d'Etudes et de Recherche Amazigh, no. 3. *Paris: Maison des Sciences de l'Homme.*

Youhana, Menassa. 1982. *The History of the Coptic Church,* 3rd ed. Cairo: Modern Cairo Publishing House.

Zniber, Mohammed. 1982. "*Sens des Médias Chez les Almohades,*" *Memorial du Maroc,* Volume II, 169.

Zouaoui, Mekki. 2005. "*L'Enseignement Supérieur depuis l'Indépendance. La dégradation de la Qualité Est Elle Inéluctable?*" In *50 ans de Développment Humain & Perspectives 2025: Systèmes Educatifs, Savoir, Technologies et Innovation,* published by *Le Cinquantenaire de l'Indépendance du Maroc,* 161–95. Casablanca: Imprimerie Najah El Jadida.

# THE ANCIENTS:
# FIFTEENTH CENTURY BCE TO
# FOURTH CENTURY CE

## *Hatshepsut*
# MY FALCON RISES HIGH

Egypt 15th Century BCE      Hieroglyphic

Hatshepsut, the favored child of Ahmos and Tutmose I, became one of Egypt's rare female pharaohs, reigning during the Eighteenth Dynasty. Following the death of her two brothers, she ruled Egypt for some twenty years, until her own death in 1482 BCE. Throughout her reign she countered challenges led by her half brother, the later Tutmose II, and produced one child, Neferune. However, neither he nor any others were able to shake her claim to legitimacy, inherited through her father, or to diminish her popular support.

Hatshepsut's reign provided a rare period of relative peace that allowed for exploration and trade, which brought great wealth to her dynasty. She supported expeditions along the Nile and desert to the Red Sea coast, reaching south into Punt, present-day Somalia, which was known to the Egyptians since the Fifth Dynasty. Following the first traders, her expeditions sought to capture the sources of ivory, spices, gold, and aromatic trees of incense that had already begun to appear in Egypt.

Hatshepsut commissioned a vast number of construction projects, building new temples and restoring old ones that had been destroyed during the foreign occupation of Egypt by the Hyksos. Among these was the temple of Hathor, the Lady of Qusai, the goddess of beauty, nourishment, and sometimes destruction. Hatshepsut also endowed the festival at the temple, which was inseparable from the celebration of Egypt and the Egyptians.

The restoration of this temple is among the great deeds to which Hatshepsut lays claim in this text, which is taken from an inscription found at Speos Artemidos, the famous archeological site on the Nile that includes another temple built by Hatshepsut. The text is very much in the tradition of the inscriptions found on ancient Egyptian temples and tombs, in which the pharaohs' achievements are celebrated in grand, often hyperbolic terms.

Pharaohs were considered incarnations of the deity Horus, who was the child of Isis and Osiris and is symbolized by the falcon. In this triumphant celebration of her power, Hatshepsut situates herself at the heart of the Isis-Osiris-Horus triangle that dominated the religious life of Egypt well into the Christian period. Her voice was the voice of all whose lives touched the Nile. Her cry, "my falcon rises high . . . unto all eternity" retains the echoes of her triumphant power.

*Hassan Mohammed El-Saady and Laila Helmi*

✦

The temple of the Lady of Qusai had fallen into disuse and disrepair, the earth-swallowed up the noble sanctuary, and children danced on its roof....Its appointed festivals [were] not celebrated. I built it anew and sanctified it. I sculptured the goddess' sacred image in gold [and] to protect her city [led her to the temple] in...land-procession.

Listen, all ...well born and common folks, as many of you as there may be, I have done these things . . . from my heart. Never have I slumbered, [and become] forgetful, but have [re]made [whole and] strong what had decayed. I have raised up what was dismembered, [even] from the [earliest] time when the Asiatics were in Avaris of the North Land, [with] roving hordes . . . overthrowing what [we] had made; they ruled [lawlessly without the commands of the god,] Re . . . I being firmly established on the throne of Re . . . was foretold . . . a born conqueror. [And now] I am come as the Sole One of Horus darting fire against my enemies. I have banished the abomination of the gods, and the earth has removed their foot[-prints]. Such who came at his (appointed) times, even Re; and there shall never be the destruction of what Amon has commanded. My command stands firm like the mountains and the sun's disk shines and spreads rays over the names of my august person; and my falcon rises high above the kingly banner unto all eternity.

*Translated by Alan H. Gardiner*

## *Ankhesen-pa-Atun*
## A PROPOSAL OF MARRIAGE

Egypt  14th Century BCE   Hittite

Widowed when she was still very young by the famous Eighteenth Dynasty pharaoh Tutankhamun, Ankhesen-pa-Atun assumed control over Egypt in 1323 BCE. She had had no sons with Tutankhamun, which left the male Tuthmosid line bereft and heightened intrigue over the succession. She had rivals for power, chief among them the powerful general Horemheb and Ay, an elderly vizier who had advised the young Tutankhamun. At the same time, Egypt was in danger from warrior Hittites, advancing through present-day Turkey toward the Mediterranean.

Ankhesen-pa-Atun sought an innovative solution to both threats. The sophistication of Egyptian culture and politics, and the reach of Egyptian trade, can be sensed by her proposal to the Hittite ruler, Suppililiuma I. Reaching out with a marriage proposal to a foreigner, however, was extraordinary. The first letter offers an eminently reasonable exchange. A suspicious response from Suppililiuma, given the unexpectedness of such an offer and the possibility of trickery, was politically also quite reasonable.

Suppililiuma sent an emissary to investigate and, after receiving Ankhesen-pa-Atuns second letter, dispatched a son to marry her, but the young man was killed on the journey, perhaps by orders from Ay himself. The Hittites unleashed their armies against Egypt, and it appears that Ankhesen-pa-Atun married Ay, either willingly or unwillingly.

The exchange of letters was found on an ancient tablet in the archives of the Hittite capital of Hattusa, now Bo azköy, Turkey. The content of the letters was recorded by Mursil II, son of Suppiluliumas, who wrote the annals of his father's reign. Because the account can be found only in Hittite documents, without corroboration in ancient Egyptian documents, the incident remains shrouded in mystery.

*Amira Nowaira and Dina Abdel Salam*

✦

### First Letter

My husband has died and I have no son, but of you it is said that you have many sons. If you would send me one of your sons, he could become my husband. I will on no account take one of my subjects; to make him my husband would be abhorrent to me.

### Second Letter

Why do you say, "They are trying to deceive me"? If I had a son, would I write to a foreign country to publish my distress and that of my country? You have insulted me in speaking thus! He who was my husband is dead and I have no son. Must I then take one of my subjects and marry him? I have written to no one but you. Everyone says you have many sons; give me one of them that he may become my husband.

*Translator unknown*

## *Anonymous*
# LOVE SONGS

Egypt   14th–12th Centuries BCE    Hieratic Script

Most ancient Egyptian love poems are thought to have been written for entertainment. Some were sung at festivities and banquets, as was common throughout the ancient Mediterranean. The gods referred to in many poems represent intense or "divine" emotion between lovers, rather than specific religious affiliations. Religion was nonetheless important, if only because it was often on religious occasions that the poems were sung. While the authors of these songs are unknown, the voices are clearly female.

The first of these love songs is taken from a cycle of seven stanzas found on what is called the Papyrus Chester Beatty I—named, like many ancient papyri, for the European man who "discovered" or collected it. The stanzas are written in alternating male and female voices, expressing the feelings of lovers who are being kept apart. (As was customary, they refer to each other as "brother" and "sister.") The stanzas included here, in the female voice, reflect the social restrictions surrounding young lovers. While the young woman is ardent in her devotion, evoking "the Gold of women"—the goddess Hathor, who was the patroness of love— her mother is obviously highly protective of her daughter's virtue. Although elements of the poem's structure are lost in translation, we can see that the first and last lines of each stanza repeat a key word or words: "my brother" in the second stanza, "heart flutters" in the fourth stanza, and "passed/passing" in the sixth stanza. The repetition provides focus and may have aided memorization for the poetic singers.

In the second of these love songs (from Second Collection of the Papyrus Harris 500), the opening inscription suggests the plowing and cultivation of a field as a natural metaphor for sexuality and fertility, often found in love poetry from the ancient world. This device appears again in the third song, from the Third Collection of the Papyrus Harris 500, in which the opening line of each stanza begins with the name of some flower or plant.

Despite the sophistication of the songs' language and construction, the voices retain a feeling of sincerity and artlessness, along with a youthful vigor. Although some modern renderings of ancient Egyptian texts may exhibit a form of mannered eroticism, it is worth mentioning that such readings were quite alien to ancient Egyptians. Ancient civilizations were based on a high sense of ritual, and sought to pay homage to fertility in many of their religions and mythologies as the obviously greatest mystery and power of the world around them.

*Laila Helmi*

✦

## Song One

Beginning of the sayings of the great happiness.

### Second Stanza

My bother torments my heart with his voice.
He makes sickness take hold of me; He is neighbor to my mother's house,
And I cannot go to him!
Mother is right in charging him thus:
"Give up seeing her!"
It pains my heart to think of him,
I am possessed by love of him.
Truly, he is a foolish one,
But I resemble him;
He knows not my wish to embrace him,
Or he would write to my mother.
Brother, I am promised to you
By the Gold of women!
Come to me that I see your beauty,
Father, Mother will rejoice!
My people will hail you all together, they will hail you, O my brother!

### Fourth Stanza

My heart flutters hastily,
When I think of my love of you;
It lets me not act sensibly,
It leaps (from) its place.
It lets me not put on a dress,
Nor wrap my scarf around me;
I put no paint upon my eyes,
 I'm even not anointed.
"Don't wait, go there," it says to me,
As often as I think of him;
My heart, don't act so stupidly,
Why do you play the fool?
Sit still, the brother comes to you,
And many eyes as well!
Let not the people say of me:
"A woman fallen through love!"
Be steady when you think of him,
My heart, do not flutter!

### Sixth Stanza

I passed before his house,
I found his door ajar;
My brother stood by his mother,
And all his brothers with him.
Love of him captures the heart
Of all who tread the path;
Splendid youth who has no peer,
Brother outstanding in virtues!
He looked at me as I passed by,
And I, by myself, rejoiced;
How my heart exulted in gladness,
My brother, at your sight!
If only the mother knew my heart,
She would have understood by now;
O Golden, put it in her heart,
Then will I hurry to my brother!
I will kiss him before his companions,
I would not weep before them;
I would rejoice at their understanding
That you acknowledge me!
I will make a feast for my goddess,
My heart leaps up to go;
To let me see my brother tonight,
O happiness in passing!

*Translated by Alan H. Gardiner*

## Song Two

Beginning of the delightful, beautiful songs of your beloved sister as she comes from the fields.

The voice of the dove is calling,
It says: "It's day! Where are you?"
O bird, stop scolding me!
I found my brother on his bed,
My heart was overjoyed;
Each said: "I shall not leave you,
My hand is in your hand;
You and I shall wander
In all the places fair."
He makes me the foremost of women,
He does not aggrieve my heart.

## Song Three

Beginning of the songs of delight.

*1*

Portulaca: apportioned to you is my heart.
I do for you what it desires,
When I am in your arms.
My longing for you is my eye-paint,
When I see you my eyes shine;
I press close to you to look at you,
Beloved of men, who rules my heart!
O happiness of this hour,
Let the hour go on forever!
Since I have lain with you,
You raised up my heart;
Be it sad or gay;
Do not leave me!

*2*

Saam-plants here summon us,
I am your sister, your best one;
I belong to you like this plot of ground
That I planted with flowers
And sweet-smelling herbs.
Sweet is its stream,
Dug by your hand,
Refreshing in the northwind.

A lovely place to wander in,
Your hand in my hand.
My body thrives, my heart exults
At our walking together;
Hearing your voice is pomegranate wine.
I live by hearing it.
Each look with which you look at me
Sustains me more than food and drink.

*Translated by Miriam Lichtheim*

## *Anonymous*
## LAMENT OF ISIS AND NEPHTHYS

Egypt c. 300 BCE    Hieratic Script

The Isis/Orsirus/Horus story is a powerful tale of death and renewal that defined Egyptian metaphysics and theology, and that challenged four centuries of Christianity for the hearts and minds of ancient worshipers. The story had many variations, over time and across the ancient Mediterranean. One of the most complete renditions was written by the second-century CE Greek historian Plutarch.

The god Seth killed his brother Osiris, the earth god and husband/brother of Isis. Finding her beloved's body, Isis hid him, but Seth found and dismembered him. With the help of her sister, Nephthys, Isis found and restored all his scattered parts, then used her magical power to breathe life back into him to conceive Horus. (In some versions, she fails to find his penis, so she fashions one out of gold.)

This text is part of a series of laments found with a papyrus belonging to a woman named Tentruty (or possibly Teret). In this excerpt, the faithful Isis laments the death of Osiris. At the end of the text are instructions for the reenactment of the lamentations by two women celebrants taking the roles of Isis and her sister Nephthys.

*Heba Sharobeem*

✦

Come to your dwelling, come to your dwelling,
You who no longer have enemies,
You who are handsome, come to your house to see me.
I am your sister who loves you,
Do not be separated from me, handsome one.

Come to your dwelling,
I do not see you; [however],

My heart dreams of joining you,
And my eyes seek you.
[...]
How marvelous it is to contemplate you!
[...]
Oh, Un-Nefer, come to the one who loves you,
   the one who loves you, who loves you,
Come to the side of your sister,
Come near your wife,
You whose heart has ceased to beat!
Come near the woman of your house.
I am your sister by the same mother.
Do not stay away from me.
All the gods and men turn their faces towards you,
And together they all cry for you; for they see me
Calling for you and shedding such heavy tears
That they hear me up there in heaven,
But you do not hear my voice.
I am your sister who has loved you on earth,
You have never loved any other woman
But me, Oh my brother! Oh my brother!

*Translated into French by Christiane Desroches Noblecourt*
*Translated from French by Heba Sharobeem*

## *Philista, Daughter of Lysias*
## A COMPLAINT

Egypt  220 BCE    Greek

This document was written by a Greek woman from Egypt in 220 BCE at the beginning of the reign of Ptolemy IV Philopator (221–204 BCE), i.e. about a century after the death of Alexander the Great in 323 BCE and the start of the Ptolemaic rule in Egypt. The Ptolemaic Dynasty in Egypt had been founded by Ptolemy I Soter as a satrap (323–305 BCE) and later as the founding monarch.

This papyrus presents a woman's demand for legal action against a male bath attendant who had burned her with a pitcher of hot water. Public baths were an integral part of urban life throughout the ancient world. In larger towns and cities they were among the gathering places that served ethnically, religiously, and economically mixed populations, often including Egyptians, Greeks, Jews, Syrians, along with local resident ethnic groups. However, they were usually segregated by gender. Women bathed at designated hours, and their presence at other times signaled their sexual availability. The evolving rules regarding gender segregation among bathers and between servers and bathers, which were probably less strict in the pre-Islamic period, reflect a view of the body, especially of a woman's body, that over the centuries attributed profoundly different meanings to female modesty and public display.

The document indicates that a woman who appears to be neither of elite status nor wealthy and who was a Greek resident of Egypt succeeded in bringing a suit for damages in her own name without even the formality of a male protector. Her appeal references the chief of police; the *epistates*, or local superintendent; and Diophanes, the *strategos,* or imperial governor. Although it was customary to address such appeals to the king, it probably went to the *strategos* Diophanes. A brief reply directs Simon the *epistates* to "Bring the one accused."

*Mohammed El-Sayed Abd-el-Ghani*

✦

Greetings to the King Ptolemy from Philista,
daughter of Lysias, one of the [settlers] in Trokimia.
I am being wronged by Petechon. When I was bathing in the bathhouse of the above mentioned village on Tybi 7, year 1, and had stepped out of the bath to soap myself, he,…the bath attendant in the women's rotunda,…brought in the small jugs of hot water, emptied [it]…over me and burned my stomach and my left thigh down to the knee, with the result that my life was in danger.

Having [captured] him, I handed him over to Nechthosiris, the chief of police, in the presence of Simon the *epistates*. If seems fitting to you, great ruler, as a suppliant who has sought refuge with you, [and] a woman who lives by her hands,…I beg of you not to allow me to be treated so lawlessly, but to command Simon the *epistates* and Nechthosiris the chief of police to bring Petechon before…Diophanes so that he may investigate this matter, so that I may obtain justice . . . [from you] the common benefactor of all people, having sought refuge with you. Farewell.

*Translated by Ronald Cluett*

## *Nikaia, Daughter of Nikias*
## REQUEST FOR A GUARDIAN

Egypt 218 BCE    Greek

This petition, like the previous appeal, originates in the third century BCE, during the three-hundred-year period of Ptolemaic rule by the Greeks in Egypt. The line extended to Cleopatra VII, who sought to become coruler of the Mediterranean, first in alliance with Julius Caesar and then Marc Antony, during the Roman civil war in the first century BCE. After the defeat of Cleopatra and Antony, Egypt—for seven centuries—was a province of the Roman Empire.

Women had different degrees of personal legal autonomy under Egyptian, Greek, and Roman law. Under all three legal codes, male representatives generally acted for women in business since none of the legal codes of the period accorded women full legal independence. By and large, Egyptian private law was less restrictive for women than Greek private law; in Roman law, over time, the male representative became the women's agent, acting under her direction.

In this petition, addressed to Ptolemy but probably received by his *strategos* Diophanes, the petitioner identifies herself as a widow of Persian ethnicity who has chosen her brother-in-law as her agent after the death of her husband and son. She seeks legal ratification of her choice. This is an example of a type of petition that women frequently addressed to the ruler. The death of husbands and sons left women needing a male figure to engage in the public acts of business, and it was important that the man was a member of the husband's family. Land and wealth needed to remain securely within the family in order to protect their transmission to the next generation. The reply directs the *epistates* Dioskourides, the local superintendent, to comply with Nikaia's request.

*Marjorie Lightman*

✦

Greetings to King Ptolemy from Nikaia,
daughter of Nikias, a Persian woman.
My husband died...leaving behind a will...through which...his own son ...[was] my trustee/guardian. But it has come about that he too has died,...and that I have no male relative to be registered as my guardian. Therefore and for this reason so that...the property left to me by my husband [will] not be utterly ruined, because I lack a guardian with whom I will be able to establish [the] management of matters concerning the household, I beg of you, King, to order Diophanes the *strategos*, that Demetrios the Thracian, be assigned to...me as guardian. [He is] one of the men serving under Ptolemaios, the son of Eteoneus of the [x] hipparchy, possessor of 100 arourai of land, to whom Pausanias also gave his sister in marriage; and to order the *strategos* to make a written record concerning these matters so that they may be properly on record for me. And since I am not able to make the journey to Krokodilopolis, since I am rather old and have become weak, I have sent the aforementioned Demetrios to submit my petition. I ask that Diophanes write to Dioskourides the *epistates* to make a physical description of me and of the guardian whom I am seeking, and to submit a copy to Diophanes. With these matters accomplished, I will have attained, King, the benefit that you bestow. Farewell.

*Translated by Ronald Cluet*

# *Apollonous*
## ABOUT A LITTLE GIRL

Egypt c.100 CE    Greek

Across the Mediterranean and in all its historical eras, correspondence among dispersed family and kin was widespread and surprisingly frequent. By the first century CE, Egypt was part of the Roman Empire, and cities like Alexandria contained multiethnic populations of Romans, Greeks, Jews, and others, as well as native Egyptians. Trade was the lifeblood of the city. Sea travel was generally faster than travel by land, and merchant ships were a favored means of transporting letters, especially if they could be delivered to their final destinations by the receiving merchants. Letters were also routinely carried by individual or small groups of travelers, and entrusted to traveling traders. Along with letters, voyagers in and out of the cities brought verbal greetings, information, and gossip about people, politics, religion, and the customs of other places.

Securing mail delivery was one mark of sovereignty among ancient empires. The ability to insure safe communication for official documents and correspondence was manifest evidence of the power over geography. "Diplomatic pouches" often included private letters. Collections of letters from such men as Cicero, Pliny, Plutarch, who traveled on official business, are an important source of knowledge about the ancient world in general, and about the women in their lives in particular. Churchmen like Jerome and Chrysostum were also highly prolific letter writers, and collections of their letters make major contributions to our understanding of women in the Greco-Roman world during the Christian era.

Although we have relatively extensive collections of private letters from men of renown, we have none from women. The papyri are unique in providing us with samples of correspondence especially among nonelite women. Remembering that literacy was probably quite widespread and that scribes were available even in small towns to read and write letters for people, it is still rare to read a letter that reflects the concerns and anxieties of everyday people. This papyrus, a message to a mother from her grown daughter, expresses a great deal of tenderness and concern for a girl-child's well-being. There is a haunting quality to the papyrus, which provides an intimate glimpse into lives about which we know nothing else.

*Marjorie Lightman*

✦

Apollonous to Thermouthas her mother, many greetings.
Above all else we pray that you are in good health, together with Apollonarion. I want you to know that I have heard from those who have come to me that you have been ill, but I rejoiced upon hearing that you were better. I fervently ask and beg of you, take care of yourself together with the little girl, so that you may get through the winter and so that we may find you in good health. We too are all well. As for the Syrian woman, so far nothing bad. I do ask you if you hear anything about Thermouthas, send word to me. I ask of you—it isn't a prob-

lem—if you find anyone coming down here, send me word concerning your health and that of the little girl. I ask and beg of you, if it is possible, that you see the little girl three times per day, so that it appears that I am near to you. I shall send the earring to you soon, for mine has not yet been made.

There are twelve cured fish and twenty-two sesame cakes for the little girl, and give them to her one by one. Gaius sends you his highest regards, and Thermouthas, and Isodorus, and Diogenas, and we kindly welcome Apollonarion. We send our regards to Ammia and her child. Everyone sends their regards to you. Be well. I send my regards to Hera and her children.

Deliver to Philadelphia to Thermouthas.

*Translated by Ronald Cluett*

## *Ptolema*
## LETTER TO A BROTHER
Egypt  2nd century CE    Greek

The second century CE was one of the most peaceful and economically secure periods of the Roman Empire. Although Egypt had become a Roman province in the late first century BCE, the Greek language remained predominate. Accompanying peace and stability had also been a gradual but steady increase in women's legal rights and visibility in the public sphere, as Roman family law gradually supplanted or modified Greek and Egyptian traditions.

In Roman custom and private law the role of men as guardians or tutors over grown women had been in transition since the first century BCE, when Rome had faced a serious gender imbalance as a consequence of years of civil war. Augustus, at the beginning of the imperial period after the end of the civil wars, initiated a set of marriage laws with the Senate that encouraged women to marry and bear children, chief among them a law that granted women who had borne three live children an independent legal personality.

Throughout the empire, women always handled family matters, managed large and small estates and farms, and engaged in complicated business transactions. During periods of political turmoil and war, of which there was no end, women were often left without men and of necessity assumed their roles. Always, among wealthy families, men were gone in the service of state for long periods of time. Collections of letters from the younger Pliny speak of his wife's aunt Hispulla, who managed her own estate; and the correspondence of Plutarch and his wife Timoxena attests to the widespread presence of well-educated and capable women.

This papyrus fragment by Ptolema to her brother, or possibly her husband, suggests that women less wealthy and well placed also managed family affairs. Ptolema reports on the status of the family estate with familiarity and competence. Her letter gives her brother/husband instructions for legal action and also reports on the sale of goods and land. In some sense, it should hardly be surprising that women like Ptolema exercised their authority and management skills: Family wealth was a corporate concern and men were often away on business, military, or civil missions for long periods of time. A woman like Ptolema followed in the most ancient tradition of Penelope, surviving by her wits as she waits for the return of her husband, Odysseus.

*Marjorie Lightman*

✦

Ptolema to her brother (=husband) Antas, greetings....

You write that you are awaiting the prefect. Take note, the prefect has gone up. If your health is good, quickly be present before the prefect so that we may be able to decide our small matter. The fields are all in good condition. The embankment/area enclosed by dikes of 17 arourai to the west has been ruined by the cattle. Your cattle have eaten the [arable] land and departed to Pansoue. Everything there has been given up to the cattle. The portion from the southwest of the vegetable-garden to the feeding enclosure has been [left fallow].

We have sold the coarse grass area in the klerouche alongside the embankment [embankment 6?], the portion to the east, for 112 drachmai. The feeding-place/enclosed space is inexpensive. Three plots of your arable land have been sold through Euetranios up to the feeding-place/enclosed space for 130 drachmai. Through him the cattle have been sold for 68 drachmai. Longinus and Sarapion and everyone in the household greet you. Ouibis has gone to Psenuris to sell corn/grain. Everyone is doing well. Be well.

*Translated by Ronald Cluett*

## Saint Vivia Perpetua
# I AM A CHRISTIAN

Tunisia  203 CE    Latin

Vivia Perpetua was born into a respectable Roman family in Carthage, located in present-day Tunisia, which was the largest city in the Roman province of North Africa. A convert to Christianity at a time when such an act was punishable by death throughout the empire, Perpetua was arrested and imprisoned. She declared herself a Christian before the Roman proconsul, claiming Christ her only God and refusing to perform a sacrifice to the traditional Gods for the birthday games of the emperor. Despite the pleadings of her father to recant, she stood firm in her belief and was condemned to death along with a small group of other Christians. She died in Carthage on 7 March 203, after having been mauled by wild animals in the arena. When she died, Perpetua was twenty-two years old, married, and had recently given birth to her first child, a son.

In prison, Perpetua recorded three visions that assured her and her fellow Christians of saintly rewards. She never questioned the sacrifice of her life or the lives of those condemned with her, among them Felicita, who appears to have been a slave or freed woman in Perpetua's household. From the narrative, we know that Felicita shared Pertpetua's devotion to Christ, her fierce determination to die for her belief, and her willingness to leave the baby girl she bore in prison to be reared by a sister. Perpetua's narrative ended on the day before the group went into the arena. The story of her death was added to the narrative by a contemporary fellow Christian who helped Perpetua in prison.

During Perpetua's lifetime, North Africa was an important and wealthy part of the Roman empire. In Carthage, which was Punic in tradition, Latin literacy was widespread among the elite, including women. Perpetua wrote in a vernacular rather than literary Latin, and her images and metaphors were borrowed from well-known Biblical tradition and life around her. Her narrative was known among Christians in the period after her death and later lost, although her name and martyrdom remained a part of tradition. A manuscript of her narrative was rediscovered in the seventeenth century and published. Since then, additional copies in both Latin and Greek have been found.

*Marjorie Lightman*

✦

When . . . we were still under legal surveillance and my father was liked to vex me with his words and continually strove to hurt my faith because of his love: Father, said I, Do you see (for examples) this vessel lying, a pitcher or whatsoever it may be? And he said, I see it. And I said to him, Can it be called by any other name than that which it is? And he answered, No. So can I call myself nought other than that which I am, a Christian.

Then my father angry with this word came upon me to tear out my eyes; but he only vexed me, and he departed vanquished, he and the arguments of the devil. Then because I was without my father for a few days I gave thanks unto the Lord; and I was comforted because of his absence. In this same space of a few days we were baptized, and the Spirit declared to me, I must pray for nothing else after that water save only endurance of the flesh. After a few days we were taken into prison, and I was much afraid because I had never known such darkness. O bitter day! There was a great heat because of the press, there was cruel handling of the soldiers. Lastly I was tormented there by care for the child.

Then Tertius and Pomponius, the blessed deacons who ministered to us, obtained with money that for a few hours we should be taken forth to a better part of the prison and be refreshed. Then all of them going out from the dungeon took their pleasure; I suckled my child that was now faint with hunger. And being careful for him, I spoke to my mother and strengthened my brother and commended my son unto them. I pined because I saw they pined for my sake. Such cares I suffered for many days; and I obtained that the child should abide with me in prison; and straightway I became well and was lightened of my labor and care for the child; and suddenly the prison was made a palace for me, so that I would sooner be there than anywhere else. . . .

Then said my brother to me: Lady my sister, you are now in high honor, even such that you might ask for a vision; and it should be shown you whether this be a passion or else a deliverance. And I, as knowing that I conversed with the Lord, for Whose sake I had suffered such things, did promise him nothing doubting; and I said: Tomorrow I will tell you. And I asked, and this was shown me.

I beheld a ladder of bronze, marvelously great, reaching up to heaven; and it was narrow, so that not more than one might go up at one time. And in the sides of the ladder were planted all manner of things of iron. There were swords there, spears, hooks, and knives; so that if any that went up took not good heed or looked not upward, he would be torn and his flesh cling to the iron. And there was right at the ladder's foot a serpent lying, marvelously great, which lay in wait for those that would go up, and frightened them that they might not go up. Now Saturus went up first (who afterward had of his own free will given up himself for our sakes, because it was he who had edified us; and when we were taken he had not been there). And he came to the ladder's head; and he turned and said: Perpetua, I await you; but see that the serpent bite you not. And I said: it shall not hurt me, in the name of Jesus Christ. And from beneath the ladder, as though it feared me, it softly put forth its head; as though I trod on the first step I trod on its head. And I went up, and I saw a very great space of garden, and in the midst a man sitting, white-headed, in shepherd's clothing, tall, milking his sheep; and standing around in white were many thousands. And he raised his head and beheld me and said to me: Welcome, child. And he cried to me, and from the curd he had from the milk he gave me as it were a morsel; and I took it with joined hands and ate it up; and all that stood around said, Amen. And at the sound of that word I awoke, yet eating I know not what of sweet.

And at once I told my brother, and we knew it should be a passion; and we began to have no hope any longer in this world. . . .

A few days after, the report went abroad that we were to be tried. Also my father returned from the city spent with weariness; and he came up to me to cast down my faith saying: Have pity, daughter, on my gray hairs; have pity on your father, if I am worthy to be called father by you; if with these hands I have brought you unto this flower of youth and I have preferred you before all your brothers; give me not over to the reproach of men. Look upon your brothers; look upon your mother and mother's sister; look upon your son, who will not endure to live after you. Give up your resolution; do not destroy us all together; for none of us will speak openly against men again if you suffer aught.

This he said fatherly in his love, kissing my hands and groveling at my feet; and with tears he named me, not daughter, but lady. And I was grieved for my father's case because he would not rejoice at my passion out of all my kin; and I comforted him, saying: That shall be done at this tribunal, whatsoever God shall please; for know that we are not established in our own power, but in God's. And he went from me very sorrowful. . . .

Another day as we were at meal we were suddenly snatched away to be tried; and we came to the forum. Therewith a report spread abroad through the parts near to the forum, and a very great multitude gathered together. We went up to the tribunal. The others being asked, confessed. So they came to me. And my father appeared there also, with my son, and would draw me from the step, saying: Perform the Sacrifice; have mercy on the child. And Hilarian the procurator—he that after the death of Minucius Timinian the proconsul had received in his room the right and power of the sword—said: Spare your father's gray hairs; spare the infancy of the boy. Make sacrifice for the Emperors' prosperity. And I answered: I am a Christian. And when my father stood by me yet to cast down my faith, he was bidden by Hilarian to be cast down and was smitten with a rod. And I sorrowed for my father's harm as though I had been smitten myself; so sorrowed I for his unhappy old age. Then Hilarian passed sentence upon us all and condemned us to the beasts; and cheerfully we went down to the dungeon. Then because my child had been used to being breastfed and to staying with me in the prison, straightway I sent Pomponius the deacon to my father, asking for the child. But my father would not give him. And as God willed, no longer did he need to be suckled, nor did I take fever; that I might not be tormented by care for the child and by the pain of my breasts. . . .

The day before we fought, I saw in a vision that Pomponius the deacon had come hither to the door of the prison, and knocked hard upon it. And I went out to him and opened to him; he was clothed in a white robe ungirdled, having shoes curiously wrought. And he said to me: Perpetua, we await you; come. And he took my hand, and we began to go through rugged and winding places. At last with much breathing hard we came to the amphitheater, and he led me into the midst of the arena. And he said to me: Be not afraid; I am here with you and labor together with you. And he went away. And I saw much people watching closely. And because I knew that I was condemned to the beasts I marveled that beasts were not sent out against me. And there came out against me a certain ill-favored Egyptian with his helpers, to fight with me. Also there came to me comely young men, my helpers and aiders. And I was stripped naked, and I became a man. And my helpers began to rub me with oil as their custom is for a contest; and over against me I saw that Egyptian wallowing in the dust. And there came forth a man of very great stature, so that he overpassed the very top of the amphitheater, wearing a robe ungirdled, and beneath it between the two stripes over the breast a robe of purple; having also shoes curiously wrought in gold and silver; bearing a rod like a master of gladiators, and a green branch whereon were golden apples. And he besought silence and said: The Egyptian, if [he] shall conquer this woman, shall slay her with the sword; and if she shall conquer him, she shall receive this branch. And he went away. And we came nigh to each other, and began to buffet one another. He tried to trip up my feet, but I with my heels smote upon his face. And I rose up into the air and began so to smite him as though I trod not the earth. But when I saw that there was yet delay, I joined my hands, setting finger against finger of them. And I caught his head, and he fell upon his face; and I trod upon his head. And the people began to shout, and my helpers began to sing. And I went up to the master of gladiators and received the branch. And he kissed me and said to me: Daughter, peace be with you. And I began to go with glory to the gate called the Gate of Life.

And I awoke; and I understood that I should fight, not with beasts but against the devil; but I knew that mine was the victory.

*Translated by W. H. Shewring*
*Translation revised by Paul Halsall*

## *Aurelia Thaisous*
# A MOTHER SEEKS LEGAL INDEPENDENCE

Egypt  263 CE    Greek

This petition, presented by a woman named Aurelia Thaisous (who also used the name Lolliane) to the prefect, the Roman governor of Egypt, requests that she have the power to conduct business transactions herself and on her own behalf. The request speaks to two significant legal conditions which improved the position of women after Egypt became part of the Roman empire. The right of citizen women to full legal personhood once they had borne three live children was the first legislation of the civilizations around the Mediterranean to provide women with an avenue to legal equality in family and civil law. The law allowed women the right to enter independently into contracts; to go before the judiciary; to receive an inheritance and to make bequests; to buy and sell land; and to enter into marriage, divorce, and the proceedings for custody of small children.

This papyrus, written after the emperor's widespread grant of citizenship, also suggests the author's pride in her literacy and writing. She provides evidence of the importance accorded education, including a women's education, at this period of time.

*Marjorie Lightman*

✦

[Laws long ago have been made], most eminent Prefect, which empower women who are adorned with the right of three children to be mistresses of themselves and act without a guardian in whatever business they transact, especially those who know how to write. Accordingly, as I too enjoy the happy honor of being blessed with children and as I am a literate woman able to write with a high degree of ease, it is with abundant security that I appeal to your highness by this my application with the object of being enabled to accomplish without hindrance whatever business I henceforth transact, and I beg you to keep it without prejudice to my rights in your eminence's office, in order that I may obtain your support and acknowledge my unfailing gratitude. Farewell. I, Aurelia Thaisous also called Lolliane, have sent this for presentation.

*Translated by Ronald Cluett*

## *Statulenia Julia*
# TO THE MEMORY OF AELIA SECUNDULA

Ancient Mauretania, now modern Morocco  299 CE     Latin

This inscription to Aelia Secundula was found across a stone table over a grave at Satafi, in the Roman imperial province of Mauretania, on the coast of modern Morocco. On the original stone, the date for the inscription is 299 CE. The original, the letters at the beginning and end of each line form the words: "The children, to their dearest mother," indicating the source of this dedication.

The inscription vividly portrays the widespread ancient custom of visiting the grave and sharing food. Dated only thirteen years before the conversion of the Emperor Constantine to Christianity, the inscription captures the quality of the pagans' intimate relationship between the dead and the living, which was pervasive and which persisted, albeit transformed in meaning, into the Christian era.

The mood of the inscription is reverent rather than sad or mournful; the activity of a shared supper among family members affirms life and celebrates the departed. Among the most difficult pagan rituals for the Christians to modify or erase were feasts associated with the dead. Throughout North Africa these feasts were occasions for public revelry that bedeviled the new bishops. This reverence for the dead included both male and female family members. The famous *Laudatio Turiae*, found on a tomb outside Rome and written sometime in the late first century BCE after the death of Julius Caesar, is a lengthy inscription in which a husband praises his wife for her womanly virtue, her bravery, and her success in protecting family members and property during the Roman civil wars. In the early first century CE, the poet Propertius composed a poem in the form of an epitaph to Cornelia, a woman of notable lineage whose life reflected ancient Roman virtues.

Propertius's poem about Cornelia was composed in literary Latin, and the *Laudatio Turiae* tells the story of a woman's extraordinary life in more straightforward prose. The language of this inscription, however, is far more earthy. Any details of the mother's life are absent; it is possible that these had already been recorded on a standing stone.

*Marjorie Lightman*

✦

We have already spent much time on mother Secundula's tomb:
Now, we have decided, at the spot where she rests,
To place a stone funeral table
Where, from henceforth, being gathered together,
We shall often remember all that she did for us.

When the food is set out, the cups are filled, and the cushions
Arranged round about, we, to heal the wound that pains our hearts,
Shall talk, late in the evening, eagerly and with praise
Of our worthy mother—and the good old lady will sleep.
Yes, she who once fed us is now done with food forever.

She lived 72 years.
260 Provincial era.
Erected by Statulenia Julia.

*Translated by Marjorie Lightman*

## *Saint Syncletica*
# LET WOMEN NOT BE MISLED
Egypt   4th Century CE   Greek

Saint Syncletica was a Christian saint who lived during the fourth century in Egypt. She was born into a wealthy Macedonian Christian family who had moved to Alexandria. Some accounts cite her education at a school established a century earlier by Bishop Clement of Alexandria. After the death of her parents, she disbursed her inheritance among the poor, and with her blind sister, she left the city to lead a solitary life, first in a family tomb outside Alexandria, later in the desert. Tradition says she lived eighty-three years, and that, over the decades of her life, word of her wisdom spread. Acolytes and visitors sought her out.

She was following a century-old Christian tradition of rejecting bodily comforts and earthly wealth to go into the desert for spiritual enlightenment. A retreat from urban and urbane life in ancient Egypt had roots for Egyptians as old as the Bible stories of Moses. For some Christian Alexandrines of the late Roman Empire, such movement followed an irresistible desire to cleanse body and soul in preparation for meeting the Lord. Some of the desert ascetics lived alone; others formed monastic communities; and all eventually became known as Desert Fathers. While clearly there were women like Syncletica who followed their own vision and established their own communities, their history—until recently—has remained obscured. Only recently have scholars and others accorded such women as Syncletica the respectful title of Desert Mothers.

In the ancient world, where women's lives were inseparable from childbearing, Christian asceticism for women provided an alternative choice of life, and one that would provide salvation. The major theme of Syncletica's teaching was "how to win salvation." Like other desert fathers and mothers, she invoked vigil, prayer, and fasting, all in silence and stillness. Her sayings also focus on different kinds of virtue, including love, charity, chastity, struggle, different varieties of sadness, voluntary poverty, humility, and the perfection required for a proper monastic life. The extract that follows makes clear the importance of diligent focus on the "enemy's" war.

In the sixth century, the teachings of Saint Syncletica—known orally in the language Copts spoke—were written down in Greek, then translated into Latin, and thus she could become known in the West. Only very recently were her teachings translated into modern languages: French in 1972; English in 1990 and 1995; and Arabic in 2002 by the nuns of the Convent of St. Philopater Mercurius in Egypt.

*Marjorie Lightman and Heba Sharobeem*

✦

Let us women not be misled by the thought that those in the world are without cares. For perhaps in comparison they struggle more than we do. For toward women generally there is great hostility in the world. They bear children with difficulty and risk, and they suffer patiently through nursing, and they share illnesses with their sick children—and these things they endure without having any limit to their travail. . . .For in giving birth women die in labor; and yet, in failing to give birth, they waste away, under reproaches that they are barren and unfruitful.

I am telling you these things to safeguard you from the Adversary. . . .Since we women have grown wings like eagles, let us soar to the higher places, and let us trample underfoot the lion and the dragon . . . ; and let us now rule over the one who once ruled over us. And this we shall do if we offer to the Savior our whole mind.

We must, therefore, arm ourselves against them [adversaries] in every way, for they attack indeed from without and they are no less active from within. Like a ship our soul is sometimes engulfed by the waves without and is sometimes swamped by the bilge-water within. Certainly we too sometimes perish through sins committed externally, but we sometimes are destroyed by thoughts within us. And so we must guard against onslaughts of spirits from outside us, and bail out impurities of thoughts inside us; and we must always be vigilant with regard to our thoughts, for they are a constant threat to us. Against the storm waves outside salvation often comes from ships nearby when the sailors cry out for help but bilge waters overflow; and frequently kill the seamen, often when they are asleep and the sea is calm.

Consequently, the mind must become painstakingly diligent with respect to its thoughts. For when the Enemy wants to destroy the soul as he would a building, he engineers its collapse from the foundations, or he begins from the roof and topples the whole structure; or, he goes in through the windows, ties up the master of the house first and thus wins control of everything. "Foundation" then, signifies good works, "roof" faith, and "windows" the senses. And through all of them the Enemy wages war. And so the person wishing to be saved must be very watchful. We do not have here something to be careless about; for Scripture says: "Let the one standing firm take care lest he fall." . . .

We are sailing in uncertainty. For our life is a sea, as has been said by the holy psalmist David. . . .But some parts of the sea are full of reefs and some full also of monsters, but some too are calm. We seem to be sailing in the calm part of the sea while secular people sail in the dangerous parts. We also sail during the day, navigating by the sun of righteousness . . . , while they sail by night, swept along by ignorance. It often happens, however, that the secular person has saved his ship in the midst of storm and darkness by crying out and staying awake; we, on the other hand, have drowned in calm waters through carelessness in letting go of the rudder of righteousness.

*Translated by Elizabeth Bryson Bongie*

# Islam: Seventh Century to Eighteenth Century

## *Om Makina*
# LETTER TO A WOMAN FRIEND

Egypt   8th Century     Arabic

This text was written in Arabic and recorded on papyrus during the early century following the Islamic conquest of Egypt in 636 CE. The first Arabic papyri were discovered in Egypt in 1824, when some farmers found two inside a small jar near the Sakara pyramid. The collections of Arabic papyri now housed in the National Archives in Cairo, as well as in other libraries such as the Louvre in Paris and the National Library of Austria, contain a huge number of social documents—personal letters, emancipation documents, and marriage contracts—as well as contracts for buying, selling, and working, along with records and log books of commercial and financial transactions. Because many of these papyri have not survived intact, some existing only as fragments, they contain a number of lacunae; hence we often find incomplete sentences and omissions in the translated texts.

This letter is one of the earliest extant papyri documents in Arabic. Written in a woman's hand and addressed to a woman friend who is clearly illiterate, it is a very early example of women's literacy in the Islamic period. It is interesting to note that both women (Om Makina, the mother of Makina, and Om Rashida, the mother of Rashida) are referred to as mothers of daughters, rather than as daughters of fathers. The letter, additionally, is sent out in the names of the female members of the family (the grandmother, the daughter Makina, the granddaughter, as well as presumably another daughter called Seifa). We do not know whether the Ali referred to in the message is the husband (which is highly unlikely), the son, or somebody else. Were he the son, then the use of the daughters' names would be still more unusual.

It is also interesting to note that less than a century following the Arab conquest of Egypt, the population represented by Om Makina were already well versed not only in the newly adopted religion of Islam but in the Arabic language as well.

*Amira Nowaira and Saied Moghawery*

✦

In the name of God, the Compassionate and most Merciful.
To Om Rashida from Om Makina, Makina, and her daughter as well as from Seifa. I send you my heartfelt greetings and I thank God. I wish to impart our news to you and to tell you that we are all fine and well, and nothing but good things have come our way. I wish to tell you that I transferred Makina to [. . .] I swear by the Almighty, who is the One and Only God, that nothing prevented me from sending you the things I wished to give you except shortness of money and straitened circumstances. But take heart, my dear, and cheer up, for a lot of good things are in store for you. Please convey my greetings to Ali and ask him about the things I had asked of him.

May God bestow His mercy on the person who will read this letter to Om Rashida.

*Transcribed by Saied Moghawery*
*Translated by Amira Nowaira*

## *Anonymous*
# A PLEA FOR MONEY

Egypt c. 9th–10th Century    Arabic

"A Plea" is another personal letter written in Arabic on papyrus, this one dating back to the ninth to tenth centuries. The writer of the letter pleads with her brother to intercede on her behalf with their father to persuade him to send her funds, provisions, and clothing. Like the earlier "Letter to a Woman Friend," this letter is written in the author's own hand, and in a style that is at once literary and poignant. Even amidst her frequent expressions of respect and piety, the writer's desperation is painfully evident. The document does not make clear why the woman and her family were in dire straits. However, other evidence suggests that it was written at a time when severe taxation, combined with famine, drought, and political instability, especially toward the end of the Ikhshidid Dynasty, led to great hardships among the people. The author must have had some hope of a positive response to her letter, since papyrus was fairly expensive at this time.

*Amira Nowaira and Saied Moghawery*

✦

In the name of God, the Compassionate and most Merciful.

Dear beloved brother, may God grant you a long life of dignity and prosperity; may He show you his mercy and bountifulness both in this world and the next; may God in His Compassion bring the end of my life before yours; may He, my dear and cherished brother, keep you well and free from harm, both in this world and the next. I pray to the Almighty, the All-seeing, the All-hearing that He may grant you all these blessings. I wish to tell you, dear brother, that father, may God keep him well, wrote to the estate agent to pay the sum of a pound to Ayyoub. But the estate agent is away now. Please tell my father to send me some clothing fast, since by God Almighty, I am going about unclothed. You have already seen my state and know the life of hardship I am leading now. I swear by the Almighty that my life is nothing but sheer misery. Although I am walking around without any garments, starving, and thirsty, I thank God all the same. For four days now, there has not been a single drop of water in the house. For four days now, I have felt thirsty [. . .] The neighbors don't have leftovers every day. I do thank God nonetheless. We often go without food for two days running, and nobody in the neighborhood is doing any baking or grinding.

Dear beloved brother, please talk to father, may God keep him safe and well, on behalf of your sister. I hope he will make the utmost haste to send me some clothes because I haven't got any, as you have seen with your very eyes. My kind father is not sending me any money, so please talk to him so that he may do so. Dearest brother, I entreat you to do this as soon as you possibly can.

*Transcribed by Saied Moghawery*
*Translated by Amira Nowaira*

## *Mahriyya Al-Aghlabiya and Khadija Ben Kalthoum*
## TWO TUNISIAN POEMS
Tunisia  9th Century, 11th Century    Arabic

Records tell us of several learned women in the early history of Muslim Tunisia, but extant poetry from this era is scarce. Not until the 1990s did patient work by the well-known Tunisian scholar Hassen Hosni Abdelwaheb uncover the work of two women poets. They lived two centuries apart, and only the two poems included here have survived.

The first poet is Mahriyya Al-Aghlabiya who, as her name indicates, belonged to the Aghlabid family that reigned over parts of North Africa in the ninth century. A princess, the daughter of Sultan Hassen Ben Ghalbun Temimi, she grew up in a refined environment, and led an easy and comfortable life in the town of Rakada, close to present-day Qayrawan. Mahriya Al-Aghlabiya became famous in her lifetime for her poetry and for following the example of the paragon of female poets, al-Khansaa, who was renowned for her elegies in seventh-century Arabia. Unfortunately, only one of her poems has survived. "If I Only Knew" is an elegy written for her brother, the scholar Abi Ikal, who died in exile in 891.

The second poet, Khadija Ben Kalthoum, specialized in love poetry. She was born under the reign of the Zirids in the eleventh century, , south of Mehdia in what is known today as Chebba, a harbor town where a *bordj*—a fortified entry into the sea—still bears her name: Bordj Khadija. Khadija Ben Kalthoum was the contemporary of the Tunisian poet Ibn Rashiq who admired her poetry and mentioned her in his work *Al Munjid* (The Dictionary): "Khadija daughter of Ahmed Bin Kalthum, Khadouj is a nickname given to her, is a famous poet." Yet while Ibn Rashiq's fame endured, Khadija's work is lost, save this one poem. "They Drove Us Apart," which expresses the despair of an impossible love, reflects the poet's own experience. A young man who was fond of poetry, Abu Marwan Abdel Malek Bin Ziyad Allah, had been madly in love with her, and she ended up falling in love with him because of his education and charm. Her brothers, however, did not accept their love and would not allow her to marry him.

*Khédija Arfaoui*

✦

## IF I ONLY KNEW

O, if I only knew how
to express my pain!
After spending so many nights
fasting and sleepless
following my beloved's exile
from home and
from the loved ones.
O brother!
My love is such
that it can but
drive me mad.
As the earth eats away
the dead, so
does sorrow eat
loving women away.

## THEY DROVE US APART

They drove us apart,
and when again
we got together,
their lies and slander
tore us to pieces.
What they did
to us can only be
compared to what
Satan did to Man.

Woe to you,
O, Abu Marwan.
Nay, woe to me
whenever you go away.

*Translated by Khédija Arfaoui*

## Astour Heyoh
# FREEING A SLAVE WOMAN
### Egypt 1003 Arabic

The date of this papyrus places it within the Fatimid Dynasty, during the reign of the eccentric and erratic caliph Al-Hakim Bi Amr Allah. The text affirms the fact that a Coptic Christian free woman, Astour Heyoh, has decided to grant freedom to her slave woman. It testifies to a degree of autonomy still enjoyed by women even under Al-Hakim, who passed a series of oppressive restrictions on women's behavior. He first forbade women to appear in public with their faces uncovered, and then forbade them to go out at all (at the same time ordering shoemakers to cease producing women's shoes). Although the document records a decision made by a Christian, the text opens with the traditional Islamic statement, "In the name of God, the most Merciful and Compassionate." The young slave, Dagasha, whose name points to her Coptic affiliation, acquires a new name, Safrah, after her emancipation, probably as an indication of her new status.

*Amira Nowaira and Saied Moghawery*

✦

In the name of God, the most Merciful and Compassionate.
In God I trust.
Astour Heyoh, daughter of Sega, son of Eblida, being sound of mind and body, acting of her own free will, unforced and uncompelled, and in full command of her senses and body, states that she has whole-heartedly granted freedom to her slave woman, named Safrah in Arabic and Dagasha in Coptic, daughter of Arnia. The young woman is henceforth her own mistress. Whoever makes any claims on the young woman, Dagasha, whether they be claims of service or of ownership, and whether by Astour Heyoh's offspring or any of her heirs, such claims would be nothing but sheer lies, acts of fraudulence, deception, and blatant transgression.

*Transcribed by Saied Moghawery*
*Translated by Amira Nowaira*

## Sara, Daughter of Abboud Al-Nahid
# USING THE RIGHT OF SEVERANCE
### Egypt 1069 Arabic

This part of a court document, written on papyrus, records a woman's decision to obtain a divorce based on her personal preference. According to *shari'a* (Islamic law), a wife has the right to sever the marriage bond and obtain a divorce if, for any reason, she is not happy with her husband and does not feel comfortable in the marriage. In such a case, she has to agree to renounce all financial rights she might have had if her husband had chosen the divorce, including alimony, and return her husband's gifts. The document illustrates very clearly that women were empowered to initiate divorce proceedings even without apparent grievance. The wife here chooses divorce based simply on her "feelings of aversion" for him.

*Amira Nowaira and Saied Moghawery*

◆

In the name of God, the Compassionate and most Merciful.

Sara, daughter of Abboud Al-Nahid, is hereby requesting her husband, Abdel Ghani, son of Berlans, one of the Raihani slaves working in the city of Ash-mouneen, that she may regain control over herself through a single divorce pronouncement, the first-time divorce pronouncement to be made since the marriage was consummated. A boy by the name of Al-Janad, aged five at the time of the writing of the present document, was born by this marriage. She hereby declares that her husband has not abused her in any way. Her choice to sever the marriage is the outcome of her feelings of aversion for his person. Since both she and her husband are afraid of inviting God's wrath in disobeying His precepts, she hereby renounces her severance rights, which amount to three dinars as well as all other financial rights the husband is compelled to pay, such as allowances of wheat, clothing, shoes, house rent, water, and oil, which are a woman's right during the period subsequent to a divorce.

*Transcribed by Saied Moghawery*
*Translated by Shadia el-Soussi*

## Hafsa Bint Al-Haj Al-Rakuniya
### LOVE POEMS
Morocco 1160    Arabic

Hafsa Bint Al-Haj Al-Rakuniya was born in 1135 to a wealthy Berber family in Granada, Spain, which was then one of the primary cities of al-Andalus, the name given to the parts of the Iberian Peninsula that were ruled by North African Muslims from the eighth through the fifteenth centuries. She lived in al-Andalus under the Almohad Dynasty, and became one of its most famous poets. Later in her life she lived in Marrakesh, where she died in 1191.

Hafsa Al-Rakuniya was well-educated, and was described by biographers as a beautiful, noble, intelligent "lady," who wrote poetry with ease. She met and fell in love with Abu Ja'far Ibn Sa'id, a poet and son of the Caliph Abd al-Mumin. She also fell in love with the governor of Granada, another distinguished poet. With the first of these men, Hafsa Al-Rakuniya exchanged poems that have been preserved over time. In some of these poems, she expresses her love; in others she invokes secret fears of the consequences of this love; and in still other poems, she expresses feelings of jealousy because her lover has spent three days and nights with a black slave.

Hafsa Al-Rakuniya's love for Abu-Ja'far created problems, which she tried to resolve in her own manner. In two verses she sent her congratulations to the governor, her other lover, on the occasion of a Muslim feast, and mentioned the special relationship she has with him. A jealous Abu Ja'far wrote to her, referring to the governor as a "black slave" and demanding she explain her attraction to him. "I can buy you ten slaves like him," he declared. This statement, along with his participation in a rebellion against the Almohads, cost Abu Ja'far his life: He was imprisoned and later hung. Hafsa Al-Rakuniya was so grieved that she wore mourning clothes despite threats on her life. Then she went to live in the Caliph's castle in Marrakesh, where she was responsible for educating the princesses, and remained there until her death.

The Jamil and Butayna mentioned near the end of the poem are a very famous couple in classical Arabic love poetry, the equivalents of Romeo and Juliet.

*Nadia Laachiri*

✦

## ONE

I praise those lips
because I know what
I am talking about.
I am giving them justice.
By God, I am not lying.
From them I've drunk nectar
more delicious than wine.

## TWO

I send you greetings that open flowers,
that make the leaves on branches talk.
Never think that distance will make me forget you.
For God's sake, this will never happen.

## THREE

I'll protect you jealously against spies,
against yourself, against your time,
and the space where you live.
Even if I hide you under my eyelids
until the Day of Judgment,
it won't be enough for me.

# FOUR

Upon your life, our union makes the garden sad,
else it would have shown envy and grief.
The river isn't pleased to see us near,
and the pigeon is singing its sadness.
Do not be angry,
for anger precludes good action.
I don't think the sky has shown
its stars
except to spy upon us.

# FIVE

Shall I visit you or will you visit me?
My heart forever inclines
toward what you desire.
I hope you'll be thirsty and hot
when they announce my arrival to you.
My mouth is a fresh and delicious source,
my hair a cool shelter.
*So answer me quickly,*
O Jamil, you are too patient
towards Butayna!

# SIX

The visitor who came to see you
has a gazelle's neck;
under his black hair, emerges the moon.
His eyes are made of Babel's magic.
His kiss is sweeter than wine.
His cheeks make roses shy,
and his teeth outvalue pearls.

*Translated by Nadia Laachiri*

# *Fatma-Setita*
# CONSOLATION AND OTHER POEMS

Egypt c.1492–1494    Arabic

Fatma-Setita, sometimes known as Fatma-Najia, was the daughter of Judge Kamal El Din Mahmoud Ibn Shereen. Born in Cairo on 8 February 1451, she was taught to read and write, and studied the Qur'an and Hadith—the sayings and deeds of the Prophet, regarded as an important source of guidance on the Muslim way of life. She was married, widowed, and married again, and gave birth to several children. She made several pilgrimages to Mecca, the first time in 1479. These journeys confirm the importance for both men and women of making the pilgrimage, which is regarded as a duty for all Muslims if they can afford it; it also points to the relative wealth Fatma-Setita must have had to make such journeys possible.

All the information we have about Fatma-Setita, as well as the surviving excerpts from her poetry, are provided by her biographer, the historian and critic Shams El Din Mohamed bin Abdel Rahman Al-Sakhawi (1428–1497). Her name is included among more than a thousand women, both learned and not, in his volume of biographies of women in the fifteenth century. Al-Sakhawi devotes six pages of his book to Fatma-Setita, describing and excerpting letters they exchanged, as well as those between Fatma-Setita and other scholars. Al-Sakhawi pays eloquent tribute to Fatma-Setita as "an accomplished poet, endowed with powerful understanding, and a vigorous mind. Her learning is truly unique." He also cites a letter he wrote to her in which he addresses her in the following manner: "You are a woman whose expressive words have surpassed all others, whose learning has exceeded that of a lot of men, and whose verse is comparable to that of Al-Khansaa," thus equating her with the most revered of Arabic female poets, who was said to have impressed the Prophet Muhammad himself.

In the first poem included here, Fatma-Setita commiserates with Al-Sakhawi on the death of his two brothers. While expressing sympathy for his loss, she does not forget to pay tribute to his learning, using his name, Shams El Din, which literally means "the shining sun of religion," as a poetic device.

The second poem starts with a tribute to Al-Sakhawi, citing his wisdom and profound knowledge of Hadith. She then moves on to ask him in verse for a religious judgment concerning women who go on pilgrimage but are held back from completing the sacred rites by what she refers to as "an impediment," a reference to the limitations imposed on women in performing religious duties during menstruation. Although the term is nowhere mentioned, Al-Sakhawi understands the meaning and responds with the reassuring opinion that God grants His reward to the individual on the strength of his or her intentions. "Such is God's will," he writes to her, "and the fate ordained by Him on all womenfolk, Adam's daughters. So be assured of God's mercy and His boundless bounty. He will, if He wills it, give you the desired reward." The relative ease with which such intimate matters are discussed suggests a degree of openness between male and female intellectuals of the period.

*Amira Nowaira*

◆

## CONSOLATION

May God reward you and bless you with His favors,
On losing your loved ones and the best of neighbors.
Generous they were, righteous, rich in integrity and candor,
Their presence gave you infinite joy.
You treasured their friendship,
But, alas, having to lose them forever and ever.
So does death sever loved ones,
And suddenly remove both friends and brothers.
So keep their memory alive and their names reiterate,
For it may for beholding them with your own eyes compensate.
Though distant, in the heart's recesses they will stay, and vibrate,
Occupying a place that is secure and intimate,
And following in the footsteps of God's Prophet.
May God reward them and make Heaven their fate.
Should their moonlight grow dim and fade,
The sun of Shams El Din will shine strong and straight;
A man of learning and renown by all obeyed,
Your name throughout the globe will constantly be relayed.


## A QUESTION

Oh great scholar, you are as generous as the ocean,
Well-versed in the meanings of Hadith, old and new,
A gift to the times, praised by all. . . .
[. . .]
You are Shams El Din, the bright sun of religion;
Your endless learning has earned you renown.
You, Al-Sakhawi, lead the world,
Blessed with immense learning.
Your mouth speaks pearls.
To you I will pose a question
From a woman who desires to perform the sacred rites
Of walking the distance between Zamzam and Hateem,
But is held back by an impediment
On that crucial night of pilgrimage
Which marks heaven's bounty. Will God reward
In the same measure those who were held back?
Will those who cannot take part be rated equal to those who can?
Please tell me, for you are the hope I seek,
And your intelligence is a powerful rock.

*Translated by Amira Nowaira*

## *Ana de Melo*
# ESCAPING THE INQUISITION
### Morocco 1559    Portuguese

By the sixteenth century, the North African rulers had been driven out of Iberia, and Portugal had attacked and occupied many Moroccan ports, fueling successive famines and civil wars. Portuguese archives contain considerable reports of Moroccans who moved from Morocco to Portugal in this period, especially during the widespread famine of 1520. Some were made prisoners and sold as slaves, while others emigrated voluntarily in search of a better life, only to be met with oppression of another kind.

Seventy-nine reports deal with the arrest and trial of Moroccan residents in Portugal charged with "going back" to Islam, their original religion. The arrests of these Moroccans coincided with the establishment of the Inquisition in Portugal, aimed at punishing anyone not faithful to the powerful Roman Catholic Church. Portugal had once been known as a tolerant country where all monotheist religions lived side by side, but in the sixteenth century, religious fanaticism became a political tool in the hands of the Portuguese rulers.

Three Inquisition courts were established in Portugal, in the cities of Evora, Lisbon, and Coimbra. Inquisition court reports constitute a valuable source of historical information on the Portuguese occupation of Morocco and its intellectual and religious ramifications, as well as on Moroccans in Portugal. One report records in great detail the stages of arrest and trial of Ana de Melo, an old woman originally from Dukkala, Morocco, who had lived in Portugal for more than twenty-two years. She was accused of going back to Islam, and practicing Islamic rituals. She denied the charges, and even refused to give her original Moroccan name when asked. Her trial began on 22 May 1559, and her sentence was publicly pronounced only on 24 April 1560.

This statement was made by Ana de Melo after one year of trial and interrogation, during which she successfully defended herself against the serious charges raised against her. Although she had to pay the sum of 292 *rials* upon her acquittal, she did not have to wear the customary robe that would have marked her as a repentant heretic. Given the overall historical context and the power of public religion, the fact that Ana de Melo won the case and escaped death was in itself a tribute to the courage and persistence of this old Moroccan woman.

*Ahmed Bouchareb*

✦

I [Ana de Melo], a Christianized Muslim residing in Evora, swear in front of you inspectors against apostasy. I swear with my hand on the sacred Bible that, of my own will, and exhausting my own personal wishes, I curse and promise to keep away from all types of apostasy. I promise never to revolt against the Holy Catholic religion and the Papal Church, especially in matters relating to the sins I committed and to which I confess in front of your excellencies. These sins have been enumerated to me and I repeated them. I swear to adhere always to the Holy Catholic religion, sheltered by our Mother the Holy Roman church.

I swear to be obedient to our Father, the Holy Pope, President of God's church, and his legal representatives. I also promise never to meet them [Muslims] and to report apostasies they know of to the inspectors and priests of our Holy Mother, the church. I swear to repent of my sins whenever I am ordered to. And if ever I sin again and refuse to repent of the charges addressed to me in the present or in the future, I will happily accept apostasy for the rest of my life and, consequently, be punished according to the law. I promise that, if at any time I display anything contradicting what I confess upon oath, I accept that my repentance won't help me in anything and will then submit to punishment and the severity of the holy law. I ask the scribe of the holy institution here present to accredit everything I say and I ask the audience to be a witness to what I say and to sign in my name.

*Translated into Arabic by Ahmed Bouchareb*
*Translated from Arabic by Fatima Sadiqi*

## *Lalla Khnata Bint Bakkar*
## TWO POLITICAL LETTERS
Morocco  1729, 1736    Arabic

In 1678, Sultan Moulay Ismail Ibn Sharif of the Alaouite dynasty, which took power in Morocco in 1666 and remains its royal family today, paid a visit to Shinquit, in the deep south of the country. The leader of that region, Sheikh Bakkar, offered his daughter to "Ismail the Great" in marriage as a token of his people's allegiance to the sultan. Lalla Khnata Bint Bakkar became one the sultan's many wives, but she was far from typical. The princess was a skilled politician and diplomat and even an accomplished horsewoman, and she built a library of some twelve thousand volumes. Her husband sought her views on many occasions, trusting her intelligence and her accurate assessments. She served as a minister and adviser to the sultan and sometimes acted as his private secretary as well, since her command of Arabic was excellent.

When Moulay Ismail died in 1727 without nominating anyone to replace him, bloody riots ensued. The sultan had several hundred sons, but Lalla Khnata's wisdom and political skill helped her son, Moulay Abdallah, take the throne, although he would lose and regain it six times between 1728 and 1749 as battles over the succession continued.

Lalla Khnata was an important partner during her son's reign. She lived in the capital, Meknes, while Moulay Abdallah traveled to manage political campaigns. She inspected the army on his behalf, undertook a number of local initiatives, and was in charge of protocol and receiving foreign dignitaries. Akensus, head of the army, described her as a true scholar, as well as a "virtuous" woman with a "strong religious faith. She was a scholar and I saw her handwritten notes on the margin of a book by Ibn Hajjar." The eminent historian Magali Mursi said of her: "She is the actual, legal heir of Moulay Ismail. We can say she deserved the crown. She had the strongest personality among all the contenders to the throne, including her son." She was also praised by France's King Louis XV, who sent her a letter in which he described her as "the Great Sultan" and requested her assistance in some matters of benefit to both kingdoms.

Moulay Abdallah, however, often refused her advice, feeling it a disgrace to rely on a woman. When Lalla Khnata learned that her son was plotting against her, in 1730 she decided to go on pilgrimage to Mecca, taking along her eleven-year-old grandson. During the journey she strengthened diplomatic relations with Libya and Egypt, and saw to it that the future Sultan Mohamed III was introduced to politics at an early age. Lalla Khnata died at about the age of eighty, in 1746 in Fes, where she is buried.

In the first of two letters included here, Lalla Khnata skillfully negotiates for the release of Flemish prisoners held in Morocco. She sends a trusted emissary, a Jewish businessman, to complete the arrangements, which clearly include some payment of ransom by the Flemish.

The second letter deals with problems taking place on the border shared with Algeria. Algeria had long been part of the Ottoman Empire, and the Turks were trying to expand their hegemony. In a voice as confident as a king's, Lalla Khnata writes to the people of Oujda, reassuring residents of the border city that they are under the protection of the Moroccan sovereign.

*Khadija Zizi*

✦

## First Letter
To the Flemish States,
19 June 1729, Meknes
All Praise be to God, Peace, and God's prayer be upon the Prophet Muhammad and his companions.

To the attention of all the Flemish states, peace is upon those who pursue the path of redemption. Please be informed that your brothers have cried before our blessed son, may his crops bear fruit, and knelt at his feet, in an endeavor to talk to him on behalf of their brothers and their liberation and also in your coming to us with your presents. We then acquiesced and permitted the non-Muslim merchant Isaac Shmika to come to you and converse with you, since we trust him. So we are sending him to you. We would like you to trust him and those accompanying him in all he says regarding all matters, including the gift and the ransom. Whoever comes along with him needs to be satisfied. We hope he will accomplish this journey with success and return to us in the protection of God.

Drafted on the twenty-second Dhu Al Qi'dah al-haram in the year one thousand one hundred and forty one.

Written under the instruction and order of the protected by the will of God, her Highness, Mother of our Sovereign, may God protect him and preserve him to his fellow Muslims, Lalla Khnata Bint Bakkar, may God be with her.

*Translated by Khadija Zizi*

*Second Letter*
To the People of Oujda,
24 May 1736, Meknes.
All Praise be to God and peace be upon his Prophet Muhammad.

To our servants, the people of Oujda, peace be upon you all and God is protecting you. We implore God to grant you prosperity and health, and we implore Him to grant our Sovereign power and triumph over his enemies. We do not want you to worry. We know your strong faith in and allegiance to our Sovereign. Do not worry about what those bitter people are doing. We are, with the assistance of God Almighty, more powerful than they are. In any case, you are our subjects. So don't fear anyone, whether you go East or West, whether or not you travel. We are capable of defeating them. Whoever attacks you attacks us and will face severe reprisals. I advise you to put the Shorfa Wlad Belqaid under your protection. No one should get near them. Treat them the way we treat them. Whoever attacks them runs the risk of being defeated. By permission of the Mistress of the divine and blessed house, Lady Hajja Khnata Bint Bakkar, may God glorify us and her.

*Translated by Moha Ennaji and Khadija Zizi*

## *Lalla Fatima*
## LETTER ABOUT FEMALE SLAVES

Morocco   1764   Arabic

Lalla Fatima was the wife of Sultan Sidi Mohamed Ben Abdellah, who ruled Morocco from 1757 to 1790. Wives of sultans have rarely been public figures in the history of Morocco but a few of them—like Lalla Khnata Bint Bekkar and Shehrazad, both included in this volume—were involved in political life, and were sometimes instrumental in resolving public issues. This text highlights the hidden power of women in Moroccan royal palaces. Although a king's wife does not hold the title of queen, she may use her husband's power—and her own diplomatic skills—to get things done.

In this letter, Princess Lalla Fatima writes to a European princess, asking her to release two Muslim female slaves imprisoned in Spain in exchange for the release of Christian female slaves held captive in Moroccan prisons. Slavery was widespread in eighteenth-century Morocco and still was legal in Spain as well. Slaves were taken in the warring between the two countries, and many others were captured by the pirates that raided ships in the Mediterranean.

The tone of the letter suggests that the two princesses may have met before. Written in classical Arabic but containing words and expressions from spoken Arabic, the letter is both formal and informal. The mixture of literary and colloquial Arabic reinforces the casual and private nature of the relationship between the two princesses.

*Ali Ouahidi*

In the name of God, the Merciful, the Compassionate.

From the great Princess of the Moroccan kingdom our lady Fatima, may God perpetuate her glory, the wife of our lord, the great Sultan of Marrakech, Fes, Meknasa, Tafilalt, Souss, and Deraa, may God glorify him.

To Her Royal Highness Princess Louisa De Asturias. My sincere greetings to you. I wish you a long, happy life. Given your love for us, we have sent you in the hands of the Consul Atomas Aprim, a box of pearls, and if we still had our Christian female captives, I would have sent them to you. A number of Christian female captives have been released, some ransomed and some sold. You will receive with this letter also a pair of gold bracelets; they are from the gold that comes to us from trade and these are a gift from us to you. We would like to request the release of one or two Muslim female captives. The release will benefit both countries. With my great respect and consideration for you.

*Translated by Moha Ennaji*

## *Shehrazad*
## STRUGGLE FOR A THRONE

Morocco c.1792    Arabic

Shehrazad was another of Sultan Sidi Mohamed Ben Abdellah's many wives. After her husband's death, Princess Shehrazad relied upon her powerful nephews for support against other family factions.

This letter was written by Shehrazad to her son Salama, known as Moulay Slimane. She is writing on the eve of a decision about the royal succession. Sultan Sidi Mohamed Ben Abdellah had many sons aspiring to succeed him, and Shehrazad wanted to guarantee the enthronement of her own son. In her letter, she defends her son's right to the throne and encourages his ambitions, and relying on the language of religious and parental blessing, which had then—and still has now—high cultural resonance in Morocco.

Although written in a private tone, the letter is a rare historical document allowing a view of the involvement of princesses in political matters of the palace.

*Mohamed Kenbib*

✦

To my son, Salama, greetings and thousands of greetings.

You know, my son, that those who love God wish your victory, and those who fear God strongly support others. May God destroy them. Your nephews want to join you and stay with you until God relieves us. If they come to you, please receive them with warmth and console them. May God bless you. Please take care of them and consider them as your own children. Let me know about what is happening. Should the throne become yours, no one will take it away from you, but if it goes to somebody else, then you will not have it. Now go home and meet your children and nephews in Fes-Jdid, and let us rely on God. If God grants somebody something, he will end up having it. Please join me and take care of your nephews. We will settle down in Fes-Jdid. We will work hard and provide for our needs without pain and without anybody's help. We will wait for the time of pilgrimage, then visit the tomb of Prophet Sidna Mohamed, prayers be upon him. As for your nephews, they were deprived of everything overnight. They had nothing to eat, so I paid them a visit while waiting for your return, may God bless you.

*Translated by Loubna Skalli*

# NINETEENTH CENTURY TO EARLY TWENTIETH CENTURY

# *Anonymous*
# *LA'RUBIYAT*, OR WOMEN'S SONGS

Morocco   Early 19th Century   Arabic

*La'rubiyat* is a unique female poetic genre that originated at the beginning of the nineteenth century in urban Fes. Although the songs were sung in Arabic and handed down through generations, they remained unnoticed by historians of Moroccan poetry. In the 1920s, the Moroccan scholar, poet, and politician Mohammed al-Fassi published a small collection in French translation; in 1971, he published a larger collection of about 170 songs in Moroccan Arabic.

The songs were composed and performed only by women and were intended for an exclusively female audience. The reciting of the poems followed a patterned ritual. Girls rose one after another, taking turns before their female elders, while mothers, grandmothers, and aunts praised their beauty and charm, their confidence and power. In such contexts, a girl's name, her beauty, and her good qualities might be noted: "That's X, the light of my eyes and heart." The elders must also have been thinking about eligible men for their protégées.

*La'rubiyat* were not signed because writing poetry was not considered an appropriate female practice. The composers of these songs chose to remain anonymous because of the shame that might be brought upon a woman who expressed love even for her fiancé or husband. The poems are quite short—between two and twenty lines—and follow a certain rhythm. Hence, they are often introduced by the Arabic syllabic string "ana nana nana."

The songs ring with all love's joys and tribulations: pain, separation, reunion, rivalry, death, fate, and passion. Women often implored God to help them, and love itself was sometimes depicted as a lover asking God for help or relief. A singer might ask God's help to relieve her pain at the loss of love, or a survivor might beg God to let her die as well. The songs employ religious imagery (in song eight, *msid* is a Qur'anic school and a *fqih* is a healer) and are rich in metaphor and personification (in song four, flowers open doors and hug people).

Despite their sensuality, intensity, and power, the songs also reflect the realities of unequal gender relations: women need to be not only clever, but patient, humble, and malleable to their lovers' will.

*Moha Ennaji, Fatima Sadiqi, and Khadija Zizi*

✦

## SONG ONE

Sing, oh, bird, since you are so lucky.
You have water and grain in your cage.
But I gave up water and grain
For a song on a tree that makes the heart throb.
May God help the lover of beauty and arm her with patience.

## Song Two

Oh, my darling, why don't you love me as I love you?
Why can't you be mine, only mine?
Were you a ring, my finger would be your size.
Were you a gold Qur'an-holder, I would be the silken cord to hold you.
Were you a dagger, I would sling you over my shoulder.
Were you a book, I'd read you again and again.
I'd challenge any woman rival and let the best win!

## Song Three

Oh, my darling, if you go, God will be with me.
One day we will surely meet.
You left me drowning in sorrow and tears,
Swaying, even staggering as if drunk.
Oh, God! You who have saved people, save me!

## Song Four

I knocked on the gate of the garden. I called, Oh, gardener!
White jasmine opened the door for me and yellow jasmine
Hugged me.
I crossed the courtyard and found a young man sewing red material.
I said to him, "Oh, young man, please tailor it for me."
He said, "Wait until these people sleep, and I'll make you
Coffee in a glass,
And if it breaks, it will be a good omen!"
Two women lovers came and told me, "Oh, darling, your beloved has died."
I told them, "If he has died, you won't have to worry about his shroud
Or his coffin.
His coffin will be made of gold with silver nails and his shroud will be
    made of taffeta."
If my beloved died today, I would be with him tomorrow.

## Song Five

If you love someone with passion, give him time to learn to trust you.
Be patient, endure his coldness, and never grow angry when he humiliates
    you.
Be smart and drink from his water.
Can the defeated stand up to the winner?

## SONG SIX

Oh, God, I have a wish: Grant me just one happy day
During which all your creatures will be under my rule
And I will freely select the best of clothes;
I will wear the new and discard the old.
I will make my enemy's life miserable,
And I will welcome my beloved to my abode,
And I will say I made a wish and God made it come true!

## SONG SEVEN

Oh, you who have left me without a reason, tell me, in the name of God,
Where will you find someone as patient as I am?
I feel just like someone whose father has died, who starts clinging to men,
And no one has pity on him.
I feel just like someone whose mother has died, who starts clinging to
    women,
And no one has pity on her.
I feel just like someone who's lost his horse: His friends are riding
While he is on foot.
I feel like someone who's cooking stone, and there is no broth
To drink, nor any meat to grill.
I feel like someone who's fallen into the ocean and
Is at the mercy of the waves that flip her over and over.
I feel like someone whose hands feel rather bitter
Because she's been planting oleander forever.
Oh, God, you who have decided to separate us,
Please help bring my beloved and me together again.

## SONG EIGHT

I never thought that passion would affect someone who adores books
Until I realized that I forgot all the Qur'anic verses that I had read.
Even my slate remained abandoned at the corner of the *msid*.
They brought a *fqih* to heal my ailments,
To throw a spell and name my tormentor.
God be with my family if I die of love,
For my love lives in the neighborhood.
He is beautiful and charming, a most perfect gazelle.
The wind was blowing when I saw the person in the red vest
He raised his gaze and looked at me, then lowered his eyelashes
And went home.
He left me in my usual state: bewildered and anxious.

## SONG NINE

Oh, my darling, people insult me because of you.
They say, "Here is a fool who befriends a slave."
He who says Messouda is a slave is a fool begot by a fool!
My darling is of noble lineage and chaste.
I am pure and dress in purple, which suits me!

## SONG TEN

My heart is a grain and my lover's heart is its grinder.
The grinder is in ruthless hands.
Oh, God, may You grind him over and over.
He threw me into the air and I became light in his hand.
Love is spontaneous and should never be forced!

*Translated by Moha Ennaji, Fatima Sadiqi, and Khadija Zizi*

## *Aisha Al-Taymouria*
# POEM TO MY DAUGHTER

### Egypt 1884    Arabic

Aisha Al-Taymouria (1840-1902), distinguished poet, fiction writer, essayist, and translator, was born in 1840 to an affluent family in Cairo. Her father was Ismail Taymour, a member of the aristocracy, and her mother was a Circassian slave who, according to nineteenth-century customs, was freed once she bore the master's children.

The eldest of three sisters, Al-Taymouria displayed, from an early age, not only intelligence but a thirst for learning. In the introduction to her fictional work *Consequences in Words and Deeds* (1887), she describes how she refused to learn sewing and embroidery, and demanded instead to spend her time learning to read and write and joining the learned men who frequently gathered for literary discussions at her father's house. While her mother insisted on the girl's learning appropriate feminine skills, her father decided to engage male tutors in Turkish, Persian, Arabic grammar, the Qur'an, and Islamic jurisprudence.

Al-Taymouria married at the age of fourteen, and became almost wholly preoccupied with her duties as a wife and mother. When her eldest daughter, Tawhida, was twelve, she began to take on some of the responsibility of managing the household, thus leaving her mother time to pursue her literary activities and ambitions. Al-Taymouria hired women instructors to teach her at home. The first tutor died six months after having been hired. The other two, clearly women of a lower class who earned their livings teaching upper-class women, were Fatima Al-Azhariyya and Setita al-Tablawiyya. Both taught Al-Taymouria grammar and the principles of Arabic poetic meter, skills she needed in order to perfect her poetic abilities.

During this period, Al-Taymouria first used her language skills as a Persian translator, accompanying the royal female guests from Persia and acting as their interpreter to the women of the Court of Khedive Ismail. Her duties at court led her to spend more and more time away from home, leaving the household in the hands of Tawhida until, at the age of eighteen, this intelligent and lively young woman fell ill and died.

The trauma of Tawhida's death, apparently intensified by guilt, haunted Al-Taymouria for the rest of her life. She burned some of her poems and writings, seemingly in the belief that they were responsible for the death. She mourned her daughter for seven years, during which time she developed an eye ailment reportedly caused by relentless weeping.

The verses included here are part of a long elegiac poem in memory of the lost daughter. Published in 1884 in a collection of poems called *Heliat Al-Teraz* (Ornamental Designs), the poem is modeled on classical Arabic poetry, particularly the elegies written by Al-Khansaa, and demonstrates Al-Taymouria's mastery of a literary tradition that was largely the exclusive preserve of men. The Al-Yamama doctor in the poem, for example, alludes to a well-known classical Arabic narrative about a clairvoyant from Yamama (Yemen) who had legendary powers of healing.

Al-Taymouria wrote in Arabic, Persian, and Turkish on an array of subjects in a variety of genres. Along with love poems, eulogies, and dirges, she authored a long essay entitled *The Mirror of Contemplation* (1892) in which she discussed the situation of women in her society; and a fictional work, *Consequences in Words and Deeds* (1886), which predates any officially recognized Arabic work of fiction.

*Amira Nowaira*

✦

In the morning the doctor came, promising a cure;
But doctors are vain and cocksure.
He prescribed medicine that would, he claimed,
Heal the body of ills and leave it whole.
Struggling with pain and her eyes brimming, she said,
"Please hurry, then, and bring my body back.
Pity my youth and tenderness,
Pity my mother, already in grief, her heart fearful.
Pity my loss of nightly rest,
And pity my drooping eyelids, faint and weak."
Too soon she saw the boasts were empty,
And turned again for comfort.
"Dear mother, the doctor cannot help,
And my hopes are gone.
Should Al-Yamama Doctor come in person,
Nothing will relieve me.
My soul grows weary of pain

And soon, like a winged bird, it shall soar and climb.
Oh, mother dear, I cannot stay close to you.
Tomorrow my hearse will move like a bridal procession,
But ending in the grave, my home, my final destination.
Pray to the Lord of the universe, dear mother, to be kind to your daughter,
Who walks like a bride to her fate and does not falter.
Near my grave, mother dear, please stay a little longer.
Let my departing soul, terror-stricken, have its fill of you and be stronger.
Dear mother, we dreamed together,
All that will not be.
Those were the dreams we kept so close, so dear,
Now torn to shreds.
Dear mother, return to the empty house without me,
And keep my bridal dress, as a memento mori."

So I answered her, tears choking my throat, stopping my screams.
"No need to implore or beseech,
My grieving heart has melted in sorrow.
But as God is my witness, I shall not cease my prayers for you,
As long as birds sing in trees,
I shall not cease weeping,
Until in eternal heavens among sweet maidens,
We shall meet once again."

*Translated by Amira Nowaira*

## *Kharboucha*
## AISSA THE FOX

Morocco 1895 Arabic

Although her real name was Hadda and she was also called Hawida, as a poet, singer, and leader of her tribe, this legendary Moroccan woman was known as Kharboucha, sometimes with the title of "shikha," the feminine of "sheikh." ("Shikha" is a title now used for popular female singers, sometimes derogatively to designate "prostitute.") She was called Kharboucha because her face bore traces of smallpox. Despite illiteracy, Kharboucha was not only an artist, but a central figure in her people's fight for land and justice.

Karboucha lived in the region of Doukkala-Abda, in west central Morocco, at the time that Aissa Ben Omar was *qaïd*, the regional state authority. In 1894, following the death of Sultan Moulay Hassan when his son and heir was just ten years old, looting threatened officials' homes and property. Aissa Ben Omar ordered his men to disarm the Wlad Zayid people, to whom Kharboucha belonged, and to confiscate their land and horses. Kharboucha wrote songs that attacked Aissa Ben Omar and urged people to fight him, becoming a voice for the silent and subdued. The Wlad Zayid people rebelled against the sultan in July 1895, and large numbers were killed by Aissa Ben Omar's army. The *qaïd* was known to be cruel, ruthless, and a pawn of the local administration (he would later side with the French colonialists); he was also famous for his love of music, his revelries, and his entertainment of tribal leaders.

After the defeat of her tribe, Kharboucha fled and Aissa Ben Omar ordered his men to capture and jail her. While he entertained people, he would ask her to sing for him all the songs that she had sung to her people. She would oblige gladly, since she was always looking for ways to take her revenge. Her singing ultimately infuriated him so much that he tortured her, and finally killed her by locking her in a grain cellar and lighting a fire around her.

Kharboucha created a new type of singing now known as *aita*, from the verb *ayyat*, which means to call. All *aita* songs begin by invoking Allah and his saints, in mystical outbursts. The cry becomes a song, which becomes a call to witness suffering, and to surpass oneself. The *aita* is traditionally sung exclusively by women; when women are unavailable, men dress as women in order to sing it. The *aita* of Kharboucha have become part of a Moroccan oral tradition.

The songs included here tell Kharboucha's story, and capture her invincible defiance of Aissa Ben Omar's authority. In Song One, Kharboucha declares that she will never give in to Aissa Ben Omar, and that she will never stop defending her people and her land, Abda. In Song Two, she addresses Aissa Ben Omar directly, denouncing him for killing people who are his "brothers," and declaring his home cursed because it stands across from a mausoleum, Maashat.

In Song Three, Kharboucha calls upon the people of her tribe to rise against Aissa Ben Omar. *Bukshur* refers to the well inside his kasbah, which provided water for the land, and Si Qaddur is the guard of Aissa Ben Omar's house. The horses that are the subject of Song Four have special significance because Aissa Ben Omar had ordered that horses be taken away from her people, although he was reported to have more than four hundred of his own—their color reflecting the *qaïd's* black heart, his ruthlessness. In the equestrian tradition of North Africa, thoroughbred horses were used in the fantasia, or *laab el baroud* (gunpowder game), a display of synchronized riding and shooting performed on special occasions.

In Song Five, Kharboucha asks her people to witness the suffering she has had to endure over many months as she stood up to Aissa Ben Omar. Song Six includes her most famous lines, adopted by many Moroccan singers and songwriters: When she asks, "Where are you from? / Where am I from?" she is reminding her torturer that they share the same roots, which he has betrayed. In her final line, "Nothing lasts forever," she also reminds him that everyone will eventually get his or her fair judgment before God.

*Khadija Zizi*

✦

## Song One

I am a slave to Abda,
But no, not to Aissa!

## Song Two

Aissa Ben Omar,
Killer of his brothers.
Aissa Ben Omar,
Oh, you little fox,
Oh, dog-face.
They say the house of Si Aissa was destroyed
It stands across from the Maashat so it is cursed.

## Song Three

Let's rise in rebellion until we reach the *bukshur*.
Let's rise in rebellion until we reach the door of Si Qaddur.

## Song Four

Didn't you see what I saw?
Did you see the horses of Ben Aissa?
Black and thoroughbred they were.
In a row they came, all aligned they were

## Song Five

Tonight is a night of physical suffering.
Oh, father, how I am suffering.
Nothing lasts forever.
Oh, father, how I am suffering.
The ultimate end is dying.
Oh, father, how I am suffering.

The Kharboucha Song
Blue-eyed, thick and dry-haired, Kharboucha, you have hurt me.
Oh mother, who is going to console me?
Oh gray-haired old man! Treachery of my *qaïd* is bad.
Where are you from?
Where am I from?
Don't we come from the same place?
Nothing lasts forever, oh, Sidi.

*Translated by Fatima Laauina and Khadija Zizi*

## *Labiba Hashim*
# THE EASTERN WOMAN:
# HOW SHE IS AND HOW SHE SHOULD BE

Egypt  1898   Arabic

Labiba Hashim (1882–1952) moved to Cairo with her family after graduating from the American College in Beirut. Among the first of many Arab intellectuals who came to live in Egypt in the last years of the nineteenth century, she became both a well-known writer and a leading figure in the Egyptian feminist movement. Her first novel, *The Merits of Love*, was published in 1899, and her most famous, *A Man's Heart*, in 1905. In 1906, Hashim founded a feminist magazine, *Fatat Al-Sharq* (The Girl of the East), in which she herself published essays on education and a column that presented the stories of renowned female figures who had made significant contributions to their societies. One of her goals was to give women a voice—a forum where they could express their opinions and talk about important issues. In 1911, she became the first Arab woman to lecture at the new Egyptian University.

"The Eastern Woman" was published in 1898 in *Anis Al Galis* (The Friendly Companion), a magazine founded by Alexandra Afrino, the official spokesperson of the feminist movement in Egypt at that time. The essay calls for women to participate actively in society, especially by learning, thinking, writing, and expressing their own ideas and opinions. It is aimed at upper-class and middle-class women, some of whom did, at that time, receive at least basic education in foreign religious schools, or by private tutors at home. Hashim believed it was the duty of these women to make use of their education and serve as models for other women. She urges them to shed their trivial concerns, such as their emulation of Western fashion, and to place their priorities on further education and work. In her attempt to drive women out of the complacency and intellectual void of the domestic sphere and into the public sphere, she chastises women for being lazy and frivolous, and encourages them to pursue knowledge and put it into use.

Hashim clearly believes that in order to combat their inferior status in society, women must move beyond blaming their oppression on others, and seize responsibility for their own progress.

*Heba Sharobeem and Radwa El Barouni*

✦

One day, while I was wandering in the wilderness of thought, torn between boredom and anticipation, as I was expecting the visit of a woman who is the pride of all women, I came across it. Sensing my boredom, this magazine had revealed itself to me. I found it a wonderful companion, so I flipped through its pages, noticing its merits, and contemplating its brilliant material until I found an article, in the third edition, entitled "The Calamity of the East," written by the eminent writer Labiba Shamoun, who has often tickled people's ears with her eloquence and intrigued many minds with her elegant style. In this article, the writer complains of the injustice suffered by the Eastern woman and the tyrannical community that hampers her progress. I therefore saw fit to take on this subject, which I regard as one of the most important and useful topics of discussion for women writers, in the hope of reaching solutions that may lead to the improvement of Eastern women.

People need to know that the Eastern woman is still on the brink of ignorance and backwardness, despite all the tools made available for her education. She is still lagging far behind her Western neighbor, a thing that leads to the criticism and demeaning of Eastern women. This applies to women of all classes and ranks, there being no difference between the rich and poor, the commoners and the elite. Our women, except for a rare few who cannot be considered the norm, have offered nothing, so far, that is worthy of praise or that puts an end to the blame leveled against them.

I find that most of the blame is well-deserved by those women who were fortunate enough to be educated in the sciences and literature, and yet neglected their talents and were so nonchalant about it all. These women regarded school education as a mere duty, and their education ended once they left school. Nothing remains of what they have learned save a smattering of foreign phrases and the imitation of Western fashion, which can neither cause harm nor help them shine. The most they can make of these "accomplishments" is to participate in a dance, adorn themselves with fake ornaments, or place some books in their bookcases to suggest intelligence, while in truth the books only embellish the shelves, for the minds of their owners are inactive. If this is the case for those fortunate ones whom life has aided in the pursuit of knowledge, what then are we to expect from the poor, who can neither attain the reality nor aspire to it?

In all this, I find that the blame lies squarely with Eastern women alone and with no one else, since schools are open, the books are at hand, and the means of making use of all this are readily available. Nothing stands in the way of the education of women. The only problem lies in the women themselves, who consider the education received at school or from the few books they have read to be sufficient. Moreover, should a woman wish to write or explore areas of knowledge, she will feel inadequate and will either have to give up the whole endeavor or be replaced by another. Such consequences are signs of ineptitude and failure. It would be commendable for women to join intellectual circles and pursue writing and composition, even if they had to seek the assistance of men. With such assistance, women would gradually be able to learn what they need to learn beyond school, until they can present their own ideas themselves and thus become role models for others, who will then seek help from them instead of from men. Women should not imagine that this is difficult, or that it is disgraceful in any way. On the contrary, it is a route to perfection, and the means by which such perfection can be achieved. Most of those women who have progressed in the attainment of knowledge, so that they rival men and can dispense with their help, followed this method at the beginning. It is seldom that we find an article by a woman who did not initially have help from someone, until she could come into her own. Unfortunately, however, even these women are, thus far, too few to become models for others or to elevate the status of the Eastern woman.

Therefore, I believe it is the duty of every woman who has been favored by fate and has been given the tools to attain knowledge to follow the path of education, so that her knowledge may become a source of pride for her. She will realize that, just as she was capable of imitating foreign customs and the fashions, she is also capable of learning and putting her knowledge to work. Moreover, thank God, we have a large number of women who are capable of achieving this if they really set their minds to it. There is no reason for us to complain of the lack of girls' schools or the small number of women being educated; our only complaint should be that they are not adequately educated and that they do not use their education to achieve their aims.

Furthermore, this women's magazine, *Anis Al Galis*, has been published for a long time now, and I have only come across two or three articles written by women. This raises the question of whether only three Eastern women have been educated. Or is it that only three women are capable of writing? Certainly not, for we have many educated women who can gradually begin to write, if they would only begin. However, it is most unfortunate that they are often prevented by their laziness or sidetracked by their imitation of Western women's fashions, which makes them forget what they had previously learned and turns them into bad role models, since women are prone to emulate one another. If women only displayed the same zeal they express in imitating fashion in their pursuit of knowledge and education, they would be no different from men. I hope that women writers, though few in number, will continue to write and encourage their sisters to follow in their footsteps so that, with the passage of time, the habit may spread and the tradition thrive, and the number of literary women increase. We certainly have the capacity and the potential to shine, and God is the best of guides.

*Translated by Radwa El Barouni*

# Zeinab Fawwaz
## THE CHOICE OF A HUSBAND

Egypt 1899    Arabic

Little is known of Zeinab Fawwaz's early life. Even her date of birth is uncertain; variously cited are 1840, 1845 or 1846. She came from a modest family in Lebanon and was twice married and divorced before she moved with her father to Alexandria, where she studied Arabic grammar with religious teachers. Unlike the Syrians living in Alexandria, she did not speak foreign languages nor was she exposed to European culture, despite the fact that Egypt was by then under British occupation, which had begun in 1882.

*Zeinab* Fawwaz's early writings were newspaper articles, published as early as the 1890s, calling for the emancipation of women and arguing that nations will progress only insofar as women are liberated and respected. In this sense she predates Qasim Amin, author of the 1899 book *The Liberation of Women*, who has been generally acknowledged as the first feminist in Egypt. She is also the first novelist in the Arab world. While Mohamed Hussein Heikal, whose novel *Zeinab* appeared in 1914, was long accorded this distinction, it rightfully belongs to Fawwaz. Her novel *Ghadet al Zahira* (The Beautiful Woman of al Zahira) was published in 1899, and comments in the book's foreword suggest that the novel was written even earlier and circulated among friends. In 1893 she published another novel, *Al Hawa wal Wafa'* (Passion and Loyalty), as well as a compilation of biographies of 450 important Arab and non-Arab women, entitled *Al Durr al Manthour fi Tabakat Rabat al Khudur.*

In the foreword to *Ghadet al Zahira*, Fawwaz explains that she turned to the novel because it both entertains and instructs, and serves as a mirror for ideas. The plot of the novel revolves round two cousins, Prince Tamer and Prince Shakib, who compete for the leadership of the area of Jabal Shamekh, and also for the hand of their cousin Fari'a. Prince Tamer is the villain who will go to any lengths to get what he wants, Fawwaz's example of the kind of tyranny that must be rooted out of society, while Prince Shakib is the model of noble princely behavior. Fari'a, who has grown up in an ideal family where the opinions of all are respected, falls in love with Shakib, and realizes that Tamer wants to marry her only for political reasons. When she turns Tamer down, he kidnaps her along with her friends Samira and Habiba. Many breathtaking episodes ensue, but all ends happily, with Fari'a and Shakib finally married. Throughout the novel, Fawwaz depicts strong women who are capable of making decisions and standing up to injustice, but at the same time loving and considerate.

The first of the two brief excerpts included in this volume makes clear that, in the family of Fari'a, women have the right to choose their husbands and violence is not a solution. In the second selection, Fari'a stands up to the kidnappers and shows that she is willing to die to protect her honor.

*Sahar Hamouda*

✦

When he [Aziz, Fari'a's brother] read the letter and understood its contents, he went to his mother and told her of the matter. Her heart was gladdened and she said, "Let him have what he has requested." She sent for her daughter and told her that her cousin had asked for her hand. Fari'a was surprised at the news, and thought that it was Shakib who was meant. She wondered why he had not told her when they were in the village of Hisn with her mother at the mourning rituals of her uncle Hamed. She attributed it to the noise and crowds, which had not given them the chance to talk, since they could only see each other from a distance. When she met her mother, she asked her about the source of the news. Her mother told her about the messenger who had come from Al Jabiya with a letter from her cousin Tamer. Fari'a frowned when she heard the name Tamer. But she stood firm and turned to her mother, saying, "And what did my dear brother say, I wonder?"

She said, "He has left that matter to you. That is why I sent for you, to inquire from you about that."

"But I do not want to be betrothed to him. So, please, mother, do not mention this matter to me ever again. I do not like to hear about it."

Her mother was distressed at the news, and said, "I do hope, my dear, that you will fulfill my wish, since there is none in the family more worthy of you than Tamer."

She said, "I do not want to get married."

"But why, my dear, when marriage is your lot, as it is for all girls."

The girl fell silent and did not answer, then rose quietly and went to her room.

Her mother sent for Aziz and told him what had happened. He, too, was annoyed by the news, and said, "I think she wants to make me become harsh and force her into acceptance."

His mother said, "My son, there is no need for force; we can resort to wiles." As soon as the words were out of her mouth, Khaled came in. He was the youngest of her children and so he was never consulted on any matter. His mother told him, "See, Khaled, how your sister has turned down the proposal of her cousin Tamer."

He said, "She has done the right thing. I stand by her decision, because her intuition has shown her what he is like and that he must be turned down."

She said, "And why is that? Is there anything wrong with him?"

He said, "Yes, all his actions are ugly and there is nothing lovable about him. My sister cannot be blamed for hating him, because he is mean, selfish, and sly. He is not attracted by anything good, and will not exert himself over anything unless there is a personal gain in it for him. I know that from him. So please do not cheat Fari'a. She has been brought up to be decent and honorable."

Aziz had been silent all the while. He looked at Khaled and listened to him without offering a reply. When Khaled finished talking, Aziz turned to him and asked, "Who told you of Tamer's behavior and deeds?"

Khaled said, "His deeds have traveled ahead of him. But you don't hear of them because you do not keep company with those who will give you such news. And even if you do sit with them, they will not dare tell you any of this because they are in awe of you. But I sit with whom I wish, and learn from them what I wish."

Aziz said, "And what is to be said to him now?"

Khaled said, "Write and tell him that she does not consent to marry him. You are excused in that, because earlier you had told him that you would not marry her without her consent, and so you are not to blame since the matter is not in your hands."

[. . .]

Then she [Fari'a] took Samira and Habiba and went to the shepherd's house, unaware of what was lying in store for her there. When they arrived, Samira went in before her, and she followed. They were met by a fearful looking Taleb.

Fari'a said, "Who are you, and what are you doing here? And where is Sadek?"

He said, "He is coming."

He banged on the door, at which six heavily armed men entered, took hold of Fari'a, and gagged her mouth. She tried to escape but couldn't. Samira screamed. Jaber stabbed her in the shoulder with his dagger, causing blood to flow. Then he gagged her mouth with a kerchief. Fari'a turned round to look for Habiba, but found no trace of her. A *howdah*, prepared for Fari'a, was waiting outside the door. The men carried the two women to it, lowered the curtains, and quickly carried it away. Since the shepherd's house was at the edge of the village, no one in the village knew what had happened. The men walked until they had passed the village. Then they set the women free, raised the curtains, and gave them some water to drink.

After the two women had rested, Fari'a asked, "Where are you taking us, and who was it who gave you these orders? Is it the accursed Tamer, or somebody else?"

When she got no answer, she roared in an imperious voice, "In the name of God, if you do not tell me, I will kill myself, and will not allow any of you to harm me. Do you not know who I am? Do you not fear my brother's power? Do you not know that he will not let me fall prey to your tyranny and aggression, even if you impale me..."

Nobody answered her and she shouted again.

Taleb said, "Enough of these threats, Princess. If you do not keep quiet of your own accord, I shall silence you with this sword."

She said, "And do you think I fear death, you lowest of men? You shall not gain what you want!"

She rose to throw herself from the *howdah*, but Samira held her back, crying and wailing, and said, "Wait a while, my friend. God must surely send us help. We have men who are looking for us and are following our trail. Do not despair of God's mercy, for He is always with those who are patient." When Fari'a heard that, she calmed down.

*Translated by Sahar Hamouda*

# Malak Hifni Nassef
## POLYGAMY

Egypt 1910    Arabic

A leading Egyptian writer and feminist of her time, Malak Hifni Nassef was born in 1886 to a family that greatly valued education. The eldest of seven children, she began publishing essays in Egyptian magazines at the age of thirteen. She attended the Saneya School, and becoming the first Egyptian girl to receive a primary school certificate from a public school and, in 1903, to pass the teachers' certificate examination.

Writing under the pseudonym Bahithat Al-Badiya, which means "Seeker in the Desert," Nassef contributed many articles to *Al-Jarida*, the newspaper of the nationalist Umma Party, eventually writing a regular, widely read column called "Al-Nisa'iyat" (Feminisms). A collection of her lectures and essays was published in the 1910 book of the same name.

A daring, educated, and devoted social reformer, she founded several organizations devoted to women's development, and took part in the first lecture series by and for women. In 1911 she presented the Egyptian parliament, a gathering of nationalist men, with a list of demands to improve the status of women (which were rejected). These included greater access to education and the professions, protections for women in arranged marriages, and a somewhat less restrictive style of public dress. Nassef was a devout Muslim and a supporter of Egyptian independence; hence, her list also included teaching girls the Qur'an and "dispensing with foreign goods and people as much as possible."

In this essay, originally published in her newspaper column, Nassef objects to polygamy on practical, human, and feminist grounds, describing it as "a corruption of men, of health, of money, of moral values, of children, and of women's hearts." She explores at length polygamy's adverse effect on women, the family, and on society in general. Although she is examining a social and cultural issue, Nassef's language is often poetic. She frequently uses the trope of fire, flames, and burning to emphasize the agony of women. After her fierce attack, Nassef ends the essay on a hopeful note, praising the "educated and well-to-do" classes for recognizing the negative effects of polygamy and its incompatibility with "modernity and enlightenment." The essay as a whole presents polygamy as harmful to all forms of social development or progress.

While she does not refer to her own situation, Nassef had herself become victim of the practice she so bitterly decries. Nassef died of influenza in 1918 when she was just thirty-two, and was eulogized by her feminist compatriot Huda Shaarawi.

*Azza El Kholy*

What a horrifying word that almost causes my fingers to freeze as I hold the pen to write about it! It is women's worst enemy and their sole devil. Many are the hearts it has broken; the minds it has distracted; the families it has destroyed; and the evils that it has begotten. Many are the innocent who have been victimized by it and many are those it has led to imprisonment. Many are the brothers who, were it not for polygamy, would not have been in conflict or estranged or eaten up by strife, full of ill will and hatred for each other, seeking revenge, like the Wael tribe, when they could otherwise have lived in harmony.

What a hideous word connoting brutality and selfishness! A word that has often embarrassed a man, taught him to lie, and thus ruined his character, and driven him to spend money he had saved from his livelihood. How often has it hardened the heart of a father toward his son? How often has it taught envy and calumny? So if you were to have your fun, dear man, remember, before rejoicing in your new wedding, that you are leaving behind a miserable creature full of sighs, raining tears like the pearls of your new bride, only these have melted, scorched by grief! Fear God and pity those youngsters crying to see her cry, who have been taught by her to grieve and have thus borrowed the gems of your wedding to forge stone-dead eyes. While you listen to drums and pipes, they can hear in their eardrums only grief, although they have once been merry.

In this nomadic land, where I live now, I would not be exaggerating if I said that all women have experienced having a second wife among them, since polygamy is common among their men. Moreover, my acquaintance with them confirms this.

I have often asked women of the neighborhood the following question: "Do you still love your husband the same way you used to before he married another?" The answer is always in the negative. Some have confirmed this themselves, and I have heard about others who would, in fact, have preferred to see their spouses carried off in their coffins rather than see them married to other women. Dear God, is it to that extent that a woman hates her rival? Let men then ponder!

I find the "old" wife sad and so too the "new." If you ask first about the reason for the "old" one's sorrow, she will answer, "What saddens me most is my degradation and the breaking of my heart when, as you can see, I am not less in beauty or character than the new wife. Besides, I have always done my best to please my husband, but now I do not, despite the fact that he continues to appease me by telling me that he loves me more, and that I am the first to capture his heart, etc. He says that he has not married for the lack of anything in me, but that it was, simply, thus fated."

Similarly, when I ask the new wife about the cause of her distress, she says, "It pains me to have a partner in, and a competitor for, my husband, although he perpetually confirms that he is indifferent to her. He tells me that, had he been convinced that she was the one for him, he would not have married another, and that he wants to divorce her, but keeps her only out of compassion and to raise his children." How resourceful is the husband of two! Indeed, were there to be any fairness at all, it might take the appointment of a politician or a colonial administrator to manage the affairs of a husband of two! (Pity, we don't have colonies.)

When a woman is doomed to bear the catastrophe of her husband's second marriage, her joy disappears, and in its place burn the flames of envy, weakening her body and planting the seeds of evil inside her. Furthermore, if she is not pious, the devil will incite her and teach her the methods of revenge and intrigue. It is not uncommon that we hear of a woman poisoning her husband, or his wife, or a son of the other woman, thus bringing about destruction for all. Nor is it uncommon that a woman spreads lies about her rival to her husband, or mars her reputation among people. Such women may even sell their jewelry and spend their money on soothsayers who promise to disrupt the life of the husband or his new wife, as they claim.

The husband of two is not as happy a man as he may imagine. For when he is late at work, one will accuse him of having been with the other and, sometimes, it does not stop at the accusation but extends to include a change of heart, hatred and, at times, slander. Moreover, if he once buys a handkerchief for one and not the other, the verbal whip lashes him, and he is then forced to double and even quadruple the value of the gift. Wouldn't he have been much better off with peace of mind rather than such torment? Indeed, polygamy is a disease that, once ingrained, is very hard to excise.

I give no excuse to a man who marries two wives, unless a happy life with the first wife becomes impossible for legitimate or illegitimate reasons. In that case he may be forced to marry another. Yet, the sensible man will not let his happiness allow him to forget his children or his first wife, especially if she is not at fault. However, if he feels that her staying with him is disturbing his life, or if he actually hates her, he should then divorce her because he may find satisfaction in another and she, too, for is it not common that many have had a change of heart?

To my mind, divorce is easier and less painful than taking a second wife. The first is unhappiness with freedom whereas the second is misery and bondage. For if unhappiness is inevitable, why should a woman bear with it and also undergo a blazing heartache and the rending of her soul? Besides, a free unhappy person is much better off than an unhappy captive. Some deceive the first wife by giving her full control of the house, with all the keys to the storage rooms. But, alas, what good are the keys of storage rooms and the control over ghee and honey compared to the keys to the heart and the love of a husband?

Polygamy is a corruption of men, of health, of money, of moral values, of children, and of women's hearts. A wise man is one who can win over the hearts of others and thus, is it not even wiser to be able to win the heart of one's kin?

Polygamy is a corruption of money because a man, apart from having to support two families, finds each wife trying to squander money to undermine his ability to spend on the other or prevent him from marrying a third. Here, we cannot blame either for overspending; it is quite normal. Each woman might say: "What use is my thrift? Why deprive myself of what I desire while my husband is spending what I save on the other woman? It is indeed best to indulge in what my heart desires like my rival." As for the children, their number is doubled, being born from two women rather than one and, if we were to exclude the well-to-do from our judgment, the middle-class man or the poor man could become destitute. Meeting the heavy expenses of life, supporting two families, and educating children are no easy tasks.

Polygamy corrupts moral values because the husband of two is forever dissembling, sweet-talking, and deceiving to win the love of each woman. As a matter of fact, polygamy is covetousness and greed.

Furthermore, it corrupts children, for I have seen with my own eyes how each wife instills her hatred for the other woman through her children. Children then grow up full of pointless hatred for half brothers and sisters, and for the other woman simply because their mother has filled their consciousness with her own principles. Therefore, no matter what the stepmother does to appease her stepson, no matter how well she treats him, he will inevitably accuse her of hating him and will think that what good she does comes from fear of his father or is simply an attempt to hide what she really feels toward him! You'd often find the children of the same man jealous and envious of one another as a result of what their mothers have taught them. This is duly confirmed by the common phrases and popular proverbs of the day.

Polygamy corrupts women's hearts because the first wife hates the man for angering her and hurting her feelings, and the second wife never trusts him because he is committed to another. The result is that he achieves nothing and becomes, like a jack-of-all-trades, master of none!

It is, however, to my great relief that the habit of polygamy is shrinking now, especially among the educated and well-to-do, because modernity and enlightenment prohibit it, even though they may still claim that jurisprudence permits it. Because living has become a competitive race, today's man—unlike our grandfathers, whose ownership of ten *feddans* of land allowed them to have a restful sleep in their houses and marry two or three—does not find two hundred *feddans*, along with his effort and sweat, enough to support one home in this modern age, where appearances matter.

*Translated by Azza El Kholy*

# Tawgrat Walt Aissa N'Ayt Sokhman
## RESISTANCE

Morocco   Early 1920s   Berber

Tawgrat Walt Aissa N'Ayt Sokhman was blind and illiterate, yet became a renowned professional poet, a master of the ancient Berber tradition of oral poetry and song. Her birth and death dates are not known, although records show that she was very old by 1930. She grew up as an orphan and never married, spending most of her life in the Berber village of Ayt Sokhman in the Middle Atlas, the westernmost of Morocco's Atlas Mountain ranges. Tawgrat celebrated her blindness as a mark of beauty, and her courage and force of personality left a powerful impression on those who met her. Her poetry, recited at performances of the Berber dance *ahidus*, was cherished by her people and recited throughout the Middle Atlas.

Tawgrat's gifts even won the admiration of the French, who came to Morocco in ever larger numbers after 1912, when much of Morocco became a French protectorate. The French historian François Reyniers said that "she was neither a prophet nor a witch, but she had an imagination that astonished people with its extraordinary power," while others compared her to the blind Greek poet Homer.

Tawgrat's poems are a vital record of the armed resistance to French domination in the Middle Atlas region. The resistance movement in the Rif region, bordering the Mediterranean, is far better known, in part because of its proximity to Europe and in part because its leader, Mohamed Abdelkrim Khattabi, was a well-educated and highly cultured man who rubbed shoulders with Europeans and was acquainted with their propaganda strategies, and managed to draw international attention to the cause. The armed resistance in central and southern Morocco, in contrast, remained largely unknown and almost forgotten, because these more remote areas were completely controlled by the French, who managed to keep hidden the fierce battles that took place throughout the 1920s and 1930s. The French used the strategy of separating "rebellious" areas from "subdued" ones, and stopped ammunition from reaching the fighters, who were often isolated in the harsh mountains.

The anticolonial struggles of the Middle Atlas and High Atlas were accompanied by a wealth of oral and written poems in both Arabic and Berber. The official history of this poetry consists primarily of written poems by men. But resistance poetry in Berber was by definition oral, and included women, both literate and illiterate, who were clearly marginalized despite their participation in the fight for independence.

Tawgrat's poems of resistance were composed in the 1920s, often in a Berber genre called *thimawayin*. In this poetry, she incited women to resist the enemy and defend their country, especially after the men of their tribes were overpowered by the French. She clearly sees the independence struggle as a form of *Jihad*, a battle to defend Islam and Islamic principles. Tawgrat was devastated by the defeat of her own tribe, and toward the end of her life she left her home to move to the village of Tunfit, near Midelt. She died feeling bitter hatred in her heart for the colonizers, their Moroccan collaborators, and whoever did not fight them. In the poem below, she uses her words as weapons to attack a man named Moha Urriban, apparently a village blacksmith, who was one of the runaways from the battle. The texts of Tawgrat's poems were collected from living people of her generation by Mohamed Chafik and published in 1982.

*Fatima Amhennede*

✦

You, Moha Urriban,
You surely stained the tribe when you escaped like a rabbit
In front of dogs.
Keep your smithy and shut up.
You are qualified only to touch coal.
How could one be a Muslim
*If you visit the unfaithful's office?*
The unfaithful came and drank from the oak spring,
And without fear, tied up their horses,
They fixed the stakes and said now we are neighbors.
Look up Itto, Thuda, and Izza; call women to carry the flag
To war, since many Berber men have become inert!
Young men, attack,
Attack the unfaithful!
Advance forward!
Because he who dies in *Jihad*,
Has a shelter in paradise,
And to his relatives
He will leave honor and glory.
Shame on you; you have no manhood,
For you love to be the slaves of the unfaithful.

*Translated by Moha Ennaji*

## *Saphia Zagloul*
## LETTER FROM EXILE

Egypt   1922   French

Saphia Zagloul was an important figure in the Egyptian nationalist and feminist movements—which for her, as for many Egyptian women of her time, were powerfully intertwined. Born in 1878 into a wealthy family in Cairo, she was also daughter and wife to prominent men in Egypt's history: Her father, Mustafa Fahmi Pasha, who was Turkish in origin, served as Egypt's prime minister in 1891 and again in 1895. Her husband, Saad Zagloul, was a nationalist leader who dedicated his life to the struggle for independence from the British.

The Zaglouls' residence became the meeting place for the Egyptian Wafd Party, chaired by her husband, and soon acquired the expressive title *Bayt el-Umma*, House of the Nation. It became the cradle of the 1919 Revolution, the largely nonviolent uprising that introduced the most intense years of struggle against colonial domination. The uprising broke out when Saad Zagloul and other nationalist leaders were arrested and exiled to Malta. Saphia Zagloul was denied permission to join her husband. Instead, she organized demonstrations and protest marches against British repression and British goods, rallying Egyptian women to public political activity for the first time in modern history. British authorities did allow her to join her husband during his second exile, which extended from 1921 to 1923.While Egypt was declared independent in February 1922, not until decades later would it be truly free of British occupation and domination.

Her nationalist endeavors soon earned Saphia Zagloul the title of *Um el-Masriyyeen*, the Mother of Egyptians.She continued to support her husband through his brief term as Egypt's first prime minister, while at the same time continuing her own political work. She pursued her struggle for women's liberation and national autonomy well after her husband's death in 1927, until her own in 1946.

The letter included here was sent from Gibraltar. Saad Zagloul had recently been transferred from the distant Seychelles, where his health had deteriorated. Written in French, the letter is addressed to Madame Balta, who had once been Saphia Zagloul's piano teacher and later a close friend. Like other daughters of upper-class families, Saphia Zagloul had been educated at home in a variety of subjects, including French, which was the language of communication of the Egyptian upper class and especially of women. In her correspondence with Madame Balta, Saphia Zagloul gives an account of her daily life, alluding to her hardships and grievances without expressing them openly.

*Madiha Doss and Laila Helmi*

◆

Gibraltar 5/11/22

My dearest friend,

I wanted to write to you upon my arrival, but I have been very busy these days. I found my poor husband in a sorry state, badly looked after, and appallingly served. All his clothes are torn and in poor condition. Only with great difficulty did I manage to establish order. At last we are settled. Our lodging is reasonable, considering that it is a prison. The house is built on a steep mountain, surrounded by large rocks and fortresses filled with English soldiers. We are also surrounded by a badly kept garden, which is almost a wilderness. In actual fact, my husband greatly needed my care and I have found him very changed. He has lost ten kilos since our last trip to Vichy. He has slept badly and has hardly eaten at all. Thank God, that since our arrival he is sleeping much better and is starting to eat more. I hope that with good care and company he will soon regain his strength.

I hope, dear friend, that my letter will find you all in good health. Fortunately, I myself am well.

I beg you to write to me as often as possible. You know perfectly well the pleasure I get each time you write. My correspondence is not censored, so write to me directly at my Gibraltar address.

Here it often rains, fortunately for this country. Otherwise there would be insufficient fresh water. In the houses, there is only sea water at the tap, which is salty and very unpleasant. Getting fresh water is quite a to-do. It has to be brought up from the garden, so you can imagine all the bother.

Finally, dear friend, I must not complain too much. I give thanks to the Almighty and am resigned to bear our exile with patience.

My husband joins me in sending our deepest felt regards to you and Mr. Balta as well as to charming Léonie.

My fondest, heartfelt kisses to you dear friend,
Saphia Zagloul

*Translated by Carole Escoffey*

## *Helmeya Yousry*
## RESPONSE TO REACTIONARIES

Egypt 1925    Arabic

We know nothing of Helmeya Yousry. *Al Amal* (Hope) magazine, a political weekly in which this article appeared, made it possible for women who were not established writers or well-known public figures to express their thoughts and feelings on its pages. The magazine was established, along with the Al Amal Society, by the nationalist Wafd Party, the dominant party in Egypt between the world wars, as a means of defending and promoting the liberal views on women's rights.

Outspokenness became the hallmark of *Al Amal*, as is clearly demonstrated by Yousry's piece. She appears to be responding to the rising movement in Egypt that combined nationalism with a more fundamentalist approach to Islam, advocating a strict adherence to the codes of an earlier era. Yousry, like most in the Wafd Party, supports Islam, but opposes those who seek to use the religion as a pretext to disrupt social progress, and especially to demean women and deprive them of education, work, and freedom. In the course of her essay, Yousry pays homage to Kassem Amin Bek (better known as Qasim Amin), author of the 1899 book *The Liberation of Women*, who applied Islamic scholarship to argue against the seclusion and oppression of women. Her piece calls on women to defy reactionary attitudes and stand up for their rights.

*Amira Nowaira and Azza El Kholy*

✦

You claim that you are motivated by overzealousness for religion when, in reality, religion denounces your smugness. Since the day the Egyptian woman has called for her right to education and freedom, each one of you has feared losing his concubine, the woman he has monopolized by his means and power and by virtue of her weakness and submissiveness.

You raved and ranted and attacked those who wanted to open the door and lead her onto a better road. The first to take the blow and endure your scorn, with great tolerance and a heart full of hope, was the late Kassem Amin Bek, who transformed the idea of women's freedom from an idea to reality, and was, indeed, the liberator of women from the bondage of slavery. Kassem Amin who, God bless his soul, once said: "I call upon every lover of truth to investigate with me the status of Egyptian women, and I am sure that they will arrive, on their own, at the conclusion I have arrived at: the necessity of reforming women's status." And, on another occasion, he said: "Some will say that what I call for today is a novel idea and I say yes, I have introduced a novel idea, not in Islam, but rather in the traditions, habits, and attitudes, areas in which perfection is most welcome."

True, Kassem has died, but his ideas live on. He has planted the seed and it has borne fruit and this is the tree of "hope" from which we pick the fruit of great advancement and progress. Women are half the world and the mothers of the other half, and thus in their education lies the education of the whole population, and in their deterioration, the misery and backwardness which will befall all people. Saad Zagloul Pasha was right when he said, in a conversation with Mounira Thabet Hanem, the editor of *Al Amal*, and a working woman herself: "Had the number of our educated women been more than they are now, it would have been a magnificent blessing and a greater benefit. I believe fully that it is impossible for a nation to progress in life without the education and advancement of women."

And so, what do you think, you back-tracking reactionaries? I think your answer is predictable: You would say that this is an imposition on Islam and a great tyranny on our part. However, the only reply to your narrow opinions and your evil allegations is that your reactions are no more than evasions of the effort to comprehend, escapes from the drudgery of research and knowledge. You make it seem as if God created Muslims from a special substance that is exclusively theirs and removed them from the natural laws that inform all other humans and living things.

Unmask, and show your ulterior motives and leave religion aside. The editor of *Al Amal* has asked for no more than reform, a reform that will lead to resolving the ongoing strife between the sexes and end the humiliation of women, which has needlessly put them in the power of those who have no mercy or compassion. Those who cast a woman and her weeping children within the confines of poverty leave her to suffer from oppression, without sanctuary or aid, while they live in affluence without blame, reprimand, or even a call for reform. If this is what you reactionaries claim that jurisprudence has decreed,

I say that is impossible. Jurisprudence has dictated doing good and avoiding evil. Are you pleased, now that your motives have been uncovered and your aims exposed? All you really want is to fill your bellies and lead your nation into backwardness by falsely using Islam as a pretext to conceal your intentions and achieve your aims and desires.

You people of darkness have filled the earth and its corners with whining and archaic and rigid ideas, but have found no response and certainly no audience. Yet, have you ever once considered repairing what you have ruined? We asked for the removing of the veil, and you said, "God forbid." We said marry only one woman and eschew polygamy, and you said, we are "violating religious laws." We called for the education of girls, and you answered that women were "created for the home." For God's sake, tell us honestly whether you intend to reform.

Is our reveiling today what you want and admire, now that, in keeping with changes in traditions, we have all become unveiled? No women are veiled today, even among those you claim still wear the veil. As for marrying one woman, Allah has decreed in His great book: "Marry as many women as you please; two, three or four, but if you fear you cannot be fair to all, then marry only one." This issue is not debatable; that one wife is enough if you cannot maintain fairness is no matter for discussion. Besides, where was fairness ever to be found with the "stronger" sex?

As for education, well, this has been decreed for men and women alike, and women have rights and duties as men do, for women have been ordered by God Almighty to perform the same duties as men. After all, in God's eyes people are not favored except by what they have acquired in knowledge, reason, and piety. We will, therefore, leave you to sink into your reactionary world, while we move on to achieve our aims. As for the editor of *Al Amal*, she must raise the flag of hope and lead the way and we shall follow…So forward let us move….

*Translated by Azza El Kholy*


## *Mounira Thabet*
# WOMEN'S RIGHTS

Egypt 1925    Arabic

Mounira Thabet (1902–1967) was an Egyptian journalist and activist born and reared in Alexandria, where she learned Arabic, English, and Italian. Thabet was the first Egyptian woman to attend the French Law School in Cairo and obtain a *license en droit*. Prejudice presented obstacles to her career as a lawyer, and she soon turned to journalism, where she carried forth her battle for women's rights. She became widely known for pieces published in the nationalist weekly *Al-*

*Ahram* in the years immediately following Egyptian independence in 1922. Thabet chastised the leading Wafd Party and its renowned leader Saad Zagloul for failing to include women on the committee charged with drafting a new constitution. After women's key role in the anticolonial struggle, she argued, they were entitled to full participation in the new government, including the right to vote and stand for parliament. Her demands highlighted some strategic differences within the Egyptian feminist movement: While there remained a basic sense of common cause, some older leaders, including Huda Shaarawi, took a more gradualist approach, while others, like Thabet, believed in fighting for immediate and sweeping change.

Mounira Thabet also founded her own publications, which made the struggle for women's right a primary concern: first a weekly political and literary newspaper in French entitled *L'Espoir*, and then an Arabic magazine called *Al Amal*. (Both titles translate to "Hope.") She also published several books, including a response to the contentious 1939 plan for the future of Palestine and in 1946 an autobiography, *Revolution in the Ivory Tower: My Memoirs of Twenty Years of Fighting for Women's Political Rights*. Thabet continued to write and campaigned for women's suffrage and other feminist issues throughout her life.

"Women's Rights with Reference to the Principles of *Al Amal*" appeared on 12 December 1925, in response to two letters Mounira Thabet had received from two men. The two letters addressed to Thabet reprimanded her and other like-minded advocates of women's political rights for their revolutionary spirit. The first, not alone among "progressive" men of his time, apparently supported greater social freedom for women, but opposed women's suffrage, which Thabet believes is fundamental to women's equality. The second has clearly accused her of "rebelling against" Islam—to which Thabet replies with citations from Shari'a (Islamic jurisprudence) and the declaration that feminists "respect religion and the Qur'an more than those who pretend to be advocates of religion, and we understand it more thoroughly."

*Naglaa Abu-Agag*

✦

Women demand their rights so that they may be able to live as men do. But some would deny women these rights. In other words, some would deny women their "lives." We have compiled a list of women's rights, which has formed the basis of the program of *Al Amal*, and has caused much turmoil and generated an unexpected number of debates. We are regarded as the source of this turmoil, and the turmoil itself has been ridiculed. To make our position clear, we write weekly with data and arguments.

Yet, today we wish to give a brief description of our stance, especially in relation to two letters I have received, each on the same issue. The first is from Dr. Mohamed Mahmoud Metwally, dated 15 November, addressed to me along with a copy of his recently published book in French, *Divorce in the Islamic Shari'a*. I am planning to write on the book in the very near future. The second letter, which is from Dr. Aziz Merhem, was published in the last issue of *Al Amal*.

I cannot publish Dr. Metwally's letter since it is a personal letter addressed to me and permission to use it publicly has not been granted. Yet the letter contains opinions that will interest the readers of *Al Amal*, and consequently I am asking for permission to discuss them here.

The letter offers some encouraging comments for *Al Amal* and its editor in its introduction. Then the writer expresses his anger about the unjust treatment of women. He states that he (in collaboration with colleagues who have just returned from Europe) will contribute to the rise of women. The writer also reprimands reactionaries and those who use religion as a weapon against women's demands. He accuses these (rightly of course) of being responsible for the decline of Egyptian society. In short, the letter's tone is that which would appeal to a revolutionary woman like the editor of *Al Amal*. Then, the writer surprises us at the end of his letter by saying that, although he supports the cause of women as put forward by *Al Amal*, there is one point of difference between him and *Al Amal*. He believes that political rights are to be enjoyed only by men, since that has always been the way the world has worked. Men have acquired much experience and unique talent in politics, while women…

Great!

This is a new and strange example of an advocate for women's rights.

Our friend wants to take pride in his being an advocate for "women's rights" and announces that he is a well-educated person who enjoys engaging in profound intellectual debate. He gives the impression that he supports new ideas and believes in the concepts of development. Yet, he does not have enough courage and is ultimately directed by selfishness. He states that he does not approve of granting women political rights and that politics has always been the domain of men—not realizing that he is contradicting himself. Why so? Simply because he is a selfish man. If asked to present his argument, he answers: "Enjoying political rights has been the privilege of men ever since history began." As such, Dr. Metwally holds fast to the way things were conducted in the past. In that case, his position is much more dangerous than that of religious men whom he blames for keeping the country behind.

The only piece of advice we can give to Dr. Metwally, whose card carries half a dozen degrees and diplomas in such fields as criminal law, financial law, administrative law, work law, political economy, and legislation concerning wine, is never again to use the discourse of the advocates of women's rights as long as he continues to believe in antiquated systems.

Political rights are part of the general rights of women's lives. Intelligent, educated, broad-minded women, who want the responsibility of leading dignified lives, cannot do so without enjoying their full rights.

If we turn to Dr. Merhem's letter, we see that he blames us for some weaknesses that he has detected in our program. We would have been appreciative had he described these weaknesses. We might have agreed with him, since concepts of "weakness" and "feebleness" do not fit the principles of a revolutionary person who advocates significant change.

Yet, how would Dr. Merhem comment on the fact that this "weak" and "feeble" program has allegedly created turmoil and agitation?

Our political opponents, who would not rise above using the meanest weapons, have intentionally misunderstood item number nine of our program. They have ignored the meaning of the words "just treatment of women," mentioned in the item and claim that we are rebelling against religion. What an accusation!

We take advantage of this occasion to tell those who care to know that we respect religion and the Qur'an more than those who pretend to be advocates of religion, and we understand it more thoroughly. Those who use religion as a slogan have a mentality different from ours and consequently have a specific objective to achieve, which blinds them to the truth. They are so confused that they end up harming themselves as well as religion.

What are their objections to our demand for the just treatment of women in financial matters? Are we not living at a time in which women are often required to support men? What should women do when men seek their wealth and not their beauty, education, or upbringing? Men simply look for women's fortunes. If a woman is wealthy, she attracts men's attention and they court her. If she is not, she is not worth the effort.

This is not to mention the fact that men employ devilish and despicable techniques to deny women their financial rights, granted them by the Shari'a.

These facts indicate the obstacles we face. We are willing to present all the sacrifices needed to achieve our objectives. May God help us accomplish our task.

It is our pleasure to note here that the ideas of the editor of *Al Amal*, fiercely attacked at the beginning, have now won over many advocates and gained the recognition of entire institutions.

*Translated by Naglaa Abu-Agag*

## *Mririda N'Ayt Atiq*
## TWO DEFIANT POEMS

Morocco 1927    Berber

Mririda N'Ayt Atiq was a poor, nonliterate Berber woman, born sometime near the turn of the century in the Tassaout Valley, in southern Morocco. She sang her improvised poems in public markets, where she attracted large audiences, and was given the nickname "Mririda," after a kind of songbird. Although her poems are today cherished by Moroccans, they reached the larger world only through recordings made in 1927 by René Euloge, a French civil servant based in the area. Euloge also published the poems, in French translation, in a 1959 book, *Les*

*Chants de la Tassaout*, from which these versions are taken. In the preface to his book, Euloge explains that he heard stories of a woman poet who performed regularlyin the region's *souq*. His meeting with Mririda was the first visit of a European to Tassaout.

These two poems, translated from the French, are reminiscent of European ballads, but they also carry a strong Berber flavor. Their attention to the poet's own identity and emotions renders them rather unconventional within a culture that emphasized the collective self, even more so in a period when women were denied autonomy. "Mririda" focuses on the poet's construction of herself as a woman and an artist, using the materials of her rural life. *ZRarit* are women's cries of joy, and *baraka* is a blessing. In "The Affront," Mririda voices her condemnation of a husband who exploited her and stripped her of dignity, but clearly did not destroy her spirit. Her divorce from this husband is depicted as a regaining of freedom. The poem is addressed not to her former husband, but to her mother-in-law, a notoriously powerful figure in that time and place. In both poems, the originality of Mririda's language and the strength of her personality can be felt in every line.

*Fatima Sadiqi*

✦

## MRIRIDA

People call me Mririda, Mririda,
Mririda, the agile wren of meadows,
With eyes like gold;
But the wren's white chest is not mine,
Nor do I have her green tunic.
Yet, like her, I have my *zRarit*, my *zRarit*,
Which reaches the sheep-folds;
My *zRarit*, my *zRarit*,
Of which people talk all over the valley,
And even on the other side of the mountains.
My marvelous and exciting *zRarit*,
Since my first steps in the fields,
When I calmly held the lively wren in my hands,
And pressed her white chest close to mine,
And then to my maiden lips.
That is how I seized the wren's lovely voice,
The *baraka* which makes her sing
A song so clear, so vibrant, so fine,
On summer nights clarified by the moon,
A song as pure as crystal,
Like the clear noise of an anvil
In the resonant air that precedes rain.
And thanks to the gift that the wren gave me,

They call me Mririda, Mririda.
He who marries me will feel
My heart beating in his hand,
As I often felt under my fingers
The crazy heartbeats of the wren.
During nights lit by the moon,
He will call me Mririda, Mririda,
The soft nickname that is so dear to me.
For him I will release my sharp zRarit,
My long, resounding zRarit,
That men admire and women envy,
And that the valley has never before heard.

## THE AFFRONT

You are wrong, mother of my ex-husband,
If you think that I suffer.
Say to your son who repudiated me
That from my memory and my heart
Are gone the good and bad days
Of our once-shared life.
They are gone
Like straw in the wind.
Not the smallest souvenir have I kept
Of my exhaustion from work in the fields,
Of the loads that bent my back,
Of the pitchers that left marks on my shoulders,
Of burned fingers from making bread,
Of the leftover bones that your son
Used to give me on feast days.
He took back my jewels?
Did he ever give them to me?
Didn't he give me blows?
Did he ever take me in his arms?
Not the smallest souvenir do I keep.
It's as if I never knew him.
You who once were my mother-in-law,
Say to your son that
Even his name I do not recall.

*Translated into French by René Euloge*
*Translated from French by Fatima Sadiqi*

## Blanche Bendahan
# VISITING A DEAD MOTHER

Algeria 1930　French

Blanche Bendahan was born in 1903 in Oran, Algeria, to a Jewish family native to the Spanish-occupied city of Tétouan, on the Moroccan coast. She spent much of her childhood in France, and later moved there permanently. In her writing, however, she returned often to her North African origins, and along with Elissa Rhaïs, stands as one of the first writers to write about the condition of Maghrebian Jewish women in fiction.

Bendahan's first poetry collection, *La Voile sur L'eau,* was published in 1926. Her novel *Mazaltob* appeared in Paris in 1930 and received *Le Prix de l'Académie Française.* Like most North African literature in French, the novel was written for a metropolitan French audience rather than for the local readership, which explains its late republication, twenty-eight years later, in Oran. Bendahan published two additional collections of poetry, *Poèmes en Short* (1948), which was awarded *Le Prix de l'Académie de l'Humour,* and *Poèmes du Mzab* (1955). Her last novel, *Sous les Soleils qui ne Brillent Plus* (Under Suns That No Longer Shine), was published in 1970, eight years after Algerian independence, and depicts the experience of exile, a theme that is common to many writers of North African Jewish descent. This last work received the Prize of the City of Nice, where Bendahan lived until her death in 1975.

In *Mazaltob,* from which this extract comes, Bendahan turned to her family's place of origin in Tétouan, which had a large population of Jews living in what was called in Spanish a *Juderia,* and in Arabic a *mellah*—a walled Jewish quarter, analogous to a European ghetto. She documents with great precision, humor, and quiet pathos the lives and customs of the Jewish community of Tétouan, composed mainly of the Sephardi from Spain, who, along with Muslims and other non-Christians, had fled persecution after the Catholic reconquest of Iberia and settled in Morocco. During the second half of the nineteenth century, many members of this community, especially those of modest means, emigrated to Algeria, where they sought to obtain French citizenship, granted to all the Jews of this French colony by the famous *Crémieux Decree* of 1870. This may, indeed, explain the history of Blanche Bendahan's own family.

The title of the novel, also the name of the heroine, is a form of the Hebrew *mazel tov,* which means "good fortune." It is clearly ironic, for Mazaltob endures the unhappy lot of many young Jewish North African women of her time, forced to marry men chosen for them by their families—often rich émigré men much older than they were. Many of the male members of the Tétouan's Jewish community migrated to South America, especially to Brazil and Argentina; in this excerpt, there is mention of a large sum of money coming from Mazaltob's husband, who has gone to Buenos Aires and appears to have no intention of returning. The excerpt also touches upon the relationship between the local Sephardim and the Ashkenazi Jews from Eastern Europe, who were rare in Tétouan. The chapter begins in the Jewish cemetery of Tétouan, where Mazaltob and her elder sister Précieuse have gone to visit the grave of their recently deceased mother, Massiah.

*Larbi Touaf and Fatima Bouabdelli*

✦

Not far from Tétouan, high up on a hill, there is a silent town.

Seen beneath the sun, it is painful in its brightness, and even in gray weather, it still seems to hold light.

There are no cypress trees—those flags at the half-mast of hope—but a motionless stairway of stone rises toward the azure sky.

It is the Israeli cemetery.

No flowers, no wreaths, no vain monuments—only the bareness of death itself.

The graves, made of smooth stone, are all the same, and to the passerby who looks upon them, there is nothing to indicate wealth, nothing to indicate poverty.

Death is egalitarian, and the Jews remember this.

All the paupers who rest there have their corners of earth permanently assured, because Israel rejects the horrors of the communal grave. In order to accommodate the last sleep of the destitute, does not the rich man pay twice for his place in the cemetery?

No walks, no paths. The living must struggle, gasping and breathless, to follow the crowded ascent of the graves.

Sometimes, at the head of the body—always turned towards Jerusalem, the Holy Land—there are five books, the Five Books of the Law, sculpted in stone: some Rabbi is buried there.

Not far from Tétouan, high up on a hill, there is a silent town.

On this Friday afternoon—the best visiting-day for the deceased—two women are climbing the slopes of the necropolis. One, fine and slender, with an elegant bearing, is supporting the other, who pushes before her an enormous belly: they are Mazaltob and Précieuse.

It is eighteen months since Mrs. Massiah died giving birth to a daughter, who survived her.

The epitaphs on the gravestones are written in Spanish and Hebrew. The contents are all the same: the name, the date of death, and a few words of praise for the life of the deceased—because in Tétouan, as in all the countries of the world, one only has to die in order to become virtuous.

The mother of Mazaltob, however, like many other women of other races, truly deserves to have these words written on her gravestone:

> Throughout her whole childhood she worked, helping her mother to raise a large family. Married very young, she continued to work, but this time on her own account.
>
> Between her fifteenth and her thirty-eighth year, she baked more than ten thousand kilos of bread. She prepared more than eight thousand lunches and dinners. She spent more than seventeen ousand hours mak-

ing jams, *alkhlié* (fried meat preserved in oil), pastries in the shape of worms called *gousanitos* syruped with cooked grape juice, and distilled figs which were used to make alcohol.

She devoted more than seventeen thousand hours to cleaning the house. She devoted seventeen thousand others to sewing the linen and the clothes of her family. She devoted seventeen thousand more to soaping and bathing the numerous offspring that, between other tasks, she gave to Israel. She darned more than three thousand pairs of socks. Early to rise, late to bed, disdaining all distractions even to a simple walk, she sacrificed to this Minotaur—the home—her youth and her beauty, and night and day, unceasingly, she suffered, suffered.

Now may she rest in peace.

What sorrow in the family!

Not only because the Lord had not seen fit to reward so many virtues by giving Mazaltob's mother a contented old age, but also because he had inflicted upon this pious woman the ordeal, the bitterness, of dying on a Saturday!

What grief to think of this pour soul in pain until the following Friday, the only day of the week when the gates of heaven are open!

It's not the way it was for Yomtob Choeron, who died worn out by his years, and at just the right time to avoid any wait for the great joy of paradise!

Mazaltob and Précieuse stop near the grave of Mrs. Massiah.

Having heaved her burden of flesh this far, Précieuse, thoroughly worn out, would like to give in to her weariness and breathe for a while.

But see, there are the others—all the mourners who, that Friday, fill the cemetery with their cries and their sobs. In Israel, the phrase "great sorrows are silent" is meaningless.

As for most Oriental peoples, for the Hebrews, everything is out in the open. For them, sorrow is measured by the scale of the voice: the louder the voice, the greater the pain is deemed to be.

So Précieuse, who was always afraid of the judgment of others, set herself to howling at the top of her voice, giving rhythm to her lamentation by swinging her swollen body.

"Ouo... Ouo... Ouo... Dearest mother! ... Ouo... my eyes! ... Ouo... my light! ... What did we do to you to make you leave us like this? ... Did we let you want for anything? ... Didn't we give you good chicken soup when you were ill? ... O mother, when you left us, you took away our soul!"

Précieuse has a high-pitched voice that pierces the ears like a drill.

Impressed, enthralled, groups of *abélim*, mourners at neighboring graves, turn admiring glances toward Massiah's eldest child.

"What a good girl!" they say. "How she loved her mother!"

Indeed, Précieuse loved her mother very much, and as soon as she realized, once she was alone, that would never see her mother again, it was as if she had been stabbed in the heart.

But for the moment she hoped only to fulfill scrupulously the obligations of mourning.

Mazaltob, however, stood pale and upright, and with her eyes half shut, and didn't move a muscle.

"Really, you'd never think that she and her sister were cut out by the same pair of scissors," sniggered the women.

"The day that she shows some feeling will be the day frogs grow hair."

It is without a doubt because Jews love life too much that their mourning is so rigorous.

For the one to whom this terrible thing has come to pass—*the loss of existence*—the survivors cannot impose upon themselves enough mortification and abstinence.

Shiva, the first eight days of mourning, of acute mourning; shiva, which dresses the whole family in black; shiva, which enjoins men to grow their beards and their hair; shiva, which, on cold winter's days, requires the parents of the deceased to sit on mats on their patios; shiva, which lays on the ground the frugal meal of the *abélim*; shiva, which weeps for you with many tears, and which claws, sometimes until blood is drawn, at the cheeks of the impassioned; shiva, known also as Abel—have you, in honor of death, killed forever the smile on the lips of Mazaltob?

As the innumerable rites of mourning unroll—it is a sign of suffering that they are not counted—ten months of the necrological year go by.

In memory of Mrs. Massiah, the men recited the Kaddish prayer, because however great the sorrow of women, their prayers are worthless in the discriminating eyes of Adonai.

And the women? Once the light representing the soul of the departed was lit in the mortuary chamber, they kept watch, humble vestals, until the day of the funeral, to see that this sacred fire did not go out.

They received visits of condolence, during which every man, and particularly every woman, seemed intent on making the *abélim* cry.

Words of consolation and gentleness are, without a doubt, the most beautiful words in the Christian vocabulary.

In the Massiah home, it is Mazaltob who must now replace her mother.

Nothing can be expected from Précieuse. Her first pregnancy led only to a stillbirth —Uou! It was a boy!— The second was interrupted by a miscarriage.

So, pregnant for a third time, Mazaltob's sister no longer dares to move.

She is afraid of everything: of the cold, of the breeze, of the smallest shock; of chairs that were low when one had supposed them to be high and upon which one sat down roughly; of the recently soaped tiles of the patio upon which one could slip.

To stay calm—if this was indeed possible—she kept her belly under a cover, like a melon.

Of all her fears, only one was justified: the fear of what people would say.

So, rather than fall foul of public opinion, she preferred rather to fall from exhaustion at the cemetery when she went there to pray for her mother that Friday.

They wrote to Buenos Aires to announce the death of Mrs. Massiah to José.

In reply, the courier brought a few terse lines of condolence, and after a period of time a large sum of money was sent in Mazaltob's name.

A large sum of money— like a compensation for betrayal.

Since then, despite the sending of many astonished letters, no more has been heard from the man who once slipped a wedding ring onto Mazaltob's white finger.

In Mazaltob's gray life there is, all the same, a faint light. This light is Léa.

Léa, the Alsatian, the daughter-in-law of Dr. Bralakoff, the much-loved wife of his son Serge.

The delightful creature with her childlike appearance, round-cheeked, with pink and perfect skin!

Her feet and hands are minute. Even her head, which is a little too large for her body, increases her resemblance to a baby!

And then there is Léa's smile, a smile always lurking at the corners of her lips, on the watch for a chance to appear—for a yes or for a no. A good smile, without ironic insinuation, without a trace of bitterness. A true smile, the only smile that would suit this baby face: the smile of a child..

Because Léa, to use a time-honored expression, wears her heart on her sleeve. And even though the sleeve is very small and the heart is very large, this generous girl is always ready to offer her heart to those who are not happy.

As a result of that mysterious law of opposites attracting—which doesn't only apply, as is believed, to the difference between the sexes—Mazaltob, with her night-filled eyes and her sadness, wept immediately with Léa.

And the two girls are friends.

It was nearly eight months ago that Léa arrived in Tétouan in the arms of her husband. In the arms of her husband! That was something that was not done around there! Then, while Dr. Brakaloff, eager to retire, introduced his successor, his son, to his friends and patients, Mrs. Serge ran all over town.

"She went out alone… She might as well have been English," they muttered about her excursions. For this reason, she was met with pursed lips—but they could not be kept up. Léa had such a straightforward way of endearing herself to everyone! She also had such respect for the opinions of others that she could almost be forgiven for a liberalism that was judged, by the severe devoutness of the women, to be excessive: her religion did not go beyond fasting for Yom Kippur.

But then, could one expect the same from this foreigner, this Ashkenazi Jew, as one would expect of a Tétouan woman? She was already unfortunate enough, poor thing, to belong to the plebian branch of the Israelites!

Because the Sephardim (from Sephard, the Hebrew name for Spain) considered themselves to be aristocrats among their co-religionists spread throughout the rest of the world.

And when a Sephardim is asked to give a reason for this prejudice—as paradoxical as it may seem, prejudices often have their reasons—here is what they say:

"Our own ancestors, Spanish Jews, left Palestine well before the destruction of the second Temple. They never knew the terrible siege of Jerusalem. They never knew the searing humiliation of bending beneath the yoke of the conqueror. Up until the Spanish exodus—the edict of March 1492—their history had been brilliant. They participated in royal councils. When the armies were at war, they pitched their campaign tents. Ennobled, they had coats of arms and vassals.

"They administered the public good, like Samuel Lévy, who was made a minister. Some became doctors to the king, some became famous astronomers, still others became philosophers or poets.

"While the Ashkenazi disappeared into the ghettos of Hungary or Russia, the gold of our ancestors chartered the caravels of Christopher Columbus, who was himself, in all probability, of Sephardic origins.

"During our long stay in Spain, numerous alliances infused Jewish blood into Iberian veins, and Latin blood into our own.

"We disdain the Yiddish of the Ashkenazi of the north, we often disdained the Arabic of the Ashkenazi of Africa. Our own language, the language of the Sephardim, is Spanish, or Ladino (from Latino or Latin). This Ladino—this Haquetia dialect with its base in the people of Tétouan, which is spoken on the Mediterranean coast from Tangiers to Salonica—this Ladino that comes from the Spanish of 1492, and because of this seems adulterated to our modern ears; this Ladino is our rallying cry among our co-religionists in the rest of the world; it is the language of our homes, it is the sacred tongue into which our prayers are translated.

"We others, we Sephardim, who often carry Spanish names such as Perez, Soto, or Toledano, we Sephardim who, according to certain writers, have mixed our blood with all those Spaniards whose names end in 'ez' (who are none other than the descendants of those Jews who converted at the time of the Inquisition), we Sephardim, who believe that we proceed directly from the line of King David, we have given to the world, among other celebrities of lesser brilliance, one Heinrich Heine, one Disraeli, and one Spinoza."

To which an Ashkenazi could reply:

"We have suffered more than you, the Sephardim. We have known the Hungarian hordes, the Russian pogroms, and the fanaticism of the Arabs. Despite captivity, despite pain—which is the most beautiful initiation into nobility—we have also, we too, our great poets and our great musicians.

"If our Yiddish or our Arabic is less melodious than your Spanish, if our Hebraic pronunciation is more guttural than yours, if our homes are far from sacred Palestine, blame only our sad destiny."

But the Ashkenazi is silent, because he knows full well that the gentle disdain in which he is held is less a matter of feeling than an amorphous tradition and that, in view of the legendary solidarity of Israel, the word Jew includes no modifier.

Séty, the third daughter of the Massiahs, a little girl of ten years, rocks the last-born, who cries tirelessly.

So Mazaltob takes the baby in her arms and starts singing, to lull it to sleep. What does she sing, this beautiful young woman?

She sings what was sung by her distant grandmothers in Castile, because Jewish-Tétouan folklore is an essentially Latin folklore.

Mazaltob sings of Don Guëro, who walks through Seville with a bar of gold in his hand. She sings of the city of Toledo, in which a frail being is born one day, "small in body and wicked in intention." She sings of the valiant girl who won a battle in the clothes of a man and, as a reward, married the son of King Léon. She sings of Count Velo who, having lost a bet of love, had his heart pulled out. She sings of the queen of the Moors, who wished for a Christian slave and who, in this slave, recognized her own sister.

And then, it is the turn of *"Escuchis, Señor Soldado"*—Listen, Soldier— the beautiful song of woman's faithfulness:

Seven years have I waited;
Seven years more will I wait;
And if at the end of fourteen years he does not come,
I will become a nun.
A nun like Saint Claire,
A nun like Dona Inès.

"Oh, Mazaltob!" cries Léa, who has just come in, "the quality of your voice is so moving! But where does this perfect knowledge of the art of singing come from?"

"I took lessons once, with Mme. Gérard, the wife of the previous French consul."

"And you hid this from me?"

"I have had so much sadness that I have not sung for a long time."

Was the young woman alluding to her marriage, or to the death of her mother? Léa hoped that one day Mazaltob would make this clear.

While Mazaltob, with hesitant movements, laid the baby in her wicker cradle, where she slept at last, the Alsatian picked up the conversation again.

"Did you know that I'm having an excellent piano brought from Tangiers? You can sing, Mazaltob, and I will accompany you. What beautiful moments lie ahead for us, for Serge, and for my father-in-law, who has been deprived of music for so long!"

"It's just that I don't really have leisure time."

"Hush hush hush… I will come to help you with your work. But you will sing, my beauty, you will sing, you hear me?

Gently authoritative, Serge's wife scolded Mazaltob with her finger; but Mazaltob shook her head sadly from right to left.

So Léa, not in the least disconcerted, insisted.

"You will sing, you will sing, I'm telling you. And Jean, my brother-in-law, who will be here in a few weeks; Jean who has become, so I hear, a violinist of great talent; Jean, your dear childhood friend, will be very happy to find in our dreary Tétouan an unexpectedly artistic environment."

Mazaltob didn't reply, but her beautiful face finally fell still.

And beneath the Moorish arches of the patio, Léa's smile signaled victory.

*Translated by Belou Charloff*

## *Asma Fahmy*
## HIGHER EDUCATION FOR WOMEN

Egypt 1934    Arabic

Asma Fahmy was born in the Sudan to Egyptian parents. She graduated from the Saneya School in Cairo in 1920, entered Cairo University as an external student, and was one of four women sent to England by the Ministry of Education in 1925 for training as a secondary school teacher. This was the same year the Shubra Secondary School for Girls opened, the first of its kind in Egypt. Asma Fahmy spent most of her life teaching at Hilmiyya Secondary School for Girls, which opened in the early 1930s to meet the demands of the Egyptian Feminist Union.

Fahmy wrote many articles and stories for Egyptian literary magazines. Her essay "Higher Education for Women" was published on 22 January 1934 in *Al Rissala* (The Message), a cultural weekly that published articles, essays, and poems by leading writers. *Al Rissala* was used by Egyptian intellectuals in general as a forum for expressing their views, and by women intellectuals in particular as a relatively liberal platform for sharing ideas about women's status.

Here Asma Fahmy voices the opinion of many enlightened women at the time, arguing for the need to make higher education available to all young women. She suggests, in fact, that women may need higher education even more than men do, since their confinement to the home has prevented them from partaking in the "free exchange of ideas" so vital to personal, social, and intellectual development.

Written just a short time after the graduation of the first group of Egyptian women from the university, the essay brings to the fore the heated debate, which persisted even among intellectuals, on how the education of women would affect society. To counter assertions by "reactionaries" that women's education would undermine family, social, and economic structures, Fahmy insists: "Humanity needs women's work and their independent talents outside the home as much as it needs their work inside it." Fahmy's controlled tone and her cogent and persuasive arguments demonstrate by example that women are capable of logical and independent thought.

*Amira Nowaira*

✦

Higher education for women in Egypt is still in its infancy. Most minds are not ready yet to give up the old notion that women are born only for home and children, needing therefore no more than the bare minimum of education to fulfill their responsibilities. As one Egyptian educator expressed it at the ceremony held last month by the Feminist Union in honor of the first women graduates of the university, the admission of women into the university in 1928 took place only because of intrigue and conspiracy. In truth, the education of women in Egypt is still a young shoot that may prove too weak to withstand the upheavals of political change and the storms of reactionary ideas.

With these fears and apprehensions in mind concerning the future of higher education for women in Egypt, I thought fit to champion this cause by placing it on the table for discussion, starting with the goals and results of higher education not only for women, but for all.

One of the salient features of higher education, when properly conducted, is that it frees students from all sorts of shackles. Relying as it does on independent research and on the ability to come to rational conclusions based on proofs and logical arguments, it brings out students' talents and gives them opportunities to develop their personalities. If undertaken properly, education has the merit of establishing bridges between students and their society, encouraging them to study its history and its various aspects whether political or economic. It also trains the young to engage in teamwork and to rally under the same leadership by teaching them how to work in groups, whether for research, games, or other goals, under the umbrella of the university. In this way, they learn how to work cooperatively, which may reduce selfish tendencies and help turn young people into useful members of the community.

Women urgently need this kind of education. A woman's mind, like that of her male counterpart, is what sets her apart from senseless beasts. This mind, nurtured by knowledge, will only develop if it is used constantly. A human being first and foremost, a woman should not be hampered by motherhood or domestic life from fulfilling the most basic of human needs: the enjoyment of an adequate and liberating higher education. From the point of view of social interaction and connectivity, women need education far more than men, since they have long been deprived of it. Confined at home and prevented from participating in the free exchange of ideas and discussion, women have been prevented from developing their own social faculties. Cultivated men are accustomed to teamwork and have the tolerance necessary for conducting conversations and arguments based on rational thinking. Were women to acquire these characteristics in addition to their natural tenderness and sympathy, the whole society no doubt would move forward, and family life would become far happier.

Nothing but a university education is capable of endowing women with these skills. In the course of her university education, a woman mingles with people of various tendencies and attitudes, of different ideas and creeds. She learns to overcome a limited view of life, which is the effect of too subjective an outlook. In fact, university life is no less important than scholarly achievement in preparing students for a sophisticated practical life afterwards. This is why such venerable universities as Oxford and Cambridge have paid great attention to it, producing as they have done the most distinguished of politicians and reformers. One might object, asking, "What has a woman to do with all that? After all, she is not expected to become an eminent politician or reformer!" It is true that in the near future there is little likelihood of this happening. We cannot, nonetheless, despair of its ever occurring in our country, since it has already occurred in other advanced societies. Of course Egyptian women still lack some essential social qualities for this work. A proper university education, however, could prepare them to assume responsibilities in the field of social reform. Certainly, no one would deny the existence of innumerable social ills in our society. Why should women, then, be deprived of their rights to higher education that would both improve their minds and allow them to serve in the field of social reform, bearing in mind that they are by nature self-sacrificing, sensitive, and very sympathetic to those suffering pain?

These, then, are the purposes of higher education. It remains for us only to mention some of the consequences of higher education for women, which reactionaries sometimes mention, but only in order to disparage them. They say, for example: "Isn't it clear that one of the results of women's education, if we are to believe statistics, is that more than 50 percent of the highly educated women in Europe and the United States refuse to marry, preferring a more productive, lucrative, and independent life to a life in the home that does not allow for the proper investment of their talents? Wouldn't then the number of offspring decrease as a result of leaving this very important task only to women who are not properly educated? Wouldn't those rebels against domestic life become then a dangerous faction, further complicating economic problems by competing with men in the workplace, increasing the numbers of the unemployed and the deprived?"

A superficial look at these objections might show women as rebels against nature, as working for the destruction of the human race and aggravating economic crises. However, a superficial look is not enough. Let us agree for the sake of argument that 50 percent of female university graduates will prefer not to marry when they find that they are sufficiently satisfied by the pursuit of knowledge and the use of their talents. But we will be admitting only a half-truth. In all fairness to women, we must admit that the woman who does not marry serves her society in a direct manner: through scientific and practical means and by helping improve society. The biological function of women cannot alone lead society to progress and prosperity. Humanity needs women's work and their independent talents outside the home as much as it needs their work inside it. A great deal has been said about university-educated women who marry. All we need say is that the crux of the matter lies not in the quantity but the quality of the offspring. If women are not educated, we may gain a greater number of offspring. But, on the other hand, we will lose the improved qualities of mind and moral strength as well as the excellent children who can only be produced by a highly educated woman.

As for the problem of educated women competing with men in the job market, it will be sufficient to argue in refutation that this objection arises only out of men's selfishness. Were men less selfish, they would see most clearly that they could not afford to sacrifice all the advantages of women's education for the sake of safeguarding their own material benefits by keeping women away from the job market. Far worse is that by guaranteeing women's inability to compete with men, men deprive women of the satisfaction to be gained from higher education and from the spiritual fulfillment it brings. Men's opposition to women's higher education hardly compliments their integrity or chivalry.

*Translated by Amira Nowaira*

## *"Al Fatat"*
## ON YOUNG WOMEN'S EDUCATION

Morocco 1935    Arabic

In Arabic, *"al fatat"* means "young woman." In March 1935, Abdelkbir El Fassi, the director of the Association of Translation, Editing, and Publication, introduced an author called Al Fatat on the front page of *Majallat Al Maghrib* (Morocco Magazine) as "The First Young Woman Writer in Morocco." He also claimed her as the first young Moroccan to study Arabic—in her home—and to be inspired by education to advocate emancipation for other women. Al Fatat, he says, is not yet twenty and belongs to a wealthy and highly educated family. El Fassi explains that he suggested she sign herself simply as *"Al Fatat,"* indicating that she is a kind of Everywoman, educated as all young women should be.

While it is not possible to know her identity with absolute certainty the Moroccan intelligentsia and media widely believed that Al Fatat was Malika El Fassi, whose essay "An Important Step for Girls' Education" (see 1934), is also included in this volume. Malika El-Fassi was not yet twenty years old in 1935, and might have been advised to use a pseudonym because she was writing in a heavily patriarchal society in which women had no public voice. She mentions writing in newspapers as emancipating for women, and this is something that Malika El Fassi did throughout her life. Perhaps a positive reaction to her very first article encouraged her to write under her real name.

"Al Fatat" is both visionary and shrewd, arguing for women's progress in ways least likely to threaten men's power. She urges fathers to send their daughters to school not only for the sake of their own emancipation from "the chains of ignorance and illiteracy," but in service of the family and the nation. She harkens back to a revered historical era—the Umayyad (661–750) and Abassid (750–1258) dynasties, and the age of Al-Andalus (711–1492)—which marked the peak of Arab-Muslim civilization, then points out that in these times, educated women were highly valued for their contribution to society. She also refutes any notion that Islam is opposed to women's advancement, calling the education of every woman "a right that God grants her."

*Zakia Iraqui-Sinaceur and Moha Ennaji*

✦

When I consider the situation of women in Morocco, I find an abundance of ignorance and backward-looking traditions, which have nothing to do with Islam. Islam refutes these traditions. I devote this article to women because they live in decadence and inertia. I call upon you to rescue and free women from the chains of ignorance and illiteracy and provide them with a proper education.

Let us ignore the talk of egoists who underestimate women and undervalue their purpose, and let us consider the problems of this task, hoping that we will reach a solution. Whoever has studied the past or present of civilized nations, and has witnessed the culture and advantages that women enjoy, will realize that women are essential in all human societies, that women form the cornerstones of rebuilding a nation. They are the first teachers of children and bear responsibility for the future generation. Therefore, we must first ask how this generation should grow and what objectives it should attain. Should our children acquire cowardice, a mean spirit, and useless traditions, which will prove harmful to any nation? Or should they acquire virtue and self-reliance? The answer is self-evident. The education of young girls should then be compulsory, and only dull minds would resist this on the grounds that girls' education is an outrage. Women are considered by many to be ignorant and feeble-minded, higher in status only than animals. Yet, one cannot deny that many women are strong, well-educated, and tactful, albeit in a few limited circles.

That is why I feel sad about the present state of Moroccan women. And therefore, I have thought of a solution: I call on all Moroccans to open the doors to girls' education so that they may acquire religious and literary knowledge in the Arabic language, so as to develop noble skills and wisdom.

I am not in favor of allowing a girl to reach high levels in education. I prefer that she does not study past the secondary school level, but that she be able to read, write, acquire handicraft skills, do housekeeping, live in a community, and bring up her children. These skills are sufficient for her and most suitable for our environment. She may cease studying at the age of fifteen or sixteen, when she will have acquired a reasonable amount of knowledge. She may, afterward, decide to enlarge her understanding by studying books and reading newspapers and magazines. Undoubtedly, if she is able to reach this level, she will grow more educated and experienced, and thus be ready to join other young people in strengthening modernization and development. This is the dream of all Moroccan women. I trust that these wishes will materialize.

Fathers, your daughter is entitled to education, so grant it to her. You should not deprive her of a right that God grants her. Neglecting your daughter's education is a great disgrace. Hence, you need to strengthen your nation with young women who are equipped with high moral standards that will benefit their society. If you look at the past and consult histories, you will find that women were prominent especially during the Umayyad and Abassid periods and during the flourishing of Arab civilization in Andalusia, when they enjoyed learning, and when educated women were celebrated for performing noble deeds.

In conclusion, I wish to say that I am optimistic about the suggestions and enthusiasm of the youth about girls' education, and pleased with the campaigns serving this aim. Your sister is addressing you—the youth—thanking you for the praiseworthy work you are contributing. I call upon your intelligence to support women with the strong determination you are known for in order to liberate them from the chains of ignorance.

*Translated by Zakia Iraqui-Sinaceur*

## *Soheir El-Qalamawi*
## A FURIOUS WOMAN

Egypt 1935    Arabic

Soheir El-Qalamawi was born in Cairo in July of 1911. She received her schooling at the American Girls' College in Cairo, then went on to Cairo University and eventually the Sorbonne. After obtaining a Ph.D. in literature in 1941, she pursued an academic career. In addition to becoming, in 1956, the first female professor of modern literature at Cairo University and later chairperson of the Department of Arabic Language and Literature, Soheir El-Qalamawi held several other cultural and academic posts. She was a member of the Supreme Council for Arts, Literature, and the Social Sciences, member of the Shakespeare Translation Committee in the Arab League, and Chairperson of the Egyptian Organization for Writing and Publishing. Her own publications include fiction, criticism, scholarly articles, and translation. Her first book was *My Grandmother's Stories* (1935), followed by *A Thousand and One Nights* (1943), and *The Devils at Play* (1946). She translated into Arabic works as varied as *My Antonia* by Willa Cather, *The Ion* by Plato, and *The Taming of the Shrew*. Among her many awards are the Arabic Language Academy prize in 1941, the State Research Award in 1955, and the State Achievements Award in 1977.

*My Grandmother's Stories* is a collection of five stories narrated by a grandmother to her granddaughter, El-Qalamawi herself. The stories deal with the life of the grandmother, who came to Egypt with her father, married, and settled there. Some of the stories deal with personal tragedies; others deal with national ones, such as the Abyssinian-Egyptian wars of the late 1870s, and the 1882 bombardment of Alexandria, carried out by the British Navy to quash a nationalist uprising, and support subsequent British occupation of Egypt. The grandmother displays the sentiments of a fervent nationalist. The extract here is taken from a story that deals with her life following her husband's death in battle.

*Sahar Hamouda*

◆

There lived near us a middle-aged man who was a friend of my husband. Indeed, he was one of his closest friends. As soon as he heard of your grandfather's death, he rushed to pay his condolences. He wept as he kissed the children, so that his streaming tears mingled with theirs. He was a generous, kindly man. It became a habit of his to pass by us whenever he could, looking after our needs and bringing the children toys or fruit or anything they had asked for. A servant would announce that he had arrived at the door to pay his respects and ask whether there was any service he could give me or my children. I hated to burden him with my needs, and only asked for what I was in dire need of. But the children often had demands, which he gladly fulfilled, content that he was doing his duty by his departed friend.

But then, my child, one day my two sons, Ibrahim and Ismail, came to me and said, "Mother, this friend of our father's asked us to put a case to you." I said, "What is it?" The elder boy looked uncomfortable, but Ismail laughed and appeared to want to hide his laughter. My eldest said, "Mother, he is asking for your hand in marriage, as this will be a comfort to you and your children."

I felt the hot blood rise to my face and head, setting them on fire. I cursed the man freely. Then I rushed to my husband's room, which had remained locked since his death. From a box in which I had placed his clothes, I took out a Sudanese whip that he used to carry. I hurried out with the whip, intending to give my husband's friend a beating that would remind him what loyalty to one's husband was!

That devil, Ismail, had seen me bring out the whip and had guessed my intention. He rushed to the friend and told him, "Hurry, Sir, run. My mother is coming to beat you with my dead father's whip." My son Ibrahim described to me how the man turned pale with amazement, then ran off before I could reach him.

He had thought it was perfectly ordinary, what he had asked for. Since I and my children needed to be looked after, and since I was all alone in this country and needed someone to take care of my external affairs, then it made perfect sense for him to do all these things, considering it his duty to marry me.

How I resented that man and cursed him. I went about fuming for weeks on end. And since that day, my child, I sent him word never to cross our threshold again. He had thought that my need for someone to look after our affairs justified a betrayal of my husband's memory. My husband had died a glorious death on the battlefield for the sake of his country, in a strange country far from his family. He had lived honorably and died nobly, and was faithful to me and my children. He loved us deeply and harbored a great respect for me. No, my daughter, had my husband been any less, I would not have married after his death. And to imagine that I could do it, when he was the man I describe! And my children, do they not have rights? How could I have abandoned them to care for a new husband?

But my son Ismail *would* make of this proposal a funny story to tell my friends. No sooner had the devil gone to one of their houses, than he would say, "Auntie, do you know what Mother did to So and So?"

She would say, "No."

So he would say, "She was going to beat him with my late father's whip, because he asked her to marry him." He would then imitate me and exaggerate the description of my fury and the man's astonishment. My friend and those with her would laugh.

When my friends met me later, they reproached me for what I had done, saying, "Could you not have turned him down gently?"

And I would answer, "No, I do not know how to be gentle when I am furious. Nor can I curb my anger when the memory of my husband is insulted."

The days flew past. My friends all ended up like me: widows who never remarried after their husbands had died in the Abyssinian war.

They would jokingly tell me, "It's all your fault. If you hadn't done that to So and So, men wouldn't have run away from us. Nobody's proposed to us because they all think we'll beat them with the Sudanese whip, as you were about to do."

I would answer back, "No, you did well. It is only one life we have, and we must live it in the best possible way. The rights your children have over you are more important than the rights of a new husband. No, you did well. One day, your children will remember that you placed their rights above all else."

*Translated by Sahar Hamouda*

## Nahed Taha Abdel Ber
# THE LOST HOPE

Egypt 1936    Arabic

Nahed Taha Abdel Ber was born in 1920 to a family that valued knowledge and education. However, in spite of the fact that her father was a scientist and a literary figure, he refused to allow her to attend college after finishing high school. Her father's decision caused her deep anguish and depression, which, coupled with a mysterious disease, hastened Abdel Ber's early death, in 1950.

Abdel Ber published only a few poems during her lifetime, chiefly in literary magazines and journals. "The Lost Hope" is included in her only collection of poems, which she titled *Inspired by Pain*. The collection was never published, although in her will she requested that this be done. The poem is a poignant plea from a soul that is dying—perhaps literally—for want of liberation and learning.

*Heba Sharobeem*

◆

Lord, have mercy upon me and hear my lament.
Lord, pray release me from a life in torment.
Release me from despair, oh Lord,
For my soul trembles before its destiny.

Crushed by ungratified desire,
Night after night my feeble body lies sleepless,
Yet dreaming of all I want,
Of a life in that great place of learning,
Of a life of study and fruitfulness.

They refused my admission, leaving me in pain,
Leaving me close to madness,
And yet I live on, bearing my grief,
Refusing to drown in melancholy.

Thus, I keep to my prison house without the joy of learning.
But, dear God, can one thus shackled be counted as living?
Or, with all hope of freedom lost,
Is not my life but a senseless waste?

*Translated by Heba Sharobeem and Radwa Barouni*

# Nabaweya Moussa
# YES TO EDUCATION AND NO TO MARRIAGE

Egypt 1937    Arabic

Nabaweya Moussa was a leading feminist educator, writer, and poet of her time. She was born in the small village of Kafr El Hekma, near the town of Zagazig in the Eastern Province of Egypt, into a middle-class family. Her father was a small landowner and an officer in the Egyptian army, who was sent on a mission to the Sudan two months before the birth of his daughter, Nabaweya, and never returned home. Moussa grew up with her mother and brother, ten years her senior, in Cairo, where he went to school.

Like other girls of her class, she was expected to stay at home waiting for the right match. Her education at home was at best sporadic, but when she was thirteen, she insisted on attending the Saneya School for Girls. In 1907, she became the first Egyptian woman to earn a high school diploma. She also became the first Arabic woman teacher appointed to the Abbas Primary School, in the girls' section, and later she worked as an educational inspector at the Ministry of Education. Eventually she resigned her government post and established her own school in Alexandria, a pioneering model for women's education in Egypt.

As a leading activist in the Egyptian women's movement, Moussa wrote for newspapers and magazines, and in 1922, she founded the Association for the Progress of Women. She represented Egypt at the International Women's Conference in Rome in 1923, the first conference to be attended by a representative of the Egyptian feminist movement. In 1937, she established a magazine called *Al Fatat* (The Young Woman). Moussa's publications include two educational readers (1911), a book called *Woman and Work* (1920), a collection of poems, and her memoir, first published in installments in *Al Fatat* in 1937, and later as *My History by Me*.

In these two selections from her memoir, Moussa demonstrates her refusal to accept for herself the "feminine," submissive image of women prevalent in Egypt in the early decades of the twentieth century. Her challenge to the dominant patriarchy was both spontaneous and original, developed in the absence of any models to emulate. Unlike many of her intellectual male contemporaries, who traveled to Europe and encountered European culture and ideas, her defiance was not based on Western models, but on an innate sense of justice, grounded in Arab Egyptian culture. Moussa herself described her memoir as "the psychological analysis of a girl who spent all her life in constant struggle."

In the first extract, Moussa describes the lengths to which she went in order to obtain an education, against both prevailing cultural prejudices and fierce objections from her family. In the second, she insists upon remaining single in a society that regarded unmarried women either as nonexistent or as pitiable freaks. She finds sex—what she calls "the filthy side of marriage"—distasteful, but seems even more determined to avoid the state of sexual servitude to which most married women had to submit, being used by men "for their pleasure" in exchange for monetary support. She clearly views financial independence, which in turn depends upon access to education and work, as an essential component in the process of women's liberation.

*Amira Nowaira and Azza El Kholy*

✦

## How I Was Admitted to Saneya School

As I mentioned earlier, I had a yearning for education and was not satisfied only with reading and learning the Qur'an. What I wanted was to be properly educated at the Saneya School. I learned through my brother that if I wished to join grade three, I would have to study the mathematics syllabus of grade two, which included the addition, subtraction, multiplication, and division of whole numbers and fractions. I was thirteen at the time. When I asked my mother for a teacher to help me, she consulted my uncle and he reiterated to her the well-known proverb: "Teach girls to spin but don't teach them to write." My mother thus dismissed the idea of a teacher, nor did she teach me how to spin, and so I am still as unskilled in this respect as I had been then.

Greatly disappointed, I turned to my brother. Since he was then totally engrossed in his own schoolwork, he simply gave me the mathematics book for grade two. Fortunately for me, the text fully explained the four basic rules of whole numbers and fractions. Although I had tremendous difficulty trying to understand fractions, I did manage in the end. At the same time I tried to learn the English alphabet during the little time I spent with my brother, although I had continually to put up with his reluctance and sarcasm.

At last, my heart was set on entering the Saneya School. When I confided my wish to my mother, it was as if all hell were let loose. She considered this wish a transgression against the rules of decency and modesty, as well as against propriety and religion. She kept telling the story of my wish to members of her family as an absurd anecdote. Everyone listening to her story rallied with her in disapproving of this wild desire. She was as adamant in her refusal as I was adamant about trying to enter school without telling her, understanding that if I were to succeed, I would still have to deal with her.

I guarded my secret and stole my mother's signature seal. At school I filled in an application form using the seal. I cannot deny that my handwriting on the form was shaky and terrible since I had not yet mastered the skill of holding the pen in writing.

The secretary of the school and the teachers were truly amazed by the daring girl who came alone to apply for admission. To get them to accept my application, I applied as a fee-paying student. Because the great majority of families were not particularly keen to send their daughters to school, most of the women students at the Saneya School in those days were offered free education. So I thought that a fee-paying student would not likely be turned down.

I sat for the admission examination, but consider how difficult it was for a thirteen-year-old girl who had never been to school before and could not even hold a pen properly! The pen seemed to have control over me and not the other way round. Oh, the number of pages I soiled and the pens I broke during that exam! My writing in Arabic was highly skilled but my handwriting was childlike. The teachers wondered about the elegance of the composition and the terrible handwriting: My composition was too sophisticated even for a secondary school pupil and my handwriting was too childish even for a first grade primary pupil.... When I learned of my admission to school, I was overwhelmed with joy. But when I broke the news to my mother, she said that if it were true, she would wash her hands of me. I told her that it was true and that I was most certainly going to school. I told her that if she persisted in refusing to help me, I would join the school as a boarder with the support of my allowance from my father. "Are you serious?" she asked.

"Absolutely," I said, "I will be leaving on Saturday."

So she said I could go as a day student and not as a boarder.

On Friday, my brother came to visit and told me that, were I to persist in my plan of going to school, he would no longer want to know me.

I smiled and said, "Never mind! I'll have one family member fewer, then!"

*Translated by Amira Nowaira*

## MY VIEW OF MARRIAGE

After I received my high school diploma... nearly a month later, I received a letter from an officer in the Sudan. The letter was addressed to me at the Saneya School although I was, by then, a teacher at Abbas Girls' School. All this officer knew about Nabaweya Moussa was that she had graduated and, therefore, that she must have been a former student at the Saneya School.

The letter revealed an eloquent writer. He said he was a decent man, and was not writing to violate the limits of Eastern custom, but rather to ask for my hand in marriage. He added that, since he did not know the identity or address of my guardian, he was compelled to write to me, especially since he admired my published writing, and thus begged me to direct him to my guardian in order to approach him about marriage.

I was impressed by the man's politeness and straightforwardness, and I also admired his distinguished writing style. In fact, had I any inclination toward marriage, I would not have hesitated to accept his offer. However, I hated the idea of marriage and viewed it as filth, and I had vowed not to profane myself with such grime, and, thus, I had no choice except to refuse his offer.

I showed the letter to my brother and asked him to write a note of refusal. Yet I also asked him to be nice about it so as not to hurt the man's feelings. Moreover, I suggested that he write the following: "Had you seen my sister, you would not have proposed to her because she is very ugly and you would not want her. Please accept my best wishes and please forget about your offer, keeping in mind that I will always be your friend." And although my brother did not approve of this language, he was obliged to use it.

About three or four days later, at the most, my brother received a letter from the intended groom, saying that he did not care about beauty and that he loved my spirit for its closeness to his. He added that he would surely love the author of the articles that he had read, regardless of her looks, and that he would, in fact, like to see her. My brother read the letter and said: "Now you have no excuse. The man accepts you anyway, and as your guardian, I would like you to marry this person." We argued for so long that my brother might have turned to nonverbal means, except that that was not his habit. At this point, my mother's relative, Mustapha Effendi Abdel Razek, entered and asked about the argument. My brother told him that I was refusing to marry a man whom he had already written to with some kind of promise. I said: "You had no right to make such a promise. The man my brother wants me to marry earns 24 pounds a month, and I, as you know, do not relish the idea of marriage. Were I to accept the filthy side of marriage, then my new economic status after marriage should be more tempting. My salary now is 12 pounds, and if I want to maintain my financial position, then the salary of my husband should be 48 pounds—12 pounds for me, 12 for him, and 24 for the children. Therefore, how can I accept marriage, which in principle I detest, and in this case also accept an inferior standard of living? Is that sensible?"

Mustapha Effendi brought me victory when he said that I had a point. My brother then remarked, "This means that she will never marry. Really, who will want to marry her with the salary she demands?"

In answer to this I said: "That is exactly what I want. I want my demand to be an obstacle to marriage."

My brother had to submit, reluctantly, to our will, and finally he said, "I will write to the man and maybe he is blessed by God, after all." Pen in hand, he started to write, reading aloud what he had written: "Best regards and sorry, dear friend, that I told you in my previous letter that my sister is ugly and forgot to mention that she is also rude, arrogant, and impossible to live with even for a single day. As a friend, I advise you not to ask me for her hand in marriage again, since she looks down upon the likes of you and me, so please do not mention her to me again."

My brother read the letter aloud just to upset me, but I laughed and said, "That is the best thing to write in such situations." We gladly returned the present the man had sent with his letter....

I had formed my views rejecting marriage when I was a child. Never oblivious to the world around me, I knew what went on between a man and a woman. Although there was no man in our house, I knew about sexual relations through hearsay or from observing animals. I saw sex as filth, especially the woman's share in it, and the whole matter revolted me. Perhaps my leaving home for school at the age of thirteen was motivated by my abhorrence of sex, since without education I would have no means of supporting myself. Thus, I abandoned the idea of marriage altogether. Furthermore, it seems as though God's will intervened to accentuate, clarify, and emphasize my resolution not to marry, when once I heard a man quarreling with a woman on a street corner and practically telling her, "How dare a woman, like you, whom I use for my pleasure, speak to me like that?" This sentence said it all to me, and I knew I would loathe having a man speak such filthy words to me. That is why I detested the word "marriage" in my youth and, as I grew older, the mere suggestion of marriage became the worst insult anyone could throw at me.

*Translated by Azza El Kholy*

## *Bchira Ben Mrad*
## HONORING DR. TAWHIDA BEN CHEIKH

Tunisia    1937    Arabic

Bchira Ben Mrad was born to a well-off Tunis family in the early twentieth century, at a time when newborn girls' birthdates were not officially recorded. Her father taught at the famous Al-Zaytuna University, a religious institution in the heart of the Medina. At that time, some fathers had come to see the importance of sending their daughters to school, particularly as educated young men increasingly refused to marry illiterate women; the first school for bourgeois Muslim girls had been founded in Tunis in 1900. When BchiraBen Mrad was made to leave school quite early by decision of a conservative uncle, her father had private tutors teach his daughter the rudiments of language and grammar, as well as music and the Qur'an. Although Sheikh Ben Mrad wanted his daughter to live according to the precepts of Islam, he also believed women's education to be essential, provided they did not follow the example of their European counterparts in colonized Tunisia. .

Sheikh Ben Mrad also encouraged his daughter's activism on women's issues, offering her advice, renting her an office, and providing a forum for her in his review *Chams el Islam* (The Sun of Islam). She later wrote for *Tunis al Fatat* (The Young Woman of Tunis), a magazine founded in 1938, contributing articles in support of Tunisian nationalism and women's emancipation and education. In 1936, Bchira Ben Mrad founded the Muslim Union of Tunisian Women, which she continued to lead until independence in 1956, when the new government established the National Union of Tunisian Women.

As in other parts of North Africa, the women's movement in Tunisia was closely allied with nationalist struggle. Bchira Ben Mrad traveled throughout the country giving speeches and organizing meetings of the Women's Union. Her goal was to raise women's consciousness and encourage them to take part in the life of their country, in particular in the struggle for independence and the resistance of colonial culture. Under her leadership, the Women's Union took a strong stand against colonialism, and found common cause with the main nationalist party, the Destour. The French colonists saw her activities as a threat, and along with her female colleagues, she endured harassment and imprisonment.

The first meeting of the Women's Union took place in 1936, ending with a sale of pastries, the profits of which were to be used to help young Tunisian men study in Europe. On April 18, 1937, a great meeting was organized to pay tribute to Dr. Tawhida Ben Cheikh, the only Tunisian woman who had volunteered to go and study abroad in order to help her Tunisian sisters, whose culture did not allow them to be examined by male doctors. It was for Bchira Ben Mrad an opportunity to present her point of view on the importance of education and knowledge. Dr. Tawhida Ben Cheikh followed with her own speech, stating that she considered it a duty toward her country to have chosen medicine, and urging the women present at the meeting to send their daughters to school so that, they, too, could be of use to their country. The meeting proved an important event in the history of Tunisian women's education, fueling the creation of schools for girls.

*Khédija Arfaoui*

◆

Ladies, this is indeed, one of the happiest days for Tunisian women. Today, women can raise their heads. Women have embarked on the road to greatness and regard. They have proved that no obstacle could prevent them from moving ahead. They have thus been able to show that they deserve every praise and deference, and that no one could be more capable of acquiring stature and knowledge.

But why am I speaking about Tunisian women here? It's because, right in front of you, on this very platform, you can all see the usefulness of science in serving the nation.

Why should I make a long speech when you have in front of you an example of will, greatness, virtue, perfection, and majesty: Dr. Tawhida Ben Cheikh.

Ladies, here is Dr. Tawhida Ben Cheikh, to whom all the women in this country have decided to pay a tribute today, in acknowledgment of her fruitful efforts and her successful work for the nation.

This honorable daughter of Tunisia had seen that her sisters needed someone to take care of their bodies and health and to treat any illness they might have. She did her national duty and answered to that need. She went abroad, far away from her family and country, until she was awarded the title of medical doctor. Doing so, she was able to fill a huge gap and an urgent need. Her nation needed her very much: Indeed, Tunisian women did not have anyone who could deal with their intimate health problems, because of the nature of tradition and religion. Tunisian women could not show their bodies and their health problems to male doctors. If that proved necessary, it was often already too late, and things could come to a tragic end.

Today, however, thank God, this honorable doctor is among her fellow citizens.

Ladies: This doctor knew what God expected her to do. Seeking knowledge is a religious duty for every Muslim man and for every Muslim woman. This Tunisian doctor chose to live in exile in order to fulfill her religious duty. She left her family and country to solve the great problem of having no Muslim female doctor, to do her duty for the daughters of this country, complying with the poet's saying: "I aspire to have the highest positions and would be satisfied with no lower ones. I must either get the best of what I am looking for or die."

But, thank God, this female doctor has come back to us with her head proudly raised, proving that, if they really want to work, Tunisian women can be successful and acquire the knowledge they wish for; nothing will stop them, neither hardships nor hard work.

Honorable doctor, you fulfilled your duty toward your religion, your country, and your sisters. Here we are today, paying tribute to your good deeds, thanking you warmly for your fruitful work. May you remain with your faithful sisters, cared for by Providence, enjoying utmost happiness.

Having said that, honorable ladies, you know that we should take this opportunity to make our celebration one that both thanks the doctor for serving her country and helps the poor and unfortunate people. They are waiting for the charity with which your generosity can provide them.

People like you have helped by offering charity and rescuing the needy. Honorable ladies, the poor of this country need your assistance; I do not need to remind you that women are compassionate and merciful; they are kind to the needy.

Ladies, do take the initiative, you who were born from noble women, and help those needy brothers of ours. And do your best in collecting money; be swift in doing good deeds. You will gain by this generosity, as you will be thanked for it.

You have got to know that helping people is a gift from God to you. "Nothing equals good deeds: they have a sweet taste and a beautiful face."

Long live the benefactresses who seek the honor of their people! Long live science! Long live Tunisia!

*Translated by Khédija Arfaoui*

# MID-TWENTIETH CENTURY

## Bady'a Sabbah-Allah
# LETTER TO A FRIEND

### Egypt 1942 Arabic

Bady'a Mohammed Sabbah-Allah was born in the town of Mahalla El Kubra in 1912, and died in Alexandria in 1969. In her childhood, she suffered both an attack of fever that caused a lifelong heart problem and a fall that left her with a permanent limp. In spite of these disabilities, and additional hardships caused by poverty and the early loss of her parents, she remained determined to cultivate her mind and to gain an education. In 1926, at the age of fourteen, she managed to go alone to El Fayyum Teacher Training School, a boarding school for women, to present her application and to sit for an interview. Such schools were the only available sources of education for young women from the countryside who wanted to qualify as teachers. In 1928, the minister of education paid the school a visit and Sabbah-Allah, sixteen at the time and already noted for her oratorical skills, gave a welcome speech and read out a few lines of verse of her own composition, to the delight of the minister and other visiting dignitaries.

After qualifying as a primary schoolteacher in 1931, Sabbah-Allah was forced to stay at home for four years because her uncle, who was then her legal guardian, still regarded women's working as socially unacceptable. She finally began teaching in 1935 at Al Manshiya Elementary School in Alexandria. She joined the faculty of the school for the deaf in Al Mattariah in Cairo in 1941, and in 1952 moved to the school for the deaf in Alexandria.

Bady'a Sabbah-Allah was keenly interested in classical Arabic literature, religion, and psychology, and had high literary ambitions that were never fulfilled. She left unpublished letters, short stories, and lists of books she was reading, as well as accounts of her own dreams.

This excerpt from a letter to a woman friend is dated 1942, at the height of World War II, a European conflict that was fought partly on Egyptian soil, to the resentment of most Egyptians. It was a time of political instability, with the presence of a large number of British troops in the country fueling already fervent nationalist feelings, and conflicts among Egypt's own parties and leaders as well. For Sabbah-Allah, as for many Egyptian feminists, the country's desire for liberation from foreign domination paralleled women's wish for a freer form of personal existence. She mentions the nationalist hero Saad Zagloul in the same breath as Esther Wissa and Mayy Ziada, well-known activists advocating women's rights (the use of their first names indicating some familiarity on the part of the writer, and presumably of the recipient as well).

The letter also reveals a shackled soul, fretting in its bondage and yearning to break free. Sabbah-Allah's urge to make her voice heard was repressed by the prevalent social restrictions, here represented once again by her uncle.

*Amira Nowaira*

✦

...But as human beings we selfishly care for our own happiness even if it comes at the expense of other people's misery. Is it possible for a human being endowed with reason ever to be happy? With a rational mind and a feeling heart, one is likely to feel miserable even while living in luxury and abundance. But the ignorant can feel happy even when surrounded by misery. I believe the highest degree of happiness is to have knowledge. Knowledge is in fact a complicated but delicious puzzle, whose beauty urges us to unravel its secrets. And we understand nothing of it, beyond the struggle for freedom. Good God! My pen seems to stray once more and I find myself harping on the word "freedom." I could swear to you that I feel my heart burning and my tears dropping, because nothing makes me more miserable than the sight of an English soldier walking on the soil of my country. You may think that I've written this on the spur of the moment, but no, my dear, I've loved my country from the cradle, and I've studied the Egyptian question all on my own through reading. When I was ten, I used to get excited and filled with enthusiasm and admiration whenever I read the speeches of Saad Zagloul, Esther, or Mayy. I remember that, in those good old days, I once got so full of self-confidence that I wrote an article on freedom and patriotism and I gave it to my uncle, entreating him to send it to one of the newspapers for publication. He read it, shook his head, and said, "What would you do if some writer picked on you and poked fun at your article? How would you then answer him? Better stay clear of all this mess." Now don't ask me about my feelings of pain and dismay. I said to myself, am I not created equal to these writers? Don't I have the right to make my voice heard along with theirs? Because it was so hard for me to accept the fact that no one would read my article, I sent it to a friend of mine living in the countryside.

*Translated by Amira Nowaira*

## *Malika El-Fassi*
## AN IMPORTANT STEP FOR GIRLS' EDUCATION

Morocco 1943    Arabic

Malika El-Fassi was born in 1919 in the city of Fes into an aristocratic family of judges, theologians, and university professors. El-Fassi benefited from the guidance of her father, El Mehdi El-Fassi, a brilliant scholar and a magistrate for whom education was a religious duty. Through him she met eminent professors from Al-Qarawiyin University. She attended an Islamic primary school where she received the same education as her brothers, but was later obliged to finish her education at home.

At a very early age, Malika El-Fassi began writing articles denouncing the marginalization of women; these stand as the first modern journalism by a woman in Morocco. At that time, it was considered shameful for a woman to sign her own name to an article in a public periodical, so she wrote under pseudonyms—initially Al Fatat (The Girl), and later Bahitat Al-Hadira (The City

Scholar). El-Fassi went on to publish many articles in Moroccan newspapers, including *Al-Alam*, and also wrote short plays and novels.

In the late 1930s, Malika El-Fassi became deeply involved in the nationalist struggle, along with her husband, father, brothers, and cousins. She was the only woman among the nationalist party's initial members and became leader of its women's section. Malika El-Fassi was also the only woman among the fifty-nine Moroccans who signed the historical manifesto delivered to the French authorities on 11 January 1944, demanding the independence of their country. She was a member of Morocco's first women's association, Akhawat Al-Safaa (Sisters of Purity), founded in 1946. During the extraordinary party congress held in 1955 as independence approached, she called for women's participation in the political life of the country and demanded that women be allowed to vote and run for office.

Throughout her political life, El-Fassi also worked to promote the education of women. In 1947, a group of nationalist men enrolled their daughters in high school, and in 1955, the first six female students graduated from Al-Qarawiyin University. After independence was won in 1956, El-Fassi became very active in the battle to reduce the high rate of illiteracy among women. She served for many years as president of the philanthropic association Al Mouassat (The Middle). Malika El-Fassi died on 12 March 2007, after this headnote had first been drafted.

The following excerpt comes from an article entitled "The Sun Has Risen for Moroccan Women," published in 1942 in the magazine *Risalat Al-Maghrib*. It celebrates girls' graduation from a primary school as an important national event, and encourages all Moroccan parents to allow their daughters to reach their full potential through education.

*Zakia Iraqui-Sinaceur*

✦

I felt happy and hopeful when I saw young girls leaving Bab El-Hedid school in Fes with their primary education certificates in their hands, testimony to their talents and abilities. I felt as pleased as their teachers and their parents, who were patiently waiting for their children, walking up and down in front of the school gate. It's an important step for girls' education and it must be applauded and fostered. This year, many young girls have obtained their primary school certificates, among them our dear Princess Lalla Aisha, who received both the Moroccan and the French certificates. These achievements strengthen our hopes and our confidence in girls' education.

We believe that a girl who has earned her certificate this year must not repress her knowledge and consign it to oblivion. She must not stay at home, nor forget what she has learned through her school years. It is difficult for a young girl to continue education at home alone, merely by reading books. As people say, "Knowledge comes out of the mouths of men." A person holding only a primary certificate may not be able to appreciate the beauty and the benefits of reading on her own. It is important to pursue one's education in order to study science and expand one's learning. Being educated enables a person to be an active and useful citizen. Men must ensure women's training, ignoring reactionary arguments that discourage their education.

Being educated and cultured will help women to behave morally and well. A good teacher considers his female students as if they were his daughters or sisters, and gives them the same consideration and attention as he does boys. A young girl can achieve virtue and success if she has self-confidence, knows her own value in life, and understands her duty to society. All this cannot be acquired without education and knowledge.

Dear friends, the future of your young daughters depends on you. You must show concern and work hard to realize a better future for them. Discussing this matter during meetings and writing articles in magazines are not sufficient to promote young women's education. A young woman who aspires to attain progress and knowledge wishes to turn these ideas into realities.

Are not many of you pleased to hear your daughters speak, using their education and learning? Your daughters are the mothers of tomorrow, and the wives of husbands who should praise the capacities of women and their understanding of values and duties. The voices of women are calling you; answer their call and think seriously about the consequences of your decisions.

For men, His Majesty King Mohammed V is the role model to follow; he has, on several occasions, insisted on girls' receiving schooling, taking great interest in his daughter's education. Evidence from this comes from the school achievements of Princess Lalla Aisha. His exceptional speech testifies to his great ambitions for a better education for women. I would like to emphasize the importance of the guidelines and advice this speech included.

*Translated by Zakia Iraqui–Sinaceur, Fatima Sadiqi, and Moha Ennaji*


## *Fatma Ne'mat Rashed*
# SHOULD WOMEN ENTER AL-AZHAR?

Egypt 1946 Arabic

In 1942, Fatma Ne'mat Rashed founded Al-Hizb al-Nisa'i al-Watani, the National Feminist Party (NFP). It was the second major feminist body to emerge in Egypt, after the Egyptian Feminist Union (EFU), established by Huda Shaarawi in 1923, and the first feminist political party. The party called for equal political and social rights between the sexes, including enfranchisement, female representation in parliament, further reform of personal status laws (including the abolition of polygamy), the promotion of the intellectual abilities of women, as well as a strengthening of the bonds between Egyptian women and their counterparts throughout the Middle East. Furthermore, the NFP advocated the unconditional acceptance of qualified women in paid employment and attacked discrimination against women workers, advocating their admittance into professional unions.

Fatma Ne'mat Rashed and three other women were among the first one hundred founders of the Syndicate of Journalists in Egypt. Rashed was also the first editor of *Al-Masreyya* (The Egyptian Woman), a fortnightly magazine published by the Egyptian Feminist Union. This magazine was a radical departure from other women's magazines, eschewing pieces on cooking, sewing, and home decorating, to focus only on the topics relevant to women's liberation and development.

The following text was occasioned by a debate about whether women should be allowed to enter—and thus enroll in—Al-Azhar, a mosque established in Cairo in 972 CE. By the 1940s, it was the best-known mosque in the whole Muslim world, as well as a renowned university. When Abdel Hamid Bek Saleh, a member of parliament from the Constitutional Liberal Party, was interviewed about his views on the subject, he vehemently opposed women's right to study at Al-Azhar on the grounds that they would have to mingle with men, which he regarded as forbidden by the code of female behavior according to Islamic jurisprudence. Instead, he believed that women should limit themselves to dutifully managing their households, and adorning their homes like flowers. He also claimed that men were delaying their marriages because women had begun to appear unveiled in society, prematurely satisfying men's needs and thus keeping them away from marriage.

Both the interview and Rashed's response appeared in a journal called *Fatat al-Ghadd* (The Young Woman of Tomorrow) on 15 February 1946. Rashed offers a concise and impassioned manifesto, supporting women's equality as both a practical necessity and a basic human right that cannot be suppressed by patriarchal laws or customs. "Give all human beings the freedom to choose their futures and goals," she demands, "so long as these goals are noble." This particular struggle would continue for twenty years, but due to the perseverance of women like Fatma Ne'mat Rashed, Al-Azhar eventually founded several colleges for women, the first of these in 1962.

*Dina Mohamed Abdel Salam*

✦

The honorable member's opinion comes as no surprise to me. In fact, I find his attitude very much in keeping with the prevalent beliefs and views of men in our society, which hold that if women, even as few as two, were to embark on a career in a particular field, they would soon be followed by countless other women, thus making the workplace exclusively their own. This theory, however, is completely groundless, since women in our country still have little social and cultural experience, and little moral courage. Even the most highly cultured and socially refined women are often not permitted to enter a new field.

As for those women who will receive the same education at Al-Azhar as men, they will constitute a minority, perhaps even a very small minority. The truth is that our theory is quite different from that of the venerable MP, since we believe that everybody, be it men or women, should be free to choose the intellectual and educational areas they prefer, and should have the right to take whichever direction they desire without being manipulated spiritually or mentally. We totally support women's progress and emancipation without any constraints.

Contrary to the claims of conservatives who uphold meaningless traditions, women's employment, like men's, has become a necessity in these difficult times. Everybody, men and women alike, must work hard and fast to earn a living, or risk being trampled upon and completely wiped out by the vigorous and rapid pace of the new generations that will compete for excellence and perfection in all areas. Whether women are fond of their domestic duties or not, they will still return to them after they have ventured into other fields outside the domestic sphere.

Another reason for demanding women's equality with men is that not all women are married. Many of them are divorced or widowed, so why should their lives be wasted? Why should they not participate with men who contribute to the progress of Egypt in particular and the East in general? Why should we suggest that women remain inactive at a time when all members of our community are encouraged to become energetic, effective, functional, and extremely active?

Give women the right of choice. Allow them to choose either to be mothers and housewives, or engineers, physicians, and lawyers. Give all human beings the freedom to choose their futures and goals so long as these goals are noble. After all, women are human beings, are they not?

As for the laws of jurisprudence, well, we cannot say that we now adhere more strictly to religious laws, nor can we claim that we are more pious than the early Muslims, in whose times Arab women were very prominent and active. In those days, women inspired warriors in the battlefields. Let me merely add that no matter how extreme the *hijab*, eyes and hands can still achieve much.

The progress of women, moreover, cannot be the cause for a declining marriage rate, since this is a global problem rooted in the social and economic structure of modern society, not caused by the progress women have achieved. Even in the West, the marriage rate has similarly declined, and this trend cannot obviously have anything to do with the *hijab*!

*Translated by Dina Mohamed Abdel Salam*


## *Huda Shaarawi*
## LETTER TO THE PRIME MINISTER

Egypt 1946   Arabic

Huda Shaarawi was an early twentieth-century Egyptian nationalist and women's rights activist whose life and works have had a profound influence on Egyptian and other Arab women. She was born into a wealthy family in Minya, in Upper

Egypt, in 1879, and educated by tutors in a variety of subjects and languages. Her father died when she was still a small child, and at age thirteen, she was betrothed to her much older cousin as a second wife. The marriage was not a happy one, and Shaarawi lived apart from her husband for several years, then rejoined him when she was twenty-one and had two children.

An upper-class woman, Shaarawi was educated in the harem system, designed, in principle, to confer respect upon women and to separate them from men. In public, women were expected to cover their hair and faces with a veil known as the *hijab*. Shaarawi resented such restrictions on women's dress and movement, and began to organize a lecture series for women, which brought women out of their homes and into public places for the first time. Eventually, the lecture series grew into the Intellectual Association of Egyptian Women.

In 1909, Shaarawi convinced the royal princess, Ain Al Hayat, to help her establish a women's charitable association to raise money for poor women and children. In 1910, she opened a school for girls, the Mabarat Muhammad Ali, which offered classes in infant care, family hygiene, home management, and other practical skills.

After World War I, many women left the harem to take part in political action against British rule. In 1919, Shaarawi helped organize a large women's anti-British demonstration, which established her own reputation as a champion for her country's freedom. To coordinate women's efforts in the independence movement, she founded the Wafdist Women's Central Committee.

In 1923, Shaarawi helped found the Egyptian Feminist Union (EFU), the first national feminist organization in Europe, which she would lead for twenty-four years. Soon afterward she attended an international women's suffrage conference in Rome. Shaarawi had made a decision to stop wearing her veil in public after her husband's death the previous year. In what was the first public defiance of the restrictive tradition, Shaarawi, returning from the conference, stepped off the train in Cairo and removed her veil. Her companion Saiza Nabarawi, editor of the EFU journal *L'Egyptienne*, followed suit, and the crowd of women waiting to welcome them applauded this unprecedented act, some taking off their own veils in support.

The EFU campaigned for various reforms to improve women's lives, including raising the minimum age of marriage for girls to sixteen, increasing women's educational opportunities, and improving health care. She was a member of the International Alliance of Women for Suffrage and Equal Citizenship, serving as Vice-President in 1935; was founding President of the Arab Feminist Union from 1945 to 1947, and supported the founding of *Al-Maraa Al-Arabiyya*, the newsletter of the Arab Feminist Union in 1946. She also founded the magazines *L'Egyptienne* (1925) and *Al-Misriyya* (1937). Popular as a speaker throughout the Arab world and Europe, Shaarawi also led Egyptian women's delegations to international conferences and organized meetings with other Arab feminists. In 1944 she founded the All-Arab Federation of Women.

The following letter, addressed to Egypt's Prime Minister, illustrates Shaarawi's continuous struggle for Egyptian women's political rights. Although the letter is undated, we can surmise that it was written after the UN General Assembly met in New York in the fall of 1946, and some time before her death on 12 December 1947. The letter was written in response to a December 1946 UN resolution stating that, in view of the UN's commitment to "promoting and encouraging human rights and fundamental freedoms for all without distinction as to sex," all member states that had not already done so should move to grant women "equal political rights with men." The letter demonstrates Shaarawi's sophisticated command of the Arabic language and deep understanding of the political scene of the time, as well as her persuasive powers. It appeals not only to the prime minister's sense of justice but also to his concern for his country's stature in the eyes of the Arab world and the larger international community.

*Nadia El Kholy*

✦

Your Excellency, Prime Minister, Mahmoud Fahmy Al Nokrashy Pasha:

It is the honor of the Egyptian Feminist Union (EFU) to approach your Excellency in connection with the suggestion of his Excellency, Senator Mohammad Aly Allouba Pasha, to grant women their political rights. The Egyptian Feminist Union is confident that the government will give this suggestion the attention it rightly deserves, based on the firm belief that women should shoulder their share of responsibilities in an equal manner with all citizens who enjoy the same political rights in a democratic country. Furthermore, as a member of the United Nations, Egypt is now bound by the resolution passed by the General Assembly of the United Nations in New York in December 1946. This resolution was based on the UN Charter calling on all states that have not yet granted women citizens such rights to take all necessary measures in that direction.

We believe that Egypt's approval of this resolution clearly expressed through the words of its representative at the UN's General Assembly is evidence enough of the government's willingness to implement it in effect, especially in view of the fact that the representative neither abstained from nor objected to the voting.

The Egyptian government in the current state of affairs will no doubt be particularly keen to implement UN resolutions since it had previously appealed to the UN to secure these fair demands. The time is ripe right now, Mr. Prime Minister, for such a request since there is an ongoing plan to alter the election law.

We have strong hopes that, in considering the proposed amendment, the government will go a step beyond what was originally proposed by his Excellency Allouba Pasha, and will grant women their full political rights, not only in elections, but also in representative councils. This will put them on an equal footing with men in a manner that would enforce the UN resolutions.

Your Excellency is no doubt fully aware that, at the present time and in view of the importance of the UN Charter, which calls for equality between the sexes, the Egyptian cause will benefit immensely. Not only will Egypt be applauded for upholding the Charter's principles of justice, equality, and respect for human rights with no discrimination on the basis of sex, language, or religion, but it will also demonstrate its implementation of these same rights to include women, emphasizing their rights as well as responsibilities.

The most important of these rights from a democratic perspective are political rights. Consequently, the Arab countries that place Egypt at the forefront will undoubtedly see, in the initiative of implementing the General Assembly's decisions, a motive for them to follow suit. Egypt, as always, will continue to be in the lead and not fall behind others. Surely your Excellency would not accept that another state, which has not yet adopted the idea of equality between men and women, should be the first to apply a resolution that all countries have contributed to and the whole world has welcomed as a true application of the UN Charter.

Should these steps be taken, the Egyptian government will not be embarrassed to respond to the inquiries of the United Nations concerning the steps taken by Egypt to put into effect this unanimous resolution.

As we wait for our country to reap the benefits of granting women their right to equality with your Excellency's support, please accept my warmest regards and gratitude.

*Translated by Nevine Rateb and Nadia El Kholy*

## *Lalla Aisha*
## A PRINCESS SPEAKS, UNVEILED

Morocco 1947   Arabic

Princess Lalla Aisha is the daughter of King Mohammed V (the present king's grandfather) and the eldest sister of King Hassan II. She is widely recognized as a pioneer of Moroccan women's emancipation, and her speech in Tangiers in 1947, nine years before independence, is a memorable event in the struggle for women's equal rights. In a powerful symbolic gesture, to deliver this speech, Lalla Aisha stood unveiled and unashamed in public by the side of her father, then the Sultan of Morocco. Taking courage from this display of feminist leadership from the royal family itself, thousands of women all over the country cast aside their own veils and began talking of emancipation.

In her speech, Lalla Aisha exhorts young Moroccans to "work together for the sake of the country" at this pivotal time in its history, when it is struggling to become an independent nation. She makes a point of including girls and women in her call for young people to participate in the public sphere. Moroccans must make sure, she asserts, that "no obstacle remains to the nation's revival, no veil to blind citizens from the paths they have chosen." Thus she positions women's education and emancipation as not only a right, but a patriotic duty.

Lalla Aisha alludes to the important connections between Morocco and Egypt. She pays homage to two great nineteenth-century leaders, King Moulay Hassan I in Morocco and Muhammad Ali Pasha (whom she refers to as Mohamed Ali Akbar Khediwy) in Egypt, both of whom led their countries on a path toward modernity and prosperity, and presided over a flourishing Arabic and Islamic culture. She also compares Al-Qarawiyin University in Fes with Al-Azhar University in Cairo, one of the most prestigious centers of Islamic learning in the world. She also praises Egyptian women as leaders in the quest for women's education and empowerment, and calls upon Moroccan women to "follow in their footsteps."

Lalla Aisha's rousing call resonated throughout Morocco's elite, where a few women had already surmounted difficulties in order to participate in the national struggle for independence. As a direct result of Lalla Aisha's speech the *Istiqlal* (Independence) Party, the oldest political party in Morocco, created its first women's cells, an action followed by other political parties.

As Lalla Aisha's speech makes clear, her father both encouraged and served as a focus for the nationalist spirit in Morocco. In 1953, the French decided to send the sultan, Lalla Aisha, and the rest of the royal family into exile in Corsica and later, Madagascar. She hated her two years in exile, but while she was away, her star waxed ever brighter in the Moroccan firmament. When at last the French were forced to bring the family back to Morocco, Lalla Aisha's return was celebrated with almost as much jubilation as that of the Sultan himself. After the Sultan became king of a newly independent Morocco in 1956, Lalla Aisha continued her life of public service. In the 1960s and early 1970s, she served as ambassador to the United Kingdom, Greece, and Italy. She also directed Morocco's *Entraide Nationale*, the administrative headquarters of all Moroccan welfare agencies and wellspring of Morocco's campaign against illiteracy.

*Zakia Iraqui-Sinaceur and Moha Ennaji*

✦

Ladies and Gentlemen,

Peoples and nations go through many stages in their lifetimes. They also may endure confusing times. A country in decline, for example, may live in a state of disruption and chaos. Its people may become selfish, seeking only to fulfill their personal interests. Spiritual links and social bonds that ordinarily unite people may dissolve, while intellectuals may become lazy and indulge in illusions, praising some glorious deeds of the nation's past or a victorious struggle of their ancestors, in order to hide their weakness and lethargy. According to these intellectuals, the nation's present and future, the common interest of the people, the sacrifices made by our forefathers, the endeavor to restore the nation's magnificence and glory—all these are far beyond them. They leave such matters to others because they are convinced that it is not their responsibility to find solutions for them.

Such are the characteristics that distinguish a nation in its decline, until it forgoes lethargy and enters a phase of renewal. When a nation's younger generation is reborn, the young may build the nation's grandeur by personal and collective effort, and they may lay the foundation for future glories. Only then can nations consider the present with courage and its future with optimism. Such a moment may determine when a country can rise above others, with pride and confidence in its own worth. A nation should recall its history simply to remember the experiences of its forefathers and to learn from them. Only then may a nation enter a stage of creation that leads to mastery of the future.

At which stage is Morocco right now? Is Morocco still living in laziness with a dark veil covering its perceptions? Or has Morocco finally taken steps to reassert its pride and to ward off its sluggishness and to call upon people to reunite and work together for the sake of the country?

To be truthful, we can here emphasize clear signs that a thorough change has occurred in the nation's thinking and behavior. That ominous time when Moroccans were preoccupied only by their own well-being, pursuing only their private interests, has fortunately lapsed. Today, every Moroccan, coming from the upper or lower classes, is ready to sacrifice everything in their possession for the sake of others, for Moroccans' general happiness, for their pride and glory.

Moreover, all citizens have demonstrated their readiness to work for the nation. If evidence is needed, one need only look around and see the increased numbers of schools that have been built in a very short time, in towns and villages. These are the work of Moroccan citizens and the implementation of Moroccan programs supported by Moroccan funds with a Moroccan purpose.

Now, can we truly say that Moroccan people are lethargic and idle, prone to indulge in old tales and superstitions?

In fact, experience has made Moroccans develop a keen awareness of their surroundings and has enlightened their minds. Nationalism has conquered their hearts and behavior. Hence no obstacle remains to the nation's revival, no veil to blind citizens from the paths they have chosen, no hindrance to prevent them from reaching their ultimate goals. Now the nation is heading toward the fulfillment of great expectations.

Moroccans have achieved their aims through three elements inherent to success: a firm religious belief, a clear goal, and an experienced leader. Islam is our religion, the right of the nation is our goal, for which we are ready to sacrifice all, and the Sultan of Morocco is our leader, whom we obey and whose wise governance we follow, because the throne of Morocco is the symbol of our unity, our pride, and strength. Moroccan monarchs were among the first to call upon Arab countries to acquire knowledge and education as modern weapons to fight for freedom and preserve their sovereignty. If we go back to the beginning of the last century, we shall find that among the Islamic nations which were still living in ignorance and darkness rose two glorious leaders, two experienced politicians who called upon their people to awaken to their potential and to build a prosperous future for their countries. Those leaders were Mohamed Ali Akbar Khediwy of Egypt and Moulay Hassan I of Morocco, both of whom urged their people to move onward with courage and in struggle. These two great leaders prepared their nations to meet the challenges allowing them to enter the contemporary era. They also provided their people with the necessary tools required for such challenges and so ensured the success of this enterprise and enhanced the position of their nations in the world.

Moulay Hassan I deployed all his might to transfer to Morocco the torch that shone in Egypt. Indeed, this great innovator was not yet twenty when the fame of Ali Akbar Khediwy collapsed. Moulay Hassan's youth, however, did not deter him from setting into motion the mechanisms to propel Morocco forward. Actually, his father had earlier sent a group of Moroccan students to Egypt for study. When Moulay Hassan was crowned, he immediately planned programs, with financial backing, that would modernize Moroccan institutions. He was inspired by successful experiences both of the East and West. The students who had been sent abroad formed the elite of the contemporary nation. They contributed to all fields of knowledge, setting up the foundations for success. . . .

Egyptian women have contributed enormously to the liberation of Moroccan women. I also want to express greetings to all women and to female students at schools and universities in Egypt. They have been the true leaders of women's reform movements in Muslim and Arab countries. To them, we express our gratitude and we pledge to follow in their footsteps. In fact, following their lead and responding to our Sultan's call, Moroccan girls and women have moved with courage and determination to set the foundations for a Moroccan cultural revival. They have begun to spread the message of learning to all social classes, introducing education and culture everywhere, so as to make every home a heaven of light, peace, and happiness.

Moroccan girls are going to schools inaugurated by our Sultan, God bless him, to get educated, learn about culture and good behavior, gain knowledge of other cultures, and improve their natural skills in studying the Arabic language, history, and foreign languages. Such knowledge will provide them with a clear understanding of other people's civilizations and societies, and should improve their own status as well. . . .

Our Sultan is expecting all Moroccan women to invest in their education and to expend all their efforts to gain an education, which is the standard by which a nation's civilization and progress can be measured. It is also the best tool that will ensure the success of the royal program of reforms that will lead Morocco to progress and reduce the distance that separates us from the prosperity everybody enjoyed under the reign of Moulay Hassan.

Our Sultan will turn the university of Al-Qarawiyin into the Al-Azhar of Morocco. He will train an elite made up of Moroccan university graduates, and he will work to transform all Moroccan citizens into brothers and sisters, sharing clean hearts and souls. We nourish great hopes that we will succeed very quickly, because we are a nation of people with generous hearts. We have a reformer who has accurate perceptions and a thinker with loyal intentions. We have a lively and enthusiastic population that has chosen to unite and stand as one person behind their brilliant sultan and leader. We have a nation with great expectations and aspirations!

Long live the Sultan,
Long live the Moroccan nation,
And long live the revival.

*Translated by Anissa Salhi*

# Doria Shafik
# THE BEST TYPE OF PUBLICITY

Egypt  1947   Arabic

Poet, journalist, publisher, and political activist Doria Shafik was a prominent fig-
ure in the Egyptian women's movement. She was born in Tanta in 1908 and was
educated at French schools in both Tanta and Alexandria. In 1928, she wrote to
Huda Shaarawi and met her in Cairo. Shaarawi invited Shafik to speak at the
Azbakeya Gardens Theater, where she made her first public speech for the
Egyptian Feminist Union in May of 1928. Later that year, Shafik also received an
Egyptian government grant to study at the Sorbonne in Paris, where she earned a
B.A. and a Ph.D. degree.

In 1945, Doria Shafik founded the magazine *Bint Al-Nil* (Daughter of the
Nile), the first postwar woman's magazine, and in 1947 she founded the Bint Al-
Nil Union. One of the actions for which she will always be remembered is her
march into the parliament building in 1951 together with more than a thousand
women. Their demands included political rights for women, the reform of the
personal status law, and equal pay. Addressing a congregation of women feminists
earlier on the same day, she told them in no uncertain terms and in words that
became the hallmark of the feminist movement: "The men are meeting just a
stone's throw away from us, so I suggest we go there now, fully aware of our
rights. We should tell the members of parliament that their meetings will remain
illegal until our women representatives are allowed to sit with them. The Egyptian parliament is not a faithful representative of the whole nation without the
presence of women in it."

Doria Shafik had tense and difficult relations with the regime of Gamal Abdel
Nasser, who overthrew the Egyptian monarchy in 1952. In 1954, together with
eight women, she went on a hunger strike to protest against the exclusion of
women from the political decision-making process in the new Egyptian republic.
She is widely considered to have been instrumental in bringing about the legislation giving women the right to vote in 1956. Her exploits became known around
the world, but at home she was increasingly regarded by the political establishment as a militant troublemaker, and often attacked in the newspapers. In 1957,
when she went on a hunger strike inside the Indian Embassy to protest what she
saw as Nasser's increasingly dictatorial rule, she was placed under house arrest. All
her publishing enterprises were halted, her name was officially banned from the
press, and even many feminist and progressive activists were afraid to support or
contact her. In 1975, after a long period of intense depression and solitude, she
died in a fall from the balcony of her apartment. The true cause of her death
remains a mystery.

Shafik published the following essay in her magazine *Bint Al-Nil* , a publication aimed at educating and "awakening the consciousness" of Egyptian and Arab
women. The magazine's declared objective was to focus on the difficulties and
problems facing women, and to counteract the biased interpretations of Islam
that were detrimental to them. The article was published at a time when Egyptians were demanding an end to the British occupation, which persisted for three

decades after Britain nominally granted Egypt its independence in 1922. The newly established United Nations was seen as an important arena in which to promote the cause of true independence for Egypt. Shafik presents as a model Khedive Ismail, who ruled from 1863 to 1879 and was known for modernizing Egypt and for advancing his country's interests in both Europe and the Ottoman Empire. She then deftly unites the nationalist cause to the quest for women's equality, pointing out that including women in the UN delegation—and, more broadly, in the public life of the nation—is vital to winning Egypt respect and support in the West and throughout the world.

*Amira Nowaira*

✦

Publicity has become an important factor in government and a principal means of promoting the national struggle. Although publicity techniques have developed only recently in the West, they have a long history in the East. Since the early days of Islam, we have been expert publicists, and the task of propagating the Islamic faith has always been a serious and highly respected vocation, greatly venerated by the public in Egypt and abroad.

Publicity was not used only in classical times in Egypt. Modern Egypt also employed the best type of publicity during the reign of Khedive Ismail, a ruler who knew how to use the media in the service of promoting Egypt's cause, both locally and in Europe. If the radio had been invented in those days, it would have been included as one of his methods of publicity, as he eloquently and tactfully promoted Egypt's cause with the governing elite in Europe and Istanbul. In spite of all the crises that plagued his rule, he managed to put Egypt on the map of civilized nations and promoted its image as a part of Europe and a link between East and West.

After a quarter of a century, the Egyptian government has at last realized that promoting Egypt's image is a national duty dictated by the current state of affairs. About two months ago, it embarked on the course of forming a commission with this objective in mind. This commission, however, has not yet begun its work, so the Egyptian delegation is preparing to go to the Security Council without any publicity preceding it and paving the way for its work. Those delegates will be working with people who understand publicity well, and who have themselves been subjected to our adversaries' publicity. Our task will therefore be twofold: waging a publicity campaign to counteract our adversaries' efforts while presenting an image of our hopes for freedom and independence to the members of the United Nations.

The government, moreover, has begun this endeavor without considering the inclusion of a single woman in this commission. Had the government included a woman, it would have secured for Egypt a vivid image among civilized nations. Egyptian women have taken their rightful positions in public life and should not, therefore, be barred from promoting the cause of their country. Ignoring the existence of educated women promotes the mistaken view that women in Egypt are nothing more than a means of pleasure for men, or that the system of the harem still survives along the banks of the Nile.

In these difficult times, a well-educated woman is the best ambassador of her country.

If the government is fair, it will include women in this delegation. They should be chosen well and be sent to the United States, where the Security Council and the representatives of the whole world will gather. By selecting educated women with wit, eloquent and elegant wit, the Egyptian delegation will make a lasting impression.

It is the custom here in Egypt to praise a husband for his good taste in choosing a beautiful wife. If she combines elegance, education, and charisma, the husband usually takes even more credit. We hope that our women ambassadors—should the government include them in this delegation—will have all the attributes of beauty, elegance, education, and good sense, and will thus be a credit to the nation. Our adversaries and our friends alike will then admit that Egypt has presented an extraordinary delegation. Egyptian women will seem equal to men, not only in Egypt but in the world as well. They deserve to take their rightful position in life and they have the right to claim complete and unfettered freedom.

*Translated by Amira Nowaira*

## *Habiba Guessoussa*
## AN OPENING SPEECH

Morocco 1947    Arabic

*Akhawat Al-Safaa* (Sisters of Purity), the first women's association in Morocco, was created in Fes in 1946, while Morocco was still colonized by the French. Its founders were urban women whose fathers, husbands, and brothers were involved in nationalist politics. The association was created within the *Al-Istiqlal* (Independence) Party, which promoted the view that women were men's partners in all aspects of social life and that the development of any nation could not be achieved without women. Aware of the priority of struggling for independence, the women who formed *Akhawat Al-Safaa* were nonetheless determined to dissociate their demands for equality as women from their nationalist demands as citizens.

The main objective of the association was to pursue legal and political rights for women, and its work in the years prior to independence launched the Moroccan feminist movement. Shortly after independence was won in 1956, members of *Akhawat Al-Safaa* became bitterly disillusioned by the new nation's passage of a reactionary family law. Some of the women withdrew completely from politics, while others joined the opposition, which at that time was on the left and sustained the feminist movement through several difficult decades.

*Akhawat Al-Safaa* held its first General Assembly on 23 May 1947 in Fes, drawing women from cities throughout Morocco. The speech that appears here was delivered during that meeting by Habiba Guessouss, of whom nothing is known other than the fact that she had been elected the association's first president. The speech itself is rather restrained, which is understandable given the political tensions of that time and the fact that women did not want to sound as if they put their own concerns before the concerns of the nation. Nevertheless, she identifies the quest for women's rights as "our movement," distinguishing the particular goals of *Akhawat Al-Safaa* from the common goals of the *Istiqlal* Party as a whole. She also connects the association's mission to the larger "struggle launched by our sisters" in nearby countries, thereby positioning it as part of a larger regional feminist movement.

*Fatima Bouabdelli*

✦

Honorable Ladies,
On this happy day, we want to thank all of you, on behalf of the association, for your presence in this General Assembly. We appreciate your support and your willingness to help us carry out our noble mission. Your beautiful faces attest to our women's optimism and forward-looking spirit, despite the heavy burden of living under backward traditions.

On this occasion, we would like to express our thanks, allegiance, and gratitude to His Majesty the King. He was the first to claim women's right to education so that they might be freed from the darkness of ignorance and brought into the light of knowledge and prosperity. He set the example by educating his daughter, Princess Lalla Aisha, whom we consider as the leader of our movement.

We also wish to thank the *Istiqlal* Party, which has welcomed the creation of this association and provided us with the appropriate means and encouragement to fulfill our mission.

Our motivation in creating this association is to inscribe ourselves in the struggle launched by our sisters in other countries in the region. We are neither less intelligent nor less educated than our sisters elsewhere, nor are we badly brought up. We merely lack the appropriate conditions. This does not mean, however, that it is now impossible for us to accomplish our mission because we do not have the same circumstances. Our duty is to join together, work hard, and thus bring about our own great rebirth.

The similarities between the first stages of our movement and those in other countries have motivated us to move forward. We are full of hope that we will succeed in the near future. We believe that we will overcome backward traditions with determination, patience, and wisdom. Today, many Moroccans accept the idea of promoting women's rights. This is why we believed that creating a woman's association composed of qualified women would help to fulfill our mission and thus contribute further to women's emancipation.

With the full support of the *Istiqlal* Party, we have been able to invite eminent figures from the city of Fes to take part in the preparatory meetings that have led to naming this association *Akhawat Al-Safa*. Its administrative board, which has been constituted through democratic consultations, has honored me by appointing me president of the association.

*Translated by Fatima Boubdelli*

## Eugenie Sinano Horwitz
## TALES FROM THE ZOGHEB SAGA

Egypt 1949    French

These selections are part of the multigenerational saga of an aristocratic Alexandrian family, written in French in 1949 by one of its younger members, Eugenie (Janie) Sinano Horwitz. Born in 1900 and educated in a French boarding school, she spoke English and French fluently, had a working knowledge of Italian and Greek, and knew some German, too, as her husband Hugo Horwitz was Swiss. Although she was a fourth-generation immigrant of Syrian origin, her knowledge of Arabic was limited to a few words. Like most upper-class women in the early part of the twentieth century, she did not work outside of the home.

In these excerpts, the author recounts stories from the lives of her grandfather and grandmother; of her mother, Marie, who married a Greek by the name of Sinano; and of her mother's two sisters, Rosine and Isabelle. The text vividly reflects Alexandria at the height of its unique position in Egypt, which lasted from the middle of the nineteenth to the middle of the twentieth centuries. During this period, Alexandria was in Egypt, but not quite *of* it. In the classical period it had been called *Alexandrea Ad Ægyptum*, meaning "Alexandria next to Egypt," and the appellation once again held true. During the first half of the nineteenth century, under the modernizing vision of Muhammad Ali Pasha, foreigners had flocked to Alexandria in pursuit of wealth and opportunity. Descendants of these early adventurers later made up much of the city's aristocracy. The presence of these foreigners gave Alexandria its unique character as part of the Mediterranean culture, vibrantly combining East and West, and the city's multi-ethnic nature encouraged a mood of pluralism that influenced all areas of life.

In the early excerpts, Eugenie Sinano Horwitz focuses on the indeterminacy of many things in her family's story: their origins, their wealth, their nationality, history and fiction, past and present, the real and the imagined. Although the bulk of "Arab" immigrants to Alexandria were Syrian or Lebanese, they considered themselves Levantines rather than Arabs or Egyptians. Because borders and nationalities were fluid in the Ottoman Empire, Levantines and Jews living in Alexandria could hold nationalities other than Egyptian and buy titles from European countries. Horwitz goes on to describe her mother and aunts, who permanently ascribed to what she calls the "Ismailian mentality"—a perspective on the world formed during the time of Khedive Ismail, who ruled Egypt from 1863 to 1869. Renowned for his modernization of Egypt, Ismail is also remembered for the extravagant projects—-such as the huge festivities surrounding the inauguration of the Suez Canal—that bankrupted the country and helped pave the way for increased European domination.

From today's perspective, these passages describe a a city that has almost vanished. The *Place des Consuls*, where the "palace" of Horwitz's grandfather stood, still exists as Manshieh Square, but those palaces were burned in 1882, when the British navy bombarded Alexandria in response to the uprising against European control. The Capitulations, agreements that had given foreigners in Egypt consular protection and special privileges, allowing them to amass fabulous fortunes, were abolished by the Montreux Convention of 1937. Although they lost their special status, their departure came later, when World War II, the Suez Aggression of 1956, and the subsequent sequestrations of the property of foreigners caused many to leave Egypt.

*Sahar Hamouda*

✦

**To the children of the house**
**Christian, Rudy, Cyrille, Doreen, and Molly**
**I dedicate these memories of yesterday**
**To those who are tomorrow**

"I am going to recount the story of my family to you. Don't pull a face, it's an extraordinary family."

"All families are extraordinary. Mine for example…"

"But my family is not out of the ordinary just on account of its members; its setting, climate and epoch are also extraordinary."

"All right then. Let's listen to this story."

"I forgot to warn you: It isn't a story in the normal sense."

"Why tell it to me?"

"To save from oblivion those grandmothers, aunts, houses, epochs, and antediluvian mentalities."

"A historical account? That sort of thing reads well and sells well nowadays."

"It's nothing like that. This book will never be read, even less published. At least not in my lifetime.…The action takes place in Egypt. No, not the Egypt of the pharaohs, but that of the khedives. However, compared to present-day Egypt, it seems just as distant. But that isn't exactly correct: The action does not take place in Egypt, but in Alexandria. It's not the same thing. Alexandria may not be Europe, but it's not Africa, either. It's the Levant. It's one of the ports of the Levant, and a gateway to the Mediterranean. This city has been a meeting place for people of all races for twenty centuries or so. It's a city with a renowned past of which there remains nothing, neither lighthouse nor library."

"So there is neither light nor culture?"

"You're obliging me say it: What there is, is commerce —onions, rice, and later on cotton. It's a city whence people from all over Europe, Syria, Palestine, and Armenia come to try their fortune. A city where Greek, Armenian, Spanish, Italian, and all the European languages, as well as Arabic of course, are spoken. However, the aristocracy speaks French (or more precisely 'Franquette,' a language made up of borrowings, Mediterraneanisms, with a lilting accent full of flavor).... These are the houses of the great Alexandrian families, whose more or less penniless offspring constitute our aristocracy and adorn our drawing rooms. In front of this house, which you insist on not calling a palace, you must take off your hat and make a deep bow: This is my grandfather's house."

"At last I've understood. It's the story of your grandfather that you are going to recount."

"I've already told you, it isn't a story. Where would it begin? And where would such a story end? At the birth of the ancestor? Of the grandfather? Or better, the day he made his fortune? Or better still, the day of his ennoblement, when he became a count? Or would it be better, for clarity's sake, to explain the distant and forgotten origins of the family in its birthplace, Damascus. (Descendants of Ubaldine, a Florentine crusader, according to the jokers and the gullible; a peanut seller, claim jealous and malicious tongues.) But how can one speak of something one doesn't know? And when would it end, this story? At the death of the grandmother? What a shame... for it would have hardly begun. And anyway, she passed away only to be replaced by the next generation, who automatically had the same ideas, habits, and mannerisms. And we, the third generation, now that we've at last reached that age, don't we catch ourselves also adopting their ideas, habits and customs?"

So it will have to be a slice of that family's life, not chosen by chance, nor because it seems the most interesting, nor the most essential. But because it is the one we lived through: our childhood, our youth, and our adulthood. Sifting through these three stages, it will be the most characteristic memories that are chosen.

Grandfather passed away well before I was born. Who was this grandfather? He was the forefather, full stop. He wasn't the one who left his native Damascus, but the one who made his fortune, was ennobled, and had ten children. So I stand corrected: He *was* the forefather, but that is not all there is to be said in the matter.

To me he was a legendary figure who appeared in portraits. Each house has its own portrait of him. Each one faithfully reproduced the same sallow, Asian features with high cheekbones, the same drooping moustache, the same cold, dark eyes. But the portrait that his widow, my grandmother, had of him, was the most beautiful one, because while all the portraits had the coat of arms and the coronet somewhere on the canvas, in hers he was wearing his consul's uniform. (My grandfather, of Syrian origin, living in Egypt, with an Italian passport, was consul of Portugal. His brother was the Danish consul. I never discovered why those countries chose them or how they came into the family's sphere of influence.) His chest was studded with innumerable medals, insignia, crosses, and ribbons. A sword hung by his side. Yet despite these obvious symbols of prestige, whenever we found ourselves alone in front of the portrait, disrespectful and mischievous children that we were, we would with the greatest pleasure carry out what we called the "Salute to the Forefather": All together, in three grand gestures, we would place our thumbs on our noses and waggle our fingers at him in style. It gave us the greatest of thrills. At a recent dinner party, a foreign guest speaking about the Egyptian nobility, the counts and barons, said that they had all arrived barefoot from their villages. I tried to defend my grandfather's origins, but merely succeeded in completely embarrassing the blundering guest. And anyway, what did I know about what my grandfather was wearing on his feet when he arrived from distant Syria? (And anyhow, it wasn't he, but his father who came from faraway Syria. It was my great-grandfather who was the immigrant.) I don't even know how he made his fortune. Before writing this book, I consulted all the uncles, aunts, and cousins who remained from the older generation. No one could help me. Various opinions were put forward. Even money-lending was suggested. But I dismissed this suggestion because money-lending doesn't make one rich. Well, not very, anyway. Grandfather was incredibly wealthy. You can judge for yourself: His two elder sons having lost a million on the stock exchange, he covered their debts without the slightest discomfort, and shortly after this, his legacy, divided between the ten children, left each one very comfortably off.

Someone suggested that the khedive had given him lots of land. Actually, he did receive some. Ah well, that was the *belle époque*, when plots of land were distributed just like cups of tea: "Would you care for another? Can I give you some more?" However, the khedive was distributing these plots of land so that the burgeoning towns of Cairo and Alexandria would expand quickly. The basic condition was that these plots should be built upon, and one had to be wealthy to build. So my grandfather must already have been rich.

What probably happened is this: My grandfather must have speculated on cotton during the American War. Those were the days when the price of cotton was so dear that everyone was emptying their mattresses to sell the cotton.

Oh cotton! The lifeblood of Alexandria! Everything goes into decline and dies, or becomes abundance and wealth, according to your rate on the exchange. In my grandfather's hands, you were transformed into property and luxury, into a large and powerful family. You became a coronet.

Grandmama used to talk about the house, which had burned down during the Orabi events of 1882. It used to have a blue drawing room, she would say, as well as a red one, a green, a yellow, and a white one, in addition to an enormous ballroom....

The family fled in 1882. People used to take flight periodically in those days. When it was not on account of "events," it was due to pestilence or cholera. There were a variety of scourges. I imagine people would greet each other by saying: "Good morning, how are you? When are you fleeing?" The family returned to find the house in ashes (according to general rumor, it had been pillaged by Hassan first) and my grandparents went to live in another of their properties, the one I described, where I would visit my grandmother, and where she later died.

Now is the time to mention a family anecdote that is supposed to be true. It's a priceless anecdote at dinner parties, where it has enabled me to outshine everyone, and I never miss a chance to relate it whenever the conversation turns to the mysteries of spiritualism, second sight, telepathy, and premonitions, each guest recounting his or her limited experience in the matter.

So here it is: My grandparents used to live in one of those "palaces" that was later burned down. Their second son, Gabriel, was living in the house I knew, which later became my grandmother's. Gabriel's first child was born there, and my grandfather was asked to hold the child over the baptismal font. The ceremony took place in the large drawing room (the one with the gilded furniture, gigantic chandelier, and ornate portrait). Suddenly, my grandfather turned pale and staggered. We rushed up, surrounding and questioning him, upon which he explained: "I saw myself dead, lying in state on a catafalque in this drawing room." "Rubbish," said my grandmother. "Even if the Almighty decided to take you from us, there's no reason why your body should be laid in state here and not in your own house."

"That may be so," replied my grandfather, "but that's what I saw."

Then, in 1882 the Orabi events took place. My grandparents' house, or "palace," had burned down, and Gabriel had offered them his. The bedrooms faced south and grandpapa couldn't take the heat, so his bed was taken down to the large drawing room. He fell ill and died there. Then his body was laid in state there, making his vision come true....

The years passed, people were born and others died, regimes changed and towns grew. Mentalities were transformed.

My grandmother was no longer with us. She had been replaced by a triumvirate of her three daughters. (This triumvirate, just like the three musketeers, was in fact four, because it included a niece, Aida.)... When I start speaking of them, I have to put my pen down with emotion. Will I be able to do it? I feel too nervous. For in addition to being interesting individually, as a trio they were priceless. I will start by trying to sketch the main traits of their personalities.

The oldest, Rosine, no doubt was once a child, a young bride, a mother and all the rest. At least that's what they say. But I do not believe a word of it. How could I? When I first knew her she was a grandmother, then she became a great-grandmother, then finally a great-great-grandmother. When I congratulated her upon the latter occasion, she answered, "Darling, let us not speak of it, let us forget these sad things." For she considered that it aged her. Becoming old was her worst fear. She had taught her granddaughters to call her aunt, because she thought that that gentle word, grandmother, made her look old. Oh vengeful gods! You transformed one of those who called her aunt into a grandmother herself. These newcomers, these great-great-grandchildren—how the devil were they supposed to address her without aging her too much?

Rosine was a thrifty, selfish, harsh realist. When her husband Emile's illness prevented her from going on holiday to Stresa, she complained bitterly about this tiresome, unforeseen impediment. (It was Emile who was the tiresome impediment.) Then she was seen showing off a new diamond and sapphire bracelet to those around her. She had christened it "Stresa." It consoled the young sixty-year-old bride.

When Emile passed away after several hours of agony, Rosine asked someone to telephone Bon Marché. She wanted to know whether the shop would agree to take back the newly delivered pajamas.

Rosine has always been heartless. She must have a stone in place of a heart. But stones do not wear down, and that is why she carries her ninety-four years so cheerfully. The one who does not wear her years so cheerfully is her poor daughter, whose life is paralyzed and consists solely of looking after her mother: getting her up, putting her to bed, feeding her, and giving her doses of the stimulant Coramine. For she naïvely believes that Coramine has an effect on stones.

Having a stone in place of a heart is infinitely practical. The hearts of mothers bleed dry if death takes their child away, but a stone does not bleed. A mother's heart is wrung with anguish, and she makes sacrifices for her child if it does not have the same comforts she does. But you cannot wring a stone.

So that is why Rosine has reached the age of ninety-four, plump, serene, blissfully happy and full of the joy of life. One day, when everything seemed to be going wrong, her daughter Aida said: "The agent is claiming that the apartment blocks need repairs, the cook is sick, I've got a migraine, and I've had to do accounts all morning. I've had enough of this life." Then, too, Christine said, "I have got to give a dinner party next week, so I must have a new dress made. My three canary chicks have died. Oh, I've had enough of this life." And Marie was saying, "The children came home at midnight yesterday, I was sick with worry. And tonight they are invited to go all the way to Ramleh. Oh, I've had enough of this life." Then, from the depths of her armchair, and of her ninety-three years, Rosine declared, "Well, I haven't."

One morning, Aida found her shining like a reliquary, wearing all her sparkling jewels. When she showed surprise at this unusual early morning display of wealth, Rosine explained, "I have so little time left to make the best of them."

Ah yes! Full of the joy of life, she eats well, sleeps well, and smiles at everything around her. She is completely senile, but that is her right and the condition hardly bothers her. The doctors take the greatest of care at her slightest indisposition, and she recovers quickly. The world marvels at her miraculous constitution, but it does not know her secret. When she dies, if she dies, which I greatly doubt, the autopsy will reveal it: A stone in place of a real flesh-and-blood heart.

Now Isabelle is the family's crowning glory. She has everything, simply everything. She is beautiful, blond, rich, and she is a lady-in-waiting. She started under the khedive, then under the sultan, and finished under the king. Isabelle is a slice of Egypt's history in her own right. I told you she has everything. Ah, but I was forgetting… She has the most beautiful house in town. Ask her if you do not believe me. She is the most prestigious person in Egypt. Her receptions, her elegance, and her graciousness are well known. Isabelle is such a brilliant character that I deliberated for a long time over whether I should make her the central focus of the book, the focal point in whose orbit the other characters would revolve.

She has had one big love in her life: Antony. On his account she refused the millionaire who asked for her hand. Because of him she married on the rebound a humble cousin, since the man she loved could not make up his mind to ask for her hand in marriage.

Actually, she lived a happy life with this humble cousin. In the beginning he was a mere civil servant, then she swept him into her glory and he died a pasha. Widowed, she had a superb mausoleum built for him in the main alley of the cemetery. However, some ghastly nouveaux riches built their tomb right next to it. "It's inconceivable," she said. "Dreadful people whom no one knows. And they want to be on the main alley next to my poor Joseph."

Her new widowhood gave her a burst of hope: Would Antony make his mind up? He almost did. Isabelle awaited his announced visit throughout the morning. But Antony had met Jacques the previous day, and Jacques—the swine, Isabelle told me as she recounted the story—had warned Antony: "You know women. When they bury one husband, they always bury the next one, too." Antony took this as a certainty, and Isabelle waited in vain.

It did not matter; she continued to live happily all the same. He was always there. He would send her sweets and flowers and attend her lavish receptions. He suddenly died of heart disease, and she was grief-stricken.…

Isabelle has presided over one of the salons of Alexandria, if you will pardon the expression. She adored everyone and everyone adored her. All the princes and princesses, all the crowned heads who came to Egypt, visited Isabelle's house. Each of these royal personages has left his or her mark in the form of an autographed photo on Isabelle's piano.…

Now that the moment has arrived to describe Marie, I find myself perplexed. I observe that the three sisters, whom we always judge as a whole—saying, "They have the same character, same tastes, language, habits, customs, and values"—are actually very different.

We have seen that Rosine went through life guided by her love of money, that Isabelle was mainly concerned with worldly vanities. Marie, on the other hand, was a mother, and likewise a grandmother. Her life was consumed by anxiety that a misfortune (heaven forbid) might happen to her daughters, their children, or their spouses. Yet do not imagine for a moment that her daughters were missionaries or worked in an explosives factory, or that they had married explorers. Both of them live, together with their families, calmly under the same roof as their mother. Nevertheless, Marie is in a continual state of anguish.

When they go out, she has to know at what time they will be back. And what of the children? They often go to the cinema without specifying which one. So she also wonders when they will come home.

She sees herself as the central nervous system of this organism, as the administrative headquarters of this regiment, or the transmitting relay station that has to keep in perpetual contact with all parties. And this effort has aged her. Although the youngest of the three sisters, she looks the oldest and is in ill health. Nevertheless, although ill and powerless, she still sees herself as the nerve center, the headquarters, or the Eiffel Tower as it were, wanting to organize each person's day, knowing their arrival and departure times, preparing the daily schedule of each family member....

I close my eyes to visualize more clearly. I can see Marie climbing the stairs with difficulty, supported by her daughters. The rest of the family follows in procession, with the dog leading the way. This scene would occur twice a day. Marie would clamor for all of them and they would all come. She would call out, "Come to help me." Although it was only possible for two people to support her, she demanded that they all come. She would only be content and happy with all of them there. I can only remember this scene, I can not conjure its image because my eyes are filled with tears. It is the very essence of Marie, of maternal love.

So that is a brief sketch of the three sisters. Now, Dora, help me to quote all those fleeting remarks that would fill us with joy at the time, and that it would be criminal to allow to be forgotten in the depths of time. Remind me how they used to meet daily to take tea at the fashionable tearoom of the day. They were ninety-two, eighty-five, and seventy-five years of age respectively, and would be covered in silk, fur, feathers, and diamonds. Rosine and Isabelle would be wearing competing coats. For some time these coats would be a source of rivalry, but their escort, Nicolas, restored harmony by telling them, "Mink suits blonds, whilst otter-skin is perfect for brunettes."...

Isabelle orders her dresses from the masters of couture in Paris. She receives them with transports of delight and then stuffs them into the wardrobe. But Isabelle is eighty-five. The era of her youth, when she would be invited and herself invite people, is over. The world has a short memory. Receptions are few and far between. So, while waiting for an opportunity to wear the dresses, every morning Isabelle rings briskly three times to summon her three chambermaids. They come running and take the dresses out of their place of safekeeping. The dresses are spread out. Isabelle gazes at them, comments on them, studies them, and tries them on. Then the unhappy dresses shudder with horror, for they know that they will not escape the torture.

Isabelle arms herself with a pair of giant scissors. Just as mute as the dresses, the chambermaids also shudder with horror. Although the ritual is repeated each day, they cannot get used to it. Isabelle cuts and cuts and cuts. She slashes the precious fabric that the dressmaker has so laboriously designed. The steel blades cut away in a wild zigzag, and scraps of fabric are strewn all over the carpet. The morning is over. Each afternoon the three chambermaids try to sew together the pieces of their mistress's puzzle. Each night the dresses sleep in the wardrobe to recover from the shock of the operation. The following morning a new day is born and it all begins again....

So these are the three sisters, whom you have now seen one by one and as a group. I have tried to show you their individual character traits. Now I want to concentrate on the very important traits that they had in common and that are, I believe, the key to all their actions and to their perfect mutual understanding.

The first is their Ismailian mentality.

At the time of the Khedive Ismail, rich families had slaves. These *sais* would run flat out ahead of the carriages. The Capitulations were working wonderfully, without anyone giving a thought for what was happening in a lakeside town called Montreux. The Europeans enjoyed a prestige without equal. The khedive was trying at any price to obtain the protection of a great power. Life was simple and easy. If by chance an untoward complication arose, one simply had to make one's identity known. One would say, "I am so-and-so and I will speak to my consul...".

Then the native would bow respectfully. Words such as union, socialism, communism, and Bolshevism were unknown. In fact, fifty years later they still haven't penetrated into the minds of our three heroines. The mind must be young and flexible to absorb new concepts—but theirs was young and flexible back in the reign of Ismail. Just like a stamp or a coin, their minds received the imprint of the sovereign's effigy. Today, stamps and coins bear a different image, but the minds of the three sisters still clearly bear the rare, precious, and old effigy of a past mentality. For example, in Italy the plebiscite was about to happen. Isabelle is a royalist, having dined a few times in her life with members of the House of Savoy. That is why she is a royalist and she felt certain that the country would choose the monarchy. Incidentally, the country did not choose the monarchy, but maybe that is because not all the voters had dined several times in their lives with members of the House of Savoy. Janie, on the other hand, did not believe in the return of the king, for, she said, "I interviewed the man in the street in Milan and Naples: chauffeurs, workmen, waiters...."

"Do those kinds of people count?" came the reply.... During the [Second World] war, on an occasion when an air raid bombing had been especially violent and unpleasant, Rosine, who was taking tea at the Yacht Club in the port, said, "It's intolerable. We should complain to the board. The subscription fees are high enough without having to put up with this."

In order to flee the air raids, Isabelle and Rosine went to live in the suburbs.... In a neighboring field a Bedouin had some goats. It was the mating season. The goats knew it and were proclaiming it loudly. Very loudly. So loudly in fact that Isabelle sent Aida to the Bedouin on the following astounding mission: "Tell him who I am. Show him my visiting card with lady-in-waiting to the queen printed beneath my name and make him silence his goats."

Isabelle bought a motor car. She drove it for a week all over the place in every corner of Alexandria. At the end of the week, she discovered that really, a saloon car would be much pleasanter than this open touring car. "Aida darling, go and tell the agent who sold me the car to return the money and take it back." When Aida, who was taken aback, began to object, her mother continued, "Tell him that the king forbids me to go out in an open car because I might catch cold."

That is the Ismailian mentality.

The other character trait that should be evident from the previous pages—and if it is not, it must be my fault—is that, in a nutshell, they did not know they were old.

Do you remember, Dora, the day you admired Isabelle's earrings? "My darling, when I am old, I shall give them to you," kindly replied Isabelle, who was approaching her eighty-sixth year....

Oh, Dora, how kind they were, how funny, and how they did not deserve to suffer the implacable law that dictates that all things must pass. You see, Dora, you have made me really laugh with all these old stories, and now I am left with an infinite sadness. Tomorrow is drawing near, is approaching with a sure and steady pace. I do not want to think of tomorrow. (Tomorrow came a few days after I had written the last anecdote, when Isabelle passed away peacefully. Six months later Marie followed her, and the bell tolled for Rosine a few years later.)

*Translated by Carole Escoffey*


## *Alia Khsasiya*
## WOMEN'S EMANCIPATION

Morocco 1950    Arabic

Alia Khsasiya, whose date of birth is unknown, grew up in a wealthy family in Fes. She received an education, mainly in Arabic, and became a journalist. Like many other educated women of her generation, she grew up in a nationalist environment in which Egypt was viewed as a model of cultural development, and expressed resistance to ancestral traditions that kept women homebound and powerless.

"Women's Emancipation" takes the form of a discussion between two young women, who focus on Egyptian women's activist work to advance women's rights. The text calls for Moroccan women to learn from the experience of Egyptian women, and confirms the importance of education as a tool for empowerment and emancipation. The two women also make reference to the Egyptian male feminist, Qasim Amin, whose pioneering 1899 book, *Tahrir Al-Mar'a* (The Liberation of Women) is considered a key work of Arab-Muslim feminism.

*Zakia Iraqui-Sinaceur*

♦

Night had unloosed its curtains and the city was hidden from sight. Moonlight glowed on the horizon; its rays played upon mountain peaks and tree branches, and penetrated into houses scattered here and there. The landscape enchanted me. It allowed my imagination to move freely toward the furthest horizon, and permitted my mind to linger on the beauties of nature. I could see this view through the eastern window of my office. Although I wanted to continue reading the book in my hands, I moved my chair closer to the window and sat looking out at the scene. My eyes moved from the pages of my book to the leaves of nature. I felt wondrously rewarded both by the natural beauty that delighted my senses and by the book's information about Arab women in Egypt. Two important motives had urged me to pursue reading this pleasant book near the window: a desire to enjoy the captivating landscape outside, and inside, a desire to understand the evolution of educated Arab women.

A moment later, I heard someone walking to the door, and then a knock. I stood up slowly because I wanted to leave neither my book nor the magical landscape. Reluctantly I walked to the door. My guest was Miss Bahia, a classmate and a neighbor. I politely welcomed my dear visitor and invited her to sit in the best chair in my office. By coincidence, she was holding the book I had been reading. I then became more interested in my friend and still more hospitable toward her. I was sure we were going to share the pleasures of the same book and the inspiring scene. I asked politely, "What book are you carrying, my dear friend?" She asked to postpone her answer until she described the reason for her visit. I listened to her with interest and satisfaction.

She stopped smiling and said, "You and every young woman who has spent a part of her life at school knows what I am going to say." She continued, "The school year has now ended. As you know, before leaving school, I prepared a special program for my summer holidays. In addition to my vacation, I decided to undertake some research on literacy and to write articles on women's living conditions. I began this work by reading two important books by Qasim Amin. I realized the important achievements of this professor who pleads for women in general and for Arab women in particular. Through these two books, I began to understand Qasim Amin's great interest in women's emancipation and in their active participation in public life. When I finished the two books, I decided to write a short paper to express my gratitude to Qasim Amin's thought and to his incessant struggle for women's education. Now I plan to send this paper to the press or the radio. So I would be grateful if you would read this paper before anyone else sees it. And of course, I'll tell you the name of the book you've asked about."

Yes, it was exactly the same book I was reading. Then she gave me the essay she had written. I began reading it eagerly, expecting to admire her style and the coherence of her organization.

But I was disappointed by her essay, which I thought would have been more interesting had she attempted to outline the different stages of women's emancipation in Egypt. Such historical information would have been extremely useful to

Moroccan women, who are eager to understand Qasem Amin's important ideas. It wasn't at all necessary to thank Qasim Amin, who had only done his duty.

While watching me read, my friend guessed what I was thinking. She asked, hesitantly, "Does my essay displease you?"

I answered that I was pleased and displeased at the same time: I felt pleased because her essay was excellent; but I felt displeased because I would have preferred her to write about a more essential subject. She asked for more details.

"You should have shed light upon the degree of emancipation of Egyptian women. This would have helped to make Moroccan women optimistic and confident about their possible success. They might then decide to spend more time in study and the acquisition of knowledge until they reached Egyptian women's levels of education, development, and emancipation. But it is too late now. No need to speak longer about that subject."

I stopped talking for a while, and then I changed the topic of our conversation and opened the window, which the wind had shut. I asked her opinion about woman's status in Morocco. According to her, "Young women in Morocco have not made an impact on their society until quite recently, because of the traditional social order in which they lived amid the plagues of illiteracy and ignorance. Young women often seem to lack intelligence and motivation and seem unable to adapt to the process of modernization. As a result, they are not viewed as useful members of society.

"Ignorance makes women's lives harder, and traditional social beliefs are responsible for their troubles. This situation is slowly changing thanks to the new solid links between Egypt and Morocco. Women's education is one of the reasons for women's emancipation in Egypt. Moroccan women must follow suit under the leadership of His Majesty King Mohammed Ben Youssef, who stresses the need for girls' education in modern Moroccan culture. He laid the foundations for such advances by establishing schools and institutes of education for women. The first product of this great change is Princess Aisha, who is a symbol of hope for women. All Moroccan young women consider their dear princess a role model. With a great thirst for learning, young Moroccan women now go to school in order to acquire knowledge, and later, to enable them to participate in the development and modernization of their country."

Then my friend stood up to relax and continued, "From this short presentation, you can conclude, my dear friend, that Moroccan women have already attained some cultural and educational progress. They are now about to experience a great literary rebirth. I am sure you would agree with me."

Then she stopped talking and listened to my point of view. I gave vent to my feelings and ideas. I confirmed all that she said. It was for me an opportunity to address a message to young girls: "Some young girls take much more interest in their appearance than in their qualifications. Our nation needs educated women, who are able to help men and society; it does not need superficially emancipated women. Finally, as a young Moroccan woman, I am sure that women in our country will achieve their goals and rights if they are dutiful, and decent, and ethical. Here's to your achievements, young women of Morocco!"

*Translated by Zakia Iraqui-Sinaceur and Moha Ennaji*

## Aisha Abdel Rahman
# THE HEIRESS

Egypt 1953    Arabic

Aisha Abdel Rahman—better known under her pen name, Bint al Shati'—was born in 1912 in Damietta, a town east of Alexandria on the Mediterranean coast. Both her parents came from religious families, and her father was an Azhar scholar, schooled in traditional Islamic theology and jurisprudence at Al-Azhar University, as well as a Sufist, a practitioner of the mystical dimension of Islam that emphasizes a deep, personal communion with God. In such a conservative environment, girls were not allowed to go to school, and Aisha Abdel Rahman received an education at home along Azharite lines: she learned the Qur'an by heart and studied Islam and the Arab sciences (the scientific method developed during the Islamic Golden Age, from the eighth through the thirteenth centuries). In 1929, she became one of the first young women in Egypt to earn the special women teacher's degree, and in 1950 she earned a doctorate. Throughout she had her mother's support, though not her father's. She was appointed to the Department of Arabic Language and Literature in Cairo University in 1939, and also, at various times, worked for the Ministry of Education, the Center for the Authentication of Heritage, and as visiting scholar at several Arab universities in Algiers, Rabat, Riyadh, and Khartoum.

Possibly as a result of her father's influence, Abdel Rahman was enamored of Sufi poetry and learned whole volumes by heart. At the age of eighteen, she began to publish short stories and articles for Egyptian newspapers and women's magazines, using the name Bint al Shati' (Daughter of the Riverbank) to hide her identity from her father—who discovered it eventually, but encouraged her to continue writing. She was deeply concerned with women's lives and with the lives of all Egyptian peasants, both of which figure in the story included here. Later she also became known for her work in Arabic literature and Islamic studies. Her nonfiction publications range from Qur'anic studies to literary, linguistic, and sociological research to a travel book on the Arabian Peninsula (*The Land of Miracles*, 1952) to an autobiography (*On the Bridge*, 1967). Her works of fiction include the short stories collections *The Secret of the Coast* (1952), *A Mistaken Woman* (1958), and *Snapshots of their Lives* (1959), and the novels *The Master of the Farm* (1944) and *The Return of Pharaoh* (1949).

*Sahar Hamouda*

When the servant announced the arrival of the health inspector, a sullen, watchful silence cloaked the bedroom. All eyes were fixed on the young doctor as he gravely walked over to inspect the dead body and determine the cause of the death.

It seemed as if the young woman was trying to withdraw from the bedroom. But a powerful invisible force paralyzed her movements and fixed her to the spot, pale, eyes wandering.

Suddenly, the silence was pierced by a low, mute gasp. It came from the young woman, who was standing next to the shrouded body. All eyes turned to her for a second, then moved away when the doctor began the process of inspection.

She did not have to wait long, for the doctor soon finished his task and announced that it was undoubtedly a natural death. The family of the deceased could begin to prepare for his funeral and his burial.

He then left, as he had come in, with slow, steady steps, a somber figure. It seemed that he was making an effort to avoid looking at the young woman who had gasped when she had seen him. But as soon as he got to his car, he threw himself into the back seat and gloomily began to remember....

Along the road from the palace of the old man who had died to the city of Mansoura forty kilometers away, his memory turned—in spite of himself—to the not too distant past, when the young woman he had seen a few hours earlier had worked as a maid in his family home.

In those days he did not know much. He was too involved in the study of medicine in the capital to concern himself with the trivial lives of unimportant people or to pay attention to what was happening in the limited world of his family, with its small events. He spent the academic year in the capital, and if he left it in the summer, it was to head for seaside resorts overflowing with friends.

And so the years followed one another, and he remained unaware of what most of the people of the area knew about the life of Zoheira, the lively maid. Her glowing youth and unique beauty were a curse to her. She moved from house to house with this curse dogging her steps, for in each house she worked, the envy of the mistress raised a cloud of suspicion about her.

She finally found a haven in the home of a generous merchant, who was willing to take her in despite the evil rumors surrounding her. The mistress of the house was a pious old woman who was charitable toward this poor hapless girl, and thought it a sin to pay attention to malicious tongues. And so the mistress provided a home and a refuge for the girl, unafraid that she would seduce the reclusive old man. Nor was she worried that the girl's beauty would bewitch her only son, who was studying medicine in the capital.

When the venerable woman died in the Holy Land, Zoheira felt there was no longer a place for her in the house. The son feared his father's feelings for her. He feared that if she remained close to the widower, in his loneliness and old age, she would end up marrying him and bringing shame and scandal upon the family. And the maid could even bear his father a small brood of children, who would gobble up a share of the awaited inheritance. These inferior brothers and sisters, born of the maid, would be a blemish upon his future. Thus, the doctor cruelly sent Zoheira from the house she had considered her refuge. That was the last he knew of her. He hadn't seen her again until today, during his examination of the dead rich man. He had ignored her, and knew nothing of her position in the palace. Only there, at that scene, had he begun to think of her again.

In the meantime, Zoheira remained in the bedroom of the deceased. She thought about the hardships she had faced after the doctor had expelled her from his father's house, the rejections and the wanderings and homelessness. She had decided never again to serve others in their homes. She chose a remote place on the outskirts of a town, where she lived with an old poor widow. She worked in the cottage, making brooms out of straw and fibers, which she sold to wandering vendors.

The poor widow was a kind aunt and a good friend to Zoheira, and in turn Zoheira drove away her loneliness and helped her with her modest business. Every week Zoheira would go out to the rice fields and palm groves on the outskirts of the town and return at nightfall laden with free materials, ample stock for at least ten days of hard work.

The young woman was content with her new life, which spared her the humiliation of service and bestowed upon her a blissful freedom. It seemed to her that she would never accept any other kind of life. She returned exhausted from her weekly rounds, but she always regained her vitality and health after a deep sleep.

Then, one day, she went out as usual to the palm groves in the suburbs. The time for her return came. She did not.

Her old aunt stayed up all night, sleepless, prey to all sorts of thoughts and worries.

With daybreak, the news spread in the neighborhood. People started making guesses as to the girl's whereabouts. Some said a demon had abducted her; others that she had been seduced by a young man on one of her trips; still others, that she had had an accident, or that night had fallen while she was far from home and she had had to spend the night with people she knew. . . . And anyway, soon things would come to light.

Things did come to light three days later, but not as people had guessed. A man from a remote region hurried toward the old widow and gave her a message from the missing girl. She said she was all right, that she was working in the palace of the master of the region, and that nothing marred her new life except sorrow at parting with her dearest friend and kindest aunt.

All were surprised by the news. The old aunt locked her cottage and set off with the messenger to the palace, to reassure herself that all was well with her darling niece. She came back two days later, bursting with happiness and the news that soon her girl Zoheira would rise very high indeed! Everyone knew that she was hinting, or hoping, that the young girl would get more than compassion from the old master.

They waited for days for news to arrive from the palace, but the days stretched to weeks and then months, and no news arrived. All they heard about her was that she was living in dignity and leisure under the patronage of the master, and that she supervised all the affairs of his palace.

Two years passed, and the abundance she enjoyed in the palace overflowed to the aunt and all the people of the neighborhood.

Then a surprise followed the death of the master.

Or maybe it was not a surprise, but people had stopped thinking about it after so much waiting for it. Finally, they heard that Zoheira had been the legal wife of the departed master. Their marriage had remained a secret until his death.

The details of how and when this marriage had taken place were lost in the latest news, that Zoheira had inherited from her husband 250 acres of the best arable land.

Since then, all eyes and tongues concentrated on the heiress. As soon as the months of mourning had passed, people began to list the names of those who had proposed to her—the wealthy ones and the fortune hunters. But she turned them all away. She spent a whole year in her widow's weeds, until people began to think that she had decided to remain a widow throughout her lifetime, out of loyalty to her benefactor.

But she disappointed them. As soon as she had commemorated the first anniversary of his death, she took off her mourning clothes, which was tantamount to the announcement of approaching nuptials.Who could the heiress have chosen from so many suitors? people wondered. Some said it was the doctor, who had in the past thrown her out of his father's house, humiliated and bereft. They didn't believe their ears, for they knew how Zoheira had suffered from that mortifying rejection. But those who visited the palace recounted how she laughed at the naiveté of those who dismissed the possibility of a match between her and the man she was bent on marrying as soon as he had finalized the procedures of terminating his engagement to his high-born fiancée, who did not own half the land that Zoheira the maid had inherited.

Those who found the whole thing suspicious only had to go to the palace—whose doors were open to all those she had known in her days of misery and homelessness—to hear from her what she delighted in repeating: How eagerly she awaited her wedding to the man who had expelled her from his family's home, for fear of the shame that would follow should his father marry the maid!

The wedding was held with great pomp and ceremony, and an obscene lavishness never before seen in the region.

The doctor invited his friends, who came from good families. They were greeted by a crowd of poor farmers and small manufacturers and wandering vendors, invited to the wedding by their own friend, the bride. To soften the blow, the groom claimed before his well-bred friends that his good bride had wanted to make the poor happy on this memorable night.

But that day was followed by others like it. Every time he invited an aristocratic guest, his wife shocked him by behaving like a low-born, nouveau riche, vulgar woman. When he objected to this behavior, which embarrassed him in front of his colleagues and guests, she would say that she was—as he well knew—only a lowly maid!

She promised a thousand times that she would try to improve her manners, but it was a cynical promise that ended, every time, with the declaration that she could not resist deep-rooted habits, or conquer her instincts and hereditary forces.

He advised her to, among other things, cut her ties with her wretched past and with those she had known in her days of wandering in the region to gather straw and fiber. She promised him she would, but it was no more than a promise.

She was certain he could not escape from the hell of life with her. The lands she had inherited tied him to her with thick chains from which there was no escape, except by death or madness.

The torture exhausted him. His nerves were stretched beyond endurance and his reason wandered. In his unholy madness, he tried to put an end to his suffering without allowing the heiress, who had led him to this purgatory, to escape.

His polluted soul urged him to poison her, drop by slow drop. But her intelligence and caution overcame his instability and dementia, and she escaped unscathed. He was carried off to the sanatorium, incurably mad.

The curtain came down on this chapter of the story. Later raised, the view revealed the heiress as a well-mannered free woman, and the doctor as a poor madman who had lost everything.

*Translated by Sahar Hamouda*

# *Zhor Lhiyania, Fatima Ali Mernissi, Hiba Elbaqali, Aziza Kerzazi, and Fatima Bourqadia*
## TO LALLA RADIA, OUR ETERNAL LIGHTHOUSE

Morocco 1955    Arabic

The woman to whom this letter is addressed, Lalla Radia Ouazzani Chahdi was born in 1919 into a wealthy family in Fes and received a religious education at the hands of a *fqiha*, a female teacher of religious matters, who was brought to the house by her family. Although illiterate, Lalla Radia had a sharp mind and a wide knowledge of life. She was very much aware of the circumstances of her country, and chose to contribute to Morocco's independence and state-building by financing the nationalist movement. One of her deepest concerns was women's education, and she helped many poor women by paying for their study and their marriages. After witnessing the suffering of young women who earned a primary school certificate and were unable to continue their studies because the city had no secondary school for them, she decided to pay for the building of a house in Fes to be transformed into a high school for girls. Working together with Malika El-Fassi, she found volunteer teachers for the high school and enabled many young female students to earn their diplomas.

Some of the women Lalla Radia's efforts helped educate became primary school teachers and dedicated themselves to educating other young girls. Among these were the five signers of this letter, which was found in the archives of the Fes city council. These five women were born in the second decade of the twentieth century and educated in private schools built by Moroccan nationalists. All were acquainted with Lalla Radia, who may have been instrumental in funding their own educations. As a token of their gratitude and admiration, the five teachers decided to contribute money to Lalla Radia's initiative. They read this letter and presented the money to Lalla Radia on 18 November 1955, which is celebrated as Independence Day in Morocco because it marks the triumphant return to Morocco of the monarch, Sultan Mohammed V, after his exile by the French. They associated their nation's freedom from the shackles of colonialism with women's freedom from the bonds of illiteracy

*Jouhara Filali Baba*

✦

11 November 1955
To the honorable Lalla Radia, may you continue to be our eternal lighthouse.
Dear Lalla Radia, the honorable president, may God protect you.

We are very pleased with your noble and sustained help and service to the people. We appreciate your good deeds, which give evidence of your vision and charity. Your qualities make us all proud and grateful. On the occasion of the independence of Morocco, we are very happy to write to you as one of the fervent supporters of an independent Morocco. You built schools and encouraged education, although you have not yourself benefited from education. God has realized the hopes of Muslims in general and Moroccans in particular. He has also made our dreams come true through education. In honor of your memorable deeds, we are contributing a small amount of money to support the work you have begun.

May God preserve you, your work, and your good deeds.

Signers:
Zhor Lhiyania
Fatima Ali Mernissi
Hiba Elbaqali
Aziza Kerzazi
Fatima Bourqadia

*Translated by Moha Ennaji*

# Djamila Débêche
## ALIENATION
Algeria   1955   French

Djamila Débêche remains an underappreciated author, despite her major contributions both to early Algerian Francophone literature and the beginnings of the Algerian feminist movement. Born in Setif, on the eastern side of the Atlas Mountains, in 1926, she was educated in French schools.

In 1947, she launched the review *L'Action*, which was dedicated to women's issues. She also published the nonfiction books *Les Musulmans algériens et la scolarisation* (Muslim Algerians and Education) in 1950 and *L'Enseignement de la langue arabe en Algérie et le droit de vote aux femmes algériennes* (The Teaching of the Arabic Language in Algeria and Women's Right to Vote) in 1951, both advocating education, suffrage, and other political rights for women.

Djamila Débêche was one of the first Algerian women to write novels in French, and to reflect upon the alienated lives of Algerian women. In the 1940s and 1950s, nationalist male intellectuals in Algeria were writing about the alienation inflicted by French colonialism, which imposed itself in an increasingly brutal way in response to the growing Algerian independence movement. Débêche was unique, however, in subtly conveying the dual alienation suffered by Algerian women, as subjects of both colonial and patriarchal oppression.

In her first novel, *Leila, jeune fille d'Algérie* (Leila, a Young Woman from Algeria), published in 1947, Débêche voices the contradictions born of receiving a French education while living in a traditional Muslim society. The protagonist is both bewitched by the principles of the French "civilizing mission" and disgusted by her people's traditional way of life, while at the same time hoping that the two societies will come together in harmony. In *Aziza*, published in 1955, Débêche presents a protagonist whose sense of alienation runs even deeper than Leila's. As the following excerpt from the novel illustrates, Aziza feels alien among both her own people and the French. This novel reflects the paradoxical situation in which Algerian men, who were struggling against foreign domination and racial inequality, nonetheless opposed their countrywomen's struggle against gender inequality. *Aziza* clearly reflects women's position as "the colonized of the colonized."

Débêche's whereabouts became unknown after Algeria won its independence in 1962, undoubtedly because she had chosen to become a naturalized French citizen during the colonial period and thus had little choice but to leave the country. Apart from an article on Isabelle Eberhardt published in 1964, there is no record of any literary production during her later life.

*Zahia Smail Salhi*

✦

It was at a European party that I was reunited with Ali Kemal after so many years. I was working for a very busy press agency, which left me with so little leisure time that I hesitated for a while before deciding to accept Laura Berthier's invitation. As soon as she had settled in Algeria, a little over three years ago, Laura B., wife of a senior civil servant, became friends with a group of people among whom I figured. Invitations to her receptions were in great demand. for on each occasion, she treated her guests to a pleasant surprise. This time, the visiting card announced a concert by the great Anne Lires, an old high school friend.

It was six o'clock when I reached the Berthiers, whose apartment overlooked the Parc de Galland in the center of Algiers. Dressed in a blue jersey dress that suited me rather nicely, I entered the lounge, where people were already gathering in small groups. A sharp note of female laughter pierced through the great hullabaloo.

Laura Berthier came over to greet me.

"Nice to see you," she said. "Your Muslim female compatriots do so rarely accept invitations."

I glanced around and recognized several people. I complimented my friend. "Your party is a success. Ah! Here comes Mme. Brahil. ..."

Fakia Brahil, an Algerian Muslim like myself, was in possession of a spirit that I found most displeasing. She had changed her name to "Francine." As for me, I have never considered camouflaging my origins.

On one occasion—toward the end of 1944—I had to go to the Maritime Health Service in order to take care of some formalities for my passage to Marseilles, where I wanted to visit some relatives.. The place was crowded and it was announced that the travelers should split into two groups: the Europeans on one side and the Muslims on the other. I naturally joined my female compatriots wrapped in their white veils. Unhappy with what he took to be an error, a young male nurse began heading toward me. "Come on Mademoiselle! Go to the other side. Can't you see that this side is for the Muslims?"

I handed him my identity card.

He read my name and left without comment. My compatriots, on the other hand, scrutinized me, but with great surprise rather than sympathy. I was overwhelmed by a strong feeling of embarrassment. I belonged in neither of the two groups. Fakia, on the other hand, had chosen the West, and in excess. Always overdressed, and in the latest Parisian manner, she discarded Muslim customs and severed all ties with Arab families she knew. She was not especially concerned with other people's opinions of her. The immense wealth that her aging husband bestowed upon her allowed her to live as she pleased.

Together with Laura Berthier, I headed toward a group of people that included the novelist Cécile Laurane. She greeted me effusively. This was in marked contrast to the polite reception I received from some gentlemen in the group.

We soon realized how difficult it was to maintain a conversation in the presence of Cécile Laurane. She was quite deaf, and in order to follow the discussion, kept asking questions without being able to understand the answers. I tried to avoid a university lecturer known for his harshness toward Muslim students. His complacency disgusted me. It was said that he dyed his moustache and his hair on a regular basis. This thought amused me, especially because his physical appearance remained repellent nonetheless.

I also tried to avoid Irène Durer, a journalist chattering to a group of people. She was too proud of her influential friends and her professional status, which had followed the publication of a series of newspaper reports. I had particularly begun to dislike her after an incident that occurred between us at a charity bazaar, where we were distributing clothes and sweets to Muslim children.

At a certain point during the distribution, Irène Durer leaned toward me. "We will never succeed in civilizing these people," she whispered.

I was about to object to her claims when she added, "You do not know them well enough, dear Mademoiselle! Believe me, it will take another century or perhaps even two before we will be able to raise them to an acceptable standard of living."

Not long after her assertion, someone called my name. Irène Durer stared at me. She was both dumbfounded and furious because of her mistake. From that moment on, she has harbored a merciless resentment toward me, particularly because I left without saying good-bye.

She was conspicuously made-up and rather overdressed, which only added to her imposing height. I passed her by without so much as a greeting. From a distance, I saw Mlle. Cordier. She was famous for her extravagant flower hats and her cane. Mlle. Cordier's stick was notorious in the quarter of La Rue de Tanger, where she had resided since her retirement as a professor. She continuously threatened the small *yaouleds*, street boys, who howled at her window. All to no avail, however, as it was always the *yaouleds* who proved victorious, for after a few small whacks of her cane, she invariably ended up giving them sweets and coins.

I wondered, as I looked at the magnificent white piano, what was making Anne Lirès so late. At that moment I sensed someone observing me. I found myself being scrutinized by a young man. He was standing alone near the patio door, a bit taller than average, slim, and dressed in a dark gray suit and white shirt that stood out against his brightly colored necktie. I turned away briskly. Fortunately, I somehow managed to hear my companion's last words and answer her question.

The arrival of Anne Lirès, escorted by Mme. Berthier, gave rise to a prolonged murmur. I was just about to tell my high school friend how happy I was to see her again when she greeted me with her charming smile. I felt the gaze of the unknown man passing over me. He was standing by a window facing me. He was talking to Judge Cartier without taking his eyes off me. Cartier, whom I knew, approached me. "One of your countrymen would like to be introduced to you. He is from your region."

The young man in a gray suit and red tie came toward me.

"M. Ali Kemal," said Cartier.

"We, in fact, are both natives of the Beni-Ahmed, Mademoiselle!"

I frowned, giving the appearance that I was trying to remember. "Really!"

"Mme Berthier has told me a lot about you. Our families were once close. We knew each other as kids. I hope your memories will resurface."

He was smiling all the time, a rather wry smile. In fact, I did have some recollection of the Kemal belonging to our tribe.

"What a surprise!" I said nonchalantly to Laura.

Mme Berthier looked satisfied. She was about to say something when the pianist, Anne Lirès, sat down, gathered herself for a moment, and began to play a Brahms sonata.

I was dreaming....Yes, I do belong to the Beni-Ahmed, just like Ali Kemal. As a child, I used to curl up in my father's *burnus*, a woolen cloak, in the evenings and listen to long tales about our Arabian ancestors, who had descended from the noble tribe of Quraysh. But for me, the *douar*, our tribe, represented neither the glorious ancestry of which he was so proud nor the immense desert crossed only rarely by small caravans heading toward some milder region. I could not even hear the gallop of the horses as they brought the chief and his men back to the tribe.

Beni-Ahmed for me was Ali and my young friends. Ali did not mingle very much with our noisy clan, but he remained my favorite companion. My exuberance as a child stood in stark contrast to his seriousness, which he displayed at the early age of seven. He used to play nostalgic melodies on his flute for me and I would listen for a long time. One day, he left with his parents for the city. Zina, Djerid, and I were stricken with sadness and dismay. He never returned. Some months later, I lost my mother, then my father, and so I too left the *douar*.

Anne Lirès completed the sonata. I was trying to observe Ali discretely. At one stage, our eyes met. He, too, was remembering!

As soon as the pianist reached the last chords, she was greeted with applause. Some of the guests rushed toward my friend to give her their compliments. I did not move. Ali Kemal leaned toward me. I heard him whisper in my ear, "What are we doing here? This is not our milieu. Shall we leave now? We can talk about our childhoods."

I accepted his invitation. Had it come from another, I would surely have refused. We left without being noticed. A short time later, we sat with cups of tea in a small but very smart tearoom on the Rue Michelet. We were both troubled. It was Cartier who had invited him to Laura Berthier's party. Ali told me that he lived in Saint-Eugène, on the outskirts of Algiers, and that his father, Sheikh Mostefa, was a high official in the Islamic legislature. His mother, Lalla Farida, was still fit and healthy. His sister had been given in marriage to a courtroom interpreter and his brother, Allel, who had married Zina, lived with them. Djerid, our childhood playmate, was a chemist in the city of Blida.

"As for me," he added, "I am a solicitor with the Algiers bar."

I, too, spoke. Ali listened with great interest. He seemed happy to meet me again. I narrated my life story from the time I left the *douar*. In the end he made me promise to see him again.

This time, too, I accepted. The young boy I had known twenty years ago could still exert his power over me.

Our meetings became very regular. I rediscovered some of Ali's traits. He remained the calm and reserved person he had always been. Yet in his eyes I could clearly see a kind of tenderness that moved me deeply each time he looked at me with his smiling face....

Ali made me meet Djerid by surprise....I had a long conversation with him. It did not take me long, however, to realize that he had become embittered. He disliked everything related to the West. Right from the beginning of our conversation, I was refuting some of his arguments, which I found to be a rather amusing game. I gave special attention to his French education, which was responsible for his liberal, honorable, and lucrative profession. He quickly became upset and his voice rose. "I am a fervent supporter of the political groups who defend our customs," he said. "You admire everything Western," he added.

Allel, who was sitting with us, looked both interested and amused by our conversation. With his mocking air he observed me and watched my reactions.

I promptly responded, "I am not talking politics."

The two men looked at each other. I sensed that they were not speaking their minds and that they did not like me.

For weeks on end, I led a happy life. Many small things enriched my existence....

Gradually, Allel began to show a great interest in me. One day, he asked me about my plans and feigned respect for the love that linked me to his brother.

"I know that Ali loves you," he said. "But you see, we live in an Arab fashion. As for yourself, you had better marry a European man."

The elegant Western outfit he was wearing made me doubt the sincerity of his words. He wasn't even wearing a fez.

*Translated by Zahia Smail Salhi*

## *Fatima Kabbaj*
## REMOVAL OF THE VEIL AND DECENCY

Morocco 1956    Arabic

Born in Fes in 1932, Fatima Kabbaj learned the Qur'an at Dar Fqiha, a religious school for young girls, and went on to attend secondary school, where she undertook an intensive program of Arabic language and literature. In 1955, after a women's section had been established at the Al-Qarawiyin University, Kabbaj became one of its first six graduates, and she taught briefly at the Lycee Lalla Nezha in Rabat. from 1960 to 1968 Kabbaj worked with the minister of culture, Mohammed El-Fassi, the husband of writer, educator, and activist Malika El-

Fassi, and. From 1972 to 1985 she was an inspector of education. At present, she is a member of the philanthropic association Al Mouassat, set up in 1956 and led for many years by Malika El-Fassi.

"Removal of the Veil and Decency," which appeared in the daily newspaper *Al-Alam*, was Fatima Kabbaj's first published article. In it she presents Islam as a "religion of tolerance" that is "compatible with modern life," rather than reactionary and oppressive. She believes that while women should strive to observe true moral principles—virtue, honor, wisdom, and respectability—they need not be bound by burdensome traditons such as the wearing of the veil. Written in 1956, the article remains highly relevant in light of the widespread return to veiling as a mandatory practice in the last decades of the twentieth century and the first years of the twenty-first.

*Zakia Iraqui-Sinaceur*

✦

Far from any fanaticism, Islam was and is still a religion of tolerance. It doesn't force the individual to bear what is beyond her capacity. What is interesting about the principles of Islam is that they are compatible with modern life and they help us follow the right path.

This characteristic is reminiscent of the early times of Islam, during the life of the Prophet and the orthodox caliphs, when women were active in private and public life. Women used to go into the mosques to attend meetings, participate in cultural associations, and enjoy evening lectures. They used to appear publicly, beside men. Did they appear veiled? Of course not! Let us review the Qur'anic verses one by one. There is no single verse that orders women to be veiled, except in the verse specifying that the Prophet's wives could wear the veil if they feared mixing with people or being attacked. This information was noted by my sister Souad Kabbaj, who stated that the veil makes no sense today. Her address was an enthusiastic call to all Moroccan women to discard the veil, which burdens our girls and women. I have been recommending this idea myself for a long time. However, I disapprove of her failure to address the manner in which the veil should be removed.

Although Islam did not order women to veil, women must never ignore its teachings or neglect its norms. Islam teaches us to lead lives of decency, honor, and virtue, and to do all that may help us to rise toward perfection. Is it commendable to reject or to tread on such sacred teachings? Certainly not! We should direct our attention to the virtues recommended by Islam, which stop us from following only our desires and pleasures. Today I must add that I am especially alarmed by women's shameful behavior in public.

Muslim women should understand that displaying their bodies by appearing publicly with their chests, backs, and arms uncovered is a sign of their deviation from virtue, honor, dignity, and respect, which are associated with Islamic law. Islam teaches us not to display our charms. The Qur'an says, "Don't display your charms, as women used to do in pre-Islamic times....Women should show their beauty only to their families or husbands." These principles have been prescribed because displaying women's beauty generates their degradation and harms their reputation and honor.

Let us dress modestly with decency and dignity. We should not be embarrassed before foreigners or anyone who asks us to reject our traditions. Long live all my sisters. Let us raise our heads high, and feel proud of Islam and our religious constraints. In that way, we can be certain that everybody will respect us and appreciate the preservation of our honor. Are you not pleased, my sisters, to be the best examples of wisdom and propriety? Are you not delighted to eschew the immorality and libertinism of profligate women and choose another path that is worthier and better suited to our religion?

Indian and British women are well known for their fine reputations and high levels of respectability. Everybody praises them for their solemn discretion in the choice and style of their clothing. Why have we not heeded these women, whose behavior is congruent with the precepts of our religion, and why have we, instead, begun imitating Western women with bad manners? Such behavior is neither approved by our nation nor accepted by our religion and society. Let us consider the consequences and endeavor to avoid falling into the void. We should be aware that we do not live for ourselves, but for our nation. We must, then, preserve our reputation and dignity and behave in accordance with our values and our religion. Let us remove the veil from our faces! But this removal does not entitle us to exceed all limits. Let us go out unveiled but with decency and in respectable attire.

*Translated by Zakia Iraqui-Sinaceur*

## *Baya Hocine*
# SENTENCED TO DEATH

Algeria 1957    French

Baya Hocine is the name Baya Mamadi adopted after she joined the armed struggle against French colonialism in Algeria, becoming the youngest freedom fighter in the Algerian War of Indpendence, which lasted from 1954 to 1962. Born in 1940 into a modest but militant family, Hocine grew up in the Casbah of Algiers, and was orphaned at the age of five. She did well at school, but the historical situation in her country made her leap abruptly from adolescence to militancy. She joined the National Liberation Front (FLN) at the age of fifteen, following the arrest of her two brothers and the imprisonment of one of them in the camp of Paul-Cazelles, which was notorious for torturing and murdering prisoners. At sixteen she became a liaison agent, and during the brutal Battle of Algiers, in which hundreds of civilians were killed, she took arms to fight the colonizers.

Hocine was arrested, and was condemned to death shortly before Christmas 1957. She courageously stood in front of the judges and told them that she could not understand how France, which placed human rights at the top of its Constitution, could treat Algerians in a barbarous way. She was then seventeen, the youngest prisoner sentenced to death during the Algerian liberation struggle. This letter to her mother is dated 24 December 1957. The phrase *condamnée à mort* (sentenced to death) is written across the letter in Hocine's hand. The handwriting on the first page is regular and strong, but it becomes weaker on the second page. Her thoughts and her style are straightforward, lucid, and stoic, expressing more concern for her mother than for herself, and making plans for an appeal. It stands as a testament to the fact that women in Algeria paid the same price as men for their nation's independence, a fact often deliberately ignored in official recorded history.

On 20 March 1958, the French military tribunal declared that Hocine could not be executed because of her youth. She was transferred to the Oran civil tribunal for minors, and in 1959 was sentenced to life imprisonment. In the Oran civil prison, she lived in hellish conditions—cut off from the world, in a cell that was alternately freezing and sweltering, with no bed and only a daily piece of bread, and subject to regular beatings and humiliations. She was transferred to the prison in Caen, France in 1960, and released after the March 1962 signing of the Evian Accords, which laid out the terms for Algeria's independence from France.

Back in Algeria, Hocine earned a B.A. in political science and an M.A. in law, married, and had three children; her daughter was named Zuleikha, after one of her closest friends who had died in the independence struggle.. From 1979 to 1982 she was a member of parliament, and in 1985 she was appointed cultural attaché at the Algerian embassy in Brussels. She wrote articles for the *People* and *Al-Mujahid* newspapers, often focusing on the plight of the poor and the marginalized.

*Malika El Korso*

✦

Mother darling,
I am writing to you for the first time after my death sentence. My sisters and I received the sentence with calm and dignity. I hope you will have the same attitude. I know your courage and I trust you; I am confident that you will adopt the right attitude. I have immediately asked for an appeal; you know now that I will sit for another trial.

The lawyer saw me yesterday after she met you during the trial. She was shocked at the sentence that was pronounced against me. In any case, she promised to come and see you.

I am well and have everything. You can come and visit me on Thursday.

I am close to you, aren't I?

I leave you now so that I can make an inventory of my clothes because our clothes have been changed to prison clothes.

Kiss the children, Hadjila, my aunt.

My best to the neighbors.

I kiss you tenderly.

Baya

*Translated by Malika El Korso*

# Assia Djebar
# THERE IS NO EXILE

Algeria  1959  French

Assia Djebar was born Fatma-Zohra Imalayen in 1936 in the coastal city of Chechell. As the daughter of a teacher in a French colonial school, she was educated at a time when few Algerian girls attended school. In 1955, she became the first Algerian woman to attend France's elite *École Normale Supérieure* in Paris. She participated in the student strikes for Algerian independence that began the following year, and contributed to for the FLN newspaper *El-Moujahid*. Djebar went on to teach at the University of Rabat, Morocco, and the University of Algiers. Since 2001 she has held the Silver chair in French and Francophone Studies at New York University.

Djebar published her first novel at the age of twenty and continues to write fifty years later. She is by far the most prolific Francophone woman writer in North Africa, and one of the most famous and influential writers in the region. She has written novels, short stories, plays, poetry, and essays. Her books include the novels *La Soif* (The Mischief), published in 1957; *Les Enfants du nouveau monde* (Children of the New World) in 1962; *Les Allouettes naives* (The Naïve Larks) in 1967; *Les Femmes d'Alger dans leurs apartement* (Women of Algiers in their Apartment) in 1980; *L'Amour, la fantasia* (Fantasia: An Algerian Cavalcade), 1985, *Ombre Sultane* (A Sister to Scheherazade) in 1987; *Loin de Médine* (Far from Medina) in 1991; *Le Blanc d'Algérie* (Algerian White) *in 1996; Les Nuits de Strasbourg* (Strasbourg Nights) in 1997; and *La Disparition de la Langue Francaise* (The Disappearance of the French Language) in 2003; all but the last translated into English. She ceased writing for a decade in the 1970s, in part due to her ambivalence about writing in French, which she called "the language of the Others," rather than Arabic, the language of independent Algeria. During this time she wrote and directed films about the lives of Maghrebi women, including *La Nouba des femmes du mont Chenoua* (The Nouba of the Women of Mont Chenoua) in 1979), which won the International Critics Prize at the Venice Film Festival. She has also received several prestigious literary prizes, including the Maurice Maeterlinck Prize in 1995, the Neustadt International Prize for Literature in 1996, the Yourcenar Prize and the Fonlon-Nichols Prize of the African Literature Association in 1997, the International Palmi Prize in 1998, and the Frankfurt Book Fair Peace Prize in 2000. In 2005, she was elected to the *Académie française*, the highly prestigious institution charged with guarding the heritage of the French language, becoming first writer from the Maghreb to achieve such recognition.

Throughout her career, Djebar has written about Algerian women's struggles to liberate themselves from both colonialism and patriarchy. While the early novel *Children of the New World* depicts women fiercely involved in the anticolonial struggle, later works have exposed the betrayal of Algerian women by their own government, which, despite all their sacrifices during the war, rendered them second-class citizens afterward. In *Algerian White*, she writes of the ongoing struggle in her country's Islamic fundamentalism and of the postcolonial civil society, in which terrorist violence claimed the lives of three beloved women friends. Djebar suggests that Algerian women's reluctance to fight for their own liberation as fiercely as they had for the liberation of their country made it easier to send them back to the private sphere, and later on deprive them of their legal rights. Only with courage and solidarity, she submits, can they defeat the barbarities of patriarchy and be truly free. Her own courage and determination in expressing the concerns of Arab women in general and Algerian women in particular have sent her to live in self-imposed exile. For Assia Djebar, writing is a form of direct action, of bearing witness, of commitment and transgression. Above all it gives voice to those who are forgotten by official forms of discourse, the marginalized, betrayed and forgotten women, whom she urges to advance with both defiance and hope.

Djebar wrote "There Is No Exile" when she was 23. This elegant, understated story, whose title belies its theme, focuses on a still-intact Algerian family in exile. Through the dour perspective of the middle daughter, we view the mother in fragile health, the beloved father, the older and younger sisters, and the brother; and we hear the grief of the family next door, mourning the day's accidental death of their only young son. It is the day not only of death next door, but of a marriage proposal for the narrator, who has lost her children and divorced her husband and does not want to be married once more. Like the master-artist she has become, the early Djebar captures both the domestic interior of women trying to lead a "normal" life in exile, and their intense need to remain connected to the wider world of Algeria's national turmoil.

*Zahia Smail Salhi*

✦

That particular morning, I'd finished the housework a little earlier, by nine o'clock. Mother had put on her veil, taken her basket; in the opening of the door, she repeated as she had been repeating every day for three years: "Not until we had been chased out of our own country did I find myself forced to go out to market like a man."

"Our men have other things to do," I answered, as I'd been answering every day for three years.

"May God protect us!"

I saw Mother to the staircase, then watched her go down heavily because of her legs: "May God protect us," I said again to myself as I went back in.

The cries began around ten o'clock, more or less. They were coming from the apartment next door and soon changed into shrieks. All three of us, my two sisters—Aïcha, Anissa, and I—recognized it by the way in which the women received it: it was death.

Aïcha, the eldest, ran to the door, opened it in order to hear more clearly: "May misfortune stay away from us," she mumbled. "Death has paid the Smaïn family a visit."

At that moment, Mother came in. She put the basket on the floor, stopped where she stood, her face distraught, and began to beat her chest spasmodically with her hands. She was uttering little stifled cries, as when she was about to get sick.

Anissa, although she was the youngest of us, never lost her calm. She ran to close the door, lifted Mother's veil, took her by the shoulders and made her sit down on a mattress.

"Now don't get yourself in that state on account of someone else's misfortune," she said. "Don't forget you have a bad heart. May God shelter and keep us always."

While she repeated the phrase several more times, she went to get some water and sprinkled it on Mother, who now, stretched out full length on the mattress, was moaning. Then Anissa washed her entire face, took a bottle of cologne from the wardrobe, opened it, and put it under her nostrils.

"No!" Mother said. "Bring me some lemon."

And she started to moan again.

Anissa continued to bustle about. I was just watching her. I've always been slow to react. I'd begun to listen to the sobs outside that hadn't ceased, would surely not cease before nightfall. There were five or six women in the Smaïn family, and they were all lamenting in chorus, each one settling, forever it seemed, into the muddled outbreak of their grief. Later, of course, they'd have to prepare the meal, busy themselves with the poor, wash the body. . . . There are so many things to do the day of a burial.

For now, the voices of the hired mourners, all alike without any of them distinguishable from the other if only by a more anguished tone, were making one long, gasping chant, and I knew that it would hang over the entire day like a fog in winter.

"Who actually died over there?" I asked Mother, who had almost quieted down.

"Their young son," she said, inhaling the lemon deeply. "A car drove over him in front of the door. I was coming home when my eyes saw him twisting one last time, like a worm. The ambulance took him to the hospital, but he was already dead."

Then she began to sigh again.

"These poor people," she was saying, "they saw him go out jumping with life and now they're going to bring him back in the bloodstained sheet."

She raised herself halfway, repeated: "jumping with life." Then she fell back down on the mattress and said nothing other than the ritual formulas to keep misfortune away. But the low voice she always used to address God had a touch of hardness, vehemence.

"This day has an evil smell," I said, still standing in front of Mother, motionlessly. "I've sensed it since this morning, but I didn't know then that it was the smell of death."

"You have to add: May God protect us!" Mother said sharply. Then she raised her eyes to me. We were alone in the room, Anissa and Aïcha had gone back to the kitchen.

"What's the matter with you?" she said. "You look pale. Are you feeling sick, too?"

"May God protect us!" I said and left the room.

At noon, Omar was the first one home. The weeping continued. I'd attended to the meal while listening to the threnody and its modulations. I was growing used to them. I thought Omar would start asking questions. But no. He must have heard about it in the street.

He pulled Aïcha into a room. Then I heard them whispering. When some important event occurred, Omar spoke first to Aïcha in this way, because she was the eldest and the most serious one. Previously, Father used to do the same thing, but outside, with Omar, for he was the only son.

So there was something new; and it had nothing to do with death visiting the Smaïn family. I wasn't curious at all. Today is the day of death, all the rest becomes immaterial.

"Isn't that so?" I said to Anissa, who jumped.

"What's the matter now?"

"Nothing," I said without belaboring the point, for I was familiar with her always disconcerted answers whenever I'd start thinking out loud. Even this morning . . .

But why this sudden, blatant desire to stare at myself in a mirror, to confront my own image at some length, and to say, while letting my hair fall down my back so that Anissa would gaze upon it: "Look. At twenty-five, after having been married, after having lost my two children one after the other, having been divorced, after this exile and after this war, here I am busy admiring myself, smiling at myself like a young girl, like you . . . ."

"Like me!" Anissa said, and she shrugged her shoulders.

Father came home a little late because it was Friday and he'd gone to say the prayer of *dhor* at the mosque. He immediately asked why they were in mourning.

"Death has visited the Smaïns," I said, running toward him to kiss his hand. "It has taken their young son away."

"Those poor people," he said after a silence.

I helped him get settled in his usual place, on the same mattress. Then, as I put his meal in front of him and made sure he didn't have to wait for anything, I forgot about the neighbors for a while. I liked to serve Father; it was, I think, the only household task I enjoyed. Especially now. Since our departure, Father had aged a great deal. He gave too much thought to those who weren't with us, even though he never spoke of them, unless a letter arrived from Algeria and he asked Omar to read it.

In the middle of the meal I heard Mother murmur: "They can't possibly feel like eating today."

"The body is still at the hospital," someone said.

Father said nothing. He rarely spoke during meals.

"I'm not really hungry," I said, getting up, to excuse myself.

The sobs outside seemed more muffled, but I could still distinguish their singsong. Their gentle singsong. This is the moment, I said to myself, when grief becomes familiar, and pleasurable, and nostalgic. This is the moment when you weep almost voluptuously, for this gift of tears is a gift without end. This was the moment when the bodies of my children would turn cold fast, so fast, and when I knew it. . . .

At the end of the meal, Aïcha came into the kitchen, where I was by myself. First she went to close the windows that looked out over the neighboring terraces, through which the weeping reached me. But I could still hear it. And, oddly, it was that which made me so tranquil today, a little gloomy.

"There are some women coming this afternoon to see you and to propose marriage," she began. "Father says the candidate is suitable in every way."

Without answering, I turned my back to her and went to the window.

"Now what's your problem?" she said a little sharply.

"I need some air," I said and opened the window all the way, so that the song could come in. It had already been a while since the breathing of death had become, for me, "the song."

Aïcha remained a moment without answering. "When Father goes out, you'll attend to yourself a little," she said at last. "These women know very well that we're refugees like so many others, and that they're not going to find you dressed like a queen. But you should look your best, nevertheless."

"They've stopped weeping," I remarked, "or perhaps they're already tired," I said, thinking of that strange fatigue that grasps us at the depth of our sorrow.

"Why don't you keep your mind on the women who're coming?" Aïcha replied in a slightly louder voice.

Father had left. Omar too, when Hafsa arrived. Like us, she was Algerian and we'd known her there, a young girl of twenty with an education. She was a teacher but had worked only since her mother and she had been exiled, as had so many others. "An honorable woman doesn't work outside her home," her mother used to say. She still said it, but with a sigh of helplessness. One had to live, and there was no man in their household now.

Hafsa found Mother and Anissa in the process of preparing pastries, as if these were a must for refugees like us. But her sense of protocol was instinctive in Mother; an inheritance from her past life that she could not readily abandon.

"These women you're waiting for," I asked, "who are they?"

"Refugees like us," Aïcha exclaimed. "You don't really think we'd give you away in marriage to strangers?" Then with heart and soul: "Remember," she said, "the day we return to our own country, we shall all go back home, all of us, without exception."

"The day that we return," Hafsa, standing in the middle of the room, suddenly cried out, her eyes wide with dreams. "The day that we return to our country!" she repeated. "How I'd like to go back there on foot, the better to feel the Algerian soil under my feet, the better to see all our women, one after the other, all the widows, and all the orphans, and finally all the men, exhausted, sad perhaps, but free—free! And then I'll take a bit of soil in my hands, oh, just a tiny handful of soil, and I'll say to them: 'See, my brothers, see these drops of blood in these grains of soil in this hand, that's how much Algeria has bled throughout her body, all over her vast body, that's how much Algeria has paid for our freedom and for this, our return, with her own soil. But her martyrdom now speaks in terms of grace. So you see, my brothers . . . .'"

"The day that we return," Mother repeated softly in the silence that followed . . . "if God wills it."

It was then that the cries began again through the open window. Like an orchestra that brusquely starts a piece of music. Then, in a different tone, Hafsa reminded us: "I'm here for the lesson."

Aïcha pulled her into the next room.

During their meeting, I didn't know what to do. The windows of the kitchen and of the other two rooms looked out over the terraces. I went from one to the other, opening them, closing them, opening them again. All of this without hurrying, as if I weren't listening to the song.

Anissa caught me in my rounds.

"You can tell they're not Algerian," she said. "They're not even accustomed to being in mourning."

"At home, in the mountains," Mother answered, "the dead have nobody to weep over them before they grow cold."

"Weeping serves no purpose," Anissa was stoic, "whether you die in your bed or on the bare ground for your country."

"What do you know about it?" I suddenly said to her. "You're too young to know."

"Soon they're going to bury him," Mother whispered.

Then she raised her head and looked at me. I had once again closed the window behind me. I couldn't hear anything anymore.

"They're going to bury him this very day," Mother said again a little louder, "that's our custom."

"They shouldn't," I said. "It's a hateful custom to deliver a body to the earth when beauty still shines on it. Really quite hateful. . . . It seems to me they're burying him while he's still shivering, still . . .". (but I couldn't control my voice any longer).

"Stop thinking about your children!" Mother said. "The earth that was thrown on them is a blanket of gold. My poor daughter, stop thinking about your children!" Mother said again.

"I'm not thinking about anything," I said. "No, really. I don't want to think about anything. About anything at all."

It was already four o'clock in the afternoon when they came in. From the kitchen where I was hiding, I heard them exclaim, once the normal phrases of courtesy had been uttered: "What is that weeping?"

"May misfortune stay far away from us! May God protect us!"

"It gives me goose bumps," the third one was saying. "I've almost forgotten death and tears, these days. I've forgotten them, even though our hearts are always heavy."

"That is the will of God," the second one would respond.

In a placid voice, Mother explained the reason for the mourning next door as she invited them into the only room we had been able to furnish decently. Anissa, close by me, was already making the first comments on the way the women looked. She was questioning Aïcha, who had been with Mother to welcome them. I had opened the window again and watched them exchange their first impressions.

"What are you thinking?" Anissa said, her eye still on me.

"Nothing," I said feebly; then, after a pause: "I was thinking of the different faces of fate. I was thinking of God's will. Behind that wall, there is a dead person and women going mad with grief. Here, in our house, other women are talking of marriage . . . I was thinking of that difference."

"Just stop 'thinking,'" Aïcha cut in sharply. Then to Hafsa, who was coming in: "You ought to be teaching *her*, not me. She spends all her time thinking. You'd almost believe she's read as many books as you have."

"And why not?" Hafsa asked.

"I don't need to learn French," I answered. "What purpose would it serve? Father has taught us all our language. 'That's all you need,' he always says."

"It's useful to know languages other than your own," Hafsa said slowly. "It's like knowing other people, other countries."

I didn't answer. Perhaps she was right. Perhaps you ought to learn and not waste your time letting your mind wander, like mine, through the deserted corridors of the past. Perhaps I should take lessons and study French, or anything else. But I, I never felt the need to jostle my body or my mind. . . . Aïcha was different. Like a man: hard and hardworking. She was thirty. She hadn't seen her husband in three years, who was still incarcerated in Baberousse prison, where he had been since the first days of the war. Yet, she was getting an education and didn't settle for household work. Now, after just a few months of Hafsa's lessons, Omar no longer read to her her husband's infrequent letters, the few that might reach her. She managed to decipher them by herself. Sometimes I caught myself being envious of her.

"Hafsa," she said, "it's time for my sister to go in and greet these ladies. Please go with her."

But Hafsa didn't want to. Aïcha insisted, and I was watching them play their little game of politeness.

"Does anyone know if they've come for the body yet?" I asked.

"What? Didn't you hear the changers just now?" Anissa said.

"So that's why the weeping stopped for a moment," I said. "It's strange, as soon as some parts of the Koranic verses are chanted, the women immediately stop weeping. And yet, that's the most painful moment, I know it all too well myself. As long as the body is there in front of you, it seems the child isn't quite dead yet, can't be dead, you see? . . . Then comes the moment when the men get up, and that is to take him, wrapped in a sheet, on their shoulders. That's how he leaves, quickly, as on the day that he came. . . . For me, may God forgive me, they can chant Koranic verses all they want, the house is still empty after they've gone, completely empty. . . ."

Hafsa was listening, her head leaning toward the window. With a shiver, she turned toward me. She seemed younger even than Anissa, then.

"My God," she said, emotion in her voice, "I've just turned twenty and yet I've never encountered death. Never in my whole life!"

"Haven't you lost anyone in your family in this war?" Anissa asked.

"Oh yes," she said, "but the news always comes by mail. And death by mail, you see, I can't believe it. A first cousin of mine died under the guillotine as one of the first in Barberousse. Well, I've never shed a tear over him because I cannot believe that he's dead. And yet he was like a brother to me, I swear. But I just can't believe he's dead, you understand?" she said in a voice already wrapped in tears.

"Those who've died for the Cause aren't really dead," Anissa answered with a touch of pride.

"So, let's think of the present. Let's think about today," Aïcha said in a dry voice. "The rest is in God's hand."

There were three of them: an old woman who had to be the suitor's mother and who hastily put on her glasses as soon as I arrived; two other women, seated side by side, resembled each other. Hafsa, who'd come in behind me, sat down next to me. I lowered my eyes.

I knew my part, it was one I'd played before; stay mute like this, eyes lowered, and patiently let myself be examined until the very end: it was simple. Everything is simple, beforehand, for a girl who's being married off.

Mother was talking. I was barely listening. I know the themes to be developed all too well: Mother was talking about our sad state as refugees; then they'd be exchanging opinions on when the end might be announced: " . . . another Ramadan to be spent away from home . . . perhaps this was the last one . . . perhaps, if God wills it! Of course, we were saying the same thing last year, and the year before that. . . . Let's not complain too much. . . . In any event, victory is certain, all our men say the same thing. And we, we know the day of our return will come. . . . We should be thinking of those who stayed behind. . . . We should be thinking of those who are suffering. . . . The Algerian people are a people whom God loves. . . . And our fighters are made of steel. . . . " Then they'd come back to the tale of the flight, to the different means by which each one had left her soil where the fires were burning. . . . Then they'd evoke the sadness of exile, the heart yearning for its country. . . . And the fear of dying far from the land of one's birth. . . . Then. . . . But may God be praised and may he grant our prayers!"

This time it lasted a bit longer; an hour perhaps, or more. Until the time came to serve coffee. By then, I was hardly listening at all. I too was thinking in my own way of this exile, of these somber days.

I was thinking how everything had changed, how on the day of my first engagement we had been in the long, bright living room of our house in the hills of Algiers; how we'd been prosperous then, we had prosperity and peace; how Father used to laugh, how he used to give thanks to God for the abundance of his home. . . . And I, I wasn't as I was today, my soul gray, gloomy and with this idea of death beating faintly inside me since the morning. . . . Yes, I was thinking how everything had changed and that, still, in some way everything remained the same. They were still concerned with marrying me off. And why exactly? I suddenly wondered. And why exactly? I repeated to myself, feeling something like fury inside me, or its echo. Just so I could have worries that never change whether it's peace or wartime, so I could wake up in the middle of the night and question myself on what it is that sleeps in the depths of the heart of the man sharing my bed. . . . Just so I could give birth and weep, for life never comes unaccompanied to a woman, death is always right behind, furtive, quick, and smiling at the mothers. . . . Yes, why indeed? I said to myself.

Coffee had now been served. Mother was inviting them to drink.

"We won't take even one sip," the old woman began, "before you've given us your word about your daughter."

"Yes," the other one said, "my brother impressed upon us that we weren't to come back without your promising to give her to him as his wife."

I was listening to Mother avoid answering, have herself be begged hypocritically, and then again invite them to drink, Aïcha joined in with her. The women were repeating their request. . . . It was all as it should be.

The game went on a few minutes longer. Mother invoked the father's authority: "I, of course, would give her to you. . . . I know you are people of means. . . . But there is her father."

"Her father has already said yes to my brother," one of the two women who resembled each other replied. "The question remains only to be discussed between us."

"Yes," said the second one, "it's up to us now. Let's settle the question."

I raised my head; it was then, I think, that I met Hafsa's gaze. There was, deep in her eyes, a strange light, surely of interest or of irony, I don't know, but you could feel Hafsa as an outsider, attentive and curious at the same time, but an outsider. I met that look.

"I don't want to marry," I said. "I don't want to marry," I repeated, barely shouting.

There was much commotion in the room: Mother got up with a deep sigh; Aïcha was blushing, I saw. And the two women turned to me, with the same slow movement of shock: "And why not?" one of them asked.

"My son," the old woman exclaimed with some arrogance, "my son is a man of science. In few days he is leaving for the Orient."

"Of course," Mother said with touching haste. "We know he's a scholar. We know him to have a righteous heart. . . . Of course. . . ."

"It's not because of your son," I said. "But I don't want to get married. I see the future before my eyes, it's totally black. I don't know how to explain it, surely it must come from God. . . .But I see the future totally black before my eyes!" I said again, sobbing, as Aïcha led me out of the room in silence.

Later, but why even tell the rest, except that I was consumed with shame and I didn't understand. Only Hafsa stayed close to me after the women had left.

"You're engaged," she said sadly. "Your mother said she'd give you away. Will you accept?" and she stared at me with imploring eyes.

"What difference does it make?" I said and really thought inside myself: What difference does it make? "I don't know what came over me before. But they were all talking about the present and its changes and its misfortunes. And I was saying to myself: of what possible use is it to be suffering like this, far away from home, if I have to continue here as before in Algiers, to stay home and sit and pretend. . . . Perhaps when life changes, everything should change with it, absolutely everything. I was thinking of all that," I said, "but I don't even know if that's bad or good. . . . You, you're smart, and you know these things, perhaps you'll understand. . . ."

"I do understand," she said, hesitating as if she were going to start talking and then preferred to remain silent.

"Open the window," I said. "It's almost dark."

She went to open it and then came back to my bed where I'd been lying down to cry, without reason, crying for shame and fatigue all at the same time. In the silence that followed, I was feeling distant, pondering the night that little by little engulfed the room. The sounds from the kitchen, where my sisters were, seemed to be coming from somewhere else.

Then Hafsa began to speak: "Your father," she said, "once spoke of exile, of our present exile, and he said—oh, I remember it well, for nobody speaks like your father—he said: 'There is no exile for any man loved by God. There is no exile for the one who is on God's path. There are only trials.'"

She went on a while, but I've forgotten the rest, except that she repeated "we" very often with a note of passion. She said that word with a peculiar vehemence, so much so that I began to wonder toward the end whether that word really meant the two of us alone, or rather other women, all the women of our country.

To tell the truth, even if I'd known, what could I have answered? Hafsa was too knowledgeable for me. And that's what I would have liked to have told her when she stopped talking, perhaps in the expectation that I would speak.

But it was another voice that answered, a woman's voice that rose, through the open window, rose straight as an arrow toward the sky, that rounded itself out, spread out in its flight, a flight ample as a bird's after the storm, then came falling back down in sudden torrents.

"The other women have grown silent," I said. "The only one left to weep now is the mother. . . . Such is life," I added a moment later. "There are those who forget or who simply sleep. And then there are those who keep bumping into the walls of the past. May God take pity on them!"

"Those are the true exiles," said Hafsa.

Tunis, March 1959

*Translated by Marjolijn de Jager*

## *Djamila Boupacha*
# TESTIMONY OF TORTURE

Algeria 1960    French

Djamila Boupacha is one of the heroes of the Algerian War for Independence. She endured horrible torture at the hands of French authorities and then courageously fought to make the details of her ordeal known and even bring her torturers to justice. In doing so, she revealed to the world the brutality of the methods employed by the French colonial machine in its suppression of the Algerian independence struggle, and helped turn pubic opinion against the colonizers.

Boupacha, who had worked as an FLN (National Liberation Front) liaison agent, was arrested and detained in February 1960, when she was twenty years old, and accused of planting a bomb (which had been defused before it exploded). A confession was extracted from her by means of extreme physical torture, which included electrical and cigarette burns, a version of what is now called "waterboarding," and rape with a broken bottle. As was—and still is—common practice, the torturers targeted the sexual organs of their victims, which caused both excruciating pain and deep humiliation. Despite being in a state of traumatic shock after this savage treatment, and despite threats of further torture of herself and her family, when she was brought before a magistrate in May 1960, Boupacha maintained that she was innocent of the bombing and openly declared: "I have been tortured. I insist on a medical examination." Boupacha's case came to the attention of Gisèle Halimi of the Paris Bar, who took on the task of defending her in the face of obstacles created by the colonial authorities—who, for example, granted her a visa to Algiers for just forty-eight hours. Her cause was also taken up by Simone de Beauvoir, who organized a committee to pressure French officials. In a June 1960 letter to *Le Monde*, Beauvoir described the details of Boupacha's torture and confronted the French population with their own complicity in such acts, supposedly being performed on their behalf. Beauvoir received death threats, but her work helped bring worldwide attention to Boupacha's case.

At a court hearing in Algiers later that month, Boupacha filed a countersuit against the police and military official who had tortured her, whose actions were in violation of the French penal code. The account included here comes from this civil indictment against her torturers, which was reported by the press and included in a 1962 book on the case by Simone de Beauvoir and Gisèle Halimi, *Djamila Boupacha: The Story Of The Torture Of A Young Algerian Girl Which Shocked Liberal French Opinion*, published in French and English.

Boupacha's case was eventually transferred to Caen, France, but military officials refused to release records that would have supported her allegations of torture. She was finally released from prison in April of 1962, following the signing of the Evian Accords. Because of blanket amnesties passed in the 1960s, none of those who committed torture—which was ordered or condoned at the highest levels of the French state—could ever be brought to justice.

Very little is known about Djamila Boupacha in post-independence Algeria, where she has not taken part in public life. This is indicative of the veil of silence thrown over the lives of women freedom fighters of the Algerian War. As they fought and died alongside of men, many believed they were securing their own liberation as women, as well as the liberation of their country—only to be rewarded with the status of second-class citizens by successive governments of Algeria.

*Zahia Smail Salhi*

◆

During the night of 10/11 February, 1960, a party of about fifty *gardes mobiles* [security police], *harkis* [Algerian collaborators], and police inspectors drove up to my parents' house at Dely Ibrahim, Algiers, in jeeps and army trucks, and dismounted there. One of them was Captain D., on secondment to the El Biar Center. I was living in my parents' house at the time. I was beaten up savagely there even before being taken away. My brother-in-law, Abdelli Ahmed, who was present that evening, suffered a similar ordeal, as did my father Abdelaziz Boupacha, who is seventy years old.

All three of us were removed to the classification Center at El Biar. There I received a second beating, so violent that I was knocked off my feet and collapsed. It was then that certain military personnel, including a captain in the paratroops, kicked my ribs in. I still suffer from a costal displacement on my left side.

After four or five days I was transferred to Hussein Dey. This, I was told, was where I would get a taste of the "third degree." I found out what this implied: torture by electricity. Since the electrodes would not stay in place when affixed to my nipples, one of my torturers fastened them on with Scotch tape. I received similar electrical burns on my legs, face, anus, and vagina. This electrical torture was interspersed with cigarette burns, blows, and the "bath treatment": I was trussed up and hung over a bath on a stick, and submerged till I nearly choked.

A few days later I was given the most appalling torture of all, the so-called "bottle treatment." First they tied me up in a special posture, and then they rammed the neck of a bottle into my vagina. I screamed and fainted. I was unconscious, to the best of my knowledge, for two days.

During the earlier part of my time in El Biar, I was brought into the presence of my brother-in-law Abdelli Ahmed, who also bore the most frightful marks of the beatings and tortures he had undergone. Nor was my father spared, despite his great age.

On 15 May 1960, I was formally committed and charged with attempted willful murder and consorting with malefactors. When brought before the examining magistrates I repeated the confession that had been forcibly extracted from me, under torture, by my inquisitors. I was then, and am still, severely shocked and shaken by my terrible ordeal. To my own sufferings must be added my father's experience—a most frightful shock for an old man—of seeing his twenty-year-old daughter still disfigured by the tortures she had endured.

My father is at present interned in the camp at Beni-Messous, but earlier his condition gave rise to such anxiety that he had to spend nearly a week in the Maillot Hospital.

My brother-in-law is under detention in the Civil Prison, Algiers, and his case is being dealt with separately from mine. Yet they are intimately linked: we were arrested on the same day, and the "malefactors" we stand accused of "consorting with" are the same men on the run. The reason for this separation is obvious. My brother-in-law and I are each witness to the fact of the other's torture, and the authorities well might fear that if we were brought into a public courtroom together, we should testify to our common experience.

*Translated by Peter Green*

## Zhor Zerari
## TWO PRISON POEMS
Algeria 1960    French

Zhor Zerari was born in 1937 in the eastern port city of Annaba, to a nationalist family that was deeply involved in resisting French colonialism in Algeria. Her father, who had been active in *Hizb Sha'b* (The People's Party), disappeared after being arrested by French paratroopers. Zhor Zerari began her own career as a freedom fighter in the Algerian War before she was twenty years old. Following the execution of four militants in Barberousse in February 1957, Zerari planted the first of several bombs, at the entrance of the Algiers radio station.. In August of that year she was arrested in her home and interrogated in Sarouy School, where she underwent torture that included being stripped, beaten, shocked, gagged with a rag filled with excrement, and urinated upon. (In 2005, she was one of several former prisoners who told *Le Monde* that Maurice Schmitt, who later served as chief of staff of the French army, oversaw her torture.) Zerari is still haunted by the specter of torture, which permanently damaged her health: She walks with great difficulty and suffers from balance problems, and says, "A fragment of my brain is not functioning properly."

Condemned first to fifteen years in prison and then to life, Zerari was imprisoned in Barberousse in Algiers and later transferred to Pau, France, and finally released in April 1962 following the Evian Accords. After independence, she became a journalist for the Algerian weekly *Algérie Actualité*. Zhor's two poems, written while she was in prison, express deep anger in response to the French colonizers. By 1960, French president Charles de Gaulle had made movements toward self-determination for Algeria, but renegade French officers resistant to these plans were still fighting the FLN. Both poems were written during a visit by de Gaulle in early December of 1960, which triggered massive demonstrations by Algerians.

"My Brother" was written after the following description of an incident in Algiers appeared in *Le Monde* on 14 December 1960: "Around 11.30, in this area [Maison Carrée], a Muslim climbed a pillar to hang the banner of the FLN. Invited to come down, he refused and was hence brought down with one shot. His body, enveloped in the white and green flag struck with the red star and croissant, was put at the back of a military truck and paraded in the Muslim district."

"The School of Freedom," also composed in December 1960, evokes the alienation inherent in colonial education. Zerari depicts Algerian children playing among books about the "glorious" history of France. "Our ancestors the Gauls," referring to the ancient inhabitants of France, is a phrase from a popular history book used throughout the French colonial empire. Charles Martel was an eighth-century French military hero who prevented a Muslim expansion into southern France by defeating armies from al-Andalus, and is credited with "saving" Christian Europe from Islamic rule. The Tafna Treaty was an 1837 agreement between French imperial forces and Amir Abd al-Qadir al-Jazairi, acknowledging the Amir's control of large portions of Algeria; it was broken by the French two years later.

The fact that these poems about cultural and political oppression are written in French, the language of the oppressors, makes them all the more poignant—for both express defiance in the face of tragedy.

*Malika El Korso*

✦

## My Brother

My brother,
I have no tears left to shed.
I do not know
Your name.
I know only that you were young
and I speak of you
In the past tense.
Still,
You are Algerian,
You are dead,

And you are free.
Drunk on freedom,
You climbed the pole,
Agile as
A gazelle
Of the Sahara.
Against the odds,
You realized
The exhilaration
Of unfurling
Our country's flag.

Then
It took
Just one bullet,
Just one bullet
Shot by one man
Into your young body
Longing for freedom.
It took
Just one man,
Just one man
Assured
Of his own country's freedom
To bring you down.
Your dislodged body
Compelled your enemies
To honor you,
For, with your fallen body,
Draped in that same flag,
They made slow progress through
Streets you played in
As a child.
I want to cry,
I really do,
But I have no tears left.
Like your body,
My heart is dislodged.

Forgive me,
My dead brother,
I have no tears left to shed.

A jettisoned schoolbag
On a street corner.
Books...
Selected High Points
Of the History of France
Peek out meekly
From an abandoned schoolbag
On a street corner.
As kids scurry
On their little legs,
A naked foot stumbles
On a history book—
"Our Ancestors the Gauls ..."
The wind ruffles
The pages—
"Charles Martel,
Conqueror of the Saracens..."
Another little foot,
Also naked—
"The Tafna Treaty ..."
The wind takes part
In the dance
Under the children's naked feet.
The children of today
Do not study in the classroom.
They are writing the history
Of a Free Algeria.

*Translated by Abena P.A. Busia and Moha Ennaji*

## Galila Reda
# I NO LONGER LOVE PASSIONATELY

Egypt 1965    Arabic

One of Egypt's most distinguished modern poets, Galila Reda was born in Alexandria in 1920. She received part of her education in a French boarding school in Cairo, where she studied Arabic and French literatures. She dreamed of a working life, but her father and brother pulled her out of school before she acquired her certificate and forced her to marry a man she had not seen until the marriage contract was signed.

Galila Reda overcame the pain of her difficult personal life—which included unsuccessful marriages and love affairs and a son with developmental disabilities—through writing poetry. Her best poems focus on the relationships between men and women, often reflecting her rebellion against the traditions of a conservative culture that restricts women's lives. She also wrote elegantly and daringly about unconventional subjects, including the memory and taste of a first kiss.

Reda published six collections of poetry; a play in verse, *Port Said*; a novel, *Under the Sycamore Tree*; and several critical studies of poetry. Having been the target of many rumors by different poets, especially those whose love she rejected, she withdrew from public view in the 1960s. In 1983 she won Egypt's Award for Encouraging Arts and the Medal of Arts and Literature, First Class.

"I No Longer Love Passionately" is included in Reda's collection of poems *The White Wings*, published in Cairo in 1965. The poem is an indictment of men who silence women—a warning to such men that by demanding subservience from women, they will destroy their character and their love. Reda's style is characterized by transparent language that reflects deep and complex feelings.

*Heba Sharobeem*

✦

Be assured this day, my voice shall not utter a word,
And through all your days, you will hear no discord from me.
All now to me is contentment and bliss,
Just as to those who rest in eternal peace.
Like them, I shall not contend, nor dispute, nor revolt . . .
If you say left or right, so shall I wander.
Any distress of yours shall I at once repair.
My stubbornness will no longer endanger your love,
For I shall be calm, transformed, a stranger.

Henceforth shall I revere my lord and master,
My liege and sovereign I shall regard with honor.
He who is innocent of all feeling, of all emotion. . .
As God is my witness, not from me shall he feel rebellion.
But, despite my surrender, it is you who will know repentance.
You will long for my heart's insurgency, for my tongue's defiance.
I know my heart . . . it is naïve and foolish;
But should it soften, or yield and feel merciful,
Then know, I no longer love passionately.

*Translated by Carole Escoffey and Heba Sharobeem*

# Wadida Wassef
# AUNT NOOR

Egypt 1965     English

Wadida Wassef was born in 1926 in Alexandria. She was a Copt, an Egyptian Christian, and therefore a member of a religious minority, who make up ten percent of Egypt's population. Her father, a prominent educator, sent her to primary school in Alexandria to acquire a strong foundation in Arabic, while her mother, a member of an Alexandrian merchant family who looked toward Europe for style, had her attend a French convent school. Because her father's work involved constant moves, Wassef was eventually sent as a boarder to the American Mission College in Cairo, where she was often punished for the most trifling reasons by some teachers and forbidden to go home on weekends to see her parents; her rebellion against such injustices strengthened her resolve to stand up for herself. She went on to study English literature at the University of Alexandria, and was fluent in Arabic, English, French, and Italian.

Wadida Wassef started her working life after marriage, teaching history, English, and translation at English schools in Alexandria. She began to write in the 1960s, and published several short stories and autobiographical essays, including "Hasan's Wives," which appeared in *Opening the Gates: A Century of Arab Feminist Writing* (1990) and "Memories," published in *Méditerranéenes Alexandria en Égypte* (1996). She is also known for her English translation of *The Cheapest Nights and Other Stories* (1978) by the distinguished Egyptian fiction writer Yusif Idris.

Part of Wassef's unfinished, unpublished autobiography, this narrative was probably written between the 1960s and the 1970s. In a series of contrasts, it depicts the lives of several generations and classes of Egyptian women in the Alexandria of the author's childhood. The lady of the house, Wassef's mother, represents a well-off woman of her time, a curious product of the conservative East, with fierce pride in its traditions—whether they be morality or the preservation of jam—and the highly stylized West, with its convent education and piano playing. The family's wealth supports an atmosphere of security and conventionality that was nevertheless stifling for the young daughter of the house, who was being shaped in the image of her own mother whose highest aspiration was to be acknowledged as *comme il faut*—proper and correct. Aunt Noor is of an older generation and represents the matriarchal roots of families that had migrated from village to city in search of wealth and a Western lifestyle. The other villager is the humble Om el Hana, who, like the two older women in the narrative, preserves the memory and traditions of her nation. She too has aspirations for her daughter—but, unlike the lady of the house, she does not look to the West for instruction, but to the Persian Gulf for its money.

Though historical references in the piece are vague, they do form a background for the narrative, and bracket it within two significant events. The first is the Orabi Revolt of 1879 to 1882, in which the Egyptian Minister of Defense Ahmed Orabi led an uprising against foreign intervention, which resulted in the British naval bombardment of Alexandria in 1882 and eventually in the British occupation of Egypt. The second event is Nasser's 1952 Egyptian Revolution, which deposed the king and ushered in an "era of workers and peasants" that the author believes Aunt Noor would have been happy to see. The revolution and the subsequent nationalization of land and industry put an end to the kind of lifestyle enjoyed by wealthy Westernized Egyptian families like Wassef's. While the text was written in English, the author included some Arabic words, perhaps to lend a local flavor. *Ya Sitt* means "Madam"; *W'Allah* means "By God" or "I swear"; *tante* is the French for "aunt"; a *souffragui* is a native butler dressed in traditional clothes; and *fellaheen* are peasants. *Samna* is ghee, or clarified butter, and *molokheya* is a traditional dish made of the leafy green plant called Jews mallow, chopped finely and cooked in a soup. Wassef also mentions the French dishes *lapin a la crème a l'estragon*—rabbit with tarragon cream sauce—and *savarins*—rum cakes. The "Mrs. Beaton" to whom she refers must be the author of the famous Victorian British cookbook and domestic manual, *Mrs Beeton's Book of Household Management*.

*Sahar Hamouda*

✦

The days followed peacefully upon one another. Father went to work every morning and when he came home at lunchtime the kitchen smells that filled the house were delicious and closely identified with the seasons. Lentil soup on cold days in winter, and stuffed cabbage and sweet lemons and tangerines, seemed to blend with the raindrops hitting the panes and the smell of naphthaline from our woolens just removed from storage. They were the essence of winter and we were snug and warm inside. In summertime there was *molokheya* and red onions and grapes and watermelon. Mother was a full-time housewife with no sidetracks, wholly devoted to running the house and looking after her family. Certain things she allowed no one else to do. In spring she made the year's stock of strawberry jam; in autumn she would spend a whole day peeling dates with Abdallah preparing them for jam. Then, one by one, she would stuff each with an almond, a clove, and a thin strip of tangerine skin. In winter she spent hours slicing bitter oranges into paper-thin strips. Her jams were always perfect because she prepared them strictly according to age-old traditions and closely supervised the cooking.

When spring came it would be time to make the yearly stock of *samna*. Om el Hana would appear at the kitchen door with our ration of butter, which she carried on her head in a huge flat basket all the way from her village. In an initial first operation in the village, the butter was kneaded with salt then shaped into fat sausages, then loaded onto Om el Hana's head. Then she and her basket were placed on a donkey who took them to the railway station, where she boarded the goods train that stopped here and there to pick up all manner of passenger, animal or human. When she reached our house the second operation began. Mother, sitting on a low stool, and Om el Hana, on the floor, placed the butter in a huge copper cauldron and took turns stirring it. … [The] butter settled at the bottom; the *samna*, without which no food cooked in Egyptian homes was worthy of the name, floated on top. It was then poured into big earthen jars and stored in the pantry to last until the next spring. The operation lasted from early morning until sunset. *Samna* is a classic of Egyptian cooking. Egyptian women are extremely fond of it, as their volume indicates. The thought of food cooked in oil or vegetable fat made their stomachs turn.

For days after Om el Hana departed the rank smell of *samna* stuck to the house. Wherever she would be, we had the windows wide open in order to create a draft to blow away her smell. She must have been the forerunner of the modern computer. Illiterate and unschooled, she could do complicated mathematical operations with amazing accuracy and she was never wrong. One could almost hear the clickety-click of figures in her brain as she calculated the exact amount she expected to be paid.

Om el Hana had a daughter whom she did not intend to raise as a dealer in *samna* like herself. The ambitions she'd had in store for the son she never had were shifted on to Warda, and Warda became a hospital nurse. She got a job in Bahrain. Om el Hana went there to see her every year. "Ya Sitt," she told mother of her first flight, "I don't know how we got to Bahrain. The plane never flapped a wing. I looked out to the right and there was the wing, standing stiff as a plank of wood. Then I looked out to the left, and there was the other wing as stiff as its brother. And I said to myself, my God, are we flying or not. W'Allah, Ya Sitt, I don't know how we got to Bahrain."

When she was not making jams or syrups, or distilling orange flowers for the extract that was her magic remedy for all afflictions, or squeezing rose petals to extract the water which was essential for her skin care, Mother would be in the kitchen trying out recipes from the *Woman's Journal*. She had a blind faith in Elizabeth Craig, the cooking editor of the journal. For the rest, in addition to traditional ways, she relied on the Comtesse de Qencé's *Encyclopédie de la Vie Pratique*, a turn-of-the-century publication that dealt with every simple aspect of housekeeping: the "feminine arts," as she called them. A plump lady with a top-knot illustrated the cover, wearing a frilly white apron tied in a large bow in the back, stirring something on a coal stove. Like Mrs. Beaton, the Comtesse could not bake a cake with less than a dozen eggs. The *Encyclopédie* was intended for the upper class. It tells people how to pick their servants, and points out the characteristics of servants who are *bien stylés*. It tells people how to give orders and see that they are obeyed, and informs them about the use and abuse of bells. It propounds a typical highly sophisticated French cuisine, requiring special herbs and long and complicated procedures for cooking. Accordingly my mother's *lapin a la crème a l'estragon* and her *Savarins* were proverbial.

When she was fifteen, Mother was removed from the convent school she attended and made to finish her education at home with private tutors. In addition to tutors for English and French, to help her perfect those languages, she was to perfect the "feminine arts." So Mademoiselle Luodovico was engaged to teach her embroidery at a very advanced level. She taught her to embroider with human hair, and to recognize and execute every type of lace. The *point de Paris*, the *point Turque*, and tulle Breton held no mysteries for her. I own a very precious piece of *point d'Angleterre*, a gossamer piece of lace she made in those days. Now it is priceless because it cannot be replicated in this machine age, either by her or anyone else, neither here nor elsewhere in the world. For music she had Signor Emiliano Rossi. She played salon pieces for entertainment: the Paderewski minuet, the "Gavotte Stéphanie," dedicated to the wife of the Crown Prince of Austria, the "Rêverie de Marguerites," full of bravura passages. Unlike my muddy notes, hers came like a ripple of crystal beads, each note clear-cut and sparkling. She played with ease and mastery. Her music notes were adorned with beautiful vignettes depicting Arcadian scenes: woods and lakes, troubadours, serenading romantic ladies leaning out of romantic balconies with bluebirds fluttering above and rambling roses creeping up the column and full moons peeping behind a sea of clouds....

We had lace on our sheets and the tablecloths were of heavy white damask for everyday and hand embroidered pure linen when we had company. They had the fragrance of perfect laundering and the linen cupboard smelled of heliotrope.

Sometimes Mother's friends came round in the morning with their knitting and their needlework. They sat out on the terrace in summer, in the drawing room in winter. Of all the ladies who gathered in mother's drawing room, whose kisses we had to endure, I did not mind Tante Arda. (Mother's close friends were called *tante* because French was the language of good society.) She had the redolence of the highborn: Fine glossy hair, creamy skin smooth as velvet, and slender limbs, the personification of her aristocratic past. Her loveliness fascinated me like a beautifully wrought object. I never tired of gazing at her, observing her movements. The way she set her feet, the way she crossed her legs, the way she picked up a teacup, the way she blew her nose. Even to that crude gesture she managed to lend style with her white hands and delicate ringed fingers with the almond shaped lacquered nails. When she kissed me I was never in a hurry to draw away. I loved the feeling of her soft cheek next to mine, and I drank in the expensive odor of her body that whispered of patchouli and amber and jasmine. Perhaps I half hoped that some of her loveliness would rub off on me. That's how I would be when I grew up, I promised myself.

I can only make a close guess as to what those ladies talked about when they gathered. We were not allowed to stay with them. It was not *comme il faut*. We were called in for inspection and warned to leave without being told. We ignored that, sometimes, when we judged the company promised to become interesting. Some of these ladies were outspoken and had no compunction about mentioning what was not to be mentioned before children. Then we would take care to sit where we would not be directly exposed to Mother's meaningful looks, which after a while turned to plain glowering.

The *souffragui*, beturbaned and in a spotless white caftan with a red sash, specially set aside for waiting at table or on guests, brought them coffee and biscuits in a silver dish with a lace doily. Serving biscuits or cake without a doily was a breach of good form my mother deplored. She was most fastidious over such matters and she took inordinate pride in the quality of her tableware. I remember when her friends came to tea: the darkened room, smelling of delicate pastries; the Richelieu tea cloth with the lace edgings, exquisitely embroidered by the nuns. The Limoge teacups with their soft colors and delicate pattern of flowers, and the apostle spoons I loved to twirl in my fingers....

When Father's Aunt Noor came to stay, all the time she was with us she kept us on tenterhooks. She was the oldest woman we had ever seen, in spite of her vitality and her constant bustling up and down the stairs. Her face looked like a crumpled piece of paper. Wrinkles and gray hair were the yardstick by which we measured a person's age, and accordingly we estimated Aunt Noor to be at least a hundred. She was terribly offended when she got wind of this and was very keen to correct the error. Except that when she got down to it she discovered she hadn't a clue as to the date of her birth. She had documents, of course, bundled up somewhere in one of the large handkerchiefs where she kept her papers folded and tied with pieces of string—but she could not tell one from another since she couldn't read. Her only clue to her age was that, at the time of the Orabi Revolt, she must have been sixteen and pregnant with her second child. Renewed attempts to calculate her age made her out to be even more than a hundred. After this estimate, we found her muttering to herself that the Orabi Revolt was only yesterday.

She had the funniest walk. With her arms bent at the elbows and stuck to her sides, she shuffled along, paddling with her hands. In profile, what with the odd shape of her back and hindquarters, she looked like a tortoise in a vertical position. But we had become so used to her that we hardly noticed her oddities, until one day when Monique from next door came to play. She took one look at Aunt Noor and gasped.

"You let *fellaheen* stay in your house?" she asked, aghast.

Monique's remark was fairly justified. On re-examining Aunt Noor with Monique's eyes, we had to admit she looked distinctly provincial. Before bad times had forced her to give up her home in the country and come to live in Alexandria, she had always lived in the villages. She was deeply attached to her rural ways, the only ways with any good in them. To have changed her manner of dress now or at any other time was nothing short of heresy. She had no use for those indecent creations that only half covered you. And she stubbornly clung to her black head kerchief and the flowing robes that reached to her ankles, cut in the peasant style with a yoke. Her earthly goods she carried round her arms in the form of twenty-four carat gold bracelets that jingled pleasantly when she moved. Their number diminished with her need for money. Her only other ornaments were a necklace of very big amber beads worn close round her throat, and a pair of diamond drop earrings tied to each other behind her neck with a red silk cord as a precaution against hazards.

It was not in dress alone that Aunt Noor was an anachronism. Modern inventions and the devil were twins. She would have nothing to do with the telephone, and listened to the radio sitting well away, provided someone else was sitting with her. Of mechanical devices she was deeply suspicious. But her greater terror was automobiles. Nothing would induce her to go out into the streets in heavy traffic. If she had to go on a visit she would be up and out at the crack of day before the streets were too crowded with cars. People were used to her ringing their doorbells at the break of day. They were also used to having her stay the whole day and part of the night until dawn of the following day, when she would start on the return journey. Having no car, she was forced to use public transport. Getting herself in and out of a bus was a complicated business where everyone who could lent a hand. People waiting at the bus stop supported her rear as she clambered up, holding her long robe by the hem. In getting off she counted on equally kind passengers to steady her down the aisle while she gathered her many veils about her and picked up the hem of her gown, calling to the bus driver in a panic to be patient, he was not to move before she got off. She was going to remember him in her prayers, she promised, as a reward for his patience.

Aunt Noor's rustic upbringing had kept the fundamental decencies intact. Untouched by the complexities of town life, she deeply believed in the brotherhood of man. Which made her a great favorite with the servants. She addressed a *souffragui* as "my son," and when they were particularly nice to her she called them *"ya habibi"*—"my darling"—and patted them gratefully on the back. Older domestics were simply "brother" or "sister," which infuriated Mother who compared poorly in this light. What a pity Aunt Noor did not live to witness this era of workers and peasants. It would so have gladdened her heart.

In view of Aunt Noor's apparent senility, we reckoned she did not have much longer to live and we eagerly looked forward to the time of her death. It was thrilling to think of the things we would be able to report at school. The event promised grand doings. It was going to provide us with a wealth of incidents to relate to classmates. At last we should be able to prove we were every bit as worldly as they. Mother's fanatic obsession with what was *comme il faut* had the result of relegating us to the lower orders in the hierarchy of the school. Naïve, gullible, and incarcerated in the narrow world of children, we were no match for our sophisticated companions with their tremendous range of experience. Obviously they played with "bad" children and picked up bad language and were allowed to sit in the drawing room when there were guests. The result was very enviable. The disadvantages of our tame and uneventful existence were all too obvious, and we longed for something to shatter its peaceful flow. That's why we pinned great hopes on poor Aunt Noor. How wonderful it would be if she died at home and we could actually observe a funeral from close up. Perhaps even actually see her close her eyes and die. Maybe we would be made to wear mourning, and we would go to school with long sad faces and all the other children would gather round and ask what happened. We would be noticed. Then the roles would be reversed and it would be our turn to dominate an awed audience and speak of great things. Here was our chance of promotion to the ranks of the worldly, like those girls always flaunting married sisters and nieces and nephews and stepmothers. We could hardly wait.

When eventually Aunt Noor died in hospital and cheated us of our funeral, we almost hated her for it. Our dreams of greatness never took off the ground and we stayed where we were, abject inferiors, though terribly *comme il faut*.

## *Fadhma Ait Mansour Amrouche*
## OUTCAST AND EXILE

Algeria 1968 French

Fadhma Ait Mansour Amrouche is perhaps best known as the mother of the novelist Taos Amrouche and the poet Jean Amrouche, who were greatly influenced by her artistry. A member of the Berber Kabyle people, she was born in 1882 in Kabylia, a mountainous region in northern Algeria. As an illegitimate child, she was shunned and tormented in her village. Her mother entrusted her to the French boarding school at a time when most Algerians refused to send their daughters to French schools. It became a refuge for the young girl, who spent ten years of her life there, studying with Madame Malaval, a Frenchwoman passionately dedicated to the cause of female education in Algeria.

Forced to leave the school when it closed, she went to work in a Catholic mission hospital, where she met Belkacem-ou-Amrouche, a devout Catholic who worked as a teacher. They married when she was sixteen and newly baptized. She said that, once she had met husband, she never felt lonely again: "From now on, there were two of us, for better or for worse." They lived together for sixty years and raised eight children. The family moved first to Tunisia and then to France, where she died in 1967.

Amrouche began writing her autobiography, *My Life Story*, in 1946 and completed it in 1962. It was published posthumously in 1968, and stands as one of the first narrative works by a contemporary Maghrebi woman. In the first excerpt included here, "Outcast," she describes her early life as in colonial Algeria, documenting the cruelty of local customs that branded her a "child of sin" and caused her to be separated from her mother, and providing a rare glimpse of French education for Algerian girls in the nineteenth century. In the second excerpt, "Exile," she reveals the alienation felt by Christian Kabyles living among Muslims, and the pain felt by exiles living far from their homeland. Her memoirs embody the many hardships suffered by Algerian women, then and now, and also testify to their strength and endurance.

Amrouche's poem "Song of Exile" is a prayer that her precious daughter be spared some of the pain she herself experienced in exile. Unpublished in her lifetime, the poem was published by her daughter, Taos Amrouche, in a volume that included her own poems and her mother's. Taos Amrouche also published *Le Grain magique* (*The Magic Grain*), a collection of Berber tales, proverbs, and songs transmitted to her by her mother, and recorded *Chants berbères de Kabylie* (Berber

Songs from Kabylia), an album of traditional Kabyle songs that had been translated into French by her brother Jean Amrouche, one of the leading Francophone North African poets of his time.

*Zahia Smail Salhi*

✦

## OUTCAST

On the night of my birth, my mother was all alone with her two small children: There was no one to assist her or to go for help. She delivered by herself and bit through the umbilical cord. The next day, an old woman brought her a little food.

When I was nine days, old my mother tied me firmly to her breast, for it had been snowing, and set out with a child in each hand to lodge a complaint against my father with the public prosecutor. She wanted my father to recognize me and give me his name. He refused. . . . The case dragged on for three years. During this time, through heat and cold, my mother returned again and again to plead with and harass the magistrates. . . . After three years he was sentenced to pay damages—the sum of 300 francs!—which my mother refused to accept. Since the law at that time forbade the establishment of paternity, he could not be forced to recognize me, and so the seal of shame was branded on my forehead. In despair, my mother plunged me into the icy waters of the spring. But I did not die. The world is a cruel place, and "the child of sin" becomes a scapegoat of society, especially in Kabylia. I cannot count the blows I received. What endless bullying I suffered! If I ventured into the street, I would risk being knocked down and trampled upon.

My mother became frightened. What was she to do with me? How was she to protect me from people's cruelty? She heard that at the Ouadhias there was a convent of the white sisters who took in little girls and looked after them. She thought that if she entrusted me to these nuns, she would have no more worries on my account, that no one could hurt me any longer.

I am haunted by a dreadful picture from this period of my life: a tiny girl standing against the wall of a corridor, covered with filth, dressed in sackcloth, with a little mug of excrement hung around her neck. . . . In addition to this punishment, the child was also flogged until she bled. When my mother came the following Wednesday, she found me still covered with the marks of the whip. She stroked my bruises, then sent for the nun and, pointing to the weals, she said, "Was it for this that I entrusted my daughter to you? Give her back to me!" The nun undressed me, even stripping me of my chemise. My mother took off her headscarf, knotted two corners together over my shoulder, pinned the material together on the other shoulder, . . . untied her wide woolen girdle, which she fastened round her head, and lifted me onto her back.

In the autumn, the *Qaïd*, a Muslim judge who fulfilled civil as well as religious functions, sent for my mother and said, "Your daughter Fadhma is a burden to you. Take her to Fort-National where a school for girls has just been opened. She will be happy there and treated well."...My mother held out for a long time, but . . . the village people, who still considered me the child of sin, were disapproving. In October or November of 1886, she agreed to give me up. Once again she took me on her back and we set out. I cannot recall this journey; I can only remember that as we climbed down toward the river we picked arbutus berries to eat—I can still see the red fruit. This brings me to the end of the first part of my childhood. I returned to the village from time to time for holidays, but I was never ill-treated again.

## EXILE

I had only two days in which to finish all the preparations, and though it was midwinter, I had to get all the laundry that Lla Djohra and I had washed in the river. In the distance I watched the mill turning for the last time. I said all my farewells and we left this house where we had thought to spend the rest of our lives. I will never forget that nightmare journey, on hard wooden seats, next to Arabs who kept on singing the same tune, over and over again.

We slept over at Constantine....The next day we had to leave for an unknown city. After traveling for a whole day and half the night, we finally reached Tunis. At the station we were met by friends from home: Lhoussine-ou-Boubachi and his cousin picked up our luggage between them and took us to our lodgings. Lhoussine had ordered a meal from a cheap restaurant, but I couldn't touch anything.

We were right in the middle of the Muslim quarter, and I didn't speak a word of Arabic. My husband made some essential purchases that same day: a rope and a small barrel for drawing water from the well, some kitchen utensils, and a bucket for fetching water from the tap, as the well water wasn't fit for drinking.

The next day, Belkacem went to his office. Paul, a child of seven and a half, had to go to buy the bread, vegetables, coffee, and sugar, and fetch water from a tap that was a few yards from the house. Fortunately everything was quite close by. Sometimes Henri, who was four and a half, tried to help his brother carry the bucket, or else a larger boy brought it as far as our door and I took it inside. I would have made myself too conspicuous if I had gone out, with my face uncovered, among all those veiled Muslim women.

I felt very lost, not knowing a word of the local language, Arabic....No one can ever imagine my misery in that period of my exile; when the children were at school and my husband at the office and Jean asleep, I would go up onto the roof, which faced the avenue, to listen avidly to the language of the Moroccan *Chleuhs*, which was very similar to the language of my country!

When the six months lease was up, I told my husband that the best thing would be for us to go to live in the European district, so that I could go out like the other women. He rented a little flat in the rue Sidi-el-Morjani, right in the Sicilian Italian district. With the modest sum at our disposal, we hadn't much choice....The Sunday after we moved my husband went to the auction rooms and bought a sideboard and two beds, one for us and the other for the children. There was nothing to worry about: I had running water in the little kitchen and a flush lavatory that didn't risk getting stopped up like the one in the Arab house.

*Translated by Dorothy S. Blair*

## SONG OF EXILE

Saints of the West, be kind
To my child who comes to you.
Extend to her your protection.

Her hair is jet like a raven's wing,
Her pupils and eyebrows more intense,
Her eyelashes long and curled back.

Her skin is like blossoming roses
On which the dew has dropped
In the still of the night.

Her parted lips
Are a pomegranate
And her teeth a necklace of pearls.

The shade of her neck is such transparent
Limpid amber, as she drinks
You see the waters flow.

Her hands, so small,
Like a child's,
So soft, so silken.

The Lord formed her full of grace;
On days when jewels enhance her beauty,
Oh Lord, preserve her from evil glances.

Oh, dear Lord, take care of her, and fill her with joy,
Open wide all doors for her, and clear her paths,
People her solitude, bring relief to her exile,
And glorify her in everyone's eyes.

*Translated by Abena P. A. Busia and Zahia Smail Salhi*

# LATE TWENTIETH CENTURY

## *Khnata Bennani*
# COME BACK IN TWO WEEKS

Morocco 1975 Arabic

Khnata Bennani was my mother. Born in Fes in 1925, she was orphaned at an early age and was brought up by her uncle, then by her brother, in Fes, Tara, Oujola, and Rabat. She and her sisters spent their time at home doing needlework, which later became a kind of informal job for her. She married a man chosen by her relatives and had eight children, one of whom died in infancy. During times of war and civil unrest, she was sometimes left to manage on her own, while her husband was away working.

Although Khnata Bennani never went to school or learned to read or write, she fiercely defended her daughters' right to education. When her eldest daughter graduated from primary school and was asked by her father to stay home, Khnata Bennani managed to sneak her daughter out of the house and send her to take the exams for secondary school, which girls rarely attended at that time . When she passed her exams, her father had no choice but to let her attend school, and she went on to earn a Ph.D. and become a world famous researcher in molecular physics, and enabled her sisters to follow in her path..

This text is an excerpt from an audio recording made in 1975 by another daughter, Assia, who was then working on the dialect of Fes for her M.A. thesis in linguistics and asked our mother to speak on any subject in order to collect a sample of her speech for phonetic analysis. She found that the recorded material also had historical and literary significance.

Khnata Bennani talks about life in Morocco during World War II and the 1948 Arab-Israeli War that followed the creation of the state of Israel. She also refers to the exile—in August 1953—of Sultan Mohammed V (whom she calls Ben ("son of") Yusef, after his father Moulay Yusef), after he refused to denounce the nationalist movement and consent to French domination of Morocco. The popular uprising that followed, known as the Revolution of the King and the People, continued until his return in 1955 and eventually led to Morocco's gaining independence, with Mohammed V as its first king.

What is most striking about Khnata Bennani's testimony is the fact that she uses the plural "we" to refer to herself. She also uses the word *rajel*, which in Arabic can mean both "the man" and "the husband," to refer to our father. Such usage suggests that she does not define herself as an individual, but rather as a wife, mother, sister, and a member of her family, her community, and her people. Her arranged marriage proved to be quite close and loving: Khnata Bennani died in May 1999 and her husband died only three months later, unable to live without her.

*Khadija Zizi*

✦

I am fifty years old. I was born in Morocco and grew up in Fes. My parents are dead and we were five girls. Two were married when our father was still alive, but three of us, along with our brother, were really young when our father died.

Our uncle brought us up until we were able to work at *dar lamaâlma* [the needlework teacher's house] doing *tarz algharza* [needlepoint].

We used to go every day and learn needlework, a little bit every day. It took us ten years of learning at *dar lamaâlma* before we could actually start doing needlework on our own. At first we stayed home and embroidered: We would set up the loom, buy plain white fabric and silk, and start embroidering on our own, without having to go to the *maâlma* [needlework teacher]. We would do needlework night and day.

We had afternoons off, and we would go up on the terrace and make friends with girls, visit with them, and spend the whole afternoon playing cards. That's the time when people usually went out, but we didn't; we didn't go out. Sometimes for a month we would not leave the house. So at sunset we would come down from the terrace, have dinner, and resume our needlework until bedtime. Then in the morning we would go back to embroidering. Doing needlework was what today you might call entertainment.

Our ancestors were from a branch, called *firâwn* [pharaoh] of the Bennani family. Our forefathers were religious scholars who studied science. People used to consult them on many issues. They used to give judicial decisions. One of our great-grandfathers studied so hard that he could no longer lift his eyelids. Someone had to do it for him: His wife used to take tweezers and lift his eyelids so that she could see the inside of his eyes. He used to provide legal counseling to a large number of people, but he would never accept payment. People would bring gifts because he didn't accept money. They would bring a leather pouch full of honey or pure butter. When he was not in, his wife would accept the gift for him. She would transfer the honey or butter into jars. Upon his return, she would inform him of the gifts, and he would send for the people who had brought the gifts and ask them to take them back. He did not want to do legal counseling as a job; he wanted to do it out of religious belief and not for material reward. So they would come and take back their gifts, along with the jars. At night, just before going to bed, he would give away all the leftover food to the poor. He would buy everything all over again each day. He would not accept payment of any kind.

This great-grandfather's grandfather was a saint, and there is a mausoleum in his name with a dome and a *darboz* [folding screen], which people come to visit, but he does not have a money box. He, too, did not want to be paid. All our ancestors refused to take money. They worked for the love of God and not for any material reward. . . .

When we grew up, we started getting married one after the other, the eldest first, then the next in age, and so forth. . . . People started coming to see our brother, our guardian, to ask for us in marriage, while we were busy doing needlework. Often we did not like these men: They were either too old, too poor, or we didn't like the work they did. So we rejected several of them until this Zizi fellow [laughter] came. When he came, we told him: "We don't know anything about you; come back in two weeks; we will inquire about you." So we did, and when we asked people who knew his family, they said that they were serious and decent people.

So when he came two weeks later, we said "yes." But there was another problem. We had never seen him and we needed to know what he looked like. So we requested that people send him to us so that we could see whether he was tall or short. They asked him to bring us a steel hammer. He did bring it to our family, and that's when we were able to see what he looked like. Still, neither of us had seen each other. So when we found that he was of a good family and that his age was about the same as ours, that's when we were able to say another yes.

So his family came and met ours and proposed, and we decided on a date for the engagement party. On that day he brought us fabric for caftans, along with henna and dates. Still, even at this point, neither of us had seen the other. Four months later we signed the *sdaq* [marriage contract], at which time he also brought gifts: *bahja* [silk fabric], a set of eleven gold bracelets, henna, and dates. So the families got together and the *aduls* [notaries] came. Since his father was still alive, the *aduls* did not have to ask him. But since my father was dead, they had to ask me whether I agreed to marry him. So we signed the marriage contract and held a party with music for lots of guests. Six months later they asked us to set a date for the wedding. During that time we prepared the trousseau: We bought wool, and with needlework we embroidered bed sheets, tablecloths, and napkins. We embroidered the gifts for his parents in needlepoint.

When the time of the wedding approached, I was living in the city of Fes and he was living in Taza. So he sent a car and a bus to help us carry all the furniture, the trousseau, and everything else. My relatives went to Taza, put all the furniture in the rooms, hung the wall carpets and curtains, and placed the pillows. This all took place amid the music of drums and the *yuyus* [ululation of joy destined to chase the evil eye from the house] of the *neggafas* [women who are hired to decorate and sing praise songs to the bride]. There was a big party. Two days later, he sent a car to take the bride to Taza. So my family members accompanied me to Taza, where the big wedding party would take place, accompanied by a big Andalusian band. That was the *dkhul* [wedding night] and the following day the *sbuhi* [morning after the wedding]. In fact, the ceremonies lasted seven days and we celebrated each day in a different way. One day we would put on one caftan with a set of pearls and another day we would get dressed in a different caftan and different jewelry. At the end of the week the guests started leaving, and that's when we went to our house. . . .

My wedding took place in the midst of the war [1939] and people could not stay long: They wanted to go back home, but they were scared to leave.

When I was seven months pregnant with my second child, Si Mohammed, my husband had to take a job in Oujda. So he left when I was seven months pregnant and our little girl was still a toddler. I delivered Si Mohammed in Taza while his father was in Oujda. We were not able to move to Oujda because during the war there were no buses or trucks with which to move the furniture. We applied for a train car, but we obtained approval the day I delivered the baby. So we moved to Oujda by train, with all the furniture and other household things, when the baby was six days old. We had the naming ceremony in Oujda. From then on things grew worse because of the war: Products were scarce; we were rationed and we had to use food vouchers. Food, clothing, and household furniture were extremely limited.

Four years later [1948] war broke out in Oujda. Emotions were running high and Muslims started killing Jews and Jews killing Muslims. There was complete chaos. They broke into homes, killed people, and looted. People were going around stabbing anyone and everyone. I was very scared and took my little daughter and stayed with my in-laws because I was afraid they would break into my house and kill me. . . .

We were faced with the frightful event of Ben Yusef [Mohammed V]. When they decided to send him to exile [August 1953], people took to the streets of Oujda and there was chaos and killings. Over 600 people were killed in Oujda. My son Si Mohammed was still quite young and one afternoon, he went to fetch a bottle of milk. That day, my husband was away in Sâidiya. I was alone in the house with the children and kept expecting the return of Si Mohammed and my husband. I locked the house and kept waiting for them, but they stayed out all night. . . .

My son Si Mohammed was carrying the bottle of milk. He was told that there was no way he could reach home because there were roadblocks. The gates to the city and many roads were closed off and people were carrying corpses. My husband was told to stay in Sâidiya overnight because the road to Oujda was closed and there was much violence. It wasn't until the following morning after that they both returned. The boy had stayed overnight with a woman who had offered shelter and had brought him home that morning. The husband was able to come back from Sâidiya once the gates opened. So from then on we were all involved in the chaotic situation of Ben Yusef. Everyone was crying over him, even the baby in the womb was almost crying. People of all ages were hailing him and calling his name. The climax of this event was that people started seeing his face in the moon. They killed most "traitors" and there was chaos. Two years and three months later, we were glad to have Ben Yusef back and people started throwing parties and celebrating. We became independent and gained our freedom. When Ben Yusef returned, people celebrated everywhere and flew into Rabat from all over the country. Everyone was extremely happy and, thank God, life got better.

*Translated by Khadija Zizi*

# Rabha Moha
# I WANT TO TELL YOU

## Morocco 1977   Berber

Rabha Moha was my husband's paternal grandmother. Born around 1900 in a small Berber village of the Middle Atlas called Timoulilt, she died in 1982 in the nearby city of Beni-Mellal. Moha lost her husband at a young age and had to struggle, alone and poor, to support and protect her family in a difficult, often hostile, rural environment. Of her three children, only one survived. She lived with her son all her life, never hesitating to follow him wherever his military career took him, and helped care for her son's seven children whom she dearly loved and was proud of. She liked adventure and once traveled to the Moroccan Sahara alone.

Rabha Moha faced hardships, including semiblindness, with courage and an extraordinary sense of humor, and never admitted weakness, even in her old age. She refused to be impressed or intimidated by others, whoever they might be. A famous storyteller, she excelled in outsmarting her interlocutors and always made sure that she had the last word; people carefully avoided making mistakes in her presence. Moha had an inquisitive mind, and although she had never been to school, she had a rare flair for news and was capable of relating facts with great acuity. Most of all, she loved reciting and singing poetry. She improvised all the verses recorded and transcribed here.

Moha's poems touch on topics ranging from colonialism, freedom, tribal affairs, and love, to hospitality and circumcision. In her poems about colonization and the French army, which she encountered when she was living in the historic city of Meknes, she brilliantly expresses the humiliation she felt, using sarcastic wit, for example, to express her willingness to eat French food, since it was free. Although she was impressed by French material wealth, she was angry to be dependent on the French, and even more angry to see her sons and grandsons in subservience to the colonial powers (as when she describes them being forced to carry *tishbriyin*, or jugs). Highly conscious of the paradox, she voiced such anger in simple but powerful verse.

Rabha Moha speaks about real people of her time and local affairs in her tribe, the Ayt Uherda. Courageously, she rages against the authorities and wants to complain to the Sultan—who was a symbol of Moroccan nationalism and pride—about the *pacha* (rural sheriff) and *qaïd* (tribal chief). The rebellious songs of this old, almost blind, illiterate Berber woman, at a time when free speech was dangerous, inspire admiration. Love is also a recurrent theme, through which Moha expresses her passion for life even when she sings of the longings or sorrows of romantic love. She also sings of love for her family, including Fatima, her eldest granddaughter, and a son who is undergoing male circumcision. Moroccan boys are usually circumcized between the ages of one and five. The ritual celebrates boyhood as the boy's father and one or two paternal uncles gather around the child and the surgeon, and the women gather around the boy's mother and sing.

*Fatima Sadiqi*

## Song One

I want to tell you
What big buildings
The French have built
In Meknes city.
They have decorated the buildings
With rich-looking marble floors.
Let us take buckets
And ask for food
From the French,
And eat soup since
They give it to us
For free.

## Song Two

In the name of God
And the Prophet Muhammad,
Who are the Best,
They told me
You are not so generous.
I came back from the French office and
I found my sons
Carrying *tishbriyin*
Like women.
I said, Oh, God, what is happening to me?
Oh, please help me, God.
This is my destiny.
I will not have children any more
Who will work for the French
When they grow up.

## SONG THREE

The French army
Has killed civilian women
And left with their bags
On their backs,
Thinking that they had defeated
The German army.
I would like to tell you,
O, dear friend,
May God help us all.
O, my tribe, Ayt Uherda,
Where are you heading?
Ahmed ou Baha is now
The pasha.
Moha ou Bami is the *qaïd*.
The barracks of Touzdiyin are busy.
I pray God give us more rain;
I pray God help me
To send letters
To the Sultan
And tell him the *qaïd*
Is dead.

## SONG FOUR

O, God, were I a bird,
I could go out at night.
O, God, were I a car,
I would take my lover
For a free ride,
And we would be happy
Together.
O, God, were I a bird,
I would fly over the mountains;
I would take a walk on the mountains;
I would search for a suitable companion.

## SONG FIVE

Love grows solidly
On a base like the wall
Of a building.
Love is growing every day
In my heart.

We're quite happy.
Fatima, you're like
A palm-tree on water.
I love you.
A girl went to bring water
From the spring.
A young man went to accompany her.
They started to have a chat.

## SONG SIX

I feel really sick,
But it is not really apparent
On my face.
God knows what the matter is
With me.
Is this sickness or love
For my boyfriend who has jilted me?

## SONG SEVEN

You have caused me trouble,
You broke my heart.
O, enemy, say good things
About me.
If you own the sky,
Let it fall on my head.

## SONG EIGHT

Come back, love,
O, come back, my love,
You have many brothers,
Come to our place,
Even if you are in power.
If you don't like someone,
Tell her, may your brothers die.
Before you die,
O, come back, my love,
And drop in.
O, Muslim woman,
You are a nice person.
I was crying at the same time as the donkey.
O, come back, my love
To my place.

## Song Nine

Come without any fuss.
Come and see me at home.
You people I love,
I would like to see you.

## Song Ten

Come back, darling.
My lover's house,
If only you were on
My way back home.
Come over, darling.
Come back home.
My lover and I
Are crying.
Come back, darling.
No one has won.

## Song Eleven

O sorcerer, do something!
Help me find
My companion.
He left me without
A warning.
I'll give you shelter.
I'll give you a milk cow.
O my lover's kiss,
You are the pure waters of the mountain,
If I could find it,
And drink it when it's hot.

## Song Twelve

In the name of God
We start.
May the pain die out
For my son.
What a nice boy I have.
I'm proud of my son.
I'll give him full support
In the name of God
The Just,

The Compassionate.
O, God, help us.
O, angels, protect my son.
May the pain die out
For my son.
Some fresh air
Is moving my son's hair.
What a lovely son I have.
I give him all my love and care.
Go away, surgeon!
You have scared my son.
Go away, surgeon!
May the pain die out
For my son.
May the pain die out
For my son.

*Translated by Fatima Sadiqi*

## *Saida Menebhi*
# TWO POEMS: PRISON AND THE PROSTITUTES
Morocco 1977    French

Saida Menebhi's involvement in politics began in 1972, when she was a twenty-year-old student majoring in English language and literature at Mohammed V University in Rabat. The Moroccan government, originally a constitutional monarchy, had become increasingly repressive, with King Hassan II dissolving parliament, rigging elections, and cracking down on political dissent. (The King, in turn, survived several coup and assassination attempts.) Menebhi joined the labor movement and the Marxist-Leninist organization called *Ila Al-Amam* (To Go Forward), which opposed the regime. In 1973, the Moroccan Students' Union was dissolved, and on 16 January 1976, Saida Menebhi was arrested, along with many other students.

Jailed in Casablanca, Saida Menebhi went on several hunger strikes to demand a hearing and denounce the violation of prisoners' rights. At the notorious Casablanca trials in early 1977, she was sentenced to five years in jail and two more for contempt and imprisoned in the civil jail in Casablanca. On 8 November 1977, she started a forty-day hunger strike to denounce the treatment of prisoners and claim her right to be called a political prisoner. This led to her death on 11 December 1977, in Ibn Rushd hospital in Casablanca. She was twenty-five.

Saida Menebhi was victim of the era of fear and repression known as the Years of Lead, after the lead bullets used by the Moroccan security forces against perceived dissidents. Political activists and thousands of others who opposed the regime were imprisoned, exiled, or simply disappeared. By the early 1990s, with Morocco moving toward a greater measure of democracy, King Hassan created a Royal Advisory Council on Human Rights (*le Conseil Consultatif des Droits de l'Homme*, or CCDH) to look into allegations of abuses by the government, including the treatment of political prisoners. When King Mohammed V came to power in 1999, he made human rights reform a top priority. The Equity and Reconciliation Commission (*Instance de l'Equité et de la Réconciliation*. or IER), was created in 2004. The "truth"commission collected statements on violations of human rights occurring between 1960 and 1999, and invited victims and their families to file claims for compensation, although it did not identify or prosecute human rights offenders. The president of the IER from 2004 to 2007, Driss Benzekri, was a former member of *Ila Al-Amam* and a former political prisoner. He died on 20 May 2007.

Saida Menebhi was a devoted communist who supported oppressed people in Palestine, Chile, and Bolivia. She also spoke for women who were oppressed by social forces and by their husbands, and is commonly referred to as the "martyr of the feminist movement" in Morocco. Between January 1976 and November 1977, she wrote twenty-six poems and fourteen letters to her family from her cell, in which she describes her arrest, the hunger strike, and her rage at the system. They were first published in France by the human rights group *Les Comités de Lutte Contre la Répression au Maroc.*

"Prison" is a letter in the form of a poem that Saida Menebhi wrote to her boyfriend, Aziz, who had been sentenced to thirty years. It evokes the intensity of both her love and her political commitment. She alludes to the popular hero Abdelkrim al-Khattabi, the Berber leader from the Rif Mountains who fought against Spanish and French colonialism from 1921 to 1925, winning a decisive battle against the Spanish that is considered the symbolic start of the war of independence. Menebhi also cites Abdellatif Zerwal, the poet, philosopher, and activist who served as president of *Ila Al-Amam* and was arrested and tortured to death in 1974. His famous declaration, "We are losing our blood drop by drop," resounds in Menebhi's wish to write her words of love and defiance in blood. It is clear that she is willing to become a martyr to her cause like Zerwal, "whom they killed / But who shall never die."

"The Prostitutes" expresses Menebhi's empathic view of women who have no choice but to sell their bodies, and lose their souls as well. Some of these women were her cellmates, and told her that they had turned to prostitution in order to survive and feed their children. The original French title, "*Filles de joie*" (Girls of Joy) is a popular euphemism for prostitutes; the usage here is clearly ironic, since the lives Menebhi depicts are anything but joyful. She refers to the 1964 song about the grim lives of prostitutes, "*Au Suivant*," or "Next," by the legendary Belgian singer-songwriter Jacques Brel.

*Khadija Zizi*

✦

# PRISON

In your last letter
You were telling me,
I feel that our love is strong,
Stronger than repression,
Than the thick darkness
Of jail.
These words make my blood spurt.
They water my thirsty body
And fill it with invincible strength.
These words I want to carve
On the gray wall
Of my jail cell.
But how?
I own no nail, no knife;
These are banned;
They are thought to be dangerous.
How then, my darling,
Whose face shines
Like the summer sun,
You whose eyes
Are a huge meadow
Where red poppies, daisies, and lilies grow,
How then shall I proceed?
Shall I cut my veins
To write these words in my blood?
Or shall I sharpen my nails
To etch the words?
Don't worry, my darling,
I am a communist.
My perseverance, together with yours
And that of all others,
Runs in our blood.
It comes from the People;
We take after Abdelkrim, the hero of the mountains,
After Zerwal, the unforgettable martyr,
The man whom they killed,
But who shall never die,
The man whose heart
Never knew fear.

## THE PROSTITUTES

When I look at these girls,
I see faces with scars;
I see bodies that bear witness to an entire life.
Yet they are still under twenty,
These girls who people call prostitutes.
I don't know why,
But I keep hearing Jacques Brel's song
In which he hollers "next!"
Forgive my forgetfulness,
Because song titles are
One of those things
That jail erases
When memory becomes frail.

When I look at these girls
I see sun-wet eyes
That desperately try to shine.
I think of them
When they make love
And sell kisses,
Just like the flower-shop girl
Sells flowers.
I think of them
Naked,
Outdoors or in bed,
A place that retains only a shred of their souls,
Or a pool of blood
From their dilated bodies.

When I look at these girls,
I see weighted-down breasts
Like two cathedrals
That have long since been erected
Under a sky loaded with bitterness,
Clouds, and haze.
I think of them
When they take off their clothes
And then quickly get dressed.
They don't want to miss the next customer,
The bus,
For they need to keep feeding their children.

When I look at these girls,
I see statues.
Can they make love?
Do they bend? Do they break? Do they like it?
Every day,
"Next" hammers in my head.
When I look at these girls,
I see a row of icons,
Even though they are still under twenty.

*Translated by Khadija Zizi*

## Zainab Al-Ghazali
# TORTURE IN PRISON

Egypt  1978  Arabic

Zainab Al-Ghazali is one of the most prominent Muslim women leaders of the twentieth century. She was born in 1917 in Egypt's Dakahleya province. Her father was an Al-Azhar scholar who gave her an Islamic upbringing. In her memoir, she writes of how in her childhood he told her stories of the heroic women of early Islam, who had fought fearlessly on the battlefields for their faith. Encouraging her to emulate them, he even made her a wooden sword, and would draw a circle on the ground and ask her to stand inside and brandish the sword to fight the enemies of God. When she was ten, her father died, and the whole family moved to Cairo, where her elder brother lived. Sensing and fearing her outspokenness even at this early age, her brother decided not to allow her to finish her education, but she managed to circumvent his decision and attend school.

After Al-Ghazali received her secondary school certificate, she joined the Egyptian Feminist Union under the leadership of Huda Shaarawi, engaging in the struggle for women's political and social rights while keeping within Islamic principles. She became a prominent member of the Union, impressing Huda Shaarawi with her eloquence. She was also receiving religious instruction from prominent Al-Azhar scholars, including Sheikh Ali Mahfouz and Mohamed El Naggar, who tried to persuade her that feminist principles as advocated by Huda Shaarawi were at variance with Islamic teaching.

Then one day, while cooking, the stove exploded and Al-Ghazali suffered extensive burns to her face and body. Overhearing the others talking of her imminent death, she vowed to sever all her ties with Shaarawi's group, to dedicate her life to the service of God, and help bring society back to the glories of the early Islamic era and women back to the examples of early faithful women. After regaining her health, Al-Ghazali resigned from the Egyptian Feminist Union, and in 1936, at the age of eighteen, she established *Jamaa'at al-Sayyidaat al-Muslimaat*, the Muslim Women's Association. Her lectures for women at the Ibn

Tulun Mosque in Cairo drew thousands. Al-Ghazali advocated for an Islamic state governed by Islamic law, which, she believed, would grant women all essential rights. She encouraged women to be educated and involved in public life, but believed their first duty was to their husbands and children.

While Al-Ghazali resisted any formal affiliation, the Muslim Women's Association was linked with the Muslim Brotherhood, whose leaders were calling for a radical application of Islam in which, according to their stated principles, the Qur'an would become the "sole reference point" for "ordering the life of the Muslim family, individual, community . . . and state." Both groups affirmed the legitimacy of using violence in certain circumstances in the cause of Islam. Both stood in opposition to secular socialist ideology, which had found expression in the nationalist rhetoric and policies of the Nasser regime after the revolution of 1952.

In response to what it regarded as the seditious political agenda and growing power of the Muslim Brotherhood, the Egyptian government began a crackdown in the mid-1960s. Islamist women were not spared either. On 20 August 1964, Egyptian intelligence officers broke into Al-Ghazali's house, searched it, and took her to prison, with the claim that the Muslim Brothers were involved in a conspiracy to murder President Gamal Abdel Nasser. Al-Ghazali was brutally tortured in an attempt to force her to confess to involvement in such a plot. She received a sentence of twenty-five years of hard labor, but was released from prison soon after Nasser's death in 1971. Until her death in 2005, she continued to teach and write in the Islamist cause, and to be involved in the turbulent politics that straddle the tenuous line separating politics from religion in North Africa and the Middle East.

The following two extracts are from Al-Ghazali's memoir *Ayyam min Hayati* (Days in my Life), published in Arabic in 1978, and in English under the title *Return of the Pharaoh: Memoir in Nasser's Prison* in 1994. She describes what she clearly believes are miracles, which allowed her to survive torture in prison—first an attack by dogs, and then another by a man sent to rape her, a method of degrading women prisoners and forcing them to admit wrongdoing. Although Al-Ghazali claims she killed the attacker with her own bare hands and teeth, unconfirmed accounts speak of the man's fainting.

*Amira Nowaira*

✦

A door leading to a dark room was opened and I was let in. A bright electric light was suddenly switched on. This was the torture room and I saw that it was full of dogs. So many of them, I could not tell the number. Out of sheer terror, I closed my eyes and crossed my arms on my chest. I heard the door being bolted with chains and locks. The dogs pounced on me, on every part of me: my head, my hands, my chest, my back. They were all over me and I felt their fangs digging into my body. I opened my eyes, but closed them from the terror around me. I stuck my hands in my armpits, and recited God's names, beginning with "Allah, Allah" and moving through the other names, one after the other, while the dogs clambered all over me. I felt their teeth dig deep even in my scalp. I called to my God out loud: "Dear God, let my mind be wholly absorbed in you and make everything else sink into oblivion. Let me think of nothing but you, you are the one and only. Take me unto you alone. Transport me away from the world of images, place me in your presence, and bestow your peace on me. Take me away from the world of fickleness and change, and clothe me in the robes of your love. Make me breathe my last in you, find love in you, and get satisfaction and relish with you. Make me stand firm and steadfast, Oh, God, like all those who have faith in you." I said all this to myself, while the dogs worked their teeth into my body. Hours passed before the door was opened again and I was taken out of the room. I had thought my white garments would be all soaked in blood, but to my amazement, they were not stained, as though not a single fang had touched them. "Oh, God, how great you are! You have been with me all along. Oh, God, am I worthy of your kindness and generosity?" I said to myself, while the Devil, holding me by the arm, whispered, "Why haven't you been torn to pieces by the dogs? Why?" . . .

✦

The man, sitting in front of me, implored me to admit to anything they wished me to admit, because he did not want to harm me. On the other hand, however, if he did not carry out what they had ordered him to do, he would be punished, severely and mercilessly. So I told him with all the force I could muster, "Don't even think of taking a single step closer to me. If you did, I would kill you. I would, I would, I would. Do you understand?" I could see that the man shrank and lost heart, but he took a couple of steps toward me. Unaware, I found my hands pressing on his neck, and I was yelling at the top of my voice, "In the name of God. God is great." I planted my teeth in his neck, and he dropped from between my hands, completely lifeless, white soap-like froth issuing from his mouth. The monster fell before my feet, a motionless corpse, frothing at the mouth. I could hardly believe that I, who had suffered unendurable pains and whose body was inscribed by the wounds inflicted by the whips all over, I, who was scarred in every part of the body, was able to overcome the monster commanded to ravish me. God has infused me with his might. It was a brutal battle in which virtue scored a victory over the ferocity of vice. It was a true sign, a good omen for the saved. Praise be to Allah, the only God. The tyrants are scared and defeated, while those with a calling, though incarcerated behind prison bars and having no sustenance except the power of their faith in God, emerge victorious.

*Translated by Amira Nowaira*

## *Amina Wahib*
# THE ROSE

Morocco   1980   Arabic

Amina Wahib was born in 1940. Her father prevented her from going to school because she was a girl., but her courage and ambition drove her to acquire knowledge in her own way. She would sit in a corner and listen discreetly to her brother as he recited his lessons aloud. As a married woman, Wahib experienced another kind of injustice, since her husband saw poetry as "the work of the devil." To him, she is just *ulia*, a woman under the responsibility of a man, who must obey him and satisfy his wishes. In this way, Amina Wahib is no different from millions of Moroccan women who are reduced to subservience and silence.

In spite of these obstacles, Amina Wahib insists upon expressing herself and asserting her identity through writing. She writes *zajal*, a very popular genre of Moroccan Arabic poetry. In "The Rose," she conveys the frustrated feelings of a silenced woman. The rose-woman she describes is hardly a blooming flower. Rather, she is fading away, and will never have the opportunity to bloom and spread her enchanting perfume. The author's anguish is present in every line, along with strength and dignity.

*Fouzia Baddouri*

✦

Life is both easy and difficult for her;
She lights a candle to brighten her way,
Then walks and turns round,
Prepares her tomb,
And takes out the veil.
The trip is too long for her:
She'll travel the whole world.
Her rose is fading away;
Its odor has gone.
On her door there are too many keys.
Her fingers are like pens.
Trees scrape against walls.
Her inheritance cannot be shared.
Her walls have become colorless,
And her cheeks tattooless.
Her pain has reached its peak.
She cries with no tears.
With her hair she makes belts.
Like a man, she can slaughter an animal.
The burden is too heavy for her.
She spends endless nights thinking.
Her torment is endless.
And with her help the dove has built its nest.

*Translated by Fouzia Baddouri*

# Aicha Mekki
# ON PROSTITUTION

Morocco  1980    French

Aicha Mekki was born Rokia Fetha in Taza, Morocco, in 1950. She came from a modest background, and her father died when she was a child. She attended school in Taza before moving to Rabat to study French at the university. Mekki chose to write in French because it was for her a language of dreams and escape, and also because she was drawn to the West and its culture: "I am eager to discover the West," she said in one of her articles.

Mekki began her career as a journalist at the Moroccan radio station in Rabat. She then moved to the Moroccan Francophone daily *L'Opinion*, where she would remain for seventeen years, writing primarily in the section called "*Au banc de la société*"[On the bench of society], which chronicled judicial matters. She depicted Moroccan society in depth, describing the hardships of the poorest and most disadvantaged segments of society. She wrote of people who were usually marginalized and ignored, including battered wives, maids, drug addicts, alcoholics, prostitutes, and illuminated such problems as violence against women, obsolete traditions, social exclusion, and the ravages of poverty. Her work reflected her belief in the nobility and dignity of all human beings, and often took her to forgotten corners of society where few journalists, much less female journalists, had ever dared go.

Mekki led a humble life in a small, shabby apartment in Casablanca with neither electricity nor running water. For two years before her death, she wrote her sad and shocking newspaper stories by candlelight. In May 1992, she was found dead in her apartment at the age of forty-two. The authorities ruled it a natural death, but rumors persisted that she had been murdered, and her death remains an enigma. She was buried in Casablanca in the Cemetery Al-Shuhada (Martyr's Cemetery), reserved for those who made sacrifices or gave their lives for greater ideals. Aicha Mekki was widely recognized by colleagues and readers as a dedicated and outstanding journalist. She was also known for her humility, simplicity, and love for others, as well as her remarkable courage. In 1994, the Aicha Mekki Prize was established to recognize the best crime reporting by young journalists.

In this article, Aicha Mekki turns her uncompromising gaze on a problem that most Moroccans wish to ignore—the world of prostitutes, the "go-betweens," or pimps, who exploit them, and the corrupt officials who permit and even profit from their business. Mekki describes a famous prostitution scandal that erupted following the arrest of a notorious pimp and important members of his network. In her reference to pimps who cater to "petrodollars"—wealthy men from the oil-producing Gulf states who come to Morocco for sex—she raises an early warning against sex tourism, which would only become more widespread in Morocco in decades to come. Mekki's aim is to force people in general, and decision-makers in particular, to confront the dangers of prostitution and the corruption linked to it.

*Moha Ennaji*

✦

In recent times, prostitution has been spreading quickly through all layers of Moroccan society. This phenomenon has produced something like secret associations of pimps. In the past, the work of pimps was restricted in duration and scope. Now, some of them have even amassed great fortune and fame. The sensational example of Joseph Ben David, nicknamed Ku Ku, is still vivid in people's minds. Fortunately, this despicable person is in prison now. Much has been written about the Ku Ku scandal, and the problem has been widely debated in the Casablanca tribunal, where the case was tried.

The debate suggests that the phenomenon of prostitution is far from being constrained or limited. Rather, it has been expanding for years. Those involved in "the production of paid love," including pimps and all those who encourage prostitution, lead well-off and stable lives, for they are protected by influential officials in the government. The Ku Ku scandal will undoubtedly be followed by other similar scandals, for prostitution and pimps are still important in our young society. Only naive people would be surprised to learn about the growth of prostitution in our society. Persons involved in prostitution are immoral and ought to be punished. Only in fiction, on television, or in the cinema, does one ordinarily see these disgusting people.

But the question I want to ask here is, what is the role of pimps in our society? The French *Petit Robert Dictionary* defines a "go-between" as a person who works as intermediary in a love affair or sexual liaison in exchange for money, or a person who earns a living from the prostitution of others.

Our penal code distinguishes at least seven types of involvement in prostitution that are punished by law. A person is involved in this activity if he or she helps or participates in prostitution or protects prostitutes or go-betweens; similarly, a person who encourages prostitution or makes money out of it, or a person who lives with a prostitute or a pimp, or who uses another person (adult or minor) in prostitution.

This is the theory, but in reality many prostitutes and go-betweens continue to work and make a lot of money by bribing those functionaries who should indeed be the protectors of the law, rather than assisting dishonorable people. One may see prostitutes and pimps in the streets or on the sidewalks. Prostitution takes place in rented houses or hotels that are often protected by those who should be the first to denounce such misbehavior.

Despite all this, I still believe that it is possible to eradicate prostitution and to destroy its dirty roots. In my previous article, in which I dealt with the problem of a bar-owner named Omar, I outspokenly denounced the new wave of pimps who have become very active and have become thirsty for foreign currency, especially petrodollars.

I made an appeal to the authorities to clean up this social mess, which is an insult to morality. My appeal has been well received, thank God. Many famous pimps have been arrested, and many brothels have been closed down.

Recall that on Saturday 9 February 1980, the tribunal of Casablanca held a session to examine still another case of prostitution and inciting prostitution and drugs. The defendant, Fatima Zairit, nicknamed Al-Abdia, aged forty-one and a widow, was found guilty. She was sentenced to two years in jail and a fine of 10,000 dirhams. This was not the first time that the court found Al-Abdia guilty of being a go-between, for the same tribunal had sentenced her in 1975 to one year's imprisonment. Al-Abdia was arrested this second time on 22 February 1979 in her Casablanca home by the morals police "while she was busy working."

Al-Abdia stood up wearing her black *djellaba* [traditional cloak] before the audience in the court, to which she paid little attention. When the judge asked her about her involvement in prostitution, she replied: "I have been a go-between since 1975. I have received in my house men and women of different ages and from all social levels. I have served them alcoholic drinks and drugs."

On 4 March 1980, a male go-between named Mohamed Bennani was arrested for the same reason and was sentenced to eighteen months' imprisonment.

I hope that this campaign against prostitution will continue. I hope the network of this campaign will grow in intensity so that it can catch more and bigger fish. The precepts of Islam and our values will be in danger if we do not eliminate such horrific misconduct and punish people who are leading a whole generation into total decline. We want to preserve our honor and dignity, which have always characterized Muslim women and men, and without which our lives would be worthless.

*Translated by Moha Ennaji*

## El-Hajja Rqia
# FATMA AND THE OGRESS

Morocco   Mid 1980s   Berber

In Moroccan culture, the most common type of female narratives are folktales, an oral discourse in which older nonliterate women often combine their storytelling with self-empowerment. The original authors of folktales may be unknown, but the tales are transmitted from generation to generation, usually by older women.

"Fatma and the Ogress" was told in the 1980s by El-Hajja Rqia, an elderly, nonliterate Berber woman who lived in the Ayt Warayn region, south of Taza. El-Hajja Rqia enjoyed a good reputation in the village as a respectable woman who had gone to Mecca for pilgrimage. Her social prestige among the villagers gave authority to her words, and her easygoing nature facilitated her interaction with Michael Peyron, a French-British scholar fluent in Berber, who collected this folktale.

The tale mixes elements of the real and the supernatural as the storyteller invokes a strange and timeless world in which wild beasts can speak. In spite of the presence of the Muslim pattern of invoking God, the tale is reminiscent of a pre-Islamic era. Its female protagonist, Fatma, defies conventional gender expectations: She is not only the family provider, but also stronger, wittier, and more intelligent than her husband, who is depicted as foolish, inconsequential, irrational, and irresponsible, with no effect on family unity. The theme of old age is important in Moroccan women's tale-telling. In this story, incompetence in old age is associated with old men. The woman is presented as somewhat ruthless, suggesting that some amount of ruthlessness is needed to guarantee balance in a harsh and patriarchal environment.

*Fatima Sadiqi*

✦

Once upon a time there was a couple with no children. The woman was still young, having been married at an early age to a man considerably older than she. They had had children, but as the years went by they had all fallen on hard times. Such were the young woman's circumstances that she was reduced to working as a servant or even to begging. They remained thus in dire straits as she earned barely enough to keep her family fed.

One day, she saw smoke issuing from a hillside cave. "In Heaven's name!" she cried, "I shall go and see where this smoke is coming from!" On drawing near she saw an ogress appear. The ogress approached the cave entrance and uttered the formula, "Open wide, O earth!" A door opened, the ogress entered, deposited her booty, and set things in order. On exiting, she said: "Close up again, O earth!" then went on her way.

Emerging from her hiding place, the young woman pronounced the magic formula, then entered and helped herself to chickpeas, beans, oil, figs, and money before returning home. Seeing such a rich haul, her husband was beside himself with joy.

"My dear, where did you obtain all this?"

His wife answered, "None of your business! Ask no questions, eat and be content with God's bounty!"

The very next day the young woman again crouched in hiding near the hillside cave. She saw the ogress return and pronounce the magic words before entering and eating and drinking her fill. On leaving, she repeated, "Close up again, O earth!" and the entrance was sealed. Once she had moved off, the eager young woman entered.

She helped herself to beans, chickpeas, other delicacies, and money. She returned home, and the old man asked again, "Fatma, wherever did you obtain such booty?"

She answered, "Eat and drink. It's none of your business! It's only God's bounty!" So he held his peace and joyfully they feasted. Though there were some leftovers, the next day she returned and again crouched outside the cave entrance. Would you believe it? That stubborn old husband had followed her and remained concealed beside her.

Back came the ogress and began reciting the formula, "Open wide, O earth!" The entrance opened, she entered, and ate and drank her fill. On leaving, she repeated the formula, "Close up again, O earth!"

Her back turned, Fatma said, "Open wide, O earth!" and entered the cave. Once inside she found that the old man had followed her in.

"Woe betide you!" she said. "What are you about? Soon the ogress will be back to eat you! Now begone with you!"

She helped herself to beans, money, and the rest. Before leaving she again warned her husband to be off.

"Go on, I will follow you shortly!" he replied, all the while gorging himself on figs, raisins, and other delicacies.

Deciding it was time to leave the cave, he stuttered, "Close up again, O earth, close up again," but all to no avail. Finally, in despair, he sat down cross-legged and waited.

The ogress eventually arrived and cried out, "Open wide, O earth!" The old fool said, "Praise be to God, those were the very words Fatma spoke!"

She entered and found him. "And what are you doing here? How did you get in?"

The naïve old one answered, "It was Fatma who first came here and brought fortune to our home. She's left now, and when I wanted to follow her, I didn't know how to go about it!"

"And where is this Fatma?," came the rejoinder, to which the old fool replied, revealing his wife's whereabouts. The ogress bade him accompany her.

They returned together to their home, entered, and the ogress said to Fatma, "Why did you come and rob my storehouse?"

"Nothing of the sort!" replied Fatma.

"Tut-tut, he told me you brought him there. How else would this old fellow have come there, since he did not know the place?" And then the ogress added, "Now, tomorrow I want to find one of your children cooked and ready for my breakfast!"

Well, Fatma went outside and burst into tears. Just then a dove drew near and inquired about the cause of her weeping. "It's a sad day! I weep for my child, whom the ogress must have for breakfast tomorrow morning!"

"You simpleton!" said the bird, "Run up that hill where you will find the carcass of some mule or horse. Take some of that meat, cook it, hide the bones, and the ogress will be none the wiser!"

Shouldering an axe, she went up that hill, brought back some meat, cooked it, and hid her child. When the ogress arrived, she called out to her, inquiring whether her child had been cooked and made ready for eating. Fatma served her the dish, the ogress ate and drank, and then, before leaving, said, "Tomorrow, I want to find your other child cooked and ready for my breakfast!"

Fatma complied readily, returning to the hill, chopping off more meat with the axe, and cooking it for serving. When the ogress returned, she called out, inquiring whether Fatma's other child had been cooked and was ready for eating and Fatma replied in the affirmative. The ogress ate and drank her fill. Before leaving she declared: "Tomorrow, I'll have *you* for breakfast!" To which Fatma agreed.

Once the ogress had departed, Fatma returned to the hill and removed a goodly portion of horsemeat. Then she cooked it, left it in a dish, and went to hide with her children. The ogress returned, ate the meat, thinking it was Fatma she was eating, then told the old man: "Tomorrow, *you* are the one I'll be having for breakfast!" To which he agreed.

Fatma came the next morning and lit a fire beneath the cooking pot, whereupon the stupid old fellow came and put his hand on the pot, saying, "Our children, Fatma, what have done with our children?"

When he insisted on putting his foot into the pot in order to be cooked, she answered impatiently, "Away with you, you old dodderer! Go up the hill, return with some horsemeat, cook it, then hide yourself!"

Off he went, brought back some meat, cooked it, then found a hiding place. Along came the ogress, who ate and drank her fill. As she was about to leave, the old fool came out and taunted her, saying, "Ah, so you think it's Fatma and her children you've eaten!"

"Why, where is she?" the ogress asked.

"That's where she is! She and her children are well hidden!" the old fellow answered. In a frenzy of rage she snatched him up and devoured him. Then she started searching for Fatma and the children. She clumsily entered a tangle of wire and wooden stakes and managed to impale herself, so that her stomach burst open and she sank down, staring at her would-be prey with the light going out of her eyes. The children, who were by now very hungry, said to Fatma, "How are we going to get out of here?"

Then back came the dove, wanting to know the cause of their weeping. "Why do you weep thus?"

Fatma replied, "Why, see the ogress watching us, ready to eat me and my children!"

The dove replied, "O foolish one! Don't you see that the ogress is dead?"

Fatma refused to believe this, and so the dove asked, "What will you give me if I go and peck out her eyes?"

"I will give you anything you ask me," replied Fatma, "Only peck out her eyes!"

This the dove willingly did, so Fatma came out, and moved with her children and belongings to the storehouse of the ogress, where she led thereafter a life of abundance.

*Translated by Michael Peyron*

## *Fatima Tabaamrant*
# WAKE UP, SISTERS

Morocco 1983    Berber

Raissa Fatima Tabaamrant was born in 1962 in Id Salm Idawchqra, in the Anti-Atlas, the southernmost of Morocco's Atlas Mountain ranges. Her tribe is called Ayt Baamrane, and is renowned for its resistance to French colonization. She is the first woman in the south of Morocco to write, compose, and sing her own texts, and dance while singing. She sings about nature, love, and youth, as well as such contemporary issues as women's literacy. For writing consciously about the revival of Berber culture, she has gained immense popularity among a young and energetic Berber constituency. In 1996, the Journalists' Club of Tiznit, a nearby town, named her the first Berber artist of the southern region. She was given the name of Raissa, a title customarily bestowed on distinguished Berber singers, and a silver ribab, a classical musical instrument. Accompanied by her own group, from that point forward Tabaamrant became a popular singer. In 2007 she was nominated by King Mohammed VI to sit on the Administrative Board of the Royal Institute of the Amazigh (Berber) Culture.

"Wake Up, Sisters," was composed in 1983. In this song, Tabaamrant urges illiterate Berber women to acknowledge their need for literacy if they wish to improve their lives and those of their children. She knows that books provide precious knowledge useful to women. In the village of this region, many men migrate to big cities or to Europe to find work; the women left behind become the real heads of families. Addressing these women, Tabaamrant notes that one of the many advantages of literacy is that it enables women to read their husbands' letters themselves, and even write letters to them.

While the proportion of illiteracy among Moroccan women is especially high in rural areas, the demands for literacy have generally been made by urban intellectual women, in Arabic or French. Here Tabaamrant expresses that demand in the Berber language, understood by a majority of rural women.

*Fatima Bouabdelli*

✦

Wake up, sisters! Let us unite, sisters!
Life is no longer as it used to be.
Now we all need knowledge,
Even if we've never been to school.
Wake up and grab your chance,
For it's never too late for learning.
We all need learning, from cradle to grave.
Wake up, sisters, and enjoy learning.
Knowing the world is also your duty,
And together we will know the world.
Wake up, sisters, and help others who need help.
Don't fear those above us—they are no better than we are.

They know we have the wisdom of our people.
O women, wake up to embrace knowledge!
Wake up to enjoy reading!
People with book knowledge are strong people!
When your husband goes far away
And sends you a letter full of secrets
That no one but you should know,
Wake up, women, so that you may read his letter.
And when you have news to tell him,
Your handwriting will make you stronger.
God bless those who trust my words.

*Translated by Fatima Bouabdelli and Fatima Sadiqi*

## *Fatima Mernissi*
# WOMEN AND POLITICAL ISLAM

Morocco 1987　French

Born in 1940 to a wealthy family in Fes, Fatima Mernissi received her primary and secondary education in one of the first coed private schools in Morocco. She studied sociology in Rabat, continuing her education in France and the United States. Back in Morocco, she taught sociology at Mohammed V University in Rabat, and was chosen to serve in the University Research Institute and on the UN University Council.

Growing up in a harem, Mernissi became aware of the dynamics of male-female segregation very early in life. Her 1995 memoir *Dreams of Trespass: Tales of a Harem Girlhood*, which was met with wide acclaim and translated into more than twenty languages, describes her attempts to understand and trespass the *hududs*, or frontiers, of Arab Muslim patriarchy. Although most of her writing consists of nonfiction essays, Mernissi often uses the techniques of a fiction writer, combining scholarly analysis and literary artistry, creativity with shrewd intelligence.

Mernissi has argued that, while gender inequality is a prominent feature of both Western and Islamic societies, there are significant differences in the underlying assumptions about women in the Christian and Muslim traditions. While in Western Christian cultures, women have generally been seen as weak and inferior beings, in Islamic societies they are seen as powerful, but dangerous. Women's sexuality is viewed as a threat to civilized society, something that needs to be controlled and repressed. Thus, in Islamic societies, women are oppressed out of fear, rather than some belief in innate female inferiority.

Mernissi also argues that because women's liberation—especially from traditional customs such as veiling—was associated with Western colonialism, it came to be seen in opposition to Muslim self-determination, and even to Islam itself, as did democracy and other institutions of modernization. Reflecting on these contradictions, Mernissi sets out, with rare courage, to tackle the most sensitive topics in Arab Muslim societies, including the absence of democracy, political repression, the lack of global power, and the dependence on the West.

Mernissi's first book, *Beyond the Veil: Male–Female Dynamics in Modern Muslim Society* (1975)—now a classic, although a controversial one—was followed by *Sex, Ideology and Islam* (1983). Mernissi became famous for her 1987 book *The Veil and the Male Elite: A Feminist Interpretation of Women's Rights in Islam*, which in the original French was titled *Le Harem politique: Le Prophète et les femmes* (The Political Harem: The Prophet and Women). For the first time, a Muslim woman scholar was wielding her right to investigate and interpret her own history, going back to its prestigious origin. Through close study of the Qur'an and Hadith—the words and deeds of the Prophet—Mernissi argues that Islam's founder supported women's equality and accepted their sexuality. The ideal of the silent, passive, obedient woman was invented by male Muslim clerics and scholars in order to preserve the patriarchal system, she writes, and has nothing to do with the true message of Islam. Although she did not attack Islam itself, many viewed Mernissi's findings as scandalous or blasphemous, and she received threats from various fundamentalist groups.

Mernissi's subsequent books include *Shehrazad Is Not Moroccan (1987), The Forgotten Queens of Islam* (1990), and *Islam and Democracy: Fear of the Modern World* (1992). In 2003, she received the prestigious Prince of Asturias Prize for Literature for her "prolific and profound œuvre" and for the "aesthetic quality and depth of her ideas."

The text included here is an excerpt from *The Forgotten Queens of Islam.* In the introduction, Mernissi notes that she decided to write the book after Benazir Bhutto was democratically elected as prime minister of Pakistan in 1988, and her defeated male opponents, in an attempt to disqualify her, brandished the argument that in the Islamic tradition women never governed a Muslim state. Mernissi took it upon herself to challenge this view.

The text deconstructs the myth of men as the "natural" rulers of the state. She begins by pointing out that the original Arab Islamic model of development was based on the notion of *umma*, or community. This idea, established by the Prophet Muhammad in the seventh century, offered a holistic and comprehensive political and social system aimed at providing Muslims with a way to balance their spiritual and material lives. Along with this deeply democratic tendency, Mernissi finds in early Islam an historical foundation for women's participation in political life as independent agents, and even as rulers, providing such examples as Egypt's Sitt al-Mulk, Queen Arwa of Yemen, and the sultanas of Persia and India.

Mernissi also describes the painful relationship between women and political Islam, maintaining that men have always used religion to obtain and maintain power and exclude women. The exploitation of *khutba*, religious speech, in the Friday prayer is a strong political tool, which maintains fear and establishes order. Resistance to including women in the *khutba* is one way of excluding them from political power. The regularity of the *khutba*, delivered in the mosque and through the media every Friday, is a way of perpetuating and reinforcing male power, a power that tolerates women's intelligence, but not their will. Women's will, Mernissi underlines, has been encouraged by modern globalized development.

This paradox may be seen, for example, in the official adherence of Arab-Islamic countries to the universal Declaration of Human Rights, and its legal and political definitions of women's status.

Mernissi shows how these original tenets of Islam came to be distorted and exploited by elite men, to the exclusion of both women and the 'amma, the common people. These men have seized control of Islamic doctrine and history—expunging women from it, for example—in order to turn religion into a "political weapon," and have created "societies ruled in the name of God, but where not everybody has the same right to speak or rule in God's name." Mernissi draws a startling comparison between the *hijab* (the veil) that Muslim society imposes on women, and the veil that Muslim rulers place between themselves and the masses. "The contemporary desire to veil women," she writes, "is really a desire to veil resistance." In this context, it is easy to see why the writings of Fatima Mernissi have been deemed revolutionary.

The text carries an empowering message for women in the sense that it does not attack religion as faith, but rather attacks the use of religion to achieve political goals, a use that may materialize in various forms of national and international terrorism. In this sense, the text may be seen as predicting the use of religion for extremists' ends.

*Fatima Sadiqi*

✦

Women do not have the same political rights as men. Given their difference, women are seen as foreign to politics. Because of their very essence, they must be strangers to politics. . . . The logic of belonging to the harem imposes the mask, the veil, for all those who violate the *hudud*, who go beyond the limits and find themselves on the other side, on the caliphal scene. The veil relates to theater and ritual, and in that way it is more troubling than absence and death. Whatever you may say about absence or death, it is existence that is important. The dead and the absent do not exist—although in varying degrees, it is true. But what is involved in the ritual of the veil is the annihilation of the free will of beings who are physically present, of women who are here and who look at you with wide open eyes. It was not the presence of Sitt al-Mulk on the throne of Egypt that was disturbing. It was rather her sovereign will, which the *khutba* is designed to magnify.

This is the reason why the Arab man is not upset by intelligence in a woman. A very intelligent woman is always something to be admired, and the huge infiltration of women into universities in the Arab world in less than 30 years of educational opportunity corroborates this. The access of women to knowledge, to the universities and academies is not upsetting, provided that this phenomenon does not spill over into politics. What is disturbing is the decision of a woman to exist as an independent will. A woman's intelligence can always be put at the service of the one who owns her, but a sovereign will can never be. A will is or is not. And if it is, it can only be in competition with another, above all with that of the man to whom she owes obedience.

This is the reason Arabic has a word, *al-nashiz*, to define a woman who rebels against the will of her husband. The concept of *nushuz* is only applied to women. It is a declaration by a woman of her decision not to follow the will of her husband. A *nashiz* is a woman who declares herself to be an individual, and no longer just a being who aligns herself with the will of someone else. And *nushuz* is obviously synonymous with *fitna*, disorder.

The definition of citizenship in the Universal Declaration of Human Rights is of the individual, whatever the sex, as sovereign on the political scene. The individual will and its place on the political chessboard of modern Islam is the key problem around which all debates revolve, whether those of imams or of secular men of the left, whether speeches of heads of state or writings by political prisoners. So in the Arab world all discussion about women is a discussion about the development of the individual and his or her place in society. As long as our will is veiled, that of the men who do not live in the entourage of the prince and who do not participate in its privileges will also remain so.

In the realms of the women who took power in Islam, only the women close to the prince, whether he was father, brother, husband, or son, succeeded in infiltrating the political scene. The women who did not live within the privacy of the palace had no more chance of access than did ordinary men. And it is this aristocratic essence of the political process that is called into question by the right to vote and universal suffrage. That is why, as the fundamentalists well understand, the election of Benazir Bhutto constituted a total break with caliphal Islam. It represented the dual emergence on the political scene of that which is veiled and which is obscene: the will of women and that of people.

Universal suffrage tears away two veils, two veils that give substance to the two thresholds of political Islam in its cosmic architecture: the *hijab* of women and that of the caliph. For, paradoxical as it may seem, women are not the only ones to hide themselves behind a *hijab*. The Muslim caliph, the ultimate concentration of all the wills of the faithful, of those who choose submission, who choose negation of the will for the benefit of the group, needs more than anyone else to protect himself. The *hijab* of the caliph, his veil, is an institution just as fundamental to political Islam as is the veil of women, and if it is never directly invoked in the desperate cry for the return of the veil, it is because it hides the unmentionable: the will of the people, the will of the *'amma*, the mass, which is just as dangerous as that of women.

*Translated by Mary Jo Lakeland*

*Amina Arfaoui*
# THE GRAMOPHONE
Tunisia 1987  French

Amina Arfaoui was born in 1947 in Sousse, Tunisia. Now a respected academic, she is a lecturer in Germanic studies in the Faculty of Arts at the University of Manouba. Her first short story, "The Gramophone," was awarded a prize by the Tenth Radio Contest for the best short stories, organized by Radio France Internationale (RFI). It was published, along with twelve other winning stories, in *Le Requin Borgne* in 1987.

The story, which depicts the life of a Tunisian woman in the very early twentieth century, is based on the life of the author's grandmother. The setting is Sousse, in the center of the Tunisian Sahel. The story reveals a great deal about Tunisian women's lives at that time. In the early years of the twentieth century, well-to-do women married young, and without being permitted to choose their partners. Women seldom went out, and if they did, they were completely covered up by a *haik*, a white or black wool veil. Arfaoui's protagonist, Zeineb, had been married in the traditional manner, and is expected never to reproach her husband, however violent or unfair he might be to her. Zeineb knew her husband had affairs, but she could not quarrel with him about them since she did not want to be repudiated—cast off by her husband—which would bring shame on her family. Yet, she was clever enough to make a proposition to her husband, one that he could not possibly refuse: "Take me to her," she says of his mistress. For her, it was a victory, for she made her husband acknowledge his weakness without reproaching him.

By a sort of magic, a sense of women's solidarity emerges, which makes Zeineb reconsider and sympathize with Rachel's real situation. The meeting even becomes an occasion for the proper, repressed Zeineb to express herself, and to discover a new kind of power over her husband.

*Si* is a term used by women in Tunisia when addressing a man. It is the equivalent of *Sidi* or *Saied*, and roughly means "My Lord." It was very common in the years preceding independence for a woman to address her husband or a girl to address her elder brothers in this way. One of the few places Tunisian women could once go after the *hammam*, the Turkish bath, was the *marabout*, or shrine. *Marabouts* remain popular today, though much less so than in the past.

*Khedija Arfaoui*

✦

The light four-wheeled carriage dropped Ali in front of his home. The door was unlocked. He kicked it open, for his arms were full of packages, and called to his wife from the threshold. She came over to welcome him, but rather reluctantly. She used to be more loving whenever he came back from a trip. But he did not seem to notice her distracted attitude, and started to open the packages he had brought.

"Here, look! This fabric with gold embroidery is for you. How do you like it?"

He also showed her a pair of shoes he wanted to offer his son and a large shawl he meant to give to Zobeida, his sister-in-law.

Zeineb did not show any interest in his presents. She looked at them without seeing them and thanked him absent-mindedly. Ali was annoyed by her indifference and asked with some irritation, "What is it? Why do you look like that? Did anything happen while I was away?"

"No, Si Ali. Nothing happened, thank God! I have only one request of you. I beg you to promise to grant it to me."

Ali thought for a few minutes. What was she trying to get out of him? A jewel? A visit to her family's *marabout*? He couldn't imagine what she could want, and tried to procrastinate.

"Listen, Zeineb, it is not the right time for that! You do see that I am tired. We will talk again about it another time."

But Zeineb insisted. She had, in fact, noticed that her husband, who was ordinarily not very conciliatory, proved to be particularly malleable whenever he came back from a "trip." She could, then, get almost anything she wanted from him. She had, therefore, learned to reserve her most delicate wishes for those very moments. This time she got what she wanted rather quickly, for Ali was tired and had only one wish: to sleep. He would have promised anything to be left alone. Besides, how could he refuse when, unconsciously, in spite of his male selfishness, he could not avoid feeling guilty toward his wife, whose concerns he could guess? So he pledged on their son's head, as she had begged him to, to fulfill her wish. Zeineb then crossed her arms and told him, with a resolute tone he had never heard from her before, "Si Ali, I want you to take me to her place."

Ali caught his breath, and pretended not to understand what she meant.

Zeineb continued, without getting upset. "I have for a long time been informed that you are seeing other women. I know that you are neither in Tunis nor in Nabeul for business, but right here in Sousse, at that female singer's. Well, I want to know her. Introduce us to one another."

She interrupted Ali, who had been trying to say something, and added with a wry, forced smile, "Don't worry, I won't create a scandal. I am a woman in an important social position!"

Then she left him standing there and went about her usual chores as if nothing had happened, though she reminded him as she left, "Don't forget that you have sworn on our son's head! You have to keep your promise now."

Ali couldn't believe his ears. This meant she knew everything, and had kept silent until now. He realized how little he knew her. When he was in a bad humor, he often said hardly a word to her. In such cases, he would drop by in a hurry to eat, change clothes, or go to bed, without expressing any interest in her thoughts or concerns. He had always considered her a naïve and trusting woman, if not somewhat stupid. But here she was showing him that she was far less stupid than he had thought, and moreover she was bossing him about as she pleased! She simply wanted to go to Rachel's, and drink a cup of tea at her place as she would at anybody else's! Too tired to think any more, he went and flopped onto his bed to sleep like a log.

Naïve and trusting, so had Zeineb been indeed, at least in the early days of her marriage. Then, after some time, insignificant details had allowed her to understand that she had a fickle husband.

He would mistake her first name, for example, calling her Zakia or Souad instead of Zeineb. Or he would contradict himself when speaking: He happened to forget that he was supposed to have gone on such or such a day to Tunis, and showed that, in reality, he had not been out of town. Something else: Each time he came back from his mistress, he was in an excellent mood and he would bring plenty of gifts, probably wanting to be forgiven for his escapades. Having finally guessed what was going on, from then on, Zeineb automatically associated the presents she received with her husband's extraconjugal affairs. Instead of making her happy, they would make her feel miserable, since they were the very proof of Ali's unfaithfulness.

It was for this reason that she had on that day welcomed her husband without much eagerness. She was happy, however, to have gotten that promise out of him. But was she certain she would be able to behave herself at Rachel's, as she had said? Yet she was dying to know her. She had always wanted to see up close those loose women who are talked about only in whispers and through the use of euphemisms, the word referring to them being so shocking. How did they behave? How did they dress? And how was it that despite their vulgarity and their ill repute, some of them were able to lay hold of other women's husbands? Zeineb had lived such a drama in her own family; her sister Zobeida had one day awakened to find herself on the street, supplanted by a lower-class prostitute nicknamed Dhahbia, the Blonde. Zeineb had taken her sister into her home. She knew what her sister had gone through; she had shared her pain. Ever since her husband had begun seeing Rachel, she had been afraid the same thing would happen to her. So it was not mere curiosity that led her to want to know her rival, but also fear. Indeed, this affair had been going on for several months already. Her husband had had other affairs, but they had always been short-lived, and Zeineb had not really been worried about them. But now she was consumed by a strong fear: Was he going to marry that woman, or was he to make her his concubine? What did she look like? She thought that the best thing to do would be to go and see Rachel so as to have a clear idea about what might happen. She had thus waited for the propitious opportunity—that is, Ali's return from his "trip."

Ali was hoping that they would both forget this promise and that the incident would end quietly. But Zeineb was not forgetting anything. On the following days, she renewed her request, harassed him, and he was compelled to deal with it. Wasn't he tied to this pledge, which he could not go back on? For Ali was superstitious, and he feared that if he didn't keep his word, something bad would happen to his only son. So he informed Rachel, and told his wife that Rachel was expecting them the following Tuesday.

The invitation day arrived. Ali was amused to see that Zeineb had dressed in her finest clothes and her jewels. "Look here," he darted at her, "you look as if you were about to go to a wedding!"

Zeineb gave no answer. She had also put on *kohl* and lipstick, things she used only on special occasions. After all, this was not an ordinary visit, and she did not want to be outshone by her rival! Ali watched his wife from the corner of his eye. He had no desire to see this visit give way to a sordid dispute. But Zeineb seemed calm and had even been kind to him during the days that had followed their conversation.

And so they went. The four-wheeled carriage dropped them before a little house whose door opened as soon as he gave four brief knocks, probably a signal. Because of her stout figure, Zeineb had some difficulty getting through the half-opened door—both sides had to be opened. This in no way made her feel uncomfortable. On the contrary, she was rather proud of being plump: Wasn't that a sign of good health and wealth? She thus went in, her head up and at ease, more so especially since the woman who had opened the door was a thin person.

The room they entered after the usual greetings smelled musty. It contained a sofa, a chair, and two somewhat used armchairs. A lute had been placed on the chair. Hanging on the wall, a lightly yellowed photo showed a smiling couple. Zeineb also saw, placed on a small table, a strange box topped by a funnel, and she wondered what it could be.

A few commonplace sentences were exchanged—on the heat that prevailed during that month of June—interrupted by ill-at-ease silences. Then the young woman who had opened the door for them stood up, probably to go and get something to drink.

So this was Rachel. Zeineb, who had been examining her carefully, could not help thinking she was ugly. Rachel was not very tall; she had black eyes that emphasized the paleness of her face. The beauty spot she had on her left cheek might have given her face a certain charm, had she not looked so sad. Zeineb was wondering whether it was a real beauty spot or what was called a patch, when Rachel came back, carrying a tray. She obviously had prepared the tea in advance. In the midst of all this, far away in the lane, they could hear a peanut salesman's call. Zeineb, who liked to drink her tea with toasted peanuts, asked in a loving tone that her husband go and buy them some.

Ali knew this habit of his wife's. Yet he hesitated to leave her alone with Rachel, for he did not trust her calm exterior: Who knew how she might behave during his absence? On the other hand, he also knew that this was not the moment to refuse anything she asked, for would she not feel offended were he to say no before Rachel? He thought it more sensible to obey. "I'll be back very quickly!" he said before going out, in order to reassure his mistress.

Ali had been right to worry. Zeineb had sent him away because she wanted to satisfy a long-held desire. How often had she dreamed of finding herself alone with her rival, of calling her bad names, scratching her face, spitting in her face! These actions would go some way toward revenging her husband's unfaithfulness, and would make her power felt. But curiously, once she was inside the space she had so often dreamed of, she felt no longing for such actions. Instead, Zeineb felt confounded. She had not expected to find in her husband's mistress a person like Rachel. She had expected a vulgar, outrageously made-up woman, with perhaps even, like Dhahbia, a gold tooth that could be seen shining as soon as she opened her mouth.

The reality did not correspond to what she had imagined. That confused her and made her feel ill-at-ease. Rachel was simply wearing a *seroual*, loose trousers that Tunisian women often wore, under a sari-like skirt and a large-sleeved embroidered blouse. She talked little, she was sad-looking, and above all, she was so very thin!

What could he see in her, good God! By the time Rachel sat next to her after putting the tray down, Zeineb had already given up her quarrelsome intentions. To feed the conversation, she pointed to the picture hanging against the wall and asked about the two people in it. She was surprised to hear that they were Rachel's parents. Curious and emboldened by her husband's absence, Zeineb asked a few more questions. She thus learned that Rachel was Algerian, which she had guessed by her accent, and that her parents, dead for a decade, had been café-concert singers.

Zeineb was a sensitive person who was easily moved by other people's misfortunes. Here she was discovering that Rachel was a poor orphan! The hostility she had felt toward her disappeared as if by a miracle. She felt pity for the young woman as she thought about all the misfortunes she must have endured through her youth.

Ali came in at that moment. He looked at them with concern and was relieved to see that nothing serious had happened. Zeineb took the peanuts eagerly and assumed responsibility for distributing them between the glasses. She even served the tea, to the great surprise of her husband, who had not in the least expected such a kindness. Wishing to take part in the heartiness that seemed to prevail, he asked Rachel to play the lute. She took up her instrument without much eagerness. She did not feel like playing or singing. What a strange idea already of Si Ali to have his wife visit them! This visit was very unpleasant, but her lover had insisted that she should accept, promising that they would not be staying long. And now he wanted her to play the lute! She started to play a few notes, then stopped rather quickly. She hadn't the heart for it. She looked at Ali appealingly. He did not insist, for she was always melancholy during the daytime, and only in the evening did she begin to feel herself, particularly after she had drunk one or two small glasses of *boukha*, a Tunisian white wine made out of figs. Her melancholy would disappear then, and her paleness, too. Her cheeks would glow, and she might even burst out laughing. She would sing and dance as soon as she was asked to, and then her presence excited the men in her circle.

Having failed in his attempt to dissipate the uneasiness that prevailed among them, Ali thought that it might be possible for Rachel to dance, since that was also her gift. He thought that would satisfy Zeineb's curiosity so that she might leave him alone afterward. Rachel had a gramophone he had bought at the beginning of their affair, which allowed them to spend many pleasant moments together. In her ignorance, Zeineb had seen only a big, strange box! Si Ali placed a record on the machine—for he was responsible for operating it—and he asked his mistress to dance. This time Rachel could not escape; a signal had made her understand that he did not want to be thwarted.

She started to dance, since she could not do otherwise. Ali had chosen music she liked, to which she often danced, so it wasn't difficult for her to follow the rhythm. She danced in a charming way. It was a pleasure for the eyes to see with what visible ease she harmonized her movements with the beatings of the *darbouka* drum. She spun around, moving her hands gracefully and lightly, as well as her shoulders, her feet, and also her hips, which she had encircled with a scarf in order to highlight her movements. Quickly, she forgot her irritation and let herself enjoy the pleasures of the dance. Then the rhythm of the music accelerated and Rachel danced more quickly. Her hair, which had been pulled up in a bun, fell down upon her shoulders. She continued to dance this way, her hair unknotted. Happy, Ali encouraged her by clapping his hands.

When he stood up in order to reset the machine, something happened that neither he nor Rachel expected. Zeineb stood up as well, and declared that she too wanted to take part in the dance. She asked Rachel to lend her two scarves, took one into each hand, and started to follow the music by taking small steps—once forward, once to the side—while waving the scarves. Ali was so surprised that he stood open-mouthed looking at her. Then, realizing suddenly that his wife's reaction was obviously a peace signal, he resumed clapping his hands all the more.

Rachel tried without success to coordinate their movements so as to create a harmonious duo, but their styles were too different. So she sat down, perhaps out of respect for Zeineb, who continued to dance on her own, a scarf in each hand. While Rachel's sensual dancing enhanced the beauty of her body, Zeineb danced in a reserved and very chaste manner. She hardly moved her hips. The fact is that she was not accustomed to that kind of dance. She rather preferred to dance at a *souleymia*, a ceremony organized for the celebration of an important event through religious singing. She enjoyed those feasts, during which, made to feel giddy by the smell of incense, the pulsating rhythm of the tambourines, and the singers' monotonous voices, women shook their heads forward and backward so much while dancing that they sometimes fell into a trance.

If Zeineb had been moved to dance at Rachel's, it hadn't been in order to outdo the young woman, whose talent she was aware of, but rather because she had suddenly felt good, as if she had been liberated from a weight. Her dance then expressed this feeling of relief, this good feeling.

Anyone passing the house and hearing the music and Rachel's and Si Ali's hand-clappings accompanying the singer might have thought that very happy people were celebrating a pleasant event. They would have been surprised had they been told that the group consisted of a man, his wife, and his mistress!

Yet, once the recording ceased, the enchantment was broken. Uneasiness reappeared again among them. There was a moment of silence. Si Ali looked then at his wife and made her understand that it was time to leave. When she was about to walk out of the house, as he was preceding her to signal the coach driver, already muffled up in her black *haik*, Zeineb grabbed Rachel's arm and whispered a question to her: "When are you going to give back my husband, Rachel?"

Rachel answered in the same tone, "When God decides it, Zeineb."

Then, they separated in a perfectly polite way.

The return journey took place in silence. Ali was dreamy. He was, on the whole, satisfied by this visit, which had not gone badly. He felt that he had got out of it rather well. The dancing, however, had kindled his senses, and he was already thinking up a pretext to use so that he might be able to join Rachel as soon as possible. As to Zeineb, she was thinking that she knew nothing that could prevent her husband from having mistresses, from repudiating her, and from remarrying if he so wished. This visit had allowed her, however, to see that the situation was not dangerous. She felt that Rachel was in no way trying to make Ali marry her. Zeineb had decided to make the best of the situation and, even to profit from it if possible.

She had intended to celebrate her son's circumcision very soon. Just as everyone else did, she was planning to call a small female group together to celebrate the event. But it would be very pleasant as well to have, like Rachel, a marvelous machine that allowed one to have music at will! She had certainly heard about it, but she had never before seen one. She had admired the ease with which Ali had operated it. Its handling seemed so simple! With just a single turn of a crank, one could listen to the song of one's choice. She, too, had to get one! Then she would be able not only to astound her female neighbors, but also to celebrate, as she wished, during seven days and seven nights. Since her husband was particularly cooperative and generous each time he came back from Rachel's, she said to herself: "Next time he goes to see her, I will ask him to offer me a gramophone." Who knows? She would perhaps even invite the young woman to come and dance during her son's feast.

And the jolting four-wheeled carriage carried them toward their home.

*Translated by Khedija Arfaoui*

# MOTHER GOAT: A FOLK TALE

Egypt 1989    Arabic

Handed down by word of mouth from one generation to another, folktales serve to amuse and, sometimes, to instruct. These stories reflect the behavior and beliefs of the cultures they portray. The historical and cultural values reflected in the stories serve as precious analytical tools for understanding the societies that generate them.

This story from rural Egypt presents a mother as protector and teacher of her children. She is the sole provider and protector of the family, and when her children are taken away, she fights alone to bring them back. She clearly possesses the qualities of courage, intelligence, and perseverance. In contrast to the mother goat is the wolf, a male figure who is the central enemy in the story. In the end, he is defeated by this brave and wily female. The story also conveys the idea that a single parent family headed by a mother can be successful, happy, and secure. The playfulness, affection, and warmth depicted in the mother's treatment of her young children complement her presentation as the main source of power and life in the family.

Storytelling has been, and still is, a very popular pastime in rural Egypt. It is customary for villagers to gather in the cool summer evenings after a long, hot day of toiling in the sun, to listen to folktales. Egyptian women have been and still are the principal narrators of tales that deal with traditions of the land. However, these stories can be narrated by anyone in the community, including elderly men and women and young children. This tale was narrated by a ten-year-old girl to Mohamed Hussein Hassan Hilal, who was collecting folktales of the Al Ayyat district, on the Nile in Upper Egypt, for a master's thesis in Arabic literature at Cairo University. Samira Tolba Abdel Tawab had probably heard the story many times, and was therefore ready to tell it herself as an act of initiation into the popular culture of her people.

*Nadia El Kholy*

✦

Once there was a mother goat who had seven little billy goats. Every day she would go out to the fields to get grass for them, and she would leave them at home. On her return she would knock on the door chanting:

Open for me, O my kiddies,
Milk is in my teats
And grass is on my hornies.

Every day before leaving she would warn them: "Beware of the bad wolf. If you let him in he'll swallow you up. You know my voice, my looks, and my white legs. Do not open the door when I am away."

One day the wolf came and saw the mother leaving the house and telling her little ones not to open the door to anyone. He knocked on the door and said in his husky voice:

Open for me, O my kiddies,
Milk is in my teats
And grass is on my hornies

The little billy goats shouted back: "No! You are not our mother! Her voice is not coarse like yours and her legs are not black." The wolf went away, softened his voice, whitened his legs, and once again knocked on their door:

Open for me, O my kiddies,
Milk is in my teats
And grass is on my hornies.

This time they were tricked into thinking he was their mother and they opened the door. On discovering that he was the bad wolf, they all tried to hide. One little billy goat went up to the roof, another hid under the bed, a third went down to the cellar, but the wolf found them all and swallowed them whole. The only one who managed not to be found was the youngest. His name was Clever.

A while later the mother goat arrived and knocked on the door:

Open for me, O my kiddies,
Milk is in my teats
And grass is on my hornies.

In tears, little Clever billy goat opened the door for her. She asked him, "Where are your brothers?" He replied, "O, mother, the wolf came and swallowed them up! But I was able to hide from him."

On hearing this, mother goat went to look for the wolf and for her children. She reached the wolf's house and knocked on his door.

"Who is it?" he asked.

"I am the mother goat."

The wolf was busy eating his porridge. "What do you want?"

"You swallowed my children"

"No, I haven't," said the wolf.

"Come, let us have a contest. If you win, you eat me up; but if I win, you give me back my children."

The wolf then asked, "Over what are we going to have the contest?"

She said, "Let us see who of us can drink the river dry."

They went to the river. The wolf kept on drinking and drinking until his belly became like an inflated balloon. As for her, she only pretended to be drinking. She would only stick her muzzle into the water and snort. When she realized that he was unable to drink all the water, she said slyly, "No one can win this contest. Let us have a ramming contest instead."

The wolf protested by saying, "You have horns, but I don't."

She replied, "You can have horns, too. You can make them of mud."

Then she backed up and came charging at him with all her might. She aimed her horns at his belly. It ripped open right away and a torrent of water gushed out, and her children came out bleating; "Ma-a-a; Ma-a-a, we all ate porridge and you had none!"

She took them home and they all lived happily ever after.

*Translated by Nadia El Kholy*

## Salwa Bakr
# WORMS IN THE ROSE GARDEN

Egypt 1992 Arabic

Salwa Bakr, one of the most widely acclaimed Egyptian novelists and short story writers, was born in Cairo in 1949. She earned degrees in business management and drama criticism, and worked as a government inspector and as a film and theater critic for several Arabic language publications, living for some years in Cyprus before returning to Egypt in the mid-1980s to focus exclusively on creative writing.

Bakr's first collection of short stories, *Zinat fi Janazet El Raies* (Zinat at the President's Funeral), was published in 1986. Her first novel, *Al-Araba ada habiyya la tas'adu ila as-sama'* (1991), published in English in 1995 as *The Golden Chariot*, was set within the walls of a women's prison, and was focused on a group of women from diverse backgrounds, thwarted in one way or another by the constraints of Egyptian society, and dreaming of a better life that they are unlikely to achieve. Like many of Bakr's works, it gives voice to women marginalized in contemporary Egypt, and makes inventive use of colloquial Arabic.

Bakr has published seven novels and seven collections of short stories, including *Wasf El Bolbol* (Describing the Nightingale) in 1993; *Araneb* (Rabbits) in 1994; *El Bashmoury*, a two-volume novel, in 1998 and 2000, translated into English as *The Man from Bashmour* in 2007; *Sawaki El Wakt* (The Water Wheel of Time) and *Sho'or el-Aslaf* (Feelings of the Ancestors) in 2003. A selection of her short stories was published in English as *The Wiles of Men* in 1992. Her only play, *Helm El Seneen* (The Dream of the Years) was published in 2002. Since 2001, she has taught at the American University in Cairo. She is a member of the Egyptian High Council for Culture and the Egyptian Writers Union.

"Worms in the Rose Garden," from her 1992 collection *Ajin al-Fallaha* (The Peasant Woman's Dough), is one of Bakr's most original and experimental stories. It captures the point of view of a young Egyptian woman who fears descending into madness, her mind driven to paranoia and delusions by the repressive and superficial social conventions that circumscribe her life. It exhibits many of the qualities that have won Bakr praise: confronting taboos, unmasking political and cultural oppression, and exploring social relations between the genders in an Egyptian context, without adopting the rhetoric of Western feminism.

*Noha Nadder Hamdy*

◆

She hates madness; she is terrified of the mind's losing control over the body, allowing the tongue to utter what it pleases, the eye to see what it chooses, and the soul to free itself from all boundaries of time and space. Farha would hate to become, one day, like her neighbor Fatheya El Arnaaoutia, who went raving mad when her son died in war. She started to eat dirt and to dance in the middle of the road, though she had formerly been a steady source of wisdom and pride. Farha does not want to talk to the stars and birds, or stay up most of the night uttering horrifying screams so that the neighbors rush to close their windows to prevent their children from waking up terrified.

That is why she has come, of her own choice, to the psychiatrist's clinic to ask his advice, to learn for certain whether she is descending into madness, or whether she has simply been incapacitated by the devil and is done for—and, if the latter, whether there is a medication or a cure. She has thought a long time about coming to this place, without telling anyone in her family, because she wants to know herself, before anyone else does, what the doctor has to say, especially whether there is hope for recovery. From his words, his expression, or his attitude toward her, she hopes to discover whether she will ever be the person she used to be: the calm, docile, and joyful young woman who neither saw worms nor was scared of them. Should she learn that there is no going back, no hope of turning from the path she has begun to walk, she will end the whole thing immediately by killing herself willingly and consciously.

She will not leave herself prey to swallowing dirt and screaming, or allow all to see her like that. She will die by a means from which there will be no return. She will open her mouth wide, and devour, at one swallow, and without closing her eyes, a large number of spongy white worms, which will surely be enough to end her life immediately, out of sheer disgust. For as soon as these ghastly creatures settle in her stomach, there will be no time for nausea or fainting because the sudden shock will be instant. Without regrets, Farha will bid farewell to this gelatinous life, which she has hated, and in which she has found no meaning. Anyway, there she is, waiting to meet the doctor, so let her not foretell events at this point.

How she hates doctors and their depressing clinics, which inspire extreme loneliness in the soul and serve to forever remind human beings that they are minute, weak creatures who are ultimately not much different from worms, even if they are called something different! Farha will wait patiently until the nurse, who is sitting in the farthest corner of the room behind her desk, allows her to go and see the doctor, who will say his final word about her condition. Therefore, she has started to think about what she will say when she meets him, trying to direct her vision away from the high gray walls that remind her of a hall of execution, and trying also to avoid the contrived smile painted on the nurse's face and her bright red-smeared lips that look like two attached worms separating occasionally to reveal a narrow abyss.

Farha forces herself not to look at the nurse and instead to think about things. Would it be better to start her conversation with the psychiatrist from the perspective of her relationship with her family? Or perhaps talk to him about her problems with her colleagues at work? Maybe she should tell him about her constant inability to cope or come to terms with people, how she feels intensely forlorn, infinitely estranged, how she feels that no one around her can ever understand her. However, more important than all this is the problem of sleep: She wants to sleep and is afraid she will break down because she has not slept, but she also does not want to fall asleep, lest she be attacked by the ghoulish nightmare that awaits her every time she closes her eyes and falls into a deep sleep.

She clenches her teeth out of sheer vexation and lets her eyelids droop, but soon becomes alert again and opens her eyes wide, trying to forget her desire to sleep. She starts watching the patients waiting their turn to meet the doctor. She notices a young woman who has not stopped spitting, in the most irritating manner, since she entered the clinic. The girl has a thin, pale face and a sharp, angry, and contemptuous expression that she fixes on everything around her. Beside her stands a man in a dark suit and tie, despite the heat, and Farha guesses that he is her father, for he keeps patting her shoulder patiently, in an attempt to convince her to stop spitting. However, the girl simply will not stop, so Farha begins to feel dryness in her throat and a strong desire for water.

She stares at the ground trying to forget about the ingenuity it takes to spit. She looks at the old carpet that fails to cover all the colorless floor tiles. It has withered bluish red flowers that have lost their contours from feet continuously treading on them.

Farha thinks again about her conversation with the doctor. She will begin with the time she began to feel that she was ill. She will tell him about the inexplicable feelings of suffocation that beset her from time to time. Moreover, she will confide in him about her chronic desire to distance herself from people and her desire to avoid speaking with any human being. She will also tell him that these feelings became more acute when she went off with her family to a summer resort, where they lived with her maternal and paternal aunts and their children in a large apartment her father had rented for that purpose. She will tell the doctor about their repulsive appearance round the lunch table as they ate fish, when their fat bodies, variously bellied, and their full, expressionless faces made her feel that they were bloated corpses. An enormous heap of grilled and fried fish had stood on the table, and they had extended their fingers to grab and sever the little fish heads, open their bellies, and devour their flesh, leaving behind their flimsy bones and empty staring eyes. They continued to eat, gulping a variety of drinks and talking about their memories of other fish meals. Her paternal aunt—whose neck, Farha could then see, resembled a huge worm like those preying on the stomach of a corpse beside a waterway in a village when she was young—said that the best fish she had ever eaten in her entire life had been in Suez, where she had been with her husband when he was employed there after the Triple Aggression of 1956.

But Farha's maternal aunt, still grinding the back of a small Nile fish with her teeth, had begged to differ with her, saying, "No, the most delicious kind of fish is the one you get in Damietta, for there the Nile meets the sea and the fish absorb the qualities of salty and sweet waters."

Soon, everyone was taking part in a violent debate about fish and the ways to cook it, even as their fingers and jaws kept on moving.

Had they only agreed to leave her behind in Cairo, as she had pleaded with them before traveling to the summer resort! She had used the excuse of not being able to take leave from her work, but her mother had vehemently refused to accept this, and her father had hurried to solve the problem by having the company doctor, who was his friend, write a medical certificate saying that she was ill and needed the summer to recover. When they had cornered her thus, she then said that she was old enough to stay at home on her own. But then her mother had resolved the issue by saying, "No matter what …you are still a girl. It is impossible for you to spend even one night on your own at home." Therefore, she had had to come with them against her will, and now she had reached this state. Had they only agreed to leave her behind, she would now be enjoying serenity and peace of mind.

She will also explain to the doctor how they had aggravated her by their insistence that she accept a man who had proposed to her some time ago and whom she had refused, ignoring her reasons for refusing him. He had a flabby figure and a slimy, gelatinous look in his eyes, which made her feel that he was crawling on the floor as he walked beside her, along with the rest of the family, as they left a restaurant where they had dined at his invitation. Her paternal aunt, who was most enthusiastic about this man because he had employed her son in one of his father's private companies, had laughed as she had gulped down, with great relish, some wobbly iced dessert, and said that what Farha had said about the man was "very droll, and no reason to refuse him as a husband because men should not be assessed for their appearance; a man is only at a disadvantage if his pocket lacks money."

On another day, they had addressed the same issue again. Farha's mother was in the kitchen, totally engrossed in thinking about the kinds of food she had to produce for lunch, and some of the others were still sitting at the breakfast table, when her sister asked their mother to listen to Farha's odd remarks about the man. At that point, Farha had wanted them all to shut up and give her a chance to tell them what she thought: "People, the truth is that our life is very stupid and devoid of any meaning. For about a year now I have been preoccupied by the idea that we resemble worms: We eat, drink, and sleep. I had hoped our lives could change. I wish we could do something meaningful, think about the world in a different way that will make us feel like people—human—different from worms."

They hadn't laughed then because she hadn't uttered a single one of these words, but had been plagued by a dreadful headache that pressed upon her head as they continued to talk about the man. Her maternal aunt said, "You have grown, Farha, and another year that passes you by will make you a spinster," a statement that was seconded by her own mother, who said, "To put it plainly, well, the truth is she is actually a spinster. After the age of twenty-five, a girl's betrothal becomes a problem because her glow fades away gradually and she enters the realm of womanhood, and her chances of finding a reasonable husband become minimal."

Her paternal aunt had then said: "The man is willing and he has an apartment—a thing we should be grateful for, considering the unavailability of apartments nowadays. It is rare to find a groom with a flat, which actually solves the most important problem." She added, "He comes from a good family and his parents are well-to-do and will not ask for any dowry or demand the furnishing of the house."

Her cousin had then suggested, laughing, that she marry this groom instead of Farha because she was ready to get married instantly and did not want to go on with her education. As she spoke, she continued to paint her long nails a bloody red color. She was severely reprimanded by her mother, who called her a brat who, at sixteen, wasn't legally ready to marry. Farha had pleaded with them to stop this bickering and shouting. She had wanted to scream at the top of her voice, but preferred to leave them and go to her bedroom to lie down. But her aunt had followed her immediately, after noticing her anger, and had tried to comfort her. She had asked her not to be upset because people are supposed to go on vacation to laugh and enjoy themselves, and offering her some roasted melon seeds to chew on and keep herself busy, she had added: "By God, Farha, I see you're in a bad mood these days and you hardly eat. What's the matter, chicken?"

She had laughed heartily as she replaced the "h" in Farha's name with a "kh," to transform it from "joy" to "chicken," as everyone liked to do by way of joking. When Farha had answered that she was fine, the aunt had decided that the girl was in a difficult state of love, and that was why she was refusing to marry. She had broached that topic, but the sad Farha had categorically denied any such thing and had asked to be left alone. Her aunt then told her she had become a person full of complexes and was really in bad shape.

The following evening, they played cards—Farha's mother, her aunts and her aunt's husband—while the refreshing sea breeze engulfed Farha's soul with a wonderful feeling. Farha had been sitting next to them, watching the waves as they embraced the shore, moving to and fro in never-ending, magnificent rhythm. Her soul had drifted far away and she dreamed of walking on the seashore with a young man she loved beside her, talking gently and compassionately about hopes and dreams that would surround them in a beautiful world where people preferred the joys of the soul to those of the body. She had been staring at the sea dreamily, but was roused occasionally by the family's commotion after someone's loss at the card game. Her aunt's husband had talked about the necessity of finding an acquaintance to help facilitate the customs procedures for the new car that belongs to his son, who was returning from the Gulf. At this instant, her father arrived with the announcement that he'd rented a new video and asked them to guess its name. After they mentioned all the names of entertaining movies currently showing in the theaters and advertised on television, they gave up. He surprised them by saying that the film was *The Terrible Incursion*, a famous horror movie. They clapped, screamed, and jumped up and down out of sheer joy. Feeling somewhat agitated, Farha left them to go to her room to lie down. Her eyes remained wide open, however, staring at a painting hanging opposite her. It was a painting of a plump woman lying on a vast bed covered by a yellow throw that concealed very little of her body. Farha felt uncomfortable looking at this, and preferred to close her eyes and sleep.

A short while later she jumped up and immediately turned on the light, shaking in fear and horror as she remembered the images of her nightmare. She was sitting alone on a vast plain surrounded by magnificent wheat fields dancing in the breeze. It had seemed as though a unique golden shawl enveloped the trees of the green plain, which abounded in the most extraordinary fruits and the strangest of humming birds, whose lovely bewitching voices she had never heard before. She had been undecided about which part of the plain she should move toward to dance joyously and gratify her soul. As she tried to decide, she saw a flower garden that extended to the horizon, indescribably rich in variety and scents. Farha began to breathe in the scents, to fill her lungs completely, telling herself how beautiful life was, and how wonderful nature. Even as she had felt consumed in comfort and ecstasy, dark clouds began to fill the sky and close off the horizon. She looked into the distance only to see huge, gray, depressing, slimy worms approaching bit by bit until they reached the vast wheat plain, devouring it all instantaneously. The worms had moved toward the birds and the trees, stripping the branches of their green and frightening the birds, who flew off, emitting melancholy sounds. When the worms had reached the rose garden, they devoured the red and the blue, the yellow and the white, erasing all that had been a pleasure to the eye and a joy to the heart. The worms had then stood erect like enormous, gray, gelatinous lumps with huge human faces, in which Farha deciphered the features of her mother, her father, and her aunts. She had then started to run in sheer terror, shouting with all her might and saying as she wailed, "Oh, birds, trees, oh, wheat as pure as gold, you wonderful roses, oh, cooling breeze." Yet only the whistling winds had echoed her words across the vast plain. And so the poor girl let out a great scream, which resounded in the wind. She fainted and fell to the ground.

When she woke up and opened her eyes, she found herself in bed. She wishes she could tell the doctor all about this dream in detail, as she had seen it and as it remained engraved in her memory. She also wants to tell him that those gloomy-faced gelatinous lumps have not stopped attacking her dreams since. Every time she feels drowsy and goes to sleep, she is attacked by them, and that causes her such pain that she is now terrified of going to sleep. More important, though, is the fact that she now sees worms during her waking hours.

A while back, her maternal aunt had come to visit them before leaving for Port Said to buy winter clothes in the Free Zone. She had brought with her some honey and butter pies and suggested that they should eat them while they were still hot to savor the flavor, and when Farha said that it was only two hours since they'd eaten breakfast, both her mother and aunt laughed and started to eat with great relish. It was then that Farha had seen four huge antenna sprouting above their heads. She had been so frightened that she had retreated to her room, sobbing in a low voice and overcome by pain and sorrow.

When she remembers that incident in the doctor's clinic, she feels like imitating the girl who was still spitting despite all the entreaties of the man with her. A thin, young man walks in, accompanied by two men wearing long gowns. His eyes are very sad, but he, paradoxically, wears a bitter yet sarcastic smile and shakes his head in a gesture that looks like utter disbelief.

Farha thinks of telling the psychiatrist that she has hated worms ever since she was a child, and that the only worm she ever liked was the silkworm that she used to keep in a cardboard shoe box at school to watch its phases of growth until it became a butterfly and flew away.

But the problem now is that she has come to see worms everywhere. About two weeks ago she had a quarrel with her boss at work. He was a man she detested because he was a thief and took bribes, and she insulted him by calling him a "worm." As she said that, her eyes had focused on his flabby belly and his short, thick neck. She had been subjected to an administrative inquest for that.

Moreover, on the following day, their neighbor, a fat woman with a flabby neck, wearing many gold bracelets on her left arm, had come to visit, and Farha had greeted her pleasantly with the phrase, "Welcome, Madam Worm." She really hopes the doctor can find a solution to this problem, which has grown to colossal dimensions, so that even when her uncle called from Saudi Arabia, where he had been working for five years, she told her father, who was in the shower, "Come out quickly, Uncle Worm is on the phone."

The spitting young lady spits again, and the sarcastic young man laughs heartily and tells her, "Your saliva is weak and of limited effect because filth is overwhelming, you poor girl." He is then overcome by a fit of bitter sobbing, and keeps repeating "filth is overwhelming," while his companions try to calm him. One of them even suggests that the nurse get him in to see the doctor quickly, after having thrust a ten-pound note into her hands. Farha sits watching the nurse as she stands up and moves from her place toward the doctor's office. She notices her wiggling behind as she walks, chafing the floor with her shoes, and then she sees two antennae sprouting slowly and extending above her head. Terrified, Farha decides to run very fast toward the street.

*Translated by Azza El Kholy*

# *Communal*
# TAKE MY BRACELET AND OTHER SONGS

Tunisia 1992    Arabic

These five songs were sung by different women who had been accused of committing adultery and forcibly placed in a special prison called *Dar Joued*. Recorded and published in 1992, the poems come from an earlier era, lasting until the 1970s, when Tunisian women were subject to confinement in *Dar Joued* or *Dar Adel* as punishment for any offense their husbands regarded as a breach of the law. In these prisons, women endured various forms of humiliation and oppression aimed at making them repent for their rebellious acts. Depriving imprisoned women of food was one form of punishment that a husband might inflict on his disobedient wife. One of the most serious reasons for sending a wife to Dar Joued was her display of sexual desire.

The first song expresses a woman's anger and resentment for being incarcerated and humiliated. The second song suggests that a husband is the real cause of his wife's transgressions. In the third song, a woman affirms her own seductiveness, showing defiance in the face of punishment and in the fourth, she remembers the pleasure of being with her lover. The final poem asks that a husband take his wife's jewelry in exchange for her freedom—from him, as well as from Dar Joued.

The word *shara'a* in the text alludes to the Islamic tribunal that rules along with the *qadi* (judge), on personal status laws. The *jaid* is paid by a husband who has brought an official request to imprison his wife. In Tunisian popular tradition, the color green denotes a woman who expresses her sexual desires.

*Dalenda Larguèche*

## SONG ONE

Oh my God,
In my prison,
Humiliated,
With no man and no meat,
With no basket,
Alone with my sighs
And the *jaid* behind the walls.

## SONG TWO

I let him down.
I will never roam about
His house.
Harm came first from him,
Leaving behind women,
Beaten and humiliated

## SONG THREE

I am still green
In the blossoming spring.
With my soft eye,
I seduce.

## SONG FOUR

Ever since we tasted
The tea of pleasures
Sadness has become our fate.
May God forgive
My lover and me.
I came before the *shara'a*—
What a misery!

## SONG FIVE

Take my bracelet,
Give me back my freedom,
You, the man I hate!
Take my earrings,
And one of my curls,
But I will never live
In the *Dar Adel* house of
Cursed women;
My father's house is waiting for me!
Take my belongings
In front of the judge and his witnesses.
I have a young lover
Who at every nightfall
Awaits me.

*Translated by Moha Ennaji*

# Latifa Jbabdi and L'Union de L'Action Féminine
## ONE MILLION SIGNATURES

Morocco 1992    Arabic

Latifa Jbabdi was born in 1955 in Tiznit, in southern Morocco. She is known for her work in reforming the Moroccan *Mudawana*—the family laws that determine the personal legal status of men, women, and children, and the relationships among them. Editor-in-chief of *8 Mars*, the first feminist magazine in Morocco, from 1983 to 1994, Jbabdi is also founder and president of *L'Union de L'Action Féminine* (UAF), or Women's Action Union, the NGO behind the One Million Signatures petition, which led to the first historic reforms of the *Mudawana*. In addition to serving coordinator of the National Council for the Reform of the *Mudawana* in 1992, she was coordinator of the Regional Conference of African women's NGOs that prepared for the 1993 Vienna Conference on Human Rights, and in 1998, became UN Ambassador of Civil Society for Human Rights and coordinator of the World March for Arab and Muslim Women. After her nomination as member of the Executive Board of the Socialist Party, she was elected a member of parliament in the September 2007 elections.

The 1992 One Million Signatures petition for the reform of the Moroccan family law is a key document in the history of the Moroccan women's movement, which began in the mid-1940s with the *Akhawat Al-Safa* (Sisters of Purity) association and still continues today. The petition, signed by the members of the Executive Board of the Women's Action Union, was sent to mainstream Moroccan newspapers, members of parliament and other government officials, and King Hassan II. The wide publicity led to numerous press conferences and television reports on the content and significance of the petition and the need for reform of the *Mudawana*. First promulgated as "The Code of Personal Status" in 1957–1958, two years after Morocco's independence, it was based on a narrow interpretation of Islamic jurisprudence, very detrimental to women's rights. It dictated that women owed unconditional obedience to their husbands and could not, for example, travel without their permission. In the post-independence period, as more and more women received education and took jobs outside the home, the law, based on an outdated vision of the family, made less and less sense.

In this context, the petition stirred public debate, and for the first time in the history of Morocco, women's issues became public issues. The debates gradually stripped the *Mudawana* of its "sacredness," and it began to be viewed as a legal text which, like any other, could be amended to serve the needs and desires of its society. This transformation in turn signaled the success of women's NGOs in bringing women fully into civil society—in effect, feminizing the Moroccan public space. Gathering one million signatures for any reason in a developing Muslim country like Morocco was an accomplishment; gathering them for the cause of women's rights was a spectacular feat.

The petition faced huge resistance from the government's minister of Islamic Affairs as well as from religious authorities. Imams circulated a counter petition in mosques, declaring that they opposed any change in the *Mudawana*. There was even a *fatwa*, a religious ruling, that criminalized UAF and threatened its members with the death penalty. Ironically, the *fatwa* helped publicize the petition more widely. UAF called for the coordinated support of all Moroccan women's organizations, unions, human rights organizations, all of which soon joined the movement, as did most of the major political parties. The petition was decisive in pressing the government, for the first time in the history of Morocco, to change key articles in the 1957 *Mudawana*. The success of the petition paved the way for subsequent victories in advancing Moroccan women's rights, including the very significant reform of the *Mudawana* in 2003.

The UAF is still active, with more than twenty branches throughout the country. It has created literacy centers and "listening-in" spaces for women in many cities. More recently, the UAF began organizing "symbolic trials" to bring private injustices such as domestic violence, divorce, and child custody issues to public attention. The first symbolic trial took place in Rabat in 1996. Since 1999, the organization has also held an annual National Campaign to Fight Violence Against Women.

*Fatima Bouabdelli*

✦

*We, the undersigned, declare that we strongly believe that only a democratization of relations within the family and society in general can lead to the construction of a real democracy. The Personal Status Law articles are in utter contradiction to the Moroccan Constitution, which explicitly guarantees equality between men and women. The present Personal Status Law is out of date and its articles are unjust toward women, as they cause unnecessary family crises and social tragedies. We, here, demand to change its articles according to the following principles:*

- Consider the family as a unit based on equity, equality, and mutual respect.
- Consider women, in the same way as men, legally recognized as soon as they reach majority age.
- A woman who reaches majority should be able to marry without a legal guardian.
- Both husband and wife should have the same rights and duties.
- Divorce should be judicial, and both husband and wife should have an equal right to file for divorce.
- Polygamy should be abolished.
- Mothers should have parental rights in the same way as fathers.
- Work and education should be considered women's pre-eminent rights; husbands should have no prerogative to deprive their wives of these rights.

*Translated by Fatima Bouabdelli and Fatima Sadiqi*

## *Fatma Kandil*
# THORNY SPACES SUDDENLY MOVING

Egypt 1993    Arabic

Fatma Kandil was born in Suez in 1958, and earned a degree in Arabic literature at Ain Shams University in 1982. She is one of the editors of the literary journal *Fusul* (Chapters) and a lecturer at Helwan University. Many of her poems and critical studies have been published in Arabic literary journals and magazines. She is also the author of a book of criticism, *Intertextuality in the Poetry of the Seventies*, published in 1999, and a poetic drama in colloquial Egyptian, *The Thousand and Second Night*, which was performed by the Youth Theatre in 1991–1992.

Her poem "Thorny Spaces Suddenly Moving" was published in a literary journal called *Ibda'a* (Creativity) in January 1993. It abounds in images of imprisonment and confinement. Longing for freedom, for a life lived in a house "with no keys, no doors," the speaker is instead trapped in a home, a marriage, and a life that she finds profoundly oppressive. A house she glimpses from the Metro, with its open door and exposed outer staircase, becomes the focus for her own dreams of escape.

*Amira Nowaira*

◆

The same keys that open doors
also close them.
The keys dangling, hanging from chains,
powerless, can only jingle
dramatically.
The key languishing in my pocket
reminds me that it's time
I became a woman
wise enough to live in a house
with no keys, no doors.

A meteor vanishes
before we can see its face,
before we can know whether
it was the same one
we have seen before.

All I perceived later in my heart
was the trace of a heavy foot.
But blood did not let me
trace it any further.

How did I happen to love a man
like a dark star,
who robbed me of other men I loved,
of all the other men I loved,
and left me with nothing
but the joy of feeling orphaned?

The darkness eats up the full moon,
which tremblingly lifts
an axe of defeat.

"Why do you enter the family scene
like water trickling down the sides of a jar?" Ziad asks me.

I answer, "I am your mother,
but you will never be mine."
I say, "My womb is full of thorns;
where can I find space for you to rest?"

Every day,
sitting in the fast Metro car,
I see a dilapidated house flash by,
with its outer wooden staircase
and its door of metal
always open.
Every day,
this house becomes mine.

*Translated by Amira Nowaira*

## *Latifa Al-Zayyat*
# IN HER OWN MIRROR

Egypt 1993    Arabic

Born in Damietta in 1923, Latifa Al-Zayyat grew up in a middle-class family and was educated in Damietta, Assiut, and Cairo. In 1942 she entered Cairo University, then rife with different and often opposing political factions, and earned her undergraduate degree in English literature in 1946. After obtaining her doctorate from the same department in 1957, she was appointed a member of the teaching staff at Ain Shams University.

Al-Zayyat was a prolific writer of novels, short stories, memoir, critical studies, and translations. Her novel *Al-Bab al-Maftooh* (The Open Door), published in the original Arabic in 1960 and in English in 2000, is a coming-of-age novel set in Cairo in the 1940s and 1950s, depicting a young woman's struggles with the constrictions placed on women's lives in that era. It proved so popular that it was turned into a hugely successful film.

Al-Zayyat was also a political activist who participated in demonstrations and expressed her views forcefully and fearlessly, leading to her arrest on several occasions. The first of these arrests took place in the late 1940s, when she was deeply involved in the anticolonial struggle as a leader of the leftist and nationalist National Committee of Students and Workers. Her last arrest in 1981 may have been the result of her activism with the Committee for the Defense of National Culture, which took a strong stand against Anwar Sadat's normalization of relations with Israel. She subsequently learned that her house had been under surveillance for the previous three years.

Latifa Al-Zayyat's autobiographical essay "In Her Own Mirror" was published in the literary journal *Ibda'a* (Creativity) in 1993, three years before her death. In it, Al-Zayyat writes of her dual passions for literature and politics, and the intersections between these two driving forces in her life. Written in an attractively simple and straightforward style, the essay is especially significant for documenting a pivotal point in Egypt's history.

In the late 1940s, many Egyptians were feeling restless after the British failed to fulfill the promises of independence made during the World War II. This period was fraught with political unrest and nationalist zeal, fomented by the lingering presence of a foreign power. During this time, Egyptian frustration expressed itself in the attempts by intellectuals to dissociate themselves from the dominant ideology of the colonial power. This was achieved, as Al-Zayyat observes, either through the adoption of a new and modernized, but extremist, version of Islam that reasserted an identity independent from Western culture, or by embracing the increasingly popular ideology of the Left. In fact, young Egyptian intellectuals of the time found themselves forced to choose between socialism and fundamentalist Islam, two poles that are in many ways diametrically opposed.

The essay also provides a rare picture of the attitudes of some women intellectuals in the 1940s, who saw their struggle within the framework of the larger national struggle and their liberation as dependent on the overall freedom of society. Latifa Al-Zayyat here gives voice to the aspirations of a generation of young Egyptians, men and women alike, to achieve the utopian dream of equality offered to them by Marxism. It is clear from this essay, written as she entered her seventies, that Latifa Al-Zayyat never entirely lost her belief in some version of that dream.

*Amira Nowaira*

✦

Whenever I think of the formative years of my life, I remember the atmosphere of the 1919 Revolution. I was born four years after that popular uprising, the year of the declaration of the Constitution. The lyrics I sang, along with all the children of Egypt, were the songs of the revolution. The celebrations held annually in memory of Saad Zagloul took place right next door to our house in

Damietta. My two brothers were keenly interested in politics, especially Mohammed Abd El Sallam Al-Zayyat. Their enthusiasm was contagious, and politics became an important element in my life.

The growing conflict between the people and the Wafd Party, on the one hand, and the king and minority parties, on the other, touched me very deeply. Beginning in the 1930s, the country entered a stage of total economic, social, and political upheaval, which Naguib Mahfouz has described in his novel *Mirrors* through the voice of the narrator: "It was an age in which morals deteriorated and hypocrisy prevailed."

My self-awareness grew in an atmosphere of popular demand for the restoration of the 1923 constitution, which had been suspended by the government of Ismail Sidky. When I was in my fourth year of primary school in Assiut, I tried to participate in a demonstration calling for the Constitution. Whether of my own free will or not, I was greatly interested in politics.

I was lucky enough to have entered the university in 1942, a time when the world was beginning to score victories over Nazism and fascism, and people were becoming more hopeful about gaining long-awaited national liberty. The atmosphere at the university was just wonderful. The love of knowledge became almost as strong as the wish for love. The whole of my being was ecstatically open to life. I remember reading at the same time the poetry of the Sufi woman Rabaa El Adaweyya, the *Communist Manifesto*, and the "Song of Songs" from the Old Testament, in addition to two books on the history of religions.

This was a time of openness and of hope. A sweeping tide seemed to carry us on golden wings and push us into that revolutionary flow. We did not create this wave; rather, it created us, as it did the rest of our generation, the generation of the 1940s that later left its imprint on all the cultural activities of society.

I entered the university an enthusiastic patriot. My hair used to stand on end, literally, when I remembered the history of Pharaonic Egypt and compared it with the presence at that time of English soldiers on the streets. Egyptian reactionary forces stood hand in hand with the king in opposition to the people. At university, two options were open to those wishing to dissent and groping for a better alternative. These were the Muslim Brothers on the one hand, and the communists on the other, since the Wafd Party was beginning to lose its revolutionary appeal. Being a woman with a special temperament, it was inevitable that I chose the communists. The ideal of equality among human beings, women and men alike, regardless of color, sex, or creed, fired my imagination. I was fascinated by the lovely future pictured by Marxists of human beings realizing their full potential as they worked to reconstruct the whole world. In short, communism offered me the image of a beautiful utopia.

My political activities and my daily struggles seemed in harmony with my intellectual and emotional being. My brothers had no objections to my involvement in politics, though they warned me of possible dangers. The activity recreated me anew, transforming me from the timid person I was into someone capable of confronting and working constructively with others.

I was twelve when I first read Tewfik El Hakim's *The Return of the Spirit*. I found in this novel a living picture of my life and the life of other Egyptians. How I wished then that I could write a similar work! I tried my hand at the short story, and some of the stories I wrote were published in the magazine *Al Hilal* and the newspaper *Al Masry*.

But I specialized in literature, and taught it at the university beginning in 1952. Writing for me was not merely a matter of talent or emotion. It became a study and a comprehensive view of things, which turned details and particulars into symbols and ideas. This intellectual experience led me to postpone the writing of a novel until I was completely ready. I read masterpieces and studied technique. I started writing *The Open Door* in 1957 and finished it in 1960, at the age of thirty-seven.

I chose to write a novel because I wanted to record my vision of life as a young woman, a vision that could not be conveyed through the short story, drama, or poetry. It was a vision in danger of getting lost as I grew older. This is why I wrote about my experience in a novel, recording in it the different stages of my development.

In the novel, we are presented, on the first level of the narrative, with the story of a middle-class girl. On the second level, we are offered a picture of Egypt's history between 1946 and 1956. On the last level, we discover the morality of the middle classes and its shortcomings. The three levels are completely interwoven in the novel, with the particular and the universal intersecting at several points. This would not have been possible in drama, since the theater mostly emphasizes one single line that deepens through conflict. To establish a connection among these three levels was not my premeditated purpose, but it became clear to me in the process of writing the novel. I was so stunned by the discovery that I thought I was either mad or a genius. Later on, I had to rewrite the first part of the novel, which makes up a third of it.

I think I read and loved all the great masters of the novel. The ones that left a lasting impression on my mind were the Russian writers of the last century: Dostoyevsky, Turgenev, Chekhov, and Tolstoy, and I discovered a connection between Egyptian and Russian characters. One of the nicest things I heard about *The Open Door* was Yehia Hakki's words on Radio Two in discussing the novel. "Laila in *The Open Door*," he said, "reminds one of Natasha in *War and Peace*."

But my attempts are obviously closer to our age than the experiences presented by the Russians. I tried to write a novel made up of the accumulation of dramatic moments. I did not stop too long for descriptions, but directed my attention to the narrative line, the building up of events that interconnected and grew to express meaning, without resorting to descriptive details. In this way, I tried to introduce something new to the Egyptian novel, which had so far depended almost entirely on description.

There was also the problem of language. But before dealing with it, I would like to describe what actually happened. *The Open Door* was shortlisted for the

State Prize for Fiction, and the committee voted unanimously to give me the prize. But Abbas El Akkad, who was a permanent member of the Supreme Council of Art and Literature, threatened to resign his post. He demanded that the prize be withheld from me on the grounds that I "overused colloquialisms." This indicates that my approach to language was fairly daring and avant-garde. I wrote in a language that was totally free from ornament, and that communicated meaning easily and directly. I believe that in the 1960s this was quite unusual in the field of novel writing.

Political activity, academic work, and literary creativity are all part of Latifa Al-Zayyat. No matter how different these fields may be, they all involve the element of self-expression. In literary criticism and in teaching, I exercise my intellectual faculties. In art, I use my intellectual, emotional, and sensory powers, and the same goes for politics when the general atmosphere is receptive, as it was in the 1940s. In the forties, I saw with my whole being that the future could be shaped by people.

Some critics consider Laila, the main protagonist of *The Open Door*, to represent me personally. This may be true up to a point. She shares with me some, but not all, traits. She is some ten years younger than I, because I intended her to represent young Egyptian women in general.

I think I have been as fulfilled as any human being can possibly be, and this is a source of satisfaction to me. It makes my old age a time of productivity and of giving, instead of a time of depression. I believe I have managed to become reconciled with myself as much as is possible for any human being. This can only happen when the undisclosed comes out into the open and when there is no rift between past and present, when one is free enough to go beyond what has happened and to recreate the present moment afresh. Human beings can only possess the future if they possess the past.

In the novel *The Man Who Knew His Charge* I tried to deal with a very harsh subject in a humorous way. This is a satirical novel in which I criticize the types of oppression practiced by the state against political dissidents, including imprisonment, forced exile, monitoring and spying on the individual, framing him, and forging evidence against him. The war waged by the state against political dissidents is actually the raw material of an epic. But when this war is waged against a simple, helpless man, a tragicomic situation arises. There is misunderstanding in every act, and the state is up against phantoms, while the poor, helpless hero has little hand in any of it. In writing this novel, I managed to overcome the personal feelings of oppression that I had in 1981 and the years just preceding it, when my house came virtually under siege.

Louis Awad once invited me to speak on a television program. He asked me why I did not lead a women's movement, since I was, according to him, well-equipped to do that. At the time, Egypt was fighting the Israelis who had occupied Sinai. So I answered that there were always priorities. The liberation of the country came before the liberation of women. I said that I believed that woman's status was a problem for the whole of society, that women could not be free unless the whole of society were free. In a deteriorating society, the situation of women becomes unspeakably worse. As a woman myself, woman's cause was mine. But I was not totally consumed by this issue because I was interested in my country as a whole, which included all its men and women.

I haven't written an autobiography in *The Search*, although some considered it a conventional, and others an unconventional, autobiography. I did use some autobiographical material, and followed the line of psychological conflict that has dominated my life, the conflict between the love of life and the wish to withdraw from it. By going forward and backward, I presented this conflict with the same minute details I myself lived through and suffered. I dealt with this theme fictionally, portraying both moments of crisis and of resolution.

*Translated by Amira Nowaira*


## Nawal El Saadawi
# WRITING AND FREEDOM

Egypt 1993 Arabic

Egyptian feminist writer, physician, and activist, Nawal El Saadawi was born in 1931 into a highly educated family in the Delta village of Kafr Talha. Obeying the wish of her father, she enrolled in the Faculty of Medicine at Cairo and qualified as a doctor, with a specialization in psychiatry, in 1955. As a medical doctor, she was witness to the inequality and hardship suffered by women in urban as well as rural Egypt. Her experience led her to write about the taboo subject of womanhood and sexuality, and she became perhaps the first woman to bring into the public sphere the social and sexual abuses suffered by a large but silent segment of Egypt's female population, including domestic violence, honor killings, and particularly female circumcision, also called female genital mutilation (FGM).

Her outspoken views regarding FGM and her criticism of the government's handling of the issue, plus her first book, *Women and Sex*, published in 1972, thrust her into a headlong confrontation with political and religious authorities that would continue throughout her life. In the early 1970s, she was dismissed from her job as director of Public Health Education in the Ministry of Health, and also lost her positions as chief editor of a health journal and assistant general secretary of the Medical Association in Egypt.

In the early 1970s she also carried out research on mental health problems among Egyptian women, focusing on women in prisons and hospitals. It was this research that inspired her well-known novel *Emra'a enda noktat el sifr* (Woman at Point Zero), published in 1973, which presents with a great deal of sympathy the story of a prostitute waiting on death row, charged with having killed a man. In 1977 she published *Al-Wajh al-'Ari lil-Mar'a al-'Arabiyya* (The Hidden Faces of Eve), which begins with a graphic account of her own experience of FGM as a child, and discusses the various forms of oppression suffered by Arab women. In the late 1970s she worked as the United Nations Advisor for the Women's Program in Africa and the Middle East.

In September 1981, in response to the vehement protests by the intellectual elite of the country following the Camp David accords with Israel, the government of Anwar Sadat rounded up a large number of intellectuals representing various and even opposing groups—Marxists, Nasserites, Islamic scholars, Coptic priests, and feminists. Saadawi was imprisoned along with many other women activists, and released a few months later, following Sadat's assassination. In *Memoirs from the Women's Prison*, published in 1983, she recounts her experiences and attacks the repressive practices of the Egyptian Government.

In 1982, El Saadawi founded the Arab Women's Solidarity Association (AWSA), an international organization dedicated to liberating women and fighting sexist practices. The group was banned in 1991 when it criticized U.S. involvement in the Gulf War. The following year, after receiving death threats from Islamic fundamentalists unhappy with her outspokenness, she went into exile in the United States, where she taught at Duke University. She returned to her homeland in 1996, still holding on to her beliefs and and denouncing all forms of injustice. Her autobiography, *Awraqi . . . Hayati* (My Papers . . . My Life), was published in 1999.

A prolific writer, El Saadawi has published more than sixty books, including short stories, novels, plays, memoir, and nonfiction. Many have been banned in Egypt at one time or another. Her work has been translated into thirty languages. Most of her books attack politicized religion and question traditional concepts of womanhood within patriarchal systems. She has also been a consistent critic of the repressive leadership in Egypt, and the dominant power of the West, especially the United States.

In 2007, El Saadawi came under renewed attack for her play "Al-Elah Yastaqeel fi Iqtima Al-Qemmah" (God Resigns at the Summit Meeting), in which she writes that God is a spirit and is therefore neither female nor male. She was accused of apostasy and contempt for the principles of Islam by authorities at Al-Azhar University, and Egyptian tribunals initiated legal proceedings against her. She felt compelled to flee her country in March 2007.

"My Experience with Writing and Freedom" is an autobiographical essay published in Arabic in *Fusul* (Chapters), a quarterly journal of literature and criticism dedicated to freedom of expression. In this essay, Saadawi characteristically describes personal reflections—including memories of the oppressive lives of her mother and grandmother—with trenchant analysis. She lifts the purda of silence that has covered Egyptian women for many decades, voicing her anger against male social, religious, and political authorities who deprive women of their freedom and agency, requiring them to submit their identity, their individuality, and their will into men's. "My Self will not dissolve in any other Self," she declares, "be it my husband, God, or the president." Ultimately, her goal is to escape socially-constructed selfhood and to find self-definition in the act of writing. By converting her own experiences and observations into words, she has woven her own identity and built her own home among silenced crowds and senseless clichés.

*Noha Nadder Hamdy and Amira Nowaira*

✦

From the moment the world of writing opened itself before me, I started to follow a route that was drastically different from the one preordained for me before birth. The history of enslavement dating back to Pharaonic times had not only laid out the path I should follow from cradle to grave, but had also created the authorities to make sure that I did. It thus provided the authority of the father and husband in the small family, the authority of the state, the legal system, social institutions, the authority of religion and Shari'a, and finally the authority of international legitimacy.

These authorities took the shape of a pyramid. At the top, you would find what we today call the New World Order, the *New York Times* and CNN, while at the bottom there would be the local governments, local television, prisons, censorship, and literary criticism.

As a child I discovered that writing was the only means by which I could breathe. But the government, the patriarchal and religious authorities, the propaganda in the media as well as the teachings of the Faculty of Medicine (which I joined to please my father), all said to me, "There is no connection between writing and the act of breathing in a woman." My experience in life, however, has confirmed a very close connection between writing and the entry of air into my lungs. These hierarchical authorities joined forces and, like an iron fist, pushed me into the conjugal bed, under the illusion of love and the "scientific" ideas, derived from Freud, that women must create babies and not ideas. At one stage of my life, I produced babies, and more than once in my life, I was married to the brim. Yet, instead of feeling the air enter my lungs, I felt suffocated.

The more a woman dedicates herself to the institution of marriage, the more suffocated she is bound to feel. I looked up the word "dedication" in the inherited dictionary of enslavement, and I found it connected with the devotion of slaves to their masters. It's a term that implies the act of getting lost in others, of self-denial and self-sacrifice, terms that come under the category of death or of self-destruction.

But creativity and writing are quite the opposite. They involve keeping the self alive, rather than destroying it. They mean the realization of self and not its denial.

And thus I discovered the contradiction between marital devotion and self-fulfillment in a woman's life, since marriage dictates that a woman's identity dissolve into that of her husband or into those of her children (after all, the children are the rightful property of the husband and his name is written on them). Thus the man of letters is blessed with a wife who cooks his food, washes his trousers, and offers him tea, while he sits to write down the story of his love for another woman. On the other hand, the woman of letters is blessed with a husband who turns her life into misery and scolds her all the time for having neglected to cook, wash, or sweep the floors, or for having allowed the children to scream out loud while he slept. The creative man has a wife who delights in his success and feels happier as he becomes more successful. The creative woman has a husband who gets depressed when she succeeds, and gets increasingly more depressed as she becomes more successful.

If the creative woman has the courage to suppress part of her brain, she may save herself from the depression of husbands, and may be able to avoid losing herself in the sacred women's kingdom inside the house. She will be able then to go out on to the streets, demonstrating along with others and shouting: God ... nation ... and king (or whoever occupies the position of a king). But she may also find herself required to identify completely with the king or the president. If she is not willing to do that, a huge wooden gate will open up before her, leading her into prison.

While in prison in 1981, I tried day and night to discover the crime I had committed, never having been affiliated with any political party, never having committed adultery, never having carried an illegitimate child, and never having insulted anyone. After eighty days and nights in my cell, I discovered that my only crime was having been unable to lose myself in the self of the president. In ancient Egypt, the pharaoh considered himself divine, and all other selves were required to dissolve completely into his. Losing oneself has been the virtue most highly appreciated from the days of the pharaohs until now. But dissolving is the opposite of creativity. Writing means expressing my Self. It means that my Self will not dissolve in any other Self, be it my husband, God or the president.

Writing means surviving and denying death. If it had not been for writing, all prophets, gods and pharaohs would have disappeared forever. If it had not been for the discovery of printing, we would not have known anything about those who had died. But for the Torah, the Bible, and the Qur'an, we would not have Moses, Jesus, or Mohammed.

Writing has the power to give life to the dead. This is why writing has become the only way I can survive. I often wonder how people who do not write manage to survive or endure life. My mother died leaving not a trace. I am one of the nine children she had given birth to. None of us carried her name. My father also died, leaving behind no mark except for his name in mine, written on my books. With the translation of my books into several languages, my father's name has become known, while my mother's has disappeared forever.

On the other hand, I feel better off than the English writer Virginia Woolf, who took on her husband's name and was known by it. A woman should use her own name on her works and not that of her father or husband. If I had to choose between my father's name and my husband's, I would certainly prefer my father's, since it is at least permanent. The husband's name may change with a change of circumstances. This is particularly true in our country. When a husband happens to fall in love with another woman, all he need to do is open his mouth and utter the words, "You're divorced," three times, upon which his wife packs her bags and leaves. In the eyes of the law and the Shari'a, she has become a divorced woman.

I consider myself lucky that I have never taken the name of any husband and never signed my books except with my father's name and that of my paternal grandfather, El Saadawi—the name of a man who is a total stranger to me, since he died before I was born. He died of bilharzia, poverty, and enslavement, the triple chronic disease afflicting our peasants from the days of the pharaohs until the present. There are times when my name is shortened to my grandfather's name, El Saadawi. This is how this strange man gets his name imprinted on me and on the covers of my books.

Nothing consoles me more than the thought that at least on doomsday, I will be able to shed that strange name and carry my mother's. When I was a little girl, my father once told me that on doomsday people would be called by their mothers' names. I asked him why this was so, and he said that maternity was certain. So I asked, "Is paternity not certain, then?" I saw the pupil of his eye quiver slightly, and a long silence followed. He gave my mother a look wavering between doubt and certainty.

My mother knew no man other than my father. How could she have, if she never left the house or, more precisely, never left the kitchen? After giving birth to her ninth child, she became pregnant with the tenth. She had an abortion.

One day while she slept, she dreamed of my father with another woman. Her grief made the milk freeze in her breast, forming a cancerous tumor. She died very young. My maternal grandmother used to sing to herself in the bathroom a song that went, "Trusting a man is like trusting that water would stay in a sieve." She used to pour water over the sieve and watch it disappear to the last drop. She would smack her lips in distress. When her husband came home late at night, she would smell the other woman in his underwear. In the morning, he would lecture her on the love of the homeland.

After the death of my grandfather, I became very skeptical of any man who chanted the song of patriotism. If he moved from the love of the motherland to the love of the peasants or laborers, my suspicions increased. If he went beyond that and held a rosary in his hand, my skepticism was confirmed beyond doubt.

Whenever I met a man who was full of religious words and clichés, and who held the rosary in his hand, I would immediately smell a rat. If this man happened to be the head of state, the problem moved from the domain of the personal to the public. And if he happened to be my husband, the disaster would still be unmitigated, because I would then have to choose between writing and living in the garden of Eden.

I have always chosen writing, Eden being rather out of reach, and its delights designed for the gratification of men. Prominent among these delights is the presence of fair young virgins. But I am a woman of a dark skin. I have long ago lost my virginity and am at the moment in the menopausal phase (to use the language of the system). In paradise, a woman like me will have none other than her husband. What a disaster! To have my husband chasing me in life and after death!

That is why I have always chosen writing. I came to realize, even as a child, that I was not going to have the same fate as my mother, my grandmother or, for that matter, any other woman. Why I had this conviction is not totally clear to me. One reason may have been that I saw my father's great admiration for the Prophet, and I wanted to get my father's admiration. One day I dreamed I became a prophet and my father looked at me admiringly. When, in the morning, I told my grandmother about that dream, she just hit her chest in disbelief. She heated some water for me to cleanse myself of the guilt. A woman could never be a prophet, she told me.

That day I took up my pen and jotted down angry words on the page. My brother, who failed his exams every year, could become a prophet, while I, who succeeded every year, could not. My anger was directed at a power I did not know. My grandmother said it was God who preferred my brother, though he failed his exams every year.

There is certainly a connection between creativity and anger. The little girl is taught to conceal her anger and draw an angelic smile on her face. But no connection exists between angels and creativity. That is why in Arabic we have the expressions "the demon of poetry" and "the demon of art."

I began to voice my anger against all authorities from the bottom up, starting with the authority of my father. My father, noticing a frown rather than a smile on my face, told me that frowning made girls lose their femininity. So I had to choose between femininity and writing. I chose writing.

In the dead of the night, I hugged my anger the way the woman carrying an illegitimate child hugged her secret. I told my mother that, if a woman did not become angry at injustice, she would not be human. She told me that being human was better than being a woman. My grandmother raised her hand to her chin and said defiantly, "I bet you won't find anyone to marry you. Obeying your father is obeying God."

In obedience to my father, I joined the Faculty of Medicine and put on the angelic white coat. For years I lived with the stool and urine of patients, the rules of the Ministry of Health and the guidelines of the general director and the minister. When my father died, I was free of my promise and started to live to please no one but myself.

Creativity only begins when one is free from the wish to please others.

After my father's death, I discovered that there were other authorities trying to dominate my life. But I promised myself that no one would have domination over me, and that I would write what my own mind dictated.

So the policemen knocked on my door, broke it open, and dragged me to prison under the pretense of safeguarding my life. I walked into prison as if into a dream. The trance was not unlike the one I had when, under the illusion of love and the marriage bond, I walked back into my second marriage.

The authority of the state and the authority of the husband constitute one iron chain, whose archenemy is writing. My husband used to fly into a mad rage whenever he saw me with pen and paper in hand.

The jailer came every day into my cell, turned it upside down, removed the tiles under the toilet, dug deep into the floor and wall, and screamed out: "If I found pen or paper, it would be far worse for you than if I had found a gun."

After the death of the president, I walked out of jail and into a prisonlike existence. My name moved from the blacklist to the gray list, the only difference between the two being the color of the paper. I saw people's faces, pale and sallow. Nobody believed anybody, and everyone accused everyone else. Accusations flew downward and upward, from the tip of the pyramid where international legitimacy resides to the bottom, to local governments, patriarchal and legislative authorities, to religious institutions, cultural institutions, the media, the press, the intellectuals, the writers and the literary critics.

Everything seemed to be receding. Even the loaf of bread, like justice, was in short supply. I realized that writing was the substitute for justice, and justice was beauty and love.

—Writing is the vain attempt to find love.

—Writing is the vain attempt to defy death.

—Both love and death are ephemeral.

—Nothing remains but the letters on the page.

—Nothing remains of gods and prophets except the books.

Without the presence of creative art to create hope from nothingness, there would be pure despair all around us. Creativity is like a spot of light in pitch darkness. It is the presence of the ray of light in the midst of this massive despair that makes our suffering in writing worthwhile.

We pay an exorbitant price for being creative, a price that may be as high as death. If the creative artist happens to be a woman, the price she pays is doubled, tripled, or even quadrupled, according to circumstances.

In addition to losing Eden, I have also lost in my life what my grandmother used to call "the shade of a man," the shade provided by a man being, as the saying goes, "better than the shade of a wall." Personally, I have always preferred the shade of the wall to that of a man who became depressed because of my creativity. This was how I lost my reputation on both the personal and public levels.

The men who tried to flirt with me and found me unyielding called me a woman without femininity and a man-hater. The men who worked for God, for the nation, and for the oil kings said that I worked for the Devil and that I was advocating permissiveness and sexual freedom. The men who loved peasants and workers said that I loved women better than peasants or workers, that I believed more in sexual freedom than in class struggle; I was therefore the ally of imperialism and Zionism. The men who loved the nation for its own sake and did not savor any talk of class struggle said I was the ally of international communism because the word class is sometimes used in my writings.

My doctor colleagues, men and women alike, who hated any talk about politics and loved nothing better than their patients, thought I was an utter faillure, having achieved none of the five goals of the profession: a clinic, a car, a house, a farm, and a bride (or bridegroom).

As for my literary colleagues of both sexes, who love to be in the limelight of the camera, the newspapers, or the state prizes, and who consider that one could criticize anything or anyone under the sun except God and the head of state, they believe I have failed in my literary career because I live away from the limelight and in the area of the gray or black lists.

More than ten years ago, in 1980, one of my books fell by chance into the hands of a small publisher living in South Africa. Although he was white, he fought alongside the black Africans against the racist regime of apartheid. He was harassed and was in danger of getting killed in Johannesburg, but he managed to escape to London and started this small publishing business. This was the first book of mine to be translated into a foreign language. With it, I stepped out of local bounds, into an English readership. And then to different languages.

From 1980 until now, in 1992, sixteen of my works, including novels, short stories and scientific studies, have been published. My books are now read everywhere in the world. This is how I escaped local confines.

In 1987, after the publication of my novel *The Fall of the Imam* in Arabic, the telephone rang at home. The voice of an official from the Ministry of the Interior told me that I was going to be put under constant guard.

"What for?" I asked in surprise.

"To guard your life," he said.

"My life?" I asked.

"Yes. Your life is under threat."

"Who's threatening it?" I asked.

"This is all the information I have. We'll send the guards in an hour," he said.

"I don't want any guards," I told him, "as long as you withhold information from me."

"We'll send you the guards all the same, with or without your consent," he said.

"Will you protect my life against my wishes?" I asked.

"Yes," he said, "your life is not yours. It belongs to the state."

The guards came to my house and stayed there for two years. Then they disappeared. Until this day I have no idea why they came in the first place, or why they left later. But I came to understand that my life was not mine.

In 1990 a journalist came to see me with the copy of an Arabic magazine published in London. In it was a list of "the dead" (or those who ought to be dead). I read my name on that list, together with the names of several other literary figures, writers, and poets.

"Who drew up this list?" I asked.

"The oil kings," he answered.

At night, while lying in bed, I saw a small butterfly, almost spiderlike, being attracted by the light of the lamp. When it came too close, it got scorched by the heat and so withdrew a little. This movement was repeated several times until finally it burnt and fell down dead.

I wondered during my sleep about this irrational attraction to the light and the flame. In the morning, opening the magazine, I realized the connection between the oil kings and international legitimacy. In the magazine I read that the oil kings had paid the Western alliance the cost of the Gulf War.

For the first time in history the slaves are paying their masters the cost of their own enslavement.

Things being what they are, isn't the connection between creativity and death more reasonable than the attraction between the butterflies and the light? And since creativity was up against all the pyramidal authorities, both internally and externally, isn't it logical, then, that the creative artist is threatened with imprisonment or death? All the more so if that artist happens to be a woman?

From the dawn of the history of enslavement and the rise of the patriarchal class system, there has always been a conflict between creativity and authority. This is why restrictions are imposed on free expression. Every creative artist, male or female, has a personal way of surmounting these limitations. But simple, clear, and direct writing remains the most dangerous, since it conveys its message directly to thousands or millions who may be incapable of deciphering more intricate literary discourse

But the creative idea imposes its own method of expression. In some of my works, symbolism and suggestiveness gain ground over directness. At times I leave meanings to be read between the lines. At others I leave spaces or even ellipsis marks. I may let out an unuttered sigh that ends up in silence or a full stop. The creative reader has the task of reading the unwritten script within the written book.

When I am overwhelmed by mad courage, I write without caution. But what I write no one will dare publish. I put these in a blue file on which I have written, "To be published posthumously." These are the writings I manage to produce away from the inner censor. This censor may hide behind a military outfit and may carry in his hand the scepter of kings or presidents.

At other times, he may wear the body of my grandfather who died before I was born. Or he may take off this body, disappearing without a trace except for a small, delicate cane, like the one that the teacher of religious instruction at my primary school used to carry in his hand.

The censor is ever present, always looking at you as though through a spyhole. There is always a price to pay for creativity, a price that may be life itself.

But for me, this is a small price to pay, because I would rather lose life than lose myself. Without this self, creativity can never be.

*Translated by Amira Nowaira*

# *Malouma Bint Moktar Ould Meidah*
## AN ARTIST WHO UNSETTLES:
## AN INTERVIEW AND A SONG

Mauritania 1993    Arabic

Malouma Bint Moktar Ould Meidah, widely known simply as Malouma, was born in 1960 in Mederdra, in the Trarza region of southern Mauritania. She is the daughter and granddaughter of celebrated male griots: Her father, Moktar Ould Meidah, is a prominent traditional musician as well as a gifted poet, and her grandfather, Mohamed Yahya Ould Boubane, was also a virtuoso poet and expert at the tidinit, a small traditional lute-like stringed instrument. She learned music from her parents at an early age, schooled first on the ardine, a multi-stringed instrument similar to a West African kora. She started performing at twelve, accompanying her parents, and by fifteen was already regarded as an accomplished solo performer, well skilled in the traditional repertoire learned from her family.

As Malouma grew and developed as a musician, her influences broadened, ranging from Arabic music, including the performances of the celebrated Egyptian singer Oum Kalthoum, to European classics and the blues. A talented artist, composer, and interpreter with an extraordinary voice, Malouma is today considered the first truly modern Mauritanian composer. Her highly innovative work reflects a unique mix of aesthetic and cultural influences, combining traditional and modern sounds—as expressed in her use of both tidnit and electric guitar—and drawing on the Moorish music of the Sahara desert as well as the rhythms of Senegal. Like Mauritania itself, Malouma's music is a place where Berber, Arab, and West African cultures meet.

In addition to being stylistically revolutionary, Malouma's compositions address certain subjects considered taboo for women, and her artistry is a part of her activism. Committed to social justice and gender equality, she writes songs for such activist causes as AIDS prevention, literacy, and the rights of women and children. Although she was at first frowned upon by the establishment, which found her unsettling, she rapidly became "the people's singer" and won a following throughout and beyond Mauritania. She has recorded three albums: *Desert of Eden* (1998), *Dunya* (2003), and *Nour* (2007).

The first text presented here was excerpted from a conversation with Ould Omer that appeared in the French-language literary journal *Notre Librarie* in 1993. Malouma speaks candidly about the three elements—formal presentation, performance length, and song content—that she uses strategically to challenge the culture of traditional music-making in her native Mauritania and make her music more accessible to an international audience. The song that follows exemplifies Malouma's frank and defiant treatment of relationships between women and men.

*Abena P. A. Busia*

✦

## INTERVIEW

I refuse to sing seated among an assembly of people who have come to listen to my music, in the traditional manner of emirs and other nobility of bygone days. I prefer to sing standing in front of an unknown audience that has chosen to come and listen to me out of love for my music, and for no other reason.

I refuse to continue to remain seated throughout the night, singing unending praise-songs. A song, to me, must be short in order not to be boring, and it must present something that is likely to be pleasing to the audience. I do not intend to continue with the tradition of praising this one or that one. My music must be committed to humanity. It must contribute to the change that is necessary for the improvement of life. My music supports the widow and the orphan; it supports the oppressed. My voice is the voice of the voiceless. Commitment, to me, is also the expression of love, of bitterness, of joy. To express these human feelings is also my commitment. To say what I want to say and to express what I feel. My commitment allows me to present to an audience something of interest, something engaging. Abroad, I can thus offer something palatable. I believe that our music must be exportable. That is why one needs to introduce the changes I propose.

As you know, there are no real composers in our country. This is a new concept, which has not yet filtered through our traditional perceptions of music. The same applies to our poets, who are still in the habit of composing poetry in pre-Islamic modes. They should be taught to compose lighter pieces, more adapted to the new form of music I am introducing. In the meantime, I have to write my own words. There, too, I am trying to innovate. I am fighting for the introduction of new themes that will express commitment on the part of the poet. Traditional poetry has always remained confined to the themes of memory and of ephemeral love. In the music I am campaigning for, the message is more important than anything else. I do conform to the norms, only in so far as they do not stifle my message. I have been accused of distorting this form of poetry, but I believe that I am rather adapting poetry to new concepts and to the contemporary environment. Some may accuse me of "desecrating" poetry, but I know that I am making the best possible use of our cultural heritage.

On this matter, I hold no grudge against the public. Everything here is new and it is difficult to understand novelty. By nature, also, a Mauritanian tends to be skeptical about whatever another Mauritanian undertakes! This is because our audience remains local. In order to become popular, one has to be successful elsewhere first. I had to first become successful in Tunisia, Egypt, Morocco, and Iraq, before I could have an audience here. Today, I believe that I am the star of youth, of those who have not been constrained by tradition and of those who are rebelling against its constraints. It is a pleasant feeling to sing in front of people who are responsive. And I believe that it is possible for an artist to share feelings with an audience. To achieve this, creative work needs only to be filled with true emotion.

*Translated by Christiane Owusu-Sarpong and Esi Sutherland-Addy*

## SONG

Arrogant, my friend,
Your friend is arrogant!

He ignores me, he hides from me, he flees
Just to hurt me.

Let me tell you,
When I talked about my
Sorrow,
My girlfriends said,
"She is crazy!"
Well, I'm not pleased.

Yes, I've loved him,
My friend,
And he's despised love.
Go find him, my friend,
And see if he has a heart.

And tell him my secret,
I'm losing patience.
Tell him,
Patience has limits.

*Translated from French by Abena P.A.Busia*

## *Mubaraka Bint Al-Barra*
## DEFIANCES: AN INTERVIEW AND A POEM

Mauritania  1994  Arabic

Mubaraka Bint Al-Barra was born in 1956 in Marzik, Mauritania, and grew up in a traditional family; her father was a teacher and her grandfather a judge. She had begun writing poems in Arabic while still in her teens—initially, poems expressing her nationalist feelings and protesting the condition of women, and later love poems as well. Although she was educated and earned a B.A. at the University of Nouakchott, in Mauritania's capital city, Al-Barra felt she had to hide the fact that she could write poetry, even burning a collection of poems in the 1980s. Only in 1984, after a poem of hers was published without her knowledge and was appreciated by readers, did she begin to publish her work. In this largely oral society, writing was male, and women who dared to write were seen as competing with men. While Mauritania is known as the "country of a million poets," female voices have been ignored and marginalized, systematically omitted from literary history.

In the following interview with Hindou Mint Aïmina, which appeared in 1994 in *Notre Librarie*, a French-language journal focusing on literature from the global south, Al-Barra discusses the obstacles she had to overcome in order to write. She also discusses traditional forms of Mauritanian poetry, composed in the distinctive Arabic dialect Hassaniya. *Legbna* are poems often composed around a theme and recited at gatherings of (usually male) *griots*. *Tebraa* is a women's genre, consisting of rhymed couplets sometimes based on a proverb.

In her poetry, Al-Barra uses rhyme in the manner of traditional male Arabic poets.

In "Caravan," she captures the landscape of Mauritania, which lies on the border of the Maghreb and the Sahel. Populated by both Arab-Berbers and sub-Saharan Africans, Mauritania retained what was in large part an essentially nomadic culture until well into the twentieth century.

*Yanserha Bint Mohamed Mahmoud*

◆

## INTERVIEW

...Let me just mention two factors which are problems for me as a poet: First, I am a woman in an Arabic and Muslim society, with all the restrictions this generally implies; then, I belong to an oral society, where writing is the prerogative of certain categories of men. There are, therefore, two fields, (as well as themes) a woman cannot, must not, talk about, precisely because she is a woman. I belong to a social category...where to be a woman poet means to question the very foundation of womanhood.

I burned a collection of poems in the 1980s, simply because it had been noticed that I was a poet and I did not have the courage to live down the consequent "marginalization." The traditional perception of the woman poet in the social milieu I belong to is that she is "like a cow that kicks": She becomes a bull. In the same manner, "a hen that crows must be killed," for she has taken on the manner of a cock. I have overcome this inferiority complex imposed upon me as a woman, but it has not been easy. Culture, and therefore writing, is masculine in our societies. A woman can only express herself in other fields, such as music or arts and crafts, but not through poetry.

The Moorish woman, despite the fact that she is quite visible and sometimes of social importance, must remain discreet. She must not compete with men in the areas from which they draw their power and supremacy, namely writing and knowledge. Because of social pressures, I have always dreaded confrontation and suffer still from a lack of confidence in my own literary production. . . .

I started in 1973 by writing nationalistic poems and poems in which I voiced my protest against the situation of women...Love is not, mind you, a theme women can talk about publicly, especially not in writing. These [early] poems were written in classical Arabic.

Because of strong social and psychological pressures, I decided not to write any more poems. But the desire to "speak out" was stronger [than the pressures]: I simply had to continue writing. This was a vital need for me, but I did it in hiding. This went on until 1984, when one of my poems, entitled "Waiting," was published without my knowledge and was well received by the general public. I must confess that this encouraged me to publish my first collection of poems, entitled *Psalms for a Single Country*.

Certain themes, in societies such as ours, are in themselves barriers that are generally not crossed by women writers. Among these are love and religion. These are themes a woman does not talk about, the first out of "a sense of decency"—for "decency makes a true woman"—and the second simply out of sheer socially dictated ignorance.

In all types of Arabic lyric poetry, the woman is presented as an object of lust, as a luxury, in short, as a body. I always believed that this perception had to be overcome. In the Arabic school of literature, the beloved woman (never the beloved man, since poets are always men) is described as an object. I do not want to talk about love as merely a physical need to be satisfied.

In Mauritania, we have the *tebraa*, through which women can express their feelings. We also have the *legbna*, in which a woman is not necessarily described as an object. I sometimes write poems and then feel that I must review them, that I must weigh each word I use. My fear of being confronted—again—is what takes away my courage; I do not want to shock. So, obviously, I do censor myself. The written word, in our societies, is very important. . . .

I do [compose *legbna*], but I do not always write the poems down, so most of them get lost. The *legbna*, mind you, is not a "woman's thing." I allow myself to compose it and sometimes my compositions are even adopted by local master-poets. I compose during sessions of verbal jousting, or of what we call "*propos*," that is, occasions on which a theme is chosen and poets meet to compose in groups or to compete with one another.

I do appreciate the *tebraa* because it is a genre through which women have demonstrated their ingenuity. It is a most expressive form of art, which produces the shortest possible poems in which one can express passion and the most profound meditation. Women have gone very far in the way in which they have exploited this, the only space they have been given to express themselves, the only loophole society has spared them. They have managed to say many things in few words. And they have managed to transgress all social barriers through the "word." I think that one must expend great effort in order to transcribe and preserve this part of our cultural heritage, which constitutes our cultural personality. It is a very dense mode of expression, which does not exist in any other part of the world.

That is what makes it difficult to translate the *tebraa*. Although the words used are, apparently simple, what they represent for their authors is usually much more profound. The *tebraa* varies in content and in mode of expression. It can be mystical or "shameless." It may use verses from the Qur'an or words or expressions generally belonging to the domain of the sacred. A translation never renders the full meaning of the words used, or one must increase the verses considerably in order to communicate the complete meaning.

[For example:] "People are dozing off / and I am thinking about the Secret." Here, the word "Secret" in Hassaniya means the "unmentionable." Evening is coming, and you have people without a care, and then you have the suffering woman who is thinking about the love she is forced to hide, to dissimulate, because of social obligations. This poem expresses the weight of social control.

A *tebraa* can be daring: "Had I been his pipe / I could be so near his mouth." "If only he felt about me / the way I feel about him."

Or, "Oh succession of children / how many *tebraa* have come before you!" [All of these] composed to express the painful and the relentless determination of her love, which has enabled her to bear the suffering of successive pregnancies to bear the children of her beloved.

"Swear to him by his name that yesterday I did not recognize him." This *tebraa* alludes to an ancient habit according to which lovers could only meet in the dark, when all the "spies" were asleep.

"My heart, calm down / it is God who decides, not us"—a whole existential philosophy.

"Cheikh Brahim / is Alive, Eternal and Ancient"—a Sufic meditation about the greatness of the Master in the eyes of his disciple.

*Translated by Abena P.A. Busia and Christiane Owusu-Sarpong*

## THE CARAVAN

In one moment I decided to be,
I wished my writing to become rain, torrents
engorging the desert sands.
I wished in the name of the nameless for the dust to disperse,
for the will to disintegrate the veil,
that, at the font of all memories, all sad nights,
all the webs of all the spiders, and the suffering
of children
would dissolve;
for all the muzzled to break free from their bits,
and all the waiting end.

I am weary of waiting.
I am weary of the caravan.

Will you always turn and turn about
your footsteps in my steps,
your footsteps hallucinatory?
And Honeïn grabbing at your sandals.

The caravan of the dispossessed encroaches outside the city gates,
their buzz arriving from a distance
like a swarm of flies.
Threading toward the horizon, their glances burning dreams spurned
by the Heavens,
and crossing all rifts, they chip at the shops of stone,
their yellow hands, raised in petition, accusations against destiny
like hollowed tree trunks.
O God, Children of the Dust,
We implore you, break our silence.

We are worn out by waiting;
We are weary of the caravan.

In the cycle of twilight Honeïn is lost in morning prayers.
The wretched returning form the six points of the horizon,
tell their beads of bitter madness.
Wisps of straw scattering in the wind
scratch faces. Two palms raise a stake and make a higher bid.
Here is Honeïn lost in prayer.
So take inspiration from this Honeïn:
exterminate all the wretched of the earth
and burn the homeless alive.

*Translated from French by Abena P. A. Busia and Christiane Owusu-Sarpong*


# *Radwa Ashour*
## ACCUSED OF HERESY

Egypt  1994   Arabic

Born in 1946, Radwa Ashour is a professor of English literature at Ain Shams University in Cairo. Her first novel, *Days in the Life of an Egyptian Student in America*, was published in 1983. Since then she has published more novels, including *A Warm Lap* (1985), *Khadija and Sawsan* (1989), and *Saddle* (1992); a collection of short stories, *I Saw the Palm Trees* (1989), and critical studies on the Palestinian writer Ghassan Kanafani and on the novel in West Africa.

*Granada* is the first novel in a trilogy of historical novels, a rare genre among women writers in Africa. It is set during and after the 1492 fall of Granada, the capital and last stronghold of the Muslim empire of Al-Andalus in southern Spain, to Castilian Christians from the north. In the years that followed, the brutal methods of the Spanish Inquisition were used to covert Muslims forcibly to Catholicism. The Moriscos, as these converts were called, led a double life, many continuing to practice their faith in secret, until they were exiled from Spain by decree in 1610. In this novel, Abu Jaafar, a bookbinder, raises his granddaughter, Salima Bint Jaafar, to love reading, "like the women scholars of Córdoba"—the seat of learning and culture in Islamic Spain. She is educated along with her brother, and turns to practicing traditional medicine, which makes her a heretic in the eyes of the Inquisition and leads to her arrest. The other characters mentioned in this extract, which comes at the very end of the novel, are Salima's husband, Saad; her daughter, Aisha; her brother, Hassan; and Hassan's wife, Mariama.

Sahar Hamouda

✦

As she sat alone in her cell, Salima tried to console herself. She did not sleep because if she stayed awake with her eyes wide open, she could drive away the rats and that horrible nightmare that always visited her during her sleep and made her scream with terror. What could ever make the inconsolable bearable? That giant of a woman who brought in her food had told her that she was a witch. It had been proved and verified. The sentence of the Inquisition, like hundreds of previous sentences, would be to burn at the stake. She imagined the scene. They would tie her and push her into a square full of expectant faces, waiting for the fire to spread from the torches to her. Like the burning of the books. How did her grandfather bear to see the tongues of flame lick one book and then the other, and one paper then another as it curled upon itself, as if to drive the fire away? And still the fire swept through them all, devouring, drying up, slicing, turning all into cinders. And then, nothing. Nothing but brittle ashes. What about all that was written in them, where would all that go? And wasn't man also, like a piece of paper, inscribed? Wasn't he but a string of words, each word carrying a meaning, and the totality of the meaning revealed by the inscribed words? In a moment of recklessness, she, Salima Bint Jaafar, had wanted to defeat death. But then she had backed away and undertaken a less unattainable task. She read books, treated patients, and removed all thought of Castilian oppression from her mind. When she walked in the streets, she did not get distracted by the markets, as other women did. She imagined the face of the woman whom she had not been able to treat with her medicine. The face of a woman, and her symptoms, would rise before her, and she would keep turning over in her mind the question: "What is the medicine?"

"Salima Bint Jaafar," the inquisitors asked, "why do people hate you?" They lied, because they had not asked the people of Biazzin. Could they bear to look at her as they put the torch to her? Would they bear what Abu Jaafar bore—and what she could not bear—that day they set fire to the books? And Aisha? She drove away the thought and the image, and hastened away from the fears that defeated body and spirit—and mind, too, since they drove one to insanity. She hastened to the image of her grandfather, Abu Jaafar, the elder who penned the first word in the book. It was not her father or mother, but her grandfather who had been the first to do it. He had announced that he would teach her just as he would teach Hassan, and whispered to his wife that Salima would be like the women scholars of Córdoba. Her grandmother laughed and repeated the words. Salima heard them. They became the first words to be inscribed in the book. She had been hard only on Saad, although she loved him. "I have made you suffer, Saad. Will you forgive me?" She repeated the words without knowing whether he was alive, or had gone there before her. And was that "there" a reality or illusion? Would she meet her grandfather and Saad and the little departed one and her father there, if that "there" was there? How would she and her father recognize each other? He would not recognize her, because the newborn babe he had left behind had aged into a woman verging on forty. She might recognize him, when she realized that he looked like Hassan. Poor Hassan. He had tried to protect his family, but the catastrophe came unexpectedly, out of he knew not where. But he was not alone. Mariama was with him, and would tend his hearth, home, and children, and Aisha, too. The tears suffocated Salima. Her body shook as she tried to stifle her sobs.

After Salima had grasped the red-hot iron bar with her two hands and walked the required distance, the inquisitors did not, as was expected, conclude that passing this test meant that the accused had been telling the truth. On the contrary, they were even more convinced that she was relying on a mighty devil that had enabled her to bear the pain.

They had once again called her before the Inquisition the day before, but she did not admit anything more than she had admitted the previous time. When the judge asked her whether she traveled by night on the back of a flying animal, she aroused suspicions by answering that she had not heard of any mortal who could do that except Mohammed, the Prophet of the Muslims. The judge requested her to explain her words, so she narrated the story of a winged animal that had carried Mohammed from a mosque in Mecca to another mosque in Jerusalem. When the judge wanted to know whether she believed that had really happened, she prevaricated by saying, "I have been baptized and become Christian."

These new details alerted the inquisitors to a new element in the case that had escaped them. The accusations of heresy and apostasy need not be limited to the dealings of the accused with the devil, but could extend to the genuineness of her belief, since it seemed that she had not abandoned her Mohammedan faith despite her baptism. In that case, her dealings with the devil were intended to harm the Catholic Church.

The inquisitors tried to force her to confess to that, and when they failed, the judge offered her a choice, saying, "You will have to carry a hot iron bar, and don't you underestimate the task." She said she was prepared. The inquisitors watched as she folded her two hands over the bar and walked. How? The question sent a shiver through them, and through the scribe for whom they had placed a table on one side of the square so he could witness everything for himself and record it.

When the inquisitors withdrew, the judge congratulated himself and his two colleagues for not having underestimated this woman and for having taken the advised precautions against her evil magic. Each of them had protected himself with an amulet of holy salt and a piece of paper on which were written the seven words Jesus Christ had uttered when he was on the cross, and each had hung the amulet round his neck. It lay there next to his skin, hidden by his monk's habit.

Father Agapeda said sorrowfully, "Torture her we must." His two assistants nodded their heads in approval. Alenzo Madeira seemed pleased at what the woman steeped in heresy would receive. Miguel Agilar's face was quiet, resigned to the fact that these were regular procedures used to extract the truth from sinners who were characterized by the pride and stubbornness that had transformed Lucifer from one of God's noblest angels into Satan the Devil.

On the day the sentence was pronounced, they tied Salima and led her to Bab al Ramla Square. The guards cleared a path for her through the crowds that had massed to follow the trial and then the execution. Salima was making a huge effort to walk on feet that had become swollen and inflamed by torture, and to avoid putting her manacled wrists, tied behind her, in contact with each other or with her clothes. Her hands still hurt her from holding the red-hot iron bar. She did not look around her, but was absorbed in her own thoughts. They were going to sentence her to death. Why, then, did her stomach not turn? Why did she not scream in fear or rebellion? Was it because she had yearned for death as an escape from a torture that body and soul could no longer endure? Or was it that she had commended herself into God's hands, like the great believers whose hearts were filled with serenity and acceptance, even if God's will was neither understood nor accepted? Maybe it was some-thing altogether different. Maybe she had, without thinking, decided that she would not humiliate herself by screaming and pleading, or even by becoming terrified like a mouse in a trap. She would not let humiliations pile on each other. It was dignified to hold on to one's sanity and pride. Now she could walk like one in possession of her soul, even if she was walking to a blazing fire. She could say, "Yes I am Salima Bint Jaafar. I was raised by a venerable man who made books and whose heart turned to ashes the day he saw the books being burned, and he proceeded in noble silence. And yes, Grandfather, it is true that at the moment of torture I screamed, when my mind and body lost balance; but only for seconds, Grandfather, only for seconds, and I never said anything that would have made you ashamed of me. I have read books, as you taught me, and relieved the pains of people when I could, and Grandfather, I dreamed that I would one day give you a gift, a book that I wrote myself and filled with the essence of what I had read and what I had felt in the bodies my hands had touched. I wished to do this, and I would have, Grandfather, were it not for the prison of time."

Salima looked around her. The crowds were strangely quiet. The three inquisitors sat on a raised platform nearby, while the judge read out in a sonorous voice that echoed around the place: "We wanted to confirm the accusations made against you, and verify whether they were true or false, and whether you walked in darkness or in light. So we summoned you to the Inquisition and made you take the oath in front of us. We questioned the witnesses and abided by all the rules that the Church canon imposes on us. In order to achieve the highest standard of justice, a revered council of theologians and scholars was gathered. After we examined and discussed all the aspects of the case and all that you said in the Inquisition, we have concluded that you, the named Gloria Alvarez, called Salima Bint Jaafar before baptism, are accused of heresy because you were the tool and servant of Satan. You kept for him the seeds that he gathered and you prepared the Satanic concoctions by which you wrought harm upon man and beast.

"In spite of your denial, witnesses have proved that you caused the death of a child in its mother's womb, and of another who was ill. It has also been proved that you foreswore the church that had embraced you and sought to save your soul. It has become apparent that in spite of your baptism, you still follow your Mohammedan religion and your loyalty is to the Prophet of the Muslims.

"In spite of all that, we wanted—and still want—to bring you back to the truth and to redeem you from heresy and allegiance to the devil who is heresy itself. We want to lead you back to the arms of the Holy Church and to the Catholic faith, so that you would be saved from everlasting hell on earth and in the hereafter. We have tried hard to convince you of that, and have postponed the pronouncement of the verdict for a long time, in the hope that you would confess your repentance. But your pride and willfulness, and your immersion in sin, have made you persist in your denial. We hereby announce, sorrowfully and sadly, that we have failed to make you repent.

"In order to set an example before all people with steadfast minds and souls, to discourage them from following the path of heresy, and for all people to know that apostasy cannot go unpunished, I, Judge Antonio Agapeda, pronounce the sentence, with God and the honor and glory of the faith as my witnesses.

"As you stand before us here in Bab al Ramla Square, we pronounce you an unrepentant heretic. Your punishment is to burn at the stake."

The din of the crowds, pushing and shoving, beats loudly like hammers in Salima's head, and jolts against her heartbeats and the pulse in her stomach. She does not want to look around her. She fears their eyes: Castilian eyes dancing with joy and preparing for the spectacle, and Arab eyes that look upon her with tenderness or fear that breaks her heart. She does not look around, but hears a voice that sounds like Saad's. She does not look. They untie some of her chains, and push her toward the flames.

*Translated by Sahar Hamouda*

## Naima Boucharef
# WHY WAS MY SON ASSASSINATED?

Tunisia 1994    French

Naima Boucharef was born in 1931 in Sousse, Tunisia. She married an Algerian in 1956, and in 1962 they both left Tunisia for Algeria. She ran a nursery school in Algiers for many years and is now retired, and enjoying caring for her grand-children.

Boucharef wrote this hearbreaking testimony following the death of her son, Fouad Boucharef, a military officer who was assassinated at a roadblock ambush in Algiers in 1994 by two Muslim fundamentalists. He was in his early thirties and was on his way to the airport, giving a ride to his brother-in-law, an engineer also in his thirties. Fouad was killed on the spot, and his brother-in-law died after two months of coma. Fouad's young wife and their four-year-old son were in the back of the car. While physically unharmed, they witnessed everything. When they got out of the car, no one would stop to help them at first, terror being such that people just drove away out of fear for their own lives. At the time her son was killed, Naima Boucharef had been living in Casablanca, Morocco, for a year or so. The event took place during the Muslim holy month of Ramadan, which is observed through prayer, fasting, charity, and self-reflection, and ends with the holiday of Eïd ul-Fitr.

Boucharef's writing expresses the suffering endured by many Algerians during the 1990s, years characterized by extreme political unrest and civil bloodshed following the 1991 victory in legislative elections by the militant Islamic Salvation Front (FIS). After the Algerian army intervened and cracked down on the FIS, some Muslim fundamentalists took up arms in a guerrilla war, perpetrating acts of terror that particularly targeted soldiers, and police, and other representatives of the secular government, although thousands of civilians were killed as well. The violence that lasted throughout the decade took a great toll in human lives, and left a legacy of sorrow that many Algerian families will have to live with forever.

*Hadhami Hached*

✦

In memory of my son, Commander Fouad Boucharef, who was the victim of a cowardly assassination on 2 March 1994, on his way to Haouari Bumeddiène International Airport in Algiers. I dedicate this humble work, in which I have expressed all my grief and sorrow, to the Algerian police, who, in spite of the massacres perpetuated against them, and in spite of the risks they run day and night, have carried on their duty with dignity. It is thanks to their bravery that my son's murderers were arrested. May God, the Almighty, help them in their hard work.

*Proverbs:*
You can always cure a wound, but the scar never wears off.
A wound does not heal on a thorn.

*Casablanca, 2 March 1994.*

My eternal nightmare is your assassination on 2 March 1994. I was in Casablanca, Morocco. I had just arrived home; it was 5:00 P.M. when the phone rang. Your father answered it. It was a call from Algiers. I suddenly saw him reel back against the wall. I was standing beside him, and I couldn't take my eyes off him. "Our son Fouad is in hospital. He was shot while he was driving his brother-in-law to the airport. The other one is injured, too," he said after hanging up the phone.

I felt a bitter taste in my mouth. It was dry. I felt I was on the verge of fainting. It was Ramadan, the fasting period, and I don't know how I managed to walk and get myself to drink some water. I was trembling all over while I dialed phone numbers, desperate for more information. Nothing was left to do except to notify the family. I could hardly speak. I had a lump in my throat.

Your father and I had a sleepless night. We remained seated in the living room all night. It was such a long and cold night! We were grief-stricken. We were in Morocco. We had to wait for the first flight to Algiers. Our neighbors had taken care of our flight bookings. We couldn't wait to go to the airport. We were there at 6:00 A.M.

What happened was too horrific. Fouad, my son, you had died on the spot. Your brother-in law followed you after a two-month-long coma. Your wife and your son were traumatized and they will remain so forever.

Both bodies were taken to the military hospital of Ain El Nahja.

Here we are, arriving home, a home I can hardly recognize as my own. I feel I am living a nightmare. There are people, so many people, relatives, friends, all in a state of shock. I couldn't see anybody, though. I was wondering all the time: "Why? Why? Why, my son? My son was so kind. My son, who had never harmed anybody...." I felt nothing but this burning, this stifling pain in my chest.

*Friday, 4 March.*

The day of your funeral. Your body was carried away to the mosque for a last prayer. It used to be your daily journey. Overwhelmed with sorrow, your brother brought your photo to show to the people, and to tell them how you had been assassinated in the most cowardly way in front of your wife and son. In the mosque, everybody said a prayer for you. They realized how unfair it is to assassinate innocent people. When they took your body out of our house, Fouad, I screamed out of grief and despair, as any mother would at the loss of her son.

My dear son, when I fall asleep, I hear a voice calling "Mom," and when I wake up, your name comes straight to my mind. People tell me not to cry anymore, but I can't help it, my tears keep flowing. May God bless your soul.

My dear son, I am writing these lines in despair, but they allow me to communicate with you, to make you somehow come back to life.

Fouad, I am heartbroken by your death. You have left a great void that nobody will ever be able to fill. Your image follows me everywhere. I talk to you.

You don't hear me, but God can hear me, and He will pass on my message to you.

On the day of Eïd, I made your son wear the new suit and shoes you had asked me to buy for him. We took some photos of him, and we took him out for a walk, as you used to do on the Eïd, and as you would have done had you been here. We did not take him to the cemetery, for we have told him that you had gone to heaven. He's still too young to be told that you are under the ground. May God bless your soul.

My dear son, when I left my native country, Tunisia, for Algeria, I never imagined the cruel destiny in store for me. Recounting your life, I remember what a beautiful baby you were. You were born on 30 September 1958. You weighed 4.42 kilos, and nothing foretold the tragic fate that awaited you.

You were my joy and my sunshine. That time appears to me today like a dream. You suffered from asthma, and the days you had attacks, I watched you, powerless and helpless. I could not regain my tranquillity until you felt better.

For many years, I watched you getting up in the morning to go to work. I used to wait eagerly for your return at midday. Then I would watch you leave again at 13:20. You used to go and pick up your son from the nursery. I would feel so happy each time I saw you coming back home.

Now you are dead, and my sorrow will be eternal. I won't be the only one who will miss you. All the people who knew you remember your kindness with great emotion.

I wish I could stay forever in the place where you were assassinated. I wish I lived by the cemetery to stay close to you, and to be able to gather my thoughts every day by your grave. I had to take sleeping pills to be able to sleep and to stop hearing about other dreadful things taking place daily in Algeria.

My son, my dear son, your tomb is now the dearest place in my heart. Death does not frighten me anymore, and my state of mind is beyond description. How could I ever bring back to life the wonderful feeling of happiness I enjoyed whenever you were close by?

I would like to return by myself to that tragic place that saw you alive for the last time. I would like to be there, on my own, with my grief and my memories.

*Translated by Hadhami Hached*

# Moufida Tlatli
## BREAKING SILENCE

Tunisia 1994 Arabic

While women filmmakers from the Maghreb are rare, their work has played an important part in breaking women's silence and giving a voice to the voiceless. In Tunisia, as in other countries of the region, women were active participants in the liberation movement that led to their country's independence from France in 1956, but were betrayed in the post-independence period by being treated as second-class citizens. Although Tunisia's first president, Habib Bourguiba granted Tunisian women legal rights unmatched by any other Arab nation, women's status in society remained largely unchanged for years after independence. Tunisian women lacked awareness of their legal rights, and strong cultural beliefs and taboos continued to exert social control.

Many Maghrebi women artists and activists have called upon women to extract themselves from the legacy of yesterday's revolutions and launch a new transformation of their societies. Such themes are prominent in the work of filmmaker Moufida Tlatli. Asked about the liberation of Tunisian women, she said in a 2000 interview: "It is not about laws; it is about changing mentalities. Things will not change in men or women's minds with a wave of a magic wand and laws. I show the combat from within."

Born in 1947, Tlatli was raised in a traditional family of modest means in the village of Sidi Bou Said. She developed a love of cinema as a member of her high school film club, and received a degree in film editing in 1968 from the *Institut des Hautes Études Cinématographiques*, France's leading film school. For twenty years, she edited the work of some of the Maghreb's most prominent male filmmakers, including Merzak Allouache, Nacer Khemir, Ferid Boughedir, and many others.

Her debut feature, *Samt el qusur* (The Silences of the Palace), was released in 1994. Immediately hailed as a rare instance of a strong female voice in Arab cinema, she won several prestigious awards, including Special Mention for the Camera d'Or at Cannes, the International Critics Award at the Toronto Film Festival, the Golden Tanit at the Carthage Film Festival 1994, and Best First Feature at the Chicago Film Festival. In 1995, Tlatli earned the Best Director citation at the All African Film Awards. Tlatli released her second feature, *La Saison des hommes* (The Season of Men), in 2000, and her third, *Nadia et Sarra* (Nadia and Sarah), in 2004. She received Harvard University's Genevieve McMillan and Reba Stewart Fellowship for Distinguished Filmmaking in 2004.

The core narrative of *The Silences of the Palace* takes place in the colonial period, when women were "the colonized of the colonized." It portrays a group of women servants in the 1950s, living in the palace of the Bey, the last in the line of Tunisian rulers who remained on the throne under the French occupation. The women are not there solely to serve, but also to submit to the Bey's right to the bedchamber. Alia, the main character in the film, is the illegitimate daughter of Khadija, who is both slave and mistress to the Bey, Sid Ali, whom Alia has always suspected of being her father. Although Alia was supposedly destined to inherit her mother's slave condition, she finds the courage to refuse her destiny by fleeing with Lotfi, a young militant hiding in the palace.

Ten years later Alia, now twenty-five, is a gifted singer, forced to earn a living by singing at weddings. She lives with Lotfi, who denies her the right to become a wife and mother. Pregnant once again, Alia is this time hesitant to have an abortion, since she has become tired of her empty life with Lotfi. The news of the death of Bey Sid Ali prompts her to revisit the palace, to offer condolences to the Bey's wife, Jneina, but most important to revisit her childhood spent in the servant's quarters. Every door she enters and every cupboard or window she opens bring back sad and cruel memories, which lead to a series of extended flashbacks. By the end of the film, Alia finally understands that, while her nation may have won its struggle for independence, women have yet to win theirs. She now realizes that Lotfi, who taught her nationalist principles, has confined her in a pattern of servitude similar to her mother's, including sexual intimacy without marriage, and serial abortions.

In this excerpt from the screenplay, written by Tlatli with adaptation and dialogues by Tunisian scriptwriter and filmmaker Nouri Bouzid, Alia has a conversation with the former head of the palace servants, Khalti Hadda, now old and blind. Afterward, she vows to transform her life: She will keep the child, and name it for her mother; and she will finally break out of servitude and silence, as her mother never could.

*Zahia Smail Salhi*

◆

**Alia:** I'm scared.

**Lotfi:** What of?

**Alia:** Of the neighbors. They stare at me all the time. Every eye accuses me, as if they could read my thoughts.

**Lotfi:** You're imagining it. They know nothing about you. It is a difficult period; the burden will be lifted tomorrow.

**Alia:** Then it will start again. Every abortion is painful. I'm losing a part of me. I want to keep it.

**Lotfi:** You are crazy! I thought we'd discussed it enough. A child needs a name, a family, marriage.

**Alia:** I'm not asking you to marry me. A failed singer!

**Lotfi:** Stop, Alia, you're torturing yourself and me. You know I love you, you mean so much to me.

**Alia:** You always have to win. Tomorrow I'll have the abortion. My head is going to explode.

**Lotfi:** I forgot to tell you. Hussein came by. Sid Ali has died.

**Alia (voice-over):** I'm dumbfounded by this news. I forget my headache, the child in my belly, these terrible wedding parties. The old torments resurface, and with them the past I thought had been buried with my mother, and I find myself in the palace I left ten years ago on that horrifying night. Your silence terrified me. Sid Ali is dead, gone with another part of my history. Now I am scared; how can I confront them?

**Alia:** Khalti Hadda, it's me, Alia.

**Khalti Hadda:** Alia? I missed you!

**Alia:** I missed you, too.

**Khalti Hadda:** We thought we'd never see you again.

**Alia:** Khalti Hadda, what did Sid Ali die of?

**Khalti Hadda:** The doctors could not do anything. They gave up. I nursed him like a baby. My eyesight was failing and I could not go on, so Mroubia took over.

**Alia:** Did he ever mention me?

**Khalti Hadda:** Your departure enraged him. He was frantic, not knowing where to get news about you. Hussein didn't want to tell him. To keep him calm, we never mentioned your name. As he saw it, you had renounced the family.

**Alia:** The family? What family?

**Khalti Hadda:** Jneina was barren, so the day you were born, he was overjoyed. You and Sarah were born the same evening.

**Alia:** Jneina could not stand me.

**Khalti Hadda:** Poor thing, she was betrayed by her womb. Is it night already, Alia?

**Alia:** There is a lump in my throat at night. I can feel death within me. I can no longer breathe. I didn't even go to her [Alia's mother Khadija's] funeral. Will she forgive me?

**Khalti Hadda:** She didn't want you to witness her despair. She was concerned for you.

**Alia:** She never wanted to tell me who my father was.

**Khalti Hadda:** Is a father simply a name? A father is sweat, pain, and joy, an entire life, daily care. Listen, my daughter; some things in life are better left unknown. What your mother went through could drive you mad, too. It is the will of God. We were taught one rule in the palace: Silence!

**Alia (voice-over):** I thought Lotfi would save me. I have not been saved.

Like you, [mother], I've suffered, I've sweated;
Like you I've lived in sin.
My life has been a series of abortions.
I could never express myself. My songs were stillborn,
And even the child inside me Lotfi wants me to abort.
This child, I feel, has taken root in me.
I feel it bringing me back to life,
Bringing me back to you.
I hope it will be a girl. I will call her Khadija.

*Translated by Zahia Smail Salhi*

## *Tassadit Yacine and Nouara*
## WHY SOME WOMEN WRITE POETRY

Algeria 1995    French

Tassadit Yacine-Titouh is known as a distinguished sociologist and anthropologist. She attended university in Algeria and worked there until 1987, when she moved to France. She is currently professor of anthropology and North African studies at the *Ecole des Hautes Etudes en Sciences Sociales* in Paris, France's leading institution for advanced education and research in the social sciences. Yacine specializes in Berber studies, with a focus on the Berbers of Algeria and Morocco. She is also the editor of *Awal*, a publication devoted to Berber issues, which she founded in 1985 with her mentor Mouloud Mammeri, the revered Kabylie writer, linguist, and ethnographer, who championed cultural pluralism and the recognition of Berber culture at a time when it was being suppressed under the Algerian government's program of "Arabization."

Tassadit Yacine, too, has devoted her life to Berber culture. Her publications center on oral traditions and on recording and translating Berber texts into French. In 1987 she published her first book on Berber poetry, *L'Izli ou l'amour chanté en Kabylie* (The Izli or Love as Sung in Kabyle), and in 1989 she published an important volume on the songs and poems of the well known Kabyle singer Ait Menguellat. Her subsequent books include *Les Voleurs du Feu: Elements d'une Anthropologie Sociale et Culturelle de l'Algérie* (Those Who Steal the Light: Elements of Algerian Social and Cultural Anthropology), published in 1993, and *Piège ou le Combat d'une Femme Algérienne* (The Trap, or the Struggle of an Algerian Woman), published in 1995, from which the following text is taken.

The book, which explores what Yacine describes as "the anthropology of suffering," is a study of Nouara, a self-educated Kabyle woman born in Algeria at the time of World War II, who has been living in France for two decades. Childless and alone in a foreign land, Nouara has turned to keeping notebooks in which she expresses her painful feelings in poetry. Yacine's book, which combines her descriptive and analytical text with selections from Nouara's notebooks, gives voice to a woman whose voice would otherwise not be heard, illuminating experience often ignored in academic circles. An excerpt from Yacine's text is included here, along with two of Nouara's poems, "The Judge" and "Yamina," in which she conveys her suffering in simple but innovative and powerful language.

*Zahia Smail Salhi*

✦

## NOUARA'S STRUGGLE

Nouara has lived in France for almost twenty years. She has told me she "suffers," and that she searches in vain for a remedy for her condition. The name Nouara means "flower" in Arabic. Nouara knows the meaning of her name even though she does not speak Arabic. However, as if by fate, Nouara has interiorized the symbolic dimension of her name: She is a little flower that smiles only for as long as spring lasts. And as Mouloud Mammeri says, "Spring in our region does not last for long... Likewise the spring of young girls does not last for long" (*La Colline oubliée* [The Forgotten Hill], 1952).

As paradoxical as it may sound, Algerian women living under the rules of traditional society increasingly feel the need to express themselves, to speak and make others speak about them, even more than their more fortunate sisters who are born to lives supposedly more favorable to women's emancipation. This is a new phenomenon, for in the past women were not allowed to speak outside of strictly designated areas and occasions, such as when they fetched water from the fountain, or when they visited shrines, or during parties, and in the Turkish baths of large cities.

Nouara was born at the time of World War II in a traditional Kabyle village, but fate took her out of her natal environment on an adventure she does not, even today, comprehend. Hers is therefore a testimony of sadness, "with no prospects," that she tries to express in her poetry. She does not describe: She laments and confides.

Nouara's itinerary seems ideal to me, for it allows me to access some domains that were up until now inaccessible. It is, in fact, easy to write about the condition of women in general, and insist that they are dominated, but it is often difficult to explain this domination and the mechanisms that govern it. I find it interesting, therefore, to describe this life, for it will inform the reader not only about various routes undertaken by women for their "emancipation," but also about the obstacles—often psychological—that hinder full emancipation. . . .

In addition, other aspects attract my attention as an anthropologist: What makes women replicate power relations, divert them, and get around them, for example? Why, in this particular case, does Nouara, despite all the possibilities that are open to her, remain a dominated woman on several levels, and why has she reached an impasse? I believe that she had believed hers was a life devoid of history and meaning, but then multiple adventures gave her life history and meaning. Once she overcame her childhood handicaps, she could rescue herself from her past and take charge of her life as a liberated woman. Several other authors describe genuinely miserable conditions they experienced during their childhood, either because they were orphans or had physical disabilities, but they managed to transform these handicaps later on in life.

What is it that makes dominated subjects likely to transcend their initial condition, to change it, or otherwise to live with it? What are the psychological factors that contribute in either case? What would be the inclinations and predispositions that might favor this rupture? And to what extent can one break off totally and permanently from one's origins, social class, and gender? What generates suffering? Is it not, at least in this case, the result of an inadequacy between the status of an individual and her expectations, which dominate and degrade her?

It is difficult to describe suffering without falling into the trap of the person speaking to us. Suffering does not *de facto* mean low status. Nouara was surely dominated while she lived within the contexts of her village, her family, and her gender, but she is certainly privileged once she begins to enjoy possibilities that women of her condition and cultural milieu do not enjoy. In short, we can say that she escaped the worst.

The suffering that can be found in her poetry and her discourse lie beyond her economic and social condition; it is of an existentialist order. Why would a woman who belongs to a traditional society protest against the tradition while, at the same time submit to it? What is the source of this hybrid position, neither totally and openly emancipated nor traditional?

If Nouara's expression is through poetry, it is that she has had no other option. Lonely, she could confide only to her notebook. This notebook, which she did not have the privilege to keep during her childhood, has now become her faithful companion. As an adult in France she effectively learned to read and write . Before she began to write, her path was full of obstacles, for two personal reasons. Nouara is an orphan, and a sterile woman who has lived through several marriages and divorces. There is also a social reason having to do with her belonging to an Islamic, Mediterranean, peasant, and ex-colonized society.

One must bear such contexts in mind when trying to understand how and why some women write poetry.

*Translated by Zahia Smail Salhi*

## THE JUDGE

Listen to me, Mr Judge.
Try to understand:
This marriage is devoid of love.

I suffered for countless years.
Reason has abandoned me.
My heart is heavily loaded.

At present I am in pain.
Patience has now run out.
Where is relief?

Lost in the midst of nowhere,
My youth is now leaving me.
You are my sole savior.

## YAMINA

He:
Yamina, listen to me.
I beg you come back to me.
I cannot live without you.
My heart has lost its happiness,
Lost its way,
And is lonely.
She:
I shall never return,
For life with you has lost its savor.
Years have passed us by,
And joy was never there.
Better for us to part,
For life has been so hard.

He:
I can never live without you.
My heart keeps yearning for you.
I fear to lose my reason,
For I cannot find another
Who could replace you.
She:
My friend, you know too well.
My life with you was hell.
For years my heart
Bore the heavy weight
Of life devoid of delight
In a foreign land.

*Translated into French by Tassadit Yacine*
*Translated from French by Zahia Smail Salhi*


## *Buthayna Khadr Mekky*
## RITES

Sudan  1996    Arabic

A novelist, short story writer, and journalist, Buthayna Khadr Mekky was born in Shindy in the Sudan in 1948, and currently resides in the United Arab Emirates. With a B.A in English literature from King Abdul Aziz University in Saudi Arabia, and two diplomas in English language teaching and folklore from the University of Khartoum, she now teaches English in a secondary school in the Emirates.

Mekky is a prolific author who writes regular columns in the Sudanese newspapers *Politics*, *Lights*, and *Unity*, and has published many of her stories in various Sudanese and Arab newspapers. Her books include three collections of short stories, *The Palm Tree and the Singer* (1992), *Town Ghosts* (1995), and *Shadows of Grief* (1996); three novels, *The Song of Fire* (1998), *Roaring of the River* (2000), and *Fields of Thorns* (2004); a collection of children's stories, *The Village Girl* (1993); and a book of essays, *The Cover of Silence* (1996). In 2003, Mekky received the Science and Literature Award from the Sudanese Presidency for her contributions in the areas of literature and education, as well as the El Zubair prize for literature. She is a member of the Sudanese Writers' Association, The Women Writers Association in the emirate of Sharjah, and the United Arab Emirates Writers' Association. Mekky's fiction typically employs a combination of classical Arabic and colloquial Sudanese to depict the Sudanese landscape and culture, and uses dialogue to enhance the local atmosphere.

In "Rites," Mekky explores the cultural divisions in the Sudan with regard to marriage and the practice of female circumcision. The first part of the story offers a lively portrait of marriage rituals in a northern Sudanese village, as the narrator attends the wedding of her husband's young sister. The joyous atmosphere is shattered when she hears the screams of the sixteen-year-old bride on her wedding night. She has to be told the next day that the same screams are a cause for rejoicing to her husband and his family. The narrator, who comes from a part of the Sudan where the practice of circumcizing (FGM) very young girls is not the norm, and she has enjoyed a healthy and happy sexual relationship with her husband. Now she finds that her own body is under siege. Eventually, she succumbs to social pressure, becoming physically, emotionally, and psychologically mutilated, transformed into a female eunuch to gratify a husband and a society that view her as an object of male pleasure.

The Sudan has one of the world's highest rates of FGM, with most estimates showing that at least 90 percent of Sudanese women have undergone some form of the procedure. The scene in which the doctor hesitates and then apparently accepts a bribe suggests that she is performing one of the more extreme forms of FGM, which involves removal of all of the external genitalia and in some cases also constructing a partial closure of the vaginal opening.

*Azza El Kholy*

✦

After my arrival at the village of Sedra in a remote area of northern Sudan, the lengthy celebration of Saadeya's marriage began. Saadeya, my sister-in-law, was to marry her cousin Abdel Mejid. At sixteen, she was exceptionally beautiful, like a glowing rose. Abdel Mejid was twenty-four years old, a radiant young man whose dark complexion had been deepened by long hours of irrigating and tilling the corn and wheat fields.

Weddings were boisterous affairs. They usually began with women applying henna to the bride, massaging her daily with perfumed oils infused with fumes from pleasant smelling wood, then combing, braiding, and perfuming her hair with musk and sandalwood extracts.

The young bride's dancing astonished me, for she had completely mastered the techniques of the huge, fair, and uninhibited woman who had been hired to teach her the rudiments of dancing and sexuality. She turned round and swayed more seductively than most professional dancers. She was in complete control of a body bursting with budding womanliness and glowing like pure honey.

On the third night of the wedding ceremony, sheep were slaughtered and barbecued and the women handed out fruit and sweets to the guests. An ornamental wooden bed stood in the middle of the courtyard, among seats for guests. The bed was covered in red Persian rugs and bright-colored cushions. On a low table by the bed, the women placed a silver tray filled with perfume bottles, bangles, silver necklaces etched with gold, and a red silk braid with a turquoise bead in the middle.

The bride was then led in, glowing like the sun, wearing a red and yellow costume, and surrounded by bridesmaids carrying incense holders. She settled onto the middle of the bed and stretched out her beautiful legs, revealing the exquisite black henna designs shining brightly on her feet, palms, and the backs of her hands. The groom then approached, wearing a short gown and a white wrap-over robe with red stripes at the hem, his feet and palms dyed dark with henna.

An elderly woman sang a traditional song that other women repeated after her, occasionally emitting sounds of joy:

Tonight is the marriage and the good fortune.
Oh, bride,
May your firstborn be a son
And may God fill your home with prosperity.

As the woman sang, other women placed the silver necklaces and bangles around the bride's neck and arms and sprinkled her hair with perfume. The singer then tied the red silk braid to the bridegroom's hand and placed a gold crescent on his forehead. The bride's aunt scattered a handful of fruit, corn, and rice as symbols of good fortune and abundance. I observed all in awed astonishment, as if I were watching a magnificent movie. Marriage rituals here differed a great deal from those in my village in the extreme south of the Sudan.

After a while, the bride stood up and began to dance on top of the bed. As she danced, one of the bridesmaids pulled off the robe that had covered her body, and she continued in a short, almost sheer, gown. She danced provocatively, while the groom watched his bride in admiration, waving a sword in the air and occasionally sprinkling the contents of a bottle of perfume toward the audience as they applauded happily.

Throughout the wedding celebration, all looked at me supportively, as I tried, often in vain, to keep the Sudanese costume carefully pinned over my chest and shoulders. I noticed that my husband had seemed rather distant that day, and felt somewhat jealous when I saw him joining the young women of the tribe in dancing and singing, while I sat in my place like a beautiful ebony statue.

After midnight, joyous cheers resounded and I learned that the women had entrusted Saadeya to her groom. Our house was close to that of the bride's family, and thus I heard a sharp scream piercing the night's silence. I sprang up horrified and woke my husband as another scream, followed by a long convulsed moan, ensued. I clung to my husband's neck, but he pushed me away in a bored manner, saying, "Go back to sleep. You wouldn't understand such things."

"But that is Saadeya's voice," I replied. "What is happening to her? Does she hate her husband that much?"

He laughed sarcastically and said, "Actually, she loves him to death."

I eyed him with fear and suspicion. Saadeya's screams stole any desire I might have had for sleep as I tossed restlessly in my bed until the morning call for prayer heralded the dawn.

In the morning I asked my other sister-in-law, "Why was Saadeya screaming? Had her husband hurt her?"

My question surprised her and she paused shyly as my husband's aunt
answered, "You will not understand this because you are—eh, uh, you are—
uncircumcised."

I understood the meaning of the word, for my husband had repeated it often
enough during our moments of intimacy, when he used to work in the city of
Waw and we lived close to my family in the village.

"You are different from the women in my village," he had once said. I was
very pleased and expected some kind of tender wooing, and so I asked, play-
fully, "How?"

He had laughed and said, "You are uncircumcised."

What a stupid, meaningless word. I searched long and hard for a synonymous term in my tribal dialect, but never found any. Gradually, I began to sense
my husband's aversion when he came close to me or whenever we were alone.
As a matter of fact, I started getting this feeling after I had given birth to my
second son. However, it became more obvious after that night we heard
Saadeya screaming.

One evening, when the moon was full and autumn invigorated the air with
the scent of fertility, I approached my husband, but he seemed quite distant,
unlike his usual self. I asked him anxiously about the reason for his reserve. He
simply replied, rather coolly, that he was tired and wanted to sleep. The following morning, avoiding my eyes, he said, "I hope you will do what my aunt
Fatma will tell you."

I said, attempting a smile, "If you already know what she is going to tell me,
why don't you tell me yourself?"

He answered irritably, "Please listen to her advice," and, adjusting his white
turban, went out.

When his aunt came by, I was anxious to hear what she had to say, but I controlled my curiosity and first performed my duties as hostess. As she eyed every
curve of my body with her wide, kohl-rimmed eyes, she slowly said, "Your husband loves you dearly, but he is complaining about the fact that you are not circumcised." Then she quickly added, "If you agree, I will take you to Dr. Sakina
to adequately circumcise you, and thus, your husband will love you more."

I was furious. If he had wanted a circumcised woman, as she was saying, why
did he marry me and bring me all the way from the remote south of the country to live among these harsh social restrictions enforced by his culture and the
traditions of his village? I had given up much for him. Why couldn't he ignore
this? What had happened to the husband who had always been captivated by
me, and keen on making love to me?

I raised my head with pride and said defiantly, "I will do no such thing. I am
twenty-four and I will not change anything about myself, and if I no longer
appeal to him, he had better leave me and go find another woman that he
likes better."

A whole week passed. We slept in separate rooms, but I could not tolerate this estrangement and so I went to him and made up. As he held me tenderly in his arms, he told me, "If you really love me, do it. You will not feel any pain; it will all be done under complete anesthesia."

I noticed a sly glee in the eyes of my husband's aunt as she accompanied me to the physician's house that day. Dr. Sakina, attempting to calm me down as she noticed that I was trembling with fear, said, "You will not feel any pain. The cut will be small and there will be a few stitches."

Aunt Fatma's face fell as she heard these words. Moving closer to the doctor, she whispered something that brought a stern frown to the physician's face. "No, no, this is prohibited now," she shouted. Aunt Fatma came closer to the doctor so that I could not hear their conversation. She then produced a bundle from her ample bosom and thrust it at the doctor. Lowering her head, the doctor thought deeply, as if she were trying to solve a riddle, and then, trying to be nice to me, said, "Do you love your husband to that extent? Do you really approve of the operation he requests?" I nodded as I tried to control my fear.

Devoid of any will, I did exactly what the doctor asked me to do. I let out a sharp scream when she injected the anesthetic; she waited for a short while then set to work on my body, cutting it with the scissors. She then began to take several stitches with a needle, pulling the thread as she knotted it. I felt the swelling and the pressure of her fingers as she worked between my thighs.

My aunt-in-law took me home and left. In less than an hour the sharp, excruciating pain began; it was like the slashing of blades. I had never felt anything like that pain before, not even in childbirth, where I felt only the normal labor pains. I tried to touch the wound with my fingers but felt as though a burning fire had penetrated my insides. I started crying and screaming like a horror-stricken child. The women around me tried to calm me down, but to no avail. When I felt like passing water, I forced myself up and approached the toilet with heavy footsteps, dragging my legs like a mule that was tied up by its master. I jumped in agony and let out a feverish moan of pain as the liquid haltingly, painfully, excruciatingly, and very slowly trickled out.

Exactly one week after this barbaric operation, my husband came to my bed pleading. Something had been shattered inside me. He seemed to me like the first cave man who had stalked a wild rabbit, enjoyed roasting it, and was now ready to devour it: I was this wild rabbit. The love, enthusiasm, and romance that had colored encounters with my husband dried up in the pinnacle of physical pain that I felt each time he came to me, whereas he seemed as vain and flamboyant as a male peacock. He considered my painful groans some kind of feminine playfulness that strengthened his feelings of virility.

What monstrosity is this? Alas, I have lost forever the beloved who resided in my heart and soul, despite having gained a man: my husband.

*Translated by Azza El Kholy*

# Fathia El Assal
## WHO IS FATHIA EL ASSAL?

Egypt 1997 Arabic

Born in Cairo in 1933, Fathia El Assal was the daughter of a well-to-do father and his first wife. Her father married several more times, moving in with each new wife and taking his first family along with him. The young Fathia El Assal experienced a cross section of Cairo's neighborhoods—and of Egyptian society— as they moved from the home of an aristocratic wife to that of a more common one. As she was beginning to learn the alphabet in primary school, a suitor proposed. Horrified by the idea of his daughter "becoming a woman," El Assal's father removed her from school and kept her at home until it was time for her to marry, denying her any further formal education. Left to her own devices, she eventually taught herself to read, starting with the newspaper.

The females of El Assal's household were not allowed outside. After an English soldier saw her sister peeping out the window and knocked at the door, asking to speak to the pretty girl, her father boarded up the windows. In 1946, during the demonstrations that had broken out against the English, El Assal was allowed to go out to see that her brother was safe. In the streets she saw the female pupils of the Saneya School taking part in the demonstration, and her imagination and passion were fired by the girls shouting at the English to evacuate their country. Thus her first taste of personal liberty coincided with the nationalist call for freedom. On another rare trip into the world outside, to check on her married sister who had gone into labor, El Assal was followed by a handsome young man who waited for eight hours until she left her sister's house and then followed her back home. He began writing letters to her, using their servants as go-betweens. Too terrified to be compromised by writing a letter, she wrote him a short story. This was the beginning of her career as a writer.

She married Abdallah El Toukhi, then a first year law student and a committed communist, who later gave up his profession to become an activist and writer. Their home became the meeting point for Leftist activists. When El Toukhi was arrested and jailed for his politics, El Assal visited him daily and kept her home open to the families whose men were also in jail. After educating herself about communism, she herself joined a cell and participated in political work and was herself jailed during the 1980s. She was one of the few women to rise in the leadership of *El Tagamoa*—also known as the National Progressive Unionist Party— which became a leading leftist opposition party in post-Nasser Egypt. She headed the Women's Progressive Union, and has championed the cause of literacy and political and social empowerment for women in both her activism and her writing.

El Assal's career as a writer began with serials for the radio, which were hugely successful and led her to write for television and the stage. One of the most widely known dramatists in contemporary Egypt, she infuses her dramatic works with political and social themes, focusing in particular on the challenges facing women, whose lives and emotions are seldom portrayed in Egyptian drama. She has said that her first play, *Women Without Masks*, "began with a cry and a question, for I felt myself pregnant with words dating back tens, maybe even hundreds of years." When she was fired by a television studio because of her political activities, she wrote under the pen name Naguiba El Assal. She has served as president of the Association of Egyptian Female Writers, and in 2004 was selected by UNESCO's International Theatre Institute to deliver the international message on World Theatre Day.

The text below is part of an interview by Attiyat El Abnoudy for a documentary film *Ayyam El Dimokrattia* (Days of Democracy). In "Zeinab and the Impossible," the television series by El Assal, in which as she mentions at the close of the extract, a young nonliterate woman ultimately learns to read and write in defiance of the seemingly impossible cultural obstacles in her path.

*Sahar Hamouda*

✦

I never got a school degree, not even a primary one. The family I was brought up in believed that boys were the ones to be educated, while girls were to be prepared for marriage. Early in life I became aware that I had been deprived of education because I was female. It didn't upset me to look female. On the contrary, I was happy to be female, and I tried to become a human being. Of course, I didn't have clarity of consciousness. But I insisted on getting an education, and I got it in the way that suited me, which was learning through books I would find in the market. So I found all kinds of reading material—literature, politics, philosophy, law, even aesthetics. And I read everything I could.

My husband is now a well-known writer and journalist, but when we first met, he was still a first year law student. He used to "take me out" to lectures in his faculty. As time went on, I joined him in political work. I did not get a formal education, but I learned what was missing in our country, especially for women. I knew what it meant for a woman not to know how to write her name, or to walk on a street without being able to read its name.

This disturbed me a great deal, until a small incident occurred that shaped the rest of my life. There was a vegetable vendor in our area. One day I found her crying bitterly. I asked her, "What's wrong, Hamida?" and she said that her husband had given her a paper and told her to press her fingerprint on it. She couldn't sign it, because she was illiterate. And because she couldn't read, she asked him what was on that paper. He told her he was giving her his mother's house. She was ecstatic at his overwhelming generosity. The following day, he brought a woman with him into Hamida's apartment, who, he said, was his wife. Hamida's husband threw her out of her home and took the children from her. He told her that the paper she had pressed her fingerprint to was an agreement to give everything up to him.

Since then, I have been involved in women's issues and public service. And because of that experience, I wrote my best work, the television series "Zeinab and the Impossible."

*Translated by Sahar Hamouda*

# Samira El Ghaly El Hajj
## THE MAGIC JOURNEY

Sudan 1997    Arabic

The poet Samira El Ghaly El Hajj was born in 1962 in the north of Cardafan, Sudan. She received her B.A in Arabic from the University of Cairo in 1985, continuing her postgraduate studies at the Omdurman Islamic University, and earning an M.A in the teaching of Arabic as a second language from the Khartoum International Institute for Arabic Language in 1993, and a Ph.D. in education from the International University of Africa in 1999.

El Hajj currently holds the post of lecturer in the Arabic department at the Sudan University for Science and Technology. She also works as an editor. Her collections of poetry include *Edhak Ayyoha Al-Qalb Al-Jarih* (Laugh Away, Wounded Heart), published in 1992, and *Lel-Nawras Oghneyaton Okhra* (The Seagull Has Another Song), published in 1993, and *Maqate' Lelbahr wa Al-Luqia* (Verses for the Sea and the Encounter), published in 1997, which includes "The Magic Journey."

*Radwa El Barouni*

The seagulls fly
over the coasts,
searching the beaches
for a wonderful nightingale to share their evening songs.
The seagulls roam,
equipped with their hymns
and dreaming of the magic journey,
yet never escaping
the temptation of the sea.

How long will the flowers continue to be overwhelmed by grief?
How long will the singing remain a wound?
We rebel within,
our desires forever eluding us.
Sorrow ages my bird,
broken wings and all.
I come closer.
I listen to the sound of my wounded tearful heart,
yet I cannot leave.
Who has the power to make the songs joyful?
Who has the power to prevent desires from echoing?
I dream of a magic journey
to take me to all those beaches.
I'm always looking for a wonderful nightingale
To share my evening songs.

*Translated by Radwa El Barouni*

# *Huda Lutfi*
# FRAMED WOMEN

Egypt 1999    English

A cultural historian by training, Huda Lutfi has emerged as one of Egypt's most versatile contemporary painters. Born in 1948 in Cairo, she studied Islamic culture and history at McGill University in Montreal, where she received her Ph.D. In 1983, she became professor of Islamic cultural history at the American University in Cairo. She has published a book on Mamluk Jerusalem and several articles on gender relations, sexuality, and culture during the Mamluk period. The Mamluks were non-Arab slaves, primarily from Turkey and the Caucuses, who were imported to the Middle East to serve as soldiers, and who developed into a powerful military caste. In 1250, the Mamluks overthrew the Ayyubid Dynasty and inaugurated a line of more than fifty independent sultans, who retained significant local power even during the Ottoman rule, and were destroyed only in 1811, in an ambush and massacre by the forces of Mohammad Ali Pasha.

Although Huda Lutfi is a self-taught artist who began to paint relatively recently, her art has attracted widespread attention and acclaim, featured in solo exhibitions in France, Germany, the Netherlands, and the United States as well as in Egypt. Lufti works in mixed media, using collage as well as painting. Among the innovative projects she has undertaken are mural paintings in two mud-brick houses she designed in Tunis, Egypt; an installation that integrates found objects from the local markets, and a program that teaches painting to Cairo street children. She has managed to present a unique artistic vision that foregrounds women's sensibilities and combines history and art in a way that is poignantly individualistic.

The cover art for this volume is by Huda Lufti. Female figures dominate in Huda Lutfi's paintings, which are inspired by a rich and varied cultural heritage, ranging from ancient Egyptian, Coptic, and Islamic motifs to Mediterranean, Indian, and African imagery. Her ability to blend different, often opposing world visions contributes to the uniqueness of her art. Moreover, her emphasis on the sensuous and the somatic in her representations of female figures underlines her rebellion against the long suppression of the female body by Arab-Muslim cultures. The women she depicts in her painting "Prayers" are defiantly naked, graphically blending and reconciling the spiritual and the physical. The text included here is an extract from an interview conducted by Samia Mehrez and James Stone.

*Amira Nowaira*

✦

I have written on women's issues, but I have also moved away from women's issues to gender, because one cannot see women's problems in isolation: Woman and man are always interacting. When you study history you never hear anything about women. As a graduate student at McGill, I started taking history more seriously, which only happens when you begin to examine primary sources. I started asking myself: Where are the women? It wasn't a feminist question; just a genuine concern: Where am I in this literature? I know I was always there; society doesn't exist without women, but where are they? I took a course on Mamluk historical literature, and for the first paper I wrote, I chose a biographical dictionary that happened to include biographies of women. It was a nine-volume dictionary: eight on men and one on women. There they were! I discovered that women were present in the historical literature. This was in the early eighties, when very little was being written on women in Arab-Muslim history. I discovered that women transmitted Hadith [the Prophet's sayings]; they used to study and teach, just as I was doing! Of course they don't appear in the literature as much as men do because historical literature is written by men, and what they considered to be historically important is not what women used to do in everyday life.

In many of my paintings, the female body is the expression of the feminine. In this sense it is very related to my historical research. In some respects my painting reinforces my historical research: Not only men, but also women must have their historical presence. My painting also contests the fact that women are rarely present in the historical chronicles. Well, here they are in image form. More recently I have been working on the symbol of birds in medieval Arabic dream texts, and during this time, I found birds appearing in my paintings. Here I used them as symbols that express freedom of movement and spirit. I always choose icons to convey feelings and emotions, and somehow it works. For example, I used the Coptic paper doll, which in earlier times (and until now, perhaps) was pricked with pins as a magical practice to get rid of bad energy. I saw one of these dolls in the museum; her hands were tied behind her back, and she was sitting nude with needles pricking her body in very vital areas. When I saw that—and at the time I was going through some personal family problems, which left me feeling helpless—I felt that the doll with the pins was me.

Women have been framed in boxes and windows. The posture in my paintings is both. That's why the confined space makes you wonder whether women are getting out of it or accepting it. Women do both: They support it but they also reject it. There are times when I feel I am trapped in a box, in a cage, and I want to get out, and there are other times when you accept the reality. However, I do feel framed in the structure. The framing is not simply external; it is internal. This is where it becomes very dangerous and problematic, because you just don't know what to do with it. The cultural frame is so engrained within us through a conditioning process that one frames oneself unconsciously. That's the big problem. And seeing it, becoming aware how it works, is crucial in terms of self-knowledge. And I have posed this question to myself: Why do I choose the frame? Is it simply a technique because I have not been trained as a painter, my inability to draw something in a complex perspective? Or does it have to do with my actual feelings of being framed? It can be both: the technique and the feeling of being framed internally. Superficially, I may be less framed externally: I am a university professor, I move, I have many friends. But what about psychological framing? This is the question. Therefore, I don't think being framed is an experience peculiar to women only. I think that human beings living in a society, be they male or female, living within structures as we all do, feel that they are framed. If we say that our natural state of being is freedom from conditioning, from structures, or relationships of power, then we are all framed. We support a social structure because we believe that it helps to produce an orderly human society, in which we are supposed to coexist as separate but related beings.

Can we get out of these frames? Women are participants in all this. Who invented such structures: women or men? Most certainly both. Not only women; we are all implicated in our frames. We have framed ourselves.

In the paintings, the posture of women with raised hands within frames reflects a state of acceptance, as if they were resigned to reality. On another level, the posture of raised hands in the paintings also reflects a spiritual state. For me, spirituality may be expressed in three movements—in flow, in rhythm, and in dance—but also in stillness, in silence. The repetition of calligraphic flow, and the standing image of the female figure, reflect the stillness of seeing, of intense seeing. Also, doing calligraphy that is highly repetitious, one becomes hypnotized. For me, stillness or silence is the absence of thought in the mind. So if your hands are working with something with no thoughts in your mind, you experience a form of stillness. It is not simply in the meaning of the words, although this is also important. I like to work in something to make the chattery mind silent. We always chatter with ourselves, and it is a great relief to silence such chatter. To experience stillness.

## *Fatma Ramadan*
# LULLABY TO A DAUGHTER

Egypt 1999   Arabic

This lullaby is widely known and sung in both the countryside and urban areas in Egypt. Many different variations of the same song can be found in areas as remote as Upper Egypt and the oases of the western desert. Evidence suggests that this lullaby has long historical roots with some older women indicating that the song was handed down to them orally by their grandmothers or great-grandmothers, which firmly establishes it in mid- or late-nineteenth-century Egypt.

The outstanding feature of this song is its quiet, melancholic rhythm, expressing the sense of oppressed resignation experienced by mothers on first learning that they have just given birth to a daughter rather than the greatly desired son. The song is charged with maternal emotions that are communicated directly and forcefully through simple words and meter. The mother's love for her daughter, despite the neglect and ill treatment she may have received on giving birth to her, is deeply moving.

This version of the lullaby was sung by Fatma Ramadan, who was born in 1937 and lives in the densely populated district of Amriya, 30 kilometers from Alexandria. She is a divorced woman who single-handedly raised her three children, working as a small peddler, domestic worker, and sometimes as a seamstress. The recording of her singing the lullaby was made on 30 June 1999. Fatma Ramadan pointed out that she had heard both her mother and grandmother sing the lullaby when she was a child.

*Amira Nowaira*

✦

Oh, my darling, little darling!
You're the moonlight of my life.
Oh, my darling, I love you so,
And I'll love all who love you!

When they said it was a boy,
I could hold up my head.
My eggs were fresh and peeled,
And my food was rich in butter.

When they said it was a girl,
The place fell on my head.
They gave me whole eggs unpeeled,
cooked in water, not in butter.

Oh, my darling, little darling,
I won't marry you off to some foreign place.
I'll marry you off close to me,
So that you'll always be near me.

Oh, my darling, little darling!
You're the moonlight of my life.
Oh, my darling, I love you so,
And I'll love all who love you!

*Translated by Amira Nowaira*

# THE NEW CENTURY

# Leila Abouzeid
# TWO STORIES OF A HOUSE

Morocco 2000    Arabic

Leila Abouzeid was born in 1950 in a small town called Qsiba, in the Middle Atlas. She began her higher education at Mohammed V University in Rabat, and went on to earn a diploma in journalism from the London Institute of Journalism, and held a fellowship at the World Press Institute in St. Paul, Minnesota. Abouzeid's earliest journalism was published under a male pseudonym. She became one of the first women journalists to work on Moroccan TV as a newscaster, and has written for various Moroccan newspapers as well as for British radio, and has worked as a press officer in the Moroccan Ministry of Information and Equipment.

Abouzeid's best-known book, '*Am Al-Fiil* (The Year of the Elephant: A Moroccan Woman's Journey Toward Independence, 1983), won critical acclaim and was translated into several languages. In the novel, she deals candidly with the predicament of Moroccan women caught between tradition and modernity. Her books also include *Ruju' ilna Al-Tufulah* (Return to Childhood: The Memoir of a Modern Moroccan Woman, 1993), an autobiography of turmoil within a family and a country in the years surrounding Moroccan independence, and *Al-Fasl Al-Akhiir* (The Last Chapter, 2003), a semiautobiographical work that deals with gender and identity. "Two Stories of a House" is a previously unpublished work, in which Abouzeid tells the true story of two elderly Moroccan women fighting for their survival. The text also captures the strong bond that can unite women even in situations of conflict: at the end of the story the younger wife becomes an accomplice of the older wife. The solidarity between co-wives in some rural areas is often perceived as a strike against male power. Yet, in this story, women appear as fighters who defy both the judge and the husband. The story also provides a glimpse into a multilingual society where the use of language has strong social significance that is difficult to convey in an English translation. The women use Moroccan Arabic in a formal setting where only Standard Arabic carries force. Modern Standard Arabic is the language used in most written materials and taught at school; it is therefore inaccessible to nonliterate women.

*Fatima Sadiqi*

◆

"Khadija Bent Ahmed! Meeluda Bent Al-Bacheer!" At this resounding call, two old women in the waiting room gathered up the voluminous folds of their veils, which bore a design of blooming red roses. They rushed to the courtroom and stood in front of the judge. He was turning over some papers on his desk.

"Khadija Bent Ahmed!"

"Yes sir!"

"Did you leave your house of your own free will?"

"I didn't sir! This Meeluda told me I could come back. She swore by Mecca that I could come back as soon as she had repaired her ceiling. Her ceiling is the floor of my house, sir. So I left everything there. I took only my clothes, because she said the repairs would take only a month. But she broke the landing and demolished the stairs. Now my two rooms are suspended in the air. I can't get to them, sir. It has been two years. And because my rooms are suspended, I go to my brother's for a while and then to my sister's. It's just two rooms, true, but it's my little home."

She burst into tears, wiped her eyes with the hem of her veil, and began to sob like a child. "I entered that house as a bride," she went on, "and I intended to stay there until the end of my days. Haven't we paid for it? Yes, we have, more than it's worth, in the thirty years we have been living there."

"Big deal," snorted the defendant. "Forty dirhams a month. What's that? It wouldn't buy a kilo of meat or even a bottle of propane."

"Stop it!" shouted Khadija. "What about the blood? Your blood from childbirth that I cleaned with my own hands? What about the meals I cooked for your feasts and your mourning ceremonies? What about your children, who grew up on my back? It's thirty years, six hundred and sixty monthly rents, two million centimes, perhaps more. Couldn't that amount have bought us your house and mine? Couldn't it? If it weren't for my late husband's carelessness and extravagance. They call it generosity! He wasted his money feeding his ungrateful so-called friends. Meat was brought to our house seven kilos at a time. If he . . ."

"Forget your late husband now, will you?" ordered the judge, "was it your husband who told you to lock the house and give the key to the defendant?"

"I didn't give her the key, sir. The key is still with me." She raised her skirts, bent over and pulled from the pocket of her bloomers a big black key. "There! But what good is it? The house has no stairs and no landing. It's suspended in the air."

"You mean you just locked the door and walked away?"

"Well, she's my neighbor, and she swore by Mecca. Wouldn't a good Muslim lock the door and walk away? I believed her. "

"What do you want now?"

"My home!" Tears overwhelmed her again, and she murmured as if to herself, "I can't stop crying when I pronounce that word." And to the judge, "I am frightened of moving, very anxious, as if I were being expatriated or were dying. It's my little home, sir." She started to cry again.

"Where have you been all this time? Why haven't you submitted your case to the court before?"

"I had it in the hands of saints, sir."

"And you took it back, I guess," said the judge smiling. The audience smiled, too. Then he asked the defendant: "What's your statement?"

"Two years ago, bless you, sir, dirt started coming down from my ceiling. So, I asked this person to evacuate her house above it, so we could repair the ceiling. But when the worker touched it, the landing collapsed, and carried the staircase with it. If not for the grace of God, the poor man would have lost his life. That's the whole story."

"What are you saying?" cried Khadija. "You swore by Mecca, Meeluda! You said to leave for a month! You said you'd do the repairs and I could come back!"

"Stop wailing! There's no way to fix it. The whole house is collapsing, for heaven's sake!"

"Enough!" ordered the judge, then pronounced the following sentence: "Tomorrow morning, if God wills it, at ten sharp, local firemen will bring Khadija Bent Ahmed's belongings from the house located in number 3A, Baker Street. She will take over her possessions, in the presence of the police, and return the key to its proprietor. Case closed. Next."

That day Khadija Bent Ahmed learned that an old divorced woman was renting a room in the house she had once lived in. The old woman now lived in a wooden hut on the roof. On the ground floor an old man occupied another room with his wife, a rough country girl hardly twenty years old, baked by the sun from work in the fields.

Khadija Bent Ahmed told her story to the old woman on the roof. "Oh! my neigh—I was going to say my neighbor. Excuse me, but I called someone by that name, and I am a fool to honor her so."

"Tell me about it," said the old lady. "There's no good neighbor in this world, no grateful people, no faithful husbands. You say that Meeluda was your neighbor for thirty years and threw you out. Well, my story is worse." She gestured to the ground floor with one earring, "I'd been married to the old man for forty years, but after he saw that country bumpkin, he ignored me completely."

"And who sent him the country bumpkin?"

"I did. I brought her to him myself. I found her shedding tears in the shrine. She was pregnant. She was scared of her brothers and was hiding there. So I said to myself, 'Well, there's a seed she's terrified to be carrying, while you have no children at all. Why don't you take her home and when she delivers, she'll go away and you will have the baby?'

"That slut said to me, 'This shrine is a witness between you and me.'

"And we concluded a pact on the saint's tomb, according to which I would hide her shame, and she would leave me the baby. She stayed with me until she gave birth, by the greatness of God, to twin boys. The old man registered them in our family records at once.

"I took care of her as if she were my own child. It was out of the question to let her go right after she gave birth. I said to myself, 'Wait one week,' and at the end of the week, I said, 'Wait another week!'

"Then the old man said, 'You've accomplished a good deed, carry it to the end. Keep her a bit longer. She'll breastfeed the babies and she'll finish her forty days. God will reward you.'

"'Amen!' I said."

"And at the end of the forty days," said Khadija Bent Ahmed in a teasing tone, "you said you'd keep her until the babies are weaned?"

"No. At the end of the forty days, I took her to the public bath, dyed her hands and feet with henna, gave her some money and presents and said to her, 'It's time for you to go.'

"'Oh no,' she retorted, 'It's time for you to go instead. I'm here in my own house, with my children.' And she pulled out a marriage contract."

"The old man had married her?"

"And repudiated me."

"What a fool! But it's your fault. You let her stay. She's breastfed her children and got attached to them."

"Well, when she waved that marriage contract at me, I ran to my chest, got out my family record, and shoved it in her face, saying, 'You can have the old man, but you will never have the babies.' I slipped the record into my shirt, took the twins in my arms, rushed up to my hut, and locked it."

"But why do you stay in the same house?"

"Where would I go? I have no family, and the life savings I earned with my sweat are in that house. You say that Meeluda swore by Mecca? Well, my country bumpkin entered a pact with me on the saint's tomb."

The twins are three years old now. When the old woman goes out, she slides a sheet of tin over the grill that covers the patio opening and then she locks the roof door. As soon as she has gone, the country girl takes a long reed pole and pushes the tin sheet away with it. She calls out: "Hassan! Hussein!" And when the boys' faces appear at the opening, she stretches the reed out to them and there are sweets tied to the end of it.

*Translated by Leila Abouzeid and Elizabeth Fernea*

## *Tafidah Mahmoud Abdel Aghany*
# GAMALEK, THE MASTER OF ALL BIRDS

Egypt 2001    Arabic

This folktale plays with the theme of sibling rivalry: the main message is that the benevolent youngest sister triumphs over the wicked elder ones through courage, perseverance, and resourcefulness. The youngest sister proves that she is a faithful lover willing to save her beloved at any price. She does not give in to her eldest sisters' deception. The central motif of the story revolves around a supernatural bird that turns out to be a handsome young man, which is a recurrent theme in Egyptian lore. The purpose of the tale is to show that true love surpasses the limitations of appearances, overcomes the destructive efforts of others, and will therefore be rewarded. The storyteller was a thirty-five-year-old housewife from the area of Al Sawfammah. (See "Mother Goat," 1989 for further information about folktales.)

This story was recorded in 2001 by Abdel Reheem and Ahmed Mohamed for a collection of tales from the area of Sawamah, which is located on the Nile in east central Egypt. The storyteller, Tafidah Mahmoud Abdel Aghany, was a thirty-five-year-old homemaker. She is likely to have learned the story from her mother or grandmother, as is the case with most folktales, which are passed down through generations as a means of transmitting the practical and moral teachings of a culture.

*Nadia El Kholy*

✦

There was once a father who had seven daughters. One day he wished to travel, so he called them all together and said, "What shall I bring back for you?" One asked for a handkerchief, another for a scarf, and a third for a silk head veil. Then the youngest said, "I want Gamalek, the Supernatural Bird." Her father replied that he would bring it if he found it.

So when he reached his destination, he went to the *souk* and bought all the presents for his daughters except for the Gamalek, which he couldn't find. He walked and walked, searching for the bird, and finally he met an elderly man and said, "Dear uncle, you are old and wise, can you tell me anything about a bird called Gamalek, and how to find it?"

The old man replied, "You have to slaughter an animal and put its meat in one pot and its blood in another. Then some pigeons must eat the meat and drink the blood. You will then hear them say, 'May the one who fed us be rewarded.' You should then reply, 'It is I and the Gamalek who have fed you. Who is he among you?'"

The father did as he was told. He slaughtered an animal and put its meat in one pot and its blood in another. Then pigeons came and they ate from the meat and drank from the blood and then they said, "May he who has fed us be rewarded."

The father replied, "It is I and the Gamalek, the master of all birds, who have fed you. Is he one of you?"

One bird answered, "Why do you ask about the Gamalek? And what do you want from him?"

The father replied, "I have seven daughters. Each asked me to buy her a present on my travels. One asked for a handkerchief, another for a scarf, and a third for a silk head veil, but my youngest daughter asked me to bring back for her the Gamalek. Is that you? Are you the master of all birds?"

The bird answered, "Take this ring and give it to your daughter. Tell her to build a small room, paint it, clean it, and then put the ring on a plate. The Gamalek will come to her when the time is right!"

The youngest daughter did as her father directed. She built a room, painted it, cleaned it, and put a ring on a plate. One night the Gamalek came, and they fell in love. He kept coming to her for a whole month, and every morning he placed a hundred pounds under her pillow. One day the eldest sister got very jealous, and so she said to the youngest sister, "Ask the Gamalek what would cause his death in his homeland."

The youngest sister exclaimed, "Why should I ask him that? He only comes and leaves at night, and neither eats nor drinks."

Her sister replied, "Do as I tell you."

So one night, when the Gamalek came, the youngest sister asked him, "What causes your death in your homeland?"

Angry, he said, "If you are tired of me, give me back my ring, and I will go!"

"No!" she said, "I am not tired of you. My sister told me to ask you that question."

The Gamalek then replied, "What kills one in my homeland is a woman no longer in love with her partner, who rubs the walls with honey and then sprinkles them with glass slivers so that when her lover comes and touches the walls, the glass slashes his body."

When night came, the eldest sister, who had been told everything that the Gamalek had said, painted the walls with honey and sprinkled them with glass slivers in order to kill her sister's lover, because she was so jealous.

That night, when the Gamalek entered, the glass slashed every part of his body, but he was able to get back to his homeland. The youngest sister waited for him to return night after night, but when her patience wore out, she decided to find him. Wearing men's clothing, she set out to search for the Gamalek, the master of all birds.

She walked for three days and three nights, and by nightfall, as she was resting on a treetop, she heard sounds coming from another tree. She listened and heard two cooing doves talking. One said to her sister, "O, my sister, we have to be careful that we are not used as a cure for the young man who was wounded by the broken glass."

When the youngest daughter heard this, she said, "Help me, God, to catch these two doves by bending the tree's branch so that I can reach out and get hold of them." And indeed, she was able to stretch out her hand and snatch the two doves. But she still did not know what to do with them. After walking for a while, she came across an old woman, and she asked her what to do. The old woman said, "Slaughter them, roast them, and grind them till they become powder, then sprinkle the powder on the wounds of the Gamalek, and he will be healed."

The young woman did as she was told, and traveled until she found the ailing young man. He was sleeping on his bed, his body all slashed. She cleaned his wounds, then sprinkled the powder on his body for two days, until he was completely healed.

He then said, "Give my ring back to me. You are nothing to me, and I am nothing to you. Why did you hurt me so? Was that what I deserved?"

She replied, "I swear to you it was my sister who did all this. I would never hurt you. Had I hurt you, I would not then have looked for you everywhere."

Then he said to her, "Go to a place far away from your envious sister, build a little house, paint it and clean it and place the ring on a plate, and I shall come back to you."

She did as she had been told by the Gamalek, and he came to her, and they lived in prosperity and begat boys and girls.

*Translated by Nadia El Kholy*

# Safia Oraho
## LOVE AND MILITANCY: ORAL TESTIMONIES

Morocco 2001    Berber

Safia Oraho was born in 1935 in El Hajeb, near Fes. In the first of these oral testimonies, she narrates the dramatic story of her own life. The daughter of a *qaïd*,
a Berber tribal governor, during the French colonial era, she was at first adored by
her father, who lavished her with material goods and appointed her his representative at *mussems*, or festivals, and on official occasions. Oraho was nonetheless
subject to the restrictions placed on women, even those of the highest stature, and
could not choose how to live or whom to love. She soon paid a price for being
both beautiful and intelligent and for daring to insult important men. She also
had the misfortune to become a pawn in quarrels between male leaders. She had
no resources of her own under the Berber *Izref* law, which prohibited women
from inheriting lest they transmit this wealth to their husbands, who might be
from a different tribe. Ultimately, Oraho fled her family home and survived as a
prostitute and then a beggar in El Hajeb, where she still lives, and where she still
speaks of her past with defiance and pride. .

In the second text testimony, Oraho describes the very different life of her
cousin, Kenza N'Hammou, who was born into a wealthy family in the middle of
the twentieth century and chose to become a *shikha*, a dancer and singer. She was
obliged to leave her home village in the High Atlas and to settle with the Ayt
Ndhir tribe, in the Middle Atlas, where she could freely exercise her art. N'Hammou's father, like Oraho's, was obliged to collaborate with the French colonizers
in order to retain power over his tribe, a fact which she resented, since she was
also a militant fighter against the French. She worked for the resistance while
entertaining the colonizers, using her beauty and talent to manipulate the enemy
and perhaps to obtain information for the benefit of the nationalists.

Historically, this Berber region was one of the most difficult for the French
army to subdue. Beginning with Moha ou Hammou Zayani, the famous Berber
leader who fought against the arrival of colonialism in 1912, the Berbers of the
Atlas mountains maintained an armed resistance movement, in which brave
women like Kenza N'Ayt Hammou played an important part. The text was
recorded by Zoubida Achahboun, who lives in the same village as Safia Oraho.

*Zoubida Achahboun and Moha Ennaji*

✦

## THE STORY OF SAFIA ORAHO

I am Safia, the "gazelle" of Ayt Ndhir. I am the daughter of *Qaïd* Oraho, who
had been the head of his tribe since 1900, since before the advent of the French
Protectorate. I was his only daughter, much spoiled, a queen whom everyone
desired. I was pretty and svelte, with a tattoo on my front. They called me "a
truly wild gazelle." Men could only look at me from a distance, since I was
always surrounded by servants. I was not like other women of the tribe, who

spent their time doing housework, weaving, and other hard work all day. I studied in a French school; I went horseback riding, and I represented my father as the guest of honor on official occasions and at *mussems* in my own tribe and such others as the Zayan [Imahzan], who were known for their nobility, wealth, and courage. Once, I had everything, but alas!

I attended all the meetings, official [tribal courts] or unofficial, and sometimes I even participated actively in decision-making. Whenever the *qaïd* needed a change, he organized an outing to which his favorite wives and servants came. Tents were built near a beautiful water fountain. He invited friends and *qaïds* and pashas from other tribes. The celebrations were marked by poets praising the *qaïd*. I was always there, beautifully dressed, bedecked with jewelry, and sitting in the grandly decorated tent. One day, one of the poets dared recite an erotic poem describing my beauty. The *qaïd* gave orders to punish the poet, who was beaten to death.

Among the friends of *Qaïd* Driss Oraho was the French General de Gaulle, who was told about my beauty. One day, the general visited the *qaïd*, and I served him milk and dates, a Moroccan way of welcoming guests and foreigners. De Gaulle, an important Frenchman, removed a heavy gold ring from his hand, gave it to me, and kissed my hand. That event is engraved in my memory. I always recall it with endless pride.

From almost all of the neighboring tribes came proposals of marriage, but I always refused, sometimes making fun of them. I believed that the man for me had not yet been born. *Qaïd* Amahrouk of the Zayan tribe near the city of Khenifra decided to marry me and swore that I would become his spouse. He visited us, offering every valuable thing: jewelry, clothing, caftans, a white horse, two slaves. But the man was disappointed when I refused him and mocked him in front of people. He went away, humiliated and offended, mainly because of his high social status and power as chief of the Zayan tribe, which all the Berbers feared at that time. After that he had only one aim: to revenge his honor and dignity. I led my life as usual, forgetting about the event, since that was the first time I had humiliated a man of stature.

But one day, when I was on the plain of Saiss accompanied by my servants and the bodyguard Mokhazni, I rode a bit farther out than I should have on my own horse. Suddenly, horsemen appeared and kidnapped me. I screamed and wept, but there was nobody to rescue me. After three days of travel, we arrived at the Zayan tribe. I understood that it was my moment to pay my debts to Qaïd Amahrouk, who was determined to take his revenge.

I was put into a small, old tent similar to those in which shepherds lived. I spent a sleepless night in this tent, desperately waiting for sunrise to know my fate. In the morning, the *qaïd* came into the tent and stared at me. He then reminded me of the harm I had done him. I knelt down at his feet, imploring him to pardon me. He was so furious and agitated that he decided to make me his slave.

Many days passed. I, the daughter of the *qaïd*, the princess of Ayt Ndhir, whom everyone had obeyed, was now receiving and obeying orders. I somehow grew accustomed to my new life and to being totally neglected by the *qaïd*, with whom I fell strangely in love. He freed me and took me back home, but I was not welcomed. My father dismissed and rejected me, claiming that I had dishonored and ridiculed him. In my tribe, people thought that I had not been kidnapped, but had escaped with my lover. Even my family rejected and criticized me. *Qaïd* Driss [Oraho], to save his honor, forced me to marry my cousin, Khoya Rahho. I became furious and felt insulted when I was forced to marry a man I didn't love. My marriage lasted only a few days, and I ended up fleeing my tribe for that of my beloved *Qaïd* Amahrouk, who welcomed me warmly and married me, and we both lived in peace, love, and tenderness.

After some years, as he grew old, my father *Qaïd* Driss became tyrannical and heartless. He decided to bring me back and to declare war on his old enemy, *Qaïd* Amahrouk. On the morning of a beautiful spring day, I got up early to prepare my husband's usual hunting trip. Surrounded by horsemen, I accompanied him to the front entrance, wishing him the best of luck and promising to take care of him in the evening when he returned, not knowing that it was my last sight of him. A few moments later, the tribe's watchmen came to inform me that a tempest of dust had covered the region. Dozens of horsemen had savagely raided the tribe and demolished everything they found in their way, and then they kidnapped me.

Since that day, I have become another person, an angry, sad woman. At first I remained isolated from the outside world and jailed in a small room, until the death of my brother, Pasha Mokhtar. I left that house without any money, deprived of my inheritance. I settled in the center of El Hajeb town, in a small, old house. The daughter of a *qaïd* and the sister of a pasha became a prostitute, to whom anyone could come and spend a night as long as they paid for it. This new move increased the anger of my family, for whom I became an everlasting dishonor. Years elapsed, and in my old age I became a street beggar.

It is with nostalgia and pride that I am now recalling my past. I was cruelly mistreated by men, although in my youth, I was a princess whom the world obeyed and whom men admired and competed to conquer.

## The Story of Kenza N'Hammou

I, Safia, am also Kenza N'Hammou's cousin. Kenza was a Berber dancer, or *shikha*. Her voice was beautiful and soothing, a voice that calmed both young children and adults. She lived through almost the whole period of French colonization. She was a pretty young adolescent when she came down from the High Atlas mountains, escaping her family, who opposed her becoming a *shikha*.

Kenza N'Hammou settled within the tribe of Ayt Ndhir. She succeeded easily in her aim, for she became the most famous *shikha* in the region. Her songs spoke of love, abandonment, and loneliness. They did not mention the political events of the day in Morocco. She formed a group of musicians and poets. For people in the region, any celebration at which Kenza N'Hammou did not perform was not really a celebration. The pashas, the *qaïds*, and the colonists—all were impressed by her songs and poems.

One evening, Kenza N'Hammou was invited by the French General Juan to celebrate his birthday. She was welcomed warmly. But while she was waiting for her band to arrive and start the party, General Juan attempted to abuse her. She was hurt and felt bitterly humiliated. She left the house immediately and swore to take revenge on Juan and all the French colonists.

After this incident, Kenza N'Hammou had only one aim: to use her artistic talents to serve the national cause of independence. She organized evenings of belly dancing for the pashas, the *qaïds*, and their French friends, but at the same time she collaborated with the nationalists and helped prepare surprise attacks on the French colonizers.

One day a French officer visited her unexpectedly. She spontaneously arranged for a dancing party. Suddenly, one of the nationalists knocked at the window, mumbling some words: Kenza N'Hammou was troubled, for she recognized the visitor. Then, in order to alert him, she started singing in Berber, "May God bless you; don't knock at the door; the way is mined; come back later." The visitor understood the message and went away. Never discovered by the French colonizers, Kenza N'Hammou continued this way of life until the day of independence.

In 1999, Kenza N'Hammou died after a long and incurable illness. Her name is still alive in the collective memory of the Ayt Ndhir tribe; she is remembered as a Berber militant woman.

*Translated by Moha Ennaji*

## Maria Bent Itto Brahim
# TWO SLAVES, MOTHER AND DAUGHTER

Morocco 2001    Berber

Maria Bent Itto Brahim was born and still lives in the town of El Hajeb, near the city of Fes. Her oral testimony describing her own life and the life of her mother provides a record of slavery during the colonial period. Although the sale of slaves was outlawed with the advent of French colonialism, the practice of owning slaves continued, largely ignored—and occasionally engaged in—by the French; in some instances it persisted until after independence. Slaves worked in the fields in rural areas and, like the mother and daughter in this testimony, were household servants to wealthy families. Women slaves, who far outnumbered men, were used as concubines as well. The slaves, who were almost exclusively of sub-Saharan African heritage, had no resources of their own, and no option but to toil for their owners or die of hunger and lack of shelter.

In this text, the author describes the life of her mother, Itto Brahmin, who was one of many slaves of a wealthy *qaïd*, a tribal leader. Itto Brahmin's life as a slave favored for her beauty and charms ended after she was raped by the *qaïd*'s son and gave birth to her daughter Maria; mother and child were thrown out into the streets with no education or resources. After her mother's death, Maria Bent Itto Brahim returned to the *qaïd*'s home and worked as a maid, caring for his children. Both women endured lives shaped by hardship, discrimination, exploitation, and violence against women, yet managed to maintain a sense of dignity, defiance, and decency.

This testimony was recorded by Zoubida Achahboun, who comes from the same village as Maria Bent Itto Brahin.

*Zoubida Achahboun and Moha Ennaji*

✦

My mother, Itto Brahim, was a beautiful slave. Her Saharan owner offered her to the *Qaïd* Driss Ou Raho. When she was seventeen years old, she was brought to the *qaïd*'s big house. Everyone admired her, for she was lovely, active, always cheerful, and at the service of everyone. She was like a butterfly. For all these reasons, the *qaïd* appointed her his personal servant; she welcomed guests and prepared tea. Itto Brahim was happy and honored to be a slave of the *qaïd*.

When she first arrived, the wives of the *qaïd* quarreled over her and sought her company. Each one wanted Itto Brahim to become her own messenger to the master. The wives were interested in knowing what took place in the large tent of the *qaïd*. Itto Brahim thus became the spoiled slave of the *qaïd*, as well as of his wives, who took good care of her and made sure she was well dressed and clean. She was faithful to her master and never talked about him. Some of his guests wanted to buy her at any price, but their demands went unanswered.

Itto Brahim was very beautiful and seemed seductive to the men who saw her. Mokhtar, the eldest son of the *qaïd*, was so attracted to her that he kept waiting for the best moment to attack and abuse her. Late at a night, when everyone was asleep, he crept into Itto Brahim's room and raped her. He threatened to kill her if she dared say a word to anyone. The poor woman wiped away her tears and concealed her secret and pain deep inside her.

But after this, Itto Brahim was no longer the same. She became very quiet and withdrawn. She did not smile often. She was lost in her own thoughts. She became thin and wore her clothes soiled. Rqia, the favorite wife of the *qaïd*, noticed the metamorphosis of the slave, and her persistent questions pushed Itto into confessing her torment, kneeling down at Rqia's feet, weeping, beating her cheeks, and beseeching her not to reveal the secret. To Itto's surprise, Rqia did not keep her promise and told the story to the *qaïd*. He decided to ruin Itto's life by marrying her to a dark Saharan man in order to hide his son's crime. Itto's dignity was deeply hurt as she faced the ordeal of marrying a man she had never seen before. This was a harsh punishment that made her lose her taste for life. Nevertheless, she accepted her fate and was patient.

She gave birth to me and named me Maria. When I was three years old, the *qaïd* took me to live with his family. I grew up amid servants with no affection or love. I hid my sadness and feelings of alienation. But one day, a maid provoked me by calling me a bastard. I could not bear the insult that had haunted my existence. I beat her without pity, taking revenge for myself and for my poor mother.

I left the *qaïd* and joined my mother, who had become a *tayaba*, a cook for big celebrations like marriages, engagements, and circumcisions. When my mother died, I returned to the *qaïd*, who had been promoted and was now a pasha. I was given the responsibility of serving my stepbrothers and stepsisters, who treated me as a bastard. I cared for their young children and ended up forgetting all about myself, my existence, and my rights. I gave all the affection I was denied as a child to these children. I remained in the big house until the death of the pasha, who had deprived me of my share of inheritance, although I was born a legitimate daughter. I kept moving from one family to another, offering my services. This was my fate and my mother's before me. May God glorify her.

*Translated by Moha Ennaji*

## *Rabea Qadiri*
## SONGS OF SEPARATION AND UNION

Morocco 2001    Arabic

Rabea Qadiri was born in 1947 in eastern Morocco and now lives in Ahfir, a culturally important eastern Moroccan city. She is the mother of one son and three daughters, one of whom is the wife of the author of this headnote, who recorded these songs in Ahfir in 2001. Qadiri's husband spent more than thirty years in Europe earning a living. During his absence, Rabea Qadiri managed to achieve her most cherished goal, which was to provide all of her children with good educations.

At the time of French colonization, some Moroccan men, especially from eastern Morocco, found it necessary to emigrate to France to earn a living, most remaining there for a year or more. Their wives had to move in with their mothers-in-law and endure derision from the family and others. If the husband failed to send money to his family for some reason, a woman might have serious problems with her mother-in-law. In this case, a postal strike in France caused difficulty for the wives left behind in Morocco. The *haïk* is a traditional cloak, usually white, that women wear outdoors; it covers their heads and bodies, leaving only their faces revealed.

The group of songs that were recorded at a wedding serves to describe the various rituals involved in marriage ceremonies in Morocco, particularly in the eastern part of the country. Qadiri sings them along with other women at wedding parties, accompanied by dancing. The songs are grouped according to three broad steps in the marriage ceremony, which often takes place over a series of days.

The first of these steps is *dfu'*, which takes its origin from the standard Arabic verb *dafa'a*, meaning "to push," "to give," or "to pay." *Dfu'* in this context means to offer gifts, presents, and food to the bride.

The henna day has derived its name from the reddish-brown dye used especially for coloring hair or skin, mainly for painting designs on the hands and feet. A deeper meaning of the term might indicate emotion—from the Arabic word *hanaan*, which means compassion—and tenderness between the bride and the bridegroom and their families. The henna ceremony that takes place prior to the wedding ceremony is an important female bonding ritual, as women gather while henna is applied decoratively to the bride's hands and feet, often by a professional woman artist hired for the purpose. When she finishes her work, the women offer prayers to the prophet and ululate to cheer the bride and chase the evil eye from the house. In response to the traditional *henna* songs, the groom's family sings songs of warm welcome.

The following day, the bridegroom, accompanied by his family and friends, arrive to take the bride to her husband's house. Before they do so, the husband and his relatives pay a sum of money so as to free the wife, whose situation is described as that of an imprisoned person. (This sum is separate from the *mahr*, or dowry.) The *neggafas*, women hired to decorate the bride and sing songs in praise of her beauty, are usually present at this ritual. Additional songs are sung while the couple is in the process of leaving for the husband's house, which completes the big day.

*Abdennour Kharraki*

✦

## THE STRIKE

Tell your son to come, mother,
Or else I'll put on my *haïk* and leave this house.
Mercy, mercy my Lord!
The strike has affected my son.
Sell your *haïk* and feed your family,
For the strike stopped the money.
O, you who used to have cakes at breakfast,
The strike has crumbled them away.
No meat, no gravy;
What would you do, madam?
I'd work and do the washing up
To keep body and soul together.
The striker sends a letter,
Mercy, mercy my Lord!

## *Dfu'* Wedding Songs

### Song One

Your brothers are coming, O, Yamina!
Bringing presents and staying up with you.
Here we come, don't say otherwise!
Spread the silk and welcome us.

### Song Two

Welcome, O, foreigners,
Who are coming with our brother.

## Henna Day Wedding Songs

### Song One

Prayer and peace be upon the prophet of God.
There is no power, save that of our master Mohammed.
May God be with the great powerful prophet.

### Song Two

We are bringing the henna
From paradise
To you, our bride.

### Song Three

Look up, sultan, to see her beauty.
The bride is like a branch of almonds,
So let her pass.
The bride is like a cluster of bananas,
So let her appear.
She is married to him
Against enemies' wishes.

### Song Four

Here the gold has fallen,
And here we search for it.

## BIG DAY WEDDING SONGS

### Song One

The bride is freed from the protection
Of her father.
The bride is freed from the protection
Of her husband.
The bride is freed from the protection
Of her brother.

### Song Two

Here is the fish,
Here it is.
Here is the honey,
Here it is.
Here is the most beautiful bride,
Here she is.

### Song Three

Look, O, bachelors,
Don't say she is not a virgin.
Such are daughters of
Noble families.
May God bring her to us with wealth.
She is another dove in our nest.
Congratulations to you, O sultan!
This is a dove coming to the house.

### Song Four

He married her; he married her.
He swears not to leave her home.
She married him; she married him.
She swears not to leave him.
May God bless her husband.

*Translated by Abdennour Kharraki*

# Lalla Mina Lamrani
# TWO FEISTY TALES

Morocco 2001   Arabic

Lalla Mina Lamrani was born in Tafilalet, in north central Morocco, in 1929. She describes her childhood as a happy one, with a mother who was very strict about housework and cooking and a father who preferred her to her sister and brother because her energy and her intelligence made her "the boy of the family." Trusting in her capacity to work, her father gave her a large plot of personal land to garden. She, like nearly all girls of her time in Morocco, was not sent to school.

When she was twelve, Lalla Mina Lamrani's parents gave her as a wife to one of her cousins, Moulay Ibrahim, who had already married and divorced two wives, was married to a third, and had two daughters from his previous wives. Moulay Ibrahim was born in 1912 (the year the French colonized Morocco, as he used to tell his children), the youngest child of a very large family. Moulay Saidi, his father and Lalla Mina Lamrani's uncle, was a renowned scholar in Boudnib, a village in Tafilelt, in southeast of Morocco. When Moulay Ibrahim's mother was pregnant with him, his father had left for a pilgrimage, spending a year walking to Mecca and then to Jerusalem, where he waited, along with a group of Moroccan pilgrims, for World War I to end so they could cross the Red Sea and return to home. But he died and was buried in Jerusalem, so that Moulay Ibrahim never met his father.

At ten, he left home to work for East Algerian Mining in colonized Algeria. Then he worked as a laborer in the port of Oran, to earn the money he needed to return to Oujda, Morocco, and start a construction business. He was a wealthy and respected businessman and a joyful musician when he and Lalla Mina Lamrani married in 1939. She bore seven children, the first two of whom died in infancy.

In both of these stories, a woman's courage and cleverness enable her to overcome hardships and reap rewards. They are among many stories recorded in August 2001 in Casablanca by the author of this headnote. Two weeks before her death in June 2003, while visiting Lalla Mina Lamrani in a clinic in Casablanca, the author told her that her stories were to be published by a press that gives space to important women's voices. She laughed quietly and seemed pleased by this expression of women's sisterly respect and love. Lalla Mina Lamrani's grave is in Sale', on the Atlantic coast in the northern corner of Africa, near the mausoleum of a saint called Sidi Benacher, who is said to have gone there to rest and feed the poor.

*Hafsa Bekri Lamrani*

◆

## BAKING BREAD

Around 1942, my husband, who had a business in real estate construction, left for a few days to go to Boudnib for a visit to his mother. He told me that if I needed money his workers would provide it. When I wanted money for the household, the workers said they could not give me any because they had a work permit problem. Here I was, I had no children of my own, the two I had

had died at a young age, and I was in charge of my husband's ex-wives' two daughters.

I had two cents, half a kilo of sugar (sugar was expensive then) and half a kilo of semolina. Instead of the few days he had promised to stay away, my husband stayed away two months. We had no money, no food! I took the half-kilo of sugar and the half-kilo of semolina I had to the market, and I sold them and bought some wheat, yeast, and condensed milk to sweeten our coffee. I made four loaves of bread, carried them to the public oven, kept one for my stepdaughters and myself, sold three, and bought some more wheat and yeast for the following day. I kept making more and more bread every day from the cash I got from selling them. For cheap vegetables and wood I would walk miles to a farm in Sidi Yahia, a village near Oujda in eastern Morocco, with my husband's two girls trotting behind me. For protein, I used to cook my vegetables with mutton legs or a mutton head.

When my husband came back, he almost walked on the bread that was rising all over the rug. I had by then reached sixty-four loaves a day!

"What's this?" he asked. "Are you having a party?"

"You'll see the party tomorrow," I replied. I sold the bread the next day. It was a time of food rationing, during World War II when Morocco was under French colonial rule, and bread was expensive, and I got a good price for my loaves. I bought some real meat that day, prepared the food, and woke him up for breakfast.

## THE SIXTY YOUNG ALGERIAN WOMEN:

I lived in Oujda during the Algerian war of liberation. Morocco was independent then. Sixty young women in the Algerian city of Oran were taken from the university on jeeps and put into jail. They were ages eighteeen to twenty-one. Because they were young women and supposedly incapable of doing anything, they weren't locked in. Reality was going to prove different.

The sixty female prisoners waited until late at night when their guardian was sound asleep and, climbing on each others' shoulders, they got to the top of the prison wall. When there were only a few left, they used their *haïk* [a long cloak of white cloth] to help the last few young women to get out. For the descent, they used the reverse process: the *haïk* first, then each other's shoulders. Then they began their flight toward Oujda, Morocco. They would walk together by night, and then separate and hide in the grass or in caves during the day, which was no easy task and meant facing all kind of obstacles, like falling into cracks or being injured by thorns. By the time they arrived at Oujda they were in terrible shape.

They went directly to Moroccan authorities and reported what had happened to them. The Moroccan authorities emptied a brothel named Aïn Meaza, moved the prostitutes out, gave the house to the sixty girls, and called for donations for them. People responded immediately by giving clothes, blankets, and money.

The event was of course reported to the late King Mohammed V, who gave instructions to take individual photographs of the young women, invite a group of young Moroccan teachers to a party, and take an individual photograph of the teachers also. Then, the teachers' pictures were given to the young women and the young women's pictures to the teachers, for eventual marriages.

The son of one of my neighbors was one of the male teachers, and his case was extraordinary: The young woman he had chosen happened to be his cousin. Amazingly enough, the young woman had also chosen to write her name on his picture. The late King Mohammed V gave a marriage allowance of two thousand *dirhams* both to the young women and to the men. The wedding ceremony and the wedding clothes were at the King's expense, the money an additional gift handed to them by the King himself. The day after the wedding, my neighbor, the male teacher's mother, started asking questions of the young bride about her family and the girl turned out to be her brother's daughter and her son's cousin!

*Translated by Hafsa Bekri-Lamrani*

## Hafsa Bekri-Lamrani
## THE CALL OF HAGAR

Morocco 2001 English

Hafsa Bekri-Lamrani was born in 1948. She studied Anglo-Saxon literature and civilization at the University of Paris VII, Jussieu Campus, and now teaches English at the American Language Center of the College Training Center in Rabat and Casablanca and at the Royal Moroccan Air Force base in Rabat Sale'. Bekri-Lamrani is a founding member of the first House of Poetry in Morocco and a member of the Union of Writers of Morocco, the Center of Mediterranean Research, and the social and cultural association *Al Madina* (The City). Her collections of poems include *East and West in Our Imaginations* (1992) and *Signs and Sounds of Maghrebi Women* (1995). She has also published one volume of short fiction, *Jellabiates* (2000), which takes its title from Moroccan women's traditional gowns; and two collections of poetry, *Sparks of Life* (2004); and *Tendresse et Autres Lumières* (Tenderness and Other Lights, 2004). She is one of the best-known Moroccan female poets writing in English.

The subject of Bekri-Lamrani's poem "The Call of Hagar" is an important figure in both Judaism and Islam. In the Hebrew Bible's Book of Genesis, Hagar is an Egyptian servant belonging to Abraham's wife Sarah. Because Sarah is barren she gives her handmaid to her husband as a concubine, and Hagar bears a son, Ishmael, who legally belongs to Abraham and Sarah. But when Sarah later gives birth to her own son, Isaac, she asks Abraham to cast out Hagar and Ishmael, and Hagar wanders in the desert with her son, searching for water, until an angel of God shows her a spring. In the Qur'an and *Qisas Al-Anbiya*—stories of the Muslim prophets—Hagar is the daughter of a pharaoh who gives her to Abraham as a wife, not a concubine. When this causes strife in his marriage to Sarah, Abraham brings Hagar and Ishmael to Mecca, seeking to resettle rather than to renounce them. The journeys Hagar takes in her search for water to save her son become symbolic as rites in Muslim pilgrimages.

Bekri-Lamrani uses the story of Hagar to address the male use of religion to construct and exploit hatred. Because the two sons of Abraham, Isaac and Ishmael, are considered the ancestors of the Israelites and Arabs, respectively, the story has resonance in modern-day conflicts between Jews and Muslims. In Bekri-Lamrani's powerful vision, Hagar reaches out to Sarah, rejecting the patriarchal discourse that has positioned them as rivals and enemies, and yielded "thousands of years of tears, blood, and hatred" between their descendants. Instead, she offers an image of female unity and love in the face of religious xenophobia, emphasizing the common experience of motherhood that binds women together. In the poem's moving conclusion, Hagar urges Sarah to join her in the desert, and proposes that they invite the Christian Mary, mother of Jesus, to live with them in peace as well.

*Fatima Sadiqi*

✦

Vulnerable, naked, unarmed,
Yet I scare them.
Armed, secured, wealthy,
They fear my bare being, and
My having nothing defies them.
An ephemeral mirror, yet so limpid,
I refuse to hate; it kindles their hatred.
FREE,
I keep escaping
The costumes of xenophobia
That they cut for me.
I am where there is Nothing and
Nothing is the kingdom of my Rebirth.
Hagar, Mother of Ishmael,
Abraham's wife;
Sarah, Mother of Isaac,
Abraham's wife;
Two mothers, two sons, one father,
And
thousands of years of tears, blood, and hatred to
soothe.
No!
Sarah, I wish you no Death!
Hasn't Europe been raped by Zeus
And hasn't she tried to stifle you
With her one thousand and one
Hitlerian hands?

No, Sarah, I wish you no Death!
Death has devoured enough of our children!
I've buried my dead, Sarah.
Come, I will show you the desert,
The stars that are lit at dusk and
Revived in the depth of night
By an invisible hand.
Come, Sarah, leave their false paradise
Behind you.
Ishmael and Isaac
Will sleep under our veils and the night's,
Caressed by the ultimate poem,
Sung in our hearts by the soul of the desert.
Come, Sarah, Mary will join us tonight,
And we shall be the same Mother.

## Ekbal Baraka
# SO AS NOT TO FORGET THE
# DREAMS OF QASIM AMIN

Egypt 2002    Arabic

Ekbal Baraka is a journalist, creative writer, and feminist. Born in Cairo in 1943, she received a bachelor's degree in English from Alexandria University in 1962, and a second B.A. in Arabic from Cairo University in 1979. Baraka is the author of twenty books. Her six novels include *Wa Lenathal Asdekaa Ila Al Abad* (Let Us Be Friends Forever, 1971) and *Al Fagr Le Awal Marra* (Dawn for the First Time, 1975), and her many short stories have appeared in Egyptian magazines and anthologies. Her nonfiction books range in subject matter from literary criticism to travel to politics to Islamic studies. She has also written scripts for radio and television. Baraka served as editor of *Hawaa*, a leading women's magazine, from 1993 to 2007, and has been a columnist for Egypt's *Al-Ahram*, a daily newspaper.

Baraka's presence on the social and political scene has increased since the publication of her controversial 2002 book *Al Hijab* (The Veil: A Modern View), which brought on attacks for its contention that the veil is not prescribed by the Qur'an. Nevertheless, Ekbal Baraka has received the National Award of Achievement in Literature from the Supreme Council for Culture in Egypt and has served as president of the Egyptian Writers Union. She continues to write for newspapers and magazines and take part in television debates on topical cultural, political, and feminist issues.

In "So as Not to Forget the Dreams of Qasim Amin," Ekbal Baraka critiques an initiative announced twelve days earlier by United States Secretary of State Colin Powell. In particular, she argues against the proposed participation of the United States in the area of women's education and development in the Middle East.. Baraka believes that any such "partnership" is doomed to reflect only Western views of what Arab women need, rather than the desires, aspirations, and cultural realities of Arab women themselves. She cites past experience with Western colonial powers, mentioning two influential colonial texts that presented the subjugation of Egyptian women as evidence of the "backwardness" of Islam and of Middle Eastern culture in general—and, by implication, as an argument for colonialism.

Baraka points out that the early Egyptian women's movement suffered from the perception of foreign interference, which became a primary cause for attacks on enlightened thinkers like Qasim Amin (1863–1908). Amin was the author of two pioneering works, *Tahrir al-Mara* (*The Liberation of Women*), published in 1899, and *Al-Mara al-Jadidah* (*The New Woman*), which followed a year later. in which he argued for the rights of women to education and work, as well as for the abandonment of the Ottoman veil, which covered even women's faces, in favor of a less restrictive form. Baraka reminds readers that although he was widely branded a blasphemer and a pawn of the West, Amin was in fact a devoted Egyptian nationalist, a friend of independence leader Saad Zagloul, and a dedicated Muslim, influenced by the famous reformist scholar and cleric Sheikh Mohamed Abdou. Along with such figures as Princess Nazli Fadel, aunt of the Khedive Abbas Helmy II (who was dethroned by the British in 1914), Amin fought for the emancipation of women in a specifically Arab, nationalist, and Muslim context.

Baraka insists that Amin's dreams have not been lost or forgotten, and that the West needs to acknowledge the fact that progress for Arab women need not be modeled on the Western paradigm. She cautions against the imposition of Western ideals on Eastern societies, while simultaneously reminding Egyptians of the advances they have made in women's rights over the past century. Finally, in rejecting the U.S. "partnership" on women's issues as one that will only impose the ideology and culture of one partner upon the other, she suggests a more general criticism of U.S. foreign policy, particularly in the Middle East.

*Azza El Kholy*

✦

The Arab peoples hail the third year of the third millennium with the initiative of the American Secretary of State, Colin Powell, which was announced on Thursday, 12 December 2002. Powell calls his initiative "The United States-Middle East Partnership Initiative: Building Hope for Future Years." An intelligent reader of this initiative is bound to feel the extent of the gap between the American government's perspective and an Arab perspective. To start with, does Mr. Powell know that the Arab people he is trying to encourage, as he claims, to take part in politics, will categorically never accept the interference of an American administration in the internal affairs of their countries?

As for women's rights—which Mr. Powell presents as something that the American government wishes to support—we sincerely hope that he ignores this question in particular. Enough harm has been done already to Egyptian women and our feminist movement by interfering colonial powers during the first half of the twentieth century. In fact, the first enlightened Egyptian feminist leaders faced much recalcitrance. They were accused of being foreign agents, deserters of Islam, and followers of Lord Cromer, the emissary for the British ambassador in Egypt at the time. This was the case especially after the great thinker Qasim Amin published *The Liberation of Women* and *The New Woman* exactly one hundred years ago. Despite Amin's dependence on references from Islamic jurisprudence, and the support he received from the *mufti*, a religious authority of the time, Egyptian men were not content with merely attacking him verbally or even with writing newspaper articles opposing the ideas expressed in his two books. Some men raided Amin's house and asked him to allow them to visit with his wife and daughter, by way of demonstrating the ideas he asserts in his books. Furthermore, demonstrations called for Amin's assassination as a renegade Muslim.

In addition, publishing houses issued more than a hundred books by various writers attacking Qasim Amin's ideas and rejecting what he had called for: education for women, and access to employment for women who had no one to support them. Among these books was one by Talaat Harb, who would become, two decades later, the leader of the film industry in Egypt! Moreover, Amin's criticism of the Ottoman Turkish veil and his call for a return to the Islamic veil, the *hijab*, which would reveal the hands and face, were considered a departure from religion and a call for licentiousness!

The publication of Lord Cromer's book, after his departure from Egypt and his return to his own country, made matters worse still. Lord Cromer, in *The Modern Egyptians* [1909], repeated the same falsehoods about Islam that had been perpetuated before him by the French judge le Duc D'Harcourt in his book *Egypt and the Egyptians* [1893]. D'Harcourt claimed that Islam was the source of the backwardness of Muslims, the prime cause of their degradation and of the-subjugation of women, and the reason behind their refusal to educate women and allow them to participate in public life! Lord Cromer also emphasized in his book, immediately translated into Arabic, that Egypt would never progress and never achieve prominence as a nation unless its women were liberated from the binding chains of the ideas, costumes, and traditions of the Middle Ages!

Now, a century after these events, the West is still criticizing the position of women in Islamic countries, and attributing the backwardness of these countries to their discrimination against, and marginalization of, half the population. Similarly, the West is still surprised by the determination of Islamic people to hold on to the ideas, customs, and traditions of the Middle Ages. To the West, it is still more astonishing to find men, some of whom belong to the intellectual and cultured class, calling persistently for the replication of the Islamic society that existed a thousand years ago.

But the fact remains that many of Qasim Amin's dreams have come true, and Egyptian women have become a functional and influential force in Egyptian society. Moreover, Egyptian women have proved their excellence in all fields of human activity, and many females have outdone males in achievement at the high school, university, and professional levels, and in diverse administrative posts. It is indeed most unfair to place such societies as Egypt, Tunisia, Lebanon, Syria, and Jordan, which have taken gigantic steps in achieving freedoms, in the same basket with all other Arab societies. Besides, it is neither essential that Arab women have dreams identical to those of Western women, nor is it mandatory that Western women be their example, model, or paragon.

Every society has its needs and its values, which are derived from and influenced by its circumstances and religious beliefs. Certainly the television series *Qasim Amin*, written by Mohamed El Sayed Eid and directed by Inaam Mohamed Aly, has shed light on the history of Egypt a hundred years ago: how some categorically refused the idea that Egyptian women should receive education, at any level, with the false claim that Islam prohibits the education of women! The series focused on Qasim Amin's patriotism, his friendship with Saad Zagloul, and the influence of Sheikh Mohamed Abdou on the two men. The series also underscored the courageous and enlightened vision of the Khedive Abbas Helmy II's aunt, Princess Nazli Fadel.

How then could this partnership that Mr. Powell talked about be established without any consideration for the circumstances, concerns, burdens, and aspirations of the other partner? How could it be founded without a serious attempt to understand and respect the independent entity of this partner?

*Translated by Azza El Kholy*

## *Hadda N'Ayt Hssain*
# O, Bride: Berber Wedding Song

Morocco 2003    Berber

Hadda N'Ayt Hsain is my mother-in-law. She was born around 1930 in Timoulilt, in southeastern Morocco, into a wealthy Berber family; her father was a *qaïd*, a local chief. She has always lived in or near her village of origin. The name Hadda comes from the Arabic word *hedd* ("limit"), and signals the patriarchal environment in which female newborns were not welcomed into the family: although she was only the second daughter, it was hoped that she would be the last. While she never had the opportunity to go to school, she has strongly supported the education of her seven sons and daughters, and admires the status of her educated daughter-in-law. During her childhood, Hadda N'Ayt Hssain learned many Berber songs, including wedding songs, and as a mother, she has in turn transmitted these songs to younger family members.

Marriage rituals and songs in Morocco, a mixture of traditional practices, religious beliefs, and acts of survival, are handed down from generation to generation, with each one adding its own flavor. Marriage is an occasion for a mother-in-law to exercise her power and for the bride's mother to negotiate some space for her daughter in the household's power network. For the female kin of the bride, especially her mother, marriage is an occasion both of joy and sadness. The joy, symbolized by the ritual decoration of the bride's hands and feet with henna, is mixed with the sadness of sending a young, inexperienced girl into a new household, where she will come under the power of a new family of women.

"O, Bride," a woman-to-woman song, is popular in Moroccan Berber rural areas. It celebrates the female bond that links daughters to their mothers and sisters, which is rarely expressed in everyday life lest the daughter fail to become a good wife and daughter-in-law when she marries. The song ends by expressing fears that female in-laws will make life difficult for the new bride.

*Fatima Sadiqi*

✦

O, bride, may God be your first assistant!
May He give you luck!
Who would believe
That we celebrate your wedding with joy?
My darling daughter!
You are better than a beautiful singer.
Give me your hand
To decorate with henna.
Give me your foot
To decorate with a bracelet.
O, my lovely daughter,
Don't let your female in-laws
Call you a dirty girl.
They will turn you
Into a shepherd or a slave.

*Translated by Fatima Sadiqi*


## Samia Serageldin
# LOVE IS LIKE WATER

Egypt 2003 English

Samia Serageldin was born into a distinguished Egyptian family of wealthy landowners. She grew up under the shadow of the Nasser regime, when some members of her family and were arrested or exiled, and their properties confiscated, along with those of most upper-class Egyptians. Serageldin's uncle, Fouad Serageldin, was the leader of El Wafd, the dominant political party before all political parties were outlawed after the 1952 Egyptian Revolution. Serageldin earned a master's degree in politics at London University's School of Oriental and African Studies. After returning to Egypt in the late 1970s, she left for the United States with her husband and children in 1980, and currently divides her time between North Carolina, Cairo, and London. She is a writer of both fiction and nonfiction, a book editor, and a literary critic, and has taught at Duke University.

Serageldin's first novel, *The Cairo House* (2000), reflects her personal experience: Her protagonist witnesses first-hand much of the political turmoil and the social upheavals brought about by the 1952 revolution, and their dramatic impact on her family and its upper-class social milieu. She also experiences the universal contradictions faced by expatriates, straddling two cultures and trying to mediate between them. The novel received wide critical praise and has been translated into half a dozen European languages. Serageldin's short fiction and her essays, many of which focus on political Islam and women in Islam, have appeared in several anthologies, including *Scheherezade's Legacy* (2004), *Dinarzad's Children* (2004), and *Muslim Networks from Haj to Hip Hop* (2005).

The short story "Love is like Water" is told through the memories of the narrator, Nadine, whose experiences closely resemble Serageldin's. The story pays homage to two grandmothers, each charming, eccentric, and powerful in her own way. It also vividly recreates the culture and customs of the lost world of aristocratic Cairo, before and just after the 1952 Revolution, and the lives of the women who lived through it.

*Noha Nadder Hamdy*

✦

I never heard either of my grandmothers addressed by her first name. For that generation, first names were not bandied about lightly. Strangers to the family would address or refer to them as *"hanem,"* a Turkish word meaning "lady"; the household help called them "the Elder *Sit*" to distinguish them from their daughters; family members, depending on relationships, called them "Mama" or some form of "Grandmother" or *"Tante."* If anyone ever called them by their unadorned first names, I suppose it would have been an intimate female contemporary of theirs, and it didn't happen in my presence.

Like other Muslim women in Egypt, my grandmothers had legally kept their maiden names after marriage. But in practice, for public matters like newspaper announcements of marriages and obituaries, they went from being referred to as *"Karimat* so-and-so Pasha," a euphemism for daughter, to *"Haram* so-and-so *Bey,"* a euphemism for wife. In our social circle, at least, they were spared the ultimate designation-by-male-relative: the ubiquitous *"Om* so-and-so" or "Mother of so-and-so." Far from seeing it as pejorative, however, married women of most social strata joyfully claimed the appellation *"Om-*somebody" as soon as they gave birth to their first son—the prejudice against using a woman's first name was that common.

So, in deference to my grandmothers' sensibilities during their lifetime, I will not now use their real first names; they might well turn in their graves. My paternal grandmother was called, within her family, *"Sit* Luli," an affectionate nickname very much along the same lines of the "Miss Elly" or "Miss Libby" that some matrons are still called in the American South. *Sit* Luli died when I was eight, so I have the rare vivid memory of her, and otherwise rely on family lore. The sight of her small, frail frame always made me wonder how she had borne my tall, strapping father, his five older brothers, and his two older sisters. The effort seemed to have drained her completely; she always seemed to have a vague air about her—although, as it turned out, *Sit* Luli could be far sharper than she was generally credited with being.

*Sit* Luli had been an heiress, but she was totally unworldly and gullible: Inexpensive trinkets pleased her more than fine jewelry. Once she had even been induced by one of her sons, the proverbial black sheep, to deed to him several pieces of her property before the others put a stop to it. In my great-grandmother's generation, women were taught to read, but not to write, specifically to forestall the possibility that they might be swindled out of their fortune—or their honor, if they wrote love letters. How it was possible to teach girls how to read, but not to write, is beyond me. My great-grandmother wore a sheer white veil, called a *yashmak*, when she went out, but neither of my grandmothers did.

The photo portrait that I have of *Sit* Luli must have been taken when she was in her forties. In the photo, her dark hair is expertly waved, and she is made up in the fashion of the times, with pencil-thin arched brows and bow lips; her manicured hands, with dark nail polish, are folded in front of her. In spite of the makeup, there is something ill-defined about her features. She is looking away from the camera, expressionless. She looks as if she had been made up and coiffed for the occasion, and as if this portrait was not her idea.

My most enduring live memory of my grandmother is of my father carrying her like a child up and down the stairs of our villa the year she died. That winter, whenever there was a particularly cold spell, *Sit* Luli showed up at our door in her outdated black Bentley, driven by her ancient Sudanese driver, with her equally ancient maid sitting in the front seat beside him. Grandmother had come to take a bath. She caught chills bathing in her own big, drafty bathroom in the family mansion, with its cathedral ceilings. The first time she visited my parents' new villa in Zamalek, she had been impressed by nothing as much as the modern bathrooms.

"Oh, how cosy they are!" She had exclaimed. "Why, one would never catch cold bathing in these bathrooms!"

Papa and Mama had immediately insisted that she must come to our house to take her baths. At first *Sit* Luli wouldn't hear of it, but having caught a chill twice already that winter, she was finally prevailed upon. Her final objection was that she could not climb the stairs in the new villa; in the family house there was a rickety old elevator between the ground floor and the second. So when she came to our house, Papa made sure to be on hand to pick her up and carry her up the stairs, with as much ease as if she had been a child. After her bath she retired immediately to bed, where hot water bottles would have been prepared, and stayed there till the next morning, when she would go home.

Whenever I visited the family house in Garden City I made a point of looking around my grandmother's bathroom. There were three tall, creaky, wooden double doors—one leading to the bedroom, one to the adjoining boudoir, now the maid's room, and one to the corridor outside. The huge old bathtub was screened off by a curtain; only its big brass claw feet were visible, and the stool that was used to climb into it. A table held loofahs, white and black pumice stones, and towels. At one end, a screen provided privacy for the W.C. with its wooden tank suspended overhead, and the bidet with its stack of washcloths.

At the other end stood a vanity with a huge gilded-frame mirror, a chair, and a wooden wardrobe. A palpable draft nipped my ankles as I stood between the door to the corridor and the door to the maid's room.

*Sit* Luli had certain phobias, and one of them was germs. She had her maid wash any coins or bills before she handled them. She also draped a sheer scarf over her hand whenever she needed to shake hands with people, under the pretext that she had washed for prayer. I was too young to see through that flimsy excuse; touching the hand of an adult male who was not a close relative would require a woman to go through her ablutions again before prayer, but my grandmother did this even when shaking hands with other women. Only close family members were exempt.

Many stories circulated in the family about her naiveté, and I'm sure most of them were embellished. My favorite had to do with the bombing of Cairo during the Second World War. Whenever the air raid sirens went off, everyone in the house had instructions to scramble down to the cellars. This included the twenty-odd family members: *Sit* Luli; her eldest son the pasha, and his wife and children; the next two eldest sons and their families; unmarried younger sons, of whom my father was the youngest; plus the thirty or so servants. But one time, when the sirens went off, *Sit* Luli was nowhere to be found.

The family had moved into this house in the new Garden City neighborhood shortly after the First World War from their house across the Nile in the old neighborhood of palatial homes, Manial. The first time the sirens sounded, the family and servants followed instructions and scrambled down to the kitchen cellars, while my eldest uncle, the pasha, directed the evacuation from a chair in the middle of the vast hall with its soaring atrium and rose marble columns. Like the captain of a sinking ship, he waited to go down to the shelter himself until every last soul in the house had been accounted for. But *Sit* Luli was nowhere to be found. The blackout was in force, and they searched for her high and low, candles in hand. They looked for her behind the high-backed velvet sofas of the outer salon and the gilt armchairs of the inner salon; behind the bookcases in the gloomy, wood-paneled study with the stained glass window; in the darkest recesses of the twenty-four-chair dining room; in each of the several bedroom suites upstairs; in the bathrooms and the boudoirs and the children's rooms; in the "lost" rooms under the twin marble staircases that swept up to meet at the mezzanine; even in the rickety wrought-iron elevator. The elevator went up to the second floor or down to the main kitchens and workrooms; there were pantries on each floor, and dumbwaiters to carry the platters up and down, but even so, food never reached the dining room warm. The basement was a no-man's land, where stray cats multiplied and the occasional nationalist revolutionary—including, one time, a certain young Anwar Sadat—took refuge to escape British colonial authorities.

*Sit* Luli was nowhere to be found. In desperation, they were about to start searching the maids' rooms on the top floor; the menservants' quarters were in a separate building. Then someone thought to look in the large armoire in her own bedroom, and found her huddled there. They brought her downstairs to the pasha, who persuaded her that it was much safer to go down to the cellar.

"But you must come too," she objected.

"Don't worry about me, Mama dear," he reassured her, quite disingenuously. "The chair I'm sitting on is the safest spot in the house."

"In that case, dear, get up and give me your seat."

As her sons and daughters married and gradually moved to villas or apartments of their own in Cairo, *Sit* Luli found herself alone in the house with her oldest son and his wife and children. But she had a regular schedule, according to which she did the rounds of her children's homes, having dinner with a different son or daughter on each day of the week. Since she had eight children and there were only seven days in the week, she never had dinner at home in the family mansion, much to the displeasure of her eldest son. "But Mama," he would try to reason with her, "all I am asking you to do is to set aside a day to have dinner with me at home, as you do with the others." The pasha was a very busy man, with many responsibilities in the cabinet and the party, so dinner— the main meal, served in the early afternoon—was the only time he had to spend with family.

But *Sit* Luli continued to make her rounds, and with her usual vagueness often seemed to confuse the days of the week. My father, the youngest, was her favorite, and sometimes she showed up at our villa when it was not her appointed day to do so, in her black Bentley with her maid, dressed all in black, and her old Sudanese chauffeur. My mother always greeted her with genuine enthusiasm, and my father would be called home from wherever he was. In those days, before the expropriation and nationalization decrees impoverished our family, my parents kept what was called an open house; drop-in guests were always welcome. The problem was the justifiable indignation of the aunt or uncle whose turn had been passed over. Whenever my grandmother was expected at someone else's house and was more than a few minutes late, her known weakness for my father made him the usual suspect, and we would receive irate phone calls from one aunt or another demanding to know if *Sit* Luli was at our house.

This is such a cynical world that a disclaimer might be necessary here: The competition for *Sit* Luli's good graces among her adult children had nothing to do with material considerations. Long before the time I am writing about, she had already deeded over to her children all her property. She had never known how to handle money—literally as well as figuratively. For that matter, she had long since turned over the running of the household, first to her oldest daughter, then, when that daughter married and moved away, to her daughter-in-law. My aunt, as tall and commanding as my grandmother was small and unassertive, ran the household with an iron hand during her tenure, disciplining her younger brothers by making them stand in a corner with the heavy bunch of household keys hanging from around their ears. One uncle, to the day he died, claimed that his ears stuck out from his head as much as they did as a result of frequent disciplining.

The affection and solicitude my father and his siblings displayed toward *Sit* Luli was genuine: partly the culturally ingrained devotion due to a mother, and partly a protective response to her childlike nature. But she could be unexpectedly observant and show surprising presence of mind.

She once came to stay at our villa, to keep an eye on things while my parents were abroad. Within days she had discovered what my parents had not in a year: that the Belgian nanny they had hired to look after my brother and me was vicious. She sneaked out of the house at night to drink and meet a man. I was just a few months old, but my brother was nearly three. To keep him from crying or trying to get out of his crib and calling attention to her absence, she threatened him with a bogeyman waiting just outside the window of his room. One night as *Sit* Luli was taking the air on the long verandah that ran from one end of the front of our villa to the other, she stumbled against a warm body in the dark. Weak-sighted as she was, she couldn't make out who it was crouching there. It would have seemed in character for her to scream or faint, but she did no such thing. She grabbed the crouching figure by its coarse hair and demanded to know who it was.

"It's me, *Sit*, the gardener's boy," whined a voice.

She made him tell her the whole story: how the *khawagaya*, the foreign nanny, had made him stand there in front of the window in the dark, his rough hair sticking up all over his head like a bogeyman, to scare my brother. *Sit* Luli gave the boy a light smack on the ears and told him to go back to his quarters. She well knew where the blame lay. She immediately telegraphed my parents to come straight home and deal with the nanny.

I wish my firsthand memories of my grandmother were not so rare. I do remember that when I was eight, I was coached to offer her my condolences on her brother's death. "May the rest of his life prolong yours," I was made to repeat, over and over, in the car as we drove toward Garden City. I was especially warned not to confuse that phrase with another formulaic phrase proffered on happy occasions like engagements and weddings: "May your turn be next." The two phrases sounded very similar in Arabic. Sure enough, when I stood before my grandmother and the dozens of ladies assembled in the salon to pay their condolences, I blurted out: "May your turn be next." There was a moment of horrified silence—Egyptians are great believers in ill omens—and then *Sit* Luli laughed.

All the same, though, she was dead within the year.

I'm sure her obituary listed her as "Karimat so-and-so Pasha," "*Haram* of . . . " and Mother of . . . " followed by a three-column list of relatives, as was proper and fitting. Even President Nasser—and this was at the height of his animosity against my uncle the pasha—sent a representative to walk in her funeral cortege and sign the book of condolences. Dying just when she did, she was spared the worst of what was to follow: her sons sent into political exile; her family's fortune expropriated and nationalized.

The best eulogy I heard anyone say about *Sit* Luli came from my other grandmother, my mother's mother. This was nearly twenty years later, when I was grown up and married myself.

"Your mother never knew what it was to have a mother-in-law," she said

"But how do you mean?" I asked. "She had *Sit* Luli. I was eight when she passed away, so Mummy must have had her as a mother-in-law for over ten years."

"*Sit* Luli was never a mother-in-law," my other grandmother repeated, giving the word its full weight in Arabic. So I understood.

Now my maternal grandmother was another proposition altogether. She was almost a whole generation younger than *Sit* Luli, and as tall and generously built as the other was small and frail. My maternal grandmother was a force of nature, a formidable woman. Although my two grandmothers were born into similar situations in life and lived under the same restrictions on women in their era, they were as different as two women could be.

We called my maternal grandmother Nanou, a corruption of grandmother—it is the fate of grandmothers to be saddled forever with the name bestowed on them by the babyish pronunciation of the first grandchild, and perpetuated by subsequent grandchildren. I have seen a photo of her as a little girl, and even then she looked determined: feet firmly planted, tummy proudly protruding, holding her father's hand as they pose for a formal portrait. She wears a large hat with a ribbon, a ruffled, low-sashed dress, white stockings, and buckled shoes. Her father cuts an imposing figure with his aloof monocled gaze and the watch fob dangling from the pocket of his frock coat.

Nanou married at seventeen and found herself a widow at thirty-six, with six children ranging in age from eighteen to six. Her father was deceased; her only brother had married an Englishwoman and was squandering away his inheritance in England. She had never been close to her husband's family. She found herself with no male relative to rely on. It was assumed she would remarry quickly; she had been a wealthy woman in her own right, and her husband's sudden heart attack left her even more so. A woman alone, in Egypt in that era, was lost. But Nanou never so much as entertained the idea of remarriage. She devoted herself to raising her six children and singlehandedly managed her considerable land holdings and property, along with her children's inheritance from their father.

It is hard to imagine that she managed to deal, on her own, with overseers and *fellahin*, with agents and the state-appointed trustees of her husband's estate, with her daughters' suitors and with her sons' peccadilloes. But manage she did, with acumen and authority. She met all the expenses of her children and her large household out of her own pocket, refusing to touch a penny of the children's trust funds. She prided herself on handing over their untouched inheritances to each of them, when they reached their majority in the case of the boys, or when they married in the case of the girls, since they married in their teens, as was the custom.

Most important, in her own eyes, she managed to do all this without a breath of scandal ever touching her or her children. But she—and they—paid a certain price for this unblemished reputation. Nanou was almost pathologically prudish; she sheltered her daughters to an extent unprecedented even for that generation. In a way, I too have paid a second-hand price for her prudishness, through my mother's inhibitions and educational policies, but that's another story.

By the time I knew Nanou, her greatest battles were behind her, and she had mellowed into the most loving and generous grandmother imaginable, but we grandchildren were still careful to use one of her many preferred euphemisms for all kinds of expressions that offended her Victorian sensibilities. I remember her as a tall, heavily-built woman who nevertheless took comically tiny steps, no doubt in an effort to minimize her stature. She was always exhorting my girl cousins and me to be more ladylike. When we were teenagers, and clomped about in the clunky shoes that were the fashion in the seventies, she would shake her head and tell us we sounded like *ghaffar*, night watchmen doing their rounds on country estates. She had learned to play some classical pieces on the piano as a child, and when we played our Beatles records for her she was shocked. "That's *Zar*," she pronounced, referring to spirit exorcism rituals practiced in certain devotee circles in Egypt. At the time we laughed and thought Nanou didn't know what she was talking about, but of course her ears had recognized the African rhythms lurking at the heart of rock music. Only recently did I learn that *Zar* rituals were imported to Egypt from sub-Saharan Africa.

After her children were grown and gone, my grandmother moved, alone, to a villa in Heliopolis, a suburb of Cairo that was in those days still constructed in strict compliance with the architectural vision of Baron Empain, the Belgian businessman and developer. Every morning Nanou telephoned each of her daughters for a chat that lasted at least an hour. Every Friday, the sabbath in Muslim countries, the entire family gathered around her table; anyone who was absent needed a good excuse. Children were kept busy cranking up batches of homemade ice cream on the verandah until everyone had arrived and the bountiful buffet in the dining room was ready. Nanou's cook was a short, middle-aged woman literally as wide as she was tall; we nicknamed her the box because of her square shape. Her enormous bulk apparently made her quite desirable in some circles; suitors would come to pick her up on a motorcycle on her days off. We children would rush to the balcony to watch, giggling, as she nimbly straddled the motorcycle's back seat and roared off, a wildly improbable sight.

Every feast, every event on the calendar was marked by my grandmother. When the Lesser Feast came around, she sent us boxes of homemade, date-stuffed cookies; for the spring festival, sweet brioche molded in the shape of ducks, with colored boiled eggs in their beaks. Nanou ran her household a little like a cottage industry, distributing the overflow to her children's homes. Every so often her driver would come to our door bearing baskets of mangoes from her orchards, or gifts of homemade jam and various specialties. She had a special jam-maker, a woman who came with her daughters by train from Nanou's farm, bearing fruits in season: the long, hard red dates in the fall; oranges for marmalade and candied peel in winter; apricots and strawberries in spring; grapes, figs, and guavas in summer. In my grandmother's kitchen they cooked up huge vats of jam and ladled them into knee-high jars; some were destined for the larder and the rest to be distributed among the family's households.

The jam-maker and her daughters also made rosewater and orange blossom essence in a special condensation contraption; my grandmother always perfumed the water she served with a drop of these attars. One year they pounded blackened almonds to make kohl; it had become fashionable again to wear kohl, and Nanou didn't want any of us girls putting impure, store-bought kohl on our eyes.

Unlike my paternal grandmother, Nanou rarely visited her children's houses; she expected them to come to her. Wherever she went, the family followed for the Friday get-together. In spring she would retire for a few weeks to her country house, and a cortege of cars would make the two-hour drive on Fridays to join her for the day. We were rewarded with farm treats of fresh clotted cream and buttery pastry, and we took long walks in the mango orchards. The summers she spent in her villa on the Corniche facing the sea in Alexandria, a rambling, humidity-ridden, three-story house teeming with aunts, uncles, and cousins. In Alexandria, Friday dinners were a feast of fresh fish and shellfish prepared a dozen different ways.

Among her grandchildren, Nanou had a weakness for boys in general, and among the girls, for the prettiest; but she spoiled us all. She always remembered birthdays with gifts of jewelry for the girls and money for the boys. I treasure the delicate Art Deco brooches and the little-girl bracelets with adjustable wristbands she handed down to me. When she went on a pilgrimage to Mecca she brought back Gulf pearls by the pound and had her jeweler make up strings of necklaces for all her granddaughters. "Love," she would say, "is like water," meaning that love flows from the older to the younger, and not vice versa, just as water flows downhill and not up.

I remember I once made Nanou an eggshell "doll"; I had hollowed it out and painted a face on it, gluing on twine for hair and dressing it up in a tiny headscarf like a babushka. She kept it on her dresser for years. Although I wasn't the oldest of her grandchildren, I was the first to get married and the first to give her a great-grandchild, and I like to think that gave her joy. She ordered delicate, hand-embroidered and lace-trimmed outfits for the baby as soon as she heard I was expecting.

I was living abroad at the time, but had gone home to Egypt to recover from severe morning sickness. One Ramadan night, my cousins and I were lounging around idly at Nanou's when it occurred to us that it would be entertaining to bring in a spiritualist medium. We sent for a man who had a reputation for being able to call random spirits into his presence. He turned out to be a sharp-eyed, scruffy-bearded fellow who right away lost some of his credibility when one of my cousins tested his psychic powers. "Is Nadine expecting a boy or a girl?" She asked.

He looked from one to the other of the group of girls; I was only four months pregnant and still flat as pita bread.

"Which one of you is Nadine?" he blurted. Then, to cover his confusion, he intoned: "The knowledge of the womb is hidden knowledge."

We went ahead gamely, following the medium's instructions to set up a table covered with a cloth in the middle of the salon and draw chairs all around it. We turned off all the lights, sat down in a circle, and held hands, the excitement building in spite of our skepticism. Just then the door opened briskly and Nanou walked in. "What's this? A séance? Well, if you want to amuse your-selves, that's fine, but not you, Nadine; you come out with me right now."

"But Nanou," I wailed, "it's just for fun. You don't really believe in spirits, do you?"

"But you can scare yourself into miscarrying or harming that baby. You come with me right now."

It's one of the disappointments in my life that I never did get to attend a spirit séance. Later my cousins swore that the tablecloth floated around the room, the chairs shook, and the windows slammed spontaneously. Knowing them, I am sure they exaggerated wildly to make me envious.

Months later, when I went to the hospital to deliver, Nanou was there. I had a very long and difficult labor, and my poor mother climbed to the highest floor of the hospital building to be out of earshot of my screams because she couldn't bear to hear them any more. When I recovered from the anesthesia, however, I bounced back quickly. I sat up in my hospital bed and announced, before the assembled relatives, that I was hungry. Nanou hushed me, embarrassed.

"What will your in-laws think!" she whispered in my ear. "You're supposed to be all washed out after the terrible ordeal you've been through. Just lie quietly until everyone's gone, and I promise I'll send the driver to get you anything you want. Almond macaroons from Lappas? You love those, and it's good for the milk."

"And pistachio *loukoum*," I whispered back. "Oh, and Nanou, *marrons glacés* from Groppi."

Nanou lived to see the rest of her grandchildren marry, and many of her great-grandchildren born; she lived to see all of her daughters widowed or divorced; she was to nurse a sick grandchild for years; she was to mediate the estrangement between two of her sons; she was to suffer through the long, har-rowing illness of a third son only to lose him in the end. As the years took their toll on her, she took to her bed for most of the day, and tended to listen more than to speak, but her mental acuity remained undiminished.

The family still gathered around her table on Fridays, and she still made the effort to have her cook prepare everyone's favorite dish. My favorite, when small green apples were in season, was a very unusual dish of chicken baked with okra and apples. It is not an Egyptian dish, and I have never eaten it anywhere but at my grandmother's. No one else has a recipe for it. After Nanou passed away, I thought of trying to recreate it from memory, but then I decided against it. It was her specialty, and it is fitting that I no longer eat it now that she is gone. Some people honor the memory of others by recreating parts of the past they associate with the loved one; others honor their memory by leaving it alone.

That is a lesson I learned from her. My father's favorite dessert was rice pudding, baked with cream and raisins. On Fridays at her house, it was invariably on the dessert buffet along with the other desserts. Nanou loved my father more as a son than a son-in-law. When he passed away, five years before her own death, she was devastated. I went abroad shortly after that, for years. The first time I came back to Cairo to visit, and came to Friday dinner at Nanou's, I looked at the laden dessert buffet and unthinkingly remarked that there was no rice pudding.

"That was your father's favorite," she replied reproachfully. "We don't make it in this house any more."

And that is how I knew when Nanou died, although I was in the States and no one told me. I had a dream that Nanou and my father were eating rice pudding, and I woke up crying, because in my heart, I knew. I started crying even before I called home and asked about Nanou, and before I heard the fatal words: "May the rest of her life prolong yours." I am not one who believes in visions or spirits; I only know that I dreamed of my father after his death, and of Nanou after hers, even though I didn't know she was dead. Those were the only times. Perhaps, if you are a person who is not particularly permeable to the spirit world, it takes great love for those departed to reach you in a vision. Great love, on both sides of the ultimate divide, even if love is like water.


## *Faiza W. Shereen*
## GIFTS OF TIME

Egypt 2003　English

Faiza W. Shereen was born in Alexandria, and emigrated to the United States as a student in 1973. She received a B.A. in English language and literature from Alexandria University, an M.A. in literature from the University of Dayton, and a Ph.D. in literary theory from the University of Cincinnati. Shereen's career as an educator and an academic began in Egypt, where she taught briefly at Alexandria University and Tanta University. In the United States, she has taught on several campuses, and became professor of English at the University of Dayton. Since 2005, she has been director of the International Center at California State Polytechnic University, Pomona.

Multilingual from childhood, Shereen has pursued her interest in languages as expressions of tradition and ways of being. This interest has culminated in her research on North African—most particularly Moroccan—writing, where she examines the intersections among Berber, Arabic, and French; oral and written traditions; the indigenous, colonial, and postcolonial; the feminine and the patriarchal. Shereen has received two Fulbright grants and an American Institute for Maghreb Studies grant to pursue her research in Morocco, and is working on a critical anthology of Moroccan writing.

Shereen has written creative fiction, poetry, and a play, *The Country Within*, which has been performed in several venues. The story "Gifts of Time" received a Literary Prize for Creative Writing in 2004 from the Radius of Arab American Writers, Inc. (RAWI). This previously unpublished story traverses continents, decades, and viewpoints as it tells the story of several generations of an Egyptian family, which is spread across the globe, but remains united by love, memory, and a very special talisman. *Akhra* is "the afterlife"; *inshallah* means "God willing"; *alhamdu-lillah* is an expression for "Thank God"; *mabrouk* is a way of saying "congratulations"; and a *hanem* is a lady.

*Amira Nowaira*

✦

I finally caught sight of his tall, lean figure as he made his way among the passengers pouring out of the jetway and into the terminal. The flight was late, and the passengers all looked drained after the long direct flight from Cairo. If they smiled, it was that tired smile of relief at finally being able to move their numb limbs. Not he. A big, warm smile and quick, long strides, and he was wrapping his arms around me with his usual bright exuberance. In the split second that he raised his arms to hug me, something caught the light, and I saw the familiar rectangular gold frame on his wrist. My heart sank. Had Father died?

As we walked to the baggage area, he talked about Mother and Father, and my moment of panic became embarrassingly unreasonable. But his account brought about the usual complicated feelings of anxiety and guilt and nostalgia—feelings usually dormant until someone returns from over there with concrete accounts of the aging loved ones, the lost realities, the absences of familiar ways and places, and the new realities that are gradually replacing our old world.

In the car I asked about the watch. "Yes," he said, "I was sitting with Father after lunch one day, in the front room, in the patch of sun by the French windows, you know, and Father asked to see the watch I was wearing. When I took it off, he took his off and said, 'let's exchange.' He put mine on, and I put on the Patek Philippe."

"What does this mean?" I asked, hardly able to say what was on my mind: Father thinks this is the last time he will see my brother. My brother remained silent. Then he sighed, and I saw the moisture in his eyes.

I kept trying to visualize the scene. They have just had lunch. Father walks slowly to the bathroom to wash his large, beautiful hands—miraculously youthful at ninety-one. He then makes his way slowly, leaning on his cane, to the front room at the end of the long corridor—the room that had at one time been

Assem's own bedroom. Now used as a sitting room, it is regularly occupied by Father in the afternoons because of the sunny warmth that fills it. It faces west, and has long French windows that open onto the balcony circling the north and west sides of my parents' home. A comfortable armchair is placed right by the window, and Father sits there and reads on winter afternoons, until the red disc of the sun disappears into the sea there at the horizon, next to Qaitbay. Assem pulls up a chair and sits across from Father. They talk about us—our life in the United States—and Father is consoled by Assem's confident descriptions and prognostications, reassured that the uprooting and separation may at least not have been meaningless sacrifices.

He sits deeply in the armchair, his woolen plaid *robe-de-chambre* neatly wrapped over his chest, in an aura of dignity born of power graciously surrendered. He rests his elbows on the armrests and holds his hands up in front of him, his fingers slightly spread, the fingers of one hand touching those of the other at the tips, in exact alignment. He hungrily absorbs what Assem brings of our lives in Ohio. His eyes are intent and focused and look larger than they are through the thick lenses of his glasses. Every now and then he nods a couple of times. Is it approval? Or the expression of a strong wish to confirm that all was for the best?

Assem picks up the paper and reads the headlines. They shift to a discussion of current events. There's a long silence, and Father is looking out of the window. He suddenly turns to Assem and, in a deliberately light and casual tone, asks him to see his watch. The exchange occurs in silence, and then Father changes the subject.

It was in this same setting that I last saw Father a year later. I had come from the States for an extended period with my family, and we were going to stay in Cairo. I took a two-day trip to Alexandria to see him, thinking to return for a longer stay once I had my children settled in school. We had had stuffed quails for lunch (of which he ate no more than a few bites). After lunch, sitting in the sun, I had told him the truth: We would be in Cairo, and I would only visit occasionally. Mother had led him to believe that we would stay with them in Alex. "He's been looking forward so much to your being here," she had said. "But he will *have* to be told!" I exclaimed. It was a painful disappointment. "I will visit every week," I assured him. He just nodded.

The next day I left for Cairo, and the following morning I received a call: He had died in his sleep.

◆

As a child, in those days before school, I used to wait for the bell ring that was Father's. I knew the time, for it was when the warm aromas of the meal, almost ready, invitingly wafted out of the kitchen, when Mohamed, the *soufragi* went into his small closet in the pantry room and changed into his majestic *shahi* caftan and replaced his skullcap with the white gauze *emma*, getting ready to serve at table. As he turned his key in the front door, Father would ring the bell, so that the servants could come and carry in the fresh fruit he brought home daily from the greengrocer's. In the winter it was oranges and tangerines, bananas, and apples; in the summer, the heavy juicy watermelons, elongated yellow melons (as I've never seen elsewhere), grapes and mangoes and pears and peaches, and sometimes figs or fresh dates. Strawberries were only in the spring.

I'd run to the front door to greet him, and I'd hold his free hand (one was always occupied with his cane) and walk with him the length of the corridor and into his and Mother's apartment on the north side. Their rooms were always remarkably cooler than ours, even in the summer months. When my father came home, he brought the outside with him: the smell of newspapers, cigars, and business conversation. As a child, I did not like any of that. I'd follow him into the soft coolness of his room (with the window open, but the shutters down—just so); I'd wait for him to take off his suit and the smell of outside. I'd stand by while he removed his fez and I'd take it to its place, and generally attend to him like a valet as he took off shoes and socks, tie and shirt (to be replaced with fresh, starched ones in the afternoon). He would also remove his wristwatch, and as a part of the solemn ritual of my duties, I would place it on the night table by his bed. He would lie down to rest for a bit as we waited to be called to lunch. And now that he mellowed in his rippling linen shirt, shedding the brittle dryness of the midday dust, I spoke to him.

I would put my head down next to his on the pillow, staring at the frosted glass in the ceiling, at the gentle light that shone through like the sky at dawn.

I often looked at the book he was reading, wondering if I would ever read like that. I wished he would leave the book and, like Mother, take me into some magically inhabited space of waterfalls and fairies and pearly treasures and song.

Instead, he seemed to be patiently waiting for the time I could meet him in his text—that place outside my comfort, where life is inscribed in the dry ink of newspapers, documents illegible, cigar ash, and serious conversation.

I feared that fantastic place. Would I survive?

Cuddling closer, with the moving breeze from the open window to remind me, I somehow knew that this borrowed comfort was not forever.

I remember when he taught me to tell the time. He picked up the Patek Philippe and explained the movement of the two arms, and the little one for seconds in the embedded circle below. And I asked, when he had explained the twenty-four hours, then the week, the month, the year, the seasons—I asked: "And then?"

"Then what?"

"And . . . forever?"

He smiled and said, "That's all we know!"

"Until the *akhra*, you mean?"

"Perhaps."

"Then there is heaven, and we all meet there? And Papa el Kebir and Nanna and everyone?"

"That's too far away to think about."

"*Umm* Saneya says we must always think about the end."

"So what else does the good woman tell you?"

"In the afternoon when she's finished her housework, I sit with her on the balcony and she tells me about the good djinn and the bad djinn. I like the stories, but I'm not scared when she says the bad djinn will come if I'm naughty!"

When did these midday encounters stop? I guess when I went to school. That new chapter must have put an end to the thousand and one nights of childhood. Later, as a teenager, I found it a tedious chore when he called me to help put things away as he removed his formal suit and tie and put on his house clothes.

✦

### The Mediterranean

It is 1932. Dr. Masry is sailing back to Alexandria on the *Esperia*. His father-in-law had insisted that they all spend the summer in Aix-les-Bains. It is a relief for him to be coming home, for though the trip had been a welcome change for all, he is a man of habit, and routine gives him comfort.

Sitting on the deck, scrutinizing the horizon for the African shore, he is enjoying a few moments of solitude when his mother-in-law, Sara Hanem, joins him. He greets her warmly. Her delicate ways, her reserve, and her kindness to all around her have always appealed to him. He has often secretly wished that his own wife—vibrant, headstrong, and daring—had been a little more like her mother. He found immeasurable comfort in her subdued and feminine ways.

"Masry Bey, *inshallah*, the trip was pleasant for you."

"*Alhamdu-lillah*. Your company made it all a pleasure."

"Farida and the child have enjoyed the beaches so much."

"Yes, she does in Alexandria, too." He is unable to hide his opinion that Alexandrian beaches were just as good. "But all the casinos and the shopping—that we can't offer at home. And Sousou, of course, is having a ball with her cousins." For their party had included two of his sisters-in-law and their children, as well. He smiles, thinking of his wife's delight at her winnings in the casino and the endless shopping at Galeries Lafayette. "The Basha bought Farida a new divan for her boudoir, and a set of St. Louis crystal. He still spoils his daughter." Was he resentful? After all, with her husband there to provide, what need had she of her father's excessive generosity? A less innocent audience would have heard a trace of disapproval in the tone, but Sara Hanem, even if she herself didn't share her husband's and her daughter's delight in some of these Western forms of entertainment, never suspected subtexts, so she fails to register the critical tone. She smiles.

"May you see your own daughter a beautiful wife, and spoil her in your turn."

"His goodness overwhelms us." And this time Masry's tone had lost its sarcastic edge, for Sara Hanem's genuineness had shamed and disarmed him.

She, changing the subject: "And your own trip to Geneva? Was it fruitful?" He had left the party to their beaches and casinos, and had gone for a week to visit a surgeon in Geneva, an old friend from his days in medical school.

"Yes. It was good to see Armand. The visit to the hospital was useful, too. Progress in the medical field is happening at such a rapid pace that I can imagine a time in the very near future when our medical practices will be as barbaric and primitive as those of the Middle Ages appear to us now." Then, lest he bored her with his professional interests: "I bought myself this wristwatch." He smiles at her. "I guess I, too, can be extravagant!" He removes the watch from his wrist and hands it to her. Up until then, he had only worn a chain watch on his waistcoat. She admires the modern watch with its rectangular shape, the curved glass, and the fine, gold frame. "It is very fine. *Mabrouk*. May you wear it in joy."

The sun is slowly disappearing on the horizon; the ship, rocking slightly on the darkening blue, is like a jewel as its lights reflect on the surface of the water, sparkling like the skin of diamonds. Dr. Masry accompanies his mother-in-law to the dining room. They are met by his wife, resplendent in a shimmering ocher evening gown, leaning on the arm of a tall, handsome man, his glossy black hair and twirled mustache set off against his fair complexion. He has an imposing presence—that, coupled with the beauty of the woman on his arm, makes heads turn to them. He is Masry's father-in-law.

✦

### Tunis

It is 1964, and Masry's eldest daughter, named Sara after her now-deceased grandmother, is the wife of Egypt's ambassador in Tunis. She is the child, Sousou, who had traveled with her parents and grandparents more than thirty years before on the *Esperia*. As Sara Hanem had predicted, Masry is now the doting father that he had resented in *Saïd* Pasha. He sits on the plane bringing him from Zurich to Tunis, where he will spend a week with his daughter and son-in-law before returning to Alexandria. He recalls with affection the mother-in-law who had died in his own house, more than ten years ago now, and once more the thought crosses his mind that he would have liked it if his own wife had been more like her: a mild-mannered, old-fashioned *hanem*. His wife, Farida, who had nothing but impatience for tradition, loved everything modern. She was, perhaps, a generation too early in the world. Where did the years go, he wonders, suddenly feeling old. And now their youngest daughter— born too late in life, he felt sadly—was only six. Would he live to rejoice in seeing her grown up and happy, as he does now with his older children? He touches his pocket and reassures himself: The pretty little watch with the beveled crystal is tucked in there for her.

✦

### Alexandria

My father was going to have surgery in Switzerland, and I just didn't want him to leave. Mother said it was going to make him all better, but I would have preferred it if he didn't have to go.

I had tiptoed out of my bedroom when I couldn't sleep, and there they were—he in the armchair by the fire, she reclining on the sofa across. I liked to see them both at home; and I suddenly felt lonely.

She saw me cowering in the hallway and called me to her.

"What are you doing up at this hour?" she said, though the tone was not chiding. Then she gathered me up in her arms, and the sweet smell of her, so familiar, made the world cozy again.

They talked the talk I didn't understand, though the voices' rhythms spoke to me. Why must he take an airplane and be alone, up there in the sky? And if the plane fell? I did not want to think of it, because something in my middle hurt when I did.

The next morning my uncle came to pick him up, when the ashes were still warm in the fireplace. I hung on the rails of the door after kissing him goodbye, and at the last minute he asked, "What do you want from Switzerland?"

"A watch, Papa, a pretty watch!"

And he was gone. I waited for twenty-eight days, for he went to visit my sister afterward in Tunis. I waited for him and for my watch.

✦

### Tunis

For weeks Sara has been preparing for her father's visit. She would take him to visit the very neighborhood from which her maternal great-great-grandfather had originally come. He had traveled with a thousand camels bearing goods to trade in Egypt, riding along the Mediterranean coast. But once in Egypt, he had married and settled in Cairo for good. She has even found the street bearing the family name in the town of Sidi Bou Saïd, just outside Tunis on the way to old Carthage. She orders the meals she knows her father loves, and holds a huge banquet at the embassy in his honor. But she feels somewhat disappointed when he is finally there. He is mostly tired, and simply wants to stay at home with her. Was it the surgery and the awful radiation treatment that discolored his skin and spoiled his good looks forever? He still has that charming smile, with the dimple in the chin. And the bright, sharp eyes. And the gentle yet confident surgeon's hands—long, smooth fingers, beautifully shaped nails, and the youthful skin—no spots, no veins.

Dr. Masry is just happy being with his first-born. Her husband is a demanding man, but a real *seigneur*, he would later tell his wife. Still, he is glad when at last it is time to go home. The evening before his departure, they attend an open-air concert. It is to his liking; much less commotion and crowds than the same kind of occasion in Egypt. He feels a certain warm pride, sitting next to his daughter, as she graciously fulfills her public role, *Madame l'Embassadrice*. They drive home before midnight, and he kisses his daughter goodnight by the fountain in the courtyard.

In his room, he sits on the edge of the bed and, in an automatic gesture, touches his left wrist with his right hand to remove his watch. It is not there. He looks around him—has he already taken it off inadvertently? But it is nowhere. He calls his daughter; they look everywhere; they send the driver to search the spot where they sat at the concert. No watch is to be found. He had worn the Patek Philippe every day of his life since that day he had shown it to his mother-in-law on the *Esperia*, and he had formed one of those silly attachments one develops for things. Sara knows it and is pained that the occurrence might spoil the memory of their time together for him.

✦

### Ohio, 1996

Assem walks into the jeweler's on the corner of Ludlow and Main, where he regularly takes his watches to Bob Garbadian for repair. Bob is the nephew of the Armenian professor with whom Assem has developed a friendship over the years. Their friendship had grown over the plates of stuffed grape leaves and syrupy baklava that Hagob's wife would make for them from time to time.

"Great to see you, Assem!" Bob's warm greeting is accompanied by kisses on both cheeks, but it is the way he pronounces the fricative *A* in Assem, producing the sound deep in his throat, that adds the sense of kinship.

"My father gave me this watch," Assem explains as he hands the Patek Philippe to his friend. "I don't think it was ever opened or cleaned."

The jeweler examines the watch carefully, consults a thick catalogue, then puts the watch down on the counter and takes off his glasses. "I wouldn't touch it! Are you aware of its value?"

"I know it's a good watch."

"Bet your life it is! There's more than your house is worth here! This is a limited edition from 1932, and worth well over a hundred thousand dollars!"

"You're kidding!"

"No kidding! If you want to have it cleaned, take it to Switzerland to Patek Philippe."

Later, as he sits eating his regular lunch of soup and salad at Liz's restaurant, Assem begins planning his trip. Not a bad excuse for a jaunt in Europe!

✦

"Hello?"

"There's this great restaurant where they make an excellent Caesar salad. I could get you there, fed, and back at your desk in less than an hour. Shall I pick you up in ten minutes?" My brother's voice rang with his usual exuberance and determination on the phone.

I laughed.

"O.K. then—ten minutes, in front of your building."

They were special, those midday rendezvous with Assem; he'd whisk me off and bring me back to the office, and the space in between was like a breath of fresh air. Whatever we talked about, he was a conversation partner who brought fresh thought and passion to the subject. Sometimes his passion was overwhelming, but his convictions were those of an artist, not a politician, and that quality, coupled with his conviviality, brightened any encounter with him. That day we talked about Roman landscapes, the Alps, and *Umm* Saneya's "Mont Blanc," the chestnut dessert named after that sublime mountain.

"And so you're off to Switzerland in June?" I asked, when he told me about the visit to Bob. "Yes, I'm sure the watch needs cleaning, and it can't wait!" I smiled. We all knew how much he loved traveling, and how he could only think of a pleasure trip if it took him to Europe. Egypt he visited out of duty, for family; and traveling in the States was only, for him, more of the same.

"Absolutely! And I'll look up Father's old friend, Monsieur Horovitz, the jeweler on Cherif Street who left Egypt in the early sixties. Do you remember him?"

"Vaguely. Isn't he the Jewish guy who refused to go to Israel with his family in the forties? He alone of his family stayed in Egypt, until the events after Suez forced him to leave?"

"That's him. He settled in Zurich, and Papa visited him there."

✦

### Zurich

It's chilly, on a June morning in Zurich, and Assem is standing at a street corner, trying to figure out where he is in relation to Bahnhofstrasse. He's peering into the street map and holding a business card in his hand. The street is empty. An older gentleman in a gray hat and coat passes him, and Assem turns to ask for directions.

"What are you looking for on Bahnhofstrasse? It's a long street."

Assem hands the gentleman the card. "This jewelry shop."

The gentleman looks at the card, then quickly raises his eyes and scrutinizes Assem's face. His expression is puzzled, then searching, and then it transforms suddenly, as though a mask had dropped, and the face is full of emotion. "Dr. Masry's son!"

A moment of silence as Assem processes what he has just heard, then he laughs incredulously at this miraculous recognition. "Yes, how did you know? You knew my father?"

"I am Horovitz! I'm the person you're looking for!"

For Horovitz, the following few moments feel like hundreds of gates opening upon a history that teased them by its absent presence. For Assem, this extraordinary encounter is a manifestation of destiny. They walk together, crossing the bridge, and sit at a café on Limatquai. They sit at a sidewalk table, sipping their coffees, much as half a century before, Horovitz used to have his morning coffee with Dr. Masry at Unica, the coffeehouse across from his shop on Cherif Street in Alexandria.

"Your father was a remarkable man." Horovitz speaks now with a tone of intimate affection. "He was one of the most hardworking men I ever knew in all the years I lived in Egypt." Then, with a twinkle in his eye: "We played more than we worked there, you know." He asks many questions, about Assem and his life in the States, about the family, and gradually the talk turns to reminiscence.

"When you were a little boy, I used to carry you on my shoulders when we went to get your father from his office at the end of a day."

"Yes, I remember. Even then, your hair was silver!"

"I had to carry you on my shoulders because the clinic was so crowded that you would have been squashed and crushed by the patients. They used to call your father 'the god of eyes.' To all these poor people who came to him from all over the country, he was the giver of sight, the most precious gift of all. He only charged those who could pay, but he treated and operated on all who came to him."

"I know."

Once more Horovitz asks about Assem's work and interests, and once more the conversation drifts back to the old times and reminiscences of the cherished friend.

Assem feels a little awkward. In the presence of this old friend of his father, as always with the older generation from the old country, he feels there are rules of deference to be observed. Almost sixty, he thought, amused at himself, and still able to be humbled emotionally simply by the presence of a member of that privileged generation.

"And you . . . your family?" He asks, wondering what was proper to ask.

"My dear son, there is none. My sister died many years ago. The rest are in Israel, and I don't even know them. I never married."

"Never married?" Assem had always heard his father speak of "Horovitz and Marianne."

"There was Marianne, of course, but we never married."

"I heard my father speak of Marianne."

Leaning forward, the silver-haired man speaks slowly, articulating every syllable with precision. "She was the most beautiful woman in Alexandria."

Assem looks at him questioningly.

"Her family was Greek Orthodox, mine Jewish. We were together eighteen years, from 1944 until I left Egypt in 1962. She died nine years ago. In Athens. We should have been together. *Ah, mon jeune! Si jeunesse savait et si vieillesse pouvait!*"

After a long silence, Horovitz turns to Assem in a gesture of sudden excitement. "Do you come to Europe often?"

"About once a year. I like to spend my vacations here when I can."

"Good. Very good." Horovitz puts his hand in his pocket, pulls out a keychain, removes a key from it, and places it on the table. Then he pulls a business card and a Mont Blanc fountain pen from his breast pocket and writes an address on the back of the card. "This," he says, "is the address of a small property I own in a town near Nice on the Côte D'Azure. It's called Menton." He sits back, looking at Assem with a big smile of satisfaction. "It's a charming vacation place." He smiles again. "It's yours any time you want it. Just let me know whenever you plan to use it. I go only in the off-season myself."

The offer is made like the conclusion of a deal, and the old gentleman will listen to no argument. The place is hardly used. It would be a good thing to have some life in it. Had he had a son of his own . . . It is decided. And when Assem tries to thank him, he simply says, "It's a very small token in memory of a very generous man."

Assem spends most of his few days in Zurich in the company of the old Alexandrian, listening to his accounts of a world that had disappeared without a trace, except for those memories that erupt out of the dead past when an encounter such as theirs explodes the boundaries of experience.

At the airport, Assem shakes the old gentleman's hand. *"Je suis ravi que le hazard nous a reunis."*

*"Mon cher ami, comme l'a si bien dit le philosophe de cette époque: 'Il n'y a pas de hazard; il n'y a que des rendez-vous.'"* The watch had been duly cleaned, polished, and made to look new. Upon his return to the States, Assem places it in a safe box at his bank, and only takes it out to wear occasionally, in order to keep it running.

✦

### Alexandria, 1964

There was a lot of rejoicing when Father arrived. I remember running back and forth between the kitchen—watching as the very special lunch was being prepared—and the front hall, where I could hear the first noises that would signal his arrival. And then he was standing there, in the middle of the living room, his nose and upper lip discolored where the pigmentation had been lost as a result of the radiation treatment. Papa would never look the same again. He stretched his arms to pick me up, and I immediately noticed the bare wrist. "Where's the watch?" I asked, and putting me down, he reached into his pocket and brought out a very pretty watch with a glass face beveled at the edges. It was so grown-up!

"This is not it!"

He looked surprised. "You don't like it?"

"No, I mean your watch. Where is your watch?"

"I think I lost it. But take your gift! This watch is for you!"

I liked my watch, but I felt sad. Father's watch was somehow a part of him.

And then, his face! I wore the watch with the beveled glass until I was a teenager—that time when fathers and mothers will not even be forgiven for being parents. I spent more and more time reading through the years of puberty. I needed to separate myself from my mother's world, already clearly not one I wanted to or would join. Her eternal preoccupations with household matters, menus, dressmakers—not to mention an endless round of dinners and lunches with her lady friends—bored me to death. I also couldn't enter my father's world. His was made up of politics, crisp, starched collars, cigars, and strict timetables. I know now how much I loved them both; I didn't then. How one takes for granted a life of unshakable security! Despite all the talk at home about how we had to tighten the belt, how it would never be the way it was in "the good, old days" (days I only heard about but was not old enough to have experienced)—despite that rhetoric of loss and reduced privilege, there was never a sense that that home would not continue to be run in the same way forever. Yet time revealed this vision of constancy as the illusion it was.

✦

## Tunis, 1965

A year after Dr. Masry's visit to Tunis, his son-in-law's term there ends; he would be going to Ankara next. Just about a week before Sara leaves for a brief vacation in Egypt, the driver, Lahcen, has an accident with the embassy car, an antique Buick. No one is hurt, but it is a real nuisance for Sara, who has errands and visits to make before her final departure from this city she has made her home for four years. The car is in the shop, and there is nothing to do but rely on taxis.

Exhausted by the heat and the long waits for taxis in town, she is sitting in the courtyard, enjoying the peace of this shady interior garden one more time, when Lahcen comes in beaming.

"What is it?" She wonders at his excitement.

"We found the Bey's watch!"

"What?!"

"We found the Bey's watch," he repeats incomprehensibly. "It was in the door. When the door was taken apart, there it was! It had fallen in where the window rolls down!"

It takes Sara a few moments to figure out what the old man is talking about. Then he comes up to her and places the Patek Philippe in her hand. The filtered light of the golden dusk is caught in the gleaming shape as she stares down at the jewel in her palm—there it was, Father's watch, the gold shining as ever.

✦

## France, 1997

Assem and his wife, Ellen, arrive at the airport in Paris. This is a very special trip. He had turned sixty in February, and he is offering himself a birthday gift:

a family reunion. And upon old Monsieur Horovitz's insistence, the event is to take place in his villa at Menton in the south of France. Ellen is happy that they will at last be with all the cousins, those first childhood friends about whom he has told her so much, "a thousand and one stories." Their life in Ohio has been happy as the years passed. But something was always missing for Assem, even though he was probably just as at home as she herself was in their Midwestern town. It wasn't that he ever seemed to miss Egypt, or ever complained of any aspect of their American life; on the contrary, he never forgot the problems of home, and was a champion of American values—liberty, democracy, efficiency, all that. But as he aged, more and more, he missed the people. There were stories, memories sweet and innocent, of his childhood and youth shared with the extended family. There were in-jokes; there were perceptions of the world that they shared, and it seemed to her, that *only they* shared. Now they were—those of them who were still alive and could afford it—coming to the reunion he had planned with such joy for so many months. But his sister was back in Ohio; she could afford neither the expense nor the time, her life being consumed by her children and her job. It was all right, for his sister was now with them there, clearly for good.

Assem picks up the van he has rented and they drive south from Paris at a leisurely pace, stopping for meals at specially chosen restaurants, walks in the small towns, and a night at Aix-les-Bains, the ancient spa renowned for its hot springs, its concerts, and its gambling casino. Ellen had wanted to break the trip a little earlier for the night, closer to the mid-point between Paris and the Riviera, but Assem insists on spending the night in Aix-les-Bains.

"My grandfather, you know, liked to come here," he says as they check into the Astoria Hotel. He had picked this particular historic hotel, thinking that it may well be where his grandfather used to stay. The décor is delightfully *Belle Époque*. After a meal of bouillabaisse and sole *menière*, Assem is in his element, strolling in the balmy streets, listening to the baroque music so invitingly filling the air outside, as outdoor concerts always do.

The next morning, Assem is up early, eager to enjoy his breakfast at the café on *Lac du Bourget*. Ellen prefers room service and the luxury of a leisurely morning. He picks her up at noon, and they're soon on the road to Menton. With a breathtaking view of the sea from the hillside, Horovitz's villa is exquisite, and they spend a couple of days getting it ready for all the guests, who will be arriving individually or together over the next few days.

There are four cousins, one second cousin and his wife, and Sara, Assem's oldest sister. They form a circle of nine variations on a theme; as Ellen watches, she notices how alike and how intimate they are, despite the absence and the years. With the exception of the second cousin and his wife, they are all over sixty, and seeing them argue, laugh, talk in three languages at once—a habit she had noticed in her youngest sister-in-law whenever she was in conversation with her Egyptian friends—Ellen can imagine them as adolescents on the beaches of Alexandria.

It is their last day—come too soon—and Assem insists they drive to that special restaurant between Cannes and Nice where the seafood is "the best in the world—except for Abou Kir." The ladies try to talk him into just getting pizza at the street corner, but he won't hear of it. "This one's on me. You'll want to come back next year, just for another seafood lunch."

They drive along the coast. The sky is a magnificent blue, and the air, slightly moist and salty, makes them hungry as they anticipate the meal. Assem has his "captain's hat," on and, indeed, he was the leader and center of this circle of kin. It is simply the natural thing to let him take over; people always put themselves in his hands.

"I want some good pictures to take back to your sister. You promised her," Ellen reminds him. And she walks around the table covered with the remains of the sumptuous lunch, evidence of a communal meal well relished. In the family voices, speaking all at once and in several languages, Ellen hears an affectionate harmony even though she often cannot make out the sense. She clicks the camera again and again—pictures that remain long afterward, as testimonials of that last meal. For it was his last.

Assem gets up, crosses from their table by the beach to the main building of the restaurant, on the other side of the street. He washes his hands in the small sink and, satisfied that the reunion has had its proper closure, pays at the desk. Putting his wallet back in his pocket, he steps off the sidewalk, glancing toward the chattering cousins around their long table, where Ellen is still clicking pictures. He's overcome with love. Suddenly, the tableau—so exquisite, with the blue of the sea barely distinguishable from the blue of the sky, against which the animated figures of his family are etched, his wife making memories with her camera—strangely, this tableau, with a thunderous explosion, dims into a black hole.

Amira is watching Assem as he steps off the sidewalk in his usual long, energetic stride, and then she is struck with horror as she sees the motorcycle turning the corner, and the inevitable collision. She jumps to her feet, her hand on her mouth, screaming internally, but making no sound, and it takes a moment for the others to realize what has happened.

He lay on the ground for a long time, bleeding. When the ambulance finally came, he had been unconscious for a while. He died in the hospital eight hours later, and Ellen was given what remained of that vibrant Egyptian man, American citizen, vacationing in France. There was his wallet, car keys, a packet of Kleenex, the Patek Philippe.

✦

### Ohio

I was getting dinner ready, that terrible June day, and the children were out with their father. The phone rang and it was my nephew from Cairo. He sounded sick, speaking almost too slowly. "It's Assem. He's had an accident," he said, as though he weren't quite sure what that meant.

"Are they all right? Is any one hurt?"

"No, not in the van."

"What do you mean?" I couldn't quite follow.

"Assem was hit by a motorcycle."

"Is he hurt?" A dizzying draining of sensation, as a wave of iciness rushed through my veins.

"Yes." And after a moment's hesitation, "it's not good."

"No. No. Not my brother. No! Impossible! Tell me it's someone else. Not him, please!"

"I'm so sorry!" He was sobbing.

"No! No! No!" I hung up. I couldn't bear to breathe. I ran upstairs, then downstairs again. I could not be still. My heart was racing. When I heard my husband's car in the garage, I ran out to him, muttering something. My husband didn't pay attention, and suddenly I wanted to break something, to hurt someone, to do something violent. I started banging wildly on the door and crying: "My brother is dying!"

They flew Assem's body home, and we buried him in Glens Falls. In a hole in the ground. In a small town in upstate New York. Sara, my oldest sister, had come with him. She wept incessantly. My sons wept, for he had been all that they ever knew of family. And I—well, he seemed to be hovering around me all the time. I kept remembering big brother, who came to watch me perform in plays at school, who would take me to the movies on a Saturday afternoon, or for a ride in his big American car along the Corniche in Alexandrian dusks, when he knew I got lonely alone in the big house. Skipping at his side to make up the space between his long strides and my small ones . . . the feeling of my hand in that firm and confident grasp. Big brother, who left for America when I was twelve, and whom I followed later with my husband. His absence changed the meaning of my life. In an odd way, I felt "homeless" for the first time in my life, cut-off and alone. My American world was now devoid of any part of my past life.

I missed him. I missed his presence, his voice on the phone, the sure stroke of his pen when he wrote me a note. I missed the dinners he cooked and his midday phone calls. I was glad to have Ellen.

Over lunch at Liz's restaurant one day, about two years after Assem's death, she mentioned Father's watch.

"The problem," she said, "is that you have two sons—who would you give it to? I did think of selling it, and dividing its value between them."

"No!" It was a cry of pain. "I wish it was not worth so much!" I looked imploringly to Ellen. "I don't know if this makes any sense to you, but this watch *is* my Father."

Ellen, I think, thought I was mad.

But the following Christmas, I unwrapped her gift to me, and there was the Patek Philippe, shining as ever. No gift had ever meant as much to me. I would wear it every day, as my Father had, I thought, until my sons were grown up.

Then one would get it, to pass on to the other's son one day. But soon enough, I, too, took it to the bank, and left it with birth certificates and naturalization papers in a box.

✦

*California*
*September 15, 2003*
*Dear Sara,*

*Nagla, the daughter of Aida and Samy, was married last night. You remember them? They were the first Egyptian American couple we had met when we came to the States. That's thirty years ago—hard to believe! She and Laila had formed one of those friendships that the children of friends form, you know. Many were the week-ends when the fathers watched games on television, while Aida and I played boggle, and the girls played with their toys, or, in the summer, out in the yard. That was before the other kids were born. Aida and Samy are now planning their retirement, after having built very successful careers, both of them. Nagla finished law school and is marrying a young man from Brazil.*

*My husband would have made a longer vacation of it, as you can imagine, but I could only take two days off from work, and it was worth it. The wedding was a wonderful experience: an American style exchange of vows, an Islamic service, a belly dancer, and extraordinary South American festivities—complete with masks, samba, and mardi gras confetti!*

*I am glad we came for the wedding, though it was a hectic thing getting away. I had to buy something to wear, and was shopping till the shops closed the night before we came! I bought a simple black dress, but brought the jewelry from the bank, and mother's diamonds gave my outfit all the sparkle it needed! The Patek Philippe was in the jewelry pouch, so I'm wearing it as I write; it makes me feel closer to you and home.*

I stopped writing my letter and lay back in my hotel bed; a desire to close my eyes and recall the history of my two lives—my early Egyptian life and my American reality—overcoming me. It's an indulgence I've yielded to more often lately.

I remembered the child, Nagla—how firmly her parents controlled her then, and how the American years had shaped her. I watched them at the wedding—looking on from the sidelines, watching as their child designed her life with what seemed like a mixture of joy and surprise that she had come into her own so independently. I knew that Aida had learned, as we all had from our American children, how to let go. She had heard her daughter's unspoken "no!"—no to so much that we had taken for granted. It was a thousand and one years ago that daughters had curfews and fathers laid down the rules. As I lay there musing, I finally understood Khalil Gibran's revelation: "Your children are not your children. They are the sons and daughters of Life's longing for itself. They came through you but not from you, and though they are with you yet they belong not to you."

And my own? Have I lost them to the culture to which I brought them? I touched the Patek Philippe on my wrist and ached for the parents I left behind.

Mother's shape as she sits in her room, stitching away at her needlepoint. Warm and cottony as she sat in the sun. The scent of the room—that fresh smell of laundry that had been dried on the line in the sun. And *Umm* Saneya, cross-legged on the floor near her, listening to the concerns of the family, and occasionally providing counsel—this illiterate wise woman who had lived forever, it seemed, in my parents' house.

And the house is empty now; and Mother and Father are dead. And *Umm* Saneya, gone before them. And Assem, apple of her eye, killed in France. And me? Hanging between two worlds, belonging to neither, privileged by a double-vision that crosses continents in a flash, a privilege paid for by the time taken up in making each real to the other. How comforting to have known what was lost. My fingers trace the rectangular shape of the watch.

The return trip from California to Ohio took a whole day, with long hours in airports, long delays on board planes that taxied endlessly before taking off, and the loss of three hours as we flew back into the Eastern time zone. It was not until the following day that I finally unpacked. I planned to stop at the bank on my way to work to put the jewelry back in the safety deposit box. But it wasn't there, the gray velvet pouch, in the zippered section of my purse where I had kept it throughout the trip. I must have hidden it somewhere—as I often do—and forgotten. With no time to search, I left for work, not too concerned, for I was sure I'd find it. I must have slid it under the sweaters, or under my lingerie in the dresser.

That night I searched, but the pouch was neither under the sweaters nor the lingerie. Slowly, despair set in. My mother's and my grandmother's jewelry was all in there, but the terrible feeling of loss struck me every time I saw, in my mind's eye, the rectangular gold watch on my father's wrist.

My daughter suggested I see a hypnotist, because, she said, "Only you know where you put it; the knowledge is in your mind." Oh, my cursed memory! Right about that time, I came upon an entry for "memory" in the *Oxford English Dictionary* that struck me: "the capacity for retaining, perpetuating, or reviving the thought of things past."

Was that it? I thought to myself. Have I lost my capacity to perpetuate my past? Have I lost the means of measuring my history? Am I forever floating outside magnetic fields, imprisoned in the outside? Privileged in my freedom, doomed to give up, one by one, every vestige of belonging? The world cannot be large enough, if it cannot grant me a small token of a place that I can call my own, a place, if only in remembrance.

◆

*Ohio, 2003*

Ellen is packing her car with Christmas gifts for her nieces and nephews in Dayton, and a Christmas dinner as well, for her sister-in-law has had to leave on one of her business trips, abandoning the family at this season for togetherness. Ellen found it almost unforgivable, belonging herself to that older generation of Midwestern Americans for whom the contemporary women's lifestyle was found threatening to the very fabric of family life. Yet she knew that her sister-in-law's job was necessary for the family. It was the absences, those business trips that she thought a mother ought to be exempt from having to take. But she will make it up to the children. Indeed, this has always been the time when she spoils them. She cannot help but think of Assem at this time. He would have put up the Christmas lights outside. He would have had all these mystery packages wrapped and hidden for her in the basement. He would sing and make a lot of noise with the children—as always orchestrating a festive atmosphere. She missed him.

She parks in the driveway; the snow has not been shoveled, and she walks carefully. Ricky runs out to help her carry things inside. At the front door, Laila is shouting, "We found the jewelry!"

"Your mother's jewelry?"

"You mean our grandmother's! Yes! And Grandpapa's watch, too!"

"An angel has brought them back for your mother! It's her Christmas gift! Does she know?"

"We'll call her at noon. She'll be making her connection in Paris then."

At noon, the children all gather in their mother's study and dial her cell number, putting the phone on speaker.

"Mom? Mom!"

"Laila?"

"Merry Christmas!" they all shout in unison.

"Merry Christmas! Is Ellen there?"

"Yes! And, Mom, we found the jewelry!"

An enormous wave of joy gushes through her body; she feels a little dizzy. "The watch is in there?"

"Yes. I'm holding it in my hand. It's all there." Her daughter's voice comes through clearly.

"Where did you find it?" Static makes the answer incomprehensible.

" . . . *All cell phones and other electronic devices must be turned off at this time.*"

The voices of the children have faded off, anyway.

✦

Seat belt anchoring me tightly in my airplane seat, I rest my head on the back of my seat and look out of the window. The roaring engines, then that exquisite feeling, that rush I always feel at takeoff, and we are up in infinite blue. It is beautiful out there, from this Archimedean height. The clouds are below us, and above us, a thousand and one layers of the eternal sky.

# Azza Filali
## DUO
Tunisia 2003    French

Azza Filali has had a successful dual career as a writer and a medical doctor and researcher. While she has argued that her writing is separate from her work as a physician and that her characters are not based on her patients, she also says that she likes to observe people, something she has the opportunity to do through her work at the Rabta Hospital in Tunis.

Filali has published several novels and short stories in French, including *Le Voyageur Immobile* (*The Motionless Traveller*) in 1990, *Le Jardin Ecarlate* (*The Scarlet Garden*) in 1996, and *Monsieur L...* (*Mister L...*) in 1999. In 2007, she was awarded the *Grand Prix du Roman Tunisien* (Grand Prize of the Tunisian Novel) for her book *Chroniques d'un Décalage* (Chronicles of a Discrepancy). The establishment of this new award is meant to encourage Tunisian authors to write about life in their country, in Arabic or in French.

Filali's fiction depicts middle-class, well-educated Tunisians whose lives reflect their particular context and culture, but also evoke universal human themes. Her female characters often have university degrees and professions, which give them economic independence; they are busy both at home and at work. In contrast, men come home to eat, read the newspapers, and watch television.

"Duo" is one of the sixteen short stories in *Propos Changeants sur l'Amour* (Changing Views on Love), published in 2003. It's title, "Duo," is the Italian for "two," and can also mean a team of two musicians playing together. In this duo, a husband and wife are playing very different songs, completely out of harmony.

Filali depicts a Tunisian couple, some time after the independence of the country in 1956. The date is important, since it marks the point after which the increasing education of girls and increasing participation of women in the workforce began to change the social fabric of life. In particular, the Code of Personal Status, promulgated by President Habib Bourguiba just a few months after independence, empowered women, transforming relationships between husband and wife. The Code of Personal Status gave Tunisian women many more social freedoms and legal rights than women in other Arab countries enjoy today, abolishing polygamy and establishing judicial divorce.

In spite of significant social changes, however, men still believe themselves to be "in charge" of women in Tunisian culture. The male protagonist in this story is so filled with rage that he cannot hear his wife or even allow her to speak. The female protagonist, after years of frustration and disappointment, realizes that her husband's anger is profound and irrevocable, and develops a new strategy: She becomes "a woman without any expectations," and meets his angry words only with laughter. Whenever he begins speaking, she laughs, blind to his anger, and in so doing, she regains her sanity and strength.

*Khedija Arfaoui*

✦

He speaks, she stops speaking: It's the rule. It was years later that she understood it, this rule. If she speaks, he speaks more loudly, more violently. He spits words and they are bitter, so she stops speaking. When he speaks, it's with intense anger, a wild anger that has always been in him. That, too, she only understood later. She understood that he had no choice but to express that anger, at every instant, without respite. Every day, anger invents a new excuse. The same excuses rekindle the same anger. Then excuses run out, but anger never does. It comes back to life like an incandescent phoenix.

He speaks and it means nothing. Anger bursts out for no reason. For no reason, and on a quiet day. Nothing. In this nothing, he spews painful words, words that shock without reason, malevolent without cause. Every single day of the calendar, he vomits his tiny bit of daily anger.

She had often wondered where that anger came from. Then, seeing him tirelessly replaying the same scene every day, a pathetic and stupid scene, she understood that he was telling an unspoken story, a very old story. She understood that after a long time had passed, and also understood that she could do nothing to quell this anger and this story that had come from so far away. A dead, buried story, a story of dead people. These people had garnered anger throughout their lives, patiently, without giving in. They had put aside their daily angers. All well put aside, carefully, and in an orderly way: resentments, pettiness, trivial quarrels, all of the simmering domestic wickedness, and then the boredom, the heavy boredom of days that looked alike. They had put all of that aside for their old age. They also had had a dog, health insurance, and three sons. He was the last one, a latecomer, still very young while they had aged a lot. "Our old age mistake," they would call him. Older than he, his brothers had left the house. He had remained, so the old people had discarded him and settled him comfortably, next to the heater, not far from the shade, a little boy in an old people's story. He had a clear face and two expectant eyes that were huge, like two mountain lakes. Standing up in the shade, he was waiting for them. They had nothing to give him. Nothing but the anger of a whole life. Then he took this anger and was careful, very careful never to lose it. And every day of his life, each day, without respite, he speaks about his anger so as not to forget.

He speaks; she stops speaking; there is nothing to do about it. At first, she had listened to him. Then she realized that he wasn't speaking to her, that he had never been speaking to her. So she stopped listening. What he says is not meant for her. Words come toward her, never in the other direction; words that belong entirely to a dead story, a dead people's story, with a dead anger in which he is bound to wander, where he wanders without any desire for escape, without any hope for release.

He speaks; she stops speaking; she has learned how to stop talking. It took her a long time, but she has finally learned how to. Patiently, as days go by, she wraps herself in silence, an invisible and protective veil. She is now entirely within the veil. Neither his words nor his useless anger can reach her any more.

Inside her silence, she laughs. At herself and at the time she has spent waiting. That dull and colorless life of hers was surely not the real one, only an attempt, a blank shot fired just to explore. This discontented man beside her is certainly not the real man, only one doing a walk-on part, while waiting for the curtain to rise. But it has taken a long time for the curtain to rise and she has long waited for dreams learned by rote, for a fresh dark wind to rise and sweep the dead years away. In the meantime, she has packed everything into boxes with mothballs: her desires, her secret gardens, a remnant of raw silk, and a few stanzas in anticipation of beautiful days. All of this was waiting tirelessly for real life to turn up.

Then, one day, laughter takes hold of her and she stops waiting. Now she goes slowly through her days, and these are slow. When the evening comes, she sits down and watches the sky as it slowly disappears into the night. In spring, she watches the swallows. Their nest is above her door; she opens the door very slowly lest she frighten the small black heads. Never has a swallow made spring. From now on, she doesn't care about spring; she can only see the swallows. When they leave in the fall, when their frail figures dot the sky, she feels overwhelmed with nostalgia, for this is the season when she cannot enjoy the company of the swallows. Then she finds herself laughing even at her nostalgia.

He speaks; she laughs. The laughter has long been contained because of the stupid waiting that stretched her as a bow. Then, on a clear morning, the laughter sprang out and has never stopped. So joyful, so loud that it sweeps away the silence. When the silence fell down like a veil, it revealed a woman without any expectations, without any anger. Now, he speaks and she laughs. She laughs without being able to stop. Sometimes, when the night emits white anger, and then at her side he wraps himself in a discontented snoring, laughter takes hold of her again and she keeps laughing until dawn. She has so many laughs to make up for that she is afraid death might come before she has had time enough to issue all the laughs she holds in reserve.

He speaks; she laughs. This laughter provokes and exasperates him. They have thus moved around, he from dark wrath to white anger, she drowned in endless laughter. He often wonders where this laugher is coming from. It has taken him a long time to understand that this laughter isn't meant for him, and that she was laughing at an ancient story, a dead people's story with forgotten laughs, a story that has been given to her to keep and that she is keeping as well as she can. Now, he speaks; she doesn't hear. She laughs; he isn't aware of it. Far away, the twilight slowly darkens.

*Translated by Khedija Arfaoui*

# Nouzha Skalli-Bennis
## PROGRESS FOR WOMEN IS PROGRESS FOR ALL!

Morocco 2004    Arabic

Nouzha Skalli-Bennis was born in Al Jadida in 1950. She obtained a doctorate in pharmaceutical studies in Montpellier, France, in 1974. She began her political career while a student, and in November 1975, she participated in the march for the liberation of the Moroccan Sahara, the coastal area that had remained a colony of Spain—a major event in the history of modern Morocco. She went on to become a founder of a hotline center for female victims of violence. In August 1995, she participated in the UN Fourth World Conference on Women in Beijing, and in 2000, she participated in the Special Session of the United Nations General Assembly devoted to the evaluation of progress achieved in the implementation of the Beijing Platform. In January 1997, she represented Moroccan NGOs in a report to a committee of experts on the UN Convention on the Elimination of All Forms of Discrimination Against Women.

In 2002, Skalli-Bennis was elected a member of the House of Representatives. She also served as head of the Socialist Alliance Parliamentary Group, the first woman to hold such a position in Morocco, and as vice-president of the standing committee on social sectors and Islamic affairs. In 2004, she was awarded the Global Leaders Award from the Population Institute. Skalli-Bennis has also published articles on women's rights in the Moroccan daily newspaper *Al Bayane*.

She delivered the following speech on 23 December 2003, two months after King Mohammed VI announced major reforms to the *Mudawana*, the Moroccan family law. The new law was widely hailed as a model of progress for the Muslim world. The United Nations Development Fund for Women (UNIFEM) stated that the Moroccan reforms "were welcomed and recognized both in Morocco and abroad as revolutionary in their ability to reconcile universal human rights principles and the country's Islamic heritage." The king's announcement of these reforms in parliament had great symbolic significance, in that it made possible the public discussion of a presumed holy text.

Skalli's speech, delivered in front of the Justice, Legislation, and Human Rights Commission of the House of Representatives on the first day of the parliamentary discussion of the family law, is significant as well, as it sanctioned the authority of women's voices in the traditional male stronghold of parliament.. While highlighting the crucial role that the Moroccan feminist movement played in the reforms, Skalli presents women's issues as family issues, crucial to the well-being of children and favorable to men as well as to women. She also links the new law to the "core values of Islam: justice and equality." Such positioning rendered the new family law understandable to the majority of the Moroccan people, and helped make these sweeping reforms possible.

*Fatima Sadiqi*

✦

The main tenets of the family law reforms were announced by King Mohammed VI in the Parliament on October 10, 2003, thus crowning the success of a long struggle of more than thirty years by the Moroccan women's human rights movement and putting an end to the staunch resistance of extremists to any attempt to reform the previous family code, in spite of its being very detrimental to women and in spite of women's crucial role in the development of Morocco. Today, I am happy to highlight the benefits of the new family law.

This is an unprecedented event in the history of our country—the first time in the history of Morocco that a family code has been discussed by representatives of the people in a parliament, which, for the first time, includes thirty-five women out of a total of 325. We are witnessing the end of an era where the family code was excluded from discussion by the legislative body and submitted to an exclusively religious male reading.

At the same time, we cannot hope to complete the construction of a democratic political system based on a state of law without a reassessment and democratization of the first cell of society, the family, on the basis of universal values of human rights, equality between people, and justice, these being the fundamental values of our noble religion and of international conventions. Indeed, how can we aspire to a just and democratic society ensuring equality of opportunity for male and female citizens, and providing a fair socializing environment for our children, within a unit based on inequality, discrimination, and violence?

Our objective is justice and family stability. The new family law establishes equity vis-à-vis women, and puts an end to decades of injustice and violence against women while protecting children and preserving the dignity of men. The fate of children is directly linked to that of their mothers. Thus, wronging women means wronging four members out of five in a family composed of a couple and three children.

The new family law is innovative in considering the interests of children a priority. The relations inside the family are usually governed by affection, goodwill, and harmony. For those who manage to maintain a balance, and as long as solutions are negotiated by a couple, recourse to the law is not needed! The law has two functions: to establish a frame of reference for structuring people's mindsets, and to serve as an instrument for conflict resolution when the law is needed.

We also aim at realizing equality and fighting discrimination. For this we need the following measures for structuring public consciousness: equality between spouses, shared responsibility, and the abolition of tutorship [legal representation of a woman by a male guardian]. In the previous family code, a young woman could marry only under the tutorship of her father, whereas a young man could marry without this tutorship. The abolition of tutorship in the new family law has a strong symbolic value because it allows young women who have reached the age of majority to decide their own fate and choose the person they want to share their lives with, just as young men do. This does not at all exclude the emotional bonds that are generally manifested toward parents by both girls and boys.

Discrimination is the source of the violence perpetrated against women: Between 1995 and 1998, no less than 29,000 cases of violence against women were registered, of which 11,890 were recorded as having taken place within the family. This, however, is only the tip of the iceberg. Further, discrimination against women creates disharmony and threatens stability within the family. It pushes women to seek the means of revenge they can afford: tricks, magic, etc. The new family law seeks to transform relations within the family and to replace competition with affection and mutual help in the interest of the couple and children. The following figures show that Tunisia, where family law is the most advanced in the Maghreb, is the country where divorce is the lowest in the region. Rates of divorce for, 1997: 15.9 percent in Morocco; 13.20 in Algeria; 14.6 in Libya; and 6.2 percent in Tunisia.

The new family law gives priority to the protection of children's rights. The marriage age for both girls and boys is eighteen. It was fifteen for girls in the previous code. Children of divorced parents are now better guaranteed to stay with their mothers. The fact that the divorced mother has guardianship and keeps the family's residence ensures a home for the children and a protection against juvenile delinquency.

The new family law also ensures a good image of our religion in the eyes of the whole world. This law highlights the core values of Islam: justice and equality. It has allowed us to show to the whole world that Islam is perfectly compatible with the values of equality and human rights.

As for the debate around wealth accumulated by the spouses, the new family law allows us to create a debate within the couple on the wealth of the couple— a subject which is still more taboo than sex! It allows us to avoid injustice and avoid women's recourse to malicious tricks in order to protect their rights.

The new family law constitutes a gain for Moroccan men. The previous code was based on a false equation: an obligation that the husband provide for the wife and children in return for the wife's submission. This obliged the husband to be the stronger and the more dominant. Indeed, the stereotypes that make wives dependents are accompanied by no less constraining stereotypes vis-à-vis men. Husbands are required to be "powerful" and "rich," and the only ones to assume responsibility—an exhausting demand that men do not always have the means or the desire to fulfill! Imagine the pressures on unemployed man! By liberating women, the new family law liberates men as well. In the new law, women will certainly have more rights, but they will also have more duties and more trying responsibilities.

Finally, a family law that targets our wives also targets our daughters! If the new reforms seem to you "hard to take" with regard to the rights of your wives, imagine the joy of seeing rights being recognized for your daughters! This is an occasion for you to remember that your wife is the daughter of another man, and that your daughter will be the wife of another man! It is good to keep in mind that progress for women is progress for all. To elevate women and do them justice is a powerful way of engaging our country in modernity, progress, and development.

*Translated by Fatima Sadiqi*

## Communal ("Lalla Fatima")
# THE FLOWER OF ALL EARTHLY CREATURES

Morocco 2004 Tashelhit

The Qur'anic and prophetic traditions portray the pursuit of knowledge as a pious endeavor incumbent upon all Muslim men and women. In various parts of the non-Arabic-speaking Muslim world, didactic poetry composed in local ver-naculars facilitated the proliferation of knowledge of Islamic doctrine, rules of practice, history, and lore among local nonliterate inhabitants. Especially among women, educational chanting sessions for the internalization of this poetry were frequently transformed into communal gatherings for ritual worship, in which education constituted a significant component. Among Berber women, afternoon ritual gatherings, during which centuries-old Berber didactic poetry is still chanted, are held throughout the Sous region of southwestern Morocco. The roots of these educational ritual events can be traced back to Berber religious lit-erary tradition and educational campaigns that originated in the sixteenth cen-tury, affirming the significance of nonliterate women's often neglected participa-tion in the transmission of Islamic knowledge and culture.

This kind of popular didactic poetry must be distinguish from the *fiqh* (jurisprudence) manuals, collections of Hadith (sayings and teachings of the prophet), and *nasiha* (religious counseling). These tools of religious instruction were also in meter and verse, but they were not intended for memorization by the general public. Some of the popular didactic poems exist only in oral form, with varying versions, and many of their authors are unknown. As a result, some early twentieth-century scholars considered this genre to be of minor significance; the scholar of Berber culture Arsène Roux, for example, described the chanting or recitation of these poems as appropriate for "little celebrations or parties," and the Moroccan scholar Mohamed Al-Mokhtar Soussi rarely mentioned such chanting sessions. Nevertheless, such sessions served as important tools and constitute valid records of what was known and transmitted at a given period in a particular setting.

The extent and significance of this level of instruction is evident from the fact this poetry is still widely known, appreciated, and chanted by men and women in separate ritual gatherings throughout the Sous. Moreover, members of the Dar-qawi Sufi order have recorded some of it on cassettes available for purchase in the region today, and popular preachers have revived it by including it, together with their own similar didactic poetic texts, in their ongoing preaching missions to provide religious guidance to illiterate populations today.

In the following text, the worship of God is inextricable from women's daily chores. The chants imbue women's hard work with reverence, and with the promise of reward on the Day of Judgment. The poem has no official title, and has not existed in written form until now. We have used as title the phrase *Ajdig N-Krad Ilulni*, meaning the flower of everyone who is born, or of all earthly creatures, which is the refrain repeated throughout. Women who chant the poem today use this phrase as designation for it. Similarly, though the full name of the woman who first said the poem is no longer known, as in the past the women who chant her poem refer to her simply as "Lalla Fatima," meaning Lady Fatima. According to the ritual participants who chanted this poem on 15 May 2004, Lalla Fatima once lived in the village of Ida Gougmar in the Anti-Atlas Mountains in the late nineteenth century.

*Margaret Rausch*

✦

Peace be upon you, O Master of Lights, O Flower of everyone who is born.
Peace be upon you, O Master of Lights, O Flower of everyone who is born.
Peace be upon you. Heal us, O Lord, and grant us our due.
Peace be upon you. Heal us, O Lord, and grant us our due.
O Muhammad, you are the Master of Lights.
O Muhammad, you are the Master of Lights.
O Muhammad, we want to join you on the Day of Judgment.
O Muhammad, we want to join you on the Day of Judgment.
If only we could be your guests in the graveyard.
If only we could be your guests in the graveyard.

Peace be upon you, O Master of Lights, O Flower of everyone who is born.
Peace be upon you, O Master of Lights, O Flower of everyone who is born.
The *houris* of paradise, they are standing at the entrance.
The *houris* of paradise, they are standing at the entrance.
The women of this world, they are standing at the gate.
The women of this world, they are standing at the gate.

Peace be upon you, O Master of Lights, O Flower of everyone who is born.
Peace be upon you, O Master of Lights, O Flower of everyone who is born.
We are better than those who always have what they need.
We are better than those who always have what they need.
We are in this world, so our troubles and faults are many.
We are in this world, so our troubles and faults are many.

Peace be upon you, O Master of Lights, O Flower of everyone who is born.
Peace be upon you, O Master of Lights, O Flower of everyone who is born.
When we grind our grain, we hold our children in our arms.
When we grind our grain, we hold our children in our arms.

We take water from the well for others. We bring it to them day and night.
We take water from the well for others. We bring it to them day and night.

Peace be upon you, O Master of Lights, O Flower of everyone who is born.
Peace be upon you, O Master of Lights, O Flower of everyone who is born.
Satan, the devil, he tempts us. Satan, the devil, he tempts us.
Satan, the devil, he tempts us. Satan, the devil, he tempts us.
When we speak of the Messenger, our hearts are cleansed of sin.
When we speak of the Messenger, our hearts are cleansed of sin.
Peace be upon you, O Master of Lights, O Flower of everyone who is born.
Peace be upon you, O Master of Lights, O Flower of everyone who is born.

*Translated by Margaret Rausch*


## Yaëlle Azagury
## A JEWISH MOROCCAN CHILDHOOD

Morocco 2007     English

Yaëlle Azagury is one of the most prominent contemporary Moroccan
Jewish women writers. She was born in 1970 in Geneva, Switzerland, but
grew up in Tangier. She is a descendant, on her mother's side, of a great
family of rabbis and scholars that stretches back to Rabbi Daniel
Toledano in Toledo, Spain, before the 1492 expulsion of the Spanish
Jews. Azagury lived with her Spanish-speaking, well-off, traditional Jewish family until she was seventeen, when she left for Paris to study French
literature at the Sorbonne-*Nouvelle* and political science at the *Institut
d'Etudes Politiques* in Paris. She also holds a Ph.D. in French literature
from Columbia University, and until recently was a lecturer in French language and literature at Barnard College. Her research has focused on the
Francophone literature of North Africa and on Marcel Proust. Although
Azagury has been living in New York for the last ten years, she returns to
Morocco frequently to visit family members who still live there as part of
a shrinking Jewish community.

This excerpt comes from an unpublished memoir about growing up in
that once thriving, now almost extinct community. Azagury reflects on
the malaise of a generation of Moroccan Jews who were born after
Morocco achieved its independence in 1956, and who experienced a sense
of disorientation and displacement; while they felt somewhat discon-
nected from Morocco, they also never fully embraced the Western countries to which most eventually emigrated. Her narrative takes its place
amid the literature of Jewish exile and diaspora, reaching out to questions

about the self, about "home," even to questions about the very notion of a native language. She attempts to construct a self-narrative that moves back and forth between stability and fluidity, striving to feed one out of the other.

*Moha Ennaji*

✦

I grew up in Tangier, in the luscious landscapes of northern Morocco where the implacable African sun becomes softer, more humane, and the dry vegetation of southern latitudes slowly gives way to amazingly green forests—almost like an anachronism. It is a magical kingdom where palm trees cede ground to deliciously smelling pines, where two continents—Europe and Africa—stare at each other, where East flirts with West. Surrounded by the Atlantic Ocean and the Mediterranean Sea, Tangier has been shaped by many cultures, religions, and dreams, but until recently, none of these influences has ever been dominant.

Morocco was partially under French rule from 1912 to 1956. The north was given to Spain, but Tangier became an international city with an astonishingly long list of identities and nationalities. Jews, who were an important presence, had somehow peacefully lived side-by-side with Muslims and Christians for generations. In fact, Tangier is among the few cities in Morocco where a *mellah*, or Jewish quarter, did not exist, which doesn't mean that Jews had assimilated. Rather, they were more open to the multiple influences to which they were exposed. Tangier Jews, for instance, considered themselves descendants of Jews who fled Spain during the Inquisition in the fifteenth century, with well-known family names such as the Toledano, the Laredo, or the Marques. They had set themselves apart from indigenous Jews—the Toshavim—who had allegedly been in Morocco since the destruction of the First Temple of Jerusalem. In some regions of the Atlas Mountains, Jews lived so close to traditional Arab tribes that one could hardly tell the difference: They looked like Arabs, spoke only Arabic, and possessed a limited awareness of the modern world. They were Berber Jews—either the descendants of Berber tribes who had been converted to Judaism, or, on the contrary, Jews who had slowly undergone Berber influence, who descended from the Toshavim and must be counted among the first inhabitants of Morocco. In contrast, the Megorashim—the exiles, i.e. the descendants of the Spaniards—enjoyed an allegedly "higher" culture inherited from Spanish courts. The divide between Toshavim and Megorashim started in the sixteenth century, but according to historians, the differences slowly became meaningless as the two groups merged.

Yet the ideology remained, and I like to think of my family's history—and mine as well—as hybrid, a blend between Toshavim and Megorashim. On my mother's side, I come from the well-known Toledano family, which can be traced back to Toledo, Spain, in the fifteenth century, and to Rabbi Daniel Toledano, a learned man who was respected by the Castilian Jewry. My grandmother, Señora Ana or *Mamita* Anita was a woman of fair skin and impeccable bearing. My grandfather, Aaron Cohen, was also a descendant of Spanish Jews, but from less glorious extraction. His grandfather had traded animal horns bought in Africa and sold in Europe, but attracted by the North's growing prosperity had left Meknes, the imperial capital of Morocco where he had lived as part of a large Jewish community, and set out to Tangier on a donkey with his two young sons, Samuel and Abraham, on either side of his saddle. In Tangier, Samuel's eldest son, Aaron, started a small business trading flour and other commodities in the early years of the twentieth century, and soon managed, with the help of his younger brother Jacob, to build a decent fortune for the time. His funeral, in 1964, which coincided with the end of Tangier's golden era, was attended not only by Jews but also by a massive crowd of Muslims and Christians, which was extremely rare.

My father's family, although already an established family in Rabat by the fifties, descended from the Berbers, or Arab Jews, as they often call themselves. My last name most likely comes from Zagora, a town on the edge of the Sahara desert, in the most southern part of Morocco.

Before the French Protectorate, Moroccan Jews lived under unpredictable conditions. They paid tax—the *jizya*—to the sultan, who in return granted them political protection. If the goals of the *jizya* were not met, Jews would sometimes fall prey to persecutions or arbitrary hangings. Their situation was thus dependent on the good will of the sultan. In fact, since the beginning of the French Protectorate, Jews benefited from French presence and culture, yet never felt entirely French. The opposite was true in Algeria, which was an official French colony, and where Jews had French passports. But the situation in Morocco had always been more complex. And Tangier was even worse. Imagine being a Jew of Spanish culture, born in a Muslim country, educated in French *lycées* or at the *Alliance Israëlite Universelle*, your feet strongly rooted on North African soil but your eyes looking toward the West.

Identity seemed, for me, anyway, like a jigsaw puzzle with one piece always missing from the puzzle—a piece that I have spent a great deal of time trying to find. I have always felt I was made of endless crystallization, layers brought by winds and oceans, built through gradual accumulation, and then shattered by landslides collapsing my epicenter. And finally, after the turmoil, it is as though I had been swallowed by seas, and granted a patient reappearance, a delivery in a new shape, as an island or perhaps a volcano. I often meditate on the story of the princess and the pea. I love to read it as a quest for identity, with the pea as the missing part, thinking that there might not be any pea under the mattresses, that the princess is lying on hundreds of layers, with nothing genuine buried beneath, begging to be brought to life.

At home, Tangier Jews spoke Spanish, a language they had been intent on keeping since their ancestors fled Spain in the fifteenth century. Actually, it was rather an old Spanish, mixed with Hebrew and Arab words, which eventually became a language in its own right, called Haquetia. It has a musical rhythm of its own, with syllables drawling at the end of sentences and magical words that I took as fetishes, with the power to transform reality, or so I believed. When, as a little girl, I broke something—a glass, perhaps, or a dish—and started to cry, fearfully anticipating my mother's anger, I would hear my father articulate the secret word, *kappara*—with the extra power gained from the doubled letter "p" at its very core—a Hebrew word that conveyed a whole range of meanings. It rested first upon a ritualistic view of life whereby literal and symbolic meaning were identical: the broken object was a sacrificial lamb that could absorb like a sponge whatever evil or pain was reserved to someone. Ultimately, and ironically, the incident was actually desirable, since it meant that I had avoided some terrible harm. This mysterious word also emphasizes the vanity of worldly losses, and the need to value the spiritual over the material. Finally, it implied a submission to higher designs, to the fatalistic belief that nothing can be done to fight whatever befalls us—that whatever happens is inevitable—and that the universe is simply a vast interaction between forces upon which humans have no influence.

Other phrases, less powerful than this but no less enchanting, have stuck with me, despite my attempts to even out my language and make it more pure, less heterogeneous. Each time I wore a new piece of clothing, I recall my mother or father always greeting me with the same Spanish words, *con salud*, wishing me to wear it in good health, and the ritualized frequency of those syllables was like a blessing. It was as if clothes possessed a magical power they might confer upon the person wearing them.

The language of my childhood was thus made of words and idioms that framed my everyday life, giving meaning to each event, and I can only wonder now how other people lived without *con salud* or *kappara*. There was a rare and reassuring pleasure in knowing these words would come back with the regularity of an old relative's weekly visit.

Language has always been an important part of my life, although for a long time I felt embarrassed about my mixed tongue—whimsical, impure, and adulterated with various foreign appendices. Our Spanish—or Haquetia—seemed like a reflection on how great we had once been, in Spain, but also a testimony to our decay, like a beautiful statue chipped and full of cracks. When we took our annual trips to Madrid, I was profoundly ashamed of my accent. My inability to pronounce the letters *z* and *c* in proper Castilian fashion identified me publicly as an outsider, an impostor who did not know proper Spanish. It sounded totally out of tune, like a baritone's melody sung by a castrato. It tortured me, that lack of musicality, that shrieking in my own ears. At times I would make the effort to speak with modern Spanish pronunciation, but I felt so conscious about the unnatural attempt that I do not know which felt more appropriate, my colorful Sephardic accent or my contrived Spanish pronunciation. Often, I made every possible effort to avoid words with those cursed letters, but to my utter despair, "thank you" in Spanish contained one of the dreaded consonants. So I was caught between my fear of being ridiculed and the terror of seeming impolite.

We had the habit of mixing our Spanish—which I considered a degenerated travesty of Cervantes's language—with touches of French, in an attempt to make it more beautiful [mixing Spanish and French is regarded by most people as a bad habit]. I hated speaking that way, but was unable to stop. The results, all too often, were odd sentences that started with a Spanish subject and verb and ended with a French complement. Verbs were sometimes declined in mysterious ways, borrowing prefixes, suffixes, or endings from French grammar. French words were sprinkled randomly into a perfectly Spanish sentence. Our sudden choice of French over Spanish obeyed seemingly arbitrary reasons— sometimes we just did not know the exact modern term—but I am now convinced we unconsciously followed a hidden order. Instinctively, we understood how different languages do not seize reality in the same way; instinctively, we favored the word that was closest to what we needed to say. The result was a sentence built like those odd mythological animals with the head of a lion and the tail of a snake.

We didn't speak Arabic and didn't really want to learn. Arabic was considered unsophisticated and only for Jews from the south or the inner lands, the *forasteros* or "strangers," as we condescendingly called them in Spanish, referring ironically to the Toshavim. In fact, not speaking Arabic was considered the "right thing," since it meant we were more European. Yet, our Spanish was densely populated with Arabic sounds, words and idioms, popping into our sentences like colorful butterflies. For a long time, I recall feeling embarrassed about being able to pronounce the Arabic *haiin* or the *ja* sound, as if that talent only brought me closer to the wild beasts' reign. When, at the age of twenty-five, I took an Arabic class at Harvard, determined suddenly o speak proper *Fusha*, or classical Arabic, our American teacher played a song by the famous Lebanese diva Fairouz. It was beautiful. The teacher ended the class with these simple words: "If you don't like how this sounds, don't bother to come back." Suddenly, my longstanding rejection of Arabic seemed foolish. It was like listening to someone who had borrowed my own voice, that same strange feeling of hearing it for the first time in a tape recorder, or as Rilke would have said, like having the first text you've ever written read by someone else. Perhaps we only own something after a process of estrangement.

Juggling languages has been only one facet of my struggle with shifting identities. I remember the terror I felt when someone asked me where I came from, what nationality I was. Would I say French, or maybe Spanish? But then, I was technically lying. And if I answered Moroccan, the next question would be, "Oh! So you speak Arabic at home?" But that wasn't true either, and I anticipated the endless explanations where, apologetically, I would have to excuse myself for calling up history and my ancestors, who had left Spain in the fifteenth century, and that's-why-we-still-spoke-Spanish-at-home.

Identity, anyway, has always been a tantalizing question for me, probably since I don't look Moroccan. In fact, I grew up feeling I didn't quite belong anywhere. My accent did not sound quite French when I left Morocco to start my degree in French literature in Paris, but that soon changed, and people began to assume I was French.

Yet, even with all my efforts to assimilate, I sometimes got the dreaded French remark, razor-sharp and definitive: "*Vous êtes vraiment typé, vous*," which translates as, "You *do* look exotic." "*Typé*," in fact, has the same etymological root as *typical* or *typically*, and should be used with an adjective—one is typically Spanish, or typically Swedish—but in French the meaning has shifted, and it is used alone to designate exclusively the black, Hispanic, or Semitic type. In other words, if someone tells you in France how "*typé*" you look, take it as a decree of excommunication. And the pounding question would come back, leaving me no respite: Who am I? Yaëlle the Frenchwoman or Yael the Jew, the Arab, the Spaniard? From Morocco to France to Cambridge to New York, I felt like a space shuttle gravitating from one planet to the next, striving to understand which is more genuinely my own, searching for an orbit and a sun.

In truth, I was confused by having so many value systems to comply with. What felt right in one seemed wrong in the other. For example, I often dream of my Aunt Licy, *Tita* Licy, my great-aunt, whom, as a little girl, I used to visit with my mother every Saturday morning after my dentist appointment, with equal anticipated boredom—or fright—for both duties. *Tita* Licy, *Mamita* Anita's eldest sister, had never married, and she carried her celibacy on her frail shoulders like a burden. I remember climbing the endless stairs to her dark apartment, a cavern with her as its endearing secret monster. And there she was, trapped within those four walls, bent with age, her face crumpled and yellow like an old parchment, her gray hair tied in a ponytail, a youthful old maiden. I still have the vivid image of her back arched over a piece of eternal embroidery she never seemed to finish, and that yarn ball unraveling with vertiginous speed; her agile fingers dancing like elves on the colorful fabric, maybe waiting for an unknown Ulysses to sweep her away. A weird smell emanated from her, cleanliness mixed with a hint of the delicious scent of babies, but with something else to it, like cologne water gone bad, or skin that's been rubbed for too long and is no longer distinct. In fact, it was simply the monotonous and slightly disgusting smell of old age.

As my mother and she conversed, the cavern started revealing its hidden jewels. The dear old lady cherished me as the grandchild she never had. And she punctuated our visit with songs, old Spanish or Sephardic "romances" from medieval times. There was one in particular that was just for me, called "*Una Rubita Como un Rubi*," or "A Little Blonde Girl Precious As a Ruby," a rosy love story with flowers and altars. But embroidery and singing exquisite ballads were not her only distractions. She had a fetish for history and genealogy, and loved gathering bits of information of all kinds. She read history, gossip columns, newspapers, and magazines, all avidly. She collected odd memorabilia like invitation cards for weddings and *Tefellimes*, the Haquetia word for *Bar Mitzvah*. She was especially fond of British history, and knew everything about the complex alliances of the royal family. Apparently, she had had a British suitor from Manchester, but for some mysterious reason her father had refused to let her marry him, and since then she had consoled herself with an insatiable curiosity for anything British. I often think that her interest in history wasn't coincidental, that, lost as she was in a world that had no place for an old maid, she escaped to the past, where things had an order and a fixed identity, an identity she probably never found for herself. And I know that no matter how rational and knowledgeable and modern I become, there will always be a part of *Tita* Licy in me.

I have often considered my Westernized, rational, civilized self as an alien in the body of a more basic, authentic self; or I think of myself as double, like those androgynous beings in Plato's famous parable. But that also seems inaccurate. For if at times I long for Morocco, or Moroccan Jews, and believe the longing embodies the missing pea, I know the questioning is endless and goes far beyond a simple division between two or even multiple selves. What I love and cherish one moment, I reject the next, and so it goes, the story of the self. Perhaps I am just made with pieces to be grafted together and voids to be filled. But in the end, I like to think of myself as an all-inclusive structure, an ever-changing ocean's surface echoing the glittering kisses of Tangier's sun.

## *Mona Abousenna*
## GIRLS' HONOR AND INTELLECTUALS' SHAME

Egypt 2007    Arabic

Born in 1945, Mona Abousenna is the founder and secretary general of two international philosophical associations, the Afro-Asian Philosophy Association, and the Averroes and Enlightenment International Association. She is Professor emeritus of English and comparative literature in the Faculty of Education at Ain Shams University in Cairo. She writes extensively on various issues, including gender, Islam, language, literature, and drama.

This article appeared in *Rose El-Youssef*, a weekly magazine with liberal leanings, named for the woman who founded it early in the twentieth century. Its publication was triggered by the death of a twelve-year-old girl named Bodour, during a circumcision operation undertaken by a woman doctor in a clinic in one of the towns of Upper Egypt. The incident focused attention on the issue of female genital mutilation (FGM), also called female genital cutting. This practice, most often performed on young girls, has continued in Egypt despite a long history of activism against it by Egyptian feminists and child advocates, and despite the government's proclaimed attempts to eradicate it. Legislation also prohibits the practice, albeit in general terms, through the penal code's ban on inflicting deliberate bodily injury on any person. The law, however, remains virtually unenforced, with the government turning a blind eye and allowing the operation to be carried out under medical supervision.

Prior to the death of Bodour, FGM had also been a largely taboo subject in the Egyptian media. However, the media coverage of her case was extensive, and led to heated debates. "Girls' Honor and Intellectuals' Shame" was one of the scores of articles that appeared in various newspapers and magazines immediately following the incident, expressing shock and anger. For the first time, a *fatwa*—a religious ruling by the Egyptian Mufti, the leading scholars of the Islamic religious establishment—condemned the practice as being against Islam. In response to this wave of protest, the Minister of Health issued a decree on 27 June 2007 explicitly banning any FGM procedures in clinics and hospitals, both public and private. Abousenna, however, argues that it will take more than religious or legal decrees to eradicate this deadly practice, which is rooted in cultural notions about women's "honor" and, even more deeply, in "the view of the female body as a site of shame." She challenges Egypt's intellectuals to lead the change in public consciousness necessary to saving more girls from Bodour's fate.

*Amira Nowaira*

✦

A prominent feature of the Egyptian character is the tendency, amounting to veneration, to hold on to traditions and inherited practices. Any attempt at change is not only regarded with dread, but may also go so far as to incite many to oppose the proposed change actively. Change involves criticizing and superseding the past in order to build a different future. Such thoughts crossed my mind as I followed that painful incident that resulted in the death of an innocent girl, Bodour, during a circumcision operation. In my view, Bodour is not the first, and will not be the last, Egyptian child victim to be offered by their mothers on the altar of a outdated social practice. Bodour's case, however, is an exception because of the media coverage it has received. Although the case appeared as though it were an isolated incident, it is in fact the exception that proves the rule. The truth is that many girls die while in the process of being circumcised.

The media coverage of the Bodour incident reveals the Egyptian characteristic of rejecting and fighting criticism, because such criticism implies disapproval of our heritage. Criticizing our heritage means exposing the roots of deeply entrenched misconceptions. Instead, the media fell victim to another misconception, namely that female genital mutilation is first and foremost a religious issue. The media therefore sought out the Egyptian Mufti, who declared in his religious ruling that "Female circumcision is forbidden by Islam." The media people imagined that with this ruling they have managed to wipe out the practice of female circumcision entirely.

On the other hand, some state institutions passed rulings prohibiting this practice and penalizing its perpetrators, in the wrong belief that prohibitive regulations will eradicate the practice. In the midst of all such commotion, nobody seemed to notice that religious rulings and government regulations are nothing but repeat acts through the ages, resulting in the fact that 97 percent of all Egyptian women are circumcized.

So will this latest ruling by the Mufti or the innovative prohibitive regulations lead to a reduction in the ever-increasing numbers of girls submitting to such an operation? The answer is no. The practice of female circumcision is neither a religious nor a legal question. It is a cultural issue. Or to put it more accurately, it is a cultural question connected with the position of women in Egyptian society from one specific angle, which is a "girl's honor." The circumcision of girls, whether in the countryside or the cities, is closely linked to the concept of virginity. A girl's virginity is not complete without her circumcision, since an uncircumcized girl is by necessity a girl without honor, or more accurately, a loose girl, who will lead her family to shame and scandal. If in fact a girl loses her virginity for one reason or another, she can be subjected to a simple surgical procedure whereby the hymen is technically restored. But were a girl to stay uncircumcized, it could not be kept secret but would remain a damning proof of the girl's lack of virtue in the eyes of society.

This outdated belief is not, therefore, connected at all with religion or Shari'a. And neither will the laws, no matter how strict, be able to deter those practicing it, because, with the revival of the work of midwives, it would be possible to evade such laws. Evidence that female circumcision is an inherited Egyptian practice not connected with religion may be found in the fact that it is absent from Islamic societies applying Islamic law. The latest paradox in this practice is that some of the circumcized girls may well be morally loose, which may mean that they have sexual relations with young men their age and may go as far as prostitution without the family's knowledge. All this, however, would not worry the families as long as they were carried out in secret, without the knowledge of neighbors or family. But when such girls get married, the families make sure that they are virgins, whether the virginity is natural or artificial. Therefore, social hypocrisy becomes a prominent feature of the Egyptian personality as it preserves the illusion of a girl's honor.

The ultimate roots of female circumcision as a necessary means of preserving virginity and the good reputation of females lies in the view of the female body as a site of shame, except when functioning as a tool for reproduction. According to this view, a woman is not a rational willful being, but only a site for men's desires. Since a girl is female, she is necessarily suspect. More precisely, she is potentially rather than actually guilty, to use Aristotle's expression. The evidence supporting this view can be found in the large numbers of honor crimes committed even when the girls were proved afterward to be virgins. In the past, primitive societies dealt with this problem by burying the girls after their birth to get rid of the shame present in their femaleness. Today, however, we only circumcize girls as a symbol of buying them. A girl's honor is in fact an illusion, since a girl has no honor so long as she has lost her reason and will. What we call a girl's honor is actually the honor of the family or tribe.

Two questions impose themselves. First, how can people rid themselves of this deeply entrenched illusion that has plagued their minds since superstitious and primitive times? Second, can the Egyptian media, together with government institutions and nongovernmental organizations, eradicate the roots of such illusions "nesting" in people's minds concerning female circumcision?

A third complex question arises out of the previous two. What should intellectuals do? Are they ready to face up to their cultural responsibility to deal with this inhuman practice and eradicate it from people's minds? Or is this issue another instance of cultural reform in which intellectuals forgo their responsibility in carrying the torch of enlightenment because they are too preoccupied with their clash with the political authority to engage in fighting backwardness?

*Translated by Amira Nowaira*

## Mona Makram-Ebeid
# RIGHTS OF POLITICAL REPRESENTATION

Egypt 2007    English

Mona Makram-Ebeid, professor of political science and former member of Parliament, belongs to a distinguished Egyptian Coptic family. She is related to Makram-Ebeid Pasha, a former finance minister and the Wafd Party secretary general from 1936 to 1942, during the period when the Wafd Party dominated Egyptian politics, between the First World War and the 1952 revolution. Mona Makram-Ebeid is an academic with a degree from Harvard, and an activist who currently runs an Egyptian NGO called the Association for the Advancement of Education. She is also one of the founding members of the Arab Organization for Human Rights, an executive member of the Ibn Khaldun Center for Developmental Studies, and a member of the UNICEF Women for Development Committee. She has received numerous awards, including the *Chevalier de la Légion d'Honneur* in 1994 and *Commandeur de la Pleaide* in 1995. She was also an adviser to the World Bank for the Middle East and North Africa Region, and a consultant for the International Consultative Group for the Middle East Center for Strategic and International Studies in Washington, D.C.

Ebeid was one of the founders and a secretary general, of the Al-Ghad Party (Party for Tomorrow). She is the first woman to run a political party not only in Egypt, but in the Arab world. She regards herself as heir to a political dynasty linking the preindependence era with today's Egypt. As a liberal icon as well as a woman, she sees herself carrying a legacy of liberal thinking, which has increasingly come under attack in Egypt.

In this article, published in the prestigious English-language magazine *Al-Ahram Weekly*, Ebeid calls on women to fight for their right to be part of the political system. By invoking the figure of the political activist Doria Shafik at the end of the essay, she tries to reestablish connections with a past that seems to be unknown to the younger generations of Egyptian women. She urges this new generation to take the fight for women's political rights to the next stage by advocating the establishment of a minimum quota of female representatives in Parliament, in the hope of creating of a more equitable future for women.

*Amira Nowaira*

✦

Political participation offers opportunities to various groups in society to promote, articulate, advocate, and defend their interests and views. Women are as vital a human resource as men. Excluding them from political life risks not utilizing fully and efficiently their knowledge, skills, experience, and distinct visions of world and society. Political participation empowers people to understand and influence decisions that affect their lives.

The time has come to move from recognizing women's contribution to challenging those factors in the family, in communities, and in the country and the Arab world as a whole, that make it difficult for women to assume their full responsibilities in democracy and development. Are issues male or female? No, issues for society include both men and women. We should not forget that women constitute [at least] 50 per cent of the total population of the Arab world. Women are the foundation of the transformation under way in Arab societies. Our societies cannot ignore the fact that women are the mothers and educators of the nation, the partners of men, and also the warriors in search of prosperity and development.

In this respect, we believe that a quota system is one useful strategy to guarantee that the voices, knowledge, experience, and skills of women make an impact on the development of the nation. Resistance to women's entering politics via such mechanisms as quotas, mechanisms that would make it possible to correct [the imbalance in representation], may be seen as a result of attitudes of the politicians. They do not look favorably upon even the idea of female representatives, who are not yet considered key to efforts to bring about democracy and sustainable development. Yet evidence from around the world shows that voluntary quotas adopted by political parties and regimes in order to increase the number of women candidates in elections have been effective, especially when applied in proportional representation-based electoral systems. In the Arab world, however, there are relatively few successful examples of political parties adopting and enforcing internal party quotas, and thus the participation of women remains limited.

Although no quota is perfect, it is better to have an imperfect system than none at all. While quotas alone will not solve the problems of patriarchal systems, attitudes, and stereotypes, the mere presence of women changes the face of decision-making and provides opportunities for their substantive contributions.

As a former member of parliament, I have participated in three different elections with different electoral systems. In the 1980s a new law was introduced which reserved thirty new seats for women. In addition, three women won elections independently and two more were appointed by President Anwar Sadat, so there were thirty-five women in parliament, representing nine per cent of the body. In 1987, the reserved seats were abolished, but the government retained the proportional representation system and 18 women gained seats in parliament. The proportional representation system was also eventually abolished. In 1990, women constituted only two per cent of parliament, most of them appointed.

There has been a lot of talk lately of empowering women and encouraging their political participation, and many activists have demanded a return to the proportional representation system, or the quota system. Parliament, however, with a majority of chauvinist and shortsighted members, has registered its strong resistance to both systems. It is now up to women's associations, women politicians, party members, and writers to stand fast and demand what is their legitimate right. Women need to mobilize on a large scale within and outside of political parties. Let us remember that thanks to Doria Shafik, the courageous political activist and her supporters, women won the right to vote in 1956. Can we expect that her daughters and granddaughters be as courageous as she was?

## *Mona Nawal Helmi*
# FROM THIS DAY FORTH, I WILL CARRY MY MOTHER'S NAME

Egypt 2006   Arabic

Born Mona Helmi in 1958, Mona Nawal Helmi is a newspaper columnist, novelist, short story writer, and poet, with more than ten books to her credit. In 1993, she was awarded the literary Taymour Prize for her collection of short stories, *Al Bahro Bainana* (The Sea Standing Between Us). Her published works also include a collection of essays, *Al-Hob Fi Asr Al Awlamah* (Beauty Queens and Creative Queens, 1999) and a collection of poems called *Hatef Al Sabah* (Morning Call, 1991). She has a bachelor's degree in political science as well as a master's degree and a doctorate in development studies. Before devoting herself full-time to writing, she worked as a researcher at the National Center for Social and Criminal Research in Cairo, specializing in media studies and public opinion research.

The daughter of the celebrated Nawal El Saadawi, Mona Nawal Helmi has always been at the center of controversy. Her uncompromising views, her relentless advocacy of women's rights, and her championing of the causes of freedom of expression and combating violence against women have often made her the target of attack from religious and political establishments. Her confrontational style, both in her writings and in her frequent appearances on television and radio, has often succeeded in provoking, challenging, and exposing the prevalent orthodoxies in a society that only seems to be growing less tolerant of different views.

This article appeared in the weekly magazine *Rose El-Youssef*, where Mona Nawal Helmi is a columnist. Many found the suggestion of using a mother's name to be disturbing and subversive, and the article triggered powerful debates in the Egyptian media. Nawal El Saadawi spoke and wrote in support of her daughter's proposal. More than a decade earlier, she herself had expressed anger at having to use her father's name in the essay "Writing and Freedom," included in this volume. In January 2007, mother and daughter were called before the prosecutor general's office in Cairo, and questioned regarding the accusation that the proposal was an insult to Islam.

*Amira Nowaira*

Next Tuesday is 21 March, Mother's Day. On this particular day, I am supposed to offer my mother "something" to prove that I am neither ungrateful nor oblivious to her significant contribution to my life, or to her help in providing me with the best conditions and facilities possible so that I could realize my dreams. But my dreams have always been tricky, perhaps even impossible to attain in a society that regards "women" as beings created solely to perform the religious practices dictated by God up in heaven and the male practices dictated by "man," who poses as the God of the earth, in the shape of father, brother, uncle, or husband. Any denial or resistance is regarded as an imported sacrilege and an imitation of the corrupt ways of the women of the West who acknowledge no religion or creed. Western women, according to this view, are in alliance with their fellow countrymen in a conspiracy to demolish the virtue of Islamic countries and the innocence of obedient Muslim women, and are plotting to destroy our men's muscularity and mastery, as well as the special character of the best nation God has created on earth.

On Mother's Day, Tuesday 21 March, according to the traditions of our Arab Muslim societies, I should buy my mother a gift from one of the shops that reduce prices on this special occasion. According to the same Arab Muslim mentality, I will take advantage of such sales to choose a gift expressing my gratitude for her sacrifices, pains, and struggles to create a "good citizen" out of me.

Each year, radio and television broadcast programs that dwell on mothers' sacrifices, efforts, and patience, on maternal feelings that are unparalleled. Highlighted is a mother's willingness to forgo her own comfort and happiness for the sake of her children, as well as a mother's translucent heart, which can foretell events because it is endowed with the touch of providence.

Each year on Mother's Day, our Arab Muslim societies reiterate that a mother means "everything." She is the queen of her home kingdom, and is almost sacrosanct. It would be shameful and unethical not to appreciate and venerate her. Repeated *ad nauseam* is the quotation that "paradise lies at the feet of mothers," which grants her the highest accolade possible. Reiterated also is that mothers are irreplaceable and their love is unqualified, because it is not conditional on our obedience of their wishes, our success in life, or our fulfillment of their dreams or desires, as is the case with all other human relationships, fatherhood included. People in general do not love others for themselves, but as a means of attaining some advantage, companionship, or money.

Only the mother loves us for ourselves, and not for the traits that we possess, the position that we occupy, or because we obey her orders and warnings. With her alone, we need to exert no effort, wear no masks, fake no obedience, or undertake no action to secure her generous, freely given love. For this reason in particular, when we lose our mother, we realize that we have lost the one human being who does not demand a price in return for love. When we lose our mother, we do not merely grieve, but we go on bleeding and hurting in silence, shedding silent tears every day throughout our lives. When we lose our mother, we realize the existence of "death," of "loss that kills without a knife," and of being "broken" without the hope of being put back together again, even if we happen to own the whole world. When we lose our mother, our cheeks "wither" permanently. Cosmetics and plastic surgeries will be unable to remove the traces. When we lose our mother, we suddenly discover that our life has frittered away from between our fingers and that we have suddenly "aged."

On Mother's Day, on Tuesday 21 March, competitions usually take place to choose the model mother from among many women: those who wear either the head-cover or the body-covering *niqab*; women who are widowed or divorced; and women who had decided to depend on themselves alone in raising their children, without taking a second husband.

The model mother may turn out to be the woman who triumphed over the poverty line and struggled to support her children until they went to university, or who was instrumental in their success taking the secondary school certificate exam. The criteria for choosing the model mother, I believe, should change, and should relate to enlightened views that may help the country to develop, rather than focusing only on the challenges of poverty, raising children, and confronting an unjust fate.

Tuesday 21 March is Mother's Day. I cannot, amid all the festivities in celebration of mothers and motherhood forget the terrifying paradox that we live in. On Mother's Day, mothers receive gifts and invitations to go out and have fun; they listen to the famous "Our Mother" song while their hands are being kissed to ask for their blessings and in recognition of all their work. But reality is a different and dismal story. Mothers have no rights, and neither do they occupy the positions spoken of. They have no opinions, no dignity, no right to object to fathers or husbands. They may be beaten up, humiliated and deprived of everything should they commit the gravest sin of all, disobeying the God of the household, their husband.

There are literally thousands of mothers standing before law courts, thousands of mothers victimized by all varieties of domestic violence, thousands of mothers who cannot give their names to their children, although maternal affiliation was the original practice. In practice, a mother's name is a source of shame and scandal; it is a term of abuse, and a source of corruption and dishonor.

Isn't this self-contradictory? How is it that a mother cannot give her name to her child even though paradise lies at her feet?

Two months ago, the law in France was changed so that mothers would have a right equal to fathers to give their names to their children. Following this French law, the baby carries the names of both father and mother, as justice dictates. Maternal affiliation, whereby a mother can give her name to her child, has existed for some time in many countries, including Spain, some African states, and the majority of South American countries.

I have always wanted to carry my mother's name. But I do not live in Spain or Colombia.

On Mother's Day on 21 March, I will not buy my mother a bouquet of flowers, a bottle of perfume, or a book on philosophy. Neither shall I make her the corn pie that she dearly loves. My mother in fact hates gifts, and often describes them as "masked bribes." And because my love for my mother is boundless, and stands in opposition to everything, and because rights are never freely granted but are grabbed, and because I have always been connected to my mother's name since my conception, and because she made freedom my goal and reference point, and because I hate waiting for my rights to come on official papers, and because next Tuesday is Mother's Day: From that day on, I will salvage by force one of my rights. It will be the proper gift for my mother. From this day forth, I will carry my mother's name.

I hope that my readers, women and men alike, will get used to my new and fairer name. It is in fact more in keeping with the cant about the sacred and elevated position of mothers in our societies.

We've had enough futile, ineffectual babbling!

*Translated by Amira Nowaira*

# CONTRIBUTORS

## EDITORS

**Azza El Kholy** is professor of American literature at the Department of English at Alexandria University, Egypt. She obtained her M.A. and Ph.D. from Alexandria University and has spent some time as a visiting scholar at George Washington University in the United States. She was executive director of The TAFL (Teaching Arabic as a Foreign Language) Center, and director of the Language and Translation Unit at the Faculty of Arts of the University of Alexandria. She is currently advisor for special projects in the director's office of the Bibliotheca Alexandrina, and Deputy Director of the Institute for Peace Studies. Her academic and research interests include feminist criticism, nineteenth century American literature, translation, and peace and conflict studies.

**Moha Ennaji** is professor of linguistics and gender studies and former head of the Department of English at the University of Fes, Morocco. He is currently the director of Arabic Studies at Rutgers University. He has published extensively on language, gender, and cultural studies with a focus on North Africa. His most recent publications include *Migration and Gender in Morocco and The Dialogue of Civilizations* (translation) both co-authored with Fatima Sadiqi (2008); *Multilingualism, Cultural Education, and Education in Morocco* (2005), *A Grammar of Moroccan Arabic* (2004). He is the editor of *Language and Gender in the Mediterranean Region* (2008). He has been a Fulbright Visiting Scholar at the University of Arizona and Mansfield University.

**Amira Nowaira** is professor of English literature in the Department of English at Alexandria University, Egypt, and former chairperson of the same department. She obtained her Ph.D. from the Department of English, Birmingham University, UK, and her publications include critical studies, translations from and into Arabic, and creative writing. Her fields of interest cover a wide area that includes English literature, comparative literature, and Arab women's writing at home and in diaspora.

**Fatima Sadiqi** is professor of linguistics and gender studies at the University of Fes, Morocco. She has written extensively on Moroccan languages and Moroccan women. She is the author of *Women, Gender, and Language in Morocco* (2003), *Grammaire du Berbère* (1997), *Images of Women in Abdullah Bashrahil's Poetry* (2004), *Migration and Gender in Morocco: The Impact on Women Left Behind* (with Moha Ennaji, 2008), and *The Dialogue of Civilizations: The Self and the Other* (translation, with Moha Ennaji, 2008). Fatima Sadiqi was a Harvard Fellow in 2007.

## Associate Editors

**Fatima Bouabdelli** is presently a senior lecturer in the Department of English, Cadi Ayyad University, Marrakech, Morocco. Her thesis on the history of the Moroccan women's movement (1940-2003) will be published in 2008. Her M.A. thesis was on "Doris Lessing as a British Post Modern Writer." As an activist, she is especially committed to encouraging young girls from poor backgrounds to get educated. She is a founding member of "Dar Al Haouz," an NGO that manages a boarding institution in Marrakech for young female university students from villages in the Al Haouz region.

**Abena P.A. Busia** is associate professor of Literatures in English, and of Women's and Gender Studies, at Rutgers, The State University of New Jersey. She also currently serves as the director of the Center for African Studies at Rutgers, and the director of the Association for the Study of the Worldwide African Diaspora. In addition to being co-director and series editor of *Women Writing Africa*, she has also co-edited *Theorizing Black Feminisms: The Visionary Pragmatism of Black Women* with Stanlie James, and *Beyond Survival: African Literature and the Search for New Life: Proceedings of the 1994 African Literature Association Conference*, with Kofi Anyidoho and Anne Adams. She has published widely on black women's literature, colonial discourse, and post colonial studies and is the author of two volumes of poems, *Testimonies of Exile* (1990) and *Traces of Life* (2008).

**Nadia El Kholy** is professor and chair of the Department of English Language and Literature at Cairo University. Her research interests include writing and translation for children, comparative and postcolonial literature, and gender studies. She has also published a number of articles on the modern Arabic and English novel. She has been nominated as a member of the jury for the Hans Christian Anderson international award for Children's Literature in 2006 and has contributed to the *Oxford Encyclopedia of Children's Literature* (2005). She won the Suzanne Mubarak Award for Children's Literature in 1999.

**Sahar Hamouda** is professor of English literature at Alexandria University, Egypt. She has published several books and articles on the modern history of Alexandria, and is interested in postcolonial and comparative literature, about which she has also published extensively. She has also translated literature and biographies from Arabic into English. For her research and publications, she won the Alexandria University 2004 prize for academic research. From 1998 to 2001 she was acting chairperson of the Department of English in Beirut Arab University. She has been deputy director of the Alexandria and Mediterranean Research Center at the Bibliotheca Alexandrina since 2003, as well as the director of the Alexandria Center for Hellenistic Studies, also at the Bibliotheca Alexandrina, since 2008.

**Marjorie Lightman** is a principal in *Q.E.D. Associates LLC*, a consulting partnership founded in 1988 to address the needs of nonprofit and mission-oriented organizations. Dr. Lightman has also been a senior fellow at the Women's Research and Education Institute (WREI), Washington, DC, since 2002. She co-authored *A Biographical Dictionary of Ancient Greek Roman Women* (Facts on File Press, 1999) and a new enlarged second edition, *A to Z of Greek and Roman Women* (Facts on File Press, 2008), which profiled 510 women. Dr. Lightman authored the opening essay in *Crossing Borders* (WREI, 2004), the first publication of the Crossing Borders Immigration Project and co-authored *Ellis Island and the Peopling of America* (New Press, 1997), which the Ellis Island-Statue of Liberty Foundation and the National Park Service designated the official publication for the Ellis Island Museum.

**Zahia Smail Salhi** is senior lecturer and head of the Department of Arabic and Middle Eastern Studies at the University of Leeds in Great Britain. She teaches Arabic literature, Arab cinema, and culture and society in the Middle East and North Africa. Her research focuses on Arabic and Francophone literature, the representation of women in Orientalist discourse, and the literary and artistic expression of Arab women writers, especially in the diaspora. She has worked extensively on issues of gender and the status of women in Islam. Her publications include *Politics and Poetics in the Algerian Novel* (1999), and *The Arab Diaspora: Voices of an Anguished Scream* (2006).

**Khadija Zizi** is senior professor of Media Studies at the *Institut Supérieur de l'Information et de la Communication* in Rabat, Morocco. She earned a Ph.D. from the University of Illinois at Urbana-Champaign and was a Fulbright visiting scholar at the University of California, Santa Barbara. Her research has been on gender issues, the media, cross-cultural communication, English for Specific Purposes, translation, and interpreting. In 1991, she was elected president of the Moroccan Association of Teachers of English. She currently serves as a member of the Ministry of Communication's Committee for Gender Equity. She paints and has been holding national and international exhibits. She also enjoys writing poetry.

## Contributing Editors

**Mohamed El-Sayed Abd-el-Ghani** is professor of Greco-Roman history and civilization and Head of the Greco-Roman Archaeology and Classical Studies Department at Alexandria University, Egypt.

**Zakia Iraqui-Sinaceur** is a French-educated Moroccan scholar with interests in oral literature. She has published extensively on the various genres of Moroccan oral literature.

**Ali Ouahidi** is professor of history at Sidi Mohamed Ben Abdellah University in Fes, Morocco, where he has been teaching since 1982. He holds a doctorate in ancient history (on Africana Romana) from the same university (1995). He has participated in many national and international conferences. He has supervised a great number of M.A. and Ph.D. theses, and is the author of several articles published in national and international journals. His main research interests are the ancient history of North Africa and archeology.

**Heba Sharobeem** is lecturer and assistant professor in the Department of English at Alexandria University, Egypt. Her M.A. thesis was a comparative study of two novels by Virginia Woolf and William Faulkner. Her doctoral thesis focused on the autobiographies of three women writers: Gertrude Stein, Eudora Welty and Latifa al-Zayyat. Her research interests are in the fields of modern British and American novels, personal narratives, gender and women's studies. She has published book reviews and essays in Egypt and abroad.

## Text Editor

**Florence Howe,** one of the founders of The Feminist Press at the City University of New York in 1970, became—in 2000—emerita professor of English at the Graduate Center CUNY and emerita director/publisher of The Feminist Press, though she continued to work full-time on Women Writing Africa. In 2005, she returned to the position of publisher, retiring once again in 2008, though continuing to work full-time on Women Writing Africa and as editorial director of the new Women Writing Science series. She has written or edited more than a dozen books and more than a hundred essays. Her books include *No More Masks! An Anthology of Twentieth Century Poetry by American Women* (1973 and 1993); *Myths of Co-Education: Selected Essays, 1965-1983* (1984), and *The Politics of Women's Studies: Testimonies from 30 Founding Mothers* (2000). She is writing a memoir.

# TRANSLATOR AND HEADNOTE WRITERS

**Naglaa Abou-Agag** is a lecturer in the English literature department at Alexandria University, Egypt. She is currently teaching at Beirut Arab University in Lebanon.

**Zoubida Achahboun** teaches sociology at the University of Meknès, Morocco. She writes poetry for local magazines and is heavily involved in activist work.

**Khedija Arfaoui** has taught English, American studies, and feminist studies at Manouba University, Tunisia. She is one of the pioneer postcolonial feminists in Tunisia. Her research focuses on women's status in the Maghreb and the Arab world more generally.

**Jouhara Filali Baba** is a university Arabic teacher and a researcher in the history of Moroccan women from 1987 until 2005. She is also an author, with publications on Moroccan women, and an activist.

**Fouzia Baddouri** has taught at the University of Fes, Morocco. She holds an M.A. in English literature and is interested in the contemporary English novel. She currently teaches in the United Arab Emirates.

**Hafsa Bekri-Lamrani** graduated from the Lycée Descartes' High School in Rabat, Morocco and from Paris VII University, France with a degree in Anglo-Saxon studies. She has taught English at the Moroccan Air Force Base in Salé, the Rabat and Casablanca Teachers' Colleges, and the American Language Centers in Rabat and Casablanca.

**Ahmed Bouchareb** is a Moroccan historian with special interests in the histories of Morocco and Portugal.

**Belou Charloff** is a 23-year-old postgraduate in women's studies, specializing in women's writing. Like the heroine of *Mazaltob*, she too comes from a family of Jewish emigrants who settled in Africa in the early twentieth century. In 2007, she interned at The Feminist Press.

**Radwa El Barouni** is writing a Master's thesis on "Modernism/Postmodernism: An Attempt at Bridging the Gap through a Reading of A.S. Byatt and Don DeLillo." She also teaches in the English department at Alexandria University, at the Arab Maritime Academy, and in the TAFL program (Teaching Arabic as a Foreign Language).

**Malika El Korso** is a historian who specializes in the role of women in the Algerian war of liberation. She has published papers on the theme in both national and international journals.

**Hassan Mohammed El-Saady** has been a professor of ancient Egyptian civilization since 1999. He is currently also vice-dean of the Faculty of Arts, Alexandria University, for Community Service and Ecological Development. Dr. El-Saady is also a member of the Egyptian Exploration Society based in London, and a member of the Archeology Committee at the Supreme Council of Culture, Ministry of Culture, Egypt.

**Shadia el-Soussi** is a lecturer at Alexandria University, Egypt, with a Ph.D. in applied linguistics. Sociolinguistics and critical discourse analysis are currently her main academic fields of specialization.

**Elizabeth Fernea** was born in 1927. She is a writer, filmmaker, and anthropologist who has spent much of her life in the field producing numerous ethnographies and films that capture the struggles and turmoil of African and Middle Eastern cultures.

**Hadhami Hached** is a teaching fellow in the Department of English at Manouba University, Tunisia. Her research focuses on American studies, particularly on American immigration policy.

**Noha Nadder Hamdy** is currently assistant lecturer at the University of Stuttgart, Germany, where she is completing her doctoral thesis on image transcodings in the fiction of Don DeLillo. Her fields of research include post-structuralist semiotics, postmodern theory, and narratology.

**Laila Helmi** is a lecturer in the Department of English at Alexandria University, Egypt. Her fields of academic interest include translation studies, critical discourse analysis, and the intersections between language and literature. She is also a freelance translator.

**Mohamed Kenbib** is professor of history at the University of Rabat, Morocco. His publications include *Juifs et Musulmans au Maroc, 1859-1948* (Jews and Muslims in Morocco, 1859-1948).

**Abdennour Kharraki** is currently professor of intercultural communication and pragmatics at Mohamed First University, Oujda, Morocco. He gained an M.A. and a Ph.D. from Newcastle-upon-Tyne University, UK. In 2003, he was a visiting professor at The Australian Embassy in United Arab Emirates. In 2008, he was a Fulbright Visiting Scholar at the University of Northern Iowa.

**Nadia Laachiri** is a university professor with an interest in women's images in Andalusian Arabic literature. She has published several articles and collective books on Moroccan women.

**Fatima Laauina** has worked as a journalist and teacher. She is currently translating a novel.

**Chérif Lamrani** studied pharmacy and biochemistry in Amiens and Paris, France and has been working in the pharmaceutical industry as a production manager. In 2006 he was elected president of the National Order of Industrial Pharmacists and Distributors in Morocco.

**Dalenda Larguéche** is professor of history at Tunis University, Tunisia. She has published extensively on women's issues in Tunisia. She co-edited *Histoire des Femmes au Maghreb* (Women's History in the Maghreb).

**Yanshera Bint Mohamed Mahmoud** is a leading scholar of women's studies in Mauritania. Her interests lie in the history of Mauritanian women and its impact on the overall history of her country.

**Saied Moghawery** is associate professor of Islamic antiquities and civilization at the Faculty of Tourism and Hotels at Mounofeya University, Egypt. He currently holds the post of Vice-Dean at the same Faculty. He is a member of the The International Society for Arabic Papyrology at Princeton University, Head of the Arabic Papyrology Committee at the Higher Council for Egyptian Antiquities, and former curator of Arabic papyrology at the Egyptian National Library.

**Christiane Owusu-Sarpong** holds a Ph.D. in linguistics, semiotics, and communication from the Université de Franche-Comté, Paris. She was an associate professor at the Department of Languages, Faculty of Social Sciences, K.N.U.S.T., Kumasi, Ghana, where she taught for twenty-two years, before returning to France in 2001. She has been involved in the Women Writing Africa project for many years; she was one of the researchers, translators and associate editors of the Western Sahel volume. She is the translator of the Women Writing Africa series into French.

**Margaret Rausch** is assistant professor of religious studies at the University of Kansas, with a Ph.D. in Islamic Studies from the Free University of Berlin. She conducts research on Muslim women's rituals in Morocco and Tajikistan. Her publications include *Bodies, Boundaries and Spirit Possession: Moroccan Women and the Revision of Tradition* (2000), *Muslim Women's Rituals: Gender and Authority in the Islamic World* (with Catharina Raudvere, Copenhagen University, I. B. Tauris, under contract) and *Ishelhin (Berber) Women's Rituals and the Transmission of Islamic Knowledge in Southwestern Morocco* (in progress).

**Carole Saad-Escoffey** is a lecturer in French at Alexandria University, Egypt. She is also a consultant for the Alexandria and Mediterranean Research Center at the Bibliotheca Alexandrina where she works mainly in research, translation, and publishing.

**Dina Mohamed Abdel Salam** graduated from the Department of English at Alexandria University, Egypt in 1998, where she currently works as an assistant lecturer. She has specialized in literary theory, and is now interested in cinema.

**Anissa Salhi** studied translation in France. She works with the Royal Academy in Morocco where she translates texts from French or Arabic into English and vice-versa.

**Loubna Skalli** teaches at American University's School of International Service, Washington DC. Her research and writings are in the areas of gender, development, and communication.

**Souad Slaoui** is a linguist and gender studies scholar. She is currently in charge of the Women and Development Unit at Sidi Mohammed Ben Abdellah University, Fes, Morocco.

**Esi Sutherland-Addy** is a senior research fellow, Institute of African Studies, University of Ghana. She is co-editor of *Women Writing Africa Volume 2: West Africa and the Sahel.*

**Lynda Touchi-Benmansour** is interested in Berber Algerian women's oral literature and rituals. She has gathered, transliterated, and translated a considerable number of women's oral texts.

# Permissions Acknowledgments and Sources

For previously published texts not in the public domain, sources and rights-holders, to the extent possible, are indicated below. Original texts published with permission for the first time in this volume are copyrighted in the names of their authors. Unless otherwise noted, English-language translations commissioned for this volume are copyrighted in the names of their translators. Headnotes contained in this volume were commissioned for this edition and are copyrighted in the name of the Feminist Press. Archives and libraries that provided access to rare texts, or gave permission to reproduce them, are acknowledged below.

In the case of oral materials such as interviews and songs, every effort has been made to locate and gain permission from the original speaker(s). In the case of written materials, every effort has similarly been made to contact the rights-holders. Anyone who can provide information about rights-holders who have not been previously located is urged to contact the Feminist Press. *Those seeking permission to reprint or quote from any part of this book should also contact the Feminist Press at the following address:* Rights and Permissions, The Feminist Press at the City University of New York, Suite 5406, 365 Fifth Avenue, New York, NY 10016.

Hatshepsut, MY FALCON RISES HIGH
Text from Papyrus Chester Beatty I, in the collection of the Chester Beatty Library, Dublin. Translation by Alan H. Gardiner copyright © 1931.

Ankhesen-pa-Atun, A PROPOSAL OF MARRIAGE
Text copyright © 2001 by Maurice Cotterell, from *The Tutankhamun Prophecies*. Reprinted by permission of Bear & Co., an imprint of Inner Traditions, Rochester VT 05767.

Anonymous, LOVE SONGS
Text of Song One: Translation by Alan H. Gardiner. Text of Songs Two and Three: Translation by Miriam Lichtheim. Reprinted by permission of The Estate of Miriam Lichtheim and the University of California Press, from *Ancient Egyptian Literature, Volume II: The New Kingdom*, 2nd edition. Berkeley: University of California Press, 2006.

Anonymous, **LAMENT OF ISIS AND NEPHTHYS**
In the public domain, this extract can be found in Papyrus in Berlin no. 3008, in *"la femme au temps des pharaons"* by Christiane Desroches Noblecourt. © Stock/Lawrence Pernoud, 1986, 1998. Translation into English by Heba Sharobeem copyright © 2009.

Philista, Daughter of Lysias, **A COMPLAINT**
Text from *Papyrus Enteuxeis* 82, in the collection of the Egyptian Museum, Cairo. Translation by Ronald Cluett copyright © 2009 by QED Associates.

Nikaia, Daughter of Nikias, **REQUEST FOR A GUARDIAN**
Text from *Papyrus Enteuxeis* 22, in the collection of the *Université de Paris IV—Sorbonne, Paris*. Translation by Ronald Cluett copyright © 2009 by QED Associates.

Apollonous, **ABOUT A LITTLE GIRL**
Text from *Columbia Papyri* VIII 215, in the collection of Columbia University, New York. Translation by Ronald Cluett copyright © 2009 by QED Associates.

Ptolema, **LETTER TO A BROTHER**
Text from *Hamburg Papyri* I 86, in the collection of the *Staats- und Universitäts-Bibliothek*, Hamburg. Translation by Ronald Cluett copyright © 2009 by QED Associates.

Saint Vivia Perpetua, **I AM A CHRISTIAN**
Translation by W. H. Shewring. From W.H. Shewring, ed. and trans.1931. *The Passion of Perpetua and Felicity*. London: Sheed & Ward. Translation modernized by Paul Halsall copyright © 1996 from the Internet Medieval Source Book.

Aurelia Thaisous, **A MOTHER SEEKS LEGAL INDEPENDENCE**
Text from *Oxyrhynchus Papyri* 1467, in the collection of the British Library, London. Translation by Ronald Cluett copyright © 2009 by QED Associates.

Statulenia Julia, **TO THE MEMORY OF AELIA SECUNDULA**
Text from, F. van der Meer, Christine Mohrmann, et al. 1966. *Atlas of the Early Christian World*, London: Nelson. p. 49. Translation by Marjorie Lightman copyright © 2009.

Saint Syncletica, **LET WOMEN NOT BE MISLED**
Translation by Elizabeth Bryson Bongie copyright © 1995. Reprinted by permission of Wipf and Stock Publishers from Pseudo-Athanasius and Mary Shaffer, *The Life and Regimen of the Blessed and Holy Syncletica.*(Eugene, OR:

Wipf and Stock Publishers, 2005) pp30-32. ISBN 978-1-597524445. www.wipfandstock.com.

Om Makina, LETTER TO A WOMAN FRIEND
Text from a papyrus (no. J) in the collection of the *Musée du Louvre*, Paris. Transcription copyright © 2009 by Saied Moghawery. Translation by Amira Nowaira copyright © 2009.

Anonymous, A PLEA FOR MONEY
Text from a papyrus (no. 6927) in the collection of the *Musée du Louvre*, Paris. Transcription copyright © 2009 by Saied Moghawery. Translation by Amira Nowaira copyright © 2009.

Mahriyya Al-Aghlabiya and Khadija Ben Kalthoum, TWO TUNISIAN POEMS
Text from Hassen Hosni Abdelwahab. 1966. *Shahirat Tunussiyat* (Famous Tunisian Women). Tunis: *El Manar Editions*. Translation by Khédija Arfaoui copyright © 2009.

Astour Heyoh, FREEING A SLAVE WOMAN
Text from papyrus (record 1900) in the collection of the National Library and Archives, Cairo. Transcription copyright © 2009 by Saied Moghawery. Translation by Amira Nowaira copyright © 2009.

Sara, Daughter of Abboud Al-Nahid, USING THE RIGHT OF SEVERANCE
Text from a papyrus found in *Al-Ashmouneen*, in the collection of the *Österreichische Nationalbibliothek*, Vienna. Published by permission of the *Österreichische Nationalbibliothek*. Transcription copyright © 2009 by Saied Moghawery. Translation by Shadia El Soussi copyright © 2009.

Hafsa Bint Al-Haj Al-Rakuniya, LOVE POEMS
Text from Al-Shaikh Ahmed Ben Mohamed Al-Maqqari Al-Tlemsamani. 1294/1968. *Nafhu Al-Tib Min Ghusni Al-Andalusi Al-Rahib* (Fragrance from a Generous Branch of Al-Andalus). Repr. ed. Dr. Ihsan Abbas, Vol. 1, 172-173. Beirut: *Dar Sadir*. Translation by Nadia Laachiri copyright © 2009.

Fatma-Setita, CONSOLATION AND OTHER POEMS
Text from Shams El Din Mohamed bin Abdel Rahman Al-Sakhawi. c. 1492-94. *Al Daw' al-Lami it-Ahl al-Qarn al-Tasi* (The Bright Light Concerning the People of the Nineteenth Century), Vol. 12, in the collection of the National Library and Archives, Cairo. Translation by Amira Nowaira copyright © 2009.

Ana de Melo, ESCAPING THE INQUISITION
Text from records of the *Inquisicao de Evora*, Mco. 74, No. 686, in the col-

lection of the *Arquivo Nacional da Torre do Tombo*, Lisbon. Published in Arabic in *Majalla Al-Manahil* 21, 1981. Translation from Arabic by Fatima Sadiqi copyright © 2009.

Lalla Khnata Bint Bakkar, TWO POLITICAL LETTERS
Text of first letter reprinted by permission of Abdelhadi Tazi from1986. *At-Tarikh Ad-Diplumasi lil Maghrib* (History of Moroccan Diplomacy), Vol. 1. Mohammedia: *Imprimerie Fédala*. Text of second letter, from Abderrahman Ben Zaydane. 1931. *Athaf A'lam Ennass* (The Power and Glory of the People of Rabat). Text of Translation by Moha Ennaji and Khadija Zizi copyright © 2009.

Lalla Fatima, LETTER ABOUT FEMALE SLAVES
Text reprinted by permission of Abdelhadi Tazi, from Abdelhadi Tazi. *At-Tarikh Ad-Diplumasi lil Maghrib* (History of Moroccan Diplomacy), Vol. 1. *Mohammedia: Imprimerie Fédala*. 1986. Translation by Moha Ennaji copyright © 2009.

Shehrazad, STRUGGLE FOR A THRONE
Text from Muhammad al-Ribati al-Du'ayyif. 1818/1986. *Tarikh Du'ayyif* (The History of Du'ayyif). Repr. ed. Ahmad Al-Amari. Rabat: *Dar al Ma'thurat*. Translation by Loubna Skalli copyright © 2009.

Anonymous, LA'RUBIYAT, OR WOMEN'S SONGS
Translation by Moha Ennaji, Fatima Sadiqi, and Khadija Zizi copyright © 2009.

Aisha Al-Taymouria, POEM TO MY DAUGHTER
Text from Aisha Al-Taymouria. 1884. *Heliat Al-Teraz* (Ornamental Design). Cairo: *Sharaf.* Translation by Amira Nowaira copyright © 2009.

Kharboucha, AISSA THE FOX
Text of Songs One, Two, Three and Five from *Ma'lamat Al Maghrib* (Encyclopedia of Morocco), Vol. 11, 2000, pp. 3642-3. Text of Song Four, from newspaper *Alittihad ALishtiraki*, April 1995, p. 6. Text of Song Six from Salem Kwindi, *Kharboucha*, Marrakech, 2001, p.14. Translation by Fatima Laaouina and Khadija Zizi copyright © 2009.

Labiba Hashim, THE EASTERN WOMAN: HOW SHE IS AND HOW SHE SHOULD BE
Text from *Anis Al Galis* (The Friendly Companion), 31 May 1898, in the collection of the National Library and Archives, Cairo. Translation by Radwa El Barouni copyright © 2009.

Zeinab Fawwaz, **THE CHOICE OF A HUSBAND**
Text from Zeinab Fawwaz. *Husn al-Awaqib aw Ghadet al Zahira* (Good Conseqences, or the Beautiful Woman of al Zahira), 1899. Cairo: *Matba'at Hindiyyah*. Translation by Sahar Hamouda copyright © 2009.

Malak Hifni Nassef, **POLYGAMY**
Text ©1998. Reprinted by permission of The Women and Memory Forum from Malak Hifni Nassef. 1910/1999. *Al-Nisa'iyat* (On Women's Issues). Translation by Azza El Kholy copyright © 2009.

Tawgrat Walt Aissa N'Ayt Sokhman, **RESISTANCE**
Text copyright © 1987. Reprinted by permission of the Royal Academy of the Kingdom of Morocco. From Mohamed Chafik, *Berber Poetry and the Armed Resistance in the Middle Atlas and the Eastern High Atlas, 1912-1934*. Rabat: *Journal of the Royal Academy 4*. Translation by Moha Ennaji copyright © 2009.

Saphia Zagloul, **LETTER FROM EXILE**
Text copyright © 2009. Published by permission of Madiha Doss. Translation by Carole Escoffey copyright © 2009.

Helmeya Yousry, **RESPONSE TO REACTIONARIES**
Text from *Al Amal* (Hope), Cairo, 1925. Translation by Azza El Kholy copyright © 2009.

Mounira Thabet, **WOMEN'S RIGHTS**
Text from *Al Amal* (Hope), Cairo, 12 December 1925. Repr. in Amira Khowask, ed. *The Egyptian Woman's Struggle to Be Liberated from the Harem Age*. Cairo: The Family Library. 2000. Translation by Naglaa Abu-Agag copyright © 2009.

Mririda N'Ayt Atiq, **TWO DEFIANT POEMS**
Text copyright ©2003. Reprinted by permission of E.J. Brill. From Fatima Sadiqi, *Women, Language, and Gender in Morocco*.

Blanche Bendahan, **VISITING A DEAD MOTHER**
Text copyright © 1930 from Blanche Bendahan, *Mazaltob*. Paris: *Editions du Tambourin*, 1930. Translation by Belou Charloff copyright © 2009.

Asma Fahmy, **HIGHER EDUCATION FOR WOMEN**
Text from *Al Rissala* (The Message), Cairo, 22 January 1934, in the collection of The Municipal Library, Alexandria. Translation by Amira Nowaira copyright © 2009.

"Al-Fatat," On Young Women's Education
Text from *Majallat Al Maghrib* (Morocco Magazine), March 1935. Translation by Zakia Iraqui-Sinaceur copyright © 2009.

Soheir El-Qalamawi, A Furious Woman
Text from Soheir El-Qalamawi. *Hykayat Geddety* (My Grandmother's Stories), 1935. Translation by Sahar Hamouda copyright © 2009.

Nahed Taha Abdel Ber, The Lost Hope
Text copyright © 2009. Published by permission of Ragaa Al Naquash. Translation by Heba Sharobeem and Radwa El Barouni copyright © 2009.

Nabaweya Moussa, Yes to Education And No to Marriage
Text copyright © 1937. Reprinted by permission of Women and Memory Forum, from Nabaweya Moussa, *Tarikhi bi Qalami* (My History), 1937/1999. Translation by Amira Nowaira and Azza El Kholy copyright © 2009.

Bchira Ben Mrad, Honoring Dr. Tawhida Ben Cheikh
Text from a speech given on 18 April 1937, Tunis, Tunisia. Published in Hassen Hosni Abdelwahab, *Shahirat Tunissiyat* (Famous Tunisian Women). Tunis: *El Manar Editions*, 1966. Translation by Khédija Arfaoui copyright © 2009.

Bady'a Sabbah-Allah, Letter to a Friend
Text copyright © 2009. Published by permission of Mrs. Enaam Sabbah-Allah. Translation by Amira Nowaira copyright © 2009.

Malika El-Fassi, An Important Step for Girls' Education
Text from "The Sun Has Risen for Moroccan Women," *Risalat Al-Maghrib* 12(1): 31 August 1943. Translation by Zakia Iraqui-Sinaceur, Fatima Sadiqi, and Moha Ennaji copyright © 2009.

Fatma Ne'mat Rashed, Should Women Enter Al-Azhar?
Text from *Fatat Al-Ghadd*, Cairo, 10 February 1946. Translation by Dina Mohamed Abdel Salam copyright © 2009.

Huda Shaarawi, Letter to the Prime Minister
Text copyright © 2009. Published by permission of Laila Sharaawy. Translation by Nevine Rateb and Nadia El Kholy copyright © 2009.

Lalla Aisha, A Princess Speaks, Unveiled
Published by permission of the Royal Archives, Rabat and The Royal Academy of the Kingdom of Morocco from a speech given on 11 April 1947, Tang-

iers, Morocco, in the collection of the Royal Archives, Rabat. Translation by Anissa Salhi copyright © 2009.

Doria Shafik, THE BEST TYPE OF PUBLICITY
Text from *Bint Al-Nil* (Daughter of the Nile), Cairo, 1947. Translation by Amira Nowaira copyright © 2009.

Habiba Guessoussa, AN OPENING SPEECH
    Text from a speech given on 23 May 1947, Fes, Morocco. Published in *Amal* no. 2, Casablanca, 1992. Translation by Fatima Bouabdelli copyright © 2009.

Eugenie Sinano Horwitz, TALES FROM THE ZOGHEB SAGA
    Text copyright © 2005. Reprinted by permission of the *Bibliotheca Alexandrina* from Eugenie Sinano Horwitz, et al, *The Zoghebs: An Alexandrian Saga*, ed. by Mohamed Awad and Sahar Hamouda, 2005. Translation by Carole Escoffey copyright © 2009.

Alia Khsasiya, WOMEN'S EMANCIPATION
    Text from newspaper *Al-Saada*, Morocco, September 1, 1950. Translation by Zakia Iraqui-Sinaceur and Moha Ennaji copyright © 2009.

Aisha Abdel Rahman, THE HEIRESS
    Text from *Al-Hilal*, Cairo, April 1957. Translation by Sahar Hamouda copyright © 2009.

Zhor Lhiyania, Fatima Ali Mernissi, Hiba Elbaqali, Aziza Kerzazi, and Fatima Bourqadia, TO LALLA RADIA, OUR ETERNAL LIGHTHOUSE
    Text from the archives of the City Council, Fes, Morocco. Translation by Moha Ennaji copyright © 2009.

Djamila Débêche, ALIENATION
    Text from Djamila Débêche, *Aziza*. Algiers: Imprimerie Imbert, 1955. Translation by Zahia Smail Salhi copyright © 2009.

Fatima Kabbaj, REMOVAL OF THE VEIL AND DECENCY
    Text from *Al-Alam*, 24 September 1956. Translation copyright © 2009 by Malika El Korso.

Baya Hocine, SENTENCED TO DEATH
    Text published courtesy of Akila Hocine. Translation copyright © 2009 by Malika El Korso.

Assia Djebar, THERE IS NO EXILE
    Reprinted by permission of the University of Virginia Press from Assia Dje-

bar. 1992. *Women of Algiers in Their Apartment*, trans. Marjolin de Jager. Copyright © 1992 by the University of Virginia Press. Originally published in *La Nouvelle Critique*, Paris, 1959.

Djamila Boupacha, TESTIMONY OF TORTURE
Reprinted by permission of *Éditions Gallimard* and Peter Green. From Simone de Beauvoir and Gisèle Halimi, eds. *Djamila Boupacha: The Story of the Torture of a Young Algerian Girl which Shocked Liberal French Opinion*, trans. Peter Green. New York: Macmillan, 1962.

Zhor Zerari, TWO PRISON POEMS
Text from Zhor Zerari. 1988. *Poèmes de Prison*. Algiers: *Éditions Bouchène*. Translation by Abena P.A. Busia and Moha Ennaji copyright © 2009.

Galila Reda, I NO LONGER LOVE PASSIONATELY
Text from Galila Reda, (*The White Wings*). Cairo: *Maktabat Misr*, 1965. Translation by Carole Escoffey and Heba Sharobeem copyright © 2009.

Wadida Wassef, AUNT NOOR
Text copyright © 2009. Published by permission of Amir Wassef and Malak Wassef.

Fadhma Ait Mansour Amrouche, OUTCAST AND EXILE
Reprinted by permission of Rutgers University Press from Fadhma A.M. Amrouche. 1988. *My Life Story: The Autobiography of a Berber Woman*. New Brunswick, N.J.: Rutgers University Press.

Khnata Bennani, COME BACK IN TWO WEEKS
Text copyright © 2009. Published by permission of Khadija Zizi. Translation by Khadija Zizi copyright © 2009.

Rabha Moha, I WANT TO TELL YOU
Text copyright © 1977, recorded by Fatima Sadiqi in Beni Mellal, Morocco. Published by permission of The Moha Family and Fatima Sadiqi. Translation by Fatima Sadiqi copyright © 2009.

Saida Menebhi, TWO POEMS: PRISON AND THE PROSTITUTES
Text of "Prison" reprinted by permission of *Editions L'Harmattan* and the Menebhi family from *La Parole Confisquée: Textes, Dessins, Peintures de Prisonniers Politiques Marocains*. Paris: Éditions L'Harmattan. 1982. Text of "The Prostitutes" reprinted by permission of the Menebhi family from Saida Menebhi, *Poèmes—Ecrits—Lettres de Prison*. Rabat: Edition Feedback. 2000. Translations by Khadija Zizi and Abena P.A. Busia copyright © 2009.

Zainab Al-Ghazali, **TORTURE IN PRISON**
Reprinted by permission of The Islamic Foundation, from Zeinab Al-Ghazali, *Ayyam min Hayati (Days in My Life)*, 1994. Translation by Amira Nowaira copyright © 2009.

Amina Wahib, **THE ROSE**
Text copyright © 1980. Published by permission of Amina Wahib. Translation by Fouzia Baddouri copyright © 2009.

Aicha Mekki, **ON PROSTITUTION**
First published in Abdeljalil Lahjomri and Aicha Mekki. *Pleure Aicha, Tes Chroniques Égarées* (Mourn Aicha, Your Lost Columns). Casablanca: *Malika Editions*, 2001. Translation by Moha Ennaji copyright © 2009.

El-Hajja Rqia, **FATMA AND THE OGRESS**
Reprinted by permission of Michael Peyron from *Women As Brave As Men: Heroines of the Moroccan Middle Atlas*. Ifrane, Morocco: Al Akhawayn University in Ifrane, 2003.

Fatima Tabaamrant, **WAKE UP, SISTERS**
Text copyright © 2009. Translation by Fatima Bouabdelli copyright © 2009.

Fatima Mernissi, **WOMEN AND POLITICAL ISLAM**
Reprinted by permission of Polity Press, University of Minnesota Press, and *Editions Albin Michel*, from *The Forgotten Queens of Islam*. Translation by Mary Jo Lakeland copyright © 1993.

Amina Arfaoui, **THE GRAMOPHONE**
Text copyright © 1987. Reprinted by permission of Amina Arfaoui Translation by Khédija Arfaoui copyright © 2009.

Samira Tolba Abdel Tawab, **MOTHER GOAT: A FOLK TALE**
Text © 1989. From Mohamed Hussein Hassan Hilal. *Folktales: Al Ayyat District*. M.A. thesis, Department of Arabic Literature, Faculty of Arts, Cairo University. Translation by Nadia El Kholy copyright © 2009.

Salwa Bakr, **WORMS IN THE ROSE GARDEN**
Reprinted by permission of the author, from *Ajin al-Fallaha* (The Peasant Woman's Dough). Cairo: Sinai Publishing House. 1992. Translation by Azza El Kholy copyright © 2009.

Communal, **TAKE MY BRACELET AND OTHER SONGS**
Text copyright © 1992, as recorded by Dalenda Larguèche in Dar Joued prison, Tunisia. Reprinted by permission of the author and *Cérès Editions*, from *Marginales en Terre d'Islam* (Misfits in the Land of Islam). Translation by Moha Ennaji copyright © 2009.

Latifa Jbabdi and L'Union de L'Action Féminine, **ONE MILLION SIGNATURES**
First published in *8 Mars* magazine no. 57, March 1992. Translation by Fatima Bouabdelli copyright © 2009.

Fatma Kandil, **THORNY SPACES SUDDENLY MOVING**
First published in *Ibda'a* (Creativity), Cairo, January 1993. Translation by Amira Nowaira copyright © 2009.

Latifa El Zayyat, **IN HER OWN MIRROR**
First published in *Ibda'a* (Creativity), Cairo, January 1993. Translation by Amira Nowaira copyright © 2009.

Nawal El Saadawi, **WRITING AND FREEDOM**
Reprinted by permission of the author from *Fusul*, Cairo, January 1993. Translation by Amira Nowaira copyright © 2009.

Malouma Mint Moktar Ould Meidah, **AN ARTIST WHO UNSETTLES: AN INTERVIEW AND A SONG**
Text of interview and song from *Notre Librairie*, 1993. Translation from French by Christiane Owusu-Sarpong and Esi Sutherland-Addy, and Abena P.A. Busia copyright © 2009

Mubarak Bint Al-Barra, **DEFIANCES: AN INTERVIEW AND A POEM**
Text of interview and poem from *Notre Librairie*, 1994. Translation from French by Abena P. A. Busia and Christiane Owusu-Sarpong copyright © 2009.

Radwa Ashour, **ACCUSED OF HERESY**
Published by permission of Syracuse University Press, from Radwa Ashour, *Granada*. 1994. Translation by Sahar Hamouda copyright © 2009.

Naima Boucharef, **WHY WAS MY SON ASSASSINATED?**
Text copyright © 2009. Published by permission of the author. Translation by Hadhami Hached copyright © 2009.

Moufida Tlati, **BREAKING SILENCE**
Text copyright © 1994. Published by permission of the author from *Samt el qusur* (The Silences of the Palaces), *Cinétéléfilms/Mat Films*, 1994. Translation

by Zahia Smail Salhi copyright © 2009.

Tassadit Yacine and "Nouara," WHY SOME WOMEN WRITE POETRY
Reprinted by permission of Tassadit Yacine, from *Piège ou le Combat d'une Femme Algérienne* (The Trap, or the Struggle of an Algerian Woman). Paris: *Publisud Awal*. Translation into French by Tassit Yacine copyright © 1995. Translated from French by Zahia Smail Salhi copyright © 2009.

Buthayna Khadr Mekky, RITES
Text from 1996. *Shadows of Grief*. Sharjah, UAE. Reprinted in A. Rashid, et al., ed. *Thakirat al-Mustaqbal: Mawsu'at al-Mar'a al-'Arabiyya* (The Memory of the Future: An Encyclopedia of Arab Women's Writings). Cairo: Nour and The Supreme Council of Culture, 2002. Translation by Azza El Kholy copyright © 2009.

Fathia El Assal, WHO IS FATHIA EL ASSAL?
Published by permission of the author. Text from an interview by Attiyat El Abnoudy, first published in Attiyat El Abnoudy, *Ayam Al-Dimoqratiya: Al-Nisa' Al-Misriyat wa Homoum Al-Watan* (Days of Democracy: Egyptian Women in Elections). Cairo: Kassem Press, 1997. Translation by Sahar Hamouda copyright © 2009.

Samira El Ghaly El Hajj, THE MAGIC JOURNEY
Text from *Maqate' Lelbahr wa Al-Luqia wal* (Verses for the Sea and the Encounter), 1997. Translation by Abena P. A. Busia and Radwa El Barouni copyright © 2009.

Huda Lutfi, FRAMED WOMEN
Published by permission of The Department of English and Comparative Literature, the American University in Cairo. From Huda Lutfi "Women, History, Memory" in Ferial J. Ghazoul, ed. "Gender and Knowledge: Contribution of Gender Perspectives to Intellectual Formation," *Alif: Journal of Comparative Poetics* 1999.

Fatma Ramadan, LULLABY TO A DAUGHTER
Text copyright © 1999, recorded in Amriya, Egypt. Published by permission of the author. Translation by Amira Nowaira copyright © 2009.

Leila Abouzeid, TWO STORIES OF A HOUSE
Reprinted by permission of the Center for Middle Eastern Studies at the University of Texas at Austin. From *The Director and Other Stories*, 2005. Translation by Leila Abouzeid copyright © 2009.

Tafidah Mahmoud Abdel Aghany, GAMALEK, THE MASTER OF ALL BIRDS
Text recorded by Abdel Reheem and Ahmed Mohamed in Sawamah, Egypt, and published in *Tales from Al Samawah*. M.A. thesis, Egyptian Center for Media Research, Cairo, 2001. Translation by Nadia El Kholy copyright © 2009.

Safia Oraho, LOVE AND MILITANCY: ORAL TESTIMONIES
Text copyright © 2001 as recorded by Zoubida Achahboun in El Hajeb, Morocco. Translation by Moha Ennaji copyright © 2009.

Maria Bent Itto Brahim, TWO SLAVES, MOTHER AND DAUGHTER
Text copyright © 2001 as recorded by Zoubida Achahboun in El Hajeb, Morocco. Translation by Moha Ennaji copyright © 2009.

Rabea Qadiri, SONGS OF SEPARATION AND UNION
Text copyright © 2001 as recorded by Abdennour Kharraki in Ahfir, Morocco. Published by permission of the author. Translation by Abdennour Kharraki copyright © 2009.

Lalla Mina Lamrani, TWO FEISTY TALES
Text copyright © 2001 as recorded by Hafsa Bekri-Lamrani in Casablanca, Morocco. Published by permission of Chérif Lamrani. Translation by Hafsa Bekri-Lamrani copyright © 2009.

Hafsa Bekri-Lamrani, THE CALL OF HAGAR
Text copyright © 2001. Published by permission of the author.

Ekbal Baraka, SO AS NOT TO FORGET THE DREAMS OF QASIM AMIN
First published in *Al-Ahram*, Cairo, 25 December 2002. Translation by Azza El Kholy copyright © 2009.

Hadda N'Ayt Hssain, O BRIDE: BERBER WEDDING SONG
Text copyright © 2003. Published by permission of the author. Translation by Fatima Sadiqi copyright © 2009.

Samia Serageldin, LOVE IS LIKE WATER
Text copyright © 2003. Published by permission of the author.

Faiza W. Shereen, GIFTS OF TIME
Text copyright © 2009. Published by permission of the author.

# AUTHORS LISTED BY COUNTRY

## ALGERIA
Fadhma Ait Mansour Amrouche, Blanche Bendahan, Djamila Boupacha, Djamila Débêche, Assia Djebar, Baya Hocine, Nouara, Tassadit Yacine, Zhor Zerari

## EGYPT
Tafidah Mahmoud Abdel Aghany, Nahed Taha Abdel Ber, Aisha Abdel Rahman, Samira Tolba Abdel Tawab, Mona Abousenna, Mahriyya Al-Aghlabiya, Zainab Al-Ghazali, Aisha Al-Taymouria, Latifa Al-Zayyat, Anonymous, Ankhesen-pa-Atun, Apollonous, Radwa Ashour, Fathia El Assal, Salwa Bakr, Ekbal Baraka, Mona Makram Ebeid, Soheir El-Qalamawi, Asma Fahmy, Zeinab Fawwaz, Fatma-Setita, Labiba Hashim, Hatshepsut, Astour Heyoh, Mona Nawal Helmi, Malak Hifni Nassef, Eugenie Sinano Horwirz, Khadija Ben Kalthoum, Fatma Kandil, Huda Lufti, Om Makina, Nabaweya Moussa, Nikaia, Philista, Ptolema, Fatma Ramadan, Fatma Ne'mat Rashed, Galila Reda, Nawal El Saadawi, Bady'a Sabbah-Allah, Sara, Samia Serageldin, Huda Shaarawi, Doria Shafik, Faiza W. Shereen, Saint Syncletica, Mounira Thabet, Aurelia Thaisous, Wadida Wassef, Helmeya Yousry, Saphia Zagloul

## MAURETANIA
Mubaraka Bint Al-Barra, Statulenia Julia, Malouma Bint Moktar Ould Meidah

## MOROCCO
Leila Abouzeid, Lalla Aisha, "Al Fatat," Hafsa Bint Al-Haj Al-Rakuniya, Mririda N'Ayt Atiq, Yaëlle Azagury, Lalla Khnata Bint Bakkar, Hafsa Bekri-Lamrani, Khnata Bennani, Fatima Bourgadia, Ana de Melo, Malika El-Fassi, Hiba Elbaqali, Lalla Fatima, Habiba Guessoussa, Hadda N'Ayt Hssain, Maria Bent Itto Brahim, Latifa Jbabdi, Fatima Kabbaj, Aziza Kerzazi, Kharboucha, Alia Khsasiya, Lalla Mina Lamrani, Zhor Lhiyania, L'Union de L'Action Féminine, Aicha Mekki, Saida Menebhi, Fatima Mernissi, Rabha Moha, Safia Oraho, Rabea Qadiri, El-Hajja Rqia, Shehrazad, Nouzha Skalli-Bennis, Tawgrat Walt Aissa N'Ayt Sokhman, Fatima Tabaamrant, Amina Wahib

## SUDAN
Samira El Ghaly El Hajj

## TUNISIA
Mahriyya Al-Aghlabiya, Amina Arfaoui, Naima Boucharef, Communal, Azza Filali, Khadija Ben Kalthoum, Bchira Ben Mrad, Saint Vivia Perpetua, Moufida Tlati

# INDEX